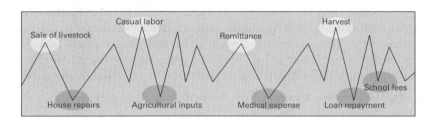

The New
Microfinance
Handbook

On microfinance and *The New Microfinance Handbook*

"Financial services help to smooth cash flows, build assets, invest productively, and, importantly, manage risks. Increasing the outreach of financial services that are affordable and meet the varied needs of poor women and men can contribute significantly to economic development and overall quality of life, key objectives of practitioners and policy makers alike."

—**Maria Otero,** former CEO, Accion International

"The journey from microfinance to financial inclusion began in earnest when we understood that clients need diverse services such as savings, payments, and insurance, as well as loans. *The New Microfinance Handbook* reflects a lesson we learned many years ago—that sharing knowledge and best practices is so important to help providers, policy makers, and others to continue to innovate, adapt, and scale financial services in order to add real value to customers in a responsible way."

—**H.R.H. Princess Máxima of the Netherlands,** The UN Secretary-General's Special Advocate for Inclusive Finance for Development (UNSGSA)

"*The New Microfinance Handbook* fills a critical gap in the current literature on financial inclusion. I am particularly pleased with the explicit focus on consumers and their needs—this, together with the onset of technology-based delivery models, has been the most important shift in the microfinance field over the past 15 years. I am sure that by taking the financial ecosystem approach and compiling all the current trends into one volume, this book will serve as a reference for the large and growing financial inclusion community for years to come."

—**Brigit Helms,** author of *Access for All*

"Financial services that support asset building, investment, and risk management are critical for people of all ages in frontier and postconflict environments. In *The New Microfinance Handbook*, the authors highlight the importance of understanding client needs and the need for a more inclusive financial sector. This work provides an excellent resource for navigating a diverse and rapidly changing microfinance sector."

—**President Ellen Johnson Sirleaf,** Liberia

"Poor people's lives are complex; the goods, services and amenities that they need to escape from poverty—and the means by which they get them—are equally diverse. One-size-fits-all solutions are an illusion. Our challenge as development policy makers, researchers, and practitioners in all fields—be that in finance, agriculture, health or education—is to understand and respond to this complexity in ways that help build diverse, resilient socioeconomic systems that are able to serve the needs of the poor, sustainably and at scale.

"*The New Microfinance Handbook* reflects this challenge. It moves beyond the original *Microfinance Handbook*'s focus on retail microfinance to deal with the imperative of understanding and strengthening the wider financial ecosystem, which is essential to making financial markets genuinely work better—inclusively and responsibly—for poor men and women. This shift has significant implications for development agencies, requiring 'smarter' subsidies, different types of partners, and more facilitative or catalytic interventions."

—**Robert Hitchens,** Director, Springfield Centre, United Kingdom

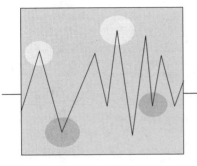

The New Microfinance Handbook

A Financial Market System Perspective

Edited by Joanna Ledgerwood
with Julie Earne and Candace Nelson

THE WORLD BANK
Washington, D.C.

CONTENTS

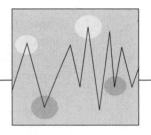

Boxes

Figures

Tables

FOREWORD

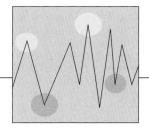

When first published in 1998, Joanna Ledgerwood's *Microfinance Handbook* was an indispensible guide for donors, policy makers, and practitioners who were working to expand access of the poor to microfinance. In the intervening years, the opportunities and pressures of commercialization have driven a reassessment of what microfinance is and whom it should serve. Today, in addition to building the capacity and ensuring the sustainability of institutions, the larger microfinance community is taking a closer look at the diverse needs of clients, the broader financial ecosystem, and the transformational nature of technology. This reassessment has become a regular fixture of global conversations about poverty alleviation.

The New Microfinance Handbook, then, is timely. The microfinance sector now reflects the multidisciplinary intersection of finance, technology, and development, where new ideas are changing the art of what is possible. The actors reflect this diverse ecosystem and include everything from mobile operators to microfinance institutions to community networks. This book has brought an impressive array of the field's experts to an area of practice in constant change.

We are pleased that this book asks the hard questions about what people living in poverty really need. This means moving the conversation beyond the walls of institutions and into the complex worlds of clients. The needs of a rural farmer are different from those of an urban microbusiness owner. A young woman embarking on a life after school has different priorities than a mother seeking to protect the assets of her family. For microfinance to deliver on its original promises, we need to put the needs of persons living in poverty at the center of this work.

It is time for us to take stock of what we have learned as we move forward. *The New Microfinance Handbook* will play an important role, helping us to advance our understanding about how financial services can serve the diverse needs of the poor.

Reeta Roy
President and CEO
The MasterCard Foundation

Tom Kessinger
General Manager
Aga Khan Foundation

PREFACE

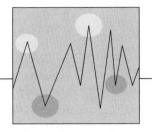

Imagine a life without access to financial services: no deposit account, no debit card, no fire insurance, no college savings plan, no home mortgage. Life would be an incredibly stressful roller coaster ride, and most dreams would remain unfulfilled. The day you get paid for work would be good, the other days rough. Any accident would set your family back. Sending the kids to college? Too difficult. Buying a house? Forget it. Nobody can pay for such needs out of cash accumulated under the mattress. For us, life without access to financial services is unimaginable.

Yet according to 2011 data from the World Bank, an estimated 2.5 billion working-age adults globally—more than half of the total adult population—have to do exactly that. They live a life without access to the types of financial services we take for granted. Of course, they cannot do without financial intermediation, so they rely on age-old, informal mechanisms. They buy livestock as a form of savings; they throw a village feast to cement local ties as insurance against a future family crisis; they pawn jewelry to satisfy urgent liquidity needs; and they turn to a moneylender for credit. These mechanisms are risky and often very expensive.

Increasingly robust empirical evidence demonstrates how appropriate financial services can help to improve household welfare and spur small enterprise activity. Macro evidence also shows that economies with deeper financial intermediation and better access to financial services grow faster and have less income inequality. Policy makers and regulators worldwide recognize these connections. They have made financial inclusion—where everyone has the choice to access and use the financial services they need, delivered in a responsible fashion—a global development priority.

A powerful vision of responsible financial market development is emerging—a vision that aims to bank the other half of the global working-age adult population by leveraging what we have learned from the microfinance story to date, using advances in technology to spur product and business model innovation, and encouraging new ways of thinking about how to create an enabling, risk-proportionate regulatory and supervisory environment.

The New Microfinance Handbook reflects the current frontier of our collective thinking and experience. It starts with the need to understand the demand side. Poor households in the informal economy are producers and consumers. They need access to the full range of financial services to generate income, build assets, smooth consumption, and manage risks. The global financial inclusion agenda recognizes these broader needs. It also recognizes the importance of financial literacy that builds consumer financial capabilities and of consumer protection regimes that take into account the conditions and constraints of poor families in the informal economy.

The *Handbook* also takes a broad look at the diversity of providers required to meet these needs and at the business model challenges of different products. The original microcredit revolution found an ingenious way to overcome the previous obstacle to providing credit for the poor. How do you manage credit risk and repayments at the local level when working with a segment of the population that has no traditional collateral? The breakthrough was the joint-liability group loan— social collateral to allow the poor to pledge for each other. But the business model challenges are different for other financial services. For small-denomination savings and remittances, transaction costs must be ultralow; for insurance, risks must be pooled and managed at an actuarially relevant scale; for pensions, micro contributions must be invested in ways that generate adequate long-term returns.

Continued innovation in products and business models is needed so that we can reach more people with a broader range of products at lower costs. No one type of provider will be able to overcome the very different business model challenges of all products. What is needed instead is a variety of financial service providers that come together in a local-market ecosystem that works for the poor at the base of the economic pyramid.

Lastly, the *Handbook* takes a fresh look at the enabling infrastructure and regulatory environment. The infrastructure requirements range from a larger number of low-cost, physical access points in harder-to-reach geographic areas to nationwide unique financial identities that facilitate consumer enrollment and protection. On the regulatory side, policy makers are recognizing that financial *exclusion* poses a risk to political stability and impedes economic advancement, and they are increasingly willing to balance the ultimately mutually reinforcing needs for financial stability, financial integrity, and financial inclusion.

With a better understanding of demand, ongoing innovation in products and business models to better meet that demand, and recognition of the need for a protective and supportive enabling environment, I believe we have the knowledge and the means to achieve full financial inclusion in our lifetime. Read on to learn how this is already happening and what more is needed.

Tilman Ehrbeck
CEO
Consultative Group to Assist the Poor (CGAP)

ACKNOWLEDGMENTS

The writing of this book has been a highly collaborative effort and there are many people we wish to acknowledge and thank for their support and contributions. First of all, our Advisory Committee, composed of David Ferrand, Steve Rasmussen, Tom Austin, Ann Miles, and Benoit Destouches, provided sound guidance and leadership for which we are very grateful. We also appreciate the significant effort and expertise of the contributing authors, without whom this book would not have been published: Ines Arevalo, Craig Churchill, Daryl Collins, Mayada El-Zoghbi, David Ferrand, Barbara Gähwiler, Alan Gibson, Susan Johnson, Kate Lauer, Joyce Lehman, Ignacio Mas, Peter McConaghy, Calvin Miller, Geraldine O'Keeffe, Stuart Rutherford, Lisa Sherk, Stefan Staschen, and Joakim Vincze. In addition, we are deeply grateful to Peter McConaghy, who conducted excellent research and provided significant draft material for a majority of the chapters. We also thank those who contributed to specific chapters, including Cheryl Frankiewicz, Liz Case, Alyssa Jethani, Linda Jones, Emilio Hernandez, and Ruth Dueck-Mbeba.

For their insightful feedback, we thank our peer reviewers of which there were many: Elizabeth Berté, Anita Campion, Liz Case, Gerhard Coetzee, Monique Cohen, Christoph Diehl, Thomas Engelhardt, Laura Foose, Cheryl Frankiewicz, Martin Habel, Michel Hanouch, Tor Jansson, Susan Johnson, Kabir Kumar, Kate Lauer, Joyce Lehman, Ignacio Mas, Janina Matuszeski, Sitara Merchant, Ann Miles, Hanif Pabani, JR Rao, Steve Rasmussen, Rich Rosenberg, Adam Sorensen, Ingrid Stokstad, Joakim Vincze, Leah Wardle, Martina Wiedmaier-Pfister, and Kim Wilson. In particular we are extremely grateful to Bob Christen for reviewing the initial draft of the book and suggesting a significant new direction that, at the time, seemed like a very big task but was exactly what was needed; we appreciate his honesty and guidance. We are indebted to Ruth Dueck-Mbeba, who reviewed the entire book, providing excellent feedback and suggestions as well as a significant portion of chapter 15.

We are very grateful to The MasterCard Foundation and the Aga Khan Foundation for the support provided throughout the making of this book, in particular Reeta Roy, Ann Miles, Ruth Dueck-Mbeba, David Myhre, Tom Kessinger, Mike Bowles, Erin Markel, Sam Pickens, Helen Chen, Jayne Barlow, and especially Tom Austin.

We greatly appreciate the efforts and patience of Paola Scalabrin for her persistence in requesting this update, ensuring that the book was published, and her patience and advice during the process. We thank Aziz Gökdemir for a brilliant job managing the publication process and we extend our thanks to Elizabeth Forsyth and David Anderson for their excellent editing, as well as to Nora Ridolfi for diligently overseeing the printing of the book. Thank you as well to Ellie Mendez and Alyssa Jethani for checking sources.

Joanna would like to thank Alan Gibson for sharing his deep knowledge and experience of the market systems framework, David Ferrand for suggesting we use the framework and his guidance in doing so, and Steve Rasmussen for his thoughtful and generous support. She also thanks Alyssa Jethani for taking on much of what needed to be done at the Aga Khan Foundation during the process of bringing this book together, for her high level of productivity, and for being a wonderful colleague. She is grateful to her family, especially Joakim, and her parents, for their consistent support throughout. In particular, she thanks her father, Doug Ledgerwood, for his guidance and advice during this project and always.

Julie is grateful for the encouragement and technical guidance from her colleagues at the International Finance Corporation, in particular Jean Philippe Prosper for his strong support and endorsement of this book to the World Bank publication committee; Tor Jansson for his numerous reviews of chapters; and Barbara Sloboda and David Crush for always finding a solution. She would also like to thank her many clients in Africa who have provided years of inspiration through their hard work and success in some of the world's frontier countries. Finally, Julie thanks the many friends who have supported her work on this book with everything from advice, shelter, and a friendly ear; and gives a special thanks to her family for keeping her close despite how far away she lives.

Candace has deep appreciation for several long-term colleagues who have done so much to cultivate and sustain her commitment to clients, including Paul Rippey, Monique Cohen, Kathleen Stack, Jeffrey Ashe, and Jennefer Sebstad. Seasoned professionals, they have inspired her with their intelligence, integrity, and passion. As ever, Candace is grateful to SEEP's Savings-led Financial Services Working Group for its high degree of collaboration; she would especially like to thank the authors of the SEEP publication, *Savings Groups at the Frontier*, from which she drew extensively in writing chapter 6.

Joanna Ledgerwood
Julie Earne
Candace Nelson

ABOUT THE AUTHORS

Ines Arevalo is a consultant to the Aga Khan Agency for Microfinance. She holds an MA in Development Economics (University of Sussex) and focuses on client research and social performance management.

Craig Churchill is the head of the International Labour Organization's Social Finance Programme, which supports the use of productive and protective financial services, particularly for excluded populations. He serves as the team leader of the Microinsurance Innovation Facility and the chair of the Microinsurance Network.

Daryl Collins is a Director at Bankable Frontier Associates, a niche consulting practice aimed at providing financial services to low-income people. She is also co-author of *Portfolios of the Poor*.

Julie Earne is a Senior Microfinance Specialist at the International Finance Corporation. She has worked extensively throughout Africa, investing in and enabling financial sector development in frontier countries for more than 15 years.

Mayada El-Zoghbi is head of CGAP's office in Paris. She manages CGAP's support to donors and investors as well as in the Middle East and North Africa Region. She holds a Master of International Affairs from Columbia University.

David Ferrand is Director of Financial Sector Deepening Kenya, a multidonor facility supporting market development. He holds a PhD from Durham University and has worked in the financial inclusion field for 20 years.

Barbara Gähwiler is a microfinance expert at GIZ in Tunisia and previously worked with CGAP's donors and investors team. She holds a Master of International Affairs from University of St. Gallen and Sciences Po, Paris.

Alan Gibson is a Director of the Springfield Centre. He has been influential in developing the "making markets work for the poor" (M4P) approach and in supporting its application in different spheres of development.

Susan Johnson is a Senior Lecturer in International Development at the University of Bath. She has extensive research experience in the microfinance field, in particular in impact assessment, gender, and the embeddedness of local financial markets in social relations.

Kate Lauer is a policy advisor to CGAP and a Senior Associate with Bankable Frontier Associates. She has a JD from New York University and has written and worked extensively on legal and policy issues related to financial inclusion.

Joanna Ledgerwood is Senior Advisor at the Aga Khan Foundation, leading its financial inclusion initiatives in Africa and Central and South Asia. She is the author of the *Microfinance Handbook* and *Transforming Microfinance Institutions* with Victoria White.

Joyce Lehman is an independent consultant focusing on financial inclusion. Previously Joyce was with the Bill & Melinda Gates Foundation, managing projects to support mobile payment platforms in Bangladesh and Pakistan.

Ignacio Mas, an independent consultant, was Deputy Director of the Financial Services for the Poor team at the Bill & Melinda Gates Foundation, and Business Strategy Director at Vodafone Group.

Peter McConaghy is a Financial Sector Development Analyst in the Middle East and North Africa Region at the World Bank, with a focus on expanding financial inclusion in postrevolutionary countries through policy reform, provider downscaling, and demand-side research.

Calvin Miller is Senior Officer and Agribusiness and Finance Group Leader in the AGS Division, Food and Agriculture Organization of the UN (FAO). He has extensive experience in agricultural and value chain finance and investment in developing countries.

Candace Nelson is a trainer, facilitator, researcher, and writer with 30 years of experience supporting microfinance, specifically financial education and Savings Groups, in Africa and Latin America. She is the editor of *Savings Groups at the Frontier*.

Geraldine O'Keeffe is the Chief Operating Officer of Software Group, an information technology company focused on the provision of solutions to the financial sector. She has over 12 years of experience working with technology for microfinance, primarily in Africa.

Stuart Rutherford is a microfinance practitioner and researcher. He is the founder of SafeSave, a Bangladeshi MFI, and cowrote two studies of how poor people manage money: *The Poor and Their Money* and *Portfolios of the Poor*.

Lisa Sherk is an independent consultant based in Amsterdam. She specializes in microfinance investment fund management, focusing on financial and social performance assessments of microfinance institutions globally.

Stefan Staschen is an economist specializing in regulation of inclusive financial sectors. He works as a consultant for CGAP, Bankable Frontier Associates, and others. He holds a PhD from the London School of Economics.

Joakim Vincze is a consultant specializing in sustainable use of technology for development, focusing on providing affordable broadband Internet to rural areas. He holds an engineering degree and an MBA from the University of Western Ontario.

ABBREVIATIONS

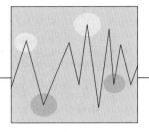

AFI	Alliance for Financial Inclusion
AKAM	Aga Khan Agency for Microfinance
ALM	asset-liability management
AML	anti-money-laundering
APR	annual percentage rate
ASCA	accumulating savings and credit association
ATM	automated teller machine
B2P	business-to-person
BCBS	Basel Committee on Banking Supervision
CAR	capital adequacy requirement
CBS	core banking system
CDD	consumer due diligence
CDO	collateralized debt obligation
CFT	combating the financing of terrorism
CGAP	Consultative Group to Assist the Poor
CLO	collateralized loan obligation
COSO	Committee of Sponsoring Organizations of the Treadway Commission
DFI	development finance institution
EFT	electronic fund transfer
EIR	effective interest rate
FAS	Financial Access Survey, IMF
FATF	Financial Action Task Force
FinDex	Global Financial Inclusion database
FIU	financial intelligence unit
FSD Kenya	Financial Sector Development Kenya
FSP	financial service provider
G2P	government-to-person
GDP	gross domestic product
GNI	gross national income
GPRS	general packet radio service
GSM	Global System for Mobile
IAIS	International Association of Insurance Supervisors

ID	identification	PSP	payment service provider
IMF	International Monetary Fund	RCT	randomized control trial
IPO	initial public offering	RIA	regulatory impact assessment
IT	information technology	ROSCA	rotating savings and credit association
IVR	interactive voice response		
KfW	Kreditanstalt für Wiederaufbau	RTGS	real-time gross settlement
KYC	Know Your Customer	SaaS	software as a service
MDB	multilateral development bank	SACCO	savings and credit cooperative
MDI	microfinance deposit-taking institution	SAR	Special Administrative Region
		SAVIX	Savings Groups Information Exchange
Me2Me	me-to-me (payment)		
MFI	microfinance institution	SEEP	Small Enterprise Education and Promotion
MFRS	Microfinance Financial Reporting Standards		
		SG	Savings Group
MII	microfinance investment intermediary	SHG	Self-Help Group
		SIM	subscriber identity module
MIS	management information system	SMART	specific, measurable, achievable, realistic, and time-bound
MIV	microfinance investment vehicle		
MIX	Microfinance Information eXchange	SMS	short messaging service
		SPV	special purpose vehicle
MNO	mobile network operator	SRI	socially responsible investing
NBFI	non-bank financial institution	STK	SIM Tool Kit
NGO	nongovernmental organization	SWIFT	Society for Worldwide Interbank Financial Telecommunication
P2B	person-to-business		
P2P	person-to-person	TCP	transmission control protocol
PAT	poverty assessment tool	USAID	U.S. Agency for International Development
PCG	partial credit guarantee		
PIN	personal identification number	USSD	unstructured supplementary services data
POS	point-of-sale	VPN	virtual private network
PPI	Progress out of Poverty Index	WSBI	World Savings Banks Institute
PRA	participatory rapid assessment	WOCCU	World Council of Credit Unions

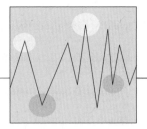

Introduction

Microfinance in 2013

It has been 15 years since the original *Microfinance Handbook* (Ledgerwood 1998) was written, and much has changed since then. Microfinance is now a household term with frequent articles in the media about its growth, innovation, and impact. The industry has grown exponentially, in terms of both the number of clients as well as the number and type of providers and products.[1] The focus is no longer only on credit for investment in microenterprises: Today there is broad awareness that poor people have many and diverse financial service needs, which are typically met by a variety of providers through multiple financial services. We know this because data have much improved in the past 15 years,[2] allowing us to better understand barriers to access and use, and we are beginning to examine impact.[3]

Over the years, the discourse has shifted from "microcredit" to "microfinance,"[4] and now widespread concern for "financial inclusion"[5] is directing attention to the broader "financial eco-system" and how to make financial markets work better for the poor. For example, a recent CGAP Focus Note looks at the financial ecosystem within the context of the supply of financial services: "Different products present different risks and delivery challenges, and it is unlikely that a single class of service providers will effectively provide all the products poor people need. A key challenge is how to create the broader interconnected ecosystem of market actors and infrastructure needed for safe and efficient product delivery to the poor" (Ehrbeck et al. 2012, p. 1).

To this end, policy makers have begun to address financial inclusion in their economic agendas with the belief that access to financial services improves the ability of consumers to access markets, which contributes to monetizing the values of products and services, enables risk pooling, and allows value storage, thus affecting economic growth and the overall stability of the system.

Increasingly, best practice in microfinance is *responsible finance*, defined as the delivery of retail financial services in a transparent, inclusive, and equitable fashion (BMZ, CGAP, and IFC 2011). Consumer protection and financial capability are now seen as important policy objectives, particularly in a context of new providers, more sophisticated products, and technology-enabled delivery channels. Recent media attention to the significant profits made through initial public offerings of microfinance banks[6] have highlighted the need for transparent pricing and appropriate interest rates.

Unlike 15 years ago, funding for microfinance today is no longer the purview of donors alone. As of 2011 more than 100 microfinance investment vehicles were managing close to US$7 billion (Symbiotics 2011), making private and quasi-private sector capital readily available. With the recognition that grant funding crowds out the private sector, responsible donors have shifted from providing funds for loan capital and operating subsidies to more of a facilitation role supporting the development of enabling environments, provision of information, and financial infrastructure.

Although significant investments have been made to reform regulatory systems to accommodate microfinance and transform microfinance institutions (MFIs) into regulated institutions complete with return-seeking investors, relatively few MFIs can absorb a significant amount of capital. "However, the pool of investment-ready MFIs is small and is not expanding at the speed of the supply of equity investment. Indeed, 52 percent of all foreign debt is channelled to only 25 MFIs, out of a total of 524 MFIs that receive foreign debt finance. At the country level, foreign investment is, to a large degree, still focused on a small number of countries in LAC and ECA[7] with only moderate levels of financial exclusion" (Reille et al. 2011, p. 10). Given the concentration of investment in relatively few institutions, the expected increase in financial inclusion resulting from the gradual substitution of donor funding with private sector capital has yet to happen. The majority of poor people remain outside the mainstream financial sector, and many MFIs continue to depend on subsidies.

Looking forward, it appears likely that technology will enable customer touch points to proliferate among nontraditional service providers. The technology drivers of financial inclusion will come from innovations in mobile money, biometric identity systems, smart phones, and wireless broadband Internet access. At the same time, however, much remains to be learned to effectively increase outreach in a substantial way, including, for example, developing appropriate regulatory frameworks for branchless banking models (Alexandre 2010). Further, it is vitally important to better understand the social dimensions of how households manage financial resources, particularly in the informal sector, and the role of technology to work within these social dynamics (Johnson 2012).

Thus, the well-documented and widely applauded achievements of microfinance are increasingly coupled with recognition of its limitations and the need to take a more holistic view. Concerns include the following:

- *Outreach*—In many countries outreach remains a small percentage of the population; only 41 percent of adults in developing economies report having an account at a formal financial institution,[8] 8 percent report having originated a new loan from a formal financial institution in the past 12 months, and 2 percent report having personally paid for health insurance (Demirgüç-Kunt and Klapper 2012); more than half the world's adult population does not use formal or semiformal services, nearly all of whom live in Africa, Asia, and Latin America (Chaia et al. 2009).

- *Sustainability*—Although figures are not precise, many microfinance operations continue to receive subsidies; commercial funding is highly concentrated in Latin America and Eastern Europe, while most of the world's poor (less than US$2/day) live in Asia and Africa (Wiesner and Quien 2010). Beyond direct microfinance operations, many other activities important in the microfinance system (for example, training, product development, and technical advice) are often subsidized.

- *Impact*—Recent research based on randomized controlled trials (RCTs) has found the impact of microcredit to be mixed. RCTs have shown that increases in consumption and business investment do not always correlate with measures of poverty reduction (O'Dell 2010). Furthermore, the distribution of gains is uneven. The broader effect of microfinance on poverty is limited by low levels of usage and persistent barriers to inclusion (Johnson and Arnold 2011).

At the heart of these concerns over the efficacy of microfinance is a better understanding of how the poor need and use financial services. Research (Collins et al. 2009; Demirgüç-Kunt and Klapper 2012) has revealed that the poor manage their financial lives with complex strategies that utilize multiple forms of savings, lending, and bartering from a mix of formal and informal providers. Achieving financial inclusion for the poor thus cannot rely on MFIs alone; rather, it requires improving the quality and frequency of services from a multitude of provider types and fully understanding client behavior and how it affects financial service needs.

Measuring Progress

At the time of the original *Handbook,* a broadly accepted assumption was that "increased access" and a "willingness to pay" provided a good proxy for impact.[9] Although today we might challenge this assumption, and are thus beginning to invest much more in assessing impact, if we just look at access figures, how has microfinance fared? Despite several decades of significant investments in the sector, access to or usage of formal financial services remains low, particularly in Sub-Saharan Africa (SSA) (see figure I.1). Data from the World Bank Global Findex database (Demirgüç-Kunt and Klapper 2012) shows that in SSA only 13 percent of individuals aged 15 years and older saved at a financial institution in the last 12 months, and only 5 percent received a loan from a financial institution. Such low usage does not, however, indicate weak demand; at the same time, 19 percent saved in a savings club, and 40 percent received a loan from family or friends in the past year. In South Asia figures are similar, with 11 percent saving in a financial institution in the last 12 months and 9 percent receiving a loan from a financial institution.[10] And yet the massively popular Self-Help Group movement in India counted 97 million households affected by March 31, 2010.[11] But even this indication of participation is weak when compared to the *potential* market of the 900 million households in India that live on less than US$2 a day (Chen et al. 2010).

One reason for low outreach is the traditional microfinance business model itself, which is based on generating revenue from primarily productive loans and other fee-based services to cover costs. Yet in microfinance, costs are high, and the revenue base is relatively low. This is especially true for the rural poor whose limited investment opportunities and capacity for debt translate into lower revenue for MFIs and banks who may lack the incentives, information, and sometimes ability to mitigate perceived risks of operating beyond urban markets or with very poor clients. Thus it is important to focus on lowering costs both for institutions to provide services and for clients to use them. And although technology will continue to push this frontier, access figures alone may offer a misleading view

Figure I.1 Financial Access Strands[a] — Country Comparisons (July 2012)

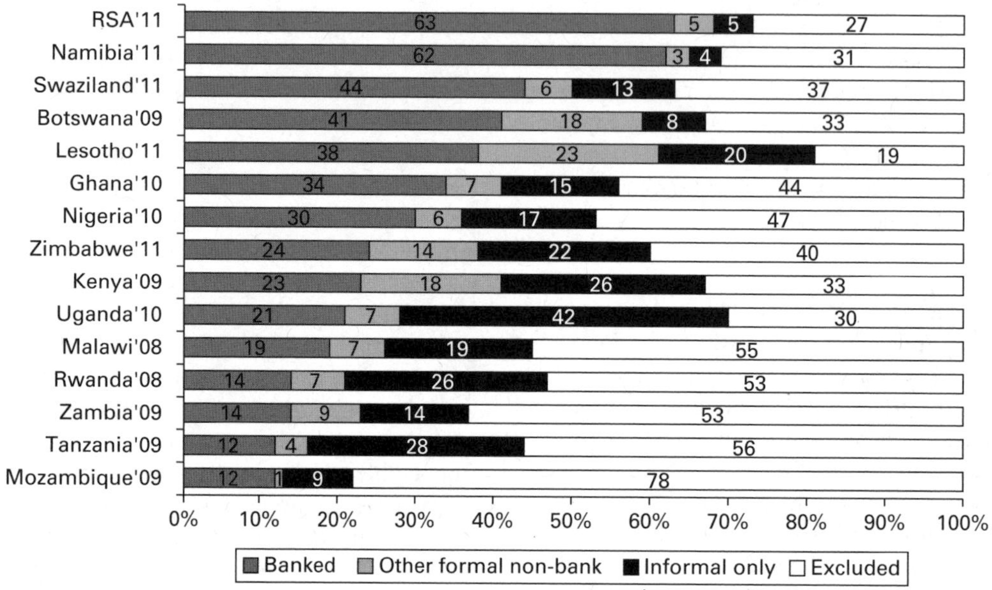

Country	Banked	Other formal non-bank	Informal only	Excluded
RSA'11	63	5	5	27
Namibia'11	62	3	4	31
Swaziland'11	44	6	13	37
Botswana'09	41	18	8	33
Lesotho'11	38	23	20	19
Ghana'10	34	7	15	44
Nigeria'10	30	6	17	47
Zimbabwe'11	24	14	22	40
Kenya'09	23	18	26	33
Uganda'10	21	7	42	30
Malawi'08	19	7	19	55
Rwanda'08	14	7	26	53
Zambia'09	14	9	14	53
Tanzania'09	12	4	28	56
Mozambique'09	12	1	9	78

Source: FinMark Trust.

Note: a. The formal sector is divided into a "banked" segment (the percentage of adults with a bank account), and a formal "other" segment (the percentage of the adult population with a formal financial product, such as insurance or a microfinance loan, but no bank account). Together, these two groups are defined as formally included. The informal sector comprises all the organizations that provide financial services but are not legally registered to do this business, for example, savings clubs, burial societies, and money-lenders. The informally serviced category in the access strand represents the percentage of adults with an informal product but with no bank account or a product from another formal financial institution. It is necessary to add the informal segment to the formally included segment to derive the percentage of the adult population that is financially served. Anyone who is not financially served is financially excluded, which means they are not using financial products (formal or informal) to manage their financial lives; for example, they may simply be using cash. See www.finscope.co.za.

of benefits; increased access and more choice do not automatically translate into effective client use. For example, the major growth in access for saving services through the Mzansi account in South Africa disguised a large number of dormant accounts, opened but often unused, because clients either found better options for their needs or were too poor to utilize the account.[12] The path from uptake (that is, opening an account) to usage is still an uncharted course.

Growth in access, especially if accompanied by access to more diverse services, may require clients with greater financial capabilities to ensure effective usage and benefits. As in any market, if

improvement in access does not develop in a competitive manner, benefits may be restricted. Clients with limited information and/or choices may not be able to exert competitive pressure on providers to improve services.

Providers and other stakeholders need to take a more proactive approach that recognizes the diversity of barriers to access, the heterogeneity of consumers, and the variety of financial service needs among various lower income segments and underserved or excluded groups. Looking for major impact from a single product or institution type risks overlooking the inherent complexity of livelihoods and financial service needs (see box I.1).

Box I.1 A Market This Big Needs Many Types of Providers

Back in 1982, when Citi made its first loan to a nongovernmental organization (NGO), the microfinance world was much simpler. There were the few global networks, and we were still using the term "microcredit." It was a much more focused, smaller community. The industry has grown tremendously since then. From a few million clients in the 1980s, microfinance now reaches more than 190 million families. We have seen tremendous growth in the size of microfinance organizations and the scale of their operations, but we are also seeing that there is a price for growing too fast—in any industry. You can grow only so fast before burning out the staff, or you cannot bring on well-trained new staff to keep up with your growth.

Most of this growth has come from organizations offering only one or two credit products. The demand, the need, and perhaps the model lent itself to consistent growth because it stayed very focused. However, fast growth of organizations using similar models and strategies in the same locations has led, in some cases, to multiple loans to the same borrower and a breakdown of lending discipline. We see these issues in Andhra Pradesh in India where institutions' client-base overlaps are putting a lot of pressure on repayments.

How do you provide financial access to the vast majority of the population? It will take more than NGOs and commercial banks—we need cooperatives, credit unions, and postal savings banks. We need cell phone companies that can make loan payments. We see opportunities for many different services and types of providers.

In most of the countries where we work, anywhere from 60 to 80 percent of the population is unbanked. This is too big a segment to cover with just one or two approaches and institutional forms. We have the ultra-poor and displaced people at one end of the scale, and the very economically active people who might even be employed on the other end. Their needs are different.

I get concerned with some of the arguments that take place in microfinance today. It seems like there is an underlying assumption that there is only one type of microfinance client and that client should be served by only one type of institution—when the opposite is true. There are many different client segments in microfinance, and MFIs would do better to focus on each segment to develop the best business models to serve those clients.

In the next few years, the innovation needs to be in designing products that fit who clients are and what they want to become; we get there by getting to know the clients, their needs, their cash flows and their aspirations much better.

Within this microfinance ecosystem, we need some institutions to work with the very difficult-to-reach and vulnerable communities, delivering social output of a very high calibre, and they cannot then be devoted just to achieving scale and even full sustainability. Their objective may never be to become a finance company, yet they may use financial tools as one of the enablers toward progress out of poverty along with health and education training.

Even as one part of microfinance becomes more commercial, we have to keep thinking about the many vulnerable, underserved, complicated communities that mainstream microfinance may not yet be able to reach.

Source: Bob Annibale of Citibank, writing in Reed (2011). Reprinted with permission.

Redefining Objectives

At the time of writing the original *Handbook,* the predominant microfinance model was an NGO MFI providing credit to microentrepreneurs for investment in microenterprises. This model was largely based on the belief that access to credit for productive investment would support entrepreneurship and economic development, empower women, and alleviate poverty by generating higher incomes and employment. However, increasing evidence of the impact of microfinance, particularly microcredit, indicates that it has some effect on the expansion of business and increased profits, very little effect on women's empowerment, and virtually no effect on poverty alleviation (O'Dell 2010).

Fifteen years later, the shift to financially inclusive systems, based in part on better understanding impact, appropriately broadens the objectives beyond economic development and poverty alleviation to include the ability of poor women and men to better manage risks, smooth income, invest in productive activities, and build assets. These broader objectives demand more of stakeholders in terms of better understanding clients and, in turn, delivering an improved value

proposition (see box I.2). "While the language changed with insights and expanded horizons, the underlying fundamental idea has remained the same: Help poor families in the informal economy realize their economic potential and give them the financial services means to manage their lives that most of us in the North take for granted" (Ehrbeck 2012).

Greater financial inclusion thus requires addressing constraints and taking advantage of opportunities in the financial ecosystem. Stakeholders are now beginning to focus on the diversity of clients (geography, income levels, livelihoods, gender, life-cycle) and their needs (growth, cash management, risk mitigation), as well as the wide range of financial services (credit, savings, payments, insurance), financial service providers (informal, MFIs, cooperatives, banks, insurance companies), and delivery channels (branches, agents, mobile phones) to meet these needs. They are paying attention to the effectiveness (social performance/impact, transparency, and client protection) of financial services as well as the knowledge and skills that clients need to use them (financial capabilities); the rules that guide financial markets (regulations, standards, norms); the financial infrastructure (payment

Box I.2 Latest Findings from Randomized Evaluations of Microfinance

"The overall message from this body of work is that poor people face various limits, and their ability to capitalize on opportunities varies greatly. ... [N]ot all borrowers want to grow a business. The variable results seen can be as much a function of borrower intent as borrower ability. A one-size-fits-all product will not bring benefit to the borrowers or profit to the providers. Instead, the microfinance industry needs to continue to mature in ways that allow it to view poor customers as individuals. Some of those individuals will leverage financial services to smooth consumption; some to manage risk; some to make investments they have the skill and resources to profit from; some will do all of the above. With a view of serving all of these needs, microfinance providers may evolve a new generation of improved services and products that reliably and flexibly help poor people."

Source: Bauchet et al. 2011.

systems and credit bureaus) required to support well-functioning markets; and the information services necessary to inform all stakeholders to better improve the system. This book attempts to address all of these issues with the objective to promote financially inclusive ecosystems that work better for the poor.

About This Book

Given the importance of both understanding and appreciating the complexities of financial services for the poor, the *New Microfinance Handbook* takes a different approach from its predecessor. In contrast to the "institutional" perspective (supply side) of the original *Handbook*, this book considers first and foremost clients and their needs (demand side) and how the market system can work better to meet these needs. It also attempts to address the rules and supporting functions required for financial markets to work well and serve ever greater numbers of poor consumers. The result is a book that is less of a "how-to" guide but rather a description of the financial market system and the functions within it and how they work, or do not work, in serving the needs of the poor. The objective is to provide a strategic guide to help assess the varied financial service needs of poor people, and to then propose how a diversified financial sector can address these needs in an accessible and beneficial manner. Ultimately it is hoped the book will contribute to greater access to and usage of financial products and services that genuinely meet the many needs of the poor through various sustainable market-based financial service providers.

The *New Microfinance Handbook* provides a primer on financial services for the poor. It is written for a wide audience, including practitioners, facilitators, policy makers, regulators, investors, and donors working to improve the financial system, but who are relatively new to the sector. It will also be useful for telecommunication companies and other support service providers, students and academics, and consultants and trainers.

Although this book is in part an update of the original *Handbook,* the growth of the sector and the complexity of the financial market system have led to a perspective much broader than the previous "financial and institutional perspective." As a result, additional chapters have been added to address issues more relevant than when the original *Handbook* was written. To reflect this complexity, we invited a number of experts to write many of the new chapters. In addition, given that this book does not go into as much detail as the previous book did, a list of key resources at the end of each chapter provides readers additional information on specific topics. Finally, although the title still uses the term microfinance, the book very much addresses the wider financial ecosystem, moving beyond the traditional meaning of microfinance to inclusive financial systems.

Book Structure and Content

The *New Microfinance Handbook* loosely follows the framework of the original *Handbook* and is organized into five parts:

Part I: Understanding Demand and the Financial Ecosystem

Part II: Financial Service Providers

Part III: Financial Services and Delivery Channels

Part IV: Institutional Management for Scale and Sustainability

Part V: Supporting Financial Inclusion

Part I—Understanding Demand and the Financial Ecosystem updates Part I of the original *Handbook* and addresses big picture issues—the financial landscape, clients, and strategies to achieve and measure financial inclusion. Given the changing landscape of the financial services sector, the book opens with *Chapter 1—The*

Evolving Financial Landscape, written by Joanna Ledgerwood and Alan Gibson, outlining three key influences in financial services for the poor that are greatly affecting the way the sector is moving: a renewed focus on clients, acknowledgment of the wider financial ecosystem, and the potential of technology. *Chapter 2—Clients* builds on the centrality of clients and financial management. Drawing from *Portfolios of the Poor* (Collins et al. 2009), authors Stuart Rutherford, Daryl Collins, and Susan Johnson examine the financial service needs of poor people and how these needs are met. *Chapter 3—The Role of Government and Industry in Financial Inclusion,* written by Stefan Staschen and Candace Nelson, addresses how key players promote financial inclusion, from the role of government as policy maker and legislator, to industry as it warms to responsible finance through self-regulation and the need for coordination. *Chapter 4—The Role of Donors in Financial Inclusion,* written by Mayada El-Zogbhi and Barbara Gähwiler, focuses on the changing role of donors in microfinance and proposes ways to facilitate the market to work better for the poor. Given that financial inclusion is on the agenda of many policy makers, much attention has recently been invested in measuring it and assessing the impact of using financial services. Supply and demand-side studies, impact assessment, and other rigorous research are addressed by Joanna Ledgerwood in *Chapter 5—Measuring Financial Inclusion and Assessing Impact.*

Part II—Financial Service Providers updates the original chapter 4 (*The Institution*), adding an additional chapter to acknowledge the numerous and varied providers in the informal sector. *Chapter 6—Community-Based Providers,* written by Candace Nelson, describes indigenous informal providers, for example, moneylenders, deposit collectors, rotating savings and credit associations and mutual aid groups such as burial societies, and other providers such as Self-Help Groups and Savings Groups that are facilitated by external agencies. *Chapter 7—Institutional Providers,* written by Joanna Ledgerwood, describes financial service providers that are more formal in nature. This grouping includes a wide variation of provider types, differing in the services they provide as well as their ownership structures, regulatory status, geographic focus, target markets, and objectives, but are similar in that they have a more concrete structure than providers in the informal sector and are thus referred to as institutions.

Parts I and II are the least technical parts of the handbook; they require no formal background in microfinance or financial theory. They will be of most interest to donors, policy makers, students, and those interested in understanding financial inclusion and the actors involved.

Part III—Financial Services and Delivery Channels expands on the original *Handbook*'s discussion of savings and credit with new chapters on agricultural finance, insurance, and payment services. It also addresses the many alternative channels that are beginning to show promise and includes a thought provoking chapter on supporting the poor through financial planning tools. *Chapter 8—Savings Services,* written by Joanna Ledgerwood, considers the various savings products demanded by the poor and touches on the institutional capacity required to offer deposit services. *Chapter 9—Credit,* written by Joanna Ledgerwood and Julie Earne, looks at pricing loans and types of credit products including traditional working capital and fixed asset loans, as well as newer products such as housing loans and leasing. *Chapter 10—Agricultural Finance,* written by Calvin Miller, acknowledges the substantial need for financial services for people working in the agricultural sector (the vast majority of the poor) and the ways in which financial products and delivery channels cater to meet these needs. Although in the original *Handbook* insurance was only briefly mentioned, in this edition, given the growing importance of microinsurance in financial inclusion and acknowledgment of the risk management needs of poor women and men, *Chapter 11—Insurance*, written by Craig Churchill, looks at the demand for micro-insurance, product characteristics, and delivery mechanisms. *Chapter 12—Payment Services and Delivery Channels*, written by Joyce Lehman and Joanna Ledgerwood, describes transaction services such as money transfers and payments as products in and of themselves, as well as the various channels for delivering financial services. In particular, this chapter considers the different ways in which clients access services through branchless touch points and the significant role played by agent networks. *Chapter 13—Beyond Products*, written by Ignacio Mas, proposes the delivery of financial products as an integrated customer experience through mobile phones.

Part III will be of most interest to practitioners who are developing, modifying, or refining their financial products, as well as donors or consultants who are evaluating financial services for the poor and want to better understand financial products and services and ways to deliver them.

Part IV—Institutional Management for Scale and Sustainability includes two chapters and provides an update of the original chapters on MFI management. *Chapter 14—Monitoring and Managing Financial and Social Performance*, written by Joanna Ledgerwood, Geraldine O'Keeffe, and Ines Arevalo, addresses core banking systems and financial and social performance management. *Chapter 15—Governance and Managing Operations*, written by Peter McConaghy, looks at various facets of institutional providers including governance, human resource management, product management, and risk management. Part IV is more technical than previous parts of the *Handbook*. Although specific institutional performance is somewhat less important given the client and financial system focus of this book, Part IV is included for the benefit of practitioners and/or funders interested in the operations and performance of institutions providing financial services to the poor.

Part V—Supporting Financial Inclusion is new and includes four chapters that focus on the roles and functions of various stakeholders supporting and promoting the overall financial ecosystem. *Chapter 16—Funding*, written by Julie Earne and Lisa Sherk, considers the significant role investors play in providing capital to financial service providers. Given the growth in the number and diversity of providers, *Chapter 17—Regulation*, written by Kate Lauer and Stefan Staschen, addresses the laws and regulatory frameworks in place to support proper oversight and safety of the financial market system and the various players. *Chapter 18—Infrastructure*, written by Geraldine O'Keeffe, Julie Earne, Joakim Vincze, and Peter McConaghy, considers the supporting functions required for well-functioning financial markets such as credit bureaus, deposit insurance, clearing and settlement systems, and unique identification systems. Outsourced services such as "software as a service," training, and security are also described. *Chapter 19—Building Inclusive Financial Markets*, written by David Ferrand, uses the market system framework to discuss the roles development agencies can and should play to contribute to financial systems that work more effectively for the poor, highlighting the different functions of market actors (service providers with ongoing roles) and those facilitating the market (donors and other development agencies with a temporary role).

Part V will be of most interest to those either providing or supporting the development of mesolevel functions in the financial ecosystem.

Notes

1. Total numbers are difficult to find, but David Roodman in "Due Diligence—An Impertinent Enquiry into Microfinance" (2011, p. 67) estimates there were close to 180 million loans outstanding and 1.3 billion savings accounts at "alternative financial institutions" in 2000 and "microfinance has grown a lot since then."

2. For example, national-level FinMark Trust's FinScope surveys, www.finmark.org.za, and Global Findex databases, http://data.worldbank.org/data-catalog/financial_inclusion.

3. For example, see Financial Access Initiative (FAI), http://financialaccess.org; Abdul Latif Jameel Poverty Action Lab (J-Pal), http://www.povertyactionlab.org/about-j-pal; and Innovations for Poverty Action (IPA), http://poverty-action.org.

4. Microfinance as defined by CGAP in CGAP Occasional Paper 15, "The New Moneylenders: Are the Poor Being Exploited by High Microcredit Interest Rates?" (Rosenberg et al. 2009), "usually refers to the provision of financial services to poor and low-income clients who have little or no access to conventional banks. The term is often used in a more specific sense, referring to institutions that use new techniques developed over the past 30 years to deliver microcredit—tiny loans—to informal microentrepreneurs. The range of services can include not only microcredit but also savings, insurance, and money transfers."

5. The ACCION Center for Financial Inclusion defines financial inclusion as "Full financial inclusion is a state in which all people who can use them have access to a full suite of quality financial services, provided at affordable prices in a convenient manner, and with dignity for the clients. Financial services are delivered by a range of providers, most of them private, and reach everyone who can use them, including disabled, poor and rural populations" (www.centerforfinancialinclusion.org).

6. See http://www.economist.com/node/11376809 for information on the Compartamos Banco IPO.

7. Latin America and the Caribbean (LAC) and Europe Central Asia (ECA).

8. Defined as "a bank, credit union, cooperative, post office, or microfinance institution" (Demirgüç-Kunt and Klapper 2012).

9. In chapter 2 of the *Microfinance Handbook* (Ledgerwood 1998, p. 49) Tom Dichter wrote, "Doing impact analysis well (and therefore credibly) can be difficult and expensive. Addressing this dilemma, there is a school of thinking that advocates certain 'proxies' for impact. Otero and Rhyne have summarized recent microfinance history by saying that there has been an important shift from focusing on the individual firm or client of financial services to focusing on the institutions providing services. This financial systems approach 'necessarily relaxes its attention to "impact" in terms of measurable enterprise growth and focuses instead on measures of increased access to financial services' (Otero and Rhyne 1994)."

10. Account at a formal financial institution denotes the percentage of respondents with an account (self or together with someone else) at a bank, credit union, another financial institution (for example, cooperative or microfinance institution), or the post office (if applicable) including respondents who reported having a debit card (Demirgüç-Kunt and Klapper 2012).

11. www.shgportal.com.

12. E-mail exchange with Gerhard Coetzee, April 4, 2012, and Bankable Frontiers Associates (2009).

References

Alexandre, Claire. 2010. "Policymakers Create Room for Experimentation with Banking beyond Branches." Global Savings Forum, Bill & Melinda Gates Foundation, Seattle, WA, November.

Bankable Frontier Associates. 2009. "The Mzansi Bank Account Initiative in South Africa, Final Report." Commissioned by FinMark Trust. Somerville, MA, March.

Bauchet, Jonathan, Cristobal Marshall, Laura Starita, Jeanette Thomas, and Anna Yalouris. 2011. "Latest Findings from Randomized Evaluations of Microfinance." Access to Finance Forum, Reports by CGAP and Its Partners No. 2. CGAP, Washington, DC, December.

BMZ, CGAP, and IFC. 2011. "Advancing Responsible Finance for Greater Development

Impact: A Stock-Taking of Strategies and Approaches among Development Agencies and Development Finance Institutions." Consultation draft, Responsible Finance Forum, Bonn and Washington, DC.

Chaia, Alberto, Aparna Dalal, Tony Goland, Maria Jose Gonzalez, Jonathan Morduch, and Robert Schiff. 2009. "Half the World Is Unbanked." Financial Access Initiative Framing Note. Financial Access Initiative, New York.

Chen, Gregory, Stephen Rasmussen, Xavier Reille, and Daniel Rozas. 2010. "Indian Microfinance Goes Public: The SKS Initial Public Offering." CGAP Focus Note 65, CGAP, Washington, DC, September.

Collins, Daryl, Jonathan Morduch, Stuart Rutherford, and Orlanda Ruthven. 2009. *Portfolios of the Poor: How the World's Poor Live on $2 a Day*. Princeton, NJ: Princeton University Press.

Demirgüç-Kunt, Aslı, Thorsten Beck, and Patrick Honohan Beck. 2007. "Finance for All? Policies and Pitfalls in Expanding Access." Policy Research Report, World Bank, Washington, DC.

Demirgüç-Kunt, Aslı, and Leora Klapper. 2012. "Measuring Financial Inclusion: The Global Findex." Policy Research Working Paper 6025, World Bank, Washington, DC.

Ehrbeck, Tilman. 2012. "More than Semantics: The Evolution from 'Microcredit' to 'Financial Inclusion.' CGAP Blog, May 16.

Ehrbeck, Tilman, Mark Pickens, and Michael Tarazi. 2012. "Financially Inclusive Ecosystems: The Roles of Government Today." Focus Note 76, CGAP, Washington, DC, February.

Johnson, Susan. 2012. "What Does the Rapid Uptake of Mobile Money Transfer in Kenya Really Mean For Financial Inclusion?" CGAP, Washington, DC.

Johnson, Susan, and Steven Arnold. 2011. "Financial Exclusion in Kenya: Examining the Changing Picture 2006–2009." In *Financial Inclusion in Kenya: Survey Results and Analysis from FinAccess 2009,* ed. Steven Arnold et al., chapter 5. Nairobi: FSD Kenya and Central Bank of Kenya.

Ledgerwood, Joanna. 1998. *Microfinance Handbook: An Institutional and Financial Perspective.* Washington, DC: World Bank.

O'Dell, Kathleen. 2010 "Measuring the Impact of Microfinance: Taking Another Look." Grameen Foundation, Washington, DC.

Reed, Larry R. 2011. "The State of the Microcredit Summit Report 2011." Microcredit Summit Campaign, Washington, DC.

Reille, Xavier, Sarah Forster, and Daniel Rozas. 2011. "Foreign Capital Investment in Microfinance: Reassessing Financial and Social Returns." Focus Note 71, CGAP, Washington, DC, May.

Roodman, David. 2011. "Due Diligence—An Impertinent Enquiry into Microfinance." Center for Global Development, Washington, DC, December.

Rosenberg, Rich, Adrian Gonzalez, and Sushma Narain. 2009. "The New Moneylenders: Are the Poor Being Exploited by High Microcredit Interest Rates?" Occasional Paper 15, CGAP, Washington, DC, February.

Symbiotics. 2011. "Symbiotics 2011 MIV Survey Report: Market Data & Peer Group Analysis." Symbiotics, Geneva, August.

Wiesner, Sophie, and David Quien. 2010. "Can 'Bad' Microfinance Practices Be the Consequence of Too Much Funding Chasing Too Few Microfinance Institutions?" Discussion paper I no. 2. ADA, Luxembourg, December.

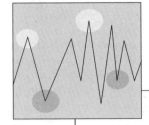

PART I

UNDERSTANDING DEMAND AND THE FINANCIAL ECOSYSTEM

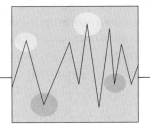

CHAPTER 1

The Evolving Financial Landscape

Joanna Ledgerwood and Alan Gibson

Historically, the promise of poverty alleviation through microcredit was tied primarily to one product—the productive loan invested in a micro-enterprise—delivered primarily by one type of provider—a microfinance institution (MFI). Yet reality belies the premise of this model: clients do not always use loans for productive purposes; they have either limited capacity to use investment credit or more pressing needs for products that support consumption or income smoothing. Today, there is broad recognition that access to capital is only one of the inputs required for economic development and poverty alleviation. Furthermore, there is wide acknowledgment that the poor, like anyone, require and use a variety of financial services for a variety of purposes. And some of these services work better than others, for reasons we are just beginning to understand.

Since the original *Microfinance Handbook* was written, the field of microfinance has changed substantially, particularly in the last few years.

Many events have influenced the landscape for financial services for the poor, but three significant "big picture" influences warrant discussion and are the subject of this opening chapter.

The first has been a shift from a narrow focus on the institution and its performance to a much broader focus on clients—understanding their behavior, financial service needs, and how various providers can better meet these needs. This shift has been brought on by the recognition—supported by significantly better data and more robust research—that outreach and, perhaps more important, impact have not been as expected. This is also the result of a widening view of microfinance. No longer limited to investing in microenterprises, microfinance now encompasses all financial services and how to provide them in a way that improves the quality of life of poor women and men.

The second important shift, which greatly influences this book, has been from a narrow supply-led view to a broader focus on the financial ecosystem. In addition to a renewed focus on consumers (demand), proponents of the "systems" approach acknowledge the variety of providers and services, including the substantial role of the informal sector. They also acknowledge the need for effective rules that govern the system and supporting functions such as credit bureaus or payment systems. The result has been a much more holistic view of the sector and a more coordinated effort by government and industry to focus on increasing financial inclusion and, ultimately, making markets work better for the poor.

The third shift has been the massive opportunity to expand outreach through new business models based on branchless banking using technology and agent networks. However, while the opportunity seems vast, to date only a few branchless banking applications have reached significant scale. At the time of writing, this area of tremendous promise requires a lot more work and testing to understand and determine ways to take advantage of the opportunities that technology presents.

This chapter considers each of these influences and places the new landscape in context. It will be of interest to readers seeking to understand some of the major influences in microfinance today. Each of the topics is introduced here and elaborated in more detail in various chapters that follow.

Focus on Clients

Almost everywhere, people involved in microfinance are talking about clients.[1] As a result, the language of microfinance is changing. Initially *microcredit* became *microfinance* with the recognition of the need for savings services; today policy makers and industry players use terms like *inclusive finance, access to finance, financial ecosystems,* and *financial inclusion* (see box 1.1).[2]

Focusing on clients is a welcome and necessary shift. However, the end game cannot simply be to develop new products or make adjustments within institutions; an institutional response alone is not enough. We need to understand consumer behavior and how it influences financial service needs and use. While the ultimate solution may be a better product or service, an easier way to access an account, or a lower-cost delivery option, to get there we need to appreciate the nuances and contextual factors that affect how poor women and men behave and which financial services are of most benefit to them, for what purpose, and why. For example, market research conducted with MFI clients in Bolivia indicates that clients identify respect as their greatest priority; product attributes are important, but they are not the most important consideration (Perdomo 2008).[3] Clients want to preserve their dignity when interacting with a financial institution, and they want to borrow without fear or humiliation. To accomplish these goals, they need to understand the services they use and the contracts they sign, and providers need to value and invest in customer service. The solution is unlikely to be simply new or more products.

Understanding how consumer behavior translates into financial service needs requires understanding the uniqueness and heterogeneity of clients and how life-cycle events, livelihoods, geography, income levels, and gender influence their behavior. The following section discusses the characteristics that define and influence client behavior and financial service needs, while chapter 2 provides an overview of how clients use financial services based on findings from *Portfolios of the Poor.*[4]

Age, Life-Cycle, and Family Structure

Financial needs and vulnerabilities change as people move through the life-cycle—from dependence on family to independence and from school to work, marriage, family responsibilities, and retirement. Sons migrate in search

Box 1.1 From Microfinance to Financial Inclusion

Financial inclusion is a multidimensional, pro-client concept, encompassing increased access, better products and services, better-informed and -equipped consumers, and effective use of products and services. Putting this concept into practice requires more than institutional expansion and portfolio growth, goals that drove early development of the microfinance industry, when the original *Handbook* was written. Balancing clients' interests and providers' viability, financial inclusion incorporates effective policies, legislation, industry and consumer protection standards, and financial capability.

Several developments have converged to refocus thinking about best practice in financial services for the poor. Commercialization of microfinance has raised concerns about mission drift, eliciting calls for paying attention to social performance and the "double bottom line," which relies on strong financial performance to fulfill a social mission. Further concerns have emerged with regard to high interest rates and private gains from public offerings of MFI shares and the concentration of investments in a small number of countries and institutions. Microfinance, as the "new asset class," may not be the newest emerging market; relatively few MFIs can absorb a significant amount of capital.

Furthermore, in some countries, client over-indebtedness is attributed in part to market saturation, with a narrow range of credit products and competition among MFIs pushing lenders to make increasingly risky loans and pursue harsh collection practices when repayment has faltered. In the first decade of the new century, delinquency rates rose dramatically in some countries, and, in 2010, the collection of loan payments collapsed in the Indian state of Andhra Pradesh (Chen, Rasmussen, and Reille 2010). These isolated crises serve as a warning that microcredit can cause trouble for clients. Over-indebtedness can increase financial and social vulnerability as borrowers take new loans to repay old ones or resort to extreme measures to make their payments, including reducing their consumption of food and selling productive assets. Such measures can lock borrowers into a downward spiral with severe consequences.

At the same time, innovation is bringing new customers and new service providers into the market. Diversification of products and services has already resulted in more choices for consumers. However, although such diversity indicates a maturing industry, increased access and more choice do not automatically translate into effective use. Simply opening an account does not mean that it will be used. Effective use is hampered by asymmetries of information as well as unsuitable product features or accessibility requirements (for example, minimum balances, age restrictions, regular contributions, affordability, and distance to branch or customer service point). This can lead to an imbalance of power between financial institutions and poor consumers, an imbalance that grows as inexperienced and ill-informed customers (for example, millions of unbanked owners of mobile phones who are potential mobile banking customers) choose among increasingly sophisticated products without recourse to adequate protective or grievance measures (Cohen and Nelson 2011).

Note: This box was contributed by Candace Nelson.

of more income; young mothers manage child-birth expenses, health care, and nutrition; parents struggle to educate their children. Widows are threatened with loss of land and other assets to their husbands' relatives. Elderly clients face acute vulnerabilities, including loss of productivity due to deteriorating health, physical immobility, and the loss of family support as children become independent and develop their own financial commitments (Hatch 2011). These

---

Box 1.2 Youth Financial Services: An Opportunity for the Future

The 1.5 billion people between the ages of 12 to 24 in the world today represent the largest number of youth ever on the planet. Of these, 85 percent, or 1.3 billion people, live in developing countries (World Bank 2011). Although the "youth bulge" is declining in East Asia and Central Europe, the youth population is expected to grow in Sub-Saharan Africa for the next 40 years. In 97 developing countries, half of the population is 25 years of age or younger. Worldwide, 47 percent of the unemployed are youth. Most young people in developing countries do not have access to the financial services and education that would help them to be productive, engaging citizens in their economies.

This explosion of youth constitutes an immense challenge and opportunity for human development. Youth is an excellent time to learn responsible habits and attitudes with regard to saving, borrowing, spending, using insurance, and investing. Appropriate financial services, tailored to the unique needs and capabilities of youth, can help young people to manage their finances better and potentially to start and expand microenterprises to support themselves and their families.

However, age restrictions, identification requirements, and relatively low profitability of small deposit accounts or loans can make it difficult for providers to meet the needs of young people. This nascent field has seen much innovation in the past few years. In most cases, the scope of the products has expanded to include interventions to provide financial education, develop capacity, and build youth skills, knowledge, and capital, including life skills training, workforce training (such as vocational education), and mentoring and internship or apprenticeship programs. Community-managed finance models, including savings-led groups and rotating savings and credit associations (ROSCAs), have been adapted for youth and have shown promise.

Some preliminary evidence suggests that access to financial services has improved the ability of young people to manage their finances and plan for their own futures. These results suggest that efforts are needed to innovate and experiment with product design as well as bundled packages of services that integrate financial with nonfinancial services. Together, these offerings support the development of a better-informed and financially savvy generation.

Youth financial services remain a niche field within the larger financial services industry, driven mainly by a few donors, large international nongovernmental organizations (NGOs), and a few innovative providers. If we are to meet the needs of this growing segment of the population and ensure that they have the skills and resources to be economically active citizens, we need to mainstream youth financial services within the financial inclusion agenda—both nationally and globally.

Source: Nisha Singh, Small Enterprise Education and Promotion (SEEP) Network. Statistics are from http://www.photius.com/rankings/population/median_age_total_2008_0.html, compiled from CIA 2008.

changes result in the need for different financial services at different life-cycle stages.

Other life-cycle events, such as celebrations, religious ceremonies, or building a home, require lump sums that are often hard to accumulate without adequate financial services. Financial exclusion is strongly influenced by age, with youth facing significant hurdles (Johnson and Arnold 2011; see box 1.2). To be relevant, financial service providers must modify products, services, and delivery channels to accommodate differences in life-cycle and age. Providers can respond to differing needs by developing age-specific products, such as youth savings accounts or pension funds.

Family structure can also affect how financial services are used. In many communities, the concept of family extends well beyond spouses, siblings, children, and grandparents. Cousins, distant relatives, and even neighbors are an integral part of a family. Polygamy further increases the size and complexity of the family structure. A large family may live together in one compound, often combining financial resources in order to meet daily needs or respond to emergencies. Similarly, income is often shared among the larger family. While saving may be difficult for an individual, sharing income facilitates risk management in the absence of formal services (see box 1.3).

In many contexts, community elders control assets and decide how they will be distributed throughout a given community. Thus an individual's ability to access services may depend on his or her social position relative to that of more senior members in the community.

Livelihoods, Geography, and Income Levels

The financial pressures of managing inconsistent income to cover daily expenses, unexpected emergencies, and life-cycle events weigh heavily on the poor. Although millions of people—from the poorest of the poor to the economically active poor to small business operators to salaried workers—face similar pressures, their responses and need for financial services vary depending on

---

Box 1.3 Gambian Family Structure and Impact on Financial Behavior and Demand

A remittance landscape study conducted in The Gambia by Women's World Banking provides insight into how family structure affects the demand for financial services (Orozco, Banthia, and Ashcroft 2011). Women often live in polygamist households and play central roles in managing the household budget. For many Gambian women, the financial goals of purchasing land or building up savings often take a back seat to the day-to-day financial needs of the extended family. Women often save in informal community-based savings clubs called *ososus* because they are close at hand, convenient, and keep money away from male family members.

In addition to earnings from small-scale economic activities, women in The Gambia also depend heavily on international remittances to feed the family, send children to school, and pay for food and clothes for religious events. In focus groups, many women said that remittance-linked savings accounts would help them to meet their financial goals, but because of the financial needs of their extended family and the cost and time of getting to a bank, consistent use of a savings account would be challenging.

Source: Banthia and McConaghy 2012.

---

their livelihoods and where they live, which, in turn, affect their income level.

Historically, microfinance has focused on microentrepreneurs, with loan products designed primarily for traders with daily or weekly cash flow and in need of short-term working capital. However, by focusing on productive credit, microfinance providers may have missed serving the majority of the potential market. As demonstrated in figure 1.1, of the 1.6 billion working poor, less than 500 million are microentrepreneurs or salaried wage workers; the rest earn their income, likely low and irregular, from farming, casual labor, fishing, and pastoral activities (Christen 2011). They, like anyone, need access to financial services to manage their daily lives, and they need a variety of products to address a multitude of financial service needs.

Geography matters as well. For example, people living in rural areas likely earn income from agricultural activities that generate very different cash flows than traditional "microenterprises." Financial services for smallholder farmers need to suit their cash flows and consider the production and marketing risks specific to a given crop (see chapter 10). However, in general, it is more expensive for providers to operate in rural areas, limiting clients' choices and challenging providers to reach scale, particularly where population density is low, access to markets or supplies is limited, and infrastructure is undeveloped. Rural areas often have higher covariance risk due to the lack of a diversified economic base and the risk of

Figure 1.1   Financial Service Needs for Different Livelihood Segments

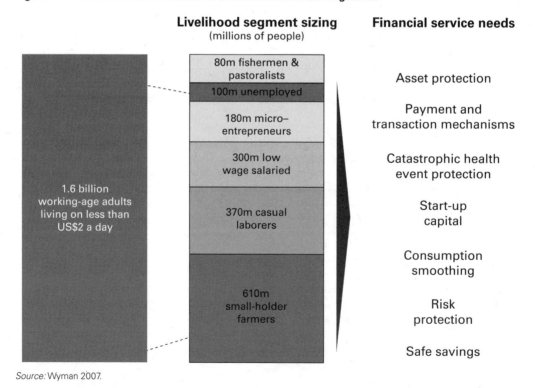

Source: Wyman 2007.

crop failure or drought; in some rural areas, a history of poorly designed rural credit programs (subsidized and/or directed credit, no savings mobilization) can affect people's perceptions of financial services.

And while having a bank account may seem more useful for an employee who receives regular wages than for, say, a laborer who is paid in cash, farmers, wage earners, and laborers would all benefit from having access to a safe place to save for lump-sum expenditures or respond to an emergency or new opportunity (see box 1.4).

In addition to *how* consumers generate income, the *amount* of income affects their access to and need for financial services. To meet varying income levels, products and services need to have characteristics—minimum balances, eligibility criteria, fees, and benefits—appropriate to each level.

Over the years, we have learned that the economically active poor rather than the poorest of the poor stand to benefit the most from access to financial services (without other interventions). "The majority of the world's estimated 150 million microcredit clients are thought to live just below and, more often, just above the poverty line" (Hashemi and de Montesquiou 2011, 1).

From the perspective of both the client and the provider, it is generally more expensive to transact in smaller amounts with greater frequency. For providers, smaller transaction amounts also result in a smaller revenue base—for example, people with lower incomes generally have lower savings balances, less capacity to take on debt, and fewer opportunities to generate income. Together, this makes it very difficult to provide financial services to the extremely poor.

Box 1.4 The Financial Service Needs of the Poor in Mexico

Although the need to save and borrow is common across all groups of people, the ability to save and pay back debt is constrained by illiquidity. Ideally, financial services should help people to create liquidity and increase their financial assets:

- Formal salaried workers who earn a stable income would value a portfolio of savings products that provide options to save with different terms, returns, and liquidity features, including simple savings products to help plan for both foreseen and unforeseen expenses and commitment savings to achieve longer-term goals. They would also value having easy access to credit or savings for smoothing shortfalls and meeting emergency needs and to transactional services for putting away money temporarily or transferring it to others.
- Entrepreneurs who earn a variable income would value a portfolio of savings and credit options that provide liquidity to respond to business opportunities and smooth out expenses across business cycles.
- Seasonal or agricultural workers have the most irregular income, often insufficient in itself. These households usually engage in multiple endeavors to supplement income and group together in extended families to pool resources and share expenses. They would value savings services, insurance, and small loans for emergencies. Perhaps the most vulnerable, this group would benefit the most from broader financial planning and literacy.

Source: Faz and Breloff 2012.

For the extremely poor, cash or asset transfers, rather than microcredit, are often a better solution, at least initially. If possible, placing cash transfers into a bank account appropriate for the poor can also support financial inclusion (see chapter 3).

While the majority of providers serve the economically active poor, an innovative model for providing financial services to the poorest in Bangladesh, developed by BRAC, is being replicated in countries around the world (see box 1.5).

Ethnicity, Caste, and Religion

Building and maintaining a level of trust in all circumstances can improve financial inclusion, and it is particularly important when different ethnic or religious groups are involved. Caste, while not solely an ethnic factor, can pose cultural barriers similar to ethnic differences. In countries where caste systems or religion are central to a community's social organization, individuals may be systematically denied access because they are from a lower caste or a different religion (see box 1.6).

Islamic finance is possibly the best-known example of religion influencing financial transactions. Islamic finance is based on Islamic or sharia law, but despite the term "law," Islamic finance is based largely on cultural norms. According to Karim, Tarazi, and Reille (2008, 6), "Indeed, sharia compliance in some societies may be less a religious principle than a cultural one—and even the less religiously observant may prefer sharia-compliant products."

A key overriding principle of Islamic finance is the need to provide for the welfare of the community by prohibiting practices considered unfair or exploitative. Fundamental to the provision of Islamic financial services is the inability to give or receive a fixed, predetermined rate of return. This principle is banned based on two sharia precepts: money has no intrinsic worth, and providers of funding must share the business risk (Karim,

---

Box 1.5   Reaching the Poorest: Lessons from the Graduation Model

BRAC works in 70,000 rural villages and 2,000 urban slums in Bangladesh, providing microfinance, schooling, health care, legal services, and marketing facilities. Realizing that its microfinance programs were not reaching many of the poorest, in 1985 BRAC partnered with the government of Bangladesh and the World Food Program to add a graduation ladder to an existing national safety net program that was providing the poorest households with a monthly allocation of food grain for a two-year period. The graduation model is built on five core elements: targeting, consumption support, savings, skills training and regular coaching, and asset transfers. BRAC worked with beneficiaries, eventually adding small loans to accelerate livelihood development. In less than 20 years, the program reached 2.2 million households. In 2002 BRAC fine-tuned its approach, both through better identification of the ultrapoor (defined as people who spend 80 percent of their total expenditure on food without attaining 80 percent of their minimum caloric needs) and through a set of more intensive, sequenced inputs.

By 2010, BRAC had reached around 300,000 ultrapoor households with this new approach, termed Challenging the Frontiers of Poverty Reduction/Targeting the Ultra Poor. BRAC estimates that more than 75 percent of these households are currently food secure and managing sustainable economic activities.

Source: Hashemi and de Montesquiou 2011.

The New Microfinance Handbook

Box 1.6 Religion and Caste in India

The caste system describes a stratification in which social classes or subclasses of traditional Hindu society are separated by distinctions of hereditary rank, profession, or wealth. Different castes engage in different productive activities according to their historical connections. Skills are passed on through apprenticeships gained through social networks based on kin, caste, and locality. Caste is least flexible where social disadvantage is most entrenched and poverty is most profound. Lower levels of technology are relegated to lower castes—for instance, the dalits have to carry heavy loads on their heads; they cannot use wheelbarrows. Workers themselves may enforce caste stratification to protect their place in the labor market.

Studies in India have found that religion can supply a collective identity, which, in turn, provides indispensable conditions for capital accumulation: "In India, religious affiliation can govern the creation and protection of rent, the acquisition of skills and contacts, the rationing of finance, the establishment and defense of collective reputation, the circulation of information, the norms that regulate the inheritance and management of property, and those that prescribe the subordination of women" (Harriss-White 2004). In addition, religious groups provide insurance and last-resort social security. Jains, for example, are often wealthy local merchants, moneylenders, and pawnbrokers who have indirect power over the local rural economy through webs of credit. The Muslim traders of Pallavaram, in contrast, are limited in their economic growth by their lack of access to finance.

Source: Harriss-White 2004, as summarized on microLINKS.

Tarazi, and Reille 2008). While these principles reflect widely held beliefs, sharia-compliant regulatory frameworks are just beginning to be developed.

Religion and ethnicity can also affect the ability of women to access services. For example, in some cultures women are home-bound for religious reasons and unable to meet with providers outside the home or to form groups with other women. Similarly, some cultures prohibit male staff from visiting female clients. Gender-based rules and norms can have a significant impact on both the financial service needs of women and their ability to access and use services.

Gender

Recognizing gender issues in microfinance, as in any project intervention, means more than targeting a programme towards women. It means recognising the position of women in relation to men as actors in society: in the context of husbands and families; local community and authority; and more broadly their position in society at the national level as governed by laws and custom. Then it is necessary to act to support women to overcome the obstacles they face in these relationships which prevent them from using financial services to achieve what they wish for themselves (Johnson 2000).

Women often lack control over cash management within their household and may be dependent on their husband to access financial services. Moreover, rules often prevent women from owning assets or participating in wage-earning activities outside the household (see box 1.7). For example, in Morocco, women's mobility outside

Box 1.7 The Embeddedness of Financial Service Use in Gender Norms in Kenya

Research in the rural areas of central Kenya indicates that the use of formal and informal financial services is strongly influenced by gender relations (Johnson 2004). Men are much more likely to have accounts with banks or savings and credit cooperatives (SACCOs), but women are much more likely to use informal group-based systems, especially ROSCAs. Men are also much more likely to use M-PESA—e-money payment and transfer—services (Johnson and Arnold 2011).

It is necessary to understand how the division of labor and control of income in the household influences the type of financial services that men and women need. While women contribute important labor to agricultural activities, men usually control the activities with the highest financial returns; women likely control smaller income streams, which enable them to pay for food and other household items needed on a regular basis. These differences in income flows result in gender-differentiated demand for financial services. For women, ROSCAs are an ideal way of turning small but fairly regular incomes into a larger amount over a period of weeks to purchase goods such as household utensils, blankets, or clothes. Moreover, the timing of these needs is not especially critical. Men's incomes are often larger and tend to be received in lump sums. Men are responsible for larger purchases, such as assets or farm inputs. They find it difficult to make regular contributions to ROSCAs at levels that would produce the size of payouts needed. Also, since some of their expenditures have specific timing, many men in a ROSCA may require access to the payout at the same time. As a result, men

are less likely to use ROSCAs and more likely to use banks or SACCOs to manage lump sums and hold them until needed or, if possible, take loans.

Social differences also affect how men and women engage with financial services. For example, men and women differ in their attitudes toward the social consequences of failing to make a payment in a ROSCA. Women said that they would experience embarrassment and shame if they were unable to pay the contribution; they would view this as "spoiling" the group. Men said that they would not be ashamed of not paying, would not trust each other to make the system work, do not like the strictness of the rules, and realize that little could be done if they did not pay. Consequently, in Kenya, women's ROSCAs are more successful than men's ROSCAs.

These differences reflect deeply rooted gender norms. Women's groups have a long history in Kikuyu society, and participation is considered an important social skill; groups socialize women in how they should act and behave. Groups also enable women to provide some of the household essentials. Additionally, since property, especially land, tends to be under men's control, to the extent that land is used as collateral, men are more able to borrow from banks than women. However, in Kenya men do not have exclusive control of land, and the family must agree to its use as collateral. Women can refuse if they think the loan may be misused. In addition, men usually hold the licenses for the production of cash crops (tea, coffee) and can open an account with a crop-based savings and credit cooperative, while their wives are usually simply a cosignatory.

Source: Susan Johnson, Centre for Development Studies, University of Bath.

Table 1.1   Gender-Based Obstacles in Microfinance and Microenterprise

Type of obstacle	Individual	Household	Wider community or national context
Financial	Women lack access to banks or financial services in their own right	Men control cash income and their expenditure patterns do not support the household	Men are perceived as controllers of money and loans
Economic	Women undertake activities that produce low returns; women have a heavy domestic workload	Households are characterized by gender division of labor, unequal access and control of land, labor, and inputs, and unequal control of joint household produce and income streams from this	Women are underpaid for equal work; women are locked in low-paid jobs; stereotypes determine the appropriate roles for women in the economy; women lack access to markets for inputs and outputs if their mobility is constrained due to social norms
Social or cultural	Women are not literate or educated; girls' education is not prioritized	Women have a limited role in household decision making; polygamy results in conflict, competition, and discrimination between wives; violence toward women is common	Banks and financial institutions do not view women as a potential market; women's mobility is constrained by social norms
Political or legal	Women lack confidence to claim political and legal rights	Women lack legal rights to jointly owned household assets	Women's legal rights to household assets are not defined in law or useful for collateral; women lack political positions to establish appropriate laws; women lack both traditional and formal legal rights to land

Source: Johnson n.d.

the home is restricted, and women's work is often associated with shame, as it reflects a man's inability to be the sole financial provider (Banthia et al. 2011).

Table 1.1 outlines the most prevalent gender-based obstacles affecting financial service access and use.

Altogether, the need for and ability to use and benefit from financial services depend to a great extent on age and life-cycle income levels, cultural context, and gender. The more we understand client characteristics and influences on their behavior, the better equipped we will be to increase financial inclusion in a meaningful way.

The Financial Ecosystem

While understanding the behavior and needs of clients is paramount, many stakeholders are also concerned with the wider financial ecosystem and how it affects financial inclusion (or exclusion). Financial inclusion efforts focus on how the supply of financial services (products and services provided by sustainable institutions) can better meet demand; they also acknowledge the functions within the wider market system that support financial transactions.

The contents of this book are shaped by the market system approach (see M4P Hub 2008).

This approach provides a practical means of assessing consumer behavior, the demand for and supply of financial services, and the rules and functions that support transactions. Whether financial service needs translate into demand that is met by a financial service provider depends on many factors, including the degree to which providers are sufficiently informed to identify client *needs*, potential clients have *information* about providers, and *trust* exists between the two. Beyond this, a provider's ability to develop and offer an appropriate product is shaped by its capacity in relation to *product development* and *delivery channels* and by its incentives to improve them. For example, do *regulations* encourage the development and expansion of services? Do the *laws* on collateral requirements promote overall financial inclusion? Can providers access *funding* to support growth? Do they have the right *legal form* and networks to do so? Do *credit bureaus* exist, and are they effective? Does the accessible *infrastructure* promote overall financial inclusion? Equally important, how do the *attitudes* and *norms* among both consumers (for example, to loan repayment) and providers (for example, to risk and reward) influence financial inclusion?

This section describes the financial market system, specifically the functions within it and the roles played by various market actors. A market system necessarily includes both private and public sector actors as well as civil society and, indeed, consumers themselves. Because the term *market* is often equated only with the private sector, the term *ecosystem* is used interchangeably with market system in this book (see Ehrbeck, Pickens, and Tarazi 2012).

Functions of the Market System

There are three main sets of functions in a market system, each carried out by various market players, including the private sector, government, NGOs, community groups, representative associations, and consumers.

- *Core*. Transactions between providers and clients (supply and demand)

- *Rules*. Informal and formal rules that shape the behavior of market players, including consumers

- *Supporting functions*. The collection of functions that provide information and services supporting the development and expansion of the core.

Understanding financial market systems involves breaking down each of these functions into more detail to identify specific elements within them and the main players who are likely to be directly engaged (see figure 1.2). Each set of functions can be viewed in isolation, yet in practice functions only have value when seen as integral parts of a wider ecosystem. By incorporating the interests and incentives of clients and other key market players and the influence of rules and supporting functions with regard to financial service provision, the market system framework acknowledges that only by understanding the entire system can we address the constraints to and take advantage of the opportunities for increasing financial inclusion (see box 1.8).

The Core

Offering a combination of the appropriate instruments and an understanding of how these can be used practically within the context of current livelihoods and existing social and cultural norms will enable and encourage people to shift towards improved management of their finances. The heart of the market systems approach is to understand the demand side and support customer-focused development and innovation driving the supply side. (FSD Kenya).

For financial market systems to work more inclusively and successfully, two characteristics must be present. First, the number of transactions

Figure 1.2 Stylized View of the Financial Ecosystem

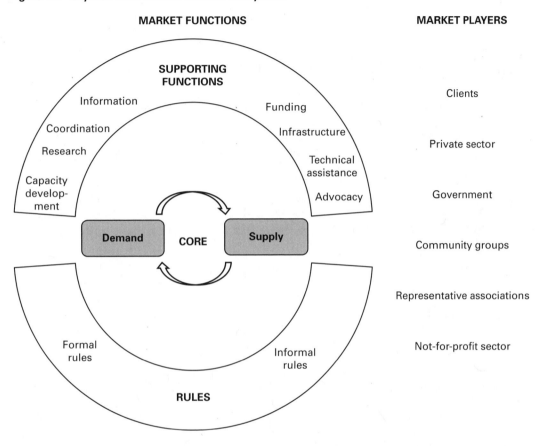

MARKET FUNCTIONS

MARKET PLAYERS

SUPPORTING
FUNCTIONS

Information

Funding

Coordination

Infrastructure

Research

Technical
assistance

Capacity
develop-
ment

Advocacy

Demand   CORE   Supply

Formal
rules

Informal
rules

RULES

Clients

Private sector

Government

Community groups

Representative associations

Not-for-profit sector

must increase; expanding the access frontier to include previously excluded people is a key indicator of financial system development and an official goal of many financial authorities. Second, products must accurately address the needs of clients, improving their lives or businesses.[5] A better-functioning core is therefore manifested in more and better-quality transactions. The key players in the core of the market are clients (demand) and financial service providers (supply), connected to each other by products (supply). The following discussion provides a brief overview of demand and supply. More detailed discussions are provided in the chapters that follow.

Demand: Clients

As discussed in the previous section on clients, poor households are in continual need of financial tools to improve their productivity and secure the best possible consumption and investment choices, all the while managing potential or existing risks. Understanding demand requires both an understanding of the financial service needs of clients and, as well, their behavior with regard to existing financial services.

Box 1.8 Understanding the Financial Market System

For any organization involved in financial market development—for-profit companies, NGOs, governments, investors, donors, and other development practitioners—an understanding of the financial market system is important when considering their objectives and roles. Building on a detailed understanding of market systems and a clear vision of the future of financial inclusion, the market systems approach guides stakeholders to address systemic constraints and bring about large-scale, sustainable change. It is through the development of inclusive and sustainable financial market systems that financial services will make a meaningful difference in the lives of poor people and promote economic growth.

The financial market systems framework recognizes how different players fit within the system, including their main functions and the relationships between them. Although the central function in market systems is to provide a space for transactions, the nature and efficiency of those transactions are shaped by formal and informal rules and a range of supporting functions. While supply-side factors (offering financial services) are crucial to making the financial system work better for the poor, achieving this goal is more complicated than a straightforward equation of supply and demand; it involves the many other functions that influence transactions—attitudes and values, skills, product and organizational development, regulations, and policies. These provide information, knowledge, and incentives that determine behavior and practices and shape relationships.

The players in the system thus extend well beyond the "simple" duopoly of clients and providers to include government, private sector service providers, associations, and communities. When the functions and players in financial market systems work well, benefits follow. When they do not, consumers, especially the poor, are likely to receive limited or temporary benefits. Sustaining the benefits of access depends on the stability of the financial system and its ongoing ability to provide services and, indeed, ensure that people's savings are not put at undue risk.

A functioning and inclusive financial market system, therefore, is characterized by strong and sustainable performance—demonstrated by size and outreach (number of clients and number and variety of providers), depth and quality (poverty level and degree to which products meet client needs)—and the capacity and competence of rules and supporting functions, allowing the market to learn, adapt, and develop in a sustainable manner.

Analyzing data from financial diaries collected across Bangladesh, India, and South Africa, Collins et al. (2009) suggests a much more complex picture of demand than previously assumed: "The authors of the book, *Portfolios of the Poor*, found that households used between eight and 10 different types of mostly informal financial instruments with very high turnovers—often 10 times the asset values through the year and more than 100 percent of their income. This reveals a remarkable resourcefulness, but when transaction costs don't scale with transaction size, fragmenting transactions over many informal instruments can be very costly. Therefore, they not only need financial tools, they need *well-performing* and *cost-effective* financial tools" (Kendall 2010, 1).

The poor often prefer the informal sector on most dimensions important to consumers (access, flexibility, product features, and service quality). However, informal financial mechanisms may entail cost, inconvenience, embarrassment, and sometimes depletion of the very social capital on which they are built. More needs to be understood about how the informal sector expands outreach, if and how those relying on the informal sector are underserved, and how the quality of consumers' lives could be improved as a result of access to formal financial services. Chapter 2 provides a more detailed discussion of demand and how we can learn from the informal sector and the behavior of clients.

Supply: Providers

While most of the first microfinance institutions were established as NGOs, the sector has evolved to include many types of providers. Specialized commercial banks providing a range of financial services have proven that the poor are "bankable," while member-based community groups have shown that financial services can be provided directly by the community on a sustainable basis. Providers are discussed in detail in part II of this book; an overview of the types of providers is included here and illustrated in figure 1.3.

While financial service providers are often characterized as formal, semiformal, or informal, traditionally referring to their regulatory status, we classify them as either community-based (generally informal with no legal status) or institutional (generally more formal and in some cases regulated).[6]

Community-based providers include both individuals (such as friends and family, moneylenders, shop owners, traders, and deposit collectors) and groups, including indigenous groups, such as ROSCAs and accumulating savings and credit associations (ASCAs), and facilitated groups trained by external agencies, such as Savings Groups (SGs) and Self-Help Groups (SHGs). While more formal than ROSCAs, these facilitated groups are not considered to be "institutions," as they, for the most part, are not legally licensed as financial service providers, have few expenses, and provide services primarily within the group itself (see chapter 6).

Institutional providers include member-owned financial cooperatives and NGOs, which are normally registered and possibly supervised, as well as banks (private and public), deposit-taking MFIs, and non-bank financial institutions (NBFIs)

Figure 1.3   The Range of Financial Service Providers

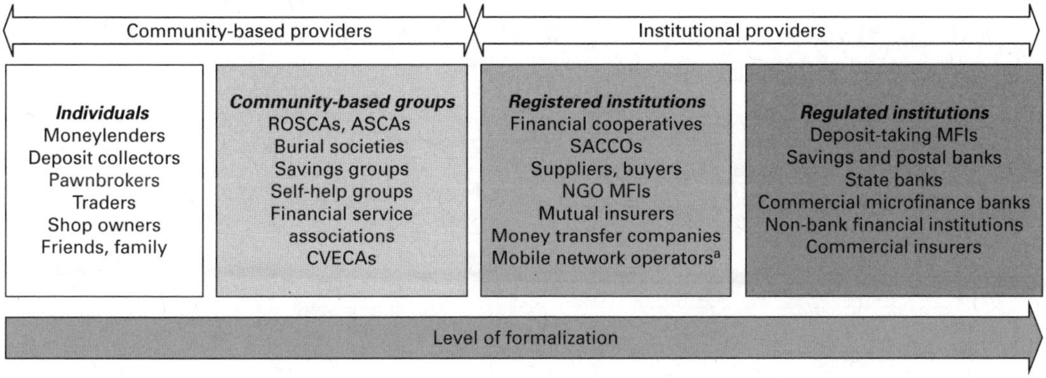

Note: ROSCAs = rotating savings and credit associations; ASCAs = accumulating savings and credit associations; CVECAs = *caisses villageoises d'épargne et de crédit autogérées*; SACCOs = savings and credit cooperatives; NGO = nongovernmental organization; MFIs = microfinance institutions.
a. Mobile network operators are regulated as communication companies; most are not licensed to provide financial services.

such as insurance companies and leasing companies, which are normally regulated in some fashion (see chapter 7).

No single type of organization presents an optimal solution to reaching all market segments with all types of financial services. In remote rural areas, the low cost structure and proximity of user-owned and managed providers constitute significant advantages over more structured MFIs or commercial banks. However, credit unions and banks have the advantage of being able to offer a wider variety of products or a broader spectrum of terms and conditions and may be more reliable than community-based providers. New entrants such as mobile network operators (MNOs) can offer services conveniently in rural areas, although relatively few have achieved scale (see box 1.9).

While recent years have witnessed a considerable increase in the commercial provision of microfinance and the emergence of publicly listed microfinance companies, informal providers remain the main source of financial services for the vast majority of the poor. For example, FinAccess data provide strong evidence that Kenyan consumers use a portfolio of financial services. Of those using regulated formal services, only 11 percent rely solely on a formal service, 31 percent use a semiformal service, 13 percent use an informal service, and the remaining 45 percent

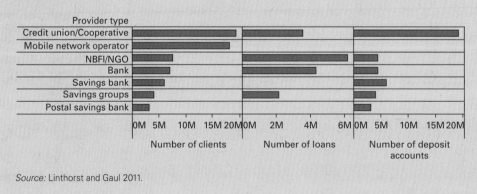

Box 1.9 The Range of Providers in Sub-Saharan Africa

In 2011 the Microfinance Information eXchange (MIX) compiled a data set on financial inclusion for Sub-Saharan Africa. The data set brought together information from more than 60 distinct industry resources along with hundreds of individual institutions, covering some 23,000 providers of financial services reaching low-income populations in Africa. Africa has a diverse landscape of financial service providers—of which specialized MFIs are an important part—but the poor also access financial services through banks, credit unions and cooperatives, postal savings banks, SGs, and many other types of providers. Figure B1.9.1 shows the outreach of different types of providers across Africa.

Figure B1.9.1   Number of Clients, Loans, and Deposit Accounts in Africa, by Type of Provider

Source: Linthorst and Gaul 2011.

use all three categories of services. Similarly, more than half of those who have a semiformal provider as their most formal source of finance also use an informal source. Furthermore, this pattern of multiple service use has increased from 2006 to 2009. In 2009, a mere 2.5 percent of Kenyans relied *solely* on the regulated formal sector (FSD Kenya FinAccess data for 2011).

Supply: Products

Clients benefit from having access to products that match the way they live and conduct business and support them in addressing challenges. The irregularity and limited size of cash flows mean that products that permit frequent, small, incremental transactions are more useful and convenient than, for example, services that require a minimum transaction amount or take significant time to access. Products provided directly in the community are generally used frequently because they are accessible, convenient, and in close proximity to where poor people live (see box 1.10).

The main financial services include savings, credit, payments, and insurance and are described in part III of this book.[7] While financial products and services are generally defined by standard characteristics such as term, size, price, returns, and eligibility, their appeal to consumers often depends on their reliability, accessibility, flexibility, safety, and affordability. For example, products are accessible when providers explain product features so that clients understand the commitment they are making. Products are safe if they are well-structured and meet client needs in a transparent way without doing harm. Increasingly, more flexible terms and conditions are being offered, including the ability to repay loans early, receive increases in existing loans, and open savings accounts with no minimum balance. Payment services, loans for housing and education, or savings accounts specifically for youth, as well as more complex products such as leasing and insurance are beginning to reach low-income populations.

Box 1.10 Savings-Led Financial Services in Bangladesh

SafeSave, one of the world's first MFIs to offer basic money management services to poor clients, takes a client-centered approach, acknowledging that the tiny incomes of poor people are often irregular and unreliable, forcing them to use a complex set of financial management strategies. With minimal access to formal sector providers, they often save in the home, borrow from moneylenders, and participate in savings clubs—devices that are accessible, but not always reliable. SafeSave tries to provide the strengths of informal finance, while redressing its weaknesses.

SafeSave offers savings and loan services to anyone living within walking distance of a branch office. Six days a week, a collector walks to households in the neighborhood, providing services to individual clients. Clients may deposit as little as Tk 1 (US$0.015) when the collector calls. Accounts with balances above Tk 1,000 (US$15) earn 6 percent interest. Clients may withdraw up to Tk 500 per day (US$7.50) at their doorstep or up to Tk 5,000 per day (US$75) at the branch office. Long-term savings products are offered as well as credit. All borrowers start with a credit limit of Tk 5,000 (US$75), but loans are not mandatory. A minimum passbook savings balance equal to one-third of the loan balance is required as collateral at all times. In March 2010, for the first time, SafeSave's savings portfolio surpassed its loan portfolio in value.

Source: SafeSave (http://www.safesave.org/).

As services become more client-centered, product delivery is also developing through innovative channels (see chapter 12).

Table 1.2 provides a simple illustration summarizing the core of the market system, that is, demand (the main financial service needs, including cash management, accumulating lump sums, risk management, and money transfers) and supply (how poor people meet those needs).

Table 1.2   Illustrative Solutions to Household Financial Management Needs

Financial management needs	Day-to-day cash management	Accumulating lump sums	Coping with risk	Transferring money
Default mechanism used by the excluded	Carry cash	Hide cash in a secret place	Reduce consumption; sell assets	Deliver in person; send by friend or family member
Benefits	Zero fees; zero transaction costs; fully liquid	Zero fees; zero transaction costs; fully liquid	Requires no planning	Cheap; possible social benefits
Costs	High risk of expropriation; no ability to borrow	Very high risk of loss; lack of savings discipline; too accessible; loss of real value	Hardship; reduce potential future income	Risk of theft or diversion; time-consuming; slow
Community-based mechanisms typically used	ROSCAs; shop credit	ROSCAs; ASCAs	ROSCAs; other community groups; moneylenders	Bus or minibus taxi
Benefits	Zero fees; very low transaction costs; social benefits	Zero fees; very low transaction costs; savings discipline; investment returns (ASCAs)	Highly flexible; very low transaction costs; social supports; very rapid response	Familiar mechanism; no access requirements
Costs	Inflexible terms; risk of loss; unpredictable; hidden costs of shop credit	Risk of loss; loss of privacy	Unpredictable availability; potentially high fees; high contingent liability	Risky; slow; difficult to access; expensive
Institutional mechanisms typically used	Bank transaction account	Bank savings account	Insurance; emergency credit	Mobile phone-based payment
Benefits	Fully flexible; secure (deposit protection); facilitates payments; can lead to credit access	Secure (deposit protection); moves savings "away from temptation"; can lead to credit access	Can cover extreme risks; no contingent liability; risk cover can be defined	Lower risk; fast; easy to access; lower cost
Costs	High withdrawal fees; day-to-day access difficult	High minimum balances; day-to-day access difficult; low returns	High premiums or interest rates; accessibility; long and unpredictable claims process	Account and subscriber identity module (SIM) card required

Source: David Ferrand, FSD Kenya.

Rules and Supporting Functions

Rules and supporting functions influence the effectiveness of transactions (the core of the market) and provide an enabling environment to allow markets to grow, adapt, and succeed in changing circumstances. Ensuring that they improve and increase transactions supports financial inclusion.

Who establishes and enforces rules and who provides supporting functions differs by function. Some functions, such as regulations, are appropriately considered a "public good"; the key players are the government and policy makers and, on occasion, business associations. Others, such as credit bureaus or rating agencies, are more appropriately provided by private sector firms (see box 1.11).[8]

Rules

A broad term used to define the *rules of the game*,[9] rules include formal rules (regulations and standards) and informal rules (social conventions and cultural norms). Formal or informal rules—the rules themselves and their enforcement—govern participation and behavior in financial market systems and strongly influence financial market outcomes. Formal rules have a defined, written set of responsibilities that are allocated to specific parties, which together create the de jure parameters that shape behavior (of clients and providers). Informal rules are usually unwritten and are invariably more nebulous and ill-defined than formal rules; they manifest themselves in attitudes, behavioral norms, social organizations, and common practices. These informal rules often drive incentives and behavior and determine the extent to which formal rules are adhered to (see box 1.12).

The key players in relation to formal rules are government organizations and industry associations. The increasing complexity of financial systems and new innovations within them—such as the emergence of mobile banking—pose new challenges for rule makers in terms of not only what rules should be, but who should make and implement them.

Formal rules play a public or collective role in market systems, leveling the playing field for providers and consumers. Formal rules affect clients by setting legal frameworks and industry standards that influence market access, the range of products, and the competitive landscape, which, in turn, affect providers and their ability to serve their markets appropriately. For example, the legal ability to enforce contracts and register assets, the existence of a national identification system, or the protection of public deposits are all critical parts of the "formal rule"

Box 1.11 Key Rules and Supporting Functions for Savings Services

- *Rules.* Prudential and supervisory regimes that balance increased access with stability and depositor protection
- *Operational and human resource development.* A combination of training services and technical consultancy aimed at building provider capacity
- *Payment systems.* Requires collaboration between public and private players, enables organizations to take deposits and transfer funds
- *Deposit insurance.* Whether public or private sector–based, requires savings organizations to agree on deposit requirements

Source: Glisovic, El-Zoghbi, and Foster 2011.

Box 1.12 Formal and Informal Rules

Formal rules consist of the written laws, government policies, formal regulations, and industry standards that are formally documented and (sometimes) enforced. They are shaped and influenced by the informal rules of the society or business community. In turn, they influence how informal rules are expressed in the performance of the market.

Informal rules are unwritten, tacit rules that define acceptable roles and activities for different individuals based on a combination of social norms, culture, and historical factors. Any specific community tends to adopt such rules, codes of conduct, and regulations based on a combination of norms associated with different social institutions. Sometimes these informal rules fill an obvious gap in the formal legislation. Informal rules are often psychologically internalized: not merely unwritten, but beneath people's conscious attention.

Source: microLINKS wiki 2010.

system. Formal rules are discussed in more detail in chapters 3, 17, and 19.

Informal rules are an integral part of local culture, value systems, and practices. By definition, they are not the responsibility of one player. Although particular individuals or organizations may exert considerable influence, informal rules emerge organically and are the result of traditions and habits influenced by social institutions, such as gender, religion, caste, tradition, inheritance rights, and landownership.[10] For example, according to microLINKS wiki (2010), "Typically these gender norms are expressed through informal (and formal) rules that lead to discriminatory property and inheritance laws, for example, different access to resources, and to restrictions on the tasks or places of work that women may occupy."

Norms suggest a standard of conduct that people believe they ought to follow to avoid sanctioning (Coleman 1994). Social and cultural norms surrounding attitudes toward money, sharing, and authority can greatly influence the type of financial services that are most useful in a given community. Trust, for example, plays an integral role in the decision to use a particular financial service or adopt a set of financial behaviors (Shipton 2007). In societies with high social

capital, where systems and structures have been developed to build trust and foster social and economic transactions beyond the family and kin group, it will be easier and less costly to build sustainable systems for financial intermediation (Bennett 1997).

Informal rules can contribute to the effectiveness of formal rules when the norm is compliance or when formal rules codify informal norms already widely accepted (microLINKS wiki 2010), such as Islamic finance principles now being incorporated into regulatory frameworks. Informal rules may also emerge in response to formal rules that do not work well for a particular group or do not exist. For example, a village leader can "vouch" for borrowers in the absence of a credit bureau or can verify property ownership in the absence of a housing registry. Given that informal rules reflect long-held beliefs and social structures, they typically are difficult to change (although some can be addressed by corrective regulation or judicial decision).

Informal rules also influence the supply side of the market. They may be manifested in, for example, industry norms in relation to innovation and risk, which, in turn, drive attitudes and practices to develop new products. And for providers of all sizes, the level of trust clients have, as well as the norms regarding repayment of loans, is critical in determining the incentives for increased financial inclusion. For example, historical experience such as conflict or disaster can create social dynamics that persist for generations, such as a lingering lack of trust, a lack of available resources, infrastructure, and opportunities, and overall difficulty in establishing relationships and creating solidarity in the community. Communities marked by significant ethnic conflict may be less receptive initially to peer-based group lending models that have historically worked very well in microfinance. Alternatively, a community where cash is less prevalent than in-kind assets potentially requires unique financial services outside traditional credit and savings products.

While some informal rules may appear unproductive, they serve an important purpose, such as providing a social safety net. These rules might include shared access to income, common understanding of property, and rigid social structures, as discussed earlier. However, social

institutions do change and evolve in response to new technologies or interaction with new cultures. For example, mobile money may make it easier to transfer money from urban to rural areas, thus resulting in less reliance on community solidarity to manage risks and deal with emergencies.[11] Understanding informal rules provides insight into what will work within a particular community (see box 1.13).

Supporting Functions

Supporting functions provide the resources, information, and services that shape financial market behavior and enable markets to grow, adapt, and succeed in changing circumstances. Weak supporting functions (and inappropriate rules) leave markets vulnerable, lacking the necessary depth to be sustainable and fit into a changing world. The composition and nature of supporting functions, and who provides them, vary from one context to another but are concerned generally with information and communication, capacity building, coordination, resource development, and innovation. All of these support

---

Box 1.13 Understanding Informal Rules through Financial Landscapes

The methodology (and metaphor) of financial landscapes seeks to examine the path through which the poor access services in relation to the world around them, including, for example:

- *Spatial.* How distance and ease of travel in locating providers affect access to services, taking into account settlement patterns and physical infrastructure
- *Historical.* How past policies and approaches have shaped existing service provision and attitudes
- *Sociocultural.* How social and personal networks develop in response to limited access
- *Economic.* How patterns of income and expenditure shape the demand for services.

This type of research seeks not only to throw light on the specific situations of households but also to examine how this affects financial service provision and access. In doing so, a more complete picture should emerge of both the core and the "informal rules" that have shaped its development.

Source: Bouman and Hospes 1994.

the core function—the exchange between clients (demand) and service providers (supply).

Because they differ from one context to another, there is no comprehensive list of supporting functions. However, the following are some of the main functional areas:

- *Capacity development.* Concerned with developing capacity of various players including policy makers and providers. It therefore may involve training services or other means by which employees learn new skills. In more established markets, capacity development for the industry as a whole may involve coordination among private and public players.[12]

- *Coordination.* The capacity (within a market system) to go beyond the limitations of individual perspectives, understand the system as a whole, and support its development. This is a noncommercial, collective, public role and therefore is likely to be the domain of government or representative industry (and perhaps consumer) associations.

- *Advocacy.* Efforts to provide an appropriate voice in the financial market system, especially for providers and consumers, and to ensure that their views contribute to public functions such as regulations and standards.

- *Information.* Refers loosely to the "information environment," for example, in relation to emerging trends and products (aimed at both providers and consumers) and to more specific information-based products and services. The key players include specialized service companies and government or associations in relation to public information on, for example, standards and legal rights.

- *Research.* The provision of knowledge-based products or services related to, for example, the demand and supply sides of the core, impact assessment and the implications of wider trends.

- *Funding.* Can take various forms, such as equity or debt. The key players here are private investors, but in practice, especially for microfinance, a range of social investors are active, often supported by donor funds, not usually seeking a commercial (or indeed any financial) return.

- *Infrastructure.* The range of technical and other support services required to enhance the efficiency of the overall system. This could include credit bureaus, deposit insurance, and accounting services. The key players are likely to be private sector companies and public regulatory authorities.

Supporting functions are described in more detail in chapters 3, 5, 16, and 18.

Implications of the Market System Framework: Providers and Facilitators

While all organizations engaged in financial inclusion may agree that development of the system as a whole represents a worthy aim, they do not all have the same role or perspective. Organizations differ with respect to several factors, for example, their legal status (for-profit business, NGO, association, government), funding sources (grants, debt, equity, client-generated revenues), scale, and motivations. However, perhaps the most basic but useful distinction is between organizations that see themselves as *market players* with a continuing direct role within the market system and *facilitators* that see themselves as external actors with a mandate to act as temporary catalysts in stimulating others in the market (see figure 1.4). Knowing your place in the financial services landscape is an important step in determining what you should do and how you should do it.

- *Market system players.* Organizations or individuals with an active and continuing role delivering functions in the financial ecosystem. This includes providers of financial

Figure 1.4 Market System Players and Facilitators

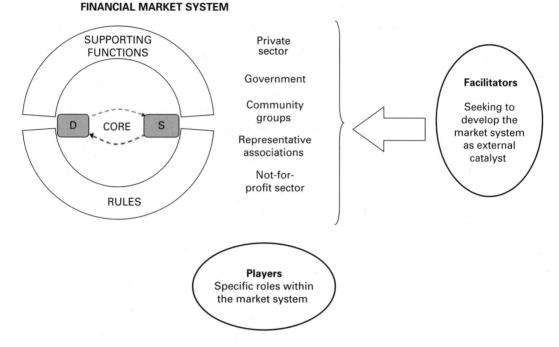

FINANCIAL MARKET SYSTEM

SUPPORTING FUNCTIONS

D   CORE   S

RULES

Private sector

Government

Community groups

Representative associations

Not-for-profit sector

Facilitators

Seeking to develop the market system as external catalyst

Players
Specific roles within the market system

services, regulators, and other developers and enforcers of formal rules and providers of supporting functions. These entities are part of the system and envisage remaining part of it in the future.

- *Facilitators*. External players, standing outside the system, whose role is to facilitate positive changes in the market system. Facilitators are most often donors and development agencies that are funded by donors. (Investors who provide debt or equity to providers are considered to be market players, as they provide funding, an important supporting function.) Grant funding is used (or should be) to facilitate the market and to develop the capacity of market players in the system. While facilitators work in a variety of ways, their role is to use resources to address constraints, allowing the system to

function more effectively and inclusively. Facilitation is therefore a public role (not commercial); it is temporary (not permanent) and requires understanding and capacity to intervene with appropriate and timely resources (financial, human, and political). And while in the short to medium term, the role of the facilitator may involve multiple activities— including direct roles in the market if required—in the longer term, the strategic purpose of facilitation is, by definition, *not* to have any continuing role in the market system.

Table 1.3 outlines the strategic differences between the two roles. In the long term, who should be a market player (that is, provide a product or service, public or private) and who should pay for those products or services? There is relatively little disagreement about who should fulfill

Table 1.3 Key Characteristics of Facilitators and Providers in the Financial Market System

Characteristic	Facilitators	Market players
Orientation and purpose	Broad. What is good for the market system as a whole?	Narrow. What is good for me and my clients or stakeholders?
Long-term role	No role in the longer term; facilitate others in the market system	Continuing role with incentives and capacity to grow
Activities	Varies with market constraints identified, for example, technical, financial, organizational, information assistance	Consistent with long-term role; provision of services, either financial services in the core or supporting functions or formal rules
Skills, knowledge	Strategic overview and (flexible) technical capacity to address constraints	Narrow technical competence to fulfill specific role
Funding	Development agencies and donors	Other players in the market, clients (revenues from services), or government (for public services)
Legal form	Development mechanisms; donors, foundations, contractors, NGOs	Appropriate to role; mainly private players (formal and informal) for service provision
Cost base	Appropriate for development agencies	Appropriate for market system

some functions in the financial system. Financial service delivery is generally accepted as appropriately provided by the private sector, while the development of regulatory frameworks, for example, merits public subsidy. Historically however, ambiguity over the nature of some functions has provided justification for extensive donor subsidy in microfinance. Donors that fund market players directly or themselves play market roles only have a valid rationale for participating in the short term (see chapter 4).

If the financial market system is to be truly facilitated and a position reached where long-term financial inclusion has been achieved and facilitation is no longer required, facilitators must figure out how to play a role without becoming a market player and how to implement their vision of how the market system should function without them in the future (see chapter 19). Figure 1.5 illustrates the evolution of taking a financial system approach rather than an institutional approach—from (a) strengthening supply to (b) understanding demand and from (c) building the core market to (d) developing the wider market system.

Banking without Branches

The third significant influence on financial services for the poor is the opportunity presented by technology to increase financial inclusion.[13] Building on the previous discussion of the financial ecosystem, this introduction to branchless banking focuses on the new market players—MNOs and agent networks—within the system and the emerging new business models that result. Chapter 12 provides a more technical discussion of each of the various transaction or access points—for example, mobile phones, Internet, automated teller machines (ATMs)—and the development and management of an agent network; it also includes a glossary of branchless banking terms.

Cost and proximity drive the delivery of financial services. Historically, providing services in close proximity to clients entailed high costs for both the provider and the client. However, financial service providers are increasingly finding innovative ways to integrate the delivery of financial services into the everyday lives of clients. While community-based providers are

Figure 1.5 Evolution of Intervention Focus from Financial Institutions to Financial Systems

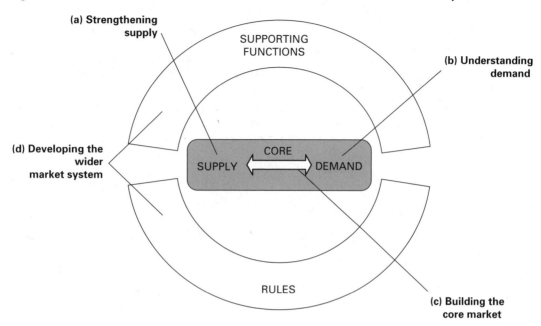

Source: Rob Hitchins, The Springfield Centre.

already largely "branchless," for institutional providers, branchless banking is changing the way clients and providers interact and is poised to lower the costs of delivery significantly and to reach financially excluded households that cannot be served profitably using conventional branch-based approaches—especially in remote, sparsely populated areas and urban slums (CGAP 2011).

Banking without branches requires alternative access points for client transactions. These include self-serve solutions such as mobile phones or ATMs, staff-based transaction points such as mobile branches that visit underserved areas on specific days, and third-party agents including retailers (or in some cases, MFIs) using card-reading point-of-sale (POS) devices, mobile phones, or Internet-connected computing devices. Branchless product offerings range from individual money transfers and government cash

transfers to full-service banking, allowing deposits, withdrawals, and, if relevant, loan disbursement and payments or even insurance premium payments or payouts.

In providing an overview of branchless banking and the associated new business models, it is helpful to define a few terms. *Mobile money* refers to a type of electronic money that can be transferred over a mobile phone. The issuer of mobile money may (depending on the local law and the business model) be an MNO or a third party, including a bank (CGAP 2011). *Mobile banking* is the use of a mobile phone to access financial services and execute financial transactions connected to a bank account. This covers both transactional and nontransactional services, such as viewing financial information on a mobile phone (Chatain et al. 2011). An *agent* is any third party acting on behalf of a bank or other financial service provider (including an electronic money issuer or distributor) in its dealings with customers. Agents perform "cash-in" (the exchange of cash for electronic value) and "cash-out" (the exchange of electronic value for cash) services.

New Market Actors: A Wider Ecosystem

Branchless banking is primarily about the emergence of different kinds of businesses, often with new kinds of players, to deliver multiple financial services to a mass market through technology-enabled business models that operate very differently from more traditional financial service delivery models. Branchless banking services require an ecosystem of players. For example, mobile banking, a subset of branchless banking, requires partnerships between MNOs and banks or other financial service providers and agents.[14] Mobile banking solutions "are hard to build because they require strong multiparty orchestration, in principle spanning several regulatory domains, and the proposition is severely weakened if any one element of the solution is not properly primed. Indeed, the commercial arrangements between the parties are what holds the system together" (Mas 2008, 8). This discussion focuses on agent networks and MNOs as the two main new entrants to financial service provision.

Agent Networks

While branchless banking channels offer clients more convenience and access points, POS devices on their own cannot accept deposits; Internet and mobile channels by themselves have no cash transaction capability; and mobile branches may not visit often enough to meet all the needs of clients.[15] Thus these channels individually cannot replace traditional channels altogether (Mas 2008). This is where agents enter the picture.

An agent network is a group of retailers with existing businesses or retail locations who (primarily) provide cash-in, cash-out services. An agent may be any retailer conveniently located

with reliable cash flow who can service clients seeking to deposit, withdraw, or send funds to a third party. Providers such as banks or MNOs often establish agent networks through a range of distribution networks, including airtime sellers, shopkeepers, retailers, traders, petrol stations, post offices, or kiosks in markets. Agents charge transaction fees, but because they serve areas where most institutional providers are unable to reach, these fees are often lower than the cost of traveling to a bank branch or using a traditional money transfer company.

Agents can facilitate transactions via several access devices, including a POS device, a mobile phone handset, a tablet, or a personal computer. A client can deposit cash with an agent in one location, and those same funds can be withdrawn immediately by another client at a different location.[16] Agents must have an account at a bank that has a secure, real-time transaction-processing capability, either online using wireless or Internet connectivity or offline using smartcards capable of updating balances and recording transactions (see chapter 12). A payments system or network (see chapter 18) is needed that allows the agent's bank to account for and settle transactions with all participating client banks. Consumer protection safeguards are also required to minimize exposure of bank clients to agent risk (Mas 2008).

Some providers use agents for more than simple transactions, such as providing account balances or notifying clients of payments coming due, delivering credit products, and, if properly licensed, delivering insurance products. Based on a representative case in the Mexican market, as much as 20 percent of the transactions coming into branches could be handled by agents (Mas and Kumar 2008).

Depending on the regulatory environment, sometimes MFIs can act as agents for larger commercial banks or for MNOs. This strategy allows microfinance customers to gain exposure to mobile banking and can also help MFIs to differentiate themselves from the competition and bring enhanced liquidity to their branches (Kumar, McKay, and Rotman 2010).

Agents provide the customer interface. Therefore, when developing a network of agents, providers must address the operational challenges in a way that fosters a positive and consistent customer experience that will create and maintain trust in the system. Strategies for enrolling, training, incentivizing, managing, and retaining agents are critical considerations for all providers that use agents to deliver financial services. Providers can hire and manage their own agents, or they can outsource this function (see chapter 12).

Mobile Network Operators

Mobile network operators provide the ability to use mobile phones for financial services—either directly to consumers or on behalf of other financial service providers, usually through an agent network. MNOs can provide money transfer and payment services directly without being linked to another financial service provider (mobile money), or they can partner with a bank or other provider to increase outreach both in terms of numbers as well as available products (mobile banking) (Kumar, McKay, and Rotman 2010).

The role of MNOs in mobile banking can vary from simply selling text-messaging services to providing a full-fledged parallel banking infrastructure (although it is still early in the process to fully understand what this involves). Which role(s) a bank or other financial service provider wants the MNO to play depends on how much it wants to integrate mobile banking services into its core business and its ability to implement technology-based deployments.[17] Customer experience is determined directly by the technology platform used and the ability to access cash-in, cash-out services (Mas and Kumar 2008). These and other issues are still being worked out, and expectations for the future are uncertain (see box 1.14).

New Business Models: Partnerships for Branchless Banking

Developing partnerships between financial service providers and MNOs is not easy. A key consideration when developing partnerships is how flexible the service will be in terms of transmitting and receiving funds from clients with other financial service providers or MNOs. MNOs may partner with multiple financial institutions, increasing the ability of clients to transact across financial institutions (interoperability), but diminishing the unique added value for the financial partners (see chapter 12). At the same time, banks and other providers that partner with only one MNO restrict the use of the service to clients of that MNO. Financial service providers must balance the need for universal, multi-MNO solutions with the practicality of outsourcing more functions to a single MNO.

At the outset, it can be expensive to engage in mobile banking; partners may be scarce and the incentives to reach a broad mass of people may not be aligned between the necessary actors. Some providers, including MNOs, do not have the high market share that might translate into the volume of transactions needed for mobile services to break even. Furthermore, adequate back-office and transaction-switching capability as well as sufficient internal controls are required, which smaller providers may not have or not have access to. To increase adoption rates, banks and others need to drive awareness of the service and ensure strong branding. While mobile banking reduces the cost of service delivery and increases convenience for both providers and clients, significant efforts are required to allay security fears and natural resistance to new technologies.

In addition, negotiations between the MNO and the financial service provider need to consider the customer service interface (for example, the MNO's customer call center) and the marketing and cross-selling of bank services to telephone customers. MNOs can use their

Box 1.14 Potential of Mobile Banking

Mobile banking has great potential to reach vast numbers of low-income, unbanked people at affordable prices with a wide range of products to meet complex financial needs. Yet early experience suggests that, although the potential is strong, it is by no means guaranteed that mobile banking will deeply penetrate low-income, unbanked segments with appropriately designed products.

First, the very qualities that endowed mobile network operators with a head start in mobile money may work against their capacity to field a more complex suite of products. The common mobile money product—a liquid, electronic wallet with the capability to transfer money—is quite simple, akin to the preexisting airtime wallet. However, MNOs know little about credit, savings, and insurance. They also lack regulatory room to offer

other services. Mobile money has often fallen between the regulatory cracks, and MNOs in several countries are offering mobile payments without being regulated as banks. Simply put, MNOs are poorly positioned on their own to offer a broader range of products. Strategic partnerships with providers that better understand the financial landscape and needs of the client are critical. For some MNOs, mobile payments do everything they want them to do: increase loyalty among voice clients and decrease the cost of distributing airtime. In other words, they have no motivation to do more unless they have strong, strategic partners. Because financial services are not their core business, MNO owners and shareholders may not be interested in investing in more services or partnerships.

Source: McKay and Pickens 2010.

extensive agent networks and retailers to provide cash-in, cash-out services and to sign up customers for banking services. The MNO's brand can be leveraged to appeal more directly to clients with stronger affiliations to mobile phones and mobile brands than to banking. This may be particularly appealing for efforts to increase financial inclusion among youth. However, using the MNOs' distribution and marketing channels also has revenue implications: fees are split among the MNO as a brand, the MNO as a transaction channel provider, and the bank as financial intermediary.

And lastly, in many countries, regulation of MNOs by the banking authorities is not yet clear, although this is beginning to change as new models emerge and the various stakeholders better understand the systemic risks inherent in mobile banking. Ultimately, significant regulatory factors

define the options for mobile banking, including regulatory restrictions on outsourcing cash-in, cash-out functions, know-your-customer (KYC) obligations, and limits on mobile money transactions. In fact, the maximum amount allowed for transfers is generally relatively low, which may limit the use of this service. Other issues include data security and customer privacy regarding e-banking, account issuance of non-banks, and taxation.

At the time of writing, various new technology-enabled business models are emerging: those that provide money transfer services (mobile money), those that link MNOs with bank services (mobile banking), and agent banking being established by large retailers. Some of the more interesting ones are described in box 1.15, although time will tell which ones will reach significant scale and longevity.

Box 1.15 New Branchless Banking Business Models

Safaricom's M-PESA: mobile money. Safaricom's M-PESA is a transfer and payment service with close to 17 million customers in Kenya, a country with 7 million bank accounts, most of which are considered active. The individual accounts only exist on the M-PESA platform, not in bank accounts. Bank accounts hold the float that backs the e-accounts one-to-one on a daily basis, which makes Safaricom a non-bank e-money issuer, though it is not licensed or regulated by the central bank or under e-money regulations (as of February 2012). In M-PESA's case, the float is held by a trust, not by Safaricom itself. M-PESA has a mixed-agent model. Some agents also sell airtime and are directly managed by Safaricom, but most agents are managed by intermediary companies under arrangements agreed with Safaricom.

M-Kesho, Iko Pesa: mobile money and bank account links. In Kenya M-Kesho links the M-PESA wallet offered by Safaricom with a bank account offered by Equity Bank, allowing customers to move money back and forth between the M-PESA wallet and the bank account. Orange in Kenya has transitioned all of its Orange Money accounts into Equity Bank accounts (Iko Pesa), which they did technically by integrating the Orange Money platform with Equity's core banking system. Rather than add a link to move money from an M-PESA account to a bank account like M-Kesho, the accounts of Iko Pesa are fully integrated, making them one and the same. Several banks and MNOs are establishing partnerships of this kind. In West Africa, Airtel Money has established a link with Ecobank in Ghana and Burkina Faso. In Madagascar, Orange has partnered with a microfinance bank to offer interest-paying savings accounts on Orange Money. It is not yet clear, however, how successful these models will be.

Telenor and Tameer's EasyPaisa (Pakistan). The partnership between Telenor, an MNO, and Tameer Bank grew out of a strategic alliance that started after Tameer Bank decided to use mobile phone banking services to reach rural clients. Telenor had 18 million subscribers in Pakistan, and Tameer Bank wanted to take advantage of Telenor's prepaid card distribution network and to act as its cash-in, cash-out agent. Tameer Bank had already decided to co-brand the new service—EasyPaisa—with the MNO in order to reach the millions of subscribers who had a strong affinity to Telenor but were not bank clients. After realizing the advantages of having a bank license to facilitate mobile money, Telenor acquired a 51 percent share in Tameer Bank in November 2008.

In 2012, millions of people were using over-the-counter services of EasyPaisa agents on a recurring basis, and more than 500,000 had mobile wallet accounts. With a network of 12,000 agents, EasyPaisa was growing quickly. Tameer's traditional core business (credit, savings, insurance) is enhanced by EasyPaisa, as Tameer holds the float from all EasyPaisa account balances, adding liquidity and dramatically reducing the cost of funds for its loan portfolio. Tameer pays all staff salaries via EasyPaisa; in the future, it could experiment with different kinds of savings and other accounts, potentially switching its good customers to receiving and paying their loans via this mobile platform. Telenor benefits from customer loyalty (reduced churn) and lower airtime distribution costs, all of which significantly enhance its core voice and text business. EasyPaisa illustrates the importance of understanding and managing partnerships in which the parties have their own core business but see advantages to joining forces for some things.

Oxxo (Mexico): agent banking. Oxxo shows how retail chains with their large retail

(*continued next page*)

Box 1.15 *(continued)*

footprint and relationship with customers across income segments can play an important role in new technology-enabled financial service business models. Oxxo is the largest retail network in North America, with more than 9,000 locations in Mexico. Oxxo claims to open a new store every eight hours and serves 7.5 million people every day. It is 100 percent owned by FEMSA, the largest beverage company in Latin America, which was originally set up to distribute beer.

Oxxo is already involved in financial services and has sizable bill payment and insurance businesses. It is negotiating with multiple banks to serve as a cash-in, cash-out merchant for their bank accounts. It is also offering its own branded electronic wallet in partnership with one of the banks, which will be accessible to customers using both cards and mobile handsets. Oxxo's main customer base is unbanked, so its offer of financial services is expected to significantly contribute to financial inclusion.

Source: Steve Rasmussen and Kabir Kumar, CGAP.

Branchless Banking and MFIs

MFIs, both regulated and NGOs, have generally not played a critical role in branchless banking; rather they have used the new technology to enhance customer service and reduce costs. For example, as MFIs become licensed, they can join the national payments system, gaining the use of ATMs and cards or POS devices to provide services through new channels. While some MFIs are able to take advantage of opportunities made available through technology, many struggle, and the expectations and hopes for what might have been have not materialized at any scale. MFIs require superior customer service skills, sophisticated back-office systems, and strong leadership and technical skills to achieve the organizational changes required, and many are simply not there yet. However, MFIs and other smaller providers can engage in branchless banking in several ways (Kumar, McKay, and Rotman 2010):

- Use mobile phones (or personal digital assistants, notebooks, or any other technology) to collect data in the field

- Use mobile financial services to update or replace practices related to the core business, for example, use mobile payments for loans and insurance premiums

- Act as an agent on behalf of a bank or an MNO.

Together, these three drivers—a focus on understanding clients better; acknowledgment of the multiplayer, multifunction nature of the financial ecosystem; and the opportunities technology presents—can support increased financial inclusion. The following chapters provide much more detail on each of these areas, describing the functions and roles within the financial market system and how they can work better for the poor.

Notes

1. For example, see the Clients at the Centre Initiative of the Consultative Group to Assist the Poor (CGAP) or the Center for Financial Inclusion of ACCION.

2. The Scottish government defines financial inclusion as access for individuals to appropriate

financial products and services. This includes people having the skills, knowledge, and understanding to make the best use of those products and services. Financial exclusion is often a symptom of poverty as well as a cause. See http://www.scotland.gov.uk/Publications/2005/01/20544/50280.

3. Findings are based on focus group discussions with 64 clients from regulated and unregulated MFIs and 20 in-depth interviews with members of the Debtors Association, the Superintendencia de Bancos, and MFI staff in El Alto, La Paz, Santa Cruz, and Montero, Bolivia.

4. *Portfolios of the Poor* is a seminal work synthesizing research findings from financial diary studies in Bangladesh, India, and South Africa (Collins et al. 2009).

5. This has become an issue of some controversy, with some believing that the microfinance industry as a whole—led by donor funding—has developed a supply-side/product-push character that emphasizes credit rather than other services, especially savings, increasing personal debt without bringing commensurate benefits.

6. There are, of course, exceptions. Some large cooperatives operate very much like regulated financial institutions, while some rural banks are tiny and somewhat informal, despite being subject to formal regulation. Furthermore, the degree of formality or legal form does not always equate with sustainability. Some state-owned banks may rely heavily on subsidies, while most commercial banks are financially independent. And while Savings Groups can have very formal operating procedures and are generally sustainable and independent of any external assistance in the long term, some externally facilitated groups such as Self-Help Groups and Financial Service Associations are designed to use outsiders on a medium- to longer-term basis, and most NGO MFIs continue to rely on donor subsidies.

7. Other products such as foreign exchange or bonds are also available in the formal sector, but they are not addressed in this book because poor populations use them so infrequently.

8. In practice, rules and supporting functions—whatever their type—are often delivered or subsidized directly by development agencies. Sustainability analysis in microfinance has historically focused on providers at the core and the extent to which their operations are financed from operational revenues, rather than extending to the wider market system as a whole. Yet if the objective is to develop functioning, sustainable market systems, sustainability analysis needs to be equally comprehensive, extending beyond the core to include supporting functions.

9. The concept of rules of the game is central in institutional economics. See chapter 19 for further discussion.

10. According to microLINKS wiki (2010), "*Social institutions* are complex, enduring structures or mechanisms of social order (and cooperation) that govern customs and recurring behavior patterns important to a society. They are usually identified with a social purpose (e.g., mitigating conflict, validating an elite). Enduring institutions such as gender, race or ethnicity, class, and religion help to shape individuals' beliefs and expectations. Social institutions exist because they serve a purpose, which is often to protect the power or privilege of particular groups."

11. Although mobile money still relies upon, and indeed may be successful because of, social institutions. See Susan Johnson's blog where she states, "These interpersonal transfers operate within social networks that involve relationships of 'give and take' that can operate over long periods of time and in which resource transfers may be given in one form, for example, cash, and returned in another, for example, support with resources of many different kinds or social connections to a job and so on. Hence mobile money transfer has brought a range of financial transactions that involve a reciprocal dimension." http://

technology.cgap.org/2012/04/19/what-does-the-rapid-uptake-of-mobile-money-transfer-in-kenya-really-mean-for-financial-inclusion/.

12. Financial literacy or education could be included within this function—or as a separate category—for the demand side of the market.

13. This section draws on various CGAP focus notes, including Mas and Kumar (2008); Mas (2008); Kumar, McKay, and Rotman (2010); and McKay and Pickens (2010).

14. The exception is that, if a bank wants to launch its own direct mobile payments system, it only needs regular data services from an MNO and could therefore launch without any real partnership. It would just require normal use of the mobile phone network.

15. This section is adapted from Flaming, McKay, and Pickens 2011 and Lehman 2010.

16. While POS devices provide access to bank accounts as well, how quickly the funds can be accessed will depend on clearing arrangements between the institutions.

17. At a minimum, banks or other providers need to buy wireless connectivity from the MNO. The next step is to seek access to the memory in the subscriber identity module (SIM) to use the encryption keys and phone service menu, which they get from an MNO. A more involved role would be for the MNO to manage the entire communications between the client and the back-office server of the bank. The bank could even have the MNO host and run the core banking system. In such a case, while the bank owns the accounts, the MNO operates the system.

References and Further Reading

* Key works for further reading.

Banthia, Anjali, Janiece Greene, Celina Kawas, Elizabeth Lynch, and Julie Slama. 2011. *Solutions for Financial Inclusion: Serving Rural Women*. New York: Women's World Banking.

Banthia, Anjali, and Peter McConaghy. 2012. *Remittances and Access to Finance in Spain and The Gambia: Understanding the Supply and Demand of Remittances between Spain and The Gambia and Its Impact on Financial Service Access*. New York: Women's World Banking.

Bennett, Lynn. 1997. "A Systems Approach to Social and Financial Intermediation with the Poor." Paper presented at the Banking with the Poor Network and World Bank Asia regional conference "Sustainable Banking with the Poor," Bangkok, November 3–7.

Bold, Chris, David Porteous, and Sarah Rotman. 2012. "Social Cash Transfers and Financial Inclusion: Evidence from Four Countries." Focus Note 77, CGAP, Washington, DC, February.

Bouman, F. J. A., and Otto Hospes. 1994. *Financial Landscapes Reconstructed: The Fine Art of Mapping Development*. Boulder: Westview Press.

*CGAP (Consultative Group to Assist the Poor). 2011. "Global Standard-Setting Bodies and Financial Inclusion for the Poor—Toward Proportionate Standards and Guidance." White Paper prepared on behalf of the G-20's Global Partnership for Financial Inclusion, CGAP, Washington, DC, October.

CGAP and World Bank. 2010. *Financial Access 2010: The State of Financial Inclusion through the Crisis*. Washington, DC: CGAP and World Bank.

Chatain, Pierre-Laruent, Andrew Zerzan, Wameek Noor, Najah Dannaoui, and Louis de Koker. 2011. "Protecting Mobile Money against Financial Crimes." World Bank, Washington, DC.

*Chen, Greg, Stephen Rasmussen, and Xavier Reille. 2010. "Growth and Vulnerabilities in Microfinance." Focus Note 61, CGAP, Washington, DC. http://www.cgap.org/gm/document-1.9.42393/FN61.pdf.

Christen, Robert Peck. 2011. "What Does Focusing on the Client Really Mean?" CGAP Blog, CGAP, Washington, DC.

CIA (Central Intelligence Agency). 2008. *CIA World Factbook 2008*. Washington, DC: CIA.

*Cohen, Monique. n.d. "The Emerging Market-Led Microfinance Agenda." MicroSave Briefing Note 25, MicroSave Kenya.

Cohen, Monique, and Candace Nelson. 2011. "Financial Literacy: A Step for Clients towards Financial Inclusion." Workshop paper commissioned for the 2011 Global Microcredit Summit, Valladolid, Spain, November 14–17.

Coleman, J. C. 1990, 1994. *Foundations of Social Theory*. Cambridge, MA: Harvard University Press.

*Collins, Daryl, Jonathan Morduch, Stuart Rutherford, and Orlanda Ruthven. 2009. *Portfolios of the Poor*. Princeton: Princeton University Press.

*Demirgüç-Kunt, Aslı, and Leora Klapper. 2012. "Measuring Financial Inclusion: The Global Findex." Policy Research Working Paper 6025, World Bank, Washington, DC.

*Ehrbeck, Tilman, Mark Pickens, and Michael Tarazi. 2012. "Financially Inclusive Ecosystems: The Roles of Government Today." Focus Note 76, CGAP, Washington, DC, February.

Faz, Xavier, and Paul Breloff. 2012. "A Structured Approach to Understanding the Financial Service Needs of the Poor in Mexico." CGAP Brief, CGAP, Washington, DC, May.

*Flaming, Mark, Claudia McKay, and Mark Pickens. 2011. "Agent Management Toolkit: Building a Viable Network of Branchless Banking Agents (Technical Guide)." CGAP, Washington, DC.

*Glisovic, Jasmina, and Mayada El-Zoghbi with Sarah Foster. 2011. "Advancing Savings Services: Resource Guide for Funders." CGAP, Washington, DC.

Harriss-White, B. 2004. "India's Socially Regulated Economy." *Indian Journal of Labour Economics* 47 (1).

*Hashemi, Syed M., and Aude de Montesquiou. 2011. "Reaching the Poorest: Lessons from the Graduation Model." Focus Note 69, CGAP, Washington, DC, March.

Hatch, John. 2011. "When Clients Grow Old: The Importance of Age in Addressing Client Needs." Workshop paper commissioned for the 2011 Global Microcredit Summit, Valladolid, Spain, November 14–17.

Hudon, M. 2008. "Norms and Values of the Various Microfinance Institutions." CEB Working Paper 08/006, Centre Emile Bernheim, Brussels, February.

*Johnson, Susan. n.d. "Gender and Microfinance: Guidelines for Good Practice." http://www.gdrc.org/icm/wind/gendersjonson.html.

——. 2000. "Gender Impact Assessment in Microfinance and Microenterprise: Why and How?" *Development in Practice* 10 (1): 89–93.

——. 2004. "Gender Norms in Financial Markets: Evidence from Kenya." *World Development* 32 (8): 1355–74.

——. 2011. "Understanding Kenya's Financial Landscape: The Missing Social Dimension." *FSD News* 17 (August): 2.

*Johnson, S., and S. Arnold. 2011. "Financial Exclusion in Kenya: Examining the Changing Picture 2006–2009." In *Financial Inclusion in Kenya: Survey Results and Analysis from FinAccess 2009*, 88–117. Nairobi: FSD Kenya and Central Bank of Kenya.

*Karim, Nimrah, Michael Tarazi, and Xavier Reille. 2008. "Islamic Microfinance: An Emerging Market Niche." Focus Note 49, CGAP, Washington, DC.

*Kendall, Jake. 2010. "Improving People's Lives through Savings." Global Savings Forum, November. http://www.gatesfoundation.org/financialservicesforthepoor/Documents/improving-lives.pdf.

*Kumar, Kabir, Claudia McKay, and Sarah Rotman. 2010. "Microfinance and Mobile Banking: The Story So Far." Focus Note 62, CGAP, Washington, DC, July.

Ledgerwood, Joanna. 1998. *Microfinance Handbook*. Washington, DC: World Bank.

*Lehman, Joyce. 2010. "Operational Challenges of Agent Banking Systems." Brief written for the Global Savings Forum, Bill and Melinda Gates Foundation, Seattle, November.

Linthorst, Audrey, and Scott Gaul. 2011. "What Do We Need to Know about Financial Inclusion in Africa?" SEEP Network, Washington, DC.

*M4P Hub. 2008. "A Synthesis for Making Markets Work for the Poor (M4P) Approach." http://www.m4phub.org/resource-finder/result.aspx?k=m4p%20synthesis&t=0&c=0&s=0.

*Mas, Ignacio. 2008. "Being Able to Make (Small) Deposits and Payments, Anywhere." Focus Note 45, Washington, DC, CGAP.

——. 2010. "Savings for the Poor: Banking on Mobile Phones." *World Economics* 11 (4).

*Mas, Ignacio, and Kabir Kumar. 2008. "Banking on Mobiles: Why, How, for Whom?" Focus Note 48, CGAP, Washington, DC.

Mas, Ignacio, and Dan Radcliffe. 2010. "Mobile Payments Go Viral: M-PESA in Kenya." http://papers.ssrn.com/sol3/papers.cfm?abstract_id=1593388.

*McKay, Claudia, and Mark Pickens. 2010. "Branchless Banking 2010: Who's Served? At What Price? What's Next?" Focus Note 66, CGAP, Washington, DC.

microLINKS wiki. 2010. "Informal Regulations under BEE." Value Chain Framework wiki page. http://apps.develebridge.net/amap/index.php/Informal_Regulations_under_BEE.

——. n.d. "Social Institutions Comprising Informal Regulations." http://microlinks.kdid.org/good-practice-center/value-chain-wiki/social-institutions-comprising-informal-regulations.

Orozco, Manuel, Anjali Banthia, and Mariama Ashcroft. 2011. "A Country Profile on The Gambia: The Marketplace and Financial Access." Women's World Banking, New York.

Perdomo, Maria. 2008. "Consumer Protection: A Client Perspective." Research note prepared for Microfinance Opportunities and Freedom from Hunger.

Pickens, Mark. 2011. "Which Way? Mobile Money and Branchless Banking in 2011." CGAP Technology Blog, CGAP, Washington, DC, March 9.

*Porteous, D. 2005. "The Access Frontier as an Approach and Tool in Making Markets Work for the Poor." http://bankablefrontier.com/assets/pdfs/access-frontier-as-tool.pdf.

Rankin, Katharine N. 2002. "Social Capital, Microfinance, and the Politics of Development." *Feminist Economics* 8 (1): 1–24.

Rotman, Sarah. 2010. "An Alternative to M-PESA? Orange and Equity Bank Launch Iko PESA." CGAP Technology Blog, CGAP, Washington, DC, December 6.

Shipton, Parker. 2007. *The Nature of Entrustment: Intimacy, Exchange, and the Sacred in Africa.* New Haven: Yale University Press.

World Bank. 2011. *World Development Report 2011: Conflict, Security, and Development.* Washington, DC: World Bank.

Wyman, Oliver. 2007. "Sizing and Segmenting Financial Needs of the World's Poor." Bill and Melinda Gates Foundation, Seattle.

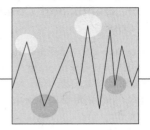

CHAPTER 2

Clients

Stuart Rutherford, Daryl Collins, and Susan Johnson

No matter how it is measured, the number of people without access to financial services is very large indeed. In 1976, when Muhammad Yunus in Bangladesh started the experiment that led to the Grameen Bank, he focused on the very poor. As microfinance grew, it attracted the "economically active poor," people who might be expected to take loans to run a small business, for example. More recently with the drive for "financial inclusion," attention has turned to the "unbanked" poor—poor people not using formal financial services of any sort (including microfinance, sometimes referred to as "semiformal" services). Just over half of the world's adult population is unbanked, most of them poor: In Africa, four out of five adults are unbanked, and in South Asia, three out of five (Chaia et al. 2009). In rich countries, by contrast, fewer than one in ten adults lacks a formal means to save or to borrow (Chaia et al. 2009).[1] All these numbers—of the extremely poor, the moderately poor, and the unbanked poor—dwarf the number of clients already served by microfinance, estimated at 190 million at the end of 2009 (Microcredit Campaign Summit 2011).

In chapter 1, "The Evolving Financial Landscape," we discussed who the poor are, how they differ, and how various influences such as life-cycle stages, geography, livelihoods, and informal rules and norms, such as gender, affect their access to financial services. This chapter examines financial services from the point of view of poor people. It looks at the kinds of tools that the poor need to manage their money, shows why they need them, and assesses the extent to which they already have access to them. It describes the key characteristics of good quality pro-poor formal financial tools and shows how and why the poor, the extremely poor, and the unbanked poor might use and benefit from such services if they were more widely available.

The Poor and Financial Services: Diverse Needs and Common Problems

The poor, as broadly defined in the opening paragraph, make up half or more of the world's population, and although they are somewhat clustered regionally, above all in Africa and Asia, in all other respects they are diverse. It follows that their financial behavior is similarly diverse. The borrowing and saving patterns of an agricultural day-laboring household are not the same as those of a farmer, let alone those of a household that depends on a small shop or workshop in an urban slum, or on low-paid wage jobs in a factory, or on domestic service. Even where livelihoods are similar, innate differences between households will generate different financial patterns, according to the age, the gender, and the health of the household members. Research shows that women and men tend to have different attitudes toward household resources and their allocation, including financial resources.[2] At an individual level, personality counts: Some people are more cautious than others and may therefore be more averse to loans and more ready to save. Conversely, there are overarching cultural traditions—for example, the preference for certain types of savings-and-loan clubs among the ethnic Chinese or among the slum dwellers of Nairobi—that give a distinctive shape to the financial behavior of whole groups of people. The degree of monetization of a country's or of a district's economy will affect the scope for financial intermediation. And, last, a household's financial service needs change over time with life-cycle events: for example, as the children are educated and leave home and productive activities in the household decline.

Nevertheless, poverty presents poor people with a number of financial management problems that cut across differences in traditions, livelihoods, and household composition. These commonalities are the subject of this chapter. Here general observations about poor people and

their money management needs are presented, beginning with the most basic question of all: Why do poor people need financial tools in the first place? To answer that question, we need to move into the villages and slums and find out more about how poor people manage their money.

The "Financial Portfolios" of the Poor

Finance is the intersection of money and time. Looking at one element in the absence of the other tells less than half the story. One-off surveys that focus on the finances of poor households may identify which savings institutions are used or what types of loans are outstanding, but say little or nothing about how the timing of cash flows is managed to accumulate savings or repay loans. To see how poor households try to reconcile constrained incomes with expenditure needs, and how financial tools, no matter how crude, are employed to achieve that end, we need to look at their household finances as a totality, as a *portfolio* of tools, each with its particular cash flow. To understand how and why poor households choose and use their financial tools, we need to observe how these portfolios change over time: "What has been missing is a close look at how portfolios function: not just how well the pieces work, but how well they work together. Focusing on *how* gives new insight into the day-to-day nature of poverty and yields concrete ideas for creating better solutions for it" (Collins et al. 2009, p. 14).

For the book *Portfolios of the Poor*, the authors conducted year-long "financial diaries" in urban and rural sites in Bangladesh, India, and South Africa, to better understand this three-dimensional view of household finances. These were not "diaries" that the households themselves kept, but reports from interviews carried out by trained investigators, speaking the local language, on a frequent and regular basis throughout a full year.[3] The investigators recorded as full an account as possible of income and expenditure, and focused especially closely on financial flows—flows in and out of savings and loan tools. At the same time, they probed for an understanding of how circumstances, preferences, and aspirations shaped the financial decisions the households made. From these "diaries" it was often possible to construct not just the balance sheets of the household accounts but also—and much more revealing—cash flow statements showing the activity that lay behind the balance sheets, all set in the context of the particular household's circumstances. Altogether, data for about 250 households were gathered, supplemented by a further 50 households from Bangladesh collected in a subsequent and slightly modified "diary" exercise.[4]

Active Money Managers

The "diary" research revealed that poor people use financial tools intensely. At first this finding seems counterintuitive. It is easy to suppose that very small incomes lead to a "hand-to-mouth" existence in which income is consumed as soon as it arrives and there is no need and no scope for intermediation and thus no need for the financial tools that make it possible. This turns out not to be the case. The poor, rather, tend to be intensive money managers, constantly seeking ways to set a bit of money aside or to borrow. This is not *in spite* of incomes being small, but precisely *because* they are small. Small incomes are often unreliable and irregular, so there is an ever-present need to make sure there is enough money to put food on the table every day and not just on those days when money comes in. Small incomes, even if they arrive regularly, also mean that large-scale but unavoidable expenditures—for marriage, education, homemaking, and festivals, for bicycles, fridges, fans, televisions, and mobile phones, and for business and bribes and so on—can almost never be found from current income, and so must be saved or borrowed, or both. The same applies to emergencies, which, no matter what form they

take, almost always require large sums of money if they are to be coped with successfully. The poor's need for ways to save and to borrow—their need for financial services—is greater than the needs of the nonpoor: not in monetary value, of course, but in intensity. Being able to take a dollar from a bank, or borrow it from a helpful neighbor, may allow a mother to take her child to the clinic and have her conjunctivitis cleared up; not being able to do so may lead to her daughter going blind in later life. Managing money well is an essential life skill that most poor people take very seriously.

To manage their money, the households that took part in the "diaries" research pushed and pulled more money through *informal* tools than through formal savings, loan, or insurance accounts at banks, insurance companies, or microfinance institutions (MFIs). This was true even where banks were near at hand (as in South Africa) or where MFIs had already reached the slum or the village (as in the Bangladesh case). This can be partly understood from the "supply side." Banks are mostly set up to serve corporate clients and wealthier individuals and were never designed to cater to the needs of the poor. MFIs *are* built to serve the poor, but so far at least, they have focused most sharply on one particular financial service they believe will help poor people to climb out of poverty—the short-term loan for small-business investment. Investing in a business may indeed provide the potential to increase incomes, but it is rarely the financial service in greatest demand. Many MFIs and other service providers now recognize this and are beginning to offer a broader range of products tailored to the poor, but most of these services are relatively new and have yet to reach large numbers of clients.

If we look at the "demand side" and see things from the point of view of poor households it is easier to understand why they rely most often on informal devices and services. They need ways to build sums of money: small sums to keep the household fed and clothed, and bigger amounts for life-cycle expenses of all kinds and for emergencies. Because such sums can be built only by capturing money squeezed from already very small cash flows, they need tools that help them do exactly that—set aside a little money each day or each week or month that can be used to build savings or to repay loans. Such tools need to be close at hand, and flexible enough to catch as many deposits and repayments as possible. The financial diaries revealed that saving at home, often in very small values, is the most common and frequent kind of transaction carried out by poor householders as they seek to protect money from many competing demands. Then comes borrowing and lending small sums in the village or slum, among family and friends, and often interest free. To build larger sums, poor people typically save through savings groups of various sorts (some of them very sophisticated) or use larger-scale informal borrowing, often from moneylenders and usually with interest.

Understanding the Poor's Financial Service Needs

Research exercises such as the financial diaries reveal the complexity of money management among the poor and the intimate way in which it shapes and is shaped by the circumstances of individuals and their households. Nevertheless, the research also provides an opportunity to look at the financial lives of poor people in aggregate, and when that is done, dominant themes emerge that respond to the set of most pressing financial needs faced by all poor people. One of these is short-term cash flow management to deal with day-to-day life—what economists might call "consumption smoothing." Another is the problem of how to deal with emergencies when they arise, or "risk management." A third is how poor households struggle to assemble the large sums of money they need to take care of major life-cycle events and to build up household assets. For some households, an important part of this last category includes the financing of productive activities, such as setting up and stocking small businesses, or buying assets for self-employment, such as rickshaws.

Cash Flow Management and Income Smoothing

When the World Bank says that a percentage of the world's population lives on US$2 a day, it means that the *average* monthly income, multiplied by 12 and divided by 365, comes to US$2. But most people who live on low incomes do not actually receive US$2 each and every day. Many poor people derive their income from one or several informal activities that produce income sporadically. An Indian slum dweller may pull a rickshaw most days, but not on days when he cannot find one to hire, or it is raining heavily, or he is too ill, or the streets are blocked by a demonstration. Meanwhile his wife has a low-grade job in a garments factory where, in theory, she gets paid monthly, but in practice she can never be sure when her floor supervisor is going to get around to paying her, or how much he is going to hold back for how long.

Income irregularity and unreliability make up one leg of a "triple whammy" of financial handicaps faced by the poor. The other legs are low incomes and the lack of adequate financial tools. The effect of all three working together and reinforcing each other is reflected most sharply in the poor's struggle to manage life on a day-to-day basis. If income really did come in at a reliable US$2 a day, not only would planning expenditures be much easier, but the poor might also be offered better financial services by lenders or deposit collectors who would know their clients could save or repay at least a small amount every day. But with US$8 coming in one day and then nothing for a week, just putting food on the table each day becomes a logistical problem that needs help from financial tools if it is to be solved.

Widening the timescale reveals an extra layer of *seasonal* problems. Farmers or traders whose income is "lumpy," arriving with the harvest or with the good trading months when festivals occur, can face two intertwined cash flow management problems. First, they have to find a way to retain liquidity throughout the year, perhaps by keeping back most of the harvest and then selling it in smaller amounts from time to time. Second, they have to make sure the money raised by such sales is stored somewhere where it can be called on for daily expenditure without being eroded by the many other demands they face. Boxes 2.1 and 2.2 illustrate this with two households from the financial diaries studies.

It is not surprising, then, that the financial diaries showed that day-to-day money management, both in towns and in villages, is the most intensive part of the poor's money management efforts. Almost everywhere housewives keep a little money back each time they shop, but they also put a handful of grain into a "reserve" bag each time they cook a meal. They borrow and lend, close by in their slum or village, both small sums of money and small amounts of rice, kerosene, salt, and soap. The disadvantages of one financial tool lead to the use of another, sometimes in a chain. For example, because saving money in the home is so hard when there are so many requests for help or for loans from family and neighbors, demands for candies or a drink by children and husbands, or the temptations offered by peddlers, people often use "moneyguards"—other trusted people in their extended family or neighborhood with whom they can keep a little money out of harm's way. Because moneyguards are not always reliable— they may not have the money on hand the day it is needed—the poor end up borrowing from other neighbors (often interest free if the sum is small), or buying goods on credit at the local shop, or

Box 2.1 Income Volatility, Week-by-Week and Year-by-Year

Pumza lives in Langa, a township near Cape Town, South Africa. She supports herself and four children by selling sheep intestines that she grills on the side of the street. Every day she buys and cooks intestines and sells them to passersby. "This can be a fairly profitable business, and indeed Pumza makes a profit averaging about US$95 per month. A government-provided child support grant of US$25 a month supplements this income, so Pumza's five-person family lives on a monthly income of about US$120. These figures show that Pumza is not among the poorest of households, but they do not reveal the fluctuations in cash flow that Pumza experiences in her business life."

Figure B2.1.1 shows these cash flows on a fortnightly basis. The dark, solid line shows her inflows of cash, that is, the cash revenues that Pumza receives as well as the collections she makes from clients who bought from her on credit. The lighter, solid line shows her business outflows of cash, that is, inventory purchases and business expenses, such as wood to cook the sheep intestines. Both lines are quite volatile, but most importantly, they do not always move in step. Sometimes business does not go well, and Pumza does not earn enough revenue to buy stock for the next day. In the time we knew her this happened twice—indicated by the arrows in the chart. She could have sold her old stock, but customers prefer fresh meat and might choose to go to one of the other several sheep intestine sellers in the area. If she's lucky, these times coincide with the receipt of her child grant,

(continued next page)

Box 2.1 *(continued)*

which helps tide her over, but on the two occasions when we observed this problem, she was not lucky in this way. However, during May, she and a group of three other sheep intestine sellers had formed a savings club. From Monday to Thursday, they each paid in US$7.70 and took turns getting the entire pot of US$30. In this way, she was able to fund her first cash flow shortfall in figure B2.1.1. Unhappily her savings club failed her during the next shortfall, because one of the club members failed to pay in. Pumza ended up going to the moneylender, where she paid an interest rate of 30 percent per month.

Figure B2.1.1 Revenues and Inventory Expenses of a South African Small Businesswoman, Daily Cash Flows Aggregated Fortnightly (Twice Monthly)
US$ converted from South African rand at US$1 = R 6.5, market rates

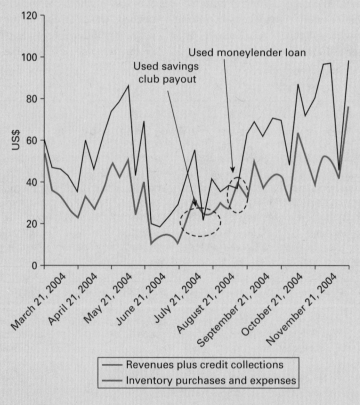

Source: Collins et al. 2009, p. 41.

Source: Collins et al. 2009, p. 42 and passim, with permission from Princeton Press.

Box 2.2 Cash Flow Management Given Volatile Seasonal Income

Sita, a widow, farmed a little land in northern India. Two of her sons lived with her, and as well as helping on the land, they took casual laboring work. Nevertheless, 60 percent of their income was earned in just four months, from June to September, and in the year that we tracked their lives, bad weather meant that that income was especially low. Averaged over the year, total household income was just under US$30 per month, or about 32 cents for each member of the household (about US$1.20 per person per day when adjusted for purchasing power).

During the household's eight-month-long "low season" it sometimes fell to less than half of that.

Astonishingly, Sita and her sons still managed to save enough grain and cash, at home, to ensure that they could eat throughout the year. To get hold of a larger sum they mortgaged land to borrow from a grain trader for whom one of the sons worked, and repaid that debt by deducting a little at a time from his wage. In these ways, over the year they saved and repaid about US$63, almost a fifth of their total income.

going into rent arrears. Then, when the rent arrears have built to the point where the landlord begins to threaten eviction, they borrow larger sums, with interest, from a moneylender. To repay the moneylender, saving efforts have to be redoubled, or assets have to be sold off. But selling off assets—for example, selling roof sheets to repay a creditor—simply creates another essential item that requires the poor to save. No wonder households in the financial diaries told the researchers that "All this keeps us awake at night," or confided that "I hate having to borrow money from other people—but there is no life without money, so we just have to do it."

But although day-to-day money management is where the majority of financial services are used, this does not show up much in the balance sheets of the poor. Year-end balances of most "diary" households revealed rather low levels of household savings and of local borrowing and lending. It is only when cash flows are examined that this intensity of use can be seen. Typically a household's annual financial cash flow was many times the value of their financial assets and liabilities. The ratio of cash pushed and pulled through

financial tools to average annual income varied between about 75 percent and 175 percent in India, a similar amount in Bangladesh, and a figure somewhat higher in South Africa (Collins et al. 2009, pp. 31–33). This is because much day-to-day management involves short-term, rapidly revolving exchanges of cash. Many of the smallest loans from neighbors were repaid in a matter of days. "Big flows and small balances" is a good general description of poor-owned portfolios, and they are matched in the experiences of MFIs that have a track record of offering unusually convenient passbook savings to poor communities. When examining the accounts at BURO, an MFI in Bangladesh, researchers found that the annual flow through the passbook savings product was four and a half times the value of the year-end savings balance (Rutherford et al. 2001). Poor people need to save short term to form small sums that can be withdrawn to cope with everyday life. Saving, for the poor, is a *verb* before it is a *noun*: something you do rather than something you possess. More often than not, saving is a way of coping with small and unreliable incomes rather than a way of building capital.

A reliable lender of small loans can also help to smooth income, as box 2.3 shows.

Dealing with Emergencies and Anticipating Risk

When emergencies strike, poor people, like everyone else, need large amounts of capital if they are to have a chance of fending off the worst effects of the event. In wealthy countries, and among the better-off in poorer ones, insurance is available to provide that capital, in the right amount at the right time. Insurance is a fast-growing and exciting part of microfinance, but it has reached few poor households so far (though many microlenders do provide insurance against debt if a borrower dies holding a loan, either as an option

for the borrower or built into the price of the loan). Lacking formal insurance, most poor people must look for other ways to anticipate risk and to deal with emergencies when they occur.

Poor households are peculiarly vulnerable to emergencies. Many live in fragile ecosystems: Pushed to the margins by poverty, they are closer than others to seas that breed cyclones or rivers that flood, or farmland prone to drought. Close to one-fifth of the burden of disease in developing countries can be attributed to environmental risk—with unsafe water, poor sanitation, and poor hygiene as leading risk factors causing premature deaths (World Bank 2005). The poor may live in provisional slums with uncertain legal status where they can be pushed out by landlords or

Box 2.3 Ramna's Top-Ups

One of several innovations that Grameen Bank introduced in 2002 in an effort to make its products less rigid was the loan "top-up." Under this provision, borrowers may top-up their loans to the original disbursed value once they are about halfway through the annual repayment schedule. In effect, they can take smaller loans every six months rather than a bigger loan once a year. Ramna and her husband provide a good example of Grameen clients who benefited from the top up loan. They were getting on in age, unskilled, uneducated, and unlikely to run any kind of business, but they still had two sons at home whose schooling they desperately wanted to continue. Their income came from whatever casual employment or self-employment Ramna's husband could find: During the three years that their financial life was tracked, he did farm labor, collected crabs from the sea nearby, and worked

in a tea stall. Ramna was in charge of keeping the home ticking and making sure everyone was fed. She found Grameen's top-up system useful. Every six months she got a usefully large lump sum that helped her keep the household stable. The researchers saw her spend these sums on stocks of rice, managing her father-in-law's funeral, buying medicines for her husband, and paying for school fees and books and clothes. Once she simply lodged her loan top-up with a moneyguard neighbor until she needed to take it back to pay off a private loan that became due. On another day she was found keeping back some of her top-up in a locked box at home because she knew that a "down" period was coming and she would need an extra source from which to make the regular weekly Grameen loan repayment—behavior that indicated the value she placed on getting her biannual infusions of useful capital.

governments at short notice, or suffer from fires ignored by the municipality. Unable to buy suitable drugs or quality feed, their animals die younger and produce less than those of wealthier farmers. Cooking over an open flame near homes built of bamboo walling or straw roofs, they experience a higher risk of destructive fires. That same wood smoke damages lungs and eyes, an example of how health problems start more often and are cured less easily among the poor than among the population in general.

In Bangladesh, half of the households studied in the diaries project suffered serious financial disruption from ill health during the study year, and in India the figure was two in five. One in five of the Bangladesh households lost a home during the year, and four out of five of the South African households had to contribute to expensive funeral ceremonies, many of them related to the HIV/AIDS pandemic.

How did they cope when these crises struck? Often they did not: The illness was never properly cured, the home or the job was lost for good, and the cousin was given only the most basic of burials. The question then becomes, How did they *try* to cope? When disaster strikes, people pull in whatever resources they can reach. Assets may be sold or, in the case of precious metals, pawned. If there is time for the deal, any land in the household's ownership may be mortgaged out. Savings may be exhausted. Social networks are called on for gifts in kind or in money, and for interest-free or low-cost loans. Nonessential spending is foregone. Without access to insurance services poor people use whatever financial tools they have available to them to manage risk (see box 2.4).

Box 2.4 Enayet's Foot

Enayet worked on building sites with his father in a slum in Dhaka, Bangladesh. When he was about 17, his parents realized he was becoming dependent on drugs. They remonstrated with him, and Enayet ran away from home and lived on the streets of Chittagong, a port city several hundred kilometers away. His father drew down their meager savings and gave up working to search for his son. He found him, but only because Enayet got into a brawl and broke his leg. He had no money to treat the injury, and it worsened: Eventually he contacted his father when he could bear the pain no longer. Back in Dhaka, Enayet's family gave up almost everything to have him admitted to the hospital. They sold their furniture, their jewelry, and their bicycle. They got loans from extended family. Enayet's younger sister withdrew her savings from a club run by women working on her floor in a garments factory, money she had planned to use for her marriage. But the sum they raised was still far from enough, and faced with a "no fee no treatment" ultimatum from the doctors, Enayet's father went to better-off people in the neighborhood—a retired teacher with a pension, a shopkeeper, and a small-time pawnbroker—to take loans on interest of 10 percent a month. Later, in the time of the financial diary research, Enayet was back home, walking with a crutch. The expensive loans had not been repaid, and very little interest had been given. Enayet's mother suffered verbal abuse from one of the lenders and did her best to ignore it. Almost certainly, the debt will not be repaid; from time to time Enayet or his father will make token interest payments, hoping that eventually the principal will be forgiven or forgotten.

Nevertheless, when a particular risk is especially expensive, or has an unusually high likelihood of happening, poor households may try to buy protection from it, using formal insurance or informal substitutes. Such is the case in South Africa of funeral insurance, where many poor households anticipate having to pay out for funerals and invest in devices specifically designed to deal with this event. Many of the "diary" households belonged to an informal *burial society* into which they pay monthly premiums and in return receive financial benefits to help cover the high costs of burials. Some of the same households also paid into formal *funeral insurance policies*.[5]

Many households used both the informal and the formal schemes, so the financial diaries authors were able to compare how well they worked. Within an overall financial portfolio of 8 to 12 financial instruments, South African diaries households usually had at least one burial society and one formal funeral insurance policy. These households spent, on average, 3 percent of gross monthly income in total on all of their funeral cover instruments.

On pure economic terms, formal funeral insurance has about the same value as informal burial insurance:[6] Formal funeral insurance tends to cost more on average per month than informal burial insurance, but it also pays out more. Looking beyond economics, burial societies have the advantage of providing a great deal of physical assistance and moral support around the time of the funeral. Fellow members take on a significant role in preparing and serving the feast during the burial, often providing the cookware and eating utensils. However, burial societies can be quite unreliable. Evidence suggests that close to 10 percent of them run out of money (FinMark Trust 2003). Therefore, although many poor households may continue to belong to burial societies for the social benefits they provide, formal insurance providers have a clear contribution to make in this market by continuing to offer good value products with reliable service.

Building Bigger Sums for Life-Cycle Events, Assets, and Businesses

The constant threat of emergencies requires households to find large sums of money *quickly*. But they are by no means the only reason why poor households need to build large sums. All of us, including the poor, need to be frequent big spenders, to deal with life's big events—annual festivals, ceremonies to celebrate birth, marriage and death, costs for education and home building, and assets to make life better, such as fans and televisions. Some will also want to build large sums to establish a new business or expand an existing one, or to invest in a large asset for self-employment, such as owning one's own rickshaw rather than hiring one on a daily basis, or buying or leasing-in more land to farm. Others will migrate to find work, in the big city or overseas, and will need to finance these often costly journeys. How do they go about building these bigger sums?

We have seen that most of the financial tools used by poor people are informal. But informal sector finance is not geared to handling large sums of money over protracted periods of time. It is not safe to hold large amounts of savings at home, or in a savings club, because the longer these savings have to be kept, and the greater their value, the greater the risk of loss or theft or misuse. Similarly, even the greediest moneylender is not willing to lend large sums to the poor because large loans need lengthy repayment periods, and the longer the loan is held the greater grows the risk of default.

So, even though these kinds of large expenditure can usually be anticipated, rather than being needed suddenly, poor people nevertheless find themselves building up sums piecemeal, just as they do when faced with an emergency. It is not unusual for a big asset to be bought with a mix of savings, loans, gifts from family, and the proceeds from the sale or mortgaging of other assets. The piecemeal approach also characterizes the way that savings for large-scale expenditures are assembled. Certain items, notably gold jewelry, roof sheets (and bricks and cement blocks and lengths of timber), and, in many households, livestock, are used as long-term stores of value, and although the terms of most informal financial tools are short, they can be used to finance these savings-in-kind. ROSCAs are particularly good at this.

ROSCAs, short for rotating savings and credit associations, are savings clubs in which members pay regularly into a pot that is taken in its entirety by one of their number in rotation and are common around the world. Pumza, the sheep-intestine seller featured in box 2.1, was in a four-member daily ROSCA, and Enayet's sister, mentioned in box 2.4, belonged to a much bigger monthly ROSCA run by fellow workers at her garments factory. ROSCAs are often deliberately designed to make it easier to obtain expensive items. In the Philippines, for example, rural school teachers use ROSCAs to help furnish their homes after marriage: They persuade their colleagues to join a ROSCA and use the proceeds to buy sofas and chairs.

Where MFIs have become common, as in much of South Asia, the short terms that characterize their lending (mostly about one year) lead to similar uses of the sums loaned. To the consternation (and sometimes disapproval) of MFI field officers, MFI clients may take a loan ostensibly for business investment and use it to buy gold jewelry. From the clients' point of view, buying such a store of savings is as legitimate a use for a loan as any other, especially when other opportunities to save (or invest) are so scarce.[7] The piece of jewelry may serve as decoration until called on to help finance something on a much larger scale, such as the wedding of the young woman whose neck it adorns.

In all three countries in the financial diaries studies, most of the rural sample owned their home and the parcel of land on which it stood, often through inheritance. The better-off also had land to farm (in the case of India and Bangladesh)

or a large compound (in the case of South Africa). In the urban areas renting a home was more common. In some cases, such as in some slums in Dhaka, Bangladesh, families owed the physical structure of a simple timber-and tin-sheet one-room home and perched it rent free on land owned officially by the government or some other institutional landlord. In South Africa some of the diaries households owned a permanent brick home, although others with shaky tenure in the urban areas could simultaneously be building a home in the rural areas.

Financing the ownership of a home, then, was a challenge being faced by only a minority of the diary households—but where that was the case, the challenge was considerable, and the solution to it required huge self-discipline, as the case of Jonas and Mimimi, from South Africa, shows (box 2.5). Although many MFIs and other providers are beginning to offer housing loans or contractual savings products to invest in a home, these tools were not available to this couple. Therefore, like many others around the world, they did their home building in a piecemeal fashion.

Much of what is observed about the financing of domestic assets is also true of productive assets. They too are often acquired through a range of sources including gifts, asset sales, remittances from family members working in the big city or overseas, and savings and loans. The savings may have been held until needed in lower-value items acquired through saving or borrowing short term in the informal sector.

Once again, community-based devices such as the ROSCA, with its simple and flexible formula, can be a powerful way of assembling cash for working assets. In Vietnam fishing communities have used "auction ROSCAs" (ROSCAs in which the order in which the lump sum is taken is determined not by lottery but by bidding for it at each draw) to raise money for boats and equipment. So high is the demand for capital that club members sometimes forego as much as 50 percent of the

Box 2.5 Building a Home Little by Little

Jonas and Mimimi, a married couple who run a *shebeen* (township bar) in Langa near Cape Town, have an impressive capacity to save. Mimimi's profits from the *shebeen* business are about US$324 per month, while Jonas works as a gardener and is paid US$185 per month, for a total monthly household income of US$509. Compared with other diaries households in Langa, which have an average monthly income of US$425, they are doing quite well. Mimimi typically manages to send about US$31 per month to her relatives in a rural area of the Eastern Cape. Their children live there with Mimimi's mother, and she sends money every month to pay for their food and school fees as well as to contribute to a home they are building there. She then manages to stretch about US$87 for their living expenses every month. A typical monthly budget is detailed below.

Mimimi's typical monthly budget (US$)	509
Source of funds	
Business profits	324
Regular wages	185
Uses of funds	486
Cell phone	6
Cigarettes	3
Electricity	16
Food	49
Money sent to Eastern Cape	31
Transport to shopping	1
Transport to work	13
Savings clubs	367
Net savings in bank	23

Jonas and Mimimi's most important savings devices are two informal savings clubs. Together, they save about US$367 with these clubs. A total of US$3,065 was paid out from one of them during the research year, and it was all used to build the house in the Eastern Cape. The other club paid out US$725 a few months later. From this payout, they spent the majority on a Christmas feast and Christmas presents when they went to the Eastern Cape for the holidays. But that still left about US$260 to buy cement for the floors and to buy doors for the house.

In the end, between the two savings clubs and the money they retained from Jonas's salary in a bank account, this young couple built up about US$4,000 in savings (not counting the money sent to the Eastern Cape every month). Of this, 12 percent was spent on Christmas, 6 percent was retained in the bank, and 82 percent was used to build the Eastern Cape house. The way they saved to build the house and the proportion of savings that went toward the house is similar to that of many other households in South Africa.[a]

Note: a. See "Housing and the Finances of the Poor" at www.financialdiaries.com for more details regarding how financial diaries households acquired housing.

sum in bidding for it. In Bangladesh rickshaw drivers run "rickshaw ROSCAs" to build a big enough sum to buy their own rickshaws. At some gathering place, often the garage where their hired rickshaws are parked overnight, each rickshaw driver in the club sets aside a fixed contribution from his daily earnings, and when there is enough in the kitty to buy a rickshaw it is decided by lottery which member of the club is to receive it. By a clever twist, which illustrates well the sophistication that often characterizes ROSCAs, after a club member has received his rickshaw he puts in double the usual amount each day: He can afford it because now he does not have to pay rent for a rickshaw. This has the effect of accelerating the ROSCA so that the next rickshaw purchase comes along sooner, reducing the length of time that members' investments are at risk. A few men have used these clubs so successfully that they have acquired fleets of rickshaws, and then graduated to motorized rickshaws.

Note, however, that not every Dhaka rickshaw driver wants to own his own rickshaw. Costs and risks are associated with owning such assets. A rickshaw needs maintenance. It needs to be stored somewhere safely at night. It has to be protected from confiscation by police officers running extortion rackets. Not every poor rickshaw driver can manage these tasks, so many prefer not to try. It is not only because they cannot afford them—or do not have access to the right financial products at the opportune time—that poor people own few productive assets or invest in few productive activities: Other aspects of their poverty may make it unprofitably hard to benefit from investment.

Nor does every self-employed person want to join a dedicated ROSCA of this sort, again for reasons to do with the financial facts of his or her life. The pressure to keep up with the payment schedule is severe, and if one cannot be sure that one's cash flow will allow one to pay on time every time, it may be better to avoid the commitment. This is not just because of the immediate consequences

of default—the shame and maybe a bit of rough treatment at the hands of other members—but, more importantly, because the inability to keep up the repayment schedule is a very good indicator that one's financial position is not strong enough to maintain the asset once it is acquired. Many rickshaw drivers who struggle to meet ROSCA dues or repay MFI loans used to buy a rickshaw end up having to sell their machine, almost always at a big discount, because they lack the means to bring financial stability to other aspects of their life.

That leads to an important observation: All poor households need financial tools to handle their basic needs—day-to-day consumption smoothing, dealing with emergencies, and building sums to pay for life's big occasions. If those basic needs are not being at least partially met, lending to poor people *exclusively* for productive investment may not be wise. At best, the loans meant for business will be diverted to the more basic needs. At worst the loan will go into a business that will prove short lived or loss making in the face of other financial demands made on the borrower.

In the case of Bangladesh, one of the world's most mature microfinance markets, MFI lenders have by and large learned to turn a blind eye to the fact that many poor clients use their MFI loans primarily or even exclusively for nonproductive purposes—even though some of these MFIs continue to insist in public that loans are given only for microenterprise investment. A set of financial diaries carried out to examine how informal devices and MFI services fit into the financial lives of the rural poor in Bangladesh sheds light on this: Productive investment is only one of a range of uses that people borrow from MFIs for, as box 2.6 shows.

Other evidence suggests that business owners can benefit from small, flexible cash infusions in a cash flow crunch, but that they may not lead to business growth. Financial diaries done with a modest sample of small business owners in

Box 2.6 How MFI Loans Are Used in Bangladesh

Out of a total of 237 microfinance loans carefully tracked through repeated visits to borrowers of Bangladeshi MFIs over a three-year period, just under half were used to stock retail or trading businesses, or to finance small-scale production, or to buy or maintain assets of one sort or another. One in ten loans were on-lent to subborrowers outside the household (neighbors and relatives), and a similar number were used to pay down existing debt (including, sometimes, debt from other MFIs). The remainder were used for consumption or for a mix of uses. Half of these MFI *loans*, then, by number and roughly by value, were used for what could broadly be called "income-generating activities." But this does not mean that half of the *borrowers* used their loans in this way, because a small number of commercially active borrowers took bigger loans and took them more frequently from more than one MFI. Imagine a small Bangladesh village: Just a few households are running shops that are anything

more than a timber hut with a few dollars' worth of stock. Then one finds only a handful of households with a more than nominally productive business: perhaps a couple of families running rice mills, and someone successfully recycling garment-factory waste into stuffing for mattresses.[a] Most of the other villagers are agricultural day laborers or are self-employed service workers, pushing rickshaws or ferrying boats or loading trucks in the neighboring market or selling tea from a microstall. The small number of better-off farmers, with landholdings big enough to produce more rice than the family can eat, are mostly not MFI clients because they dislike having to attend weekly meetings and find the loans too small for their needs: They may also have access to formal finance, particularly if they have land they can pledge. Putting this into numbers, the study found that 14 percent of the MFI borrowers were responsible for taking two-thirds of all MFI loans used for businesses.

Note: a. This was the situation in one village where these diary studies were undertaken.

South Africa[8] showed that business owners were able to start operating with fairly small sums of upfront capital. However, to keep their business in operation, they need frequent fresh infusions of capital. Rarely did these business owners dream of expanding their business, or imagine that they would make more money if they did. They were rather more concerned about just keeping it going, to provide a stable, if small, source of income.

Enterprise borrowing, then, is not for everyone. Nevertheless, a good proportion of MFI borrowers—at least one in seven in the sample from Bangladesh described in box 2.6—respond well to the microcredit dream of enabling poor

people to borrow to establish and expand businesses.

Most MFIs began with the primary purpose of providing loans to the poor to start or expand a small business, but the early hope that every poor person can become a successful entrepreneur is now giving way to an understanding that enterprise lending is best when targeted at clients selected for their aptitude for business and their stable domestic finances. As a result, the enterprise-investment side of microfinance is gradually moving away from loans with weekly repayment schedules that may not match the cash flow patterns of small business, and toward loans given to and tailored for individuals rather than group-based borrowers. This should leave room for group-based saving and borrowing for the non-entrepreneurial poor to adapt better to their wide range of nonbusiness money-management needs.

How Good Are the Financial Tools Used by the Poor?

So far this chapter has provided numerous examples of how poor people choose and use their financial tools. In this section we step back to review the overall quality of these services and devices. Understanding better the strengths and weaknesses of the present set of tools should help to structure thinking about how microfinance might, in the future, add more value to the financial lives of the poor.

Convenient, Frequent, and Flexible—But Not Always Reliable

The most convenient tools of money management are ones that can be organized by the users themselves, without the need to interact with others, without the need to travel, available at any time of the day or night, and at little or no cost. It is not surprising then that the financial diary research found almost every poor household held—or tried to hold—savings at home. But this level of convenience and flexibility comes with obvious drawbacks: It is just too easy to take back these savings, so only those with exceptionally strong willpower (and there are such people) are able to build or keep large sums at home. Security is another obvious weakness of home savings: They are vulnerable to theft or misuse, or to being lost in floods or storms, and at the very least they will lose value to inflation. Self-help home saving, then, illustrates the trade-off very commonly found in informal finance—between convenience on the one hand, and low reliability, short-termism, and insecurity on the other.

One way to mitigate these drawbacks is to form a financial relationship with somebody else.

"Moneyguards"—people trusted to hold money safely on one's behalf—are common. They may be neighbors, relatives, or employers. Often the transactions take place in both directions: The diary research found several households that both take in and put out money in this way, at the same time.[9] Moneyguarding is closely related to casual interest-free borrowing and lending among kin or neighbors. Sometimes it is hard to tell them apart: In Bangladesh diary households might say they had "put" some money that week with a neighbor, and they would give vague answers when asked to specify whether this was a loan or a savings deposit or a repayment on a loan. Nothing better illustrates the complex ways in which a community's aggregate cash savings flow back and forth between its members. This ambiguity is, like much in the informal sector, a strength and a weakness: It enables a good deal of interaction to take place, but at low levels of reliability that in turn place limits on the values and durations of this kind of intermediation.

Where greater certainty or larger sums are needed, a price is usually demanded. Village or slum moneylenders who lend as a business ask for interest, and many who lend merely to fulfill family or social obligations do likewise. The interest is often at a high rate, either to compensate for the evident risk of lending to very poor people (in the case of professional lenders) or, in the case of those lending as an obligation, to help limit the amount of money being lent. There is more on the social aspects of this kind of lending below.

One way to borrow free of social entanglements is to use a pawnbroker. The limitation here is that poor people rarely hold much in the way of pawnable goods, so very large sums cannot usually be obtained by this route. The mortgaging of land has other disadvantages: The land mortgaged may have been the household's main income source, and the larger sums that can be had from mortgaging land often prove very difficult, if not impossible, to repay, so the land is in effect lost for good.

MFIs have been much better able than banks to approximate the convenience of informal finance. They have done this in various ways. First, they got physically close to their clients, by holding meetings right in the village or slum. Soon, they settled on a form of lending in which repayments were made easy by being small and frequent—often weekly, at the meeting, sometimes even daily, through itinerant collectors. It was this level of convenience and frequency—rather than anything to do with microenterprise development, or "group solidarity"—that led to microcredit's extreme popularity in its early days. Provided that their household cash flows were strong enough to come up with a small weekly toll, people could borrow for whatever purpose was most pressing at the time. Later, when some of the disadvantages of a credit-only regime became apparent (such as the risk of overindebtedness), MFIs, where regulators allowed them to, introduced passbook savings that could be deposited into or withdrawn from at will, at the village or slum meeting. Nevertheless, most general lending to the poor by MFIs (as opposed to their lending to microenterprises) is short term and therefore of low value relative to incomes: A typical loan may have a term of 11 months and be worth the equivalent of two or three months' household income. This is very useful for consumption smoothing (as shown by Ramna's behavior described in box 2.3) but not for the bigger sums that all households need from time to time. To accumulate big sums, with most MFIs, borrowers still need to build a series of modest sums through successive rounds of borrowing, and find their own ways of storing their value—most commonly by holding them in nonfinancial assets such as jewelry or livestock.

Disciplined—But Only in the Short Term

Saving on your own is hard. Saving with a money-guard helps impose some distance but not enough discipline. Saving within a bigger group, as in a ROSCA or an ASCA[10] (accumulating savings and credit association, described in chapter 6, "Community-Based Providers"), offers much more discipline, relying on the power of group pressure and sanctions to keep the transactions flowing regularly. Many poor people are well aware of the flip side of informal finance's flexibility and convenience—its lack of discipline—and this helps to explain the popularity of devices like the ROSCA. Researchers have also suggested that when people are distracted by the problems of poverty, and have to juggle several income flows from different sources and deal with the individual cash flows of numerous financial tools, they can lose sight of their longer-term financial position.[11] By joining a group such as a ROSCA poor people may inject enough regularity into their financial lives to help them plan for and meet longer-term goals.

In earlier sections we have seen how ROSCAs help their members build sums that can be used to meet emergencies or acquire assets. ROSCAs can fail, but as well as offering a disciplined environment that encourages regular saving, they have other advantages. One is that because they never require cash to be stored (at each meeting the money goes straight to that meeting's taker) there is no risk of the treasurer dipping into the fund. Another is that the combined eyes of all the members ensure that transactions will be more than usually transparent and verifiable. These virtues offset the moderate risk of the ROSCA going wrong because a member simply fails to pay in after he or she has taken his or her turn at the lump sum. Other features of ROSCAs make them suitable for poor people: They require no bookkeeping, so the illiterate are rarely confused by more literate members of the group. They are without cost: Money goes straight from the depositors to the taker in what must be the world's swiftest and cheapest form of financial intermediation. And they are close at hand and convenient: People set up ROSCAs right where they live or work and hold meetings at times that suit them. Box 2.7 illustrates several of these ROSCA features.

Poor people find it easier to form larger sums through ROSCAs than they do through saving at home or saving with partners such as money-guards. Nevertheless, really big sums—enough to buy a home or business outright or fund a pension annuity—cannot usually be formed through ROSCAs because, like all informal schemes, ROSCAs become riskier the longer they run, the more members they have, and the bigger the amounts transacted. ROSCAs are time bound: As soon as every member has received the "prize" once, it comes automatically to an end, although the members are, of course, free to start another cycle and accumulate another modest sum. ROSCAs illustrate another typical informal-finance trade-off—security versus longevity and volume.

The group-based approach to financial services to the poor has been taken up by outsiders in various ways. The oldest and most impressive is the credit union movement, now found throughout the world.[12] Credit unions take the basic idea behind all ROSCAs and ASCAs—the idea of a group of people coming together voluntarily to pool their savings—and submit it to enough formalization to allow the credit union to become a permanent formal institution, providing the members with ongoing services and, crucially, enough security to allow members to build up large deposits over the long term, or pay steadily into insurance or pension policies. What has stopped this admirable system from becoming the obvious first choice for poor people around the world is that the degree of formal organization needed to keep a credit union stable requires levels of education and financial sophistication that are simply not available in most of the world's poorer village and slums.

Credit unions are inventions of the nineteenth century. More recently, nongovernmental organizations (NGOs) have taken up the basic idea of the savings club and used it to work with poor people on a range of development issues, not just finance. The largest endeavor of this kind is India's Self-Help Group (SHG) movement, which counts its members in millions. SHGs are basic savings clubs linked to formal banks, which recognize them as legal entities and lend to them at favorable rates. More recent still is the Savings Groups movement,[13] which has been building steadily over the last 20 years and follows a rather different course. The NGOs that promote savings groups prefer to tackle the weaknesses of savings clubs, especially problems

Box 2.7 Daisy's ROSCA

Enayet's sister's saving club (see box 2.4 about Enayet) was a ROSCA (she called it a *lotteri shomiti*). Daisy earned 1,500 taka a month (about US$25 at the market rate). In a meeting that took place each monthly payday, when she and 16 other women on her floor conducted their ROSCA, they each contributed 300 taka from their wages, and each month one of the women, in a fixed order decided by lottery on the first day of the ROSCA, took the whole 5,100 taka, a sum equivalent to two or three months' salary. When Enayet was admitted to the hospital, Daisy's turn to take the money was still a long way off, but, in return for a modest tip, she was able to get another member to swap turns with her.

of poor governance, by training members in the use of improved practices. Because these savings groups are standalone entities not linked to banks or other institutions, they are seen as particularly suitable to remote and sparsely populated areas.

Microcredit MFIs, as is well known, of course, lend through groups. But MFI groups in the fastest-growing microcredit traditions, such as that based on the work of Grameen Bank, are not mutual entities that own or share their own group funds, but simply groups of retail customers brought together by the MFI to reduce service delivery costs.

Social Embeddedness—A Strength and a Weakness

The discipline that ROSCAs offer is in part a result of the social relationships they embody: Being a member of the group creates an obligation to contribute or to be shamed in front of the group.[14] However, this discipline is often tempered by flexibility in the way in which the ROSCA responds to clients' needs. The essential feature of the group is that it represents a source of liquidity that members can access *one way or other*. This can involve direct negotiation at a group meeting to obtain the payout because of a pressing need, shock, or emergency, or members can negotiate directly with each other to change the order in which the payout is received (as in Daisy's case; see box 2.7) or borrow the payout from the member who did receive it. Groups organize themselves in many ways, and they vary in how flexible they are prepared to be, but the key feature is that by jointly creating a source of liquidity, members have a right to make claims on that resource and to be listened to by other members, either formally at the club meeting or at its margins. This feature can be referred to as "negotiability."

Although the mechanism differs, this negotiability is also a feature of moneylending. Moneylending is often seen as exploitative, but the social relationships in which people are engaged may be complex, involving labor exchange and land rental as well as money. In such contexts "moneylenders" may act as patrons who assist their "clients," and this remains true even when such help could result in cycles of debt that are ultimately damaging to the long-term welfare of the borrower. In these cases, with few competing options, poor people often prefer to retain such avenues of access to resources than to avoid them.

Another way in which the informal sector operates through social relationships is in the ways people assist each other, especially family and friends. Poor people may help their friends and relatives in ways that are quite open-ended. If a child needs school fees and parents cannot provide, another relative—or even a friend—may help. Such assistance creates a debt that takes the form of a future obligation to reciprocate. It may not be reciprocated in cash, or in school fees, but in a completely different form such as labor, lending animals, or taking care of a child. It is a form of saving with others that is not directly financial and in which the return is unknown at the time, but is indeed an obligation. In this way debts are not to be avoided: They create relationships of reciprocity that can be drawn on in the future. In the case of Enayet (see box 2.4) the loans his parents took were never repaid in full and were on the way to being "forgiven"—but public disapproval and comment ensures that the borrowers cannot forget that the obligation represented by the unpaid debt continues.

The social relationships in which informal financial services are embedded are both one of their greatest strengths as well as their greatest weakness. For those who are able to manage "negotiability" successfully they offer flexibility and responsiveness for risk management in particular, but also for productive investment and asset building. However, such relationships are not open to all, and the poorest people are less able to engage with them because they are less able to reciprocate, although they may also be the recipients of assistance from time to time.

Creating Better Financial Services for the Poor

The picture this chapter has painted of the current state of financial services for poor people has numerous implications for microfinance. They are overwhelmingly positive. Taken together, they suggest that microfinance enjoys big opportunities to grow in both quality and quantity:

- First, the picture implies a very high demand from poor people for financial services. This is seen in the intensity with which poor households use whatever financial tools they have at hand.

- Second, it implies that this high level of demand is by no means fully met, neither in volume nor in quality. This is seen in the failure of the existing, largely informal, tools to satisfy in full the financial needs of the poor, in the low levels of reliability that characterize much informal intermediation, and in the still very modest numbers of poor people reached by MFIs and other formal providers.

- Third, it implies that a great deal of the demand from poor people is *not* for the products and services that the microfinance industry has emphasized during its first three decades. In particular, the demand for savings (including insurance) may outstrip the demand for loans; the demand for general-purpose loans may outstrip the demand for loans for microbusiness investment; and the demand for long-term saving, borrowing, and insurance instruments is at least a strong as the demand for short-term savings and loans.

- Fourth, it implies that much of the methodology that microfinance has already developed will be relevant to meeting this demand. Techniques for getting close to clients and

enabling them to transact frequently, through out-of-branch banking of the sort seen in weekly village or slum meetings or in mobile-phone banking, will remain vital. Breaking the formation of sums down into small bite-size pieces, as in Grameen- or village bank–style weekly savings and repayments or via daily collection agents, will still be essential. Above all, the MFI's superior level of reliability and transparency, relative to much informal finance, needs to be retained and strengthened.

- Fifth, it shows where microfinance will have to improve and extend its products and delivery systems. Two very important goals are finding ways to introduce greater flexibility into loan terms and repayment schedules (while still offering discipline) and finding ways of enabling the poor to engage in much longer-term intermediation, through long-term commitment savings plans (including insurance and pension plans) and loan terms longer than the six months to one year common to much microlending at present.

- Sixth, it suggests that the demand by poor people for financial services may be quite similar across regions and districts, which implies that although microfinance practitioners will need to modify their work to suit each location, a core set of needs is present that can be met by broadly similar products. This is seen in the remarkable congruence of behaviors observed in the two South Asian nations and in South Africa—countries that have very different histories, cultures, and levels of economic and financial development.

A key challenge for formal service providers has been the struggle to get close enough to the poor to compete with the proximity and frequency of informal tools. Informal tools are certain to keep their advantage in this respect, and it would be foolish to think that formal services will entirely replace them. But by finding ways to contact their clients where they are, in the village or slum, and doing so as often as they can, through regular weekly or daily routines, or via cell phones and bank agents, formal services should be able to gain a much bigger share of the everyday financial intermediation of the poor than they have at present. Recent innovations that will help them do this include mobile-phone banking and legislation to allow banks to operate through agents—either peripatetic as in India's recent "banking correspondent" provisions or as a supplemental business for local shops, as in Brazil.

Another challenge for formal providers is to make products more flexible, to respond better to the irregular cash flows of poor clients. Here again there is cause for optimism: Worries about internal control, and a sensible concern to keep things simple, caused early microcredit pioneers to begin with rigid payment schedules, such as the strict weekly repayments of Grameen-style microlending. But with experience and the astute use of technology they are now able to offer "passbook" savings—savings accounts where the client can deposit or withdraw as much as he or she likes at any time—and flexible loan repayments, at least for modest value loans.

Because they are permanent institutions, it is much easier for MFIs and other formal providers to offer long-term intermediation. Formal commitment savings plans for the poor (which include endowment and other forms of insurance, and pension plans) will be a huge growth area for microfinance. They offer the discipline that poor people so often seek when they use group-based devices such as ROSCAs but add value by having much longer terms, allowing much larger sums to be formed. They can also offer a "one-stop shop" for such services. In East Africa it is common for people to take membership in several ROSCAs at once, each with its own term, frequency, and value, so that the user can ensure that different spending needs—weekly consumption, quarterly rents, or annual

school fees, for example—can be met. This range of plans can be offered, more reliably, by a formal provider that is in regular frequent contact with its clients.

These challenges are well worth formal providers tackling. Informal finance, where poor people conduct most of their financial lives, can suffer from low reliability and an inability to offer long terms to create large-value sums. These are major deficiencies, and formal services can and should offer something better. Reliability, in the sense of ensuring that agreed contracts are honored, is fundamental. The poor live in environments that are continuously changing; most have neither cash flows, nor living arrangements, nor environmental and social conditions that are static or *reliable*. Bringing more reliability into financial tools will provide a significant boost to the ability of the poor to plan and envision a future beyond the short term. This requires services that are offered in a timely manner and under clear conditions, with terms that are upheld and with opportunities to easily ask questions and seek redress.

A minimum "menu" of financial services for *all* poor clients in the second decade of the twenty-first century would ideally include passbook savings and flexible small-scale loans (for short-to-medium-term money management), medium-term loans (such as up to three years) with structured repayments suited to whatever is known about the client's household cash flow, and medium-to-long-term commitment savings. As techniques for doing so evolve, providers should aim to add pensions, and insurance cover, starting with the risks that are easiest to calculate, such as life insurance, but aiming eventually at the more difficult ones, above all health and agriculture. To carefully selected segments of clients, providers should also learn how to offer longer-term loans for productive investments tailored to business cash flow, and for big life-enhancing investments (in homes, household goods, and education) tailored to repayment capacity shown to exist by the transaction records of successive loans. There is nothing in the history of microfinance to suggest that offering these services to a majority of the world's poorest households cannot be achieved in this decade.

Notes

1. http://financialaccess.org/sites/default/files/110109%20HalfUnbanked_0.pdf.
2. Susan Johnson, "Gender and Microfinance: Guidelines for Good Practice," http://www.gdrc.org/icm/wind/gendersjonson.html.
3. Details on how the households were selected and how the fieldwork was executed can be found in Appendix I of Collins et al. (2009).
4. These diaries ran for three years rather than 12 months, but with monthly interviews rather than biweekly. The objective was to understand how households used MFI services rather than how they manage money generally.
5. For more analysis on how well both types of funeral insurance helps cover the event of death in poor households, see Collins and Leibbrandt (2007).
6. See Daryl Collins, "Focus Note: Financial Decisions and Funeral Costs," http://www.financialdiaries.com/Funerals_and_Financing.pdf.
7. For more on "borrowing to save" see Jonathan Morduch, "Borrowing to Save: Perspectives from Portfolios of the Poor," http://financialaccess.org/sites/default/files/FAI_Borrowing_to_Save_0.pdf.
8. Bankable Frontier Associates, "Small Business Financial Diaries: Report of Findings and Lessons Learned," http://www.bankablefrontier.com/assets/pdfs/Small-Bus-Fin-Diaries_Pilot-Study.pdf.
9. In Uganda a MicroSave team found two women who always "kept" a few dollars of each other's money. They explained that by doing so they could resist their husbands when they asked for cash, by saying "Oh, no, you can't have that money—it belongs to the lady next door" (Rutherford 1999, p. 23).

10. For descriptions of some of the most common forms these clubs take, see Rutherford (2009).
11. For a view of how the realities of poverty affect financial decision making among low-income people, see Bertrand et al. (2004).
12. See, for example, http://www.woccu.org.
13. See http://savingsgroups.com and http://savings-revolution.org.
14. This section was contributed by Susan Johnson, Centre for Development Studies, University of Bath.

References

Bertrand, Marianne, Sendhil Mullainathan, and Eldar Shafir. 2004. "A Behavioral Economics View of Poverty." *American Economic Review* 94 (2): 419–23.

Chaia, Alberto, Aparna Dalal, Tony Goland, Maria Jose Gonzalez, Jonathan Morduch, and Robert Schiff. 2009. "Half the World Is Unbanked." Financial Access Initiative Framing Note, Financial Access Initiative, New York.

Cohen, Monique. 2012. *The Emerging Market-Led Microfinance Agenda*. PoP Briefing Note 25, MicroSave, Lucknow.

Collins, Daryl, and Murray Leibbrandt. 2007. "The Financial Impact of HIV/AIDS on Poor Households in South Africa." *AIDS* 21 (suppl. 7): S75–S81.

Collins, Daryl, Jonathan Morduch, Stuart Rutherford, and Orlanda Ruthven. 2009. *Portfolios of the Poor: How the World's Poor Live on $2 a Day*. Princeton: Princeton University Press.

FinMark Trust. 2003. *FinScope Survey South Africa*. Johannesburg: FinMark Trust.

Genesis Analytics. 2005. "A Regulatory Review of Informal and Formal Funeral Insurance Markets in South Africa." www.finmark.org.za.

Helms, Brigit. 2006. *Access for All: Building Inclusive Financial Systems*. Washington, DC: Consultative Group to Assist the Poor.

Kuyasa Fund. 2005. *Kuyasa Fund: Community-Based Lending.* Marshalltown, South Africa: FinMark Trust.

Microcredit Summit Campaign. 2011. "The State of the Microcredit Summit Campaign Report 2011." Microcredit Summit Campaign, Washington, DC.

MicroSave. 2010a. "Borrowing to Save: Perspectives from *Portfolios of the Poor.*" PoP Briefing Note 3, MicroSave, Lucknow.

——. 2010b. "Grameen II and Portfolios of the Poor." PoP Briefing Note 7, MicroSave, Lucknow.

——. 2010c. "How Do the Poor Deal with Risk?" PoP Briefing Note 3, MicroSave, Lucknow.

——. 2010d. "Living on $2 a Day." PoP Briefing Note 1, MicroSave, Lucknow.

——. 2010e. "The 'Triple-Whammy' of Poverty: Lessons from *Portfolios of the Poor: How the World's Poor Live on $2 a Day.*" PoP Briefing Note 1, MicroSave, Lucknow.

Rutherford, Stuart. 1999. "Savings and the Poor: The Methods, Use and Impact of Savings by the Poor of East Africa." MicroSave, Lucknow.

Rutherford, Stuart, with Sukhwinder Arora. 2009 *The Poor and Their Money.* Rugby: Practical Publishing.

Rutherford, Stuart, with S. K. Sinha and Shyra Aktar. 2001. *Buro Tangail Product Development Review.* Dhaka and London: BURO and DFID.

World Bank. 2005. *Environment Matters: Annual Review.* Washington, DC: World Bank.

Wright, Graham A. N. 2005. "Designing Savings and Loan Products." MicroSave, Lucknow.

CHAPTER 3

The Role of Government and Industry in Financial Inclusion

Stefan Staschen and Candace Nelson

Tailoring a country's financial system to enable financial markets to work better for the poor involves the combined efforts of public and private players. It is relatively recent, and commendable, that both government and the financial services industry acknowledge the importance of increasing financial inclusion. But financial inclusion is not simply about numbers or attracting more clients to the range of providers. "Responsible" financial inclusion increases access to financial services in ways that are safe for consumers, enabling their participation informed by knowledge and choice. Increasingly shared by public and private actors, this vision requires coordinated efforts from both. Governments are investing authority in policies and rules that shape behavior in market systems; their imprint is wide-ranging,

from infrastructure to legally mandated outreach targets. Industry players are rallying around codes of conduct intended to increase transparency and fair treatment of consumers and are defining performance in financial, social, and environmental terms. Both spheres share the responsibility for "responsible" finance, building financial inclusion on a foundation of consumer protection.

This chapter outlines the role of government (through its policies, regulation, and other support for a stable financial sector) and industry (through standards and guidelines) in promoting financial inclusion, as both separate and sometimes overlapping arenas of activity. In addition, it recognizes coordination and advocacy as important functions within the market system. This chapter provides a high-level perspective on the

---

Contributions to this chapter were made by Kate Lauer.

roles of government and industry, largely related to formal rules that help to shape the financial market system;[1] more detailed information on the specifics of regulation is provided in chapter 17. It will be of interest to policy makers, industry associations, financial service providers, and other stakeholders seeking to understand the enabling environment for financial services.

The Role of Government in Financial Inclusion

Microfinance is now seen as an integral part of an inclusive financial system. As a result, financial inclusion has become an important policy goal that complements the traditional pillars of monetary and financial stability, as well as other regulatory objectives such as consumer protection (Hannig and Jansen 2010).

Government as Rule Maker

Governments have increasingly embraced financial inclusion as one of their policy objectives. Data from the Financial Access 2010 Survey (CGAP 2011) show that in 90 percent of economies, at least some aspect of the financial inclusion agenda is under the purview of the main financial regulator. Furthermore, "As rule makers, governments determine not only what efforts may be undertaken to promote financial inclusion, but also by whom, how, and when. In addition to prudential and consumer protection rule making, governments can enable innovative financial inclusion business models, including permitting the entry of new actors into the financial service sector" (Ehrbeck, Pickens, and Tarazi 2012, 6). Rather than provide financial services directly, the government's role is to maintain macroeconomic stability and provide appropriate regulatory and supervisory frameworks (see Duflos and Imboden 2004). And while the assumption still holds that the private sector plays the central role in providing financial services, there is much more awareness of the reasons why market forces will not—without an appropriate enabling environment, infrastructure support, and adequate consumer protection and financial capability—achieve the goal of improving financial inclusion.

Policy making is a complex process bringing together various actors who use a multitude of tools and strategies to promote financial inclusion. Policy decisions influence where resources are allocated and how priorities are established within political, economic, and social institutions. Policies are designed to guide decision makers and to achieve an intended purpose. They typically outline general principles, but they do not carry the force of law.[2]

Policy makers recognize the potential for economic growth and poverty alleviation through the development of a more inclusive financial services sector. In doing so, they also acknowledge three primary barriers to financial inclusion:

- Supply-side barriers such as transaction costs, the inability to track an individual's financial history, and lack of knowledge about how to serve poorer customers

- Demand-side barriers that restrict the capacity of individuals to access available services and products, including socioeconomic and cultural factors, lack of formal identification systems, and low levels of financial literacy (AFI 2010)

- Poor regulatory frameworks, including consumer protection mechanisms that hinder the quantity and quality of financial products and services.

The main participants in developing formal rules include the legislature (typically the parliament), the government unit (the relevant ministry and government bureaucracy), and the regulator (the central bank or regulatory authority). A legislative process in microfinance normally starts with a mostly technical discussion among the experts and the regulator,[3] but eventually depends on the support of the legislature to implement legal changes. Educating lawmakers about the rationale and objectives of proposed rules early on can help to overcome any potential resistance and create a joint understanding of what is needed to achieve an enabling environment for financial services for the poor.

Infrastructure Support

The government has traditionally played a strong role in ensuring that infrastructure is in place and providing oversight. The front-end infrastructure includes client access points, such as post offices, automated teller machines, point-of-sale devices, and retail agents, all of which are subject to specific rules and regulations. The back-end infrastructure includes automated clearinghouses, real-time gross settlement systems, retail payment switches, and cash distribution networks (see chapter 18). Not least because of the growing importance of branchless banking models, the payment system infrastructure has received a lot of attention, as it constitutes the rails for the cost-effective provision of financial services. If the government (for example, the central bank) does not run these systems, at least it nurtures them and sets the general rules of operations.

In addition to service delivery infrastructure, several other supporting functions should be considered in the government's domain for financial inclusion. For example, credit bureaus allow clients to build a credit history and help providers to reduce the risk of serving them, a deposit insurance system protects clients against loss of savings, and a land registry system facilitates access to loans using land as collateral.

Nonfinancial infrastructure also has a bearing on financial inclusion. For example, roads for traveling to the nearest service point, electricity for recharging mobile phones or running real-time communication systems between remote areas, agents, and head offices, and national identification systems all promote access to financial markets. In all these areas, the government plays a crucial role, either as provider or as regulator and promoter.

Promoting Savings through Government Payments

The government can potentially play an important role in promoting savings and catalyzing volumes by moving its social transfers, wages, and pension payments onto electronic channels and ensuring that these channels are linked to easily accessible, basic transaction accounts. Its policy with regard to social safety nets and government-to-person (G2P) payments can thus have an important impact on the viability of innovative delivery channels and draw more clients into the formal financial sector. Both the government and the poor benefit as G2P payments can often be delivered at substantially lower cost and with less "leakage" if they are delivered electronically (Pickens, Porteous, and Rotman 2009; see box 3.1).

Box 3.1 Bank and Retail Network Partnership

The Mexican government is leveraging public infrastructure for savings and G2P payment delivery. The 2010 Budget Law crafted by the Ministry of Finance stipulates that all government payments (primarily administered by the Ministry of Social Development) must be delivered electronically by 2012. The government is harnessing its public infrastructure to pursue this goal. In areas with no financial services, it is attempting to reach people by linking a network of 23,000 community-owned stores with its conditional cash transfer program (Oportunidades) and the savings services of a state-run bank.

Source: Almazan 2010.

Consumer Protection

In an environment of increasingly complex financial products and services, effective consumer protection is important for the overall sustainability of the financial market system.[4] Participation in the formal financial sector must pose fewer risks for vulnerable, low-income people who have little experience with formal finance and low levels of financial literacy and capability.

Governments have an important role in providing the legal and enforcement muscle to ensure that financial institutions do not undermine consumer protection by intentionally capitalizing on their advantages in information, knowledge, and power. Effective consumer protection legislation, applied equitably across providers, can facilitate comparison shopping and healthy competition, leading to improved products and practices. Despite limited regulatory and supervisory capacity and challenges in enforcing legal contracts in the countries where microfinance is needed most, governments can ensure that providers disclose prices and other characteristics of credit products in a consistent manner using agreed terminology and definitions; and they can set rules for client privacy, out-of-court redress mechanisms, or rigorous safety of data storage and transmission to protect customer funds and information (AFI 2011). Some examples of consumer protection regulations include the following:

- The National Bank of Cambodia requires that microfinance institutions (MFIs) state their interest on a declining balance rather than a flat-rate basis.

- South Africa's sweeping National Credit Act addresses over-indebtedness and reckless lending by defining these terms under the law. It sets clear rules governing disclosures, credit reporting, and advertising, among other practices.

- Indonesian regulators require regulated providers to have written procedures and a formal complaints unit.

For countries characterized as "low-access environments" (where levels of financial access and financial literacy are low and regulators face significant capacity constraints), the Consultative Group to Assist the Poor (CGAP) recommends that the government agenda for consumer protection pursue three basic goals: transparency, fair treatment, and effective recourse (Chien 2012; Brix and McKee 2010).[5]

Transparency covers broad disclosure of relevant product terms and conditions, including pricing, fees, and default provisions. When such disclosure rules require all providers of the same type of product to use standardized formulas as well as plain language to communicate relevant charges, consumers are better able to compare products. Disclosure requirements are considered more market friendly and effective at reducing costs to the borrower than mandated interest rate ceilings (Brix and McKee 2010).

Transparency targets two interrelated objectives—increased *consumer comprehension*, allowing consumers to understand and choose appropriate products, and increased *market competition*, stimulated as consumers engage in comparison shopping. Disclosure regulations should govern both content provided to the consumer and how it is communicated for effective comprehension. Disclosure of the various cost components and other product terms can be overwhelming to consumers and counterproductive to the objective of enhancing their comprehension. For example, creditors in Armenia are required to advise customers orally regarding terms, costs, risks, and obligations associated with a service. A standardized summary sheet of product costs and terms used by all providers is one of the most useful tools for ensuring that consumers have information they can understand and compare. Standardized forms are also easier for providers, particularly smaller and less sophisticated ones, as they save time and resources by not having to develop their own disclosure forms to meet regulatory requirements (Chien 2012).

The perspective of the individual consumer is critical to tailoring disclosure regulations. Loan pricing provides a good example. Because nominal interest rates do not reflect the total cost of a loan, regulations should mandate that pricing be expressed using one or more of the following methods: (1) total financial cost of credit, (2) repayment schedules, and (3) annual percentage rate (APR) or effective interest rate (EIR; see chapter 9). While the use of APRs and EIRs allows for greater comparability, total loan cost and the amount and frequency of repayment may be easier for low-income consumers to comprehend. Limited data suggest that borrowers tend to focus on the amount of the installment payment rather than the interest rate, because their main concern is whether their cash flow will cover loan payments (Chien 2012). For example, policy makers in Peru and Ghana standardize the calculation of APR or EIR with regulators specifically to address the capacity constraints of smaller, less formal institutions. Allowing for the monthly presentation of APRs or EIRs is another practical option introduced in the Philippines. Monthly APRs or EIRs may be more appropriate for loans of less than a year and more comprehensible to consumers (Chien 2012).

Fair treatment covers ethical staff behavior, the sale of appropriate products, and acceptable marketing and reasonable collections practices. Rules governing truth in advertising support transparency through disclosure. Codes of ethics guard against overly aggressive responses to delinquency. Zero tolerance of delinquency, a cornerstone of institutional performance, can result in abusive collections with adverse effects on poor households. In India, Ghana, and elsewhere, regulators have established rules governing fair debt collection and prohibiting intimidation and coercion.

Effective recourse is necessary for consumer trust in the formal financial system; when things go wrong, consumers need to know they have a way to communicate their complaints and resolve their issues. Consumer recourse mechanisms such as specialized help desks within financial institutions not only handle complaints, but also often handle questions and can play a role in facilitating consumer comprehension of disclosed information. Sometimes the regulatory agency takes responsibility for this function, and sometimes it assigns the role to an industry association, ombudsman, or other entity. Rules governing these processes should specify all aspects of customer complaints, including the method of submission, location, and time frame for resolution. Providers need to display such information clearly and communicate it directly to clients.

While these three goals—transparency, fair treatment, and recourse—are basic to protecting consumers, it may not be feasible or practical to address all of them at once. An incremental approach to developing a set of disclosure policies and regulations may be necessary, taking into consideration compliance costs for industry and supervisory capacity of government. A starting point might be to tackle the most critical yet discrete transparency issues in a given context. At an intermediary level, governments can target broader consumer comprehension. Finally, regulators can reinforce market competition by requiring broad dissemination of comparable metrics for total costs (such as APRs and EIRs) and other key terms through advertising and media channels, allowing market forces to apply pressure on providers. Extensive dissemination of new disclosure requirements, coupled with sufficient time for implementation, can help to reduce the industry's costs of compliance. Consumer testing can be used to refine disclosure rules at each stage and build a stronger disclosure regime over time (Chien 2012; see box 3.2).

However, even where provided for by law, broad application and enforcement of consumer protection regulations can be difficult to achieve in practice. Challenges include consistent application of rules and coordination among multiple regulators where supervisory authority is divided. Microinsurance provides a good example of this (see box 3.3).

Box 3.2 Encouraging Stakeholders to Adopt New Rules

The success of the disclosure regime in Peru can be attributed in part to the extensive efforts of the Superintendency of Banking and Insurance. Regulators spent two years discussing disclosure rules with the industry, addressing issues of compliance costs, and developing providers' familiarity with formulas for calculating EIRs. In addition, a large campaign was launched to educate consumers on EIRs and to ensure they understood the new disclosure rules.

Financial institutions in Peru are required to resolve all questions related to the content of a contract before it is signed. In addition, they must designate customer service personnel to consult with clients on the scope of standardized contracts. Such an approach shifts the burden of achieving comprehension onto the provider, but should not be viewed as a substitute for clear instructions on what and how information is disclosed.

Source: Chien 2012.

Box 3.3 Policy for Microinsurance

Policy makers need to understand the insurance needs of low-income households and ensure that policies facilitate the market-based provision of microinsurance. They can engage the insurance industry and other actors—such as unregulated insurers and networks—in a dialogue on microinsurance and involve them in educating the market and promoting

microinsurance. Government can consider treating microinsurance products differently than commercial products for tax purposes. Increasingly, central banks and finance ministries have become engaged in promoting financial literacy, as low levels of information and trust are probably the biggest barrier to uptake of insurance among low-income populations.

Source: Martina Wiedmaier-Pfister.

Building Financial Capability

Although historically governments may have focused on limiting harmful credit products through interest rate caps and debt forgiveness, the focus has shifted toward the need to empower financial service users, to inform them, and to give them tools to protect their rights (CGAP 2010). CGAP identifies consumer financial capability, government regulation, and industry codes of conduct as the three principal consumer protection strategies (McKee, Lahaye, and Koning 2011). Consumers need to know their rights in order to exercise them. These include the right to understand product choices, often offered by competing providers, and the right to choose the services that are best for them.[6] Consumers need to develop relationships with financial service providers on the basis of knowledge and choice as opposed to fear. Ill-informed consumers and unsupervised providers can undermine the impact of financial inclusion efforts; this risk is especially high in a context of rapid, often technology-driven, change in the financial service marketplace. Given the asymmetries in knowledge, as well as access to information and skills between providers and consumers, governments can help to meet the challenges—educational, regulatory, and financial—of empowering consumers to use financial services effectively and participate in their own protection. However, with limited experience in addressing this need, government strategies to support responsible finance are key to learning what works (see box 3.4).

Three overlapping terms are used in relation to the concept of consumer financial capability: financial literacy, capability, and education.

Financial literacy is the ability to understand basic information about financial products and services.

Financial capability is the ability to apply that knowledge, to make informed decisions, and to take effective actions regarding the current and future management of money. It includes the ability to save, borrow, and spend wisely, to generate more stable cash flows, and to manage the challenges associated with costly life-cycle events (see box 3.5). Challenges of money management are never static, and neither are the solutions, especially given the unpredictable and seasonal incomes that are common among the poor. Financial capability is an evolving state of competency subject to ever-changing personal and economic circumstances.

Box 3.4 Financial Capability Strategies

A Ghanaian government survey in 2007 revealed a low level of knowledge of financial institutions, services, and products among adults. As a result, the government launched a financial literacy program in 2008 to create awareness and build trust between consumers and service providers. In 2009, a national strategy for financial literacy and consumer protection in the microfinance sector was adopted that addressed three pillars of financial capability: knowing, understanding, and changing behavior. The strategy featured education materials describing key products and a road show that toured rural areas.

Source: AFI 2011.

Box 3.5 Financial Literacy in the Russian Federation

In Russia, research was conducted to study the consequences of greater financial literacy on the use of financial products and financial planning. The study found that financial literacy was positively related to participation in financial markets and negatively related to the use of informal sources of borrowing. Individuals with higher rates of financial literacy were significantly more likely to report having more unspent income at the end of the month and higher spending capacity. The relationship between financial literacy and the availability of unspent income was even more evident during the recent financial crisis, suggesting that better financial literacy may better equip individuals to deal with macroeconomic shocks.

Source: Klapper, Lusardi, and Panos 2012.

Financial education is a key tool, coupled with experience using financial services, to build financial literacy and capability. It introduces people to good money management practices with respect to earning, spending, saving, borrowing, and investing. Its power lies in its potential to be relevant to anyone and everyone, from the person who contemplates moving savings from under the mattress to a Savings Group to the saver who tries to compare account features between competing banks. Serving multiple, interrelated purposes, financial education promotes personal financial management, product uptake and use, and consumer awareness and protection.

Matching the content of financial education to the target group is essential to making it relevant. Target groups for financial education can be defined by age, gender, employment status, or relationship to a specific financial product. For example, financial education targeted to youth is likely to focus on negotiating with parents about spending money, the value of saving, and planning for the future.

Finally, to ensure financially capable consumers, financial education must be integrated with hands-on experience; consumers need to choose and use financial products and services if they are to understand their full benefits.

Financial Inclusion Strategies

A financial inclusion strategy clearly defines and aligns a shared vision among policy makers and other stakeholders for achieving an inclusive financial sector. It also raises awareness of and secures commitment to sound practices and establishes the means for communication and coordination around implementation to avoid gaps or duplication of efforts (Porter 2011). In 2010, 45 percent of the countries participating in the Financial Access 2010 Survey had a dedicated strategy document for promoting financial inclusion (see box 3.6). Regulators in countries with a financial inclusion strategy also have, on average, more financial inclusion topics under their purview and more resources and staff working on these matters (CGAP 2010).

Financial inclusion strategies are developed through a consultative process among the key stakeholders in financial inclusion (government, regulators, the industry, and consumer associations) and approved by a government body. They typically include a diagnostic of the current state of the sector to ensure "evidence-based policy making," policy objectives, strategies, and an action plan for implementation (Duflos and Glisovic-Mézières 2008). Financial inclusion strategies need to consider existing capacity as well as the need for reform and capacity building (Porter 2011).

An important element is the process itself: bringing a diverse range of actors to the same table whose only common denominator may be their potential to affect the financial ecosystem and getting them to agree on a shared vision for

Box 3.6 Financial Inclusion in Mexico

Under its National Development Plan for 2007–12, the Mexican government reformed banking laws to permit nontraditional entities such as banking agents to operate in rural areas. Niche banks were allowed to offer different services and were subject to different regulations than traditional banks. The plan also facilitated the transition of small savings and credit organizations into regulated deposit-taking entities.

Source: AFI 2011.

the sector. The action plan for implementation needs to consider all elements of the financial market system: the core (clients and providers and the products they exchange) and the rules (formal and informal) and supporting functions (infrastructure, funding, and information). Only a combined effort of all stakeholders is likely to have a significant impact on the overall goal of making markets work for the poor.

While financial inclusion strategies have the potential to lead to better structured and more evidence-based policy-making processes, they have suffered from several shortcomings (drawn on CGAP research summarized in Duflos 2011):

- *Many strategies are driven by donors.* Government must have strong interest in and ownership of the process and the outcome.

- *The outcome can only be as good as the analysis.* At times, the diagnostic does not include all relevant actors and institutions; the analysis should be conducted by a team of experts with a diverse set of skills and be updated regularly.

- *The common vision does not sufficiently consider the local context.* This is particularly the case if the document is drafted by an international consultant without much involvement of local actors.

- *The strategy is not disseminated widely or updated regularly.* The success of implementation depends on broad dissemination, a clear allocation of rules, sufficient funding, and the setting of realistic targets; the strategy should be a "living document."

The extent to which financial inclusion strategies have improved access to finance is difficult to know, as we do not know how the sector would have developed without a strategy. What we do know is that financial inclusion strategies, if taken seriously, are a powerful instrument for convening stakeholders who have a potential impact on financial inclusion and helping them to come to a common understanding on how to reach this goal.

National strategies that focus on *responsible* financial inclusion, as opposed to simply *access* to finance, might lead to significantly greater benefits for households and service providers alike. While many financial inclusion strategies may not focus on consumer protection and financial capability, they should (see figure 3.1).

Legal Mandates

Some countries use quantitative financial inclusion targets or specific product offerings mandated by law as tools to promote the provision of financial services to underserved populations or geographic areas. These *financial inclusion mandates* can be seen as a complement to other financial regulations and incentives (for example, tax advantages for providers to reach poorer segments of the population). Mandates appear to be a simple and effective tool for achieving financial inclusion targets; assuming that enforcing compliance is possible, predefined targets can be reached (for example, everybody has access to certain products or all districts are served by at least one branch). However, in practice this might not always be the case.

Priority sector lending targets are the best-known example of financial inclusion targets. Priority sector lending usually requires a certain percentage of a provider's loan portfolio to be dedicated to sectors such as agriculture, micro and small businesses, housing, or microfinance. Basic or "no frills" bank accounts, designed for low-income clients with low or no fees, are another example of financial inclusion mandates; in some countries (including Belgium and France in the European Union, Indonesia, and Mexico) banks are required by law to offer basic accounts (see box 3.7).

Expert opinions about the usefulness of legal mandates are divided. Opponents give the following reasons:

Figure 3.1   Financial Inclusion Strategies and Responsible Finance

'Responsible' financial inclusion that raises financial capability in line with financial access leads to:

- Stronger positive impacts at level of individual, firm, economy, financialsector
- Lower risk (for individuals, financial institutions, and the financial sector)
- Improved uptake of new technology

FINANCIAL INCLUSION	FINANCIAL INCLUSION COMBINED WITH FINANCIAL LITERACY, CONSUMER PROTECTION
Examples of how households/firms can benefit	Examples of how households/firms can benefit
• MICROINSURANCE: Reduces exposure to potential losses to enable business growth • BASIC BANK ACCOUNTS: Low income household access through a mobile phone or ATMs • REGULATORY REFORMS: Innovation by financial institutions to serve lower income clients	• MICROINSURANCE: Understand the risks covered, cost compared to the potential benefit, select product • BASIC BANK ACCOUNTS: Select a bank account that meets its needs, manage fees and debt levels • REGULATORY REFORMS: Harmonization of regulation to capability levels and objectives of education programs

Financial inclusion

Responsible finance

Source: Tata and Pearce 2012.

Box 3.7 Financial Inclusion in India

India's government has a long tradition of promoting financial inclusion. For more than 40 years, the central bank, the Reserve Bank of India, has been operating priority sector lending mandating a portion of banks' loan portfolios to be in the agriculture sector and to small and micro enterprises. In 2005, it required banks to offer basic no-frills accounts with no, or very low, minimum balances and affordable charges. However, use of these accounts has been very low. In 2011, banks were advised to provide at a minimum four products: (a) a savings or overdraft account, (b) a remittance product for electronic transfer of government benefits and other remittances, (c) a pure savings product (ideally a recurring-deposit scheme), and (d) entrepreneurial credit.

In a parallel initiative, in 2010 the government and the central bank set goals to provide by 2015 all 600,000 villages in India with a banking outlet (either by a branch or a retail agent, in India known as a business correspondent), with stipulated annual targets along the way. While these targets were not specified by law, the Reserve Bank of India requires all banks to report progress regularly and closely monitors their achievements.

It is still too early to say how successful the implementation of these ambitious goals will be. Some banks have risen to the challenge and opened numerous new outlets (mostly business correspondents). Others have complained that the financial inclusion targets hurt their profits.

The New Microfinance Handbook

- In a market economy, it is assumed that providers know best how to serve the market. It is also assumed that a decision *not* to offer a certain product is informed by economic factors. If mandated to do so, providers will incur losses that have to be recovered elsewhere.

- Targets can be achieved at lowest cost if they focus on those providers that are best positioned to contribute to their achievement.[7]

- On a more practical level, it is difficult to set up rules in a way that does not encourage regulatory avoidance (for example, providers choosing a different legal form, moving to another jurisdiction, or bending the rules).

- The achievement of targets has to be monitored, and an effective enforcement mechanism, including penalties for nonachievement, has to be established, which requires additional resources.

Proponents, however, argue that mandates to explore new markets are needed to counter the complacency of financial institutions. When mandates are imposed (if applied to all so that no individual provider's competitive position is compromised), financial institutions will do their best to comply with the targets at the lowest cost and eventually may even be able to cover their costs. In some cases (South Africa and Germany), the mere threat of a legal mandate prohibiting commercial banks from refusing any customer the opportunity to open a bank account was sufficient to lead the banking industry, of its own accord, to offer basic accounts to everybody.[8] The ultimate decision whether to mandate financial inclusion in law depends on the specific context of a country.

Global Standards and Standard-Setting Bodies

The term "standards" encompasses many things in the financial sector.[9] Standards may be general or specific, and they may be national or international.

Standards for supervision are largely set by international financial standard-setting bodies; they reflect national and global experience with different types of institutions and the risks and benefits of different activities. While standards represent formal rules, they are typically "soft law"; there is no technical means of enforcing them, although there may be consequences (in terms of reputation and pricing) for failure to comply with them. In some cases, the threat of these consequences can have significant impact on the actions of a government or its regulator.

Global standard-setting bodies set standards and provide guidance for the regulators of financial institutions. Due to the historical emphasis on setting standards for existing institutions and their clients and the supervision of such institutions, many standards have not yet considered the issues of particular relevance to providing the poor with financial services. Moreover, these standards may inhibit new approaches, including technical and nontechnical innovations, and new products and services that the poor need. However, the global standard setters have begun to consider how existing standards might need to be revised in order to facilitate financial inclusion. This effort requires understanding the risks of financial exclusion as well as the changing risks and benefits of increased financial inclusion. In addition, attention is required to understand the situation of poor countries with high levels of financial exclusion and weak supervisory capacity (both staffing and experience) and to adjust standards accordingly (CGAP 2011).

Of the various standard-setting bodies, the three most relevant to financial services for the poor are the Basel Committee on Banking Supervision (BCBS), the Financial Action Task Force (FATF), and the International Association of Insurance Supervisors (IAIS).

The BCBS formulates standards and guidelines for the supervision of banks and other deposit-taking institutions and is best known for its international standards on capital adequacy and its Core Principles for Effective Banking Supervision (known as the Basel Core Principles). In December 2011, the BCBS proposed revised principles intended to address the postcrisis lessons for promoting sound supervisory systems. These proposed principles are significant for the prominence given to the principle of proportionality (see chapter 16). In 2010 the BCBS issued guidelines on applying the Basel Core Principles to microfinance activities of depository institutions. The guidelines highlight the importance of a proportionate (risk-based) approach as well as the key differences between a microloan portfolio and a commercial loan portfolio. The key differences include (a) the particularities of the labor-intensive microlending methodology, (b) the licensing requirements, which should reflect different risks than those of commercial banks, (c) the particular provisioning and reserve requirements that should be applied to microloans, and (d) the need for different liquidity requirements (BCBS 2010).

The FATF is the global standard-setting body for anti-money-laundering and combating the financing of terrorism (AML/CFT) rules. It is organized as a task force–style body with 34 member countries and two regional organizations (the European Commission and the Gulf Cooperation Council).[10] The FATF recommendations articulating standards for national regimes on AML/CFT have recently been revised to incorporate a risk-based approach that is critical to financial inclusion efforts (FATF 2012). For example, under the revised recommendations, a mobile money account with strict transaction limits does not require the same customer due diligence rules as a current account with no limits. Specifically, FATF recommendations outline the measures that countries, financial institutions, and related businesses should institute. While the recommendations are not legally binding, countries that do not adhere to them run the risk of being considered a haven for illicit transactions or criminal activity. This can result in international sanctions

and higher borrowing costs, among other consequences (Isern and de Koker 2009).

The IAIS is a broad-based forum composed of insurance regulators and supervisors from some 190 jurisdictions in almost 140 countries. Its stated mission is to promote effective and globally consistent regulation and supervision of the insurance industry in order to develop and maintain fair, safe, and stable insurance markets for the benefit and protection of policyholders. The IAIS issues standards and guidance material (including *Issues in Regulation and Supervision of Microinsurance*; IAIS 2007) and has recently revised its Insurance Core Principles to incorporate the principle of proportionality. Specifically, the Insurance Core Principles state, "Supervisors need to tailor certain supervisory requirements and actions in accordance with the nature, scale, and complexity of individual insurers. In this regard, supervisors should have the flexibility to tailor supervisory requirements and actions so that they are commensurate with the risks posed by individual insurers as well as the potential risks posed by insurers to the insurance section or the financial system as a whole" (IAIS 2011, para. 8).

Coordination and Advocacy

An important element of policy and rule making for financial inclusion is the interaction of various stakeholders and how those interactions shape policy outcomes. The development and implementation of formal rules are not a one-off event; rules need to be revised regularly in light of experience and learning. As with every other part of the financial market system, the process of how rules are developed and who is involved needs to be understood and supported in a way that encourages pro-poor regulation (Gibson 2010).

How rules develop depends on the level of accountability and responsiveness among rule makers to the advocacy "voice" of different interest groups and the wider political economy around financial regulation. This means that coordinating bodies, such as the G-20 Global Partnership for Financial Inclusion, and advocacy groups, such as associations of providers or consumer groups, are important players in relation to the rules regarding financial services. Each group has its own motivation and objectives, which may or may not always result in what is best for the ultimate beneficiary of policies, the wider public.[11]

Coordination

Coordination of policy makers and various stakeholders interested in financial services for the poor is a key element in designing and implementing effective financial inclusion reforms and policies (see box 3.8). This is particularly important as new partnerships develop between providers, including banks and mobile network operators, or as retailers and agents become involved in the delivery of financial services. A lack of coordination can increase risks such as improper sequencing of regulatory changes or regulatory changes in one sector that undermine efforts in other areas (AFI 2010).

Alliance for Financial Inclusion

More and more policy makers and representative bodies are beginning to coordinate formally with

---

Box 3.8 Negotiating a Special Microfinance Law in Uganda: The Outcome of Competing Interests

In 2003 Uganda passed a special law for microfinance deposit-taking institutions. A detailed analysis of the process leading to the adoption of this law and the role of participating interest groups can explain why the law has generally been regarded as a success, despite its bias toward overregulation (which occurs at the expense of improving access to financial services) and weak emphasis on consumer protection.

The interest groups with the strongest influence on the outcome were the central bank (Bank of Uganda), donor agencies, and the most mature MFIs in the country (which planned to apply for a license under the new law). All three groups had the highest level of knowledge about what an enabling legal framework for microfinance should look like: The Bank of Uganda knew about financial regulation and acquired increasing knowledge about microfinance, but was biased toward overregulation (as regulators typically are); on

the contrary, MFIs knew about microfinance and increasingly learned about financial regulation; donor projects at the time were led by knowledgeable microfinance "champions."

Policy makers (the government and the parliament) also had a strong interest in the topic of microfinance, viewing it as a way to gain political capital, but knew much less about the rationale for and objectives of regulating it. They could easily have derailed the process, but donors, MFIs, and the Bank of Uganda prevented that. Finally, clients had the most to gain from adoption of the law because they would acquire better access to financial services (savings, in particular). However, their voice was hardly heard in the process. The absence of client consultation and the conservative approach taken by the regulator explain why the new regime has not been as successful in increasing access as hoped and is relatively weak on consumer protection.

---

one another to influence financial inclusion. For example, as of 2012, government institutions from 78 countries had joined the global Alliance for Financial Inclusion (AFI), a network of financial policy makers that promotes peer learning and the implementation of effective policies that advance the goal of financial inclusion:

A global policy response based on leadership from developing countries, closer international cooperation, and strong and coordinated partnerships between relevant public and private sector stakeholders at national and international levels could be the most effective way to support countries at all levels of policy development ... Dialogue between policy makers and the industry is also a powerful tool for deciphering and mitigating risks that help to create regulation and foster innovations in access (AFI 2010).

A good example of coordination efforts is the Maya Declaration initiated by AFI to commit policy makers to prioritize financial inclusion (see box 3.9).

Other coordination and advocacy efforts include the G-20 Global Partnership for Financial Inclusion and the Responsible Finance Forum.

Box 3.9 The Maya Declaration

Launched under the auspices of the Alliance for Financial Inclusion (AFI), the Maya Declaration is the first global set of measurable commitments, spearheaded by developing- and emerging-country governments, to unlock the economic and social potential of the 2.5 billion poorest people through greater financial inclusion. In the declaration, members recognize the key role that financial inclusion policy plays in enhancing stability and integrity, its role in fighting poverty, and its essential contribution toward inclusive economic growth. The Maya Declaration raises the profile of financial inclusion and provides public visibility to ensure that policy makers are held accountable for their commitment. Among AFI members, 24 have made specific national commitments to financial inclusion. For example,

- *Central Bank of Brazil* pledged to launch a National Partnership for Financial Inclusion.
- *Bank of Tanzania* pledged to raise its level of financial access to 50 percent of its population by 2015 through mobile banking.
- Mexico's *Comisión Nacional Bancaria y de Valores* committed to establishing banking agents or branches in every municipality of the country by 2014.
- *Reserve Bank of Malawi* pledged to introduce agent banking in 2012.
- *National Bank of Rwanda* set a target of 80 percent financial inclusion by 2017.
- Peru's *Superintendency of Banks and Insurance* pledged to enact a new law regulating electronic money within the next year.

In support of the Maya Declaration, AFI is establishing a peer review mechanism, serving as a policy clearinghouse for peer-reviewed solutions, and providing subject matter expertise to help members to implement commitments. It will award grants to support knowledge exchange, develop financial inclusion strategies, and provide advocacy tools to help institutions win the support of key partners needed for implementation.

Source: http://www.afi-global.org/gpf/maya-declaration.

Global Partnership for Financial Inclusion

In 2010 the G-20 recognized financial inclusion as a key pillar of the global development agenda and created the Global Partnership for Financial Inclusion as an implementing body open to G-20 countries, non-G-20 countries, and other relevant stakeholders (Ehrbeck, Pickens, and Tarazi 2012). The G-20 principles for innovative financial inclusion play an increasing role as a point of reference for policy makers and other stakeholders seeking to promote increased financial inclusion (see box 3.10).

Responsible Finance Forum

The Responsible Finance Forum is an interinstitutional community of practice for exchanging knowledge and building consensus on responsible finance. It was created to support participating

---

Box 3.10 The G-20 Principles for Financial Inclusion

At its first summit in June 2010, the G-20 identified a set of principles that reflect conditions conducive to spurring innovation for financial inclusion while protecting financial stability and consumers:

- *Leadership.* Cultivate a broad-based government commitment to financial inclusion to help to alleviate poverty
- *Diversity.* Implement policy approaches that promote competition, provide market-based incentives for delivering sustainable financial access, and promote the use of a broad range of affordable services (savings, credit, payments and transfers, insurance) as well as a diversity of service providers
- *Innovation.* Promote technological and institutional innovation as a means to expand financial system access and use, including by addressing infrastructure weaknesses
- *Protection.* Encourage a comprehensive approach to consumer protection that recognizes the roles of government, providers, and consumers
- *Empowerment.* Develop financial literacy and financial capability
- *Cooperation.* Create an institutional environment with clear lines of accountability and coordination within government and encourage partnerships and direct consultation across government, business, and other stakeholders
- *Knowledge.* Use improved data to make evidence-based policy, measure progress, and consider an incremental "test and learn" approach acceptable to both regulators and service providers
- *Proportionality.* Build a policy and regulatory framework that is proportionate with the risks and benefits involved in such innovative products and services and based on an understanding of the gaps and barriers in existing regulation
- *Framework.* Consider the following in the regulatory framework, reflecting international standards, national circumstances, and support for a competitive landscape: an appropriate, flexible, risk-based AML/CFT regime; conditions for the use of agents as a customer interface; a clear regulatory regime for electronically stored value; and market-based incentives to achieve the long-term goal of broad interoperability and interconnection.

Source: G-20 Information Centre (http://www.g20.utoronto.ca/2010/to-principles.html).

---

institutions, including development agencies and development finance institutions, in sharing knowledge and information on development efforts and potential collaborations, to build on responsible finance frameworks and foster broad-based dialogue and facilitate convergence of views, and to support coordinated action. The Responsible Finance Forum considers issues related to consumer protection regulation, industry action, and financial capability, with an emphasis on more transparent, inclusive, and equitable financial sectors (Responsible Finance Forum 2012; see figure 3.2).

Advocacy

Industry networks or associations often take a central role in advocating the interests of providers. As associations are formed on the premise of common interests, they can effectively communicate members' shared concerns about a particular issue. The activities that constitute advocacy are

generally developed on the basis of member needs, internal capacities, and the external political environment. For example, regional or international associations, whose membership typically comprises national-level networks and providers from multiple countries, engage in policy in a more indirect manner. Regional associations often publish information on industry practices or lobby market players on issues affecting their members across countries and markets. By doing so, they facilitate the work of local association representatives.

National associations can influence policy more directly by engaging with local authorities who can pursue direct changes to various laws or secondary legislation (for example, regulations and guidelines). They can pursue specific actions that advance an advocacy strategy—letter writing, publicity campaigns, or direct lobbying with policy makers—to communicate or publicize their support for change on a particular issue. Industry

Figure 3.2   Responsible Finance: A Multiple-Stakeholder Approach

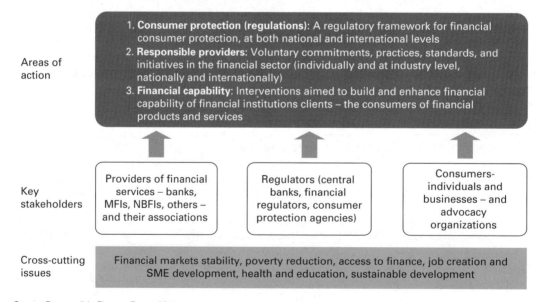

Source: Responsible Finance Forum 2011.

The New Microfinance Handbook

associations often provide policy advocacy as a service to members. If implemented effectively, advocacy can strengthen the voice of providers and their associations and thus help to design rules that are tailored to their specific needs (see box 3.11).

While clients should be the main beneficiaries of financial inclusion efforts, their voice is rarely heard; often, they lack the technical expertise to lobby effectively for their interests. In addition, their divergent interests pose a challenge to collective action. Although consumer associations try to overcome both of these challenges, they are not yet widespread in microfinance. More effective representation occurs through the intersection of client and provider interests. While the interests of providers and clients are not identical (for example, they differ with regard to product pricing), the fact that providers depend on the satisfaction of their clients creates substantial

Box 3.11 SEEP's Toolkit for Policy Advocacy

The Small Enterprise Education and Promotion (SEEP) Network connects microenterprise practitioners from around the world in efforts to develop practical guidance that supports their common vision of creating a sustainable income in every household. The SEEP Network has an advocacy planning model that seeks to develop the capacity of advocacy within microfinance. The following are the most common forms of advocacy it promotes:

- *Engagement* is a gradual process of relationship building. It is not focused on a particular policy goal, but rather on the development of greater familiarity, trust, and mutual understanding. Associations can engage stakeholders through invitations to association-sponsored events, educational opportunities, and formal and informal meetings.
- *Facilitation* and *consultation* are based on working with policy makers and affected stakeholders to create opportunities for action. Facilitation involves creating opportunities for direct contact with decision makers to promote dialogue and build awareness through conferences, workshops, field trips, and meetings. Facilitation may also involve creating strategies for policy creation more directly. Consultation with a diverse base of members and a broad range of stakeholders is required to increase the contribution of individuals and organizations, while engendering greater overall participation in policy-related discussions.
- One of the most significant contributions advocates can make to policy reform is through the dissemination of high-quality *research and information*. Association members have a direct understanding of the concerns of affected populations. By promoting credible and well-documented information on the sector, associations can build legitimacy as a representative voice. Examples include industry assessments, benchmarking reports, market studies, and focused policy investigations.

In its most direct form, advocacy is about promoting concrete solutions to problems. Advocates can promote the reform of existing laws and the creation of new ones, oppose legislative initiatives considered damaging to the sector, and promote changes to the implementation of existing policies and regulation. By lobbying decision makers as well as stakeholders who can influence them, advocates can directly affect policy outcomes.

Source: D'Onofrio 2010. SEEP Network, http://networks.seepnetwork.org/ppt-newhtml/Policy_Advocacy_mar2010_web.en_.pdf.

overlap. Furthermore, because clients constitute an important voting bloc, policy makers should be motivated to consider their current and potential interests.

The Role of Industry in Financial Inclusion

Financial inclusion calls for better outreach, appropriate products and services, and consumer trust. Responsible finance emphasizes value, respect, and protection of the consumer (McKee, Lahaye, and Koning 2011). Efforts by providers to encourage responsible finance influence institutional behavior, market access, the range of products and services on offer, and the competitive landscape, all of which have an impact on the functioning of the market and the suitability of financial services. Given that financial services for the poor are most prevalent in countries with limited supervisory capacity, often providers may need to take the lead in promoting responsible finance.

Industry Standards and Guidelines

Standards of practice and codes of conduct that financial service providers and other market actors abide by can contribute to financial inclusion and help to build the industry's commitment to consumer protection. In recent years, multilateral agencies have promulgated many initiatives to provide guidelines and principles, and the titles of their documents define the targeted areas: the "United Nations Principles for Investors in Inclusive Finance," the "World Bank Draft Guidelines for Consumer Financial Protection," and the "Organisation for Economic Co-operation and Development (OECD) Principles and Good Practices for Financial Awareness and Education." Often these are living documents, open to review and revision as members respond to issues raised by stakeholders and better understand what is missing or inadequate in the standards or codes. However, enforcement

can be challenging: There is typically no legal consequence for failure to comply, and influential financial institutions may use their power to discourage the self-regulatory body (for example, a microfinance association) from taking action. Without enforcement, such standards can only exert a weak influence.

CGAP has developed numerous guidelines for the industry based on consensus from various stakeholders, including, for example, "Microfinance Investment Vehicle Disclosure Guidelines"; "Good Practice Guidelines for Funders of Microfinance"; "Regulation and Supervision Consensus Guidelines"; "Information Systems Implementation Guidelines"; "Disclosure Guidelines for Financial Reporting by Microfinance Insitutions"; "The Role of Funders in Responsible Finance"; "Due Diligence Guidelines for the Review of Microcredit Loan Portfolios"; "Developing Deposit Services for the Poor"; and "Definitions of Selected Financial Terms, Ratios, and Adjustments for Microfinance."[12]

Other industry representative bodies such as the Social Performance Task Force, the Smart Campaign on Client Protection Principles, and Microfinance Transparency have all launched initiatives and advocacy campaigns.

The Social Performance Task Force

The Social Performance Task Force, with more than 1,000 members in 2011, represents the primary stakeholders in financial services for the poor: practitioners, donors and investors, industry associations, technical assistance providers, rating agencies, and academics. It defines social performance as the "effective translation of a microfinance organization's mission into practice in line with commonly accepted social values."[13] Its mission is to promote standards by which providers can manage the double (and, for some, triple) bottom line that is at the core of providing financial services to the poor. Seeking to ensure that services focus on clients, the

Social Performance Task Force promotes the following:

- Efforts to serve increasing numbers of poorer and more excluded people sustainably

- Systematic assessment of the target population's specific needs to improve the relevance and quality of services

- Benefits for microfinance clients, their families, and communities, including increased social capital, assets, income, and access to services; reduced vulnerability; and fulfillment of basic needs

- Social responsibility of the provider toward its clients, employees, and the community it serves.[14]

Tools covering a wide range of purposes support the measurement and achievement of strong social performance (see chapter 14).

The Smart Campaign

Under the broader umbrella of social performance management, the Smart Campaign, initiated in 2009 by the Center for Financial Inclusion at ACCION International, advocates consumer protection principles and has recruited hundreds of organizations and individuals to endorse them. The shift from assumed to explicit articulation of consumer protection measures followed debates about pricing and profits in microfinance, as well as the emerging crises related to over-indebtedness and abusive practices. The Smart Campaign has advanced seven consumer protection principles:[15]

- *Appropriate product design and delivery.* Providers will take adequate care to design products and delivery channels in such a way that they do not cause clients harm. Products and delivery channels will be designed taking client characteristics into account.

- *Prevention of over-indebtedness.* Providers will take adequate care in all phases of their credit process to determine that clients have the capacity to repay without becoming over-indebted. In addition, providers will implement and monitor internal systems that support the prevention of over-indebtedness and will foster efforts to improve market-level credit risk management (such as sharing credit information).

- *Transparency.* Providers will communicate clear, sufficient, and timely information in a manner and language that clients can understand so that they can make informed decisions. The need for transparent information on pricing, terms, and conditions of products is highlighted.

- *Responsible pricing.* Pricing, terms, and conditions will be set in a way that is affordable to clients, while allowing financial institutions to be sustainable. Providers will strive to provide positive real returns on deposits.

- *Fair and respectful treatment of clients.* Financial service providers and their agents will treat their clients fairly and respectfully. They will not discriminate. Providers will ensure adequate safeguards to detect and correct corruption as well as aggressive or abusive treatment by their staff and agents, particularly during the loan sales and debt collection processes.

- *Privacy of client data.* The privacy of individual client data will be respected in accordance with the laws and regulations of individual jurisdictions. Such data will only be used for the purposes specified at the time the information is collected or as permitted by law, unless otherwise agreed with the client.

- *Mechanisms for complaint resolution.* Providers will have in place timely and responsive mechanisms for handling complaints and resolving problems for their clients and will use these mechanisms both to resolve individual problems and to improve their products and services.

Of the seven principles, over-indebtedness and transparency receive the most attention. Efforts to prevent over-indebtedness have included more careful assessments of client debt capacity, staff incentive schemes focused on portfolio quality, and attempts to identify or limit the number of loans a client carries from multiple lenders (see box 3.12). In addition, lenders have found that the policies developed for markets with minimal competition need to be adjusted for more mature markets with multiple providers (Rozas 2011).

The Smart Campaign conducts a global campaign to garner support for these principles. It also promotes activities that help providers to move from endorsement to implementation, including developing numerous tools for assessment, training, and client protection and education (Rozas 2011).[16]

Both the Social Performance Task Force and the Smart Campaign also work with microfinance rating agencies and investors to achieve alignment between their rating frameworks or due diligence processes and consumer protection principles.

MicroFinance Transparency

Pricing is central to the debates regarding profits and the broader social responsibility of financial service providers. The true prices of microloans are not always measured accurately or reported and remain widely misunderstood. Consequently, the need for the industry to improve the disclosure of interest rates and the standardization and communication of costs is a priority. MicroFinance Transparency (MFTransparency) is a global initiative committed to promoting pricing transparency in the microfinance sector. The organization aims to achieve its mission in the following ways: data collection, standardization, and dissemination; training and capacity building for financial institutions; development of educational materials; and consulting with regulators and policy makers on price disclosure legislation.[17]

Microloans often have higher interest rates than mainstream commercial loans because they are more expensive to make and manage. This challenge has driven many providers to quote prices that are significantly lower than the effective prices. Once providers in a specific market begin to employ confusing product pricing, it becomes very difficult for any single provider to maintain transparent pricing. Standardized forms of disclosure can help to address this problem.

Compliance

Industry associations and individual financial providers have an important role to play in

---

Box 3.12 Battling Over-Indebtedness in Azerbaijan

In addition to serious internal efforts to avoid over-indebtedness among its own clients, AccessBank has been spearheading a campaign to reduce over-indebtedness at the sector level. Collaborating with the Azerbaijan Microfinance Association, AccessBank has promoted a "one-client, one-lender" strategy, in which a lender seeking to provide a loan to another MFI's client commits to paying off the client's existing loan. Thus if a lender wishes to issue a US$3,000 loan to a client who already has US$5,000 outstanding with another lender, that new lender would have to issue a US$8,000 loan, part of which would go to pay off the client's outstanding debt.

Source: Rozas 2011.

promoting responsible finance through standards. However, industry standards rely on compliance with self-imposed codes of conduct and explicit rejection of strong incentives for deceptive behavior. Furthermore, membership of industry associations rarely comprises all relevant providers, which limits the scope of protection and may place compliant providers at a competitive disadvantage (Chien 2012). For example, although the consumer protection principles advanced by the Smart Campaign are intended to benefit both financial service providers and their clients and pricing transparency initiatives are intended to benefit clients, the asymmetries between what providers endorse and what clients understand have the potential to undermine those efforts. Identifying the priorities of consumers and providers highlights potential barriers to translating principles of responsible finance into effective practice, as significant distance separates clients from financial institutions (see table 3.1).

Table 3.1 Potential Barriers to Effective Consumer Protection through Standards and Guidelines

Target group and barrier	Details
Clients	
Low literacy	Illiterate clients cannot read published lists of consumer protection principles and client rights. They may have trouble filing complaints.
High priority assigned to accessing loans	Fear of not getting a loan often drives client behavior, serving as a deterrent to asking for product information or raising issues of unethical behavior.
Lack of knowledge	Clients often do not know their rights or what constitutes a violation. Violations are not limited to cases of borrower versus lender. In Bolivia, in focus group discussions, group lending members reported the use of abusive debt collection practices—intended to shame defaulters—that violated members' rights. Clients often do not understand the products on offer. At a basic level, many do not understand that interest is charged as a percentage of the loan; few can evaluate the difference in interest cost calculated using a flat rate or declining balance.
Financial institutions	
Overestimation of consumer knowledge	Institutional investments in product development have not been matched by investments in client education about new offerings.
Potential conflict with profitability	Efficiency requirements and financial incentives can undermine staff motivation to spend enough time with clients to ensure that they understand the products they may purchase. Institutions have a bigger vested interest in product-specific marketing than in education that will enable customers to compare products across lenders. Transparent presentation of rates and fees could be a disadvantage if not done uniformly and universally by all lenders in the same market.
Implementation of consumer protection principles	Implementing new codes can be costly, involving revisions to human resource systems, new mechanisms for customer feedback and complaints, and monitoring of compliance by providers in multiple countries (for example, by an MFI network)

Source: Nelson 2009.

Box 3.13 Financial Education as Part of the Business Model

Over a period of just three years, the Kenyan financial market experienced significant growth, exposing many previously unbanked clients to an increasingly complex array of products. Without adequate information to make informed decisions about these products, clients were often confused and vulnerable to exploitation. Faulu Kenya believed that inappropriate use of financial services was leading to over-indebtedness and default. Clients lacked information on how best to use credit and how to make decisions about how much and when to borrow (or not) and from where. In 2009 Faulu Kenya embarked on a financial education project Elewa Pesa (Understand Your Money), co-funded with the Financial Education Fund. Faulu's objective was to equip nearly 50,000 clients at 26 branches with the necessary financial knowledge and skills to facilitate prudent money management, premised on the belief that educated people are better clients. Financial education was provided through a one-time training workshop complemented by video clips, comic strips, and interactive worksheets, delivered by professional trainers. Training was supported by interactive coaching sessions with loan officers. An impact evaluation, using a quasi-experimental design, revealed improvements in specific indicators of knowledge and behavior among the treatment group. Most significantly, portfolio at risk was lower in the four pilot treatment branches than in the nontreatment branch.

Training for staff was initially planned to facilitate client recruitment. Yet, with the inclusion of financial education as part of staff curriculum, the results were much greater. Staff became more knowledgeable and better equipped to answer clients' questions and more engaged in coaching and advising them; they even began saving more themselves.

Finding that financial education has benefits both for the client and for the institution, Faulu has incorporated financial education in its loan orientation training and as a key indicator of performance.

Source: Alyna Wyatt, Financial Education Fund; Jacqueline Nyaga, Faulu Kenya.

The barriers noted in table 3.1 highlight the need to understand the perspectives of both providers and consumers. They also indicate another role for industry in consumer protection—developing the financial capability of consumers. By having direct contact with consumers, some providers are actively choosing to invest in building their clients' financial capacity. Financial education is relatively new, with initial efforts emerging only after 2000, but many institutions have embraced it,[18] as illustrated by the case of Faulu Kenya, an MFI (see box 3.13).

Notes

1. As discussed in chapter 1, formal rules are generally the purview of government or industry stakeholders. They include primary legislation (also referred to as *laws*), whether statutory (that is, passed by the legislature) or established by the judiciary; secondary legislation (which may be entitled *regulations, guidelines,* or *circulars*) issued by a government agency or executive body pursuant to a law; and other legal proclamations imposed on financial service providers and other players supporting the financial system. Formal rules

also encompass consumer protection guidelines and global standards and principles that guide the actions of regulators and supervisors as well as industry standards, nonstatutory codes of conduct, and other principles that guide the actions of financial service providers, even though they may not be legally enforceable.

2. In some cases, market actors can be just as concerned about public statements (such as policies) by the regulator as about legal provisions.

3. And in many cases with donors playing a key role.

4. This section draws on Brix and McKee (2010); Chien (2012).

5. CGAP is a significant provider of information and coordination in financial services for the poor. An industry coordinating body housed at the World Bank, CGAP focuses on "policy and research representing more than 30 development agencies and private foundations who share a common mission to alleviate poverty. CGAP provides market intelligence, promotes standards, develops innovative solutions, and offers advisory services to governments, financial service providers, donors, and investors." See www.cgap.org.

6. Consumer protection is often discussed in terms of the rights and responsibilities of both providers and clients. Clients need to develop the capability to assess product offerings; to do this, they have the right to ask questions about products, and providers have the responsibility to respond respectfully.

7. This would argue for setting up a market for tradable "priority sector lending certificates," as the Rajan Committee argued for the case of India. See Planning Commission, India (2009).

8. South Africa shows that such a self-commitment by the industry can lead to the opening of many new accounts (7 million accounts within four years, bringing the banked population to 20 million by the end of 2008). The banks now offer low-cost bank accounts. See Bankable

Frontier Associates (2009); http://mg.co.za/article/2012-02-17-mzansi-accounts-reach-dead-end.

9. This section was contributed by Kate Lauer.

10. www.fatf-gafi.org.

11. For an example of an interest group analysis in microfinance regulation, see Staschen (2010, ch. 7).

12. See www.CGAP.org.

13. http://sptf.info/hp-what-is-sp.

14. http://sptf.info/.

15. www.smartcampaign.com.

16. See http://www.smartcampaign.org/tools-a-resources.

17. Contributed by Alexandra Fiorillo.

18. Microfinance Opportunities, an early champion of financial education in developing countries, reports that between May 2006 and December 2011, 469 organizations participated in financial education training-of-trainers workshops. It also reports outreach to more than 40 million end users through a combination of direct financial education training and delivery of financial education messages via mass media.

References and Further Reading

* Key works for further reading.

AFI (Alliance for Financial Inclusion). 2010. "Consumer Protection: Leveling the Playing Field in Financial Inclusion." Bangkok, Thailand: Alliance for Financial Inclusion.

*———. 2011. "G-20 Principles for Innovative Financial Inclusion." http://www.afi-global .org/library/publications/g20-principles-innovative-financial-inclusion.

Almazan, Mireya. 2010. "Beyond Enablement: Harnessing Government Assets and Needs." Global Savings Forum, Bill and Melinda Gates Foundation, Seattle.

*Bankable Frontier Associates. 2009. "The Mzansi Bank Account Initiative in South Africa." FinMark Trust.

*BCBS (Basel Committee on Banking Supervision). 2010. "Microfinance Activities and the Core Principles for Effective Banking Supervision—Final Document." BCBS, Basel, August. http://www.bis.org/publ/bcbs175.htm.

———. 2011. "Core Principles for Effective Banking Supervision: Consultative Document." BCBS, Basel, December. http://www.bis.org/publ/bcbs129.htm.

Bester, H., D. Chamberlain, L. de Koker, C. Hougaard, R. Short, A. Smith, and R. Walker. 2008. "Implementing FATF Standards in Developing Countries and Financial Inclusion: Findings and Guidelines." The FIRST Initiative, World Bank, Washington, DC.

*Brix, Laura, and Katharine McKee. 2010. "Consumer Protection Regulation in Low-Access Environments: Opportunities to Promote Responsible Finance." Focus Note 60, CGAP, Washington, DC, February.

*CGAP (Consultative Group to Assist the Poor). 2010. "Investors Implementing the Client Protection Principles." CGAP, Washington, DC.

*———. 2011. "Global Standard-Setting Bodies and Financial Inclusion for the Poor: Toward Proportionate Standards and Guidance." White paper prepared on behalf of the G-20's Global Partnership for Financial Inclusion. CGAP, Washington, DC, October. http://www.gpfi.org/sites/default/files/documents/CGAP.pdf.

Chatain, P.-L., R. Hernandéz-Coss, K. Borowik, and A. Zerzan. 2008. "Integrity in Mobile Phone Financial Services: Measures for Mitigating Risks from Money Laundering and Terrorist Financing." Working Paper 146, World Bank, Washington, DC.

*Chien, Jennifer. 2012. "Designing Disclosure Regimes for Responsible Financial Inclusion." Focus Note 78, CGAP, Washington, DC, March.

Cohen, Monique, and Candace Nelson. 2011. "Financial Literacy: A Step for Clients towards Financial Inclusion." Workshop paper commission for the 2011 Global Microcredit Summit, Valladolid, Spain, November 14–17.

*Dias, D., and K. McKee. 2010. "Protecting Branchless Banking Consumers: Policy Objectives and Regulatory Options." Focus Note 64, CGAP, Washington, DC.

D'Onofrio, S. 2010. "Policy Advocacy: A Toolkit for Microfinance Associations." SEEP Network, Washington, DC. http://networks.seepnetwork.org/ppt-newhtml/Policy_Advocacy_mar2010_web.en_.pdf.

*Duflos, E. 2011. "National Strategies for Financial Inclusion: Lessons Learned." Unpublished presentation.

*Duflos, E., and J. Glisovic-Mézières. 2008. "National Microfinance Strategies." CGAP Brief, CGAP, Washington, DC.

*Duflos, E., and K. Imboden. 2004. "The Role of Governments in Microfinance." Donor Brief 19, CGAP, Washington, DC.

EDA Rural Systems and M-CRIL (Micro-Credit Ratings International). 2011. "Of Interest Rates, Margin Caps, and Poverty Lending: How the RBI Policy Will Affect Access to Microcredit by Low-Income Clients." M-CRIL, Gurgaon.

*Ehrbeck, T., M. Pickens, and Michael Tarazi. 2012. "Financially Inclusive Ecosystems: The Roles of Government Today." Focus Note 76, CGAP, Washington, DC.

*FATF (Financial Action Task Force). 2012. *International Standards on Combating Money Laundering and the Financing of Terrorism and Proliferation: The FATF Recommendations.* Paris: FATF, February.

Gibson, Alan. 2010. "The Financial Market Systems Framework." Unpublished draft.

*Hannig, A., and S. Jansen. 2010. "Financial Inclusion and Financial Stability: Current Policy Issues." ADBI Working Paper 259, Asian Development Bank Institute, Tokyo.

*Helms, Brigit, and Xavier Reille. 2004. "Interest Rate Ceilings and Microfinance: The Story So Far." Occasional Paper 9, CGAP, Washington, DC, September.

*IAIS (International Association of Insurance Supervisors). 2007. *Issues in Regulation and Supervision of Microinsurance.* Basel: BIS.

*———. 2011. *Insurance Core Principles, Standards, Guidance, and Assessment Methodology.* Basel: BIS, October.

*Isern, J., and L. de Koker. 2009. "AML/CFT: Strengthening Financial Inclusion and Integrity." Focus Note 56, CGAP, Washington, DC. http://www.cgap.org/gm/document-1.9.37862/FN56.pdf.

Klapper, Leora, Annamaria Lusardi, and Georgios A. Panos. 2012. "Financial Literacy and the Financial Crisis." Policy Research Working Paper 5980, World Bank, Washington, DC, February.

MasterCard Foundation, Microfinance Opportunities, and Genesis Analytics. 2011. "Taking Stock: Financial Education Initiatives for the Poor." MasterCard Foundation, Toronto.

*McKee, Katherine, Estelle Lahaye, and Antonique Koning. 2011. "Responsible Finance: Putting Principles to Work." Focus Note 73, CGAP, Washington, DC, September.

*Morduch, J. 2005. "Smart Subsidy in Microfinance." *ADB: Finance for the Poor* 6 (4).

Nelson, Candace. 2009. "Consumer Protection: A Client Perspective." Brief, Microfinance Opportunities, Washington, DC.

——. 2010. "Financial Education for All Ages." *Innovations* 5 (2): 83–86.

Nelson, Candace, and Angela Wambugu. 2008. *Financial Education in Kenya: Scoping Exercise Report*. Nairobi: FSD Kenya.

*Pickens, M., D. Porteous, and S. Rotman. 2009. "Banking the Poor via G2P Payments." Focus Note 58, CGAP, Washington, DC.

*Planning Commission, India. 2009. *A Hundred Small Steps: Report of the Committee on Financial Sector Reforms*. New Delhi: Sage.

*Porter, Beth. 2011. "National Strategies: Where Do They Get Us? A Roadmap for Financial Inclusion." Workshop paper commissioned for the 2011 Global Microcredit Summit, Valladolid, Spain, November 14–17.

*Porteous, D., and B. Helms. 2005. "Protecting Microfinance Borrowers." Focus Note 27, CGAP, Washington, DC.

*Responsible Finance Forum. 2011. "Advancing Responsible Finance for Greater Development Impact." Consultation draft, BMZ, CGAP, and IFC, Washington, DC, and Berlin.

——. 2012. "Global Mapping 2012: Progress in Responsible Financial Inclusion, Terms of Reference—July 2012." BMZ, CGAP, and IFC, Washington, DC, and Berlin.

Rozas, Daniel. 2011. "Implementing Client Protection in Microfinance: The State of the Practice, 2011." Center for Financial Inclusion, Washington, DC.

*Staschen, S. 2010. *Regulatory Impact Assessment in Microfinance: A Theoretical Framework and Its Application to Uganda*. Berlin: Wissenschaftlicher Verlag Berlin.

*Tata, Gaiv, and Douglas Pearce. 2012. "Catalyzing Financial Inclusion through National Strategies." CGAP, Washington, DC, March 5.

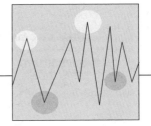

CHAPTER 4

The Role of Donors in Financial Inclusion

Mayada El-Zoghbi and Barbara Gähwiler

Financial inclusion is the state in which all individuals and businesses have the choice to access and the ability to use a range of appropriate financial services, responsibly provided by institutions permitted to offer such services. As described in chapter 1, demand and supply of financial services meet in a broader financial ecosystem that includes supporting functions and rules. Donors aiming for financial inclusion, as an end in itself or as a means toward economic development or poverty alleviation, can help make the financial ecosystem work better and be more inclusive.

Chapter 1 makes an important distinction between actors *within* the market system and organizations that are *outside* the system. For the most part, donors are outside the system, but they may enter the system temporarily to provide a catalytic role in market development. This chapter will discuss who the donors are that support

financial inclusion, what part of the financial system needs donor support, how donors can support the attainment of full financial inclusion, and the tools they have to do this (figure 4.1).

Donors That Support Financial Inclusion

In this chapter we use the term *donors* to mean entities that have an explicit mission to support development goals. A spectrum exists of these actors in terms of their ownership, where they raise their resources, and how they operate in the market. Some donors are structured as state-owned agencies, whereas others are private foundations. Some donors raise their funding from public resources such as federal or state government resources (that is, taxes). Donors may also raise their resources from private donations.

Figure 4.1   The Role of Donors in Financial Market System Development

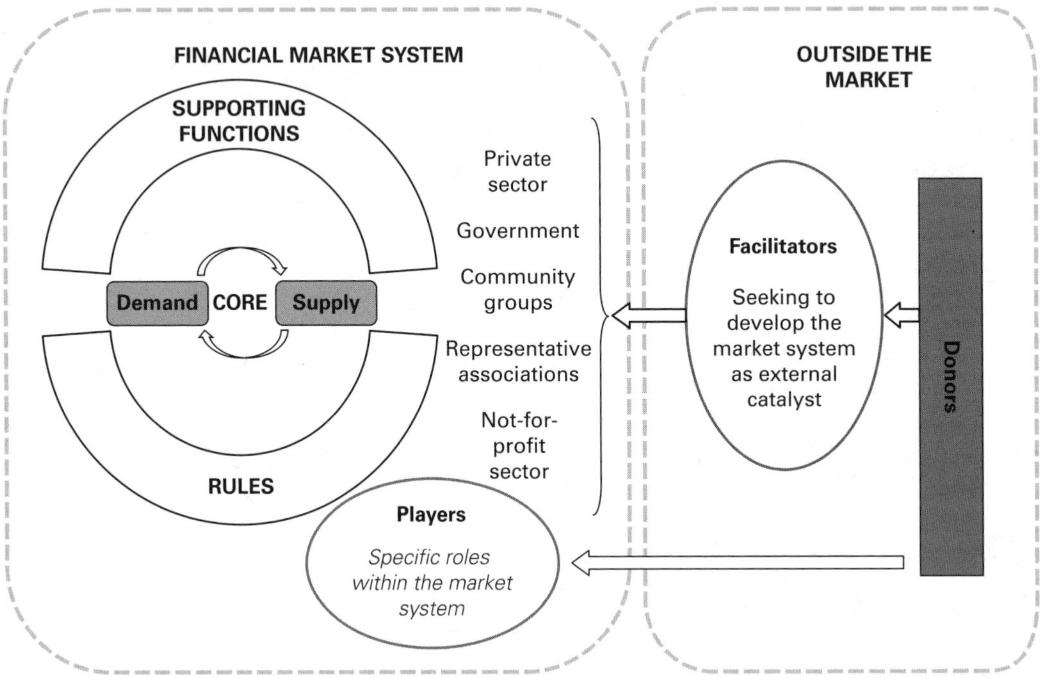

Source: Adapted from Alan Gibson, The Springfield Centre.

Some donors are highly concessional, whereas others try to mimic private investors. Regardless of where they sit along this spectrum of behavior, the fundamental role of donors in financial inclusion is to provide catalytic support to market development (table 4.1).

It is important to point out here that development finance institutions (DFIs) are a distinct category of development agency. They often see themselves as market actors (inside the market) and try to mimic the behavior of private investors. Although they may temporarily play the role of a market actor, their existence, mandate, and legal status entrust upon them the same catalytic market development role that "traditional" donors have. DFIs are part of the public system of development assistance and are able to raise money in capital markets benefiting from an implied state

guarantee. DFIs should therefore enter markets only temporarily to play a catalytic role by "crowding in" other market actors such as the local capital markets, banks, or depositors. If DFIs become permanent actors within a market, their stay defeats the purpose of their market catalytic role.

Although many international nongovernmental organizations (NGOs), such as World Vision and CARE, raise significant amounts of private donations that they either allocate to partners on the ground or use for their own development work, we do not classify NGOs as donors. The majority of NGOs rely on donor funding through either grants or cooperative agreements. However, among NGOs a large spectrum is seen of how they operate, with some acting like donors, others serving as facilitators, and others entering

Table 4.1 Spectrum of Donors in Financial Inclusion and the Way They Operate

Type of donor	Examples	Source of funding	Concessional vs. commercial	Ownership
Foundations	Bill & Melinda Gates Foundation Michael & Susan Dell Foundation MasterCard Foundation	Private donations	Concessional	Private
Bilateral donors	USAID (United States) DFID (United Kingdom) GIZ (Germany) SIDA (Sweden)	Public government funding	Concessional	Public
Multilaterals	UN agencies (IFAD, UNCDF) European Commission World Bank	Bilateral donors (member states) Capital markets	Concessional	Public
Regional banks	African Development Bank Asian Development Bank	Bilateral donors (member states) Capital markets	Mixed	Public
Development finance institutions	IFC KfW (Germany) Proparco (France)	Bilateral donors Public government funding Capital markets	Mostly commercial (some concessional)	Public

the market and delivering retail or support services directly. This chapter will not focus on the role of international NGOs, only noting where they may overlap with donors, facilitators, or market actors.

Where Is Catalytic Funding Needed?

Areas within a market system that may need catalytic support from donors tend to fall into three categories: information, capacity, and incentives.

Information

Markets are a mechanism for exchange. For exchange to occur between parties, whether this exchange is monetized or merely traded, certain information is required about the item being exchanged, about the entities engaged in the exchange, and about the terms of the exchange itself. Markets can yield outcomes that may seem

unbalanced or unfair when the level of information between parties engaging in an exchange is skewed.

With regard to the market for financial services, information asymmetry is a common malfunction in the market whereby suppliers do not have sufficient knowledge about certain segments of clients (demand) or clients do not have sufficient knowledge and information to make informed choices among suppliers.

Solutions to the problem of information in a market can include changing the rules, for example, mandating disclosure about interest rates; within the supporting functions, for example, establishing a private credit bureau with data on transaction histories of all income groups; or within the core itself, for example, making information available to suppliers about the nature and quantity of demand among specific market segments that may be excluded from current exchange.

Capacity

As described in chapter 1, the financial market system is made up of many actors (figure 4.2). These actors are at the core but are also delivering supporting functions and setting rules and norms. The capacity of certain actors within this system may be holding back the development of the system as a whole. For example, the capacity of the government may be a major constraint in allowing for enabling regulation for financial ser-

vices to reach the poor. The capacity of representative associations may be too weak to advocate for the regulatory reforms needed.

Solutions to capacity problems go beyond delivering capacity outright, but require working with those in the market who can deliver capacity development. It requires strengthening their ability to deliver long-term support on capacity development for the market as a whole. Many actors within the local market may be able to fill this role, such as private consulting firms, universities, trade associations, and training centers.

Figure 4.2   Stylized View of the Financial Market System

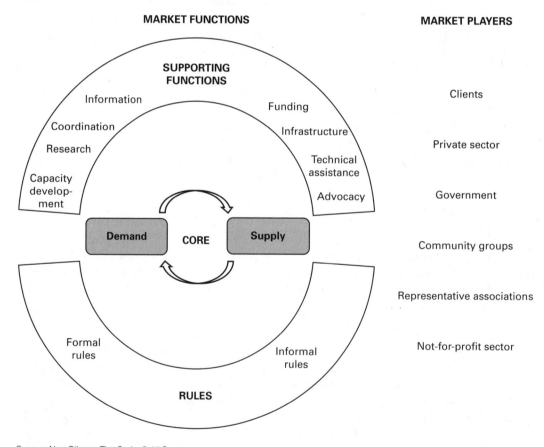

Source: Alan Gibson, The Springfield Centre.

In some instances, the local market may be too small for a viable entity to deliver capacity development on a sustainable basis; searching for regional or even global solutions may be the preferred mechanism to ensure long-term delivery of capacity development.

Incentives

Incentives, whether material or immaterial, guide choices and behavior. Incentives can be explicit in that they are offered as a reward for accomplishing certain goals or targets. They may also be implicit in the sense that the system as a whole may reward certain behavior or choices. Incentives can be both positive and negative. It is important to fully understand and acknowledge the incentives of actors to operate and deliver services on an ongoing basis; that is, donor subsidies must be designed to work to ensure long-term incentives exist to continue to deliver the service after the subsidies end.

A financial system may be plagued by negative incentives that reduce the likelihood of actors within the system to think about or deliver services to the poor. For example, the regulatory system may incentivize the banking system to serve corporate clients at the neglect of other potential market segments. A donor's intervention may be to work with regulators to change the rules that create the negative incentives for the banking system.

In many markets, financial service providers have limited information on poor clients. Often they need both information and incentives to adapt their products and services to meet these market segments. Donor guarantees can be structured in a way so that the negative incentives for financial service providers to serve this segment are reduced.

Solutions to address problems of incentives require strong awareness and understanding of the political economy in a country. Ultimately, modifying incentives often confronts entrenched power dynamics within a society. In the example above dealing with regulation, bankers may have very deep and strong relations with their traditional clientele: corporate clients and high networth individuals. Creating a new incentive system for financial service providers to serve low-income clients may be threatening to a regulatory system that is comfortable with the existing level of risk inherent in serving the upper echelons of society.

Is Current Donor Funding Catalytic?

Over the last 30 years, we have seen considerable progress toward financial inclusion in many countries. The picture will continue to evolve because of the dynamic nature of financial services markets. Markets experience the entry of new providers and supporting market actors and perhaps the exit of others. Demand evolves, and new approaches and products emerge to meet clients' needs. As markets grow and become more sophisticated, the risks and returns for different market actors change as well. Donors need to respond to these changes as they work to support the development of inclusive financial markets.

If we look at current donor commitments, data on where funding is allocated raise many questions as to whether donor funding is used in a catalytic way and allocated where it can most add value.

Majority of Donor Funding Used for On-lending

Depending on the constraints and opportunities in a given market, donor interventions might be needed at different levels in the market system, including at the core via funding for retail financial service providers. Without thorough market assessments, we can therefore not make judgments on whether donor funding is used in a catalytic way. However, the amount of global donor commitments still allocated to retail financial service providers for the purpose of on-lending to microfinance clients, a role that should be provided by funders within the market system, raises questions. Over the last 20 years, growing investor interest in microfinance as an alternative asset class has led to the emergence of more than 100 specialized microfinance investment vehicles that channel funding from institutional and individual investors, as well as from DFIs, to microfinance institutions (MFIs). The cumulative assets of those vehicles are estimated at US$6.8 billion (Symbiotics 2011). In addition to foreign private investments, mostly channeled through these microfinance investment vehicles, microfinance institutions increasingly have access to funding from local commercial banks or client deposits as a funding source. Despite the availability of funding from actors within the market system, 86 percent of donor commitments are still used for on-lending, according to a survey with the 20 largest donors and investors (Gähwiler and Nègre 2011).[1] Capacity building at the market infrastructure level (supporting functions) and the policy level (rules) account for only 2 percent of total commitments each (figure 4.3). Although it is difficult to draw any conclusions only by looking at committed amounts of a subset of donors, this allocation of funding seems unbalanced and out of touch with a catalytic approach to market development. On the contrary, the easy availability of donor funding can create disincentives for the development or expansion of savings services and undermines the borrowing institutions' financial discipline. Too much funding can push MFIs to embark on unsustainably steep growth paths, which has led to repayment crises in some countries (CGAP 2010a).

Donor Funding Concentrated on Few Institutions

Among donors, development finance institutions are the main providers of funding to MFIs. For young MFIs or those in nascent markets, DFIs can play a market development role by catalyzing private investment. Private sector investors are more likely to lend to MFIs that have received funding from a DFI. Once an MFI has established relationships with private investors, DFIs' continued investment arguably adds less value. In theory, DFIs should then move on and focus on less developed markets or riskier institutions with promising market development potential (for example, innovative business models or underserved client groups). However, as of December 2009, more than 40 percent of loans provided by DFIs are concentrated on 15 profitable MFIs, all of which receive funding from private sources (CGAP 2010b).

Geographical Concentration of Donor Funding

A CGAP survey conducted in 2010 with more than 60 donors found that donors supported projects in at least 122 different countries (CGAP 2010b). Out of the funding that can be allocated to one single country (regional and global projects excluded), 15 countries received more than 50 percent of total commitments. Among the countries receiving the highest donor commitments are some of today's most developed microfinance markets, such as India, Bangladesh, Bosnia and Herzegovina, Morocco, and Kenya,

Figure 4.3   The Purpose of Donor Commitments

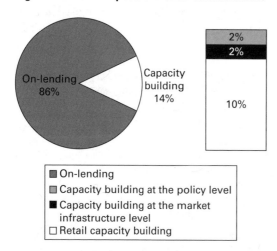

Source: Gähwiler and Nègre 2011.
Note: Percentage of total commitments as of December 2010, data from 18 public donors and one private investor.

where a variety of financial institutions offer a range of financial services to poor and low-income households, and the level of financial access to accounts with a formal financial institution is higher than regional averages (Demirgüç-Kunt and Klapper 2012). Today, local funding sources or foreign private investment are available in these countries, implying the success of the catalytic approach that many donors have had. Nevertheless, microfinance institutions in these countries continue to receive significant amounts of donor funding. On the one hand, concentration of funding is considered a positive element in the broader aid effectiveness literature because it enables countries to have sufficient resources to address a particular issue.[2] On the other hand, to develop markets, the role of donor funding is to leverage private investment, and as such a decline in donor funding should be seen over time. Thus a concentration of donor funding in any set of countries for an extended period of time is worth further exploration because it could signal "crowding out" as opposed to "crowding in."

Donor Efforts to Support Financial Inclusion

Internal incentives within some donor agencies run counter to many of the traits needed to support catalytic market development. Internal systems often reward disbursements of large amounts of funding, creating a bias toward markets and recipients of funding that can absorb large amounts easily. More challenging obstacles for financial inclusion that may require small, long-term, and patient funding are too often ignored. The trend in most donor agencies is to support larger projects in fewer countries.

To keep overhead costs low, donors are slashing staffing budgets, and the predominant staffing model is now one where generalists oversee large projects in a variety of fields and disciplines. This means that even as the field of financial inclusion requires increasingly specialist knowledge in

regulation, payments systems, credit reporting, and a host of other subspecialties, the donors that are making funding decisions have less and less knowledge about the areas in which the field needs donor funding.

Shrinking aid budgets are also demanding that donors demonstrate their effectiveness through clear results. Calls for value for money are commonplace in the media and in parliaments. For some sectors, it is easier to measure the impact of specific interventions; for example, in the health sector, one finds decades of experience and data on measuring the number of children immunized or the incidence of malaria infection. For private and financial sector development, where donors are trying to support market development, demonstrating results is challenging, and establishing attribution is even more so.

These very real constraints challenge donors to consider the models for channeling the right technical know-how, funding amounts, and oversight without unduly distorting markets. We see two alternative options for donors that aim to achieve catalytic market development with limited market distortions: (1) act as a facilitator or (2) fund a facilitator.

Different donors are equipped with a different set of funding instruments, which will be discussed in greater length later in the chapter. In understanding roles, however, it is important to know that roles will be closely aligned with instruments. For example, bilateral agencies tend to have grants as their main instrument, whereas multilateral agencies such as the World Bank or International Fund for Agricultural Development work primarily through loans to governments, but may also have mechanisms to offer grants for technical assistance. DFIs mostly provide debt, but increasingly are also able to use equity investments, and some agencies, such as the International Finance Corporation, also have significant grant funding used for building market infrastructure or technical support to investees. A few agencies rely primarily on guarantees, such as the

Overseas Private Investment Corporation and the Development Credit Authority, both part of the U.S. government.

The use of the funding instrument should be aligned with the type of facilitation that is needed rather than requiring the market to adapt to the instrument offered by the donor agency. For example, a donor that has only loans to government as its main instrument should be careful in how it intervenes in the private sector development arena more generally and in inclusive financial systems development more specifically. Ultimately, many of the actors engaged in the delivery of financial services are from the private sector and thus an ability to work directly with private institutions is first and foremost. Nonetheless, many aspects of the financial market system are public goods where government leadership is warranted. Thus donors with loans to governments as their main instruments should focus primarily on their influencing role with government on policy issues and in supporting public goods within the financial system. They should not force their instrument—loans to government—as a way to finance the private sector.

Act as a Facilitator

Provided that donors have the capacity to operate at the country level, they may be able to fill the role of facilitator directly. This role requires that the donor understands the constraints and opportunities in a given market and has the capacity and flexibility to respond to the specific needs.

Chapter 1 noted that market development facilitation must start with a mapping of the financial landscape and then an identification of the opportunities within the market where facilitation will lead to expanded usage of financial services. This very important understanding of the market and what is needed is at the heart of facilitation. Because everything starts with the condition of the market and the opportunities that lie within that unique market means that no

standard recipe can be followed. There is no blueprint that facilitators can take from one country and apply to the next. However, every financial market can be viewed within the overall framework—and its multifunction and multiplayer character—even if the detailed, constituent elements vary. Although it is not a precise or formulaic model, it is an aid to strategic analysis and decision making (see box 4.1).

The market development process is necessarily dynamic, and whether a given type of intervention is appropriate depends strongly on the market's stage of development. Although no global definition is available of what it means to be a nascent market, we can assume that it is one where access and usage of financial services are low, where the enabling environment is not conducive, and where little existing market infrastructure is in place. At the other extreme, we can assume that mature markets are where these things exist. In between are found many other market development stages. The role of the facilitator will be quite different depending on this market development spectrum.

In nascent or "frontier" markets, facilitators may need to support basic retail level capacity (the supply side of the "core"). Although MFIs and other providers may have demonstrated their success elsewhere, local actors in a nascent market would not necessarily have any information or share this knowledge. Thus, facilitators may need to address this market deficiency. Because basic market infrastructure and the regulatory environment are also likely underdeveloped, significant room exists for facilitators to intervene.

The role of facilitator becomes much more nuanced in a mature market. In these markets, we already find market actors that are functioning as well as many entrenched ways of doing business. Additionally, in these markets, facilitators may need to bring in disruptive technology or business models that threaten the existence of existing market actors. Identifying the opportunities to

Box 4.1 Shaping Intervention from an Understanding of the Market System

The FinMark Trust's approach to the development of transaction banking services in South Africa was distinctive from the outset. Faced with the challenge of how to improve access (in the core of the market), FinMark sought to identify the underlying causes of poor access in the supporting functions and rules in the financial market system; that is, it took a systemic perspective to analysis and intervention to facilitate change. Although a conventional approach might have emphasized engaging directly with providers—with financial and technical assistance—in practice, FinMark identified a number of priority constraint areas (see figure below):

*   *Rules*—Numerous weaknesses in relation to, for example, consumer credit, and problematic capital requirements for new providers.
*   *Informal rules*—A prevailing culture that did not understand or emphasize low-income consumers (the "unbanked") or consider how to innovate new services.
*   *Coordination*—Little constructive dialogue between stakeholders in relation to the low access problem and how to address it.
*   *Information*—An absence of detailed, analytical data on the low-income market as a whole, including its size, perceptions of services and providers, current use of money, and needs.

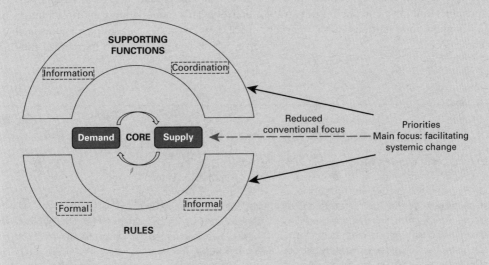

These constraints formed an agenda for action for the industry as a whole and for FinMark specifically. Its interventions focused on these as underlying causes—in rules and supporting functions—to bring about change in the core of the market and contribute to a substantial increase in access from 2003 to 2010.

Source: Alan Gibson, The Springfield Centre.

push the frontier becomes the most critical step for a facilitator to make. Facilitators may also need to directly confront political and influential actors that form the status quo.

Facilitators' ultimate objective is to get the market to work without their support. This means that their support to any one actor in the market is de facto a temporary one. Because the risk of overextending a stay is so acute, facilitators should be extremely careful to structure funding mechanisms in a way that is time bound. The litmus test of whether a facilitator is doing the right thing is to ask "what will this look like in 'X' years." If the facilitator will still be required to deliver a specific function in the market, then this is a sign that the facilitator is not intervening appropriately. The areas on which the facilitator will focus should change over time as the market develops and new opportunities arise. To ensure that an intervention is "time bound," facilitators must build in a convincing exit strategy in all of their interventions in the market (see chapter 19).

Fund a Facilitator

Although relatively few examples of this model are found, we see it as an emerging approach that has the potential to ease the internal constraints donors face while delivering catalytic market support at the country level. In this role, donors fully outsource their funding to a facilitator at the country level. One example of this is the Financial Sector Deepening Trust in Kenya funded by DFID, the World Bank, the Swedish International Development Agency, the Gates Foundation, Agence Française de Développement, and the government of Kenya (see box 4.2).

This outsourced model allows donors to place a large amount of funding, thus easing disbursement pressure, into an entity that can then take its time to understand the local market, identify which interventions can unleash market potential, and help to build capacity among market actors to fulfill their long-term role of service delivery. This model allows multiple funders to pool their resources and support a joint facilitator, which is a good way to harmonize funding

---

Box 4.2 Financial Sector Deepening Kenya (FSD Kenya)

FSD Kenya started as a DFID project in 2001 but was transformed into a multidonor trust in 2005. The creation of this independent trust was motivated by the desire to strengthen effectiveness by permitting a closer, more flexible, and responsive engagement with market actors as well as to improve efficiency by pooling donor funds within a single special-purpose vehicle. Fiduciary oversight is provided by a firm of professional trustees (currently the international accounting firm KPMG), and policy guidance and strategic direction are the responsibility of the program investment committee (PIC). The PIC comprises nominees from supporting donors as well as independent experts. A specialist technical team is responsible for developing and delivering FSD Kenya's strategy and managing its market making investments. As the market has developed in Kenya the depth of expertise in this team has expanded, with the emphasis shifting from funding to guiding market actors through research and technical assistance. For FSD Kenya to function effectively as a market facilitator, its core donors fund a single common approach, set out in its strategy paper.

Source: FSD Kenya 2012, private communication.

and increase donor coordination in a country. The structure of this entity can be similar to FSD Kenya, an independent trust, or it can be a project, an international NGO, or another structure that can fulfill this facilitation function.

Multiple facilitators can be working in any one market, each focusing on areas of core competence, as long as complementarity and a common vision on how to support market development are found. An example could be a facilitator that focuses on only capacity development.

The distinguishing characteristic of a facilitator is that it operates at the country level. The level of market knowledge that is needed precludes actors at the global level from fulfilling this role. Nonetheless, facilitators can be aided in their role by global actors who share and disseminate knowledge from elsewhere, helping to inject and cross-breed ideas in different markets.

The key to ensuring that such an entity is able to take on the role of facilitator, without the inherent internal weaknesses of donors, lies in a few key design considerations. Such entities must be able to take risks, invest in innovations with small grants, have a long-term perspective, and demonstrate their influence on the market through both direct and indirect means. We will explain below how facilitators intervene in the market to be catalytic.

Donor funding to a facilitator would need to be structured as a medium- to long-term project; however, the funding provided by this facilitator to the market would need to be able to offer many small, short-term funding agreements.

Coordination with Other Facilitators

In light of political pressures and internal incentives, some donors will not be able to outsource their funding decisions to a facilitator. Donors that continue to fund interventions directly must work closely with other facilitator(s) at the local level for access to the market knowledge that is required to identify market-enhancing interventions. This is the minimum level of responsibility

required of donors to ensure they minimize market distortions.

DFIs, some multilateral agencies, and regional development banks all may have internal incentives that make outsourcing their funding to a facilitator difficult. Nonetheless, these donors have an important influence on governments and significant funding levels and must prioritize coordination if they want to remain catalytic.

Coordination is the perennial development problem, and there are not many examples of success. Nonetheless, this fact does not alleviate the burden of working toward possible solutions to improve the ways donors interact and complement one another at the country level.

Donor Funding Instruments

The ways in which donor funding is delivered will have a profound impact on its effectiveness.[3] In using donor funding to develop the market one necessarily finds an acute risk that the resources provided could displace market-based activity. Even a relatively small subsidy can distort incentives by changing expectations. Perhaps one of the more obvious illustrations of this is in the subsidy of interest rates, which can lead borrowers across the market to expect lower rates.[4] Using the right tools can mitigate this risk. Nevertheless, regardless of which tool is used, there is no substitute for maintaining a strong awareness of how the market is developing and ensuring that the extra-market support provided by facilitation is withdrawn when market actors are able to take over.

Technical Assistance

Much know-how is about *tacit* knowledge, which cannot be readily generated and transferred outside the circumstances in which it is generated. For example, although classroom learning can play a useful role, the successful management of solidarity groups is learned by credit officers through actually doing it. Working with specific organizations to generate key aspects of know-how is often essential. However, wherever possible the aim should be to find channels to disseminate this knowledge to other players, both to increase impact and to minimize the risk of tilting the playing field in favor of the institutions receiving support.

Grants

Grants are commonly used to support the development of microfinance. On the positive side, grants can be used to deliver a time-limited nudge to the market. Beyond the requirement to use the grant for the agreed purpose and usually relatively modest reporting requirements, grants do not convey any reciprocal obligations to the donor on the part of the recipient.

However, perhaps more than any other tool used, grants carry the risk of distorting markets and incentives. Grants can be used as a simply bottom-line subsidy—enabling the survival of an activity or business where there is no real business case or, worse, providing an advantage to one player over another. It is not uncommon to see loss-making, inefficient MFIs continue for very long periods simply by acquiring a sequence of donor grants. Unlike an equity investment, a grant does not necessarily (and rarely does) tie the donor into a long-term relationship with the supported institution. This has the potential to weaken governance if there is no real owner of the capital value created in the MFI business. The role of ownership is critical within a market economy for providing a long-term incentive framework for management to use scarce capital resources efficiently.

One encounters very limited circumstances in which grants to build retail institutions remain relevant in the current financial inclusion landscape. In some nascent markets, such as postconflict countries, the use of grants to help kick-start an industry may still be relevant. Grants may also be relevant to help institutions extend outreach in difficult-to-reach market segments, such as remote rural areas. However,

grants are increasingly relevant for building market infrastructure and supporting policy and regulatory reforms, particularly when we begin to think beyond microcredit.

Challenge funds provide a valuable way to use grants, particularly for encouraging the private sector to innovate to reach the poor. The terms of a challenge fund are set up transparently in advance, seeking applications for grants on a competitive basis to undertake initiatives with specified end objectives. Applicants propose how they want to use the grants and compete for a limited pool of resources. Often the terms require that those applying for awards match the grant resources sought with their own funds and show in their applications how the development will be sustained after the award funding has been exhausted. This structuring helps mitigate some of the common problems associated with grants. Challenge funds can be especially helpful in encouraging innovation by offering a simple way to share the inherent risks, with open competition defusing the risk of unfairly favoring some players.

Grants may also be essential for research-related work, whether impact studies to understand the effects of interventions on clients or data collection on market segments and client demand. Although, in the long term, markets should be able to deliver this kind of information without donor assistance, donors may be needed to build the capacity of the research institutions or demonstrate to private actors that this information is useful for their business. It sometimes seems surprising how frequently existing market players (or those in a linked market) are simply unaware of the potential in a market. Financial sector research can be an important first step in creating greater awareness in the industry and helping to guide players toward opportunities to expand inclusion. The FinScope surveys, pioneered by the FinMark Trust in South Africa (and now used across Africa and in some parts of Asia), have been very successful in this respect, helping commercial banks in seeing entirely new areas of the market. This type of research can be argued to have the key characteristics of a sectoral public good,[5] which is likely to be underprovided without external support. Therefore a strong case can be made for its financing by donors in the short term. Ultimately information providers should also seek to be viable commercially.

Guarantees

Guarantees are very commonly used by government and donors in supporting financial markets. Many different forms of guarantee are used, but the core concept is the agreement to provide financial resources in the future contingent on specified conditions. Probably the most commonly seen form is a simple guarantee to repay part or all of a loan (or more often a portfolio of loans) should the borrower default. A major attraction to the providers is that funding is often not required up-front and a diversified portfolio of guarantees offers the prospect of considerable leverage. USAID's Development Credit Authority, a well-established and managed program, has been able to build a strong portfolio leveraging the earmarked resources 28 times. A guarantee can be used to help cautious institutions enter new markets where they lack knowledge and proven techniques to manage credit risk. The premise of their effective use to support market developments is that institutions will learn through the process and change as a result. For this to be credible one must have both sufficient incentives and realistic potential for the institutions receiving the guarantee to change. Simply reducing or eliminating the risk will not necessarily achieve this. To be effective the institution receiving the guarantee must generally bear part of the risk. Equal sharing often proves a good starting point. However, if behavior change is to occur, it may be necessary to ensure that a realistic plan is in place for this to happen. Typically this will require developing new approaches to measuring and controlling risk,

which might involve defining new processes, deploying new technology, or training credit officers and risk management departments. The risk is that without a clear development plan, the institution will simply revert to its earlier practices once the guarantee is removed.

Equity and Quasi Equity

Providing risk capital using equity or quasi-equity instruments can be valuable in supporting the development of retail (or other) institutions and avoiding some of the problems with grants relating to market distortion discussed earlier. If creating substantial new organizational capacity, whether at the retail or market infrastructure level, is essential to achieving progress, then investing by way of equity is often preferable. An objection is sometimes raised that a new institution may be loss making in the early years of its development. This can easily be overcome by simply rolling up the projected losses into the overall level of equity investment required. Many businesses are commercially financed in which investors do not expect to break even for several years.

Equity as a form of financing has important advantages over other instruments in relation to governance and creating appropriate incentives for managers (McKee 2012). It also potentially mitigates the problem of market distortion and can be more efficient allowing the eventual return of capital to the market facilitator where successfully invested. However, use of investment instruments carries substantially higher transaction costs, requiring careful structuring at the outset and ongoing management of the investment. The skills to undertake this effectively may not be possessed by many broad-based market facilitation organizations. Specialist impact investing funds that have the capacity and local presence required are better placed to manage a portfolio of equity investments and play an active role in the governance of institutions they invest in.

Planning for exit may also be problematic, especially where capital markets are thin. Quasi equity (various forms of debt with equity-like characteristics) is one way to address this difficulty if it is possible to credibly structure a repayment. A long-term engagement will nevertheless typically be required because the capital repaid will need to be replaced—through either new investment capital or retaining earnings.

The danger faced in using investment instruments is that a market facilitator investing in a company crosses the line to become, in effect, a player. A risk exists of displacing commercial capital, especially where the investment funds used derive from a concessional source. In the long term the aim should be to see concessional capital (or capital with an explicit or implicit state guarantee, as is the case with DFIs) replaced by commercial sources. It should also be noted that considerable heterogeneity exists in the sources of commercial capital. The objectives of investors vary considerably. On a purely commercial level investors will have differing appetites for risk, minimum returns, and time horizons. Beyond this there is growing interest in looking at the social and environmental impact of investment, which is clearly highly relevant to inclusive finance. The availability of long-term social investment provides an opportunity for earlier exit by the market facilitator.

Loans to Governments

Loans to governments are an instrument typically used by multilateral organizations, regional development banks, and some bilateral agencies. Overall, they represent about 25 percent of total donor commitments for financial inclusion. Loans to governments can have maturities of 11 years or more, which makes them a good tool for long-term support, but bears the risk of subsidizing functions that the local government or the market could take over. Loans to governments can be used for several purposes, including budget support, on-lending to retail financial services providers via wholesale financial institutions, or strengthening the market infrastructure and policy environment. Through their relationships with governments and/or conditions specified in lending agreements, funders can influence the use of the funds by the governments. However, loans to governments are not adapted to provide support for private sector actors, and the funder has little control of how projects are managed and implemented.

Conclusion

Donors have played an important role in much of the progress achieved in inclusive finance. The large number of private funds that serve the financial needs of MFIs are a testament to this success. This role in helping to "crowd in" private capital was arguably the market weakness that needed correcting in the past. Today it is far less common to identify a weak domestic funding market as the overarching problem that requires catalytic donor assistance.

Donors must thus respond and focus their attention on ways they can remain catalytic in building financial markets that serve the poor. This chapter presented ways in which donors can try to do this by working through or with facilitators or behaving themselves like facilitators at the local market level. In all cases a facilitator on the ground with market knowledge is key to making this role a success. Because one finds few donors who structure their support in this way today and because of the real internal challenges in being catalytic, much still can be done to realign internal incentives within funding agencies to minimize negative market distortions. Much also can be learned in practice to improve how donors can fulfill this catalytic role.

Notes

1. The largest 20 donors and investors include 10 DFIs, three multilaterals, three bilateral donors, two regional development banks, one private foundation, and one private institutional investor.

2. See, for example, work by Bill Easterly and Tobias Pfutze (2008), which uses level of fragmentation as one of the criteria to rank donor effectiveness.

3. This section was originally drafted by David Ferrand.

4. This is one reason why price subsidies should usually be avoided. Price-based signaling is a key mechanism in effective market operation, and a supply-side subsidy can disrupt the signaling. Furthermore, given that in the financial services market one rarely finds a public policy case or the resources to support universal subsidies, targeting is the norm. Practically these often prove difficult to deliver cost-effectively and to control the potential for rent seeking created.

5. Research data of this kind are certainly nonrival, and the nature of the type of information is such that it rapidly becomes nonexcludable (because it is difficult to keep the results private).

References and Further Reading

CGAP (Consultative Group to Assist the Poor). 2010a. "2010 CGAP Funder Survey." CGAP, Washington, DC.

——. 2010b. "Growth and Vulnerabilities in Microfinance." Focus Note 61, CGAP, Washington, DC.

Demirgüç-Kunt, Aslı, and Leora Klapper. 2012, "Measuring Financial Inclusion: The Global Findex." Policy Research Working Paper 3628, World Bank, Washington, DC.

Easterly, William, and Tobias Pfutze. 2008. "Where Does the Money Go? Best and Worst Practices in Foreign Aid." *Journal of Economic Perspectives* 22 (2): 29–52.

El-Zoghbi, Mayada, Barbara Gähwiler, and Kate Lauer. 2011. "Cross-border Funding in Microfinance." Focus Note, CGAP, Washington, DC, April.

FSD Kenya. 2005. "Policies and Procedures." Financial Sector Deepening Project, Nairobi, Kenya.

Gähwiler, Barbara, and Alice Nègre. 2011. "Trends in Cross-border Funding." Brief, CGAP, Washington, DC, December.

McKee, Katherine. 2012. "Voting the Double Bottom Line: Active Governance by Microfinance Equity Investors." Focus Note 79, CGAP, Washington, DC.

Symbiotics. 2011. "Symbiotics 2011 MIV Survey Report: Market Data & Peer Group Analysis." Symbiotics, Geneva, August.

CHAPTER 5

Measuring Financial Inclusion and Assessing Impact

Joanna Ledgerwood

To make financial markets work better for the poor, it is valuable to understand what is taking place in the core of the financial market system—what services are provided by whom, to whom, and how—and what is the impact. Measuring financial inclusion helps us to understand which segments of the population lack what types of financial services, why they lack access, and which financial services they use. Monitoring financial inclusion allows us to determine if inclusion is improving over time and to compare countries within peer groups. Assessing impact helps us to understand the quality of services—convenience, affordability, safety, dignity—and, ultimately, the long-term outcomes of using financial services. This provides a much better understanding of the value of increased financial inclusion and the importance of continuing to invest in achieving it.

This chapter focuses on measuring and monitoring financial inclusion—that is, supply and demand—and on assessing outcomes leading to impact. In doing so, it provides an overview of tools to measure and monitor financial inclusion and to conduct research. It seeks to inform stakeholders, including development agencies, regulators, and providers, who are increasingly modifying policies, services, delivery channels, and outreach models, to capitalize on insights provided by databases and research findings. These modifications can occur either at the macro level, initiated by governments and regulators, or at micro levels, affecting financial service structures within communities and financial service providers themselves (see box 5.1).

Contributions to this chapter were made by Ines Arevalo and Alyssa Jethani.

Box 5.1 Using Data to Increase Financial Inclusion

Better data can increase awareness of the problem of financial exclusion and motivate policy makers to enact market-expanding reforms. Data can also give the private sector the information it needs to expand and develop new products and can stimulate new research into the drivers and impacts of financial inclusion.

At the Alliance for Financial Inclusion's 2009 Global Policy Forum in Nairobi, Gerald Nyoma, director of the Central Bank of Kenya, credited the first FinAccess survey in 2006, which showed that only 14 percent of Kenya's population had access to banking services, with having a significant influence on the central

bank's decision to allow Safaricom to launch the M-PESA platform, an e-money transfer and payment system. M-PESA now reaches 55 percent of all Kenyan adults. After the first FinScope data for Zambia were released in 2005, several institutions reported being motivated to launch new ventures. Barclays reopened some of its rural branches, Zambia National Commercial Bank launched a mobile banking venture, and Dunavant, a cotton company, created a mobile payment linkage for 150,000 of its growers. Similar reports have come from policy makers and market players in other countries.

Source: Kendall 2010.

Measuring Financial Inclusion

Financial inclusion refers to people and businesses having access to appropriate and affordable financial services. Defining financial inclusion may also include factors such as proximity (being within a 20-kilometer range of an access point, for example, a bank branch, automated teller machine [ATM], microfinance institution [MFI], or agent) or choice (having access to multiple providers with varied and relevant products and services) and being financially capable of understanding the available choices and how best to use them. However, increased access and choice of financial services do not always translate into increased use. In addition to studies that measure access, studies that attempt to understand the use and quality of services, and ultimately their impact, are also important.

As discussed in chapters 3 and 4, the government, industry, and others, including development agencies, have a role to play in expanding financial inclusion. In order to achieve this goal,

it is necessary to determine the current state of the financial market and to identify population segments that are excluded from it. Measurement also indicates the frequency of services accessed from various types of providers and allows for comparisons between countries or regions and among poverty levels within an area. This enables stakeholders to be better informed and to respond with appropriate policies and regulations. According to the Global Partnership for Financial Inclusion (2011), "A comprehensive set of financial inclusion indicators should serve three purposes: i) to inform financial inclusion policy making both domestically and internationally; ii) to provide a basis for measuring the current state of financial inclusion on a global scale and at country level; and iii) to provide a basis for monitoring and evaluation of financial inclusion policies and targets, both domestically and internationally."

Measuring financial inclusion is not a straightforward exercise, however. Financial inclusion has to be clearly defined according to the needs of the country. The Alliance for Financial Inclusion (AFI) puts forth four dimensions of financial inclusion—access, usage, quality, and welfare, each requiring increasingly complex data collection and analysis—and proposes indicators for each (AFI 2010a, 2010b).

- *Access* refers to the ability to use financial services, taking into consideration physical proximity, affordability, and eligibility. Understanding levels of access may require insight and analysis of potential barriers to access. Indicators include number or percentage of people who access a certain type of service (credit, savings, payments, insurance) from whom (formal or informal provider), client touch points within a certain distance, and poverty levels.

- *Usage* refers to the actual use of financial services and products. Determining usage looks at the regularity, frequency, and patterns of use over time, including the combination of services. Indicators include frequency of use or percentage of active accounts.

- *Quality* considers the attributes or relevance of the financial service or product to consumer needs. Quality is determined by the nature and depth of the relationship between the financial service provider and the consumer, including the choices available, the financial capabilities of the consumer, and how those capabilities affect the experience. Indicators include the financial capability of consumers, choice of services and providers within a reasonable distance, and frequency of complaints.

- *Welfare*, the most difficult outcome to measure, focuses on the impact that financial services have on the welfare of consumers, including changes in consumption, business productivity, and quality of life. Indicators include increased savings, increased consumption, and increased decision making in the household.

Measuring access and usage requires assessing both the supply of and the demand for financial services. Supply-side studies and databases such as Financial Access 2010[1] or Microfinance Information eXchange (MIX)[2] use aggregate data to understand the total outreach and performance of various types of providers and to enable comparative analyses over time. Demand-side surveys such as FinScope[3] or Findex[4] seek detailed information about what and how financial services are used at the individual, household, or community level.

Demand-side research offers richer information than supply-side research and provides new avenues for analyzing how the poor manage their financial lives, highlighting the multifaceted nature of financial management. It normally requires household surveys and therefore is more costly and thus less frequent. Furthermore, demand-side information can be susceptible to sampling bias and omissions by respondents, making it less comparable over time or across countries (Global Partnership for Financial Inclusion 2011). Supply-side data can be collected more frequently and allow for comparisons; however, such information often only includes formal and regulated providers, which can miss a significant portion of what is taking place in the financial market system. Demand-side research, in contrast, can provide insight on the value and vibrancy of the informal sector, highlighting the flexibility and innovations inherent in family, kinship, and community-based financial services.

Supply-Side Research

Supply-side research collects and aggregates data on number of providers, services used (primarily credit and savings accounts and sometimes payments and insurance products), and access points (for example, bank branches and ATMs) and may also collect data on volume and costs. Supply-side data are generally gathered by regulators, other government bodies, or development agencies (such as the financial access studies conducted by the World Bank) or are self-reported by providers to global databases such as MIX. Supply-side data are, for the most part, publicly available and generally accessible online. Supply-side data indicate the scale and trending of activities of financial service providers, allowing insight into the growth, depth, and scale of outreach. Databases also provide a valuable source of secondary data to support impact assessments and understand key outcomes and may help to uncover pressing issues in the industry, for example, over-indebtedness, improper pricing, or poor financial and social performance of providers—and sometimes consumer abuse (see box 5.2).[5]

Global Supply Surveys

Two relevant global supply surveys (sometimes referred to as landscape supply data) are (i) the Financial Access 2009 and 2010 of the Consultative Group to Assist the Poor (CGAP) and the World Bank Group, which gathers data from financial regulators in about 150 countries, and (ii) the Financial Access Survey (FAS) of the International Monetary Fund (IMF), which reports on key indicators of geographic and demographic outreach of financial services in about 160 countries.

"*Financial Access 2010* is the second in a series of annual reports by CGAP and the World Bank to monitor statistics for financial access around the world and to inform the policy debate. The series was launched in response to the growing interest in financial inclusion among policy makers and the development community. The first report, *Financial Access 2009*, introduced statistics on the use of financial services in 139 economies and mapped a broad range of policies and initiatives supporting financial inclusion. Building on the previous year's data, *Financial Access 2010* reviews survey responses from 142 economies, updates statistics on the use of financial services, and analyzes changes that took place in 2009—a turbulent year for the financial sector" (CGAP and World Bank 2010). *Financial Access 2010* contributes to efforts to measure financial access at the country level worldwide, to develop a consistent database, and to present the data in a coherent manner for future analyses.

The IMF conducts the Financial Access Survey annually and makes the data available to

Box 5.2 Evidence of Over-Indebtedness through Research

Over-indebtedness has become a cause for concern and a new focus of research and data collection. Strong competition in some markets and the expectation of excessive returns on the part of some investors have led to predatory lending, with rising levels of portfolios at risk. Explanations for these behaviors are many, including the absence of credit bureaus, limited due diligence by lenders, or the assumption that clients assume more debt than they can manage. Multiple loans from an array of lenders are associated with the growing levels of default. The evidence to date is not clear-cut. The high levels of default in Bosnia in the late 2000s are proof of too much debt and a lack of financial capability to manage the credit. By contrast, in Ghana many possess the financial capability to juggle multiple loans, even when the personal cost is high. What has not changed is that over-indebtedness has long been an attribute of poverty and that a life of perpetual shocks without protection keeps many stuck in the vicious cycle of poverty.

Source: Monique Cohen, Microfinance Opportunities.

the public through an online database. The FAS database disseminates key indicators of geographic and demographic outreach of financial services as well as the underlying data. It measures outreach by bank branch networks and ATMs as well as the availability of three key financial instruments: deposits, loans, and insurance. New data on outstanding deposits and loans of households were added for the 2011 FAS. The database helps policy makers and researchers to understand the determinants and implications of financial access and usage. The financial access indicators can help researchers and authorities to identify knowledge gaps, to devise appropriate policies for broadening financial access, and to monitor the effectiveness of policies over time (IMF 2011).

About 140 countries participated in the 2011 FAS, and the FAS website now contains annual data for about 160 respondents covering a seven-year period (2004–10), including data for all G-20 countries.

Global supply surveys provide useful country-level data. As many are conducted annually, these data can indicate progress toward increasing financial inclusion. However, most supply-side surveys rely primarily on information from regulators or regulated financial institutions, which effectively excludes unregulated (or nonformal) providers. Use of services from other providers— for example, nongovernmental organization (NGO) MFIs, cooperatives, Savings Groups (SGs), and the informal sector as a whole—is not counted.[6] The resulting picture is distorted, particularly in Africa, where only five countries—the Comoros, Ethiopia, Madagascar, Mauritius, and Rwanda—report data on credit outreach to the FAS (Linthorst and Gaul 2011).

In addition, because the data track accounts rather than individuals, there is potential for double counting. Furthermore, the general lack of financial identity in many developing countries weakens the reliability of supply-side data on usage; users cannot be uniquely identified in forming country-level aggregates and are prone to multiple counting (Global Partnership for Financial Inclusion 2011). Also, generally no information is provided on income levels or livelihood segments of those accessing services (Kendall 2010).

National Supply Surveys

Regulators and others are beginning to measure financial inclusion at the national level. According to AFI (2011), "More and more, policy makers are recognizing the importance of evidence-based policy making and the critical role data play in the policy-making process, from design and implementation to monitoring and evaluation. With rigorous, objective, and reliable data, policy makers can accurately diagnose the state of financial inclusion, judiciously set targets, identify existing barriers, craft effective polices, and monitor and assess policy impact."

When determining how to measure financial inclusion at the country level, the first step is to define financial inclusion—that is, what providers and which services are considered financially inclusive.[7] The next is to define the data needs, to look at the information available from secondary sources (on both supply and demand), and then to determine how to obtain missing data. Options include enhancing an existing survey or creating a new one (AFI 2010a).

In an attempt to create a consistent set of indicators that are defined in the same manner and therefore can be tracked in national surveys and compared across countries, AFI's Financial Inclusion Data Working Group developed a "core set" of indicators for use by regulators at the country level. The AFI core set of indicators provides a framework to guide country-level data collection and to support policy making by creating a standard for what to measure and how (AFI 2011).[8]

The core set is a list of five quantitative indicators that measure the most basic and fundamental aspects of financial inclusion: access and usage:

- *Access indicators* include the number of access points per 10,000 adults at the national level and segmented by: type and by relevant administrative units; the percentage of administrative units with at least one access point; and the percentage of total population living in administrative units with at least one access point.

- *Usage indicators* include the percentage of adults with at least one type of regulated deposit account and the percentage of adults with at least one type of regulated credit account. The following proxies may be used where data for usage indicators are not available: number of deposit accounts per 10,000 adults and number of loan accounts per 10,000 adults.

It does not measure quality and welfare, which require more qualitative studies.[9]

Global Databases

While surveys continue to provide information useful for establishing scale, expanding supply-side data to include nonregulated providers remains a key challenge. Global databases and provider networks are helping to fill this gap.

In addition to supply-side surveys conducted at the global and national (or regional) levels, supply-side data are also collected through self-reported databases such as MIX, the Savings Groups Information Exchange (SAVIX), the Microcredit Summit, the World Council of Credit Unions (WOCCU), and the World Savings Banks Institute, among others.

MIX is a global, web-based platform for information on microfinance. It provides information on MFIs worldwide, public and private funds that invest in microfinance, MFI networks, raters and external evaluators, advisory firms, and governmental and regulatory agencies. Institutions self-report to MIX, with data checked by in-house analysts. While MIX collects data on nonregulated entities, the information requested is geared more toward sustainable institutions with the capacity to report prescribed indicators on a consistent basis. Consequently, the majority of smaller MFIs, savings and credit cooperatives (SACCOs), and others do not participate. However, the MIX database covers an estimated 85 percent of clients served by specialized microfinance providers (see box 5.3).

Box 5.3 Microfinance Information eXchange

Committed to strengthening financial inclusion and the microfinance sector by promoting transparency, MIX provides information on the performance of MFIs, funders, networks, and service providers serving low-income clients.

Incorporated in 2002, MIX collects and reviews financial, operational, product, client, and social performance data, standardizing the information for comparability. Its published data track development of the industry, both for its operators and for those supporting it through funding, policy, or analysis. Its primary data platform, MIX Market, has delivered MFI profiles and annual standard performance reports since 2002. Between 2002 and 2012, its public database has grown from covering just over 100 MFIs to more than

(continued next page)

2,000 providers around the world. Its platform data include benchmarks and comparative analysis, along with quarterly results. In addition, MIX publishes annual regional updates and topical analysis of the sector through the long-standing *MicroBanking Bulletin*.

The data available on MIX Market has evolved with the industry. In the early years, data focused on outreach and financial performance as the sector sought to understand the dynamics of building sustainable institutions. As funding sources and products diversified, MIX's data evolved to capture information on the nature and terms of MFI funding as well as the growing array of credit and deposit products. In recent years, a renewed focus on understanding the social mission and results of the sector led MIX to work with industry peers to standardize, collect, and analyze data on MFI social performance.

Active partners include the Small Enterprise Education and Promotion (SEEP) Network for developing financial reporting standards and the Social Performance Task Force for measuring MFI social performance. In addition, MIX encourages local microfinance associations to embed these reporting standards in local markets and connects associations with a global network of analysts working with MFIs to collect, standardize, analyze, and disseminate data on MFI performance. More than 30 associations have joined the network.

Since 2011, MIX has published country briefings, quarterly updates on market developments, and market forecasts for major microfinance markets. These additional tools and analysis are available through paid subscriptions.

Source: Blaine Stephens, MIX; www.mixmarket.org.

The SAVIX is a centralized reporting system that provides transparent, standardized data on SGs (see chapter 6). Data are collected and submitted on a quarterly basis (see box 5.4).

The Microcredit Summit database contains information on more providers than other databases but only collects information on the number of borrowers (totaling 137.5 million in 2010), the number of "poorest" borrowers, and profitability.[10] Summary information is published annually.[11]

Microfinance Transparency is an NGO established to promote pricing transparency of providers. It maintains a database with microfinance interest rate data for individual country markets and publishes the information as a series of interactive tables and graphs. The database supports the mission of promoting transparent pricing in the microfinance industry.[12]

The World Council of Credit Unions, the global trade association and development agency for financial cooperatives, promotes the development of financial cooperatives worldwide and advocates for improved laws and regulations. It maintains a database on its members, providing information annually on the number of credit unions (by country), total members, savings balances, loan balances, reserves, and total assets.[13]

The World Savings Banks Institute represents savings and socially committed retail banks or associations. It maintains a database for savings and postal banks that globally tracks total assets, loans, deposits, capital adequacy, outlets, employees, and customers annually.[14]

Box 5.4 Savings Groups Information Exchange

SAVIX is an online reporting system that provides transparent and standardized data on the performance of SGs and the agencies that promote them. In 2012 it collected and validated financial and operational data from more than 80,000 SGs representing over 1.8 million members in all regions of the developing world. Metrics include measures of outreach (for example, number of groups), membership data (for example, percentage of women members), portfolio indicators (for example, value of loans outstanding), and performance ratios (for example, annualized return on assets). As of mid-2012, 142 projects in 22 countries were reporting to SAVIX on a voluntary basis and uploading quarterly program data to the website.

SAVIX enables users to conduct comparative, trend, and geographic analysis with a choice of filters and metrics. Informed decision making improves program planning and management, and SAVIX seeks to facilitate analysis, develop norms, and improve the performance of institutions that promote SGs. The site also provides donors and facilitating agencies with industry benchmarks and analysis that support planning and investments across the sector.

Source: David Panetta, Aga Khan Foundation; www.thesavix.org.

For the most part, these databases collect information on outreach and financial performance used by various stakeholders (see box 5.5). However, some databases have recently begun to collect nonfinancial information. Since 2005, the industrywide Social Performance Task Force has developed ways to measure social performance (see chapter 14), creating 22 social performance indicators to assess how an MFI aligns its systems to its mission and measures its social performance. MIX began collecting information on these social performance indicators in 2009, with 212 MFIs reporting. SAVIX is considering adding social performance indicators once they are established for SGs.

Demand-Side Research

Demand-side research seeks detailed information about how financial services are used and from what providers. It can be carried out at the individual, household, or community level and uses a variety of tools, including national surveys, panel studies, randomized control trials (RCTs), and focus group discussions, for example. Demand-side research may identify unmet demand as well as reasons why the uptake of services offered (supply) may be lower than anticipated. Researchers may also analyze structural deficiencies in markets that prevent the poor from accessing financial services and explore the opportunities for increased financial inclusion.

Demand-side research often begins with client behavior, attempting to assess transaction volumes at the individual and household levels and identify links between use and quality of services. This is in contrast to institutionally driven information-gathering techniques that focus on provider performance as a metric for financial access.

Overall, demand-side research considers how poor households use financial services and who is excluded, sometimes also looking at the nature of household cash flow and how money is spent. Examples of demand-side studies include the World Bank's Access to Finance, Living Standards

Knowledge is power only if it is used productively. Who uses the data collected so painstakingly by hundreds of organizations? And who should be using the information?

So far, much activity on financial inclusion has taken place in the high-level policy sphere. Regulators and policy makers use data on financial inclusion to develop policy and to monitor progress. For instance, the Superintendency of Banking and Insurance in Peru uses benchmarks on financial inclusion to measure progress in reaching underserved areas. However, MFIs can also use landscape data to support business planning when expanding into a new market or a new product. What types of competition might they encounter? Which populations are most underserved? A subnational view on the data—especially at a branch or district level—can be valuable in addressing such questions.

Networks also use and potentially contribute to landscape data. Landscape data can give members the big picture and place their activities in context, whether the network itself has a broad or a narrow focus for membership. Networks can also use landscape data to highlight gaps or opportunities for donors and investors.

Source: Linthorst and Gaul 2011.

Measurement Study, Global Findex, and FinScope databases—the latter two being the most relevant. Most financial diaries studies also conduct demand-side research.

Global Findex

The Global Financial Inclusion (Findex) database is a detailed demand-side survey covering 150,000 individuals in 148 economies, measuring how adults use financial services. According to Demirgüç-Kunt and Klapper (2012), "The Global Findex fills a major gap in the financial inclusion data landscape and is the first public database of demand-side indicators that consistently measures individuals' usage of financial products across countries and over time. Covering a range of topics, the Global Findex can be used to track global financial inclusion policies and facilitate a deeper and more nuanced understanding of how adults around the world save, borrow, and make payments."

Findex provides demand-side data by gender, age, education, geography, and income levels, helping policy makers and others to understand the behaviors and constraints regarding consumers' access to and use of financial services. Key characteristics include cross-country compatibility, availability of demographic covariates, and regular measurement of the entire set of countries over time (Demirgüç-Kunt and Klapper 2012). Findex provides a baseline for benchmarking financial inclusion and tracking progress over time, leading to the identification of priorities (see box 5.6): "One of the most fascinating parts of the results are people's answers to obstacles they face in getting access to finance, which range from too expensive, document requirements, and too far to travel" (Latortue 2012).

FinScope

FinMark Trust is an independent trust based in South Africa that seeks to extend financial access by strengthening the market system. In 2003 FinMark Trust launched FinScope, a consumer survey that seeks to understand consumer demand with regard to access

Box 5.6 Core Indicators of Global Findex

The core set of Global Findex indicators addresses five dimensions of individual use of financial services: accounts, savings, borrowing, payment patterns, and insurance. Use of financial services refers to how different groups (poor, youth, and women) use financial products. Financial inclusion also refers to how easily individuals can *access* available financial services and products from formal institutions (defined as institutions that are authorized or licensed to offer financial services and that may or may not be actively supervised). The demand-side data provided by Global Findex complement existing supply-side data collected by the IMF's Financial Access Survey and the AFI's core set of financial inclusion indicators.

The following core set of indicators and subindicators of financial inclusion is based on the Global Findex database:

- *Use of bank accounts.* Percentage of adults with an account at a formal financial institution (such as a bank, credit union, post office, or MFI that is registered with the government and possibly regulated), purpose of accounts (personal or business), frequency of transactions (deposits and withdrawals), percentage of adults with an active account at a formal financial institution, and mode of access (such as ATM, bank branch, retail store, or bank agent)
- *Savings.* Percentage of adults who saved within the past 12 months using a formal financial institution (such as a bank, credit union, post office, or MFI), percentage of adults who saved within the past 12 months using an informal savings club or a person outside the family, and percentage of adults who otherwise saved (for example, in their home) within the past 12 months
- *Borrowing.* Percentage of adults who borrowed within the past 12 months from a formal financial institution such as a bank, credit union, post office, or MFI (a *flow measure*), percentage of adults who borrowed within the past 12 months from an informal source (including family and friends), and percentage of adults with an outstanding loan to purchase a home or an apartment (a *stock measure*)
- *Payments.* Percentage of adults who used a formal account to receive wages or government payments within the past 12 months, percentage of adults who used a formal account to receive or send money to family members living elsewhere within the past 12 months, and percentage of adults who used a mobile phone to pay bills or send or receive money within the past 12 months (not collected in high-income countries)
- *Insurance.* Percentage of adults who personally purchased private health insurance and percentage of adults who worked in farming, forestry, or fishing and personally paid for crop, rainfall, or livestock insurance.

Source: Demirgüç-Kunt and Klapper 2012.

to transactions, savings, credit, and insurance from both formal and informal providers.

FinScope, an initiative of FinMark Trust, "is a nationally representative study of consumers' perceptions of financial services and issues, which creates insight into how consumers source their income and manage their financial lives. The sample covers the entire adult population, rich and poor, urban and rural, in order to create a segmentation, or continuum, of the entire market and to lend perspective to the various market segments."[15]

Primarily a demand side-survey, FinScope also integrates supply-side information, leading to a more holistic understanding of usage. FinScope data sets can be used to inform policies, commercial strategies, and product development as well as development agendas (see box 5.7). Donors have traditionally financed the surveys, although costs in some countries are partially recovered by a syndication process whereby stakeholders (often commercial but also public) purchase access to the final results.

FinScope data are used to create three key access indicators including the financial access strand, the access frontier, and the financial access landscape. The financial access strand provides detailed analysis of the financial market based on customers' level of financial access (formal, informal, and financially excluded) and enables comparison of levels of financial inclusion across countries and market segments (see figure 5.1).

Once the "formally unserved" is identified through the FinScope survey, the FinScope livelihoods framework is applied to assess the individual and factors that affect usage of financial services, leading to a better understanding of the interventions required to increase financial inclusion, specifically the needs of consumers.[16] The result is the access frontier, which provides an estimate of the percentage of people who are unserved but could be financially included over time. This serves to identify both potential new market opportunities as well as specific development needs to increase financial inclusion (see figure 5.2).

Box 5.7 FinScope Surveys

The FinScope survey information supports private and public sector initiatives to improve the policy environment and stimulate commercial innovation. For example,

- Bank Windhoek in Namibia used FinScope to develop its low-income savings product called EasySave.
- In South Africa, the Financial Services Board has used FinScope to improve consumer financial literacy. According to the board, "The FinScope surveys have played a major role in identifying consumer financial education needs by following consumer financial behaviour over time and in making valuable information available to others for their consumer financial education programmes." The National Treasury in South Africa also used FinScope data to support the development of a policy of financial inclusion to feed into government processes for wide-ranging social security reform.
- According to African Life Assurance Zambia, "From the time we started using FinScope, we have been able to develop a funeral insurance policy for the informal market ... and by understanding the current coping mechanisms and the recurrent costs of such mechanisms used by the informal sector, we have been able to determine an affordable price."
- ABSA, South Africa's largest retail bank, stated, "Until FinScope there was no single source of information that provided us with an in-depth understanding of the life styles of different segments of South Africa's population ... [FinScope] really gave us that edge in terms of getting such an insight that we could really develop a customer value proposition for the mass market."

Source: http://www.finscope.co.za/new/pages/About-FinScope/Using-FinScope.aspx?randomID=d2e9237a-4bf9-4272-92ec-8c82443013ea&linkPath=2&IID=2_2; Makanjee 2009.

Figure 5.1 FinScope Financial Access Strand: Definitions

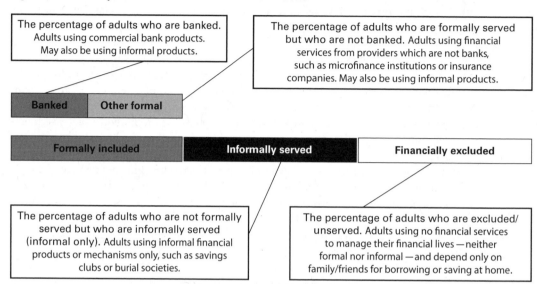

The percentage of adults who are banked. Adults using commercial bank products. May also be using informal products.

The percentage of adults who are formally served but who are not banked. Adults using financial services from providers which are not banks, such as microfinance institutions or insurance companies. May also be using informal products.

| Banked | Other formal |

| Formally included | Informally served | Financially excluded |

The percentage of adults who are not formally served but who are informally served (informal only). Adults using informal financial products or mechanisms only, such as savings clubs or burial societies.

The percentage of adults who are excluded/ unserved. Adults using no financial services to manage their financial lives — neither formal nor informal — and depend only on family/friends for borrowing or saving at home.

Source: Adapted from FinScope, "From Data to Action Brochure," http://www.finscope.co.za/new/scriptlibrary/getfile.aspx?file name=FS workshop 2011_brochureFNL.pdf&file=../module_data/71e3e62d-1eeb-412e-893b-970e98f6a3fa/downloads/03bcf1fe-0fd2-40de-95f4-ffb73c12f1f0.file.

Figure 5.2 FinScope Access Frontier

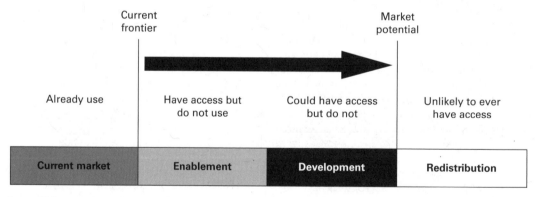

Current frontier

Market potential

| Already use | Have access but do not use | Could have access but do not | Unlikely to ever have access |

| Current market | Enablement | Development | Redistribution |

Source: FinScope, n.d.

The financial access landscape provides further information on access to specific products by creating a diagram with five axes, illustrating the percentage of adults who have used transactional, savings, credit, insurance or remittance financial products or services.

While the access strand is a key comparative measure to see how access has changed over time, it is less successful in accounting for the use of multiple products and services. For example, individuals who use both formal and informal services are only counted as formally included (see box 5.8).

Financial Diaries

Financial diaries also assess demand, albeit of a (usually) much smaller group (and thus unlikely to be statistically representative at the national level) because of the costs involved. Primarily longitudinal surveys, financial diaries are used to understand consumer behavior in the financial sector of certain geographic areas, such as the research reported in Collins et al. (2009) and summarized in chapter 2.

Financial diaries use detailed micro-level consumer data to paint a complex, realistic picture of the financial lives of the poor. Data are gathered on income, consumption, savings, lending, and investment over an extended period of time (usually one year). A team of local field workers, trained and supported by the research organization, visits every participating household each week or fortnight and asks members to recount all resources that

---

Box 5.8 Interpreting Financial Access Strands

The top-line findings for the access strands from the FinAccess Kenya 2009 survey show that the proportion of individuals included in the formal sector increased from 18.9 percent in 2006 to 22.6 percent in 2009 and that the proportion using "formal other" services (such as SACCOs, MFIs, and money transfer services) increased dramatically from 7.5 to 17.9 percent, while those using the informal sector (mainly informal financial groups such as rotating savings and credit associations, ROSCAs) declined from 35.2 to 26.8 percent. Hence services included in the "formal other" category increased, while informal services declined (see figure B5.8.1).

Figure B5.8.1 Access Strand Analysis

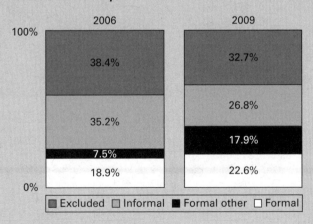

Source: FSD Kenya and Central Bank of Kenya 2009.

(continued next page)

Box 5.8 *(continued)*

However, the access strand classifies a person according to the "most formal" service used. A service-by-service analysis presents some contrasting points. Figure B5.8.2 disaggregates the "formal other" category and shows a fall in the use of SACCOs, a small increase in the use of MFIs, and a large increase in the use of M-PESA. The data also suggest an increase in the use of services in the informal sector (ROSCAs, ASCAs, buyers, hire-purchase, local shops, informal moneylenders). Although the use of formal sector services rose, so did the use of informal sector services. This is not apparent in figure B5.8.1, which does not count the use of informal services once a person uses a more formal service (moves up the continuum).

Figure B5.8.2 Service-by-Service Analysis

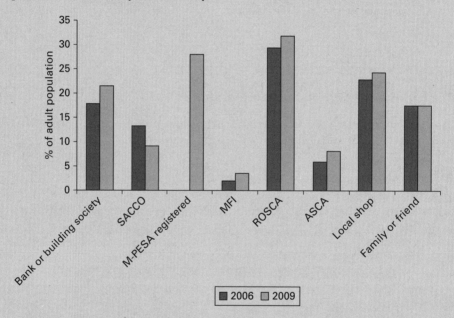

Source: FSD Kenya and Central Bank of Kenya 2009.

Thus the access strand approach needs to be used carefully. First, increased use of "formal" sector services does not necessarily mean that the use of "other formal" or "informal" services has declined. Second, it is very important to know how services in these studies are classified. In Kenya, M-PESA is classified as "formal other," which implies a significant increase in financial inclusion. However, M-PESA does not intermediate funds in the way that SACCOs and MFIs do, and research suggests that many use it simply as a cash-in, cash-out mechanism. Hence being included in the category "formal other" via M-PESA use alone does not signal the same quality of inclusion as having access to a SACCO or an MFI and may result in misleading classifications of inclusion.

Source: Susan Johnson, Centre for Development Studies, University of Bath.

entered or left the household or business over the prior period (week or fortnight). Financial diaries enable researchers to examine the dynamics of financial behavior by capturing transactions data in near "real time" and to examine data in sequence, providing a view inside the "black box" of the household budget (MFO 2010).

Financial diaries can also be used to test a new product or delivery channel for a specific financial service provider to better understand its target market, such as the work carried out by the Opportunity International Bank of Malawi (see box 5.9).

Financial Landscape Studies

Financial landscape studies combine demand- and supply-side data to document what financial services are available (both formal and informal) and how they are used, including consumer preferences and changes over time, drawing on data from both consumers and financial service providers.[17] To identify strategies for improving access, financial landscape studies focus on the needs of consumers. They do not have a bias toward any institutional form of provision; they use a supply-side survey (providers and products) and a demand-side survey (clients) to understand demand for and use of both formal and informal providers as well as the enabling environment. They also may examine the rules and supporting functions needed to develop financial markets and expand inclusion of the poor. Based on this understanding, they propose interventions to increase appropriate access. Most often, landscape studies are conducted in smaller geographic areas rather than nationally and sometimes in more than one location for comparative purposes. Financial landscape studies also may focus on one type of institution or service innovation, placing it in the context of local competition to examine how these interactions dampen or multiply its impact.

Box 5.9 Cash-In, Cash-Out: Financial Diaries in Malawi

Using financial diaries, Microfinance Opportunities (MFO) undertook research to explore the extent to which the introduction of a mobile "bank-on-wheels" serving rural locations in central Malawi provided value in areas without branch offices of the Opportunity International Bank of Malawi (OIBM). MFO collected transaction data (all inflows and outflows, including use of financial services) from just under 200 low-income households, half of whom were OIBM clients using the mobile bank, for 18 months over 2008–09. The sample was mostly a mix of poor farmers and microentrepreneurs. Eight field workers interviewed participants at the van stops and recorded their financial transactions once a week.

The study determined that the mean number of weekly transactions per household was 19. Cash exchanges between individuals were ubiquitous, largely from men to women, suggesting gender-based dependency on cash gifts and a pervasive informal safety net among family and friends. Savings transactions dominated bank use. Although the mobile van was popular initially, OIBM services rarely replaced informal finance and use of the van dropped off markedly. Yet the OIBM van added value for women clients; furthermore, the analysis of aggregate transaction data helped the OIBM to understand client behavior and develop better products.

Source: Stuart, Ferguson, and Cohen 2011.

Financial landscape studies seek to answer the following questions:

- *Supply.* What is the landscape of financial service supply? Who are the providers of financial services? What are the key products offered by existing providers? What are the key characteristics of different types of providers (for example, prices, volumes, market share, structure of products offered)? What are the limitations of providers reaching the poor?

- *Access.* What are the level and type of access to financial services? What are the key barriers, opportunities, and constraints to accessing financial services? What interventions can be considered to improve access and improve livelihoods in the proposed regions?

- *Use.* What financial products and services do the poor use? Which providers do the poor use? Are these providers in the formal or informal sector or both? To what extent do the poor use various financial services? Would the poor use certain products or services that they do not have access to? Do the characteristics of demand provide programming insights?

- *Rules and supporting functions.* What rules (formal, informal) and supporting functions (for example, infrastructure, funding) do or do not exist in the market? For example, do weak supporting functions constrain access? What role does the government play, and do opportunities exist to improve it? Is there sufficient telecommunications and physical infrastructure to benefit from innovative delivery channels?

On the supply side, as many providers as possible are interviewed to establish what products and services they offer, prices and volumes (accounts, savings, and loans), and competition and dynamics of their business. On the demand side, a one-time access and use survey is carried out on a random sample to map existing patterns of use against poverty levels (using poverty assessment tools), livelihood types, gender, and age segmentation. Data are analyzed for descriptive patterns, and regression analysis is used to establish key socioeconomic, demographic, and geographic factors determining access and use, including consumer preferences and changes over time. In addition to the surveys, a comprehensive desk review of secondary sources covering financial service outreach data (for example, FinScope studies, if available) is generally included.

The financial landscape approach provides insight into the behavior of consumers and their use of financial services and allows results to be contextualized within local profiles of provision— for example, understanding the nature of local providers and how they fit into the market system. Combining quantitative and qualitative data allows much deeper insight into consumer preferences and strategies and greater understanding of their engagement with the market (see box 5.10). Financial landscape studies begin to look at the quality aspect of financial inclusion as defined by AFI.

Financial landscape studies also examine the wider environment and supporting functions at local and national levels. Information is gathered through in-depth interviews with key informants (including policy makers, regulators, clients, private sector providers, and donors). Rules and regulations, infrastructure and delivery channels, information, and funding are all examined; secondary research is used to support information obtained from the interviews.

Sometimes financial landscape studies are supplemented with further research carried out through financial diaries, for example, or livelihood landscape studies (see box 5.11).

Monitoring and Evaluation

In addition to supply and demand research, monitoring outcomes and evaluating impact are important to understanding financial inclusion. In particular, they help to assess quality and

Box 5.10 Financial Landscapes in Kenya

Landscape research maps the supply and demand sides of financial service provision—both formal and informal—and seeks to understand the patterns of use and the reasons for them. Financial Sector Development (FSD) Kenya commissioned a landscape research study in 2010–11 to examine what was occurring in smaller towns and their rural environs. The goal was to understand to what extent and in what ways the dynamic changes in the market evident at the national level were being experienced in specific contexts and by people whom the financial sector finds it hard to reach (because of both low incomes and rural context).

The research was conducted in three towns chosen to reflect different poverty profiles. A supply-side survey collected data from banks, SACCOs, MFIs, and informal groups on product profiles, number of clients, volume of savings and loans, competition, and local market context. On the demand side, questionnaires were completed with small samples (20 households and multiple users in each household where possible) in each town and in two rural sites at different distances from the town, yielding an overall sample of 337 individuals in 194 households across the three sites. The surveys were followed by in-depth qualitative interviews with 148 individuals.

Supply-side data were compiled to develop a profile of service provision and products and provide insight into competition dynamics. The analysis involved probit regressions to understand socioeconomic characteristics most associated with the use of particular services (for example, employment type, poverty level, age, gender, marital status, and distance) and analysis of qualitative data to identify the reasons people gave for their service use and preferences.

The results revealed the following:

- Bank accounts and SACCOs are used to manage payments more than to make voluntary savings.
- Financial groups are used extensively because they offer structure but also flexibility and liquidity—in particular, easy access to loans of sizes that individuals need on a frequent basis rather than the much larger loans offered by formal providers.
- Mobile money services are used extensively because they allow access to liquidity through social networks but are not used for saving beyond an emergency reserve.

Source: Susan Johnson, Centre for Development Studies, University of Bath.

welfare, the last two dimensions of financial inclusion as defined by AFI.

Monitoring involves the regular collection of data, generally quantitative, while evaluation involves periodic or one-time in-depth analysis of performance against objectives and anticipated outcomes. Impact assessment attempts to determine if there is a change in consumer welfare and, if so, what the change is and if it can be attributed to the use of financial services (or an intervention seeking to enhance financial inclusion).

Generally four main components are included in monitoring and evaluation—inputs, activities, outputs, and outcomes. Inputs are the basic resources used, activities are the set of actions taken, outputs are the deliverables, and outcomes are the net result of the outputs over time. Long-term outcomes are sometimes referred to as impacts. These can all be viewed within a logic model (see figure 5.3).

The logic model (also known as the theory of change or results chain) links the results that we

Box 5.11 Livelihood Landscape Studies

Livelihood landscape studies are similarly qualitative in orientation and employ the same
methods as financial landscape studies, but
with a focus on the livelihood strategies of the
target population, including the range of occu-
pations and perceived advantages and disadvantages of each. Livelihood landscape studies
move beyond occupation to encompass the
full range of activities that contribute to the
subsistence of individuals and households.

Special attention is paid to understanding the
composite livelihood strategies that individuals
pursue (for example, small business, plus
farming, plus support from family), how the
pieces fit together, and the reasons for combining them. These studies also attempt to
understand differentiated access to livelihood
strategies and the factors that boost or inhibit
access to financial services—for example,
class, gender, or ethnicity.

Source: Microfinance Opportunities.

Figure 5.3 Logic Model Definitions

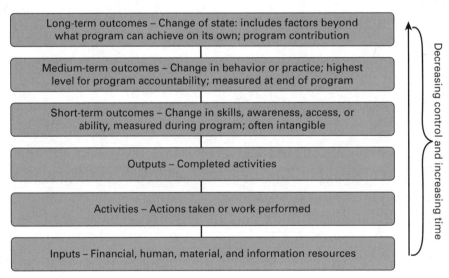

Source: Aga Khan Foundation 2011.

would like to see with the activities and inputs that are in place (see box 5.12).[18]

Assessing Impact

Impact assessments evaluate long-term outcomes. They help providers to understand the effect of their services (both positive and negative) on client welfare, help funders to understand the impact of their investments, and, coupled with measuring financial inclusion, help policy makers to adjust policies and make budget allocation decisions. Academics use impact assessments to answer rigorous academic questions regarding the role and function of financial services in the

The New Microfinance Handbook

Box 5.12 Measuring Outcomes of Facilitating Savings Groups

Facilitators of SGs generally anticipate outcomes in multiple domains that take hold within the first two years of group participation and deepen with time. The five domains of outcomes are as follows:

1. *Stronger economic capacity.* Asset accumulation, consumption smoothing, income-generating investment, income, management of finances, savings
2. *Increased social capital.* Solidarity (with other members), collective activities taken on by members, increase in leadership roles taken on by members in the community
3. *Increased self-empowerment.* Increased self-confidence, greater decision-making power in the household
4. *Greater food security.* Increased food consumption or more varied diet
5. *Other.* Changes due to targeted activities, such as increased specific knowledge or changes in behavior.

Source: Gash 2012.

lives of the poor. With the increased interest in and emphasis on financial inclusion, stakeholders' interest has moved beyond increasing the number of account holders to understanding if consumers are benefiting from financial services and if those are provided using fair and prudent practices.

Traditional impact assessment measures the developmental outcomes intended (and unintended) by the use of financial services; it tries to identify links between product use and client welfare.[19] Impacts can be economic, sociopolitical, or cultural. Economic impacts include broad changes in economic growth—for example, movements from a barter to a monetized economy (particularly in rural settings), business expansion or transformation of enterprises, net gains in income within subsectors of the informal economy, or a reduction in the vulnerability of poor people through consumption smoothing and risk management. Sociopolitical impact could include changes in policies that enhance the business environment or improvements in human development indicators within a region (such as changes in nutrition or educational outcomes). Cultural impact may include redistribution of

assets, power, or decision making at the household level. For example, if credit or crop insurance is concentrated on more profitable but risky cash crops mostly controlled by men, it is important to assess the potential welfare effects of shifting resources away from crops that are controlled largely by women (Copestake 2004).

Historically, impact assessment was often conducted to determine if a particular provider's services or delivery were having any impact on its clients. The purpose was to improve their products and services based on findings from the assessments. While there are benefits to this approach, the following section provides a broader discussion on impact assessment and research methodologies, some of which may not be used extensively by individual providers (for example, RCTs; see box 5.13).

Research

Generally all research begins with an overarching question that guides the focus, methodologies, and tools used to carry out the research. The research question may be in the

Box 5.13 The Changing Focus of Impact Assessment

The audience for microfinance impact assessments is diverse. The original stakeholder group—providers, donors, and academics—has expanded to include investors, policy makers, and regulators. Yet despite stakeholder diversity, the reasons to invest in impact assessment have not changed that much. Proving impact was, and still is, needed to justify the allocation of public and private resources. However, impact assessments can also play a role in market research because client data can help providers to improve their products and services. These two agendas form the prove-improve continuum that guides the design and use of assessment.

For those seeking to prove impact, the methodological challenges of causality, selection bias, and fungibility of money persist. In the mid-1990s, these difficulties led some to reject impact assessment, arguing that those who want to prove the causal relationship between microcredit and poverty alleviation face an uphill battle. Instead, they proposed easier, more practical proxies. Early advocates of commercialization, for example, argued that repeat loans are a good indicator of the positive value that borrowers ascribe to microcredit and can serve as a reasonable proxy for difficult-to-obtain impact data. In the intervening years, both arguments have shown their weaknesses, the welfare effects of access to credit have proven marginal, and repeat borrowing reflects the scarcity of capital available to low-income populations more than the appropriateness of the products they use.

The need for cash to smooth consumption and provide working capital trumps all.

Thus the tension persists between credibility born of research rigor and useful information. The ongoing, rapid evolution of the industry has fed the need to prove impact. Rigorous approaches to research are seen as essential to generating credible results, and, consequently, interest in conducting RCTs has exploded. An important pool of knowledge has thus been generated, albeit one that seems disconnected from the dynamics of the industry or institutional practicalities of delivering services.

Despite several recognized "good" and credible studies, the industry still has much progress to make. While it is no longer a single-product industry focused exclusively on working capital loans, the bulk of impact assessments still addresses the effects of microcredit. Recognition of market segmentation and product differentiation has yet to spawn products and services that respond to clients' changing life-cycle requirements. Broader impact assessment and financial inclusion studies are needed.

What has perhaps changed is how impact assessment findings have played out in the public arena. As the audience has grown, this information has, in some countries, become more politicized, and the results of the new critiques have been co-opted by politicians to the detriment of providers and their clients. The microfinance crisis in India between 2009 and 2011 reflected this misalignment of interests.

Source: Monique Cohen, Microfinance Opportunities.

form of a hypothesis, which is a proposed explanation for a phenomenon or a presumed correlation between cause and effect—for example, the provision of payment services will lead to a lower incidence of theft (Nelson n.d.). A hypothesis can be confirmed, denied, or proposed for further investigation via qualitative or quantitative research. A research question can also be open ended. For example, research can be conducted (or commissioned) by an investor to assess the financial landscape in an area to determine constraints and opportunities for funding, by a donor to determine the impact of a particular intervention, or by a provider to better understand the needs of their clients or potential clients.

Indicator Selection

Indicators are specific data that are linked to objectives and hypotheses (if applicable). These indicators allow defined changes to be measured or analyzed, help to develop an understanding of whether the hypotheses are correct, and highlight other unexpected changes or processes. Indicators need to relate closely to the changes that an organization or researcher hopes to observe. Wider impacts—those beyond the immediate financial and social benefits for the individual or household—are difficult to identify and assess. Since many of the wider changes examined are difficult to measure directly, proxies are often used instead.

In addition to being SMART (specific, measurable, achievable, realistic, and time-bound), indicators ideally have the following characteristics (Dunn, Kalaitzandonakes, and Valdivia 1996):

- *Valid.* Measure what they are intended to measure and capture effects due to the intervention rather than external factors

- *Reliable.* Verifiable and objective, so that, if measured at different times or places or with different people, the conclusions will be the same

- *Relevant.* Directly linked to the objectives of the intervention

- *Technically feasible.* Capable of being assessed and measured

- *Usable.* Understandable and ideally providing useful information to assess performance and inform decision making

- *Sensitive.* Capable of demonstrating changes and capturing change in the outcome of interest (national per capita income is unlikely to be sensitive to the effects of a single intervention)

- *Timely.* Possible to collect relatively quickly

- *Cost-effective.* Worth the cost to collect, process, and analyze

- *Ethical.* Acceptable to those providing the information.

Indicators help researchers to measure what they believe to be affected; however, if the focus is only on measuring indicators, the research may miss unintended or unanticipated impacts, both positive and negative. Ideally research efforts track indicators for consistency and accountability and pose a broader set of questions for understanding wider or unanticipated impacts.

Research Approaches

The overall approach taken to proving the research hypothesis or answering the research question is influenced by the research objectives, the quality of information required, the interests of various stakeholders, and the research budget.[20] Many decisions need to be made about the scope of the study, including size (number of individuals, households), time frame (a one-time survey or a longitudinal study), unit of study (transactions, individuals, households, or enterprises), and geographic coverage (local, national, regional, or global).

Choices also include whether the research should be an ongoing process of collecting information for a period of time (such as financial diaries), a one-off survey, or a survey with two or more rounds, such as baseline or endline, that is repeated after a period of time; whether the research will study the financial sector as a whole or will focus on an individual provider or a particular product (or potential product);

whether it will look at demand or supply or the overall financial landscape; and who will carry out the research. A key decision is the balance between *qualitative* and *quantitative* approaches or a combination of the two. Combining different tools can increase the credibility and usefulness of the research, but adds complexity and cost.

Qualitative Research

Qualitative research is undertaken to gain an understanding of human behavior and the reasons for it. Qualitative methods investigate the *why* and *how* of decision making, not just the *what*, *where*, and *when*. Qualitative methods capture what people have to say in their own words and describe their experiences in depth. Qualitative research helps us to discover what we do not know we do not know because it is flexible and adaptable, which allows us to follow up on interesting, unanticipated findings. Hence, qualitative research uses small, focused samples, whereas quantitative research uses large samples. Sampling is generally purposive—that is, respondents are chosen *because* they have specific characteristics and can provide information on the specific focus of the research. The type of information the researcher is looking for will determine the type of individuals chosen, the time spent with each individual or group, and the size of the sample. In cases of very small samples, selecting "information-rich" clients to interview is critical (Patton 1990).

Qualitative research is generally carried out using individual *in-depth interviews, focus group discussions,* or *participant observation.* These interviews and discussions can form the basis for *case studies*, which assess the needs, conditions, opportunities, and limitations of a small number of individuals. Participatory rapid assessment (PRA) expands on the traditional focus group discussion, making it particularly interactive (see box 5.14).

Quantitative Research

Quantitative research collects data to create generalizable results from a sample of the population of interest. It measures the reactions of many subjects to a set of predetermined questions. The process of measurement is central to quantitative research because it provides the fundamental connection between empirical observation and mathematical expression of quantitative relationships. Thus sampling (choosing which persons, households, or enterprises) must be random and large enough to represent the population adequately. Properly designed quantitative studies can provide reliable results because of the statistical validity of the findings and the lack of bias in the sampling methodology. But these approaches are not as flexible as qualitative methods, so they are best suited when there is some idea of the situation on the ground.

Quantitative research commonly uses *surveys*—predesigned and pretested questionnaires administered in formal interviews. Surveys contain questions with a limited set of answers so that the results can be quantified, compared, and analyzed statistically. Because quantitative research is associated with statistical analysis of responses from a large number of clients, it is considered a more "scientific" approach than qualitative methods. Quantitative methods allow researchers to determine how extensive a phenomenon is and if it exists with statistical certainty, but they are less able to measure unforeseen impacts or phenomenon.

Quantitative research methodologies can be nonexperimental, quasi-experimental, or experimental. Nonexperimental studies look at the differences in behavior between different people and relate the degree of access to variations in outcomes. Quasi-experimental and experimental studies look at what changes take place over time between a *treatment* group (who accesses services) and a *control* group (who does not access the service and who, otherwise, is believed to be identical to the treatment group). Baseline and follow-up surveys are conducted

Box 5.14 Participatory Rapid Assessment

PRAs are derived from classic sociological and anthropological approaches in that they involve the use of semistructured interviews with key informants, participant observation, and the methodological principles of triangulation and open-endedness. However, compared to traditional approaches, PRA techniques are more interactive. Workshop activities engage respondents by using drawings, stories, and theater, encouraging them to identify significant changes that have occurred in their lives as a result of access to financial services. PRAs use the following techniques:

- Social mapping and modeling drawn by participants, indicating which institutions and structures of their community are important in their lives
- Seasonality maps or calendars, allowing communities to show how various phenomena in their lives vary over the course of a year
- Daily time-use analysis to track how participants use their time, allowing participants and researchers to obtain a sense of responsibilities, challenges, and opportunities for structuring interventions
- Participatory linkage diagrams, showing chains of causality
- Venn diagrams, showing the relative importance of different institutions or individuals in the community
- Wealth ranking
- Product attribute ranking
- Life-cycle needs analysis
- Cash mobility mapping, providing an understanding of where the community goes to acquire or spend cash (markets, wage labor, cooperatives) and leading into a discussion of supply and demand.

Source: Ledgerwood 1998.

with both groups, and results are compared to show what happened as a result of using the financial services and what happened in the absence of using them.

Quasi-experimental studies are nonrandomized, while experimental methods, or RCTs, randomly assign groups or individuals to treatment or control groups. While no one can ever know what would have happened to a specific individual had they not participated in an intervention, a random control group forms a *counterfactual* (what would have happened in the absence of whatever is being studied) for the group of individuals or households who use the service or receive the benefit. Changes that are not due to

the use of a financial service should affect both populations equally, so any difference in how these populations change over time can be attributed to the effects of the financial services being studied.

No one method is perfect, however, because various methodological challenges are inherent in research:

- *Attribution.* The difficulty of attributing changes to a specific activity (access to or use of financial services), given the complexity of environments shaped by an array of factors, including economic forces, social and cultural norms, and the political climate

- *Fungibility.* The exchange or substitution of one thing for another—in this case, fungibility means that money can be used for many purposes, with changes in intention occurring quickly. Assessing the impact of borrowing for a business, for example, assumes that the borrower used the loan capital for the business and that the borrower did not just reduce his or her borrowing from other sources (that is, substitution)

- *Selection bias.* The systematic differences in characteristics of people self-selecting to participate in an intervention or access a financial service and whether these characteristics make them more likely to benefit from use of the service (Gash 2012)

- *Causality.* The relationship between an event (the *cause*) and a second event (the *effect*), where the second event is understood to be a consequence of the first. The difficulty of isolating a variable causal impact is commonly referred to as a *causality bias*.

While these challenges have persisted through decades of social research, some new techniques are being used to address, in particular, issues of sampling bias and causality. Overall, nonexperimental and quasi-experimental designs are generally considered better at showing association or correlation than at proving causation (Gash 2012). By randomly assigning people to treatment and control groups (experimental design), RCTs attempt to overcome the causality bias; since the selection bias is removed, it is possible to attribute the impact to use of the service (see box 5.15).

Randomized Control Trials

At the time of writing, randomized control trials are relatively new in microfinance and thus are described in more detail here.[21] In addition to overcoming selection biases, RCTs are one of the few methods (if not the only method) that can account for unobservable factors. Because the control and treatment groups are selected randomly, the households in those groups should be equivalent, on average, on all observable (for example, education levels) and unobservable (for example, an individual's entrepreneurial skills, organizational ability, or access to social networks) characteristics (Bauchet and Morduch 2010). Randomized designs make it possible to uncover the net impact of the intervention, free of selection bias.[22]

However, experimental methods only estimate the *average* impact of accessing services or other interventions. They do not provide an understanding of the median impact, and in practice they say little about the distribution of impacts. For example, if access makes one person much better off and all others a little worse off, an RCT might conclude that the average impact is positive if the positive impact for that one person is large enough to offset the sum of negative impacts for everyone else (Bauchet and Morduch 2010). That said, if the sample is large enough, data can be disaggregated into subcategories to see the impact on certain groups.

Furthermore, *spillovers* (or *leakage*) can occur when randomizing at the individual level, for example, when someone transfers from the treatment group to the control group or vice versa (leakage) or when members of the control group are inadvertently affected by the treatment. This could happen, for example, when a borrower gives part of her loan to a friend in the control group or when a client receiving training shares some of the lessons with someone not assigned to the training (Bauchet and Morduch 2010).

RCTs are very good at providing an estimate of impact, but the results may be difficult to generalize to other settings. This means they may have high internal validity (estimates are credible on their own terms), but not external validity (conclusions are applicable to a wider range of situations). For example, when conducting RCTs, researchers are sometimes forced to use a

Box 5.15 The Difficulty of Proving Causation

One significant issue to consider is the ability of a study design to prove causation or eliminate outside factors that could otherwise explain the results. A useful way to think about the link between methodologies and their ability to prove causation is to consider where the methodology would fall on a spectrum, as shown in figure B5.15.1. The farther the methodology is to the right-side arrow, the better it proves causality, and the farther it is to the left-side arrow, the less it proves causality and only shows association (or correlation). In general, the more rigorous the method, the more likely that cause can be attributed to the intervention.

Figure B5.15.1 The Spectrum of Evidence

ASSOCIATION   CAUSALITY

Field experience, anecdotes
Interviews, case studies
Client surveys
Quasi-experimental with nonrandomized
comparison group
Randomized control trials

Source: Gash 2012; provided by Kathleen Odell, Brennan School of Business, Dominican University.

Quasi-experimental and nonexperimental studies indicate where impact may lie and help to identify important questions that can be answered more confidently with experimental studies. They are more flexible in terms of identifying unanticipated impacts and can sometimes more easily incorporate the context of the situation. Their results can also hint at the "why" of results that are not explained otherwise. The longer-term nonexperimental studies give us an idea of additional impacts that may emerge as participants use services for longer than the one- to three-year span of some RCTs. On a practical level, quasi-experimental and nonexperimental studies can be less expensive and easier to implement. Quasi- and nonexperimental studies, or even monitoring systems, can be used to check for similar results elsewhere. In essence, all three designs complement each other by filling in gaps and triangulating data.

Source: Gash 2012.

nonstandard population, making the results less valid externally. While nonrandomized approaches may collect data on larger geographic areas or diversified populations, thus having fewer problems with external validity, the internal validity of these methods is often far less satisfactory. To reduce external validity problems, well-designed RCTs try to understand the "why" of impacts by gathering information on

intermediate outcomes and considering other contexts to which the conclusions would apply (or conduct multiple studies in different contexts).

RCTs are sometimes considered unethical because they require that a portion of the population does not receive access to the intervention being evaluated. Furthermore, the choice of who does or does not receive the intervention cannot be made based on who needs it the most or who deserves it the most. However, sometimes randomly selecting participants can be "fairer" than other selection mechanisms when, for example, funding is too limited to serve everyone who is eligible. In this case, publicly randomizing who benefits and who does not can improve fairness (Bauchet and Morduch 2010).

Mixed Methods

A combination of quantitative and qualitative methodologies often provides more comprehensive findings than one approach alone. Mixed methods can be carried out simultaneously, using different research teams or mixed methods in one study. For example, combining quantitative household surveys to track changes with qualitative focus group discussions and key informant interviews expands the understanding of contextual factors and may lead to unexpected ideas.

A mixed approach can also be sequential. Qualitative work can inform what questions should be measured with quantitative work or explore unusual findings from quantitative studies. Different studies can build on one another in expected or unexpected ways. For example, qualitative studies indicate that SG members seem to increase their saving rates from the first to the second cycle because, by the end of the first cycle, members have come to trust the model, understanding that they are able both to save and to earn profits on their savings. However, complementary quantitative data show that this increase in saving from the first to the second cycle is much stronger for the first group in the village than for later groups in the same village. Having learned from the experiences of the first group, later groups understand better how the model works and tend to start out with higher saving rates and thus do not experience as great an increase (Cojocaru and Matuszeski 2011).

All research benefits from *triangulation*— that is, checking data with respondents and cross-checking the information with others to confirm different points of view of the same phenomenon and to verify something as more likely to be true and not due to just one or a few respondents who could be biased. Similarly, secondary sources and desk reviews of existing findings can supplement primary research.

Table 5.1 summarizes the various research methods and their usefulness.

Poverty Assessment Tools

Poverty assessment tools (or calibrated income proxy tools) are used to determine the poverty levels of groups or individuals being studied.[23] While most often associated with social performance monitoring, they are discussed here because they are often used in various research efforts (for example, financial landscape studies or impact assessments) to assess the level of poverty of a group being studied. They allow researchers (or providers or others) to estimate the rate of poverty incidence in a population (or their clients) without having to measure income or consumption directly through time-consuming household budget surveys.

Poverty assessment tools include short, country-specific surveys with indicators that have been identified as the best predictors of whether a given set of households is very poor, according to the legislative definition of extreme poverty applicable to the country in question. Once the gathered data are entered into a template, software can estimate the share of households living below the applicable poverty line. The construction of the tool relies on a set of indicators that are correlated most strongly with poverty in the nationally representative expenditure surveys. Each tool is meant to be administered by minimally trained staff in 20 minutes or less.

Table 5.2 presents an overview of poverty assessment tools commonly used in microfinance to measure absolute and relative poverty. Absolute measures classify people as poor or nonpoor in relation to a defined poverty line (national or international, like purchasing power parity of

Table 5.1 Research Methods and Their Usefulness

Method	Application	Advantages	Disadvantages	Usefulness
Randomized control trials (RCTs) comparing treatment and control groups	Uses structured surveys to measure variables and changes attributable to the steps in a presuggested chain of results when samples are sufficiently large	Regarded as the most rigorous statistical method; avoids "selection bias" because the treatment and control groups are identical on average	Difficult to design and administer if the treatment group is self-selecting (that is, buying a service). In the case of a self-selecting treatment group, encouragement design can be used, which allows anyone to take up the treatment, but randomly assigns the encouragement. Study questions cannot be changed mid-study	Useful for measuring the effects of specific innovations where randomization is possible and for measuring the impact variables of interest (for example, specific products or services such as savings accounts, weather insurance)
Quasi-experimental research comparing before and after characteristics in treatment and control groups (before-after with control group; also control variables before-after studies)	Uses structured surveys to measure changes attributable to a step in the results chain; could be useful for pilot projects	More approximate in that the control groups method is not an exact control	Easier to implement than RCTs; results are similar, but control group is not a perfect counterfactual because it is not randomly selected. The costs of the survey design, implementation, and analysis are identical for RCTs and for nonrandom control groups. Careful design and measurement are needed to ensure accuracy. Not valid when the control group is significantly different from the treatment group, especially with regard to underlying trends in both groups	Similar to RCTs, useful for investigating specific interventions and where the sample is sufficiently large but, for operational reasons, RCTs are not feasible
Participatory approaches (for example, focus groups)	Used where the change in behavior might have been caused by different factors	Might be the only way to show attribution; can uncover unanticipated impacts	Might be subjective, open to bias	Useful for understanding access to and use of financial services at the local level; complements RCTs in understanding causal pathways
Opinions of key informants and expert interviews	Might be used when the key change is driven by one person (for example, policy change)	Low cost	Might be influenced by interviewer; open to subjective interpretation	Especially useful for understanding processes of policy change and where causes of market changes are being established (for example, demonstration effects) and are necessary for assessing development of rules and supporting functions
Case studies analyzing changes in behavior and performance	Used where qualitative understanding is needed to interpret quantitative data	Low cost; can be a good indication of attribution, if well designed and executed	Might not represent the universe of beneficiaries; can be time-consuming; might be influenced by interviewers	Very useful at all stages of logic model or results chain and especially important for understanding changing patterns of use by clients

Source: Johnson 2009.

Table 5.2 Main Poverty Assessment Tools Available for Microfinance Practitioners

Tool	Purpose	Description	Implementation	Pros	Cons
Grameen Foundation Progress out of Poverty Index (PPI)	Estimates the % of poor clients, based on one or two poverty lines and the probability of an individual falling below the poverty line; measures absolute poverty	Country-specific poverty scorecard with 10 questions (socioeconomic indicators that correlate with poverty); indicators are derived from large-scale nationally representative surveys	Scorecard can be applied to a sample of clients or to the entire client base; implemented by field staff and can be used before, during, or after service delivery	Good balance of ease of use and accuracy; can be used for targeting and for assessing changes in poverty levels;[a] results can be compared across regions	Makes no urban-rural distinction;[b] not available for all countries; validity of indicators changes over time
USAID poverty assessment tool (USAID PAT)	Estimates the % of poor clients, based on one or two poverty lines; provides an absolute measure of poverty	Country-specific poverty scorecard of 16–33 questions (socioeconomic indicators that correlate with poverty); indicators are derived from large nationally representative surveys	Scorecard can be applied to a sample of clients or to the entire clientele; implemented preferably after clients join the program	Good balance of accuracy and ease of use; results can be compared across countries and regions	Data cannot be disaggregated and are not available for all countries; validity of indicators changes over time
FINCA client assessment tool (FCAT)	Broad client assessment; allows classification of the population according to different poverty lines, based on expenditure data; provides an absolute measure of poverty	A 130-question survey divided in sections: demographic and loan information, household characteristics, expenditures, assets, access to facilities (water, electricity, health care), business types, and client satisfaction and exit	Surveys a sample of clients, interviewed at periodic intervals	Provides a comprehensive assessment of clients' well-being and a fair amount of information that can be used for management	Relies on clients' recall of past expenditures to measure poverty levels, which is prone to measurement errors
CGAP poverty assessment tool (CGAP PAT)	Assesses the poverty levels of MFI clients compared to nonclients within the operational area of an MFI, based on a multidimensional index; provides a relative measure of poverty; can use secondary data to put relative measures into a regional, national, or even international context	Questionnaire includes a range of indicators (adapted to local context): demographic characteristics; housing quality; assets (type, number, and value); educational level and occupation of family members; food security and vulnerability; household expenditures on clothing and footwear (poverty benchmark)	Surveys a sample of 200 clients and 300 nonclients; implemented by external consultants	Uses multidimensional definition of poverty	Lengthy survey; demanding of technical input (highly qualified staff that does not build internal capacity for future in-house replication

Housing index	Identifies poor households in relation to the community where they live, based on the structure and conditions of their dwelling; provides a relative measure of poverty	Uses a simple index that is adapted to the local conditions, in terms of housing conditions	MFI staff visit the communities and apply the index to identify potential clients; applied before or after service delivery	Easy to verify; can be used for targeting, monitoring, and assessment	Limited definition of poverty; accuracy depends on the actual link between poverty status and housing conditions
Means test	Assesses the level of poverty of households based on a composite index; provides a relative measure of poverty	Uses household surveys with a small number of easily verifiable indicators; includes asset ownership (land, livestock, radio, television), sociodemographic characteristics, and others	Short interviews conducted by field staff with all potential clients; applied before or after service delivery	Combines simple indicators with short survey and standard scoring system, simplifying implementation; good for targeting, monitoring, and assessing	Indicators may or may not be closely linked to poverty; accuracy is unknown
Participatory wealth ranking	Identifies the poor in a community, based on community perceptions of wealth (measures relative poverty)	Involves mapping the community, ranking individuals by level of wealth, triangulating results, and classifying individuals	Participatory appraisal carried out in the community; facilitated by experts and MFI staff before or after the program; 100–500 households	Provides a rich picture of livelihood strategies, nature, and causes of poverty; can be highly correlated with national poverty lines	Requires staff with strong participatory facilitation skills; accuracy is unknown

Source: Ines Arevalo, consultant to the Aga Khan Agency for Microfinance drawing from Social Performance Task Force (2009); CGAP (2003); IFAD (2006); Simanowitz, Nkuna, and Kasim (2000); SEEP Network (2008); www.progressoutofpoverty.org; www.povertytools.org; http://www.microfinancegateway.org/p/site/m/template.rc/1.11.48260/1.26.9234/

a. Does not establish causality.

b. While the urban-rural indicator has been tested for power of prediction, it has never been included in a PPI. It was found that adding a rural-urban indicator did not improve the PPI accuracy as much as other indicators that are also correlated with the geographic location of the household (including ownership of agricultural land, type of dwelling, access to electricity). Geographic variation has also been accounted for by adjusting the poverty line that is used to construct the scorecard to the cost of living in different regions of a country (Grameen Foundation 2008, 13; personal communication with Mark Schreiner).

US$1.25 a day). Relative measures classify people in relation to other people of the same community or geographic area. Absolute measures allow comparisons across providers, countries, and so forth and are useful for impact assessment (Zeller 2004). In general, tools that measure absolute poverty perform better at the aggregate level—that is, they are more accurate when they measure the rate of poverty in a group of people and not the poverty status of an individual. If the purpose is to target beneficiaries, relative measures are a better alternative. However, the Progress out of Poverty Index (PPI) of the Grameen Foundation, unlike the poverty assessment tool (PAT) of the USAID or the client assessment tool (FCAT) of the Foundation for International Community Assistance (FINCA), which all measure absolute poverty, can also be used for targeting because of the methodology used to derive the indicators.

None of the tools included in the table uses income as an indicator of well-being, as consumption is generally considered a better indicator of welfare than income and is preferred as a poverty measurement.[24] Of the tools presented in table 5.2, two attempt to measure expenditure as well (FCAT and CGAP PAT). However, large samples and advanced techniques that do not rely on recall over large periods of time are required to reduce the error in estimations. To overcome this issue, most tools use indicators that are correlated with poverty, such as household characteristics, dwelling structure, ownership of assets, human capital, and access to service facilities (Zeller 2004).

The two tools whose set of indicators has the strongest correlation with poverty are the Grameen Foundation's PPI and USAID's PAT, as they derive the final set of indicators from large nationally representative income and expenditure household surveys. Other tools such as a housing index rely on a single indicator to predict poverty; only when there is a very strong correlation with that one indicator can a robust relationship be expected. In general, this over-simplification of the definition of poverty leads to less accurate assessments. Other tools rely on a wider set of indicators (for example, participatory wealth ranking), but these are derived subjectively, which means that the rate of poverty cannot be compared across regions.

An important caveat applying to most tools included in table 5.2 is their validity over time. As the underlying relationship between the set of indicators and poverty changes, the accuracy of the tool is reduced. This means that tools need to be updated (more recent national surveys need to be conducted in the case of PPI and PAT or the participatory wealth ranking exercise needs to be conducted again) and extra effort made to allow inference of conclusions from the application of the tools to different points in time.

Notes

1. http://www.cgap.org/p/site/c/template.rc/1.26.14235/.

2. www.theMIX.org.

3. www.finscope.co.za.

4. http://data.worldbank.org/data-catalog/financial_inclusion.

5. For example, see http://www.themix.org/publications/microbanking-bulletin/2012/02/over-indebtedness-and-investment-microfinance.

6. Regulated financial service providers are required to report to central banks, but their reporting is not standardized across countries. The reporting of unregulated providers can be especially complicated. Credit unions often report to their own apex body. Mobile money providers are governed by specific legislation and thus may or may not be captured in reports from regulators. Further, there is no systematic method for tracking outreach and contribution to financial inclusion of NGOs and non-bank financial institutions (Linthorst and Gaul 2011).

7. AFI defines three levels of "formal" providers, each with implications for regulatory reporting: (a) registered institutions, such as cooperatives or loan companies, that offer financial services but are not required to provide information to a regulator, (b) institutions, such as remittance agents, that are authorized (or licensed) to offer financial services but are not actively supervised and have limited or no reporting obligations, and (c) institutions that are authorized and directly supervised on an ongoing basis. This is the most restrictive definition, but is also the level at which financial regulators have the most influence.

8. The Global Partnership for Financial Inclusion subgroup is proposing G-20 basic financial indicators built on the AFI core set of indicators (Ardic, Chen, and Latortue 2012).

9. *Administrative unit* is defined by each country and could, for example, refer to municipality, township, county, or other (depending on the country). *Access points* are defined as regulated access points where cash-in (including deposits) and cash-out transactions can be performed. This would include traditional bank branches and other offices of regulated entities (such as MFIs) that perform these functions. Depending on the type of transactions permitted, this could include agents of regulated entities and ATMs (only those that perform cash-in as well as cash-out transactions). *Regulated entities* are entities that are prudentially regulated and supervised. Since regulations vary by country, a country should disclose which types of financial institutions are included in the calculation (for example, banks, cooperatives, MFIs). *Adults* refer to the population 15 years of age and older; if a different age is used because of country-specific definitions, a country should disclose the age threshold used. See AFI (2011).

10. "Poorest" borrowers are defined as individuals among the lowest half of individuals living below the national poverty line or living on US\$1 or less per day. Profitability is measured as "operating self-sufficiency," which is income divided by cash costs for a given period, with no standardization of loan loss provisioning and no adjustments for the effects of subsidies. Operating self-sufficiency is self-reported by the MFIs, unverified, and not reported publicly, although the Microcredit Summit independently verifies MFIs' reported number of borrowers, where possible.

11. http://www.microcreditsummit.org.

12. http://www.mftransparency.org/.

13. http://www.woccu.org/memberserv/intlcusystem.

14. http://www.wsbi.org/.

15. www.finscope.co.za.

16. FinScope brochure, "From Data to Action," http://www.finscope.co.za/new/scriptlibrary/getfile.aspx?filename=FS workshop 2011_brochureFNL.pdf&file=../module_data/71e3e62d-1eeb-412e-893b-970e98f6a3fa/downloads/03bcf1fe-0fd2-40de-95f4-ffb73c12f1f0.file.

17. This methodology was developed for financial services by Susan Johnson, University of Bath.

18. The logic model, combined with the plan to assess progress toward expected outcomes, is often expressed in a log frame analysis or a performance monitoring framework.

19. Transactions-level analysis, for example, can isolate unusually large household expenses and study the transaction patterns surrounding them. When looking at the value and frequency of transactions, it is possible to identify previously unseen trends and opportunities to design and deliver improved financial services.

20. This section draws from Nelson (n.d.).

21. This section was contributed by Alyssa Jethani and is summarized from Bauchet and Morduch (2010).

22. Some variations of quasi-experimental research can approximate experimental methods, such as *regression discontinuity*

design, which relies on an arbitrary cutoff or rule to produce two populations that are essentially similar except that only one has access to or has used the service; *natural experiment*, which is an RCT that occurs without any intent to create a research situation; and *encouragement design*, which is a form of RCT that can be used when it is illegal or unethical to deny a service to participants. Here, the randomization pertains to who gets extra "encouragement" to take up a service that everyone is free to join (Janina Matuszeski).

23. This section was contributed by Ines Arevalo, consultant to the Aga Khan Agency for Microfinance.

24. Income is widely believed to be inappropriate as a welfare indicator because, first, it does not capture emergency coping strategies (for example, borrowing, selling assets, and consumption smoothing) and, second, it is prone to large measurement errors—in economies with large informal markets, people might find it difficult to recall their earnings or might be unwilling to report parts of their income (Haughton and Khandker 2009).

References and Further Reading

* Key works for further reading.

*AFI (Alliance for Financial Inclusion). 2010a. "Financial Inclusion Measurement for Regulators: Survey Design and Implementation." Policy paper, Data Working Group, AFI, Bangkok.

——. 2010b. "Financial Inclusion Measurement for Regulators." PowerPoint presentation, AFI, Kuala Lumpur. http://www.afi-global.org/sites/default/files/fidwg_measurementoverview_porteous_0.pdf.

——. 2011. "Measuring Financial Inclusion: Core Set of Financial Inclusion Indicators." Data Working Group, AFI, Bangkok. http://www.afi-global.org/sites/default/files/afi%20fidwg%20report.pdf.

Aga Khan Foundation. 2011. "Monitoring, Evaluation, and Learning Plan." Internal document, Aga Khan Foundation, Geneva.

*Ardic, Oya Pinar, Gregory Chen, and Alexia Latortue. 2012. "Financial Access 2011: An Overview of the Supply-Side Data Landscape." Access to Finance Forum Reports by CGAP and Its Partners 5, CGAP and IFC, Washington, DC, May.

*Bauchet, J., and J. Morduch. 2010. "An Introduction to Impact Evaluations with Randomized Designs." Financial Access Initiative, New York, March.

CGAP (Consultative Group to Assist the Poor.) 2003. "Microfinance Poverty Assessment Tool." Technical Tools Series 5, CGAP, Washington, DC.

CGAP and World Bank. 2009. *Financial Access 2009: Measuring Access to Financial Services around the World.* Washington, DC: CGAP and World Bank.

——. 2010. *Financial Access 2010: The State of Financial Inclusion through the Crisis.* Washington, DC: CGAP.

*Chaia, Alberto, Aparna Dalal, Tony Goland, Maria Jose Gonzalez, Jonathan Morduch, and Robert Schiff. 2009. "Half the World Is Unbanked: Financial Access Initiative Framing Note." Report, Financial Access Initiative, New York.

Cojocaru, Laura, and Janina Matuszeski. 2011. "The Evolution of Savings Groups: An Analysis of Data from Oxfam America's Savings for Change Program in Mali." Draft, Oxfam America, Boston, November.

*Collins, Daryl, Jonathan Morduch, Stuart Rutherford, and Orlanda Ruthven. 2009. *Portfolios of the Poor: How the World's Poor Live on 2 Dollars a Day.* Princeton, NJ: Princeton University Press.

*Copestake, J. 2004. "Impact Assessment of Microfinance Using Qualitative Data: Communicating between Social Scientists and Practitioners Using the QUIP." *Journal of International Development* 16 (3): 355–67.

*——. 2011. "Microfinance Impact and Innovation Conference 2010: Heralding a New Era of

Microfinance Innovation and Research?" *Enterprise Development and Microfinance* 22: 17–29.

Copestake, J., S. Johnson, and K. Wright. 2002. "Impact Assessment of Microfinance: Towards a New Protocol for Collection and Analysis of Qualitative Data." Working Paper 23746, Imp-Act, University of Sussex.

*Demirgüç-Kunt, Aslı, and Leora Klapper. 2012. "Measuring Financial Inclusion: The Global Findex." Policy Research Working Paper 6025, World Bank, Washington, DC.

Dunn, Elizabeth, Nicholas Kalaitzandonakes, and Corinne Valdivia. 1996. "Risks and the Impact of Microenterprise Services." USAID, Washington, DC, June.

Duvendack, M., R. Palmer-Jones, J. G. Copestake, L. Hooper, Y. Loke, and N. Rao. 2011. "What Is the Evidence of the Impact of Microfinance on the Well-Being of Poor People?" EPPI-Centre, Social Science Research Unit, Institute of Education, University of London.

*FSD Kenya and Central Bank of Kenya. 2009. "Results of the FinAccess National Survey: Dynamics of Kenya's Changing Financial Landscape." FSD Kenya, Nairobi.

*Gash, Megan. 2012. "Pathways to Change." In *Savings Groups at the Frontier*, ed. Candace Nelson. Bourton on Dunsmore, U.K.: Practical Action.

*Global Partnership for Financial Inclusion. 2011. "Financial Inclusion Data: Assessing the Landscape and Country-Level Target Approaches." Discussion paper, IFC, Washington, DC.

*Grameen Foundation. 2008. *Progress Out of Poverty Index™. PPI Pilot Training. Participant Guide.* Washington, DC: Grameen Foundation.

Haughton, Jonathan, and Shahidur R. Khandker. 2009. "Inequality Measures." In *Handbook on Poverty and Inequality,* 101–20. Washington, DC: World Bank.

*Hulme, D. 2000. "Impact Assessment Methodologies for Microfinance: Theory, Experience, and Better Practice." *World Development* 28 (1): 79–98.

IFAD (International Fund for Agricultural Development). 2006. "Assessing and Managing Social Performance in Microfinance." IFAD, Rome.

IMF (International Monetary Fund). 2011. "IMF Releases 2011 Financial Access Survey Data." Press release 11/274, IMF, Washington, DC, July 11.

Johnson, Susan. 2009. "Quantifying Achievements in Private Sector Development." Centre for Development Studies, University of Bath.

Karlan, Dean S. 2001. "Microfinance Impact Assessments: The Perils of Using New Members as a Control Group." *Journal of Microfinance* 2 (3): 75–85.

Karlan, Dean, Nathanael Goldberg, and James. Copestake. 2009. "Randomized Control Trials Are the Best Way to Measure Impact of Microfinance Programmes and Improve Microfinance Product Designs." *Enterprise Development and Microfinance* 20 (3): 167–76.

*Kendall, Jake. 2010. "The Measurement Challenge." Paper presented at the Global Savings Forum, November. http://www .gatesfoundation.org/financialservicesforthe-poor/Documents/measurement-challenge.pdf.

Latortue, Alexia. 2012. "What Really Works for Clients." Part of the (virtual) conference "Financial Inclusion: What Really Works for Clients?" CGAP, Washington, DC.

Ledgerwood, Joanna. 1998. *Microfinance Handbook: An Institutional and Financial Perspective.* Washington, DC: World Bank.

*Linthorst, Audrey, and Scott Gaul. 2011. "What Do We Need to Know about Financial Inclusion in Africa?" SEEP Network, Washington, DC.

Makanjee, Maya. 2009. "Financial Inclusion in Africa." PowerPoint presentation at AFI Global Policy Forum, September 14. http://www .afi-global.org/sites/default/files/GPF_Maya_ Makanjee.pdf.

*MFO (Microfinance Opportunities). 2010. "Financial Diaries as a Tool for Consumer Research." MFO, Washington, DC.

MIX (Microfinance Information eXchange). 2010. "Social Performance Indicators." Report, MIX, Washington, DC, January 11.

*Nelson, Candace, ed. n.d. "Learning from Clients: Assessment Tools for Microfinance Practitioners." SEEP Network, Washington, DC.

Patton, Michael Quinn. 1990. *Qualitative Evaluation and Research Methods.* 2d ed. Newbury Park, CA: Sage Publications.

Schreiner, M. 2010. "Seven Extremely Simple Poverty Scorecards." *Enterprise Development and Microfinance* 21 (2): 118–36.

SEEP (Small Enterprise Education and Promotion) Network. 2008. "Social Performance Map." Social Performance Working Group, SEEP Network, Washington, DC.

Simanowitz, Anton. 2000. "Making Impact Assessment More Participatory." Working Paper 2, Imp-Act, University of Sussex, June.

———. 2004. "Issues in Designing Effective Microfinance Impact Assessment Systems." Working Paper 8, Imp-Act, University of Sussex, January.

Simanowitz, Anton, Ben Nkuna, and Sukor Kasim. 2000. "Overcoming the Obstacles of Identifying the Poorest Families." http://www.microcreditsummit.org/papers/povertypaperH.pdf.

*Social Performance Task Force. 2009. "Poverty Targeting and Measurement Tools in Microfinance." SPTF User Reviews, vols. 8–9. CGAP, Washington, DC, October.

Stuart, Guy, Michael Ferguson, and Monique Cohen. 2010. "Managing Vulnerability: Using Financial Diaries to Inform Innovative Products for the Poor." Report, Microfinance Opportunities, Washington, DC, January.

———. 2011. "Cash In, Cash Out: Financial Transactions and Access to Finance in Malawi." Microfinance Opportunities, Washington, DC, January.

World Bank. 2011a. "Household Financial Access: Using Surveys to Understand Household Financial Access: The Research Agenda." World Bank, Washington, DC.

———. 2011b. "Living Standards Measurement Study." World Bank, Washington, DC.

Zeller, M. 2004. "Review of Poverty Assessment Tools." Report submitted to IRIS and USAID as part of the Developing Poverty Assessment Tools project.

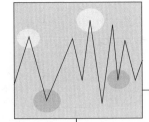

PART II

FINANCIAL SERVICE PROVIDERS

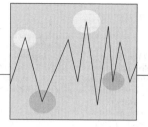

CHAPTER 6

Community-Based Providers

Candace Nelson

"There are many devices for turning small savings into usefully large lump sums—the main money-management task of the poor. Most of it is done in the informal sector" (Rutherford 2009). People often borrow from or save with a friend or a relative to help smooth cash flow, take advantage of an opportunity, prepare for a life-cycle event, or address an emergency. Informal groups, formed for the purposes of mutual aid or savings and credit, are also common. An early analysis of the Global Financial Inclusion (Global Findex) database 2012 reports, "Community-based savings methods such as savings clubs are widely used in some parts of the world but most commonly in Sub-Saharan Africa. Among those who reported any savings activity in the past 12 months, 48 percent reported using community-based savings methods"; of these, 34 percent reported having saved using only a community savings club (that is, not in addition to a formal account) (Demirgüç-Kunt and Klapper 2012).

Informal financial services tend to be flexible, convenient, and close to where the poor live; however, they may not always be available when or in the amounts needed. As discussed in chapter 1, informal financial service providers are referred to as *community-based providers* (see figure 6.1).

Community-based providers offer flexible services that can accommodate uncertain cash flows and provide discipline to encourage regular savings and loan payments. One of the greatest benefits of community-based providers is accessibility, determined by both proximity and product features (for example, minimal administrative procedures, no collateral requirements, low transaction costs, flexible terms) that suit the needs of poor women and men. However, limited product offerings and potential unreliability are some of their disadvantages. Somewhat more so than institutional providers (discussed in chapter 7), community-based providers are vulnerable to collapse or fraud, whether because of corruption,

Figure 6.1 The Range of Financial Service Providers

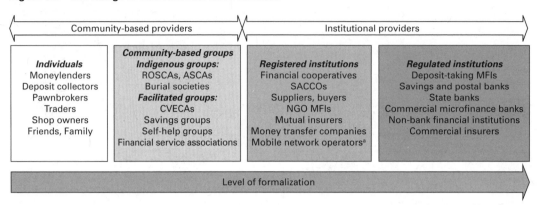

Note: ROSCAs = rotating savings and credit associations; ASCAs = accumulating savings and credit associations; CVECAs = *caisses villageoises d'épargne et de crédit autogérées*; SACCOs = savings and credit cooperatives.
a. Mobile network operators are regulated as communication companies; most are not licensed to provide financial services.

lack of discipline, or collective shocks—for example, a natural disaster or a bad harvest (Robinson 2001). Borrowing from family and friends can also be associated with stigma or loss of dignity, especially if borrowers become dependent on others or over-indebted (Ruthven 2002).

Informal or community-based financial service providers can be divided into two broad categories: indigenous and facilitated.

Indigenous providers, both individuals and groups, emerge within communities with no external input or training. Individual providers such as moneylenders generally offer basic credit services using their own capital. As local residents, they offer convenience and a rapid response. Indigenous groups are different; their most common goal is to combine small sums into bigger ones, the purpose of which varies with the type of group. A rotating savings and credit association (ROSCA) pools money to circulate among the members in turn, while a mutual aid society pools member contributions to have funds available to respond to unexpected or emergency expenses (often a specific

type of expense, such as a funeral). Group members determine the rules that govern the group.

Facilitated providers are groups (not individuals) that receive external training or assistance, typically provided by nongovernmental organizations (NGOs) or government, to develop and implement a process for saving and lending. Many forms of facilitated groups have been introduced over the years, but perhaps the largest, most well-known are India's Self-Help Groups (SHGs). Most facilitated groups follow a set of procedures designed to help them to save regularly, pool their savings, and make loans. Some operate solely within their community; others federate, borrow from banks to on-lend to their members, and take on other development activities in addition to financial services. Despite their diversity, facilitated groups serve people who typically may not have access to other financial services. They have a relationship with an external facilitator (often time-bound) that introduces an approach or model with procedures and systems to guide their financial activities.

Indigenous Providers

Individual indigenous providers include money-lenders, deposit collectors, informal traders, pawnbrokers, store owners, and informal money transfer providers. Some traders, processors, and input suppliers also operate informally, while others are more formal in nature (and thus are discussed briefly in chapter 7 as well). Indigenous groups include ROSCAs, accumulating savings and credit associations (ASCAs), and burial societies. Table 6.1 summarizes their key characteristics.

Individual Providers

Family and friends are the most common providers of financial services in the informal sector in all developing-economy regions, but especially in Sub-Saharan Africa, where 29 percent of adults report friends and family as their only source of loans (Demirgüç-Kunt and Klapper 2012). In addition to personal relations, individual community-based providers such as moneylenders or shop owners are common and operate either as licensed providers or completely informally.

As part of the local community, *moneylenders* are not only easily accessible to borrowers, but often have personal relationships that enable them to evaluate the borrower's repayment capacity. These factors allow for fast transactions in locations convenient to the client. However, moneylenders can be very expensive. For example, in many countries a standard loan from a moneylender is a "5/6 loan"—that is, for every five units borrowed, six must be repaid. This amounts to a periodic (daily, weekly, monthly) interest rate of more than 20 percent (Helms 2006). Individuals are often willing to pay high prices in exchange for receiving cash quickly and

Table 6.1   Characteristics of Community-Based Financial Service Providers: Indigenous Groups

Characteristic	Individual (money lenders, deposit collectors, traders)	Money transfer (hawala systems)	Community-based groups (ROSCAs, ASCAs, burial societies)
Legal form	No formal legal form; adhere to local customs; sometimes registered	No formal legal form, adhere to local customs; sometimes registered	May be registered with local authorities or community leaders
Regulation and oversight	Typically not regulated; sometimes local oversight or registration	Not regulated	Not regulated
Ownership	Owner operated	Owner operated	Member owned
Governance	Self-governing	Self-governing	Self-governing; sometimes an elected committee
Target market	Poor and very poor needing credit or a place to save	Poor and very poor needing quick and accessible transfer services	Poor and very poor needing small amounts of credit and a safe place to save frequently
Products	Basic credit and savings; contractual savings with some collectors	Informal money transfer across geographic distances	No capital costs; user fees to cover operating costs and profits
Funding	Own capital; interest and fees collected to cover operating costs and profits	No capital costs; user fees to cover operating costs and profits	Member contributions or savings; sometimes external borrowing; interest and fees (no operating costs)

conveniently, particularly in an emergency when there are no other options.

Pawnbrokers are also characterized by a high volume of small advances made for a relatively short period. In contrast to most moneylenders, pawnbrokers take physical possession of collateral when lending. In some countries this practice has become more formalized, with rules, standards, and registration required. Loan amounts are normally significantly smaller in value than the collateral pledged. Given the necessary processing, valuing, and storing of collateral, a pawnbroker's transaction costs may seem high given the small amounts borrowed. These transaction costs, however, are partly offset by the fact that the pawnbroker does not take time to evaluate the borrower or monitor the loan (Skully 1994). Loans are made strictly on the basis of collateral, which can be sold to recover the loan amount (most pawnbrokers also operate a retail store to sell goods that are not collected).

Deposit collectors or *money guards*—people who collect and store savings—are commonplace in the developing world. They offer a convenient way to put cash safely out of reach without having to spend money and time on travel. Deposit collectors travel to their clients, visiting their homes or businesses to collect a predetermined amount on a daily or weekly basis, while money guards generally expect clients to come to them (see box 6.1). Collection normally occurs over a specified period of time, after which the depositor's savings are returned net of fees. Fees are charged either as a percentage of the amount deposited or as a flat fee per deposit. Research shows that the amount charged is similar to the total cost, direct and indirect, of depositing directly with a bank or saving in real assets (Ashraf, Karlan, and Yin 2006). Clients may use deposit collectors for various reasons, including convenience, lack of connectivity, or cultural restrictions. Deposit collectors provide structure to accumulate savings, offering both safety and discipline. Saving with a deposit collector is not without risk, however, as clients may not be able to access funds when needed or the collector may disappear with their savings.

Shop owners sometimes hold cash they receive from clients who want it out of the house; they also often provide credit to trusted clients who take goods "on credit" and pay for them at a later date.

Especially in agriculturally dependent rural areas, *traders* may be important sources of informal credit for farmers. For example, credit may be extended to purchase raw materials with the promise that they will sell the product back to the trader.

Box 6.1 Ghana's *Susu* Collectors

Ghana is home to a large number of *susu* collectors in the informal sector who go door to door collecting savings for a fee, mostly from female market vendors and microentrepreneurs. *Susu* collectors have an average of 150–200 clients and collect deposits at homes within the village on a daily or weekly basis. The *susu* club is a variation on this collection system, wherein members go to a designated place on a scheduled day of the week to deposit their savings with the *susu* collector, who uses the group format to service a much larger number of clients.

Source: Gallardo 2001.

While credit and savings are the most common services associated with individual providers in the informal sector, *money transfer providers*—individuals specializing in transferring money from one person to another—offer a fast, usually safe, and cost-effective way to transfer funds domestically and internationally. Informal fund transfer systems vary in structure and complexity. Hand carrying cash, usually by migrants who are often family or friends, is the most basic system and especially common in situations of seasonal or circular migration, when migrants frequently return to their homes. Internationally, cash is physically transferred by couriers; domestically, it is transferred by bus companies and taxi drivers (Isern, Deshpande, and Van Doom 2005). Many senders and receivers prefer informal transfer mechanisms because they are discreet and involve little to no paperwork. They are also more accessible, especially for those without documentation in the sending country, and may seem more trustworthy because they are underpinned by personal relationships (see box 6.2).

Individual providers in the informal sector offer advantages associated with operating inside the community, including accessibility, convenience, small transactions, and familiarity. They provide direct cash-in, cash-out services, with all transactions taking place on a personal basis usually right in the village. This makes transaction costs relatively low, although the price of services is normally quite high. As individual providers are often the only option available, the poor are forced to accept both their costs and risks, including theft and fraud. Association with

---

Box 6.2 Beyond Carrying Cash: Informal Money Transfer Systems

More sophisticated informal systems exist under different names around the world, including *hundi* (South Asia), *fei-chen* (China), *hui kwan* (Hong Kong SAR, China), *padala* (the Philippines), *phei kwan* (Thailand), and *hawala* (the Middle East). Many of these systems, such as those common in African mineral-exporting countries like Angola, evolved as mechanisms for financing trade and transferring net funds against the movement of goods.

The *hawala* system used in the greater Middle East is representative of how such systems work. Typically, a migrant makes a payment to an agent (*hawaladar*) in the country where he works and lives, and the *hawaladar* provides a code to authenticate the transaction. The *hawaladar* asks his counterpart at the receiving end to make the payment to the beneficiary upon submission of the code.

After the transfer, *hawaladars* settle accounts through payment in cash or in goods and services. They are remunerated by senders through a fee or an exchange rate spread. *Hawaladars* often exploit fluctuations in demand for different currencies, which enables them to offer customers better rates than those offered by banks (most of which only conduct transactions at authorized rates of exchange). Since many *hawaladars* are also involved in businesses where money transfers are necessary, such as commodity trading, transfer services fit well into their existing activities. Remittances and business transfers are processed through the same bank accounts, incurring few, if any, additional operational costs.

Source: Isern, Deshpande, and Van Doom 2005.

---

illegal activities is also a risk, even though most people are not aware that they are taking place. Informal providers require minimal documentation and, by definition, are not regulated.

Indigenous Groups

Member-owned community groups have proven effective in providing basic financial services, especially in remote areas or urban slums characterized by inadequate infrastructure and low savings and debt capacity. They provide members mutual encouragement to save and to use money wisely, as well as an economic safety net to protect them in the event of sudden hardship. In so doing, they promote savings discipline, build social capital, increase assets, and decrease household vulnerability to financial and other shocks.

Poor women and men find these groups easily accessible because they are local and offer few barriers to entry. Members know each other and learn to rely on each other to achieve financial goals together that would be unattainable alone. A common goal of community-based financial groups is accessing a lump sum of money, either through saving or borrowing, where embedded social relations reinforce repayment. Some groups establish social funds to help members in times of crisis. This experience of managing funds together and using their collective strength both to enhance household finances and to help friends in need builds solidarity within groups— one important reason why people often maintain their membership in community-based groups even after they have gained access to formal financial services.

There are three predominant types of indigenous groups: ROSCAs, ASCAs, and informal microinsurers.

Rotating Savings and Credit Associations

ROSCAs exist in developing countries around the world and are known locally by many names: merry-go-rounds (Kenya), *tandas* (Mexico),

tontines (West Africa), chit funds (India), *kibati* (Tanzania), *stockvel* (South Africa), and *esusu* (Nigeria). ROSCAs are the simplest form of financial intermediation: several people form a group and contribute an agreed amount on a regular basis. At each meeting (or round), the money is collected, and the total is given to one member on a rotating basis. When the last member has received the lump sum, the group can choose to start a new cycle or disband.

Easy to form and manage, ROSCAs are common in many countries. A study by the Institute for Financial Management and Research in India estimates that the registered chit fund industry could be as large as 10–50 percent of all lending to priority sectors; the unregistered chit fund market could be as large as 15 times the registered market (Linder 2010).

ROSCAs are structured to allow for financial services overseen entirely by group members. Since all members contribute the same amount at each meeting, each individual member accesses the same sum of money at some point during the life of the ROSCA for use at her discretion.[1] Transactions take place only during regularly scheduled meetings (often monthly) and are typically witnessed by every member. In addition, since no money is retained by the group, often no records are required (other than possibly the list of who is to receive the funds when), and there is no need to safeguard funds. The system further reduces risk to members because it is time limited—typically lasting no more than 12 months. This mitigates potential losses should a member take the funds early and stop contributing. These characteristics make the system transparent, flexible, and simple, providing a financial service well suited to poor communities with low literacy rates. At the same time, many people who are better-off financially also join ROSCAs, both to save for a specific purpose and to take advantage of the social capital that develops. While ROSCAs typically attract more women than men, mixed ROSCAs also exist.

However, a ROSCA's simplicity is counterbalanced by risk and lack of flexibility:

- All ROSCA members receive the same amount of money in a predetermined order. Each must wait her turn regardless of need, and there is no flexibility to contribute more or less than the agreed amount.

- The fund does not grow in value, as no loans are made and no interest is paid.

- Those who are last in line risk not receiving their payout if the group disbands. When a ROSCA collapses, members who have not yet received their proceeds have no recourse.

As a result of these limitations, informal secondary markets may be created, whereby one member pays a premium to another member to switch turns. These premiums sometimes exceed 50 percent or more of the value of the proceeds.

Accumulating Savings and Credit Associations
While still indigenous, an ASCA is a more flexible and more complex group savings mechanism than a ROSCA. Like a ROSCA, group members save regularly, but the combined contributions are not distributed at each meeting; instead, savings are pooled for the purpose of lending to members. While all members save, not everyone borrows. Members borrow only when needed, in amounts that they and the rest of the members are confident will be repaid.

Since members do not all transact in the same way, ASCAs are more complex than ROSCAs. Members may borrow different amounts on different dates for different periods. Interest payments provide a return on savings that is shared fairly among the group. ASCAs may be "time-bound," with members saving, borrowing, and repaying for a predetermined amount of time, usually 6–12 months. However, given the diversity of indigenous ASCAs, the cycle can vary in length, with some choosing to operate indefinitely (see box 6.3). Depending on the time frame and the simplicity of their structure, ASCAs can operate without keeping any records by periodically dividing the accumulated funds equally. However, more complicated ASCAs require bookkeeping, particularly those that deal in large amounts or operate for long periods of time.

Box 6.3 Rural ASCAs in India

In northern India, the good ASCA leaders and bookkeepers are known in the community, so setting up a new ASCA involves little more than identifying reliable members with a shared need for financial services. Furthermore, ASCAs have adopted several measures to address the seasonality of rural cash flows:

- They start operations during surplus seasons.

- They take top-up contributions, often Rs100 per share, during start-up.
- During lean seasons members can defer contributions by converting the required savings amount into short-term loans of up to two months.
- They are much stricter about loan repayment at the end of the cycle (usually another surplus season) than they are in the middle.

Source: Abhijit and Matthews 2009.

Informal Microinsurers

The third category of community-based financial service providers focuses on the provision of insurance. Community-based organizations that provide insurance are owned and managed by their members. Their closeness to the market enables them to design and market products more easily and effectively, yet they are disadvantaged by their small size and scope of operations. They normally only operate in a limited geographic area, creating a high risk that the same misfortune will befall a large number of clients at the same time (covariance risk). The resulting simultaneous claims can deplete the organization's fund or substantially reduce individual payments. By definition, they are unlicensed and therefore cannot obtain reinsurance (see chapter 11). Some community-based microinsurers create federations with others, which can improve oversight and management, but this is not common.

According to Roth, McCord, and Liber (2007, 24), "There are numerous [types] of informal insurers throughout the poorest 100 countries, covering tens of millions of low-income people through hundreds of thousands of tiny informal groups." Two of the most common are burial societies and stretcher clubs.

Burial societies assist members during bereavement. They can consist of a few households or several thousand people from different neighborhoods in a large city. A burial society is managed at the community level; members draw up a constitution specifying operations, contributions, participation, and benefits policies. Members make their payments monthly or weekly and—similar to commercial insurance—do not receive benefits if their payments are not up to date. In the event of death, benefits are paid to the member's family to cover funeral costs. Certain burial societies lend out the money they collect in order to generate additional resources. Burial societies offer financing in times of great economic and personal uncertainty and, as such,

offer an important service at the community level. The risk of fraud is potentially high, however, as leaders may abscond with the accumulated funds (Churchill and Frankiewicz 2006).

Stretcher clubs are indigenous community groups, often found in rural areas, that address health emergencies. Members contribute small amounts weekly or monthly, as determined by club rules and the structure of the group. When a member falls ill and needs to be transported to medical care, the costs of transport and other ancillary fees associated with medical care are covered. In a few cases, members are literally carried on stretchers to the appropriate health center, but the club normally provides cash to cover other relevant costs. Stretcher clubs are managed within the community, with leaders determining formation, rules, contributions, and benefits.

Facilitated Groups

In many parts of the world, indigenous ROSCAs, ASCAs, and informal insurance schemes have been enhanced through facilitation (training and capacity-building support), often provided by nongovernmental organizations (NGOs) or other external agencies. Training supports improved governance, recordkeeping, security, and, sometimes, access to additional services. Examples of facilitated groups in the informal sector include Savings Groups (SGs), SHGs, and community associations (see table 6.2).

SGs are essentially "time-bound distributing" ASCAs. They have grown significantly since their emergence in Africa in the early 1990s. SHGs are generally not time-bound and are most often linked to banks for access to wholesale loans. They exist in various forms in many countries, but are most common in India. Less prevalent but more formalized groups include Financial Service Associations (FSAs) and *caisses villageoises d'épargne et de crédit autogérées* (CVECAs). While

Table 6.2 Characteristics of Community-Based Financial Service Providers: Facilitated Groups

Characteristic	SGs	SHGs	Community associations (FSAs, CVECAs)
Legal form	May be registered with local authorities or community leaders	May be registered with local authorities or community leaders	Registered with a central authority
Governance	Self-governing via an elected committee	Self-governing via an elected committee	Self-governing via an elected committee
Target market	Poor and very poor, requiring small amounts of credit and a safe place to save frequently	Poor and very poor, requiring credit and a safe place to save	Poor and often rural
Products	Basic savings and credit; often insurance; sometimes nonfinancial services	Basic savings and credit; sometimes nonfinancial services	Basic savings and credit products
Management and reporting	Self-managed with initial technical assistance from a facilitating agency	Often outsourced to literate members of the community or to an SHG federation	Ongoing external support provided for a fee
Funding	Member savings	Member savings and often external credit	Member savings and sometimes external credit
Sustainability: overall independence	Groups independent after 9–18 months	Need minimum of three years to function independently; often federations provide ongoing support	Varied sustainability and independence

still community-based, they are larger and behave more like financial cooperatives, remaining relatively informal. They generally rely on ongoing external management, unlike other community-based groups, where the facilitation process normally ends (although SHGs may also require ongoing assistance).

By offering financial services to members, many of whom have had limited access to savings and loans, these facilitated groups support financial inclusion. In the process, they also build members' financial capability. Through participation in groups, members have an opportunity to save and borrow, to generate more stable cash flows, and to manage the challenges associated with costly life-cycle events. Regular meetings keep financial management at the front of members' minds, leading them to think critically about their fiscal behavior. In short, they learn by doing in a relatively safe and reliable environment. Yet some advocates believe that facilitated financial groups can do more to improve members' financial capabilities and thereby increase financial inclusion. Offering financial education to group members is a proactive strategy that can enhance the benefits of facilitated groups. Financial education introduces people to good money management practices with respect to earning, spending, saving, borrowing, and investing. Thus there is a natural fit between the experiential learning linked to group participation and the content of financial education. Financial education can help to achieve the following:

- Increase members' knowledge of how to manage money, especially as they have access to small loans and lump sums that were not available to them prior to joining the group

- Enable members to plan for future expenses

- Allow members to compare products, an especially critical skill for those who use their group experience to gain access to formal microfinance institutions (MFIs) and banks

- Help members to understand the costs and benefits of the various forms of mobile money and electronic wallets to which they will increasingly have access (Ledgerwood and Jethani 2012).

Savings Groups

Savings Groups began in Niger in the 1990s to improve on traditional ROSCAs. They are now facilitated by numerous international and local NGOs, which mobilize groups, train members, and supervise their operations for a limited time.[2] These facilitating agencies introduce governance and recordkeeping systems designed to ensure effective self-management. The methodology promotes democratic participation with clear and transparent procedures that foster members' trust in the group as a safe place to save and borrow. Minimal risk, maximum transparency, a profitable structure for saving, access to small loans, and an annual lump sum of capital are the hallmarks of the SG methodology. Most SGs are in Africa, but they are beginning to spread to Asia and Latin America.[3]

Savings Group Methodology

Groups are composed of 15 to 25 self-selected individuals and generally operate in nine- to 12-month cycles. Members develop their own rules for meeting frequency (usually weekly, but sometimes fortnightly or monthly), savings requirements, and loan terms. In some variants of Savings Groups, every member saves the same amount, which the group can decide to vary during the cycle to reflect the seasonality of the local economy. In other variants, members save through the purchase of shares; the share price is decided by the group and cannot be changed during the cycle. At each meeting, every member has the opportunity to buy one or more shares, usually to a maximum of five. Their pooled savings (the loan fund) are lent to members, with loan size often limited to a maximum multiple of savings, often three times. The circulation of capital earns interest for the loan fund.

At the end of every cycle, the accumulated savings and earnings are shared among the members according to a formula chosen by the group. The "share-out" gives members access to lump sums for investment or other purposes. This end-of-cycle distribution simplifies accounting and serves as an "action audit," providing members immediate verification that their savings are intact and that the process is profitable. After each annual share-out, groups begin another cycle of saving and borrowing. At this time, members can leave and new members can join. They can make changes, such as adjusting the share price, and may decide to make an exceptional contribution (that is, a one-off contribution that exceeds the normal limit for share purchase) to recapitalize the loan fund. As groups mature, savings can easily exceed tens of thousands of dollars.

Groups elect officers annually, including positions specifically to handle money and hold keys. A treasurer or recordkeeper records member savings and loans in passbooks, a central ledger, or both, often with a symbol to accommodate illiterate or innumerate members. Some groups use memory-based systems that require no paper records at all.

Security and transparency are essential to success. Most SGs, but not all, keep their records and any extra cash in a strongbox—typically locked with keys that are kept by separate group members who open the box only during meetings and in front of all the members present—the only time that group funds are handled. Multiple locks and multiple elected key holders minimize the risk that records or money will be tampered with between meetings. Members report that they trust the group because they see what happens to their money and receive it all back at the end of the cycle.

Many SGs also have an insurance fund (often referred to as a social fund) that serves a variety of emergency and social purposes according to rules set by the group. Groups set their own policies for the social fund, notably how it is capitalized and the terms of disbursement (for example, as a grant or no-interest loan). The insurance fund is separate from the loan fund, and normally all members contribute the same amount. The insurance fund is set at a level that covers the minimum emergency needs of the group members and generally is not intended to grow.

Role of Facilitating Agencies

Facilitating agencies organize SGs and carefully train and supervise them during their first cycle. Facilitators are trainers, not service providers. They do not manage the group's activities and never touch its money or manage its recordkeeping. Facilitators train the groups intensively at start-up, after which they simply supervise procedures and routine operations as the group conducts its business. The frequency of visits diminishes as the groups demonstrate their ability to run organized, disciplined meetings and maintain accurate records. Facilitating agencies are funded by donors and do not generate any revenue from the group. While SGs are sustainable in and of themselves, facilitating agencies may continue to provide groups with other development interventions (see box 6.4).

Box 6.4 Savings Groups and Other Activities

SGs are ultimately created to provide financial services. However, where launched, they have grown, through external facilitation and spontaneous replication, into a visible network of rural groups that increasingly serve as a platform for other development (nonfinancial) services. They are natural vehicles for initiatives ranging from agricultural production and crop marketing to training in business skills, literacy, and health. Yet the addition of nonfinancial services to SGs is not straightforward. It is important to determine whether the "add-on" is truly driven by demand and to examine the incentives for adding it (that is, does the activity truly benefit members and constitute an appropriate role for the NGO to play, or is it a way for the NGO to attract additional funding?). Will it undermine the independence of Savings Groups? Additional costs, ongoing dependency on external service providers, diversion of group funds to the "extra" service(s), and spreading of group resources (members' time, energy, focus, and funds) too thinly are risks that practitioners must consider. Furthermore, with limited resources, facilitating agencies face the difficult choice between strengthening existing Savings Groups with additional programming or creating new ones.

Source: Ashe and Nelson 2012; Rippey and Fowler 2011.

Facilitating agencies have assumed the responsibility for tracking SG performance using a standardized management information system (see chapter 13). In addition, they report to the Savings Groups Information Exchange (SAVIX), an online database that provides transparent and standardized data on SG performance and outreach (see chapter 5).

Savings Group Sustainability and Replication

Sustainability and simplicity are key strengths of this model, enabling self-management and spontaneous group replication. After an initial training period, SGs manage themselves; early research indicates that most groups continue to operate indefinitely. Furthermore, members introduce the model to others, leading to the multiplication of groups; an investment in one group often results in the formation of two or three others (Anyango et al. 2007; see box 6.5).

Most facilitating agencies build into their methodology a system of purposeful replication through community-based trainers (CBTs), also known as village agents or replicating agents—individual members whom the facilitator trains to operate independently. Eventually, the paid facilitator shifts to a more supervisory role and CBTs are paid directly by the community, either through cash, shares, or in kind (such as free labor during planting season). This fee-for-service model is taking hold in many variations across multiple SG programs. It significantly reduces facilitation costs and establishes a market-based system for communities to promote new groups and support existing ones after the facilitating agency leaves (see box 6.6).

While fee-for-service seems like the next logical step from a market development perspective, it is not yet clear whether the market for training services will be sufficient in the longer term to support local trainers. If replication is robust, the most cost-effective option for supporting the emergence of SGs may be to invest in building a critical mass of them and to rely on a combination of spontaneous fee-for-service and

---

Box 6.5 Paths to Savings Group Replication

Field research in Kenya found that SGs replicate "spontaneously" without any external facilitation in the following ways:

- *Fission of large groups.* As groups add members, they get unwieldy and sometimes split into two or more groups.
- *Splinter groups.* Members object to some aspect of their group and start a new one.
- *Social entrepreneurs.* Dynamic group members form additional groups, usually as a civic service, but sometimes for a fee.
- *ROSCA upgrading.* An SG member introduces the approach to her ROSCA or another group.
- *Natal village.* Women who move to their husband's village visit their families back home and introduce the SG model.
- *Inspired by.* Neighbors carefully observe meetings and copy the procedures.
- *Clusters.* Groups often meet at the same time and in the same place, forming a cluster of groups. The visibility and dynamism of clusters attract new members, encouraging the formation of new groups.

Source: Rippey and O'Dell 2010; Digital Divide Data 2011.

Box 6.6 Fee-for-Service: Variations on a Theme

In India, the Aga Khan Foundation initially operated its SG program through local partner NGOs using paid staff. However, as the program matured, the local partners began using CBTs to ensure continued expansion and sustainability. CBTs are remunerated at a rate of Rs 1 per member per meeting and are paid exclusively by members of the groups they mobilize and train. The funds are deposited in a separate bag held in the cash box and may be withdrawn by the CBT at any meeting.

In Kenya, Uganda, and Tanzania, Catholic Relief Services has built a private commercial system for training and supporting SGs. It hires field agents who spend one year learning to perform their duties. After a rigorous certification process, these agents become private service providers. The communities in which they work are prepared from the beginning for the eventuality that they will assume responsibility for paying the private service provider.

In western Kenya CARE piloted the use of independent contractors—both individual entrepreneurs and faith-based organizations—that contracted their own CBTs to mobilize and train SGs in return for a fee per successful group trained. The pilot dramatically reduced the cost per member trained, and the critical mass of SGs created under the project has raised their visibility, whereby communities are slowly agreeing to pay the trainers to help them to establish their own groups. Further demand for CBT services comes from existing groups seeking intermittent assistance even after graduation.

Source: David Panetta, Aga Khan Foundation; Ferrand 2011.

voluntary replication to spur group expansion (Ferrand 2011).

Financial Linkages

Although advocates of SGs have championed their simplicity—locally based, accessible, transparent, autonomous financial service providers that are free of debt obligations to external lenders—as groups mature, access to formal financial services may be important. SGs do not, nor are they designed to, meet all the financial needs of their members, and some of their limitations can be addressed by linking to formal financial service providers. Among the most urgent needs is the ability to store cash assets safely; this arises primarily near the end of a cycle, when all loans are due in anticipation of the share-out. At this time, groups have been known to hold thousands of dollars in their lockbox, at significant risk.[4] However, the need for formal savings vehicles to manage liquidity may exist throughout the cycle; according to SAVIX, in the first quarter of 2012, globally, loans outstanding represented only 53.2 percent of total performing assets of SGs, indicating that there may be significant excess liquidity.[5] Innovations are emerging that will enable SGs to deposit excess liquidity through members' mobile phones (see box 6.7).

While SGs have been linked to other financial service providers for savings, credit, payments, and, in some cases, insurance products, the wisdom and benefits of doing so are still debated.[6] Advocates suggest that such financial linkages put Savings Groups one step higher on the ladder to formal financial inclusion, while others are concerned about elite capture, loss of autonomy, and group sustainability, arguing that SGs are

Box 6.7 Bank Linkages through Mobile Phones

A partnership between CARE, Equity Bank, and Orange allows CARE Savings Groups in Kenya to open an Equity Bank account (*pamoja*) and deposit cash into an interest-bearing group savings account without visiting a physical branch. This is made possible by the extensive network of Equity Bank and Orange agents throughout Kenya.

To ensure account security, CARE, Orange, and Equity Bank developed a first-of-its-kind security verification system that requires three members to provide personal identification numbers for every transaction—the electronic equivalent of the three-padlock metal lockbox that prevents any one person from accessing the group's cash. Although individuals have accessed bank accounts with mobile phones before, this is the first system that

allows groups the same type of secure mobile access.

The second feature, which was in the final stage of testing in 2012, is that all group members can register their cell phones enabling them to receive a text message announcing any transaction made to the group account. This assures them that no one has tampered with the group's resources between meetings.

Equity Bank's *pamoja* savings account offers a safe place to save, a 2.5 percent annual interest rate, no account maintenance or deposit fees, and minimal withdrawal fees. SGs have 24-hour access to their accounts using the Eazzy 24/7 mobile phone platform. Using the same system, Equity will soon offer loans to SGs.

Source: CARE 2012; www.savings-revolution.org.

---

financial service providers in their own right and should be left alone. These debates center on the following questions:

- Should linkages be created for the purposes of savings, credit, or both?

- Should the focus be on linking individual members only to formal financial institutions or on linking the whole group?

- Is there a way to preserve the original group and its characteristics, while simultaneously fostering new relationships with other providers?

- What are the roles and responsibilities of the facilitating agency in financial literacy and consumer protection as it fosters formal linkages?

Self-Help Groups

Initiated in India in the 1980s, SHGs are groups of 10–20 people—the vast majority of whom are women and marginal farmers or landless agricultural laborers—who save and borrow together. They are facilitated by a diverse set of external organizations that include NGOs, farmers clubs, government agencies, and even banks (see box 6.8). These facilitators are collectively referred to as self-help promotional institutions.

Initially, SHGs function much like indigenous ASCAs; members save regularly and use pooled savings for loans. However, within a relatively short amount of time (six to eight months), most access credit from banks. In fact, they are essentially credit driven; they save primarily as a prerequisite for a bank loan. They also serve as a community platform from which women become

Box 6.8 Banks as Facilitators

In a program of the Oriental Bank of Commerce in India, the only role of the bank's Rudrapur branch is to service SHGs. The branch's two officers oversee about 1,000 five-member SHGs and perform most support functions. The bank charges groups 11 percent a year on loans to cover the costs of funds, support services, and overhead. Individual "facilitators" provide day-to-day transaction and bookkeeping services directly to groups. Each facilitator is contracted by about 200 SHGs and is paid 1 percent of each group's outstanding loans.

Source: Isern et al. 2007.

---

active in village affairs, stand for local election, or take action to address social or community issues, such as the abuse of women, alcohol, the dowry system, schools, and local water supply (Sinha et al. 2010).

Self-Help Groups have achieved impressive outreach—by 2010, nearly 7 million groups were serving more than 80 million members, making them the dominant form of microfinance in India and perhaps the world. Although pioneered by NGOs, the SHG model was taken to scale by the National Bank for Agriculture and Rural Development (NABARD), a government wholesale lender, through its flagship Self-Help Group Bank Linkage Program, introduced in 1992 (Lee 2010).[7] The potential for this relationship was catalyzed by government-mandated, priority sector lending for banks (40 percent of all bank credit must be lent to borrowers from priority sectors such as agriculture, microenterprises, and low-income populations). Banks, most of which are government owned, maintain an active presence in densely populated rural areas, facilitating access by rural clients.[8] Since launching the program, NABARD has lent billions of dollars to hundreds of banks to on-lend to SHGs, significantly expanding their number.

SHG membership is open to all and covers all social groups, including scheduled castes and tribes. Self-Help Groups are often single-caste groups. A study of 214 SHGs in four states found that two-thirds of the groups sampled are single caste, reflecting both the practical advantages of neighborhood proximity and the greater ease of organizing people by affinity (EDA Rural Systems and APMAS 2006). The formation of SHGs—in which villages and with whom—is influenced by the targeting policies of the self-help promotional institutions. Some target only poor areas and poor people, some have a softer target of *some* poor people, and some pursue a community-inclusive approach (EDA Rural Systems and APMAS 2006).

Self-Help Group Methodology

Members join SHGs both to save (at least initially) and to access loans. During the initial months, members focus on building the group fund to increase the amount available for internal lending and, more important, to become eligible for larger, external loans. Once the group has saved the amount that the bank requires to access wholesale loans, members often stop saving with the group (Isern et al. 2007).

An SHG typically qualifies for a bank loan after it has deposited savings with the bank for a minimum of six months. Banks make one loan to the group, which on-lends to members. Initial loans usually start at Rs 10,000 (about US$186 as of October 2012), with repayment within six months to one year. Banks charge SHGs 8–10 percent interest, and groups typically charge members 24 percent. Subsequent loans can be larger and longer term (three to five years). Loan size is normally based on a ratio of the group's savings on deposit, and the average is 4:1; however, this ratio varies from 1:1 to as high as 20:1 (Isern et al. 2007; EDA Rural Systems and APMAS 2006; Srinivasan 2010).

Because members' savings are used as a guarantee against funds borrowed from the bank, they have limited access to them. Generally, SHGs "roll over" or retain some earnings at the end of the cycle. That they do not "cash out" entirely allows them to have longer loan terms, but requires more sophisticated bookkeeping (Lee 2010). The fact that they are not time-bound also distinguishes them from other types of ASCAs. Yet with millions of SHGs, diversity is a given; some SHGs do cash out on a regular basis, and many do not take external loans. An estimated 25 to 30 percent of SHGs are not linked to a bank (Lee 2010).

Self-Help Group Formation and Technical Assistance

Self-help promotional institutions train, monitor, and support SHGs and often help with recordkeeping. Most are funded by government banks to carry out this role, which varies greatly by institution; some are committed to grass-roots social mobilization and change, while others are more narrowly focused on establishing permanent financial services at the village level. Their diversity is reflected in the activities they offer. In addition to training and facilitating bank linkages, they may offer services related to reproductive health, conflict resolution, school construction, sanitation, watershed management, and social initiatives to advance the disenfranchised (for example, advocating for the rights of lower castes, against child marriage, and for educating female child laborers).[9]

Similar to participation in an SG, participation in an SHG sometimes leads to employment, as individuals can also serve as facilitators for other groups (see box 6.9).

Box 6.9 Individuals as Facilitators

Sudesh is a "promoting individual" who works directly with more than 30 SHGs, most of which she has "given" to a local bank manager or a government program to contribute to their targets:

> I was leader of a group under the government's program. The staff asked me to form a few more groups in my village ... Since then, I have promoted more than 30 groups in neighboring villages. This is my main job, since I am working with all these groups at the same time. The bank manager said that he needed a few groups, so I gave him a few [in exchange for Rs 800 for each SHG]; then DRDA [the District Rural Development Agency] needed some groups, so I gave them some [also for Rs 800 for each SHG]. Now, DRDA's targets are achieved, so they don't need any more groups, and the banker needs SHGs from time to time. I still have eight groups. I charge each group Rs 20 a month for writing the records, which gives me a good income.

Source: EDA Rural Systems and APMAS 2006.

In addition to forming SHGs, some promotional institutions contribute grants or revolving funds to member savings for internal lending (EDA Rural Systems and APMAS 2006). Although most do not intermediate loan funds from the bank to the group, they can be instrumental in establishing the linkage; on average, SHGs rely on their assistance for three years before being able to operate independently.

The government has encouraged SHGs to federate into larger organizations to ease the withdrawal of promotional institutions from their financial and nonfinancial roles. Such federations can also support banks that wish to on-lend to SHGs by serving as an intermediary and providing a single point of contact. In this role, some federations intermediate funds, borrowing from banks to on-lend to member groups (Srinivasan 2010). They also build capacity, monitor performance, and provide policy guidance.

Although several state governments actively promote and fund SHG federations (there are 1,100 in Andhra Pradesh, 12,000 in Tamil Nadu, and 7,800 in Orissa) with the expectation that banks will provide them with loans for on-lending, federations face significant financial and, especially, organizational challenges (Srinivasan 2010; Lee 2010). Furthermore, some question their added value, given that India has the largest network of bank branches in the world, and most villages are close to some type of branch. Some have suggested that the rationale for federating may be more social than financial. Federating affords groups more visibility and gives them experience with public interactions. Yet to achieve either financial or social goals, SHG federations require better governance, staffing, and organizational processes and systems (Sinha et al. 2010).

Thus SHGs receive organizational, operational, and financial support from multiple sources. The facilitating agency (NGO, government, or bank) usually employs a field agent to train and monitor the group, the federation offers technical assistance (such as help with bookkeeping), and the lender often maintains a dedicated staff for assisting SHGs.

Challenges

Well-managed SHGs can be profitable in their quest to bring financial services to the poor and marginalized. Their promotional costs compare favorably with those of other approaches to microfinance (Isern et al. 2007). Yet few are well managed, and many perform poorly. Their recordkeeping systems are complex, partly due to the exigencies of external loans and partly due to the fact that most carry on their financial activity from year to year without stopping periodically to distribute funds. Without full cash-out, SHGs need to have some level of transactional analysis to keep track of different terms and payments, arrears (sometimes exceeding one year), and the complexity of liquidity and risk management (Lee 2010). The number of records, and the amount of work to maintain them, prompts many to rely on their promotional institution or federation to keep their records. One specialized support institution for SHGs—the Andhra Pradesh Mahila Abhivruddhi Society—reported in 2002 that the records of only 15 percent of SHGs were good, while the records of nearly 40 percent of SHGs in Andhra Pradesh were grossly neglected or nonexistent (Isern et al. 2007). Furthermore, since external loans are linked to savings, SHGs have a strong incentive to overstate their savings and understate their losses (Matthews and Devi 2010). Researchers have called recordkeeping the "dark side of Self-Help Groups" (EDA Rural Systems and APMAS 2006).

Other issues challenging the performance of SHGs include high default of intragroup loans (the repayment rates on internal loans within groups are reportedly as low as 35 to 40 percent) and the equal distribution of bank loans among members, with those who receive more than they are able to invest lending the excess to others (Srinivasan 2010).

However, the Indian SHG model remains unique for its sheer size and outreach to the poor; SHGs are the link between individuals and rural regional banks, commercial banks, and cooperatives. Although community based, they illustrate how the government, formal banks, and organized poor clients can work together to respond to the financial service needs of the rural poor. In addition to providing access to credit, they are the entry point for many social activities (see box 6.10).

Other Facilitated Groups

There have been dozens of other models for community-based groups whose purpose is to

---

Box 6.10 Self-Help Groups: A Holistic View

Several key factors, rooted in India's banking policies, explain how SHGs have flourished, engaging more than 70 million people. First, the Reserve Bank of India mandates that banks must have 40 percent of their portfolios in a "priority sector," and SHGs are one of the options for meeting these requirements. Second, a NABARD directive in 1993 allowed informal, unregistered SHGs to be treated as "legal persons," enabling banks to open accounts and transact business with them. Overall, approximately 70 percent of SHGs are linked to a bank for loans, and more than 16 percent of all bank lending to priority sectors is done through them.

As one of India's national flagship programs, SHGs are a key government strategy for offering financial services to unbanked communities and expanding financial inclusion, particularly directed toward women. Perhaps more important, they are increasingly used to deliver many other development schemes and programs. As a result, they have become much more than informal financial groups. Many are engaged collectively in common livelihoods, marketing, and procurement activities. Health and nutrition workers use them to deliver services; SHGs often double as the local water management committee; schemes for low-cost housing, pensions, and group insurance are delivered through them; a large-scale employment guarantee scheme delivers payments through them; social campaigns by local leaders use them as their organizational base; and politicians of all parties and ideologies woo them in an effort to influence opinion and win elections. From the top levels of government policy and planning through to the local *panchayat* (village government), SHGs have become one of the most visible platforms for women's development and empowerment; they are a household name for public and development programs alike.

SHGs represent a counterpoint in the microfinance world—a model that is owned and managed by the members themselves, encompassing a large set of small, decentralized, informal cooperative organizations, enabled, actively supported, promoted, and resourced by the state, with women as its central focus. However, the realization of this vision varies significantly: Some civil society organizations and women's initiatives emphasize "self-help" and empowerment; others focus on a more minimalist financial inclusion numbers game, with greater emphasis on delivering loans. Capacity and performance vary vastly. While the SHG model is relatively simple, its implementation has evolved in complex ways, and the groups have become important institutions for social, political, and economic participation.

Source: Anuj Jain, Coady Institute.

facilitate saving and lending for groups who experience barriers (for example, distance, cost, trust) to accessing more formal providers. Some are very small, limiting participation to 20–30 members; others federate small groups in order to serve hundreds. Two examples are Financial Service Associations (FSAs) and CVECAs (self-managed village savings and credit banks) in Africa.

Financial Service Associations

Introduced in Benin in 1997 with support from the International Fund for Agricultural Development, FSAs are member-owned and -operated institutions at the village level. With external technical support, they have been replicated in several countries—Guinea, Mauritania, Kenya, Uganda, and Sierra Leone—producing variations to the model. Some leverage their equity base, built from member shares, with loans from commercial banks (Helms 2006). In Sierra Leone, some offer long-term credit and group approaches to marketing goods and produce (IFAD 2010). Membership can include groups and institutions, such as savings clubs, schools, churches, and health clinics. They range in size from 300 to 10,000 members.

Membership requires a purchase of shares, which can be sold to other members but not withdrawn. FSAs are governed by a general assembly of shareholders, which elects a board of directors and an audit committee. Their legal form also varies from country to country. In some countries they are not registered at all, while in others they are registered with the relevant government ministry as community-based organizations or cooperatives.

The original goal—to become self-reliant following initial training and oversight—has been compromised by poor management and weak governance. Managers often lack the basic capacity and experience needed to manage a financial institution; the absence of a clear separation of responsibilities between management and governance has led to problems such as disbursing loans to friends, relatives, or influential board members who may not feel obliged to repay them. To counter these challenges, most FSAs have management contracts under which an external service company is hired to help to manage the operations (see box 6.11). Others, particularly in Uganda, have transformed into financial cooperatives.

Box 6.11 Financial Service Associations in Kenya

In Kenya, the K-Rep Development Agency (KDA) promotes FSAs; from 1997 until 2007, 77 associations with a total of 34,000 members were established in 17 districts—including the far north, where agro-ecological conditions are very challenging, livelihoods are predominantly livestock based, and population densities are low. With support from the Financial Sector Deepening Project, the KDA registered K-Rep Fedha Services (KFS), a limited liability company, to provide both management services and supervision to the associations for a fee. In addition to training, the

KFS also assists with market research and product development, strategic planning, business development, branding, and marketing. The aim is to achieve sustainable management and oversight. Marked improvement in performance has led to increased community confidence in and use of FSAs. In 2012 the KFS network included 44 FSAs, totaling approximately 122,000 members. FSD Kenya estimates that there are an additional 80,000 members in 40 associations outside of the KFS network.

Source: FSD Kenya 2007; communication with Felistus Mbole, Financial Sector Deepening Project, June 2012.

CVECAs

CVECAs are member-based organizations with an emphasis on remote rural areas. Originally promoted by the French-based Centre International de Développement et de Recherche, they grew out of an interest in improving the traditional model of cooperatives in West Africa. CVECAS are member-based microfinance intermediaries facilitated by external technical support. They are designed to operate in rural areas with clients who are primarily subsistence farmers, with minimal nonfarm income. While most CVECAs have fewer than 250 members, they achieve flexibility and economies of scale by networking together into regional federations (Chao-Béroff n.d.). CVECAs were first developed in the Dogon region of Mali in the late 1980s and have been replicated in other countries in Africa (Cameroon, The Gambia), adapting the original model to suit the local environment. In The Gambia, they are known as village savings and credit associations. Their primary role is to provide safe and easy access to savings, offering both current accounts and term deposits, as well as loans. Some of these groups also take on external credit, distorting the savings incentives and creating another set of challenges around repayment, ownership, and vitality of the groups. Many also suffer from weak governance, a common issue for many financial service providers (Secka 2011).

Notes

1. Many ROSCAs form expressly to help members to purchase the same item—for example, mattresses, cookware, solar lamps, or iron roofing sheets.

2. At the time of writing, well-known international NGOs including CARE, Catholic Relief Services, Oxfam America, Freedom from Hunger, the Aga Khan Foundation, Plan International, and World Vision were facilitating SGs.

3. As of May 2012, SGs globally counted more than 6 million members. http://savingsgroups.com.

4. Steps for managing this risk include dividing up the group funds among members until the share-out date or storing them in a government office.

5. This result is based only on SGs that are currently trained and monitored by facilitating agencies. Over time, the level of loan activity varies significantly depending on local market opportunities and access to other financial service providers. At the same time, in a research sample tracking 332 groups in 33 projects, loans as a percentage of outstanding assets were significantly higher, at 81 percent.

6. This section draws from Ledgerwood and Jethani (2012).

7. The growth of SHGs has been most robust in the south; more than 50 percent of such groups in the NABARD program are found in the state of Andhra Pradesh, where 72 percent of households belong to one. Here, the State Credit Plan allocated 24 percent of credit for lending to SHGs, possibly the highest level of support available to any type of community-based group in the country. As much as 65 percent of the total loan exposure of some branches was to SHGs (Srinivasan 2010).

8. In a study of 214 SHGs in nine districts in India, the average distance to a bank was 3.5 kilometers (EDA Rural Systems and APMAS 2006).

9. A study of 214 SHGs found that 62 percent were engaged by their promotional institution in a "microfinance plus development" model; in Andhra Pradesh, the proportion rose to 90 percent (EDA Rural Systems and APMAS 2006).

References and Further Reading

* Key works for further reading.
Abhijit, Sharma, and Brett Hudson Matthews. 2009. "Village Financial Systems in Northeast India." Focus Note 21, MicroSave India, July.

Anyango, Ezra, Ezekiel Esipisu, Lydia Opoku, Susan Johnson, Markku Malkamaki, and Chris Musoke. 2007. "Village Savings and Loan Associations: Experience from Zanzibar." *Small Enterprise Development Journal* 18 (1): 11–24.

*Ashe, Jeffrey, and Candace Nelson. 2012. "Introduction." In *Savings Groups at the Frontier*, ed. Candace Nelson. Washington, DC: SEEP Network, November.

Ashraf, Nava, Dean Karlan, and Wesley Yin. 2006. "Deposit Collectors." *Advances in Economic Analysis and Policy* 6 (2): Article 5. http://www.bepress.com/bejeap/advances/vol6/iss2/art5.

Ballem, A., and R. Kumar. 2010. "Savings Mobilisation in SHGs: Opportunities and Challenges." Focus Note 44, MicroSave India. http://www.microfinancegateway.org/gm/document-1.1.6347/IFN_44_Savings_Mobilisation_in_SHGs.pdf.

CARE. 2012. "CARE, Equity Bank, and Orange Launch Partnership to Connect Community Savings Groups to Banks Using Mobile Phones." Press release, CARE, Nairobi, March 16.

Chao-Béroff, René. n.d. "Cooperatives and Community-Based Financial Systems." CGAP, Washington, DC. http://www.cgap.org/gm/document-1.9.2310/africaday_Theme4.pdf.

*Churchill, Craig, and Cheryl Frankiewicz. 2006. *Making Microfinance Work: Managing for Improved Performance*. Geneva: International Labour Organization.

*Demirgüç-Kunt, Aslı, and Leora Klapper. 2012. "Measuring Financial Inclusion: The Global Findex Database." Policy Research Working Paper 6025, World Bank, Washington, DC.

Digital Divide Data. 2011. "Results of Study of Post-Project Replication of Groups in COSALO I." FSD Kenya, Nairobi.

*EDA Rural Systems and APMAS (Anhdra Pradesh Mahila Abhivruddhi Society). 2006. "Self-Help Groups in India: A Study of the Lights and Shades." EDA and APMAS, Gurgaon and Hyderabad. http://www.edarural.com/documents/SHG-Study/Executive-Summary.pdf.

Ferrand, David. 2011. "Keynote Paper 1: Strengthening Financial Service Markets." PowerPoint presentation at M4P Hub conference "Developing Market Systems: Seizing the Opportunity for the Poor," Brighton, U.K., November 7–9. http://www.m4phub.org/userfiles/file/David%20Ferrand%20Empress.pdf.

FSD (Financial Sector Deepening) Kenya. 2007. *Annual Report*. Nairobi: FSD Kenya.

Gallardo, Joselito. 2001. "A Framework for Regulating Microfinance Institutions: The Experience in Ghana and the Philippines." Financial Sector Development Department, World Bank, Washington, DC, November.

Helms, Brigit. 2006. "Access for All: Building Inclusive Financial Systems." CGAP, Washington, DC.

Helms, Brigit, and Douglas Pearce. 2001. "Financial Service Associations: The Story So Far." CGAP, Washington, DC.

IFAD (International Fund for Agricultural Development). 2010. "FIDAction in West and Central Africa." *IFAD Newsletter* 18 (October).

Isern, Jennifer, Rani Deshpande, and Judith Van Doom. 2005. "Crafting a Money Transfers Strategy: Guidance for Pro-Poor Financial Service Providers." Occasional Paper 10, CGAP, Washington, DC.

*Isern, Jennifer, L. B. Prakash, Syed Hashemi, Robert Christen, and Gautam Ivatury. 2007. "Sustainability of Self-Help Groups: Two Analyses." Occasional Paper 12, CGAP, Washington, DC.

Johnson, S., M. Malkamaki, and K. Wanjau. 2005. "Tackling the 'Frontiers' of Microfinance in Kenya: The Role for Decentralized Services." Decentralised Financial Services, Kenya.

*Ledgerwood, Joanna, and Alyssa Jethani. 2012. "Savings Groups and Financial Inclusion." In *Savings Groups at the Frontier*, ed. Candace Nelson. Washington, DC: SEEP Network.

Lee, Nanci. 2010. "Community-Based Financial Services: African Savings Groups vs. Indian

Self-Help Groups." Unpublished report, Aga Khan Foundation.

Linder, Chris, with contributions from Denny George. 2010. "Who Says You Can't Do MicroSavings in India? Part 1: Community-Based/Owned." Focus Note 45, MicroSave India, July.

Matthews, Brett H., and Trivikrama Devi. 2010. "SHGs Should Balance or Break." Focus Note 19, MicroSave India.

*Rippey, P., and B. Fowler. 2011. "Beyond Financial Services: A Synthesis of Studies on the Integration of Savings Groups and Other Development Activities." Aga Khan Foundation. www.akdn.org/publications/2011_akf_beyond_financial_services.pdf.

Rippey, Paul, and Marcia O'Dell. 2010. "The Permanence and Value of Savings Groups in CARE Kenya's COSAMO Programme." Savings Groups Learning Initiative, Aga Kahn Foundation.

Robinson, Marguerite. 2001. *The Microfinance Revolution: Sustainable Finance for the Poor*. Washington, DC: World Bank.

*Roth, Jim, Michael McCord, and Dominic Liber. 2007. *The Landscape of Microinsurance in the World's 100 Poorest Countries*. Appleton, WI: MicroInsurance Centre.

*Rutherford, Stuart, with Sukhwinder Arora. 2009. *The Poor and Their Money*. Updated version. Bourton on Dunsmore, U.K.: Practical Action Publishing.

Ruthven, O. 2002. "Money Mosaics: Financial Choice and Strategy in a West Delhi Squatter Settlement." *Journal of International Development* 14: 249–71.

Secka, Ndegene. 2011. "Economic Challenges Impending Gambian Entrepreneurship." *Today—The Gambia's Quality Newspaper*, February 1. http://microfinanceafrica.net/tag/visaca/.

*Sinha, Frances, Ajay Tankha, K. Raja Reddy, and Malcolm Harper. 2010. *Microfinance Self-Help Groups in India: Living Up to Their Promise?* London: Practical Action Publishing.

Skully, Michael T. 1994. "The Development of the Pawnshop Industry in East Asia." http://library.wur.nl/way/catalogue/documents/FLR21.pdf.

*Srinivasan, N. 2010. *Microfinance India: State of the Sector Report 2010*. New Delhi: ACCESS Development Services and Sage Publications India.

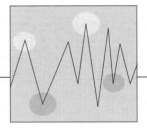

CHAPTER 7

Institutional Providers

Joanna Ledgerwood

Chapter 1 provides an overview of the types of financial service providers within the core of the financial ecosystem. Chapter 6 focuses on community-based providers that operate primarily in the informal sector. This chapter focuses on institutional providers—those that are more formal in nature; that is, they generally have brick and mortar branches (but not always), incur operating expenses, generate revenue, maintain financial accounts (including producing financial statements), and are usually registered and often regulated.

A financial institution is a collection of assets—human, financial, and other—combined to perform activities such as granting loans, underwriting insurance, or mobilizing deposits. Projects are not institutions—institutions serve a permanent function within the core of a market system. Financial institutions that provide financial services to poor women and men include nongovernmental organization (NGO) microfinance institutions (MFIs), financial cooperatives, formal commercial microfinance banks, specialized MFIs and other non-bank financial institutions (NBFIs) such as insurance and leasing companies, as well as payment service providers. They can be found on the right side of figure 7.1.

These institutions differ in their organizational structure and governance, the types of products and services offered, their legal form, and the associated supervision by authorities. Although they may lack the flexibility and proximity of community-based providers, they often can offer a broader variety of products and services. The types of financial products and services that a provider offers are influenced by its legal structure and related regulation (if applicable), capacity, mandate, and target market. Most, but

---

Contributions to this chapter were made by Julie Earne and Peter McConaghy.

Figure 7.1 The Range of Financial Service Providers

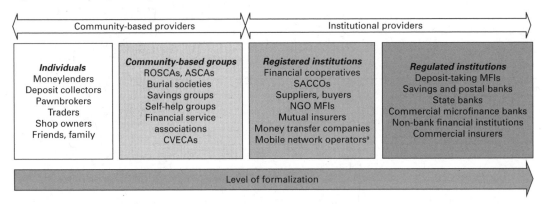

Note: ROSCAs = rotating savings and credit associations; ASCAs = accumulating savings and credit associations; CVECAs = *caisses villageoises d'épargne et de crédit autogérées;* SACCOs = savings and credit cooperatives.
a. Mobile network operators are regulated as communication companies; most are not licensed to provide financial services.

not all, financial service providers provide credit—either to their members, as with financial cooperatives, or to the public at-large, as with banks and NGOs. Most nonregulated institutions and even some regulated NBFIs (finance companies, insurance companies) are generally not allowed to mobilize and intermediate savings from the public. However, financial cooperatives can normally intermediate deposits within their membership. Although some banks, MFIs, and cooperatives sell insurance, this product is largely restricted to insurance companies, as is insurance underwriting. In some countries, banks, regulated MFIs, and some mobile network operators, in addition to institutions licensed as money transfer companies, provide payment services and other transaction accounts. Institutional providers generally require more sophisticated operations than informal providers, which often mean professional staff and relatively more complex systems. The financial sustainability and independence of different providers vary primarily in relation to time and, in some cases, objectives. NGO MFIs and transforming MFIs take time to reach sustainability, depending on their target market, support provided, and overall mission,

while microfinance banks tend to take a few years to break even because they need to invest in infrastructure and develop their market. To date, microinsurance providers have found it very difficult to reach sustainability.

This chapter discusses the types of institutions that provide financial services to poor women and men. Institutional management issues, such as human resource management, product development, social performance monitoring, and financial reporting and risk management, are discussed in chapters 14 and 15.

Characteristics of Financial Institutions

A financial institution's structure is determined by its legal form, its ownership and governance structure, the degree to which it is supervised by the state, and the types of clients it serves. These, in turn, influence an institution's product offering, financial management, reporting needs, funding sources, and overall financial sustainability and independence. Table 7.1 summarizes the key characteristics of institutional financial service providers.

Table 7.1 Characteristics of Institutional Financial Service Providers

Type of provider	Legal form	Regulation and oversight	Ownership	Governance	Client type	Products	Management and reporting	Funding	Sustainability and independence
Financial cooperatives	Registered with central authority	Credit unions may be regulated; oversight by specialized body	Owned by members	Board of directors or management committee elected by members	A range of clients, depending on members	Basic savings and credit, although inherently savings led	Professionally managed to varying degrees; report to supervisory authorities	Equity provided from member contributions; deposits and some external debt	Medium to high depending on capacity of management and governing body
NGO MFIs and multipurpose NGOs	Registered as an NGO, not-for-profit institution, or company limited by guarantee	Not regulated; may be subject to government oversight	No owners, strong ownership characteristics among founders and board	Board of directors, appointed by founders and funders	Poor, "unbanked" clients; for multipurpose NGOs, various target clients and beneficiaries	Traditionally credit led; multipurpose NGOs generally add financial services to other activities	Professionally managed to varying degrees; may need to report to registration body	Grants and debt from development institutions, foundations, socially responsible investors, or aggregators	Low to medium (high costs and lack of separation of activities can delay or prevent sustainability of financial activities)
Deposit-taking MFIs	Licensed as a bank or other form as per regulatory requirements	Regulated and supervised by central bank, ministry, or a specialized body	Mostly private shareholders; some development banks as initial shareholders	Board of directors appointed by shareholders	Unserved or underserved individuals or micro or small businesses	Credit, savings, insurance, payment services; terms may be modified for client needs	Professionally managed; report to central bank or supervisory authority	Mix of equity and debt financing from both private and public sources, deposits	Varied, costs to transform can be high; ongoing costs of regulatory requirements can be high
NBFIs: credit companies, insurance companies, leasing companies	Licensed as an NBFI or modified financial institution (determined by country-specific legal charter)	Regulated by central bank or specialized body or by one or more government units	Mix of public and private shareholders; sometimes other financial institutions or other companies	Board of directors appointed by shareholders	Clients vary depending on type of products (for example, credit or insurance)	Range from credit only, leasing, insurance; normally not able to intermediate deposits	Professionally managed; report to supervisory authority	Mix of equity and debt financing from both private and public sources	Medium to high; initial support may be required depending on target market

(continued next page)

Table 7.1 *(continued)*

Type of provider	Legal form	Regulation and oversight	Ownership	Governance	Client type	Products	Management and reporting	Funding	Sustainability and independence
Suppliers, wholesale buyers, processors	Registered as a company under primary business	Credit services generally not regulated	Varies; can be owner operated or part of larger company	Varies	Rural farmers	Basic credit embedded in purchases	Little formal structure, provider driven	Funding from working capital; may have debt	High sustainability
Rural, savings or postal banks	Licensed as a bank	Regulated by central bank or specialized body or by one or more government units	Shareholders, government and/or private	Board of directors appointed by shareholders	Broad target group: poor and nonpoor; generally rural	Primarily savings; wide distribution network leveraged for payment services	Professionally managed to varying degrees; report to regulators	Equity and debt financing, generally from public sources and savings	Medium to high
State banks	Licensed with the central authorities; incorporated as either a parastatal or shareholding company	Normally regulated and supervised by the central bank	Shareholders, generally government, some private	Board of directors appointed, influenced by government	General population; government sometimes mandates poor or rural focus	Varied; some offer a full variety of financial services, others focus on agriculture lending	Professionally managed, but may be politically influenced; normally report to regulators	Public funding; debt largely sourced from deposits	Varied; medium (benefits from public subsidies in certain cases due to often rural distribution network)
Commercial microfinance banks	Licensed as a commercial bank	Regulated and supervised by central bank	Private shareholders and some development banks	Board of directors appointed by shareholders	Commercial micro, small, and medium enterprise clients, urban, fewer poor clients	Credit, savings, payments, sometimes insurance	Professionally managed; report to central bank	Equity and debt from institutional investors; deposits	High; with greenfields, some initial support required, then independent
Money transfer companies	Licensed as a money transfer provider	Regulated by local financial services authorities	Private shareholders	Board of directors appointed by shareholders	Poor and nonpoor; rural and urban	Transfers and payments between people, government, businesses	Professionally managed	Private funders	Generally high sustainability due to user fee structure

Note: MFI = microfinance institution; NBFI = non-bank financial institution; NGO = nongovernmental organization.

Financial Cooperatives

Financial cooperatives are member-owned financial service providers, also called savings and credit cooperatives (SACCOs), savings and loan associations, credit unions, or building societies (a special form of cooperative that mobilizes member savings to finance housing). Financial cooperatives are organized and operated according to basic cooperative principles: There are no external shareholders; the members are the owners; each member has the right to one vote. Members of financial cooperatives are usually affiliated through geography, employment, or religion. To become a member, each person is required to purchase a share and is generally restricted in the number of shares he or she can own. The share purchase value is set by the cooperative and is the same for all members, although it can change over time. In addition to holding shares redeemable at par, members may deposit money with the cooperative or borrow from it. Although financial cooperatives traditionally provided simple savings and credit products, many are introducing a greater variety of products, such as contractual savings and housing loans; if properly licensed, they sometimes provide money transfer or payment services and insurance (Branch 2005).

Well-managed cooperatives often provide loans at lower interest rates than MFIs. If profitable, they either reinvest excess earnings in the cooperative or return them to members in the form of dividends, usually based on their average savings balances or share ownership. These measures sometimes translate to more affordable loans for members or higher returns on savings than are available from other institutional providers (WOCCU 2011).

Member savings and shares, the primary funding mechanism for cooperatives, constitute a stable and relatively low-cost funding of funds from which loans are made. During the 2008 financial crisis, for example, local financial cooperatives weathered the storm relatively well because local deposits proved a much more stable source of funds than external investments (Christen and Mas 2009).

Financial cooperatives are essentially a formalized version of a large accumulating savings and credit association (ASCA) that is legally registered (see chapter 6). They vary in size from very small (dozens of members) to very large (thousands of members). They are subject to the country's laws and pay taxes if required. Cooperatives are usually governed by a volunteer board of directors elected by and from the membership. In smaller cooperatives, management may also be voluntary. As with the microfinance sector, governance is one of the greatest challenges facing the cooperative sector.

Cooperatives, particularly smaller ones, may focus on rural markets, facilitating access to both savings and credit services and circulating resources within a community. With both wealthy and poor members depositing funds, excess liquidity of one household can provide credit for another. However, cooperatives can be subject to power imbalances, with elected board members or management taking advantage of their position to borrow excessively or extend credit to their supporters (see box 7.1).

Individual financial cooperatives often choose to be affiliated with an apex institution, which represents the cooperative at the national level, provides training and technical assistance to affiliated cooperatives, acts as a central deposit and interlending facility (central financing facility), and, in some cases, channels resources from external donors to the national cooperative system. Being a member of an apex institution can also mean that individual cooperatives benefit from economies of scale for purchasing or other services. Affiliation involves purchasing share capital and paying annual dues to the national or regional apex institution. Membership provides the right to vote on national leadership and

Box 7.1 Reflections on Member-Owned Financial Service Provision

Member-owned and -managed financial service providers offer several features that appeal to poor people. First, their survival depends on the degree to which they respond to their members' need for financial services. Second, a high degree of client ownership and participation is present: Users have a direct influence in determining the financial services provided, including the interest rates charged. (However, flexible terms and conditions require more detailed reports to monitor performance and hence higher levels of management skill and stronger governance mechanisms.) People assist one another and offer social support, and when a member has a genuine repayment problem, the member can appeal for more time to repay (Johnson 2004). This flexibility means that members are not as frightened of taking loans from these systems as they would be from other systems; and unlike in MFI group-solidarity systems, members are not forced to make repayments on the defaulter's behalf.

However, the very nature of these advantages leads to the problems facing user-owned systems. The element of "negotiability" allows powerful individuals to manipulate the

system to their own advantage (Johnson 2004). This arises from a more general set of "principal-agent problems" in which the investors in the organization or the shareholders (the principals) elect a board or committee (the agents) to represent their interests (fiduciary responsibility). But when these organizations become large and monitoring the performance of the board becomes more difficult, the board may tend to protect its own interests and those of management rather than those of shareholders and the organization as a whole. This results in the all-too-familiar situation of escalating costs and bad loans to board members, which become particularly problematic when board members are net borrowers whose savings cannot cover the loan losses. These problems are compounded in poorer areas where people are less well educated and poorly equipped to understand and monitor management. Where these systems are most successful, it is often because board members are skilled, such as retired civil servants and professionals, and sufficiently concerned about the well-being of the organization. Members often trust community leaders more than unfamiliar staff at another institution.

Source: Johnson, Malkamaki, and Wanjau 2005.

policies and to participate in nationally sponsored services and programs.

As institutions that intermediate member savings, larger cooperatives are normally supervised. The level and structure of supervision varies significantly from country to country (see chapter 17). In many countries, the authorities charged with overseeing cooperatives of all kinds—agricultural, marketing, transport, and others—also supervise financial cooperatives. These entities may not

have the requisite skills to supervise financial intermediaries. This general lack of financial oversight coupled with weak governance can compromise the safety and soundness of financial cooperatives, which is especially problematic when poor people's savings are at risk. Although many still struggle with poor management, financial cooperatives are significant providers of financial services in many developing countries.

NGO MFIs

Nongovernmental organizations are nonprofit organizations that provide social and economic services, which may include health or education or microfinance, among other services. They differ from financial cooperatives or community-based groups in that they are not member owned and managed. NGOs are a diverse group, including large multipurpose organizations such as BRAC in Bangladesh, international NGOs such as ACCION or Opportunity International that have fostered a network of local NGOs, and small independent local organizations.

The level of formality of NGOs varies significantly, depending on the mission, funding, and vision of the organization. NGOs are typically registered under national laws, which permit a range of activities and determine the tax treatment of incoming donor money and revenue generated from operations. NGO MFIs have no owners. Rather, they have boards with members appointed by the founders or funders, which are the functional equivalent of shareholders. NGO boards are responsible for overseeing the collective activities of the NGO and providing input on strategic activities. NGO governance structures are generally not suited for bearing fiduciary responsibility because board members do not represent shareholders or member-owners with money at stake. NGO MFIs may receive oversight from a government body or international network, but they are typically not regulated or supervised by a country's central bank or financial system regulatory authorities.

As financial service providers, NGO MFIs are limited in the services they can provide (for instance, only credit); some may also operate as agents for a bank or insurance company. They traditionally offer a standard microenterprise loan for investment in productive activities, either to individuals or to groups, often using peer guarantees, group solidarity, or village banking methods (between 5 and 30 neighbors meet regularly to save and borrow, providing a guarantee for each other's loans; see chapter 9). Although some NGOs require compulsory savings, they cannot be legally intermediated (that is, on-lent to another client). Many NGOs have broadened their product offerings in an effort to enhance access to financial services, offering credit for uses other than productive investment, such as housing or education.

The funding structure of NGO MFIs varies. Traditional NGO MFIs are generally funded by a mix of grants, debt, and accumulated equity, however, with the professionalization of and demand for sustainability among NGO MFIs, revenue from daily operations is expected to cover overall costs and provide capital for growth, while grants are increasingly spent on technical assistance and product and channel development. The equity of NGO MFIs includes grants provided by donors for loan capital and retained earnings (excess revenue over expenses). NGOs often have fairly weak leverage (the amount of debt relative to equity) because their lack of formality can limit their ability to borrow commercially, although they are increasingly accessing various kinds of debt. Where traditionally they were required by funders to hold cash collateral or pledge their loan portfolio as collateral, well-performing NGOs are able to borrow with guarantees and lower or no physical collateral requirements. Debt for NGOs is largely in the form of term loans; however, a few NGO MFIs have been able to issue bonds supported by partial credit guarantees (see chapter 16).

NGO MFIs benefit from less onerous reporting requirements and less formalized structures than regulated institutions and thus may be able to operate more informally in response to client needs; however, management is often weak, particularly as the NGO expands, which may lead to difficulty maintaining stability and growth. NGO MFIs were early, if not the first, providers of microfinance in areas underserved by formal financial institutions. Over the years, however,

NGOs have become less prominent in microfinance largely because of their inability to provide savings services and difficulty covering their costs and funding growth. Although thousands of multipurpose NGOs offer microcredit, they serve a relatively small number of clients. Given these limitations, some NGO MFIs become regulated institutions. Larger multipurpose NGOs may spin off their financial services to a separate entity (ideally self-sustaining), while other activities continue to require subsidies.

Deposit-Taking MFIs

Deposit-taking MFIs have the institutional structure and regulatory approval required to mobilize and intermediate deposits. They may be licensed and regulated as banks or operate under a special category for deposit-taking MFIs created by the regulatory authorities. For example, the Bank of Uganda created a special "tier 3" category of financial institutions, called micro-deposit-taking institutions, that intermediate deposits but do not qualify as banks. These institutions have lower minimum capital requirements and cannot provide all the services banks can. The ability of an MFI to accept deposits contributes to financial inclusion by providing clients with a secure place to save. By facilitating savings, these institutions better respond to client needs and can expand services to nonborrowers.

Deposit-taking MFIs can be set up as greenfield institutions or be transformed from an NGO MFI into an institution licensed and regulated by the central bank. Accepting deposits provides both a much valued service and an important resource base with which to fund loans. Accepting deposits also enhances the MFI's sustainability and places it in a better position to access commercial sources of funding to fuel growth and expand outreach. Given their regulated status, deposit-taking MFIs are usually shareholding institutions, with a mix of funding sources, including equity raised from shareholders and

retained through earnings and deposits, as well as various forms of debt. Deposit-taking MFIs are often able to borrow from a broad range of lenders as well as the capital markets. The ability of a deposit-taking MFI to borrow is determined by its performance.

Deposit-taking MFIs are a form of NBFI, which can be an interim step to obtaining a bank license or an end in and of itself. As with other shareholding institutions, deposit-taking MFIs need to balance the need for shareholder value and returns with the need to serve poor women and men. Furthermore, if transforming from a nonprofit organization with no owners into a for-profit company with return-seeking shareholders, a tremendous amount of work and strong leadership is required. The cultural changes—from frontline staff, to all levels of management, to the board—are very difficult to manage and require substantial commitment and involvement of the board and senior management. Transformation takes money, strong visionary leadership, institutional ownership, and time (see box 7.2).

Other Non-Bank Financial Institutions

In addition to specialist deposit-taking MFIs, which are generally not licensed as banks, other NBFIs are beginning to increase their depth of outreach to poor women and men. NBFIs include insurance companies (discussed in a separate section below), leasing companies, specialist credit companies such as finance companies, consumer credit companies, and others. NBFIs are restricted by law in the range of services they can offer and the financial infrastructure they can access. NBFIs cannot normally intermediate deposits (unless specifically licensed to do so) and may not be allowed to participate in payment and settlement systems (see chapter 18). From a legal and regulatory perspective, it is often easier to obtain a license to operate as an

Box 7.2 Transformation from an NGO to a Deposit-Taking Institution

Many NGOs have taken different routes over the past decade, with some of the larger and more professional organizations transforming into deposit-taking institutions. The transformation process is difficult and has proven to be extremely time-consuming and expensive. Thus it is not for the majority of NGO MFIs. Assuming that the proper regulatory framework is in place, an NGO MFI must modify its governance structure, develop savings products, and design new operating processes and procedures. These processes include both front-office operations—those that interface with clients—as well as back-office operations, including accounting, reporting, and treasury. In addition, upgrading infrastructure such as banking halls and vaults to comply with banking regulations, developing management information services capable of reporting to regulators, and capturing data associated with savings products are all crucial activities for a successful transformation. Furthermore, MFIs must hire and train new staff for savings products, and they often hire new senior management with experience managing a regulated institution.

Numerous institutional incentives are associated with becoming a deposit-taking institution. Client satisfaction is improved when the range of products is broad; and deposits offer a stable base of local currency funding. In addition, rigorous reporting to a regulator facilitates increased transparency and increased access to diversified investors and funding sources. There are trade-offs, however. Many institutions target large deposits, which are generally less expensive to mobilize but can be less stable than small local deposits and may undermine the original purpose of transforming; however, mobilizing only small deposits generally entails high costs and therefore is not feasible. Some institutions struggle for years to implement appropriate information systems to facilitate accepting deposits, and many underestimate competition in the formal sector. In addition, formal reporting to investors, regulators, and a board of directors is substantially greater for deposit-taking institutions. Many MFIs find it difficult to keep up with the volume of reporting and level of detail required of regulated financial institutions.

Source: Ledgerwood and White 2006.

NBFI than as a bank, because minimum capital requirements are lower and because there is less systemic risk as there is no (for the most part) intermediation of deposits.

Leasing Companies

Leasing companies and hire-purchase companies finance fixed assets such as equipment or heavy-duty vehicles and mostly provide credit under financial lease contracts. Under a leasing model, the leasing company retains ownership of the leased asset, which is generally used as collateral for the transaction. Leasing companies are licensed and regulated by the banking authorities and are generally privately owned. Although most leasing companies do not focus on the poor (there are few microleasing companies), many types of providers are beginning to add leasing products. Because the lease is granted based on cash flow with the asset itself as security, leasing provides entrepreneurs with financial resources to start a business on a limited budget or to increase productivity through new capital investments. Leasing requires processes and systems that accommodate asset ownership and residual value, specific taxation, and accounting and legal requirements. Leasing products are discussed in chapter 9.

Finance and Consumer Credit Companies

Finance companies or financiers are NBFIs that provide small, short-term loans, which are frequently unsecured and used to purchase consumer durable goods and services. Finance companies are often associated with consumer credit and installment contracts. They are normally not allowed to mobilize savings; however, their activities vary by their charters, and exceptions are found. For example, some may be able to mobilize time deposits, but not demand deposits (see box 7.3).

Organizations that provide consumer credit include specialized consumer finance companies, payday lenders, supplier credit, and retail stores. For example, some large retail outlets are applying for licenses to provide financial services, such as Grupo Elektra in Mexico (see box 7.4). Some provide short- to medium-term consumer loans to employees that are repaid through payroll deductions. Similar to MFIs, consumer credit companies often serve low-income households and microentrepreneurs, and they are becoming more and more significant in many emerging and developing markets: "For most customers, consumer credit is their first experience and first access to the financial system. Customers build up a credit history, start saving, and start using the financial system. Consumer finance stimulates the penetration of financial services in society, and a well-developed consumer finance delivery system leads to a better overall financial structure (banks and non-banks), better competition, and more access to credit for all income groups and, last but not least, at better credit terms" (FMO 2006).

Asset finance companies, which were especially popular in North America in the 1950s, have been replaced largely by finance divisions of large retail chains, but they can help the working poor to buy household assets such as furniture and appliances. This financing is similar both to leasing, where the purchaser is able to use the asset during the lease agreement, and to consumer financing, where the retailer sells on "lay away" and the purchaser pays a certain amount periodically until he or she owns the asset. However, financing costs can be quite high.

Suppliers and Buyers

Private companies such as input suppliers, buyers, wholesalers, exporters, and processors sometimes provide financial services, primarily credit, to low-income markets. Supplier credit is

---

Box 7.3 NBFIs in India

Many MFIs in India operate as for-profit NBFIs. Under Indian law, an NBFI is a company registered under the Company's Act of 1956 and engaged in the business of loans and advances and the acquisition of shares, stocks, bonds, debentures, and securities issued by the government or a local authority.

Banks differ from NBFIs: (1) NBFIs cannot accept demand deposits, (2) they are not a part of the payment and settlement system and cannot issue checks, and (3) deposit insurance facilities are not available. NBFIs registered with the central authorities are classified as an asset finance company, an investment company, or a loan company. An asset finance company, the most common type of NBFI, is a financial institution whose principal business is the financing of physical assets such as automobiles, tractors, lathe machines, or generators to support productive activities.

Source: India Microfinance Editorial Team 2009.

Box 7.4 Grupo Elektra and Banco Azteca in Mexico

In March 2002 one of Mexico's largest retailers for electronics and household goods, Grupo Elektra, received a banking license. In October 2002 it launched Banco Azteca, opening 815 branches in all Grupo Elektra stores.

From the outset, Banco Azteca targeted low- and middle-income customers, historically underserved by the traditional banking industry. Azteca began offering savings accounts that could be opened with as little as US$5. Within the first month, 157,000 accounts were opened, increasing to 250,000 accounts by the end of December 2002. At its opening in October 2002, Banco Azteca also took over the issuance of installment loans,

which were previously issued by Elektrafin, the financing unit of Grupo Elektra's retail stores. These loans averaged US$250. Although tied to merchandise, they could be used for business purposes such as the purchase of a new sewing machine or a refrigerator that could be used to start or sustain a microbusiness. In 2003 Azteca started offering US$500 consumer loans not tied to merchandise. These amounts were comparable in size to loans offered by several microfinance organizations, which in 2002 amounted to about US$360 on average. Toward the end of 2003, Azteca also expanded into the mortgage and insurance business.

Source: Bruhn and Love 2009.

provided by input suppliers and wholesalers, who provide in-kind credit or cash in return for either installment payments over a period of time or a lump-sum payment at the end of the term. For example, seed suppliers may provide seeds to farmers during the planting season with the expectation that the seeds will be paid for at the time of harvest. Financing costs are built into the price of seeds.

Credit provided by input suppliers and buyers is often embedded in another transaction and therefore is not provided without it. Credit is built into existing business relationships through a *value chain*. A value chain is a path that a product follows from raw material to consumer, from input supplier to producers, and through various actors who take ownership of the product before it arrives at its final condition and location (Jones and Miller 2010). The fact that actors are within the same value chain provides incentivized lending by input suppliers, processors, wholesalers, and others to, for example, guarantee the sale of inputs or commit producers to sell the product

back to the supplier. Value chain finance is discussed in detail in chapter 10.

Private companies that provide credit are normally not regulated or supervised by banking authorities because they generally do not pose systemic risk (and may not be licensed at all to provide financial services). Although volumes are not tracked, private companies often provide a substantial amount of credit, particularly in rural areas.

In addition to supplier credit, other private companies embed financial services within their normal business operations. For example, Patrimonio Hoy provides financial services to increase access to housing (see box 7.5).

Banks

Many types of banks are engaged in microfinance, including rural banks, postal and savings banks, state banks, and commercial banks. Banks are normally licensed and regulated by the central bank or other government agency or ministry,

Box 7.5 Patrimonio Hoy: Housing Microfinance That Addresses Market Opportunities

CEMEX, a Mexican cement manufacturer with a US$15 billion market capitalization, developed an innovative corporate social responsibility program called Patrimonio Hoy (Patrimony Today). The program aims to reduce the Mexican housing deficit—which has left more than 20 million people with inadequate shelter—while stimulating consumer demand for housing materials in the low-income urban slums of Mexico.

For more than a year, CEMEX employees and consultants immersed themselves in the urban slum of Mesa Colorada in the state of Jalisco, where they conducted a series of learning experiments and in-depth interviews. They discovered that a significant barrier to building homes was the inability to save enough money to purchase the required materials. The families explained that committing to long-term projects was difficult because employment in the area was unstable. Moreover, even when they tried to purchase construction materials, Patrimonio Hoy participants had nowhere to store them. Theft is common in such impoverished neighborhoods, and weather conditions often spoil the products before they can be used.

Participants in Patrimonio Hoy pay about US$14 a week for 70 weeks and receive consultations with CEMEX architects and scheduled deliveries of materials that coincide with the building phases. Prices on all building materials are kept stable for the life of the project, which shields consumers from sudden price hikes and supply shortages that are common in free markets. And if needed, participants can store their materials in a secure CEMEX facility. Participants found the program enabled them to build homes more cheaply and three times faster than they could on their own.

From 2000 to 2011, Patrimonio Hoy provided affordable solutions to more than 1.3 million people throughout Latin America and enabled more than 265,000 families—251,000 in Mexico and 15,000 in other countries—to build their own homes. Patrimonio Hoy operates through more than 100 centers in Mexico, Colombia, Costa Rica, Nicaragua, and the Dominican Republic. Of these 100 offices, 85 are in Mexico and 93 are completely self-sustaining.

Source: Segal, Chu, and Herrero 2006.

which ensures that the term "bank" is reserved for certain types of financial institutions. Although microfinance banks share features of standard commercial or retail banks, lending and outreach are targeted to customers not normally reached by traditional formal financial institutions.

Rural and Community Banks

Rural and community banks operate in rural areas, providing primarily savings services and agricultural loans, reflecting the main economic activity in rural areas. Rural banks can be government

owned, member owned, or privately owned and are normally licensed and supervised by the banking authorities. They are relatively small institutions, but large enough to support professional management and staff. They are normally restricted to a certain geographic area and may be limited in the products they can offer. They generally provide products similar to commercial banks, including short- and long-term savings products (sometimes with overdraft facilities) and investment and consumption loans, often focused on agriculture and trading. Rural banks may also be licensed to provide money transfers and payments. Given their small size, rural banks are often part of an association or apex institution and may benefit from technical support including, for example, capacity building, fund mobilization, and treasury management. In Ghana the Association of Rural Banks also performs important supervisory functions delegated to it by the Bank of Ghana (see box 7.6).

Rural and community banks exist predominantly in Indonesia, Ghana, Nigeria, India, China, and the Philippines. In these countries rural banks were often established as part of rural development strategies implemented by national governments. For example, in Indonesia rural banks were established during the 1960s in an effort to foster the growth of financial services. Rural banks in Indonesia are largely owned by provincial governments and used to support regional economic policies. In India regional rural banks have a mandate to improve access to financial services, including savings, in underserved, primarily rural, areas and are heavily involved in credit-linked programs to Self-Help Groups (Linder 2010a, 2010b). The Philippines has both rural banks, which are owned and organized by individuals living in a given community, and cooperative rural banks, which are owned and organized by cooperatives and other farmer associations. In the Philippines, in addition to savings and credit

services, some rural banks are also allowed to distribute microinsurance (BSP 2011).

Savings Banks

Savings banks are regulated financial institutions with a retail focus that extends across broad geographic areas. In Europe and North America, savings banks originated as early as the eighteenth century, with the objective of providing easily accessible savings services to a broad range of populations.

The universe of savings banks is very diverse; no "prototype" savings or socially committed retail bank exists.[1] However, most savings banks were set up to reach clients who are not served by commercial banks. Typically their objective is not to maximize profit (Christen, Rosenberg, and Jayadeva 2004).

Savings banks are regulated by the banking authorities and are both publicly and privately owned. They often have a broad decentralized distribution network, providing local and regional outreach. Research conducted by the World Savings Banks Institute in 2006 showed that savings banks hold three-quarters of the 1.4 billion accessible accounts provided by double-bottom-line financial institutions (De Noose 2007).[2] Furthermore, data from 2000 to 2003 show that non-postal savings banks represent close to 20 percent of total banking

Box 7.6 Rural and Community Banks in Ghana

As a network, rural and community banks are the largest providers of formal financial services in Ghana's rural areas. By the end of 2008, Ghana had 127 rural and community banks, with 584 service outlets, representing about half of the total banking outlets in the country, reaching about 2.8 million depositors and 680,000 borrowers. Although the service delivery of the network has been strong, its financial performance has been mixed. The profitability and net worth of the network have grown, but the financial performance of some members has been poor, and a small number are insolvent.

Source: Nair and Fissha 2010.

assets (Christen, Rosenberg, and Jayadeva 2004). Because of their large branch networks, in many countries, such as Kenya and Chile, the geographic proximity of savings banks enables greater access than some other types of providers. As well, savings banks offer product terms that make them accessible; their standard passbook savings account has low minimum balance requirements and low or no fees. Finally, savings banks can also contribute to developing financial capabilities because, in addition to introducing financial services to many unbanked individuals, they often provide financial education programs. For example, in Thailand the Government Savings Bank has a school-based savings program in which students create a savings bank in their class and acquire the basic principles of personal financial management (De Noose 2007).

Postal Savings Banks

A large proportion of savings banks are postal savings banks, often established by governments originating from the postal network. In addition to their core postal activity—collecting and distributing mail and parcels—postal branch networks can provide financial services. Postal financial services traditionally include payment and money transfers as well as savings services, generally in small amounts (see box 7.7). In some countries services also include credit or insurance products, either directly by the postal bank, if licensed to intermediate deposits, or on behalf of a commercial bank that partners with the post office acting as an agent. Postal banks are primarily wholly or majority owned by governments directly or through government-owned and -managed post offices. They are normally supervised by a specialized unit of the central bank or by a separate government agency altogether (Christen, Rosenberg, and Jayadeva 2004).

In 2010 post offices worldwide had an extensive retail distribution network with more than 660,000 points of sale, above twice the number of commercial bank branches; many of these are located in periurban, rural, or remote areas, presenting immense opportunities to offer entry-level banking services to the public (WSBI 2010; see box 7.8).

State Banks

State banks include agriculture banks, development banks, postal banks (discussed above), and, in some cases, even commercial state banks. The primary institutional feature is that they are owned and controlled primarily by the government and, as such, are considered public or semipublic entities. State banks often have a large number of savers and extensive branch networks. In line with their ownership structure, they are funded largely by investment of public funds as well as deposits.

Box 7.7 Post Office Banks in India

Of the 155,000 post office branches in India reported in March 2008, more than 98 percent offer some type of savings services. The post office controlled 174.7 million savings accounts (or 40.7 percent of what banks held), accounting for Rs 3.4 trillion in deposits (more than US$75.6 billion, 42.9 percent of what banks held). Even more encouraging for financial inclusion is that, unlike banks, 89.8 percent of all post offices are located in rural areas.

Source: Linder 2010a.

Box 7.8 Increased Financial Inclusion through Postal Savings Banks

The large branch and agency networks of postal banks offer valuable channels for international and domestic money transfers. Using a postal bank's network, the government and other institutions can pay salaries and pensions and individuals can pay school fees and transfer allowances to pupils in remote areas that are not being served by commercial banks. For example, in Kenya about 55 percent of the allowances for university students in public universities and 50 percent of government pensions are paid through the Kenya Post Office Savings Bank (Robinson and Anyango 2003). Postal banks often attract young people and students—either as parents seek to open a low-cost bank account for their children or as governments seek to pay student allowances across the country.

Significant opportunities exist for postal banks to become profitable, modern, client-responsive organizations. Postal banks have large networks of branches, giving them a comparative advantage over commercial banks and creating the potential for offering e-banking solutions. The postal bank networks also have a comparative advantage over shops or other agent locations. They are permitted to accept deposits and utility bill payments, are used to handling remittances and manage money, and in many cases have greater liquidity than shops with limited turnover. Indeed, in some countries, the central bank authorities do not permit shops or others to offer even a basic withdrawal service. Strategic alliances with other banks can allow postal banks to offer withdrawal and deposit services through point-of-sale devices or mobile phone–based payment systems, thus leveraging the postal banks' networks. The Kenya Post Office Savings Bank has partnered with Citibank and Stanbic Bank to do this. The network could also provide valuable outlets and agencies for insurance products, as insurance companies increasingly examine the low-income mass market and develop products for it. However, the challenges of successful linkages and strategic alliances should not be understated; to date, few examples have reached significant scale.

As postal banks start the process of reengineering themselves and their business, the threat of brand confusion with the post office will grow in importance. The Kenya Post Office Savings Bank suffered damage to its reputation as a result of being confused with the post office and its poor service quality. Postal banks often also suffer from serious overstaffing, partly as a result of their manual operations and past politicization of appointments. This phenomenon means that, at some levels, postal banks not only have too many staff, but also do not have the appropriate skills to manage cash balances and the treasury, with the result that savers must often travel to larger centers to withdraw cash. Furthermore, most postal banks are required by their enabling acts or laws to invest mainly in government instruments. Often state corporations cannot borrow without the approval of the shareholder—the government—which guarantees the amount borrowed. This can result in budgetary constraints. Fluctuating interest rates on treasury bills have meant significant variances in annual profits and in the capacity to carry out major projects.

Source: Wright, Koigi, and Kihwele 2006.

Many government-owned banks are established to serve the agriculture sector. Their primary activities include extending credit and savings services to promote small-scale farming production, cottage and village industries, and other rural livelihood activities. Individual farmers and merchants, cooperatives, or associations are the primary target market. In many cases agriculture development banks are the only formal financial service provider in rural areas.

State banks have often been established to correct market failures and provide resources to underserved or high-priority sectors of the economy. As a result, they may be susceptible to the political priorities of ruling governments and to political influences that may not serve the institutional objectives. Beyond politics, some aspects of government ownership threaten the long-term sustainability of state banks: An implicit government guarantee creates a safety net, limiting their motivation to operate profitably, and poor collection practices and frequent forgiveness schemes enable a weak credit culture, undermining the ability of the private sector to operate in rural markets (Young and Vogel 2005). State banks may be reluctant to operate under prudent financial management and accounting practices. For example, they may not write off delinquent loans, frequently understate provisions for portfolios at risk, and overstate profits and assets. Political ties may compromise full transparency of financial positions. State banks may not be "accountable" to the regulators in the same way that a private bank or financial services company should be. Furthermore, board members may be appointed based more on political or other criteria than on professional skills or business rationale, limiting effective governance and perpetuating the challenges of fiduciary responsibility. Governments have often been willing to subsidize continuing losses, weakening management discipline (Christen, Rosenberg, and Jayadeva 2004). Faced with an often massive budgetary burden, some governments have had to close or restructure state-owned financial institutions (ADB 2007; see box 7.9).

However, not all state banks suffer from governance and management problems and fail to become profitable. Bank Rakyat Indonesia provides a good example (see box 7.10).

Private Commercial Banks

Commercial banks have the most robust product offering of all financial service providers, typically providing a full menu of payments, credit, and savings services.[3] Although they are beginning to reach lower-income markets, private commercial banks generally operate in urban areas and serve a wealthier clientele than alternative financial institutions specifically targeting low-income populations.

Commercial banks tend to be more highly leveraged than other providers given their access to different sources of funding enabled by their formality, regulated status, and, by definition, commercial orientation. Equity is raised from shareholders either through private placements or through capital markets. Debt is raised through commercial sources, including borrowing from other commercial banks, development finance institutions, and microfinance investment vehicles, and through capital markets.

In general, commercial banks engage in microfinance in three ways: (1) by expanding their product offering to microclients—referred to as downscaling—either through the creation of a separate internal unit or through a new subsidiary, (2) by creating a new institution—referred to as greenfielding—for the specific purpose of offering regulated formal financial services to the poor, or (3) by establishing an agency relationship with an experienced microfinance organization or other provider.

Downscaling

When a commercial bank creates a separate internal unit or establishes a microfinance subsidiary,

Box 7.9 Privatization: The Experience of Khan Bank in Mongolia

Khan Bank was established in 1991 from the assets of the former state bank with the specific goal of serving the rural sector. In 1999 the World Bank made reforming Khan Bank a condition of its Financial Sector Adjustment Credit Program for Mongolia, and the U.S. Agency for International Development agreed to fund external support to manage Khan Bank. Management's mission was to (1) restore financial soundness to Khan Bank, (2) bring financial services to the country's rural population, and (3) prepare Khan Bank to operate independently as a precursor to privatization.

After being placed in receivership in 2000, the bank was recapitalized, put under a restructuring plan, and successfully privatized in 2003. From December 2001 to June 2006,

the loan portfolio grew from US$9 million to US$149 million. In 2006, 76 percent of the loan portfolio was in rural areas, business loans accounted for 45 percent, consumer loans for 28 percent, and agricultural loans for 26 percent. The portfolio at risk over 30 days was only 2.5 percent. During the initial transition period, Khan Bank focused on simple, standardized products in rural areas. It piloted new products in selected urban branches, only rolling them out once they proved viable. Over time Khan Bank increased its range of products and now offers a wide range of loan, deposit, and money transfer services. Loan products range from express micro loans and small and medium enterprise loans to crop and herder credit.

Source: DAI 2007; ADB 2007.

Box 7.10 Bank Rakyat Indonesia

In 1983 Bank Rakyat Indonesia (BRI) began the transformation from a dispenser of subsidized agricultural credit to a self-financed microbanking network with ever-growing deposits, loan portfolios, profits, and outreach to the lower segment of the market. In 1997 and 1998 the Asian financial crisis destroyed much of the commercial sector in Indonesia and almost wiped out the country's banking industry. However, BRI was one of the state-owned banks exempted from closure. It was restructured through a massive recapitalization effort in 2000, and in 2003 the government of Indonesia offered 40 percent of the

shares of BRI to the public in an initial public offering. Listing on the Indonesian Stock Exchange brought a new level of reporting and transparency as well as a true double bottom line, with public investors expecting a return on their shares, while the government maintained majority ownership as protection against purely commercial motives.

BRI became the most profitable bank in Indonesia in 2007 and the largest bank in terms of loan portfolio size in April 2008. In 2010 it purchased Bank Agroniaga in an effort to expand its footprint in the agribusiness sector.

Source: Seibel and Ozaki 2009.

it needs to change its organizational structure, lending methodologies, staffing, processes, and procedures to facilitate smaller transactions appropriate for microclients. For example, loan officers, who traditionally meet prospective clients at the bank branch, must usually visit clients in their home, marketplace, or village. Loan products must be modified to reflect the reality that most microclients do not have collateral, official accounts, or financial statements; instead, loan officers must focus on business and household cash flows. Savings services need to be modified to have lower or no minimum balances. Pricing may need to be adapted to reflect higher operating costs and lower balances. Similarly, auditing and accounting procedures need to be modified to analyze a portfolio with numerous small transactions. Cultural and operational changes of this magnitude require a distinct management structure to ensure, first and foremost, that the new microfinance unit or subsidiary offers a value proposition for clients under its own image and brand. The culture and brand of the commercial bank will not necessarily carry through appropriately to the microfinance arm.

If a subsidiary is created, it must be licensed and regulated separately, with its own management team and staff. The parent bank is a partial owner (usually majority) in the new microfinance subsidiary. Other investors (equity shareholders) bring microfinance experience, and specialized consulting firms often take a role in setting up and managing the new subsidiary (see box 7.11).

Greenfielding

While transforming NGO MFIs and downscaling existing commercial banks can be effective for increasing financial inclusion, greenfielding—the start-up and creation of new microfinance banks—is another approach whereby a formal bank is created with financial services dedicated entirely to the micro, small, and medium-size enterprise markets. The banks are licensed and formally regulated institutions with professional

---

Box 7.11 Subsidiary Model in Practice: ACCION-Ecobank Partnership

Ecobank is a full-service regional banking institution employing more than 11,000 staff in 746 branches and offices in 29 West, Central, and Southern African countries. In an effort to move down-market and provide banking services to lower-income clients, it partnered with ACCION to form subsidiaries in Ghana and Cameroon. As part of the agreement, ACCION brings its technical expertise and leadership in the microfinance sector, and Ecobank offers the opportunity to leverage its infrastructure and extensive network of banks to help to standardize and deliver high-quality financial services to low-income clients.

At the end of 2006, Ecobank and ACCION launched Ecobank-ACCION Savings and Loans Company (EASL) in Ghana—an institution jointly owned by Ecobank (70 percent shares) and ACCION (30 percent shares) through its investment company, ACCION Investments. The new entity received its license from the Bank of Ghana in March 2008. Since its launch, EASL has experienced significant growth, serving clients through a network of six branches and two satellite kiosks based in markets throughout Accra. EASL provides the working poor with access to credit and savings products, along with debit cards for use across the country. In particular, EASL has successfully launched six savings products addressing a variety of client needs. In May 2010 EASL opened its first two branches in Douala, Cameroon.

Source: Ecobank-ACCION website (http://www.accion.org/page.aspx?pid=2067).

---

management teams and unique methodologies for deploying small-scale savings accounts, credit, and other financial services.

Greenfielding of new microfinance banks has grown rapidly since 2006 with the creation of numerous commercial microfinance networks. These networks are structured as holding companies in which the sponsor or primary shareholder provides the technical expertise while other like-minded investors, including development finance institutions and bilateral donor institutions, provide various forms of funding. In addition to investing equity, shareholders normally provide grant funding to the technical partner, often a foreign network, to develop the capacity of the institution as well as related products and channels, support a critical analysis of the financial needs of target beneficiaries, and hire and train local staff. Over time, local employees are trained to take over virtually all functions of the new banks.

Holding companies provide standardized services to their affiliated subsidiaries such as support for fundraising, help negotiating loan and shareholder agreements, and backup support for information systems, product development, auditing, and training programs for middle and senior management. The commercial microfinance network model is founded on the principles of social responsibility, transparency, efficiency, and sustainable profitability. Banks owned by the same holding company are integrated into a worldwide network in which ideas and experience are exchanged and synergies are exploited. All network institutions are co-branded and adhere to a common set of ethical, environmental, and professional standards (see box 7.12).

Creating a new institution entails three stages:

- *Foundation stage.* A greenfield MFI is established, the license is obtained, initial capacities are developed, and operations are launched. At

Box 7.12 Microfinance Networks and Commercial MFIs

ProCredit, the first commercial microfinance network, started operations in Central and Eastern Europe. In 2011 the ProCredit group consisted of 21 banks operating in transition economies and developing countries in Eastern Europe, Latin America, and Africa. Building on the success of the network model, numerous other commercial microfinance networks were created between 2005 and 2007, including AccessHolding, MicroCred, and Advans. These networks have focused largely on filling market gaps in some of the most underbanked countries. Among all the networks, more than 20 microfinance banks were greenfielded in Africa between 2006 and 2010, largely supported by the International Finance Corporation and Kreditanstalt für Widenraufbau.

AccessHolding, a commercial microfinance holding company dedicated to investing in microfinance banks through a combination of equity and management services rendered by its technical partner LFS Financial Systems GmbH, concentrates on start-up and early-stage greenfield banks. Together with other partners, it establishes new and transforms existing non-bank microlending institutions into full-service microfinance banks. Over time, AccessHolding will transform from a holding company of associated MFIs into a controlling parent company of a global network of microfinance banks with a common brand identity. As of December 2011, AccessHolding had assets of €479.8 million and had invested in seven microfinance banks in Azerbaijan, Liberia, Madagascar, Nigeria, Tajikistan, Tanzania, and Zambia. All investments are regulated entities operating under full commercial bank or special microfinance licenses.

Source: Access Holdings (http://www.accessholding.com); ProCredit (http://www.procredit-holding.com).

this stage management consists largely of staff seconded from the technical partner or shareholder. The new bank receives continuous training and capacity building from the technical partner. Ideally a local partnership is also established at this stage.

- *Institutional development stage.* The branch network is gradually expanded, and operational breakeven is expected by the third or fourth year of operations. Funding for technical assistance is maintained but reduced as local management and staff personnel have been trained and adequate systems have been rolled out.

- *Sustainability and further advancement.* A second injection of capital is foreseen during the fifth or sixth year of operations to sustain the bank's growth. Local staff now assume most managerial positions, and the bank absorbs the costs of senior expatriate staff, if applicable.

Agency Relationships and Partnerships

The third method for engaging in microfinance is to provide services through an agency (rather than directly). Agency relationships occur when a commercial bank partners with a microfinance organization or other financial service provider to provide services to microfinance clients on behalf of the bank.

In this model the microfinance clients do not engage directly with the bank, but rather with the partner organization acting as its agent. The agent undertakes marketing, sales, and service (most direct client contact), while loans and savings are booked on the balance sheet of the bank. Often operating on a fee-for-service basis, the agent is paid by the bank for each new loan; incentives are in place to ensure loan quality. When an agency relationship is used, the primary changes in the bank occur at the senior management level to integrate microfinance assets into the bank's overall strategy and cost structure.

Microfinance organizations acting as agents for banks can offer the physical presence, experience, and agility to reach low-income populations and assess them efficiently, whereas banks offer longer-term, lower-cost sources of funds. For MFIs, agency relationships can support increased income, while expanding financial services to their clients (Miller 2011). Some agency relationships originate with the microfinance organization rather than the commercial bank, while others are hybrid, with only some services being managed by the agent institution.

Agency relationships can also include different financial service providers (most often banks or money transfer companies), to allow clients to process transactions when they cannot access their primary provider; this is referred to as "correspondent banking," where a bank performs services for another bank located in a different city or country. A correspondent bank usually conducts business transactions, accepts deposits, and gathers documents on behalf of another bank or other financial institution. Other correspondent banking services may include treasury management, credit services, or foreign exchange.

Correspondent banking services can help a financial institution to extend its geographic coverage, while lowering transaction costs for clients using the existing infrastructure of partner institutions. Correspondent banking can be used to offer services to clients without having to invest in physical infrastructure, which may prove too costly for a smaller provider. For example, money transfer companies such as Western Union or MoneyGram often arrange to have a kiosk or window located within the branch of a bank (or MFI). Normally each of the partners continues to run its businesses separately but benefits from the ability to share branch costs and to access a greater number and type of customer. Another example is where many smaller providers such as MFIs or SACCOs partner with a larger bank or group of banks to negotiate access to the larger provider's network of automated teller machines (ATMs) (see box 7.13).

Insurance Companies

Microinsurance is a relatively new area within microfinance and is still very much in the learning stage. Chapter 11 provides a thorough discussion of microinsurance products and services and addresses some of the issues and challenges facing the delivery of microinsurance. This section describes the main types of insurance providers active in microinsurance.[4]

NGO Insurance Providers

NGO insurance providers include development organizations, trade unions, federations, and MFIs that provide microinsurance (Roth, McCord, and Liber 2007). They interact directly with poor communities and are therefore close to the market. Most operate without the benefit of an insurance license and are outside the regulations to which commercial insurers must adhere. They are not driven by profits, which gives them more flexibility and propensity to experiment in providing new microinsurance products. NGO insurance providers have traditionally been the largest provider of health microinsurance, for example, in part because demand exists and in part because funding for health insurance is popular among donors.

Mutual Insurers

Mutual insurers are nonprofit organizations that are often owned by credit unions or cooperatives and are nonprofit, member-based organizations. They are distinct from other community-based groups such as burial societies (see chapter 6) because they have professional management and are typically supervised under regulations other than the insurance act. They have the advantage of operating in low-income areas and are experienced in financial activities, disbursements, and confirmation of events. After commercial insurers and NGOs, mutual insurers are the third largest provider of microinsurance (Roth, McCord, and Liber 2007).

Takaful insurers are insurance organizations that operate according to Islamic financial principles; a takaful insurer can invest only in non-interest-bearing assets and, as such, operates essentially as a nonprofit mutual. However, very few takaful insurers provide microinsurance.

Commercial Insurance Providers

Commercial insurers are for-profit insurers regulated under various country-specific insurance acts. They are professionally managed and required to maintain reserves in accordance with

---

Box 7.13 Linking Different Types of Institutions

SACCO Link is a partnership in Kenya that has increased linkages within the formal financial sector. The SACCO Link service has helped SACCOs to enhance the sophistication of financial services they offer to members. The SACCO Link debit card enables SACCO members to access their cash through Co-Operative Bank of Kenya's ATMs as well as any Visa-branded ATM. It links many rural cooperative members with the larger financial sector. The SACCOs pay for connectivity, software upgrades, and a bridge to connect to the bank's system (integrator).

Source: Co-Operative Bank of Kenya 2008.

regulations. Commercial insurers provide a variety of insurance products through established sales and delivery structures and have the potential to distribute microinsurance on a very large scale. However, in addition to modifying products to make them both appropriate for low-income clients and cost-efficient, a specific challenge for delivering insurance is establishing trust between the insurer and the client. Commercial insurers, especially, may not be accustomed to the extra effort required to ensure that clients understand the service and see the value of microinsurance. Microinsurance providers need to understand the risk profiles of clients as well as the tolerance and mitigation measures of poor people, which make the provision of microinsurance significantly more challenging than traditional insurance.

Unlike general credit and savings products, insurance products typically involve more than one organization—the insurer and the delivery channel. The insurer carries the risk, finalizes the premium and product design, and ultimately pays claims. The delivery channel sells the product and provides after-sales service (Roth, McCord, and Liber 2007).

Selling insurance, collecting premiums, and supporting policyholders to settle claims may be performed by the insurer's direct sales division or by others serving as the delivery channel, including MFIs, financial cooperatives, independent agents, churches, post offices, governments, funeral parlors, and retailers. Depending on the country, regulation may affect different delivery channels differently.

For example, although an MFI may not have the capacity or regulatory approval to offer insurance, it can act as an agent for a large insurance company, offering direct access to customers (see box 7.14). Responsibilities are separated in such partnerships, with the insurer specializing in product design and risk management and the MFI leveraging its geographic footprint and client relationships. In these cases, the MFI manages the customer relationship, handling sales, premium collection, policy administration, claims assessment, and settlement, while the microinsurance provider is responsible for the design and development of the products (Roth, McCord, and Liber 2007). In some cases a third-party service provider (such as a health care provider) is also involved.

MFIs with strong processes and systems can administer policies for insurers. However, weaknesses in these areas can be exacerbated by the responsibility for administering microinsurance policies (Roth, McCord, and Liber 2007). These relationships require much expenditure of time on building trust and capacity and providing support.

Commercial insurers also have access to reinsurance. Reinsurance is a risk management tool whereby one insurance company purchases insurance from another insurance company. Reinsurers provide insurance to insurers for catastrophic risk or excessive losses and are becoming increasingly common with microinsurance, although to date, they do not play a very large role because the size of claims is so small (Roth, McCord, and Liber 2007).

Payment Service Providers

Payment services refer to the electronic transfer of funds, sometimes called money transfers, transfer services, transactions, mobile money (when using a mobile phone), or simply payments. Although nonelectronic payment services exist (for example, paying a fee to a human courier to transport cash to another person, as discussed in chapter 6), for institutional providers these terms refer to the electronic transfer of funds between two parties.

Electronic money or e-money products (electronic or mobile payment services) are offered by numerous types of providers, including money transfer companies, post offices, banks, or other formal financial institutions as well as, more

Box 7.14 Allianz in West Africa

To reach out to the low-income market, Allianz, a commercial insurance company, looked for partners with established networks in rural areas. It teamed up with PlaNet Guarantee, an international organization that promotes microinsurance across Africa. PlaNet Guarantee has brokered nine partnerships for Allianz in different African countries. Partners are MFIs that secure their credits with standard credit life insurance. CAURIE, Allianz's partner in Senegal, provides credit to 21,000 women in 275 village banks. Within each village bank, the women split up into solidarity groups of between 3 and 10 women. To avoid the burden that the death of a member can put on the whole group, the MFI added compulsory credit life insurance to its product.

With this new service, CAURIE's loan officers had to learn how to explain microinsurance. They found that the benefit of insurance is much harder to convey than the benefit of credit, because customers pay up-front for a specific future event that may or may not happen—for example, the death of the insured. If that event does not happen, there is no payout. Moreover, customers have to trust that the insurer will keep its promise. Formal contracts are worth little in villages where people often do not have addresses,

may not have identity cards, do not know their rights, and could not enforce them even if they did. In a "cascade of trust," Allianz relies on PlaNet Guarantee's knowledge of local MFIs and ability to manage microinsurance; PlaNet Guarantee trusts the reliability of Allianz; CAURIE trusts the advice of PlaNet Guarantee; the loan officers trust CAURIE; and the women in the village banks trust their loan officers. Information about insurance and Allianz products in particular is handed down this cascade.

To provide even better service in the future, PlaNet Guarantee and Allianz initiated dialogues with 300 microcredit clients through local NGOs. Customers help loan officers to understand their needs beyond individual life insurance—such as coverage for the death of a family member and the associated funeral costs or health expenses. This information helps Allianz to develop new products that will create additional value for these customers. In Senegal Allianz added a livelihood component to its life insurance product. The insurance pays out a fixed sum for each day a borrower is unable to work to cover lost income. Although not yet a full-blown health insurance, the daily allowance is large enough to cover smaller medical expenses.

Source: Allianz 2010.

---

recently, through Internet networks or mobile network operators (MNOs) and other third-party providers. These payment services typically require the use of a cash-in, cash-out location whereby the customer making the transfer brings cash to the office of the provider or the location of an affiliated agent.

Money transfer companies are commercial networks that transfer funds domestically and

internationally for people who are unbanked or for people who prefer not to use either the formal banking system or informal systems. They transfer funds through electronic funds transfer (EFT) networks. The sender visits the company's retail or affiliated agent's location, submits the transfer amount, and pays the fee, at which point the funds are transferred and the recipient is informed by telephone or text message. The recipient is then able to collect the transfer amount by showing appropriate identification at any retail or agent location representing the money transfer company. Each major money transfer company operates in a similar manner, with a central database linking all staff or company agents who are disbursed widely in various locations, including branch offices (generally their own) and extensive networks of partner banks, postal agencies, MFIs, travel agents, change bureaus, grocery stores, convenience stores, and other retailers.

The provision of money transfer services was a highly profitable industry long before the advent of the Internet and mobile phone networks (see box 7.15). Although the profit margins for these services have shrunk as innovations in telecommunications have created other options for customers, transfer service companies remain an important financial service provider. The service points are widely accessible, and the service is efficient and convenient without much paperwork. Although expensive, money transfer services are often the only option for an unbanked customer who cannot or does not wish to rely on informal systems or is not comfortable with transferring money using a mobile phone.

Post offices offer electronic cross-border payments referred to as *giro* transfers. To make the transfer, clients must do so from a post office location; the receiver can receive the transfer into a postal account, a bank account, or in cash. *Giro* transfers take advantage of the cash float in the postal system, and although transfer times may be relatively long (two to four days), the fees are generally lower than with banks (Frankiewicz and Churchill 2011).

Banks most often conduct transfers and payments through current accounts (see chapter 12). Current account transactions may be carried out using negotiable instruments such as checks or money orders and, like other financial products, can be accessed through various delivery channels such as debit cards, ATMs, or mobile phones. Commercial banks also facilitate electronic fund transfers to another bank account; this is generally expensive and not available to persons without a bank account.

Although traditional providers of electronic transaction services are regulated financial institutions, credit unions, post offices, or commercial money transfer companies, over the past decade more than 100 mobile money deployments (that

Box 7.15 Western Union and MoneyGram

Two of the largest players in the money transfer industry are Western Union and MoneyGram. In 2012, Western Union had approximately 510,000 agent locations in 200 countries and territories, allowing consumers to send money worldwide through retail or agent locations, including convenience stores, kiosks, and the postal service. Similarly, in 2012 MoneyGram had more than 275,000 locations in 194 countries. Each company earned significant profits.

Both Western Union and MoneyGram have increasingly offered retail and agent locations in developing countries, while at the same time targeting members of diaspora communities who frequently send money back to their home countries. Migrant workers seeking economic opportunity in urban areas away from home also provide a natural target market because many migrant laborers do not use banks.

Source: Isern, Deshpande, and Van Doom 2005; Wikipedia.org/wiki/moneygram; corporate.westernunion.com/news_media_corporate.html.

is, money transfers using mobile phones) have launched in developing countries, which suggests there is significant commercial interest among MNOs in offering payment services using mobile phones.[5] Mobile network operators are becoming important players within the financial ecosystem, as a channel both for delivering financial products and services through mobile phones as well as for providing money transfer services in their own right. As experience is gained and the sector evolves, they are poised to become increasingly more relevant.

Although the regulations in Kenya permit an MNO to offer payment services to clients without a bank account, the central banks in other countries (India, Pakistan, and Bangladesh, for example) require the deployment of all mobile payments to be led by banks; in other words, the users of mobile money are customers of the bank, and the mobile device is the delivery channel for transacting through accounts held at the bank (see chapter 12). Related to this are third-party providers that are neither financial institutions nor MNOs that are also emerging as payment service providers, for example, bKash in Bangladesh and Sub-K in India. While they do provide direct interface with clients, they are discussed in chapter 12 because it is hard to differentiate them as providers or as delivery platforms; by definition they need to partner with other providers to deliver services.

Notes

1. www.wsbi.org.
2. Double-bottom-line financial institutions target the mass market, such as MFIs, credit unions, cooperatives, agricultural and development banks, and savings and postal savings banks (De Noose 2007).
3. This section was contributed by Julie Earne.
4. This section is summarized from Roth, McCord, and Liber (2007).
5. GSMA Mobile Deployment Tracker (http://www.wirelessintelligence.com/mobile-money).

References and Further Reading

* Key works for further reading.

ADB (Asian Development Bank). 2007. "Proposed Loan. Mongolia: Khan Bank. Report and Recommendation of the President to the Board of Directors." Project 41911, ADB.

Allianz. 2010. "Learning to Insure the Poor." Microinsurance Report. Allianz, Munich.

Branch, Brian. 2005. "Working with Savings and Credit Cooperatives." Donor Brief 25, CGAP, Washington, DC, August.

Bruhn, Miriam, and Inessa Love. 2009. "The Economic Impact of Banking the Unbanked: Evidence from Mexico." Policy Research Paper 4981, World Bank, Washington, DC.

BSP (Bangko Sentral ng Pilipinas). 2011. "BSDP Grants Microinsurance License to Two Rural Banks." Press release, BSP, December 22.

*Christen, Robert Peck, and Ignacio Mas. 2009. "It's Time to Address the Microsavings Challenge, Scalably." *Enterprise Development and Microfinance* 20 (4): 274–85.

*Christen, Robert Peck, Richard Rosenberg, and Veena Jayadeva. 2004. "Financial Institutions with a 'Double Bottom Line': Implications for the Future of Microfinance." Occasional Paper 8, CGAP, Washington, DC, July.

Co-Operative Bank of Kenya. 2008. "Africa Technical Workshop." PowerPoint presentation, November 26.

DAI. 2007. "Khan Bank: Bank Management Support." http://dai.com/our-work/projects/mongolia%E2%80%94khan-bank-bank-management-support.

*De Noose, Chris. 2007. "Bringing the Hidden Giants to the Footlight: The Role of Savings and Retail Banks in Increasing the Level of Access to Financial Services." *Microbanking Bulletin* 15 (Autumn).

FMO (Entrepreneurial Development Bank of the Netherlands). 2006. "Guidelines for Consumer Finance." Memo, FMO, July 6.

*Frankiewicz, Cheryl, and Craig Churchill. 2006. *Making Microfinance Work: Managing for Improved Performance.* Geneva: ILO.

———. 2011. *Making Microfinance Work: Managing Product Diversification.* Geneva: ILO.

*Helms, Brigit. 2006. "Access for All: Building Inclusive Financial Systems." World Bank and CGAP, Washington, DC.

India Microfinance Editorial Team. 2009. "NBFC—Frequently Asked Questions—RBI." India Microfinance Business News (Delhi), Financial Inclusion, Social Entrepreneurship, and Mobile Money Blog, April 7.

Isern, Jennifer, Rani Deshpande, and Judith Van Doom. 2005. "Crafting a Money Transfers Strategy: Guidance for Pro-Poor Financial Service Providers." Occasional Paper 10, CGAP, Washington, DC.

Johnson, S. 2004. "'Milking the Elephant': Financial Markets as Real Markets in Kenya." *Development and Change* 35 (2): 249–75.

Johnson, Susan, Markku Malkamaki, and Kuria Wanjau. 2005. "Tackling the 'Frontiers' of Microfinance in Kenya: The Role of Decentralized Services." Decentralized Financial Services, Nairobi.

Jones, Linda, and Calvin Miller. 2010. *Agricultural Value Chain Finance: Tools and Lessons.* Rome: Food and Agriculture Organization.

Ledgerwood, Joanna, and Victoria White. 2006. *Transforming Microfinance Institutions: Providing Full Financial Services to the Poor.* Washington, DC: World Bank.

Linder, Chris with contributions from Denny George. 2010a. "Who Says You Can't Do MicroSavings in India? Part 1: Community-Based/Owned." Briefing Note 45, MicroSave India.

———. 2010b. "Who Says You Can't Do MicroSavings in India? Part 2: Conventional Finance." Briefing Note 46, MicroSave India.

Miller, Calvin. 2011. "Microfinance and Crop Agriculture: New Approaches, Technologies, and Other Innovations to Address Food Insecurity among the Poor." Workshop paper commissioned for the 2011 Global Microcredit Summit, Valladolid, Spain, November 14–17.

Nair, Ajar, and Azeb Fissha. 2010. "Rural Banking: The Case of Rural and Community Banks in Ghana." In *Innovations in Rural and Agriculture Finance,* ed. Renate Kloeppinger-Todd and Manohar Sharma. Focus 18, Brief 5. Washington DC: International Food Policy Research Institute and World Bank.

Ritchie, A. n.d. "Typology of Microfinance Service Providers." Version 1.3. World Bank, Washington, DC.

Robinson, Marguerite, and Ezra Anyango. 2003. "Report on Kenya Post Office Savings Bank: MicroSave Africa Mid-Term Review." Background paper, MicroSave, Nairobi.

*Roth, Jim, Michael McCord, and Dominic Liber. 2007. *The Landscape of Microinsurance in the World's 100 Poorest Countries.* Appleton, WI: MicroInsurance Centre.

Segal, Arthur I., Michael Chu, and Gustavo A. Herrero. 2006. "Patrimonio Hoy: A Financial Perspective." Case study, Harvard Business School, Cambridge, MA.

Seibel, H. D., and M. Ozaki. 2009. "Restructuring State-Owned Financial Institutions: Lessons from Bank Rakyat Indonesia." Asian Development Bank, Mandaluyong City, Philippines.

*WOCCU (World Council of Credit Unions). 2011. "What Is a Credit Union?" http://www.woccu .org/about/creditunion/.

Wright, Graham A. N., Nyambura Koigi, and Alphonse Kihwele. 2006. "Teaching Elephants to Tango: Working with Post Banks to Realise Their Full Potential." MicroSave, Nairobi, Kenya.

*WSBI (World Savings Banks Institute). 2010. "A WSBI Roadmap for Postal Financial Services Reform and Development." Position paper, WSBI, Brussels, June.

*Young, Robin, and Robert Vogel. 2005. "State-Owned Retail Banks (SORBs) in Rural and Microfinance Markets: A Framework for Considering the Constraints and Potential." Development Alternatives, Inc., Maryland.

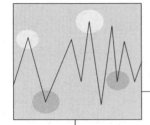

PART III

FINANCIAL SERVICES AND DELIVERY CHANNELS

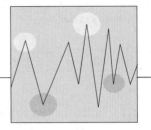

CHAPTER 8

Savings Services

Joanna Ledgerwood

Voluntary savings mobilization from the public is not a matter of adding a few products to a microcredit organization. If successful, it inevitably and irreversibly changes the institution, though not its mission. Those that are not prepared for such changes should not undertake to collect savings from the public. However, those that are willing and able to make the changes needed to overcome the risks can profitably attain wide outreach as financial intermediaries and can serve as models of the industry for other institutions.

—Robinson (2006)

Demand for savings services is diverse and robust. A small amount of savings in a secure place can provide resources to manage consumption needs, smooth irregular income, cover expenditures for health and education, or provide the capital necessary to invest in household assets or new tools

and operations that improve productivity and contribute to higher incomes. Savings also help to manage shocks through providing resources during times of crisis (figure 8.1). In recent years the volume of demand and consumer preference for safe and convenient savings services has been increasingly acknowledged, outdating a previous, widely held view that the poor do not save.

"The poor need savings services that allow them to (1) deposit small, variable amounts frequently and (2) access larger sums in the short, medium, or long term (Rutherford 2009). Like everyone else, they demand a portfolio of savings products that offer differing terms of access and generate differing returns" (CGAP 2005, p. 3). In some cases, poor people need highly liquid services, for example, to cope with emergencies or to take advantage of an investment opportunity. For other purposes, they prefer illiquid options to protect their savings and instill discipline, particularly

---

Contributions to this chapter were made by Cheryl Frankiewicz.

Figure 8.1   How Savings Can Improve the Lives of the Poor

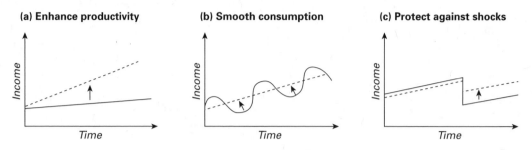

Source: Christen and Mas 2009.
Note: Dotted line denotes cash flows when people have access to savings services.

if they are saving to purchase an asset or pay an upcoming expense such as school fees. Savings services also help to keep savings secure, especially when receiving lump sums such as at harvest time or through a remittance (CGAP 2005).

This chapter provides an overview of savings services, primarily from an institutional perspective focusing on the institutional capacity required, the range of clients served, the added complexity to operations when mobilizing deposits, and a brief discussion of savings products. It will be of interest to practitioners, donors, and regulators, particularly those interested in adding savings services for the poor.

Savings Services in the Community

Poor people often rank convenience, access, and security over interest earnings, with proximity being key. For these reasons, poor savers have persistently chosen to save in the informal sector. Banks typically have limited rural infrastructure, and many find it difficult to serve small, often isolated savers profitably. Furthermore, for clients, accessing savings services from formal institutions often requires time and high transaction costs such as transportation, identification, registration, and opportunity costs. As well, given low and irregular incomes, poor people

save in small amounts, making the transaction costs proportionately even higher. Products may have complicated procedures and requirements that are difficult for poor people to meet, such as minimum balances or formal identification; intimidating banking facilities and procedures can potentially make poor savers feel disrespected (Frankiewicz and Churchill 2011). Although informal saving mechanisms have drawbacks, because of the difficulties in accessing formal providers, many poor women and men continue to save informally (see box 8.1; see also chapter 2).

Saving in cash at home or with neighbors or friends is the most liquid and accessible form of savings but also the most vulnerable to pressure for unintended or unnecessary expenditures and at the most risk of theft. To avoid such risk, many choose to save in kind—storing value in grain, animals, or jewelry—or through savings clubs or deposit collectors found in the local community.

Often women will save a store of food (such as rice) with a neighbor for use at a time when food is scarce. These arrangements are generally reciprocal between households and build on the trust and social capital within communities. Saving in livestock is common as well and can provide short-term income from the sale of products such as milk, eggs, or wool. In addition, selling animals can support the need for medium-term lump

Box 8.1 Savings Patterns in India

A study by MicroSave and the International Finance Corporation of savings patterns in India showed that challenges to saving can include cash flow volatility, unplanned expenditures, and unanticipated events such as illness and natural disasters. Examining the supply and demand of savings options for poor people in India, the study highlighted regulatory and operational challenges and opportunities for financial institutions and mobile banking platforms serving the low-income market. It found that nearly 75 percent of opportunities to save are unplanned and remain in the informal sector because of ease and access. Although bank branch density in India is reasonable, usage is low because of bad personal experiences with banks, mistrust of the banking system, inaccessibility (specifically with affordability of travel and transaction time/money listed as hindrances), and lengthy procedures to open accounts. As such, the vast majority of excess liquidity remains in the informal sector.

When respondents were asked why they do not save, volatility in cash flows was the reason cited most often. Unplanned expenditures, unanticipated events such as illness or natural calamity, and the lack of a proper place to save were all also frequently cited. Opportunities for individuals to save on a structured, regular basis were highly valued. The researchers concluded with seven key attributes that influenced the performance of service providers who mobilize deposits: security, interest, proximity, liquidity/ability to withdraw, acceptance of small savings, deposit term, and the opportunity to save in small amounts on a regular basis.

Source: Sadana et al. 2011.

sums. Yet saving in kind is not always safe and often not very liquid as market demand and values fluctuate. There are also costs associated with saving in livestock because animals require food, water, grazing land, and shelter—costs that add to household financial pressures. Saving in jewelry is popular in many cultures because it is transferable into cash and can be used to maintain value during a period of inflation. However, jewelry can also fluctuate in value and poses a high risk of theft and fraud (Robinson 2004).

Saving clubs such as rotating savings and credit associations (ROSCAs), accumulating savings and credit associations (ASCAs), deposit collectors, and others in the community are used frequently (see chapter 6). These offer more security than keeping cash or other assets at home and instill discipline with mandatory regular deposits (daily, weekly, biweekly, or monthly). However, they can also be inflexible (for example, ROSCAs) and result in a negative return (for example, deposit collectors),[1] and money may not be accessible when needed (for example, ASCAs).

Institutional Savings Services

Formal providers are beginning to make important progress in reaching lower-income markets with savings services. When savings services are offered by institutional providers, they are generally referred to as deposits. Savings is a more general term used when discussing a broad set of activities related to holding assets stored by others; deposits are the portion of savings held in financial institutions (CGAP 2005). Mobilizing deposits is very different from providing credit and much more difficult. Whereas lenders must select borrowers whom they trust to repay the loans, the situation is reversed with savings: It is the customers who must trust the service provider (Robinson 2006).

Savings services from formal providers can improve upon informal services and, in some cases, support increased incomes (see box 8.2).

Institutional Capacity

For financial institutions to offer deposit services to the public, they must be licensed to do so (see chapter 17).[2] They also require careful oversight by a competent, committed governance structure knowledgeable about financial intermediation, and strong institutional capacity including skilled management and appropriate systems and processes to manage the complexity of both lending and mobilizing savings, and to facilitate a relationship of mutual trust (see chapter 15). Infrastructure is required that provides easy access for clients (see chapter 18) as well as the capacity to

---

Box 8.2 Savings Constraints and Microenterprise Development: Evidence from Kenya

"Does limited access to formal savings services impede business growth in poor countries?" In search of an answer, Pascaline Dupas and Jonathan Robinson conducted a field experiment in which a randomly selected sample of small informal business owners in a village in rural western Kenya received access to an interest-free savings account. By directly expanding access to bank accounts, they tested the impact of these accounts on overall savings mobilization, business investment, income (measured using expenditures), and health expenditures, among other variables. The sample was composed primarily of market vendors. Dupas and Robinson relied on a data set collected from 279 daily logbooks kept by individuals in both the treatment (those with access to the account) and control (those without access) groups. The logbook data were supplemented by bank account activity information, making it possible to examine the impact of the accounts along a variety of dimensions that typically are not easily measured.

The bank charged substantial withdrawal fees, and as such, the de facto interest rate on the account was negative. Despite this,

take-up and usage of the account was high among market vendors, especially women—40 percent of female market vendors took up the savings account. The fact that these women voluntarily saved in accounts earning negative returns suggests that access to a formal savings account was highly valued.

The research found that having an account had a substantial positive impact on levels of productive investments among market vendors and within six months led to higher income levels, determined through a proxy of expenditures. The authors found suggestive evidence that the account made market women less vulnerable to health shocks. The logbook data indicated that over the period of the study, market women in the control group were forced to draw down their working capital in response to health shocks, whereas women in the treatment group did not have to reduce their business investment levels and were better able to smooth their labor supply over illness. It seems that Dupas and Robinson's initial hypothesis was correct: Limited access to formal savings services can impede business growth in poor countries.

Source: Dupas and Robinson 2011.

---

manage liquidity throughout a network of branches, outlets, or agents (see chapter 14). Additional (and sometimes substantial) reporting requirements and compliance issues (for example, strong rooms and safes, teller windows) to satisfy the regulatory body imply increased personnel costs and the need for expanded information systems and infrastructure. According to Robinson (2006), five main conditions need to be met for a financial institution to mobilize public deposits:

a. *The political economy.* Mobilizing voluntary public deposits requires at least a moderately enabling macroeconomy and some degree of political stability.

b. *The policy and regulatory environment.* A reasonably adequate policy and regulatory environment is needed—or if not immediately possible, at least consistent nonenforcement of inappropriate policies and regulations. Institutions licensed to take savings from the public and to intermediate these funds need to operate in an environment characterized by liberalized interest rates and regulations appropriate for commercial microfinance.

c. *Public supervision.* For the protection of their customers, especially savers, institutions that mobilize deposits must be publicly supervised. This generally means that their governments must be willing to modify their standard banking supervision practices so that the rules are suitable for their activities. Appropriate supervision does not mean relaxing standards; It means applying high standards in ways that are relevant for financial service providers serving the poor. It also means ensuring that the supervisory body has the capacity to monitor effectively the performance of such licensed providers.

d. *A strong institutional performance record.* An institution mobilizing deposits must have high-quality governance and management capacity that is appropriate for a financial

intermediary. The institution should have a demonstrated track record of high-level performance and transparency. It should have effective and efficient operations, maintain a high rate of loan recovery, and regularly earn good returns. It should be financially self-sufficient, with considerable outreach.

e. *Preparation for far-reaching changes.* Before becoming regulated and undertaking deposit mobilization, the institution's owners, governing board, managers, and staff, as well as the licensing authorities, need to understand that substantial changes in the institution's organization, leadership, infrastructure, information, and operations will be required—many of them in a relatively short period.

In order to be financially self-sufficient, institutions that mobilize deposits from the poor must also attract large deposits; transaction costs are too high to collect savings in very large numbers of small accounts. Providing large numbers of small savers with deposit services is labor intensive and therefore costly—even if no interest is paid below a minimum balance. By attracting larger deposits, the overall costs are lowered and liquidity risk is reduced, especially when low-income clients need to withdraw their savings at the same time, such as when school fees are due or in preharvest months. If large numbers of clients withdraw savings at the same time, the institution can easily run into liquidity problems. When savings are collected from a range of clients of different income levels, including organizations and institutions, this is unlikely to occur except in special circumstances such as hyperinflation, regional shock, or loss of trust in the provider (Robinson 2006).

Management Skills
Managing a financial intermediary, that is, an institution that takes savings and lends those savings to others, is far more complex than managing credit services only. Financial intermediation

requires significant management skills, in particular, strong financial capabilities, as well as knowledge of the opportunities and risks of providing financial services to the poor. This can be difficult to achieve. Well-qualified managers are hard to find and generally command high salaries (Robinson 2006).

When mobilizing deposits, managers and staff need to understand how local markets operate, how to locate potential savers, and how to design instruments and services for that market. They also need to understand basic finance and the importance of an adequate spread between lending and deposit services. They need to be trained in developing savings products and services appropriate for all types of savers, and adapting products when necessary. Both classroom and on-the-job training are needed in market research, including monitoring and evaluation, product costing and pricing, and operational procedures (Robinson 2006).

Managing Operations

Most providers that mobilize deposits have organizational structures that are both extensive and decentralized. Locations close to deposit customers reduce transaction costs for both the provider and its clients and are an important part of establishing a permanent relationship built on mutual trust, which is key to successful savings mobilization. "People will deposit their savings with an institution only if they perceive it to be reliable, trustworthy and professional" (Frankiewicz and Churchill 2011, p. 89; see box 8.3).

Because of this extensive and decentralized structure, savings operations can be more vulnerable to fraud and errors than credit operations. Institutions must manage the liquidity risks associated with larger amounts of cash and the unpredictability of the size and timing of deposits. Effective asset liability management (see chapter 14) and internal controls (see chapter 15), for example, as well as adequate premises are crucial. Accounting, reporting, and

---

Box 8.3 Inspiring Trust

To ensure depositors develop a trust relationship with the institution, providers must do the following:

- Deliver on promises, even if they seem insignificant or have no direct connection to a savings product; failure to deliver will create the impression the provider is unreliable.
- Serve customers in an efficient, friendly, and responsive manner.
- Provide well-defined and transparent services.
- Create a secure, attractive, and professional appearance.
- Hire and promote managers who demonstrate professionalism and are perceived by clients to be strong, risk-conscious, and trustworthy.
- Make withdrawals simple and easy to access.
- Develop marketing campaigns and promotional materials that communicate safety, reliability, transparency, and a long-term commitment to the community.
- Make public relations an important component of the institution's marketing strategy.
- Provide financial counseling or financial education to increase clients' understanding of the benefits of saving and the measures the provider is taking to ensure the safety of their funds.

Source: Frankiewicz and Churchill 2011.

audit systems must normally be approved by the regulator as well as internal controls, and often physical premises. Deposit mobilizing institutions must ensure that the product terms do not increase interest rate and liquidity risk and that the deposits mobilized are invested in assets that match their term and pricing structure. There must be sufficient reserves, capital, and operating funds to cover any operating losses or losses due to catastrophic events without using client deposits. Internal controls must be sufficient to protect savings from fraud and mismanagement and to ensure the physical security of funds. The physical premises must provide adequate protection, accommodate clients, and inspire their trust. Additional security measures are likely needed as well as reporting and information systems. Systems must be able to handle an increased number and type of transactions associated with mobilizing deposits and provide information that is sufficient, accurate, timely, and transparent. Finally deposit-taking institutions need a profitable place to invest mobilized deposits beyond those that are used for lending (CGAP 2005; McKee 2005).

Altogether, financial institutions that mobilize deposits generally have significantly more savings accounts than loan accounts. It is necessary that institutions know how to design and deliver products, including loans, for a wide variety of clients and that they have realistic business plans that demonstrate ongoing profitability. Revenues and costs need to be detailed, and plans must also consider the cost of capital in addition to the administrative and financial costs of deposits.

Pricing Savings Products

Some savings services pay interest (or a share of earnings if savings are on lent) to the saver; others do not and, in fact, may result in negative earnings (the value of savings declines) because of fees charged. The interest rate paid on savings products is often tied to the balance and length of time the savings are held on deposit; the longer the term and the larger the amount, generally the higher the interest rate paid. Fees are often levied for withdrawals and transfers that exceed the number of allowable free transactions per month, and for balances that fall below a predetermined minimum. With deposit collectors or money guards, fees are charged for collecting savings, resulting in negative returns.

The interest rate paid on deposits is generally based on the prevailing deposit rates of similar products in similar institutions, the rate of inflation, and market supply and demand. Risk factors such as liquidity risk and interest rate risk must also be considered based on the time period of deposits. Because highly liquid accounts are costly to administer, they pay lower interest. Most savers who select a liquid account are more interested in greater access to their savings than to higher interest earnings. Fixed-term deposits pay a higher rate of interest because the funds are locked in and provide a more stable source of funding than more liquid savings products.

In addition to interest paid on deposits, providers incur numerous other costs, including staff and branch costs to mobilize and administer deposit accounts. Deposits do not generate revenue for providers; rather, they provide capital, which is used to fund loans or other investments for a return. As discussed in chapter 9, credit products are priced to cover all operating costs, loan loss provisioning costs, and the cost of capital. The cost of capital includes the costs of deposits and other debt and equity. A provider needs to earn a spread between what it pays for savings and what it earns from lending services. This spread is then used to cover other costs, namely, operating costs, provisioning costs, and other capital costs. Credit and savings products should therefore be designed and priced together to enable both appropriate coverage and institutional profitability (Robinson 2006). Determining the rate of interest to pay on deposits is complicated and must be considered as part of the overall cost structure of providing financial services (see chapter 15).

Some providers organize their branches or field offices as *profit centers* and employ a method of *transfer pricing*, ensuring full-cost coverage throughout the branch network (if applicable). Transfer pricing refers to the pricing of services provided by the head office to the branches on a cost-recovery basis. For example, costs incurred in the head office to manage the overall organization are prorated to the branches based on a percentage of assets (loans) or liabilities (deposits) held at the branch. Funding costs are apportioned as well. A branch that disburses a larger volume of loans than the deposits it collects needs to receive funding from the head office (or another branch) to fund those loans. The head office (or a regional office) acts as a central funding facility to ensure that any excess deposits in one branch are "sold" to another branch to fund their loans. The branch that has excess deposits receives payment (interest revenue) for those funds, while the branch receiving them pays a fee (interest expense). If the head office determines that there is no excess

funding within the system, it will then access external funding and on-lend it to its branches for a set price.

The transfer price charged to branches (or paid to branches for excess deposits) is set either close to the interbank lending rate or at a rate somewhat higher than the average costs of funds of the provider. This provides incentives for branches to mobilize savings locally rather than relying on the excess liquidity of other branches within the network. It can also result in additional revenue at the head office level to cover overhead. Transfer pricing ensures transparency and instills accountability and responsibility in the branches.

Savings Products

In general, an institution providing deposit services does not need a large number of products (see box 8.4). A savings account permitting unlimited transactions, a time deposit account

---

Box 8.4 Savings Services—Not Only about Products

"For many years, product design was neglected in microfinance. Now the pendulum has swung, and product design is too often overemphasized by managers who sometimes appear to think that the race is won by the provider with the largest number of products. Well-designed savings products are essential, but they are only one element in a much larger set of requirements for successful mobilization of savings from the public—many of which tend to be overlooked as increasing emphasis has been placed on designing multiple products. Product delivery is far more difficult than product design. Convenience of branch location and opening hours; attitudes of managers and staff toward

clients; information systems, space use, asset-liability management, liquidity, and cash management; efficiency of operations (for example, short waiting periods for savers who want to deposit or withdraw); quality of administration; quality of the loan portfolio; trustworthiness of the institution; and many other factors are crucial to capturing and maintaining public savings. Getting the structure and operations of these interlinkages right—which requires experienced, skilled management at all levels—is far more important than a wide range of products. The race is generally won by the institution that demonstrates the best delivery of a few well-chosen products."

Source: Robinson 2006.

(which includes options for relatively short maturities), potentially a contractual savings account to support education, retirement, housing, or upcoming ceremonies, and, if necessary, one or two other deposit products are sufficient. They must be carefully designed through a balance of product features, security, convenience, and price to allow them to be used in different combinations for different purposes by all types of savers—poor and nonpoor, individuals and institutions (Robinson 2006).

Deposit products available from regulated providers include current accounts, savings accounts, contractual savings accounts, time deposits, and long-term savings or micropensions.[3]

Current Accounts

Current accounts are generally considered to be more of a transaction account than a savings account (see chapter 12). They provide the account holder with the ability to manage daily cash flows and transfer funds and make payments. Also called checking accounts or demand or site deposits, current accounts are fully liquid accounts in which the depositor may deposit and withdraw any amount at any time with no advance commitment or notice. Current accounts may be set up with automatic transfers, for example, to pay bills each month or to transfer to another account.

Customers often must deposit a minimum amount to open a current account and maintain a minimum balance to keep it active. Generally current accounts do not pay any interest but charge clients fees either on a monthly or a transaction basis or both. If clients overdraw from their current accounts, they may be charged a penalty or the payment may be rejected outright.

Passbook Savings Accounts

A basic savings account or passbook savings is an account that is fully liquid (that is, money can be freely deposited and withdrawn by the account holder) or semiliquid (that is, the number of transactions are restricted). For example, for savings accounts with no minimum balance requirement, to compensate for the small balances generally held in these accounts, providers may restrict the number of monthly transactions and/or limit withdrawals to lower-cost access points such as automated teller machines or mobile phones. Passbook savings generally offer clients interest on the funds deposited, although many providers also charge transaction and other fees associated with services.

The main advantages with passbook accounts are liquidity and higher interest rates compared to current or transaction-based accounts. Generally passbook savings accounts are used for short-term savings for cash flow management or for emergencies or unexpected opportunities. Interest paid is normally lower than that paid on time deposits.

Contractual Savings Accounts

Contractual savings accounts (also called commitment savings or target savings) require clients to commit to regularly deposit a fixed amount for a specified period to reach a predetermined date or amount. Clients are prohibited from or penalized for withdrawals before the maturity date. After the maturity date, the client can withdraw the entire amount plus the interest earned.

Contractual savings accounts help clients accumulate funds to meet specific expected needs, such as school fees or to pay for an upcoming celebration such as a marriage (see box 8.5). Generally the interest paid on contractual savings is similar to other savings accounts, the primary benefit being the discipline they provide.

Contractual savings products can be used as a first entry point for youth in microfinance. Often only small modifications are needed to tailor a regular product for youth, including, for example, low or no minimum balances or a link to a financial education program.

An innovative savings product similar to contractual savings is borrowing for the purpose of saving (see box 8.6).

Box 8.5 Saving for Education

Opportunity Bank Malawi offers a savings account designed for parents and guardians with school-age children called *Tsogolo Langa*. The account allows parents to more easily pay school fees and other related expenditures and to keep their money safe until the fees are due, ideally allowing children to go to school continuously. The account features include a minimum balance of MK 300 (US$1.85) and a contractual agreement between the parents and the bank to use the savings to pay for their children's education. Parents can open the account and voluntarily deposit money into it if the beneficiary child is a student at any of the bank's approved schools. The account offers no service charges and makes fee payments directly to the school on behalf of the depositor. Interest is paid on a monthly basis.

Source: Opportunity Bank Malawi, http://www.oibm.mw/index.php/deposit-products/62-tsogolo-langa-account.

Box 8.6 Borrowing to Save

P9 is a savings-and-loan service offered to low-income households by *Safe*Save in Bangladesh that builds on Stuart Rutherford's pioneering work on understanding how the poor manage their financial lives. P9 "lends to save" by advancing only a portion of the loan amount and holding the remainder (40–50 percent) in escrow as "savings." Over time, the client pays the entire loan amount and retains the savings. For example, if a client wants to save US$5, she borrows US$10 and immediately has use of US$5 to do with whatever she wishes. The remaining US$5 is locked away as savings. She cannot touch it until she repays the US$10 in full, at which point, she has accumulated US$5 in savings. The client is able to borrow increasing amounts in subsequent tranches, building up significant savings within a short amount of time. P9 has an initial registration fee of 200 takas (approximately US$3), a disbursement fee of 3 percent, no interest, and allows top-ups.

Jipange Kusave (JKS) builds off of the same concept, offering a savings-and-loan service through Kenya's hugely popular mobile money service M-PESA. The first loan is usually small, about US$20. Half of it is deposited into the client's M-PESA account to use as they please, and the other half goes into a savings account in a regulated bank. JKS encourages clients to set "savings goals" and commit to a number of smaller commitments—a goal of US$50 for example, could involve five rounds of US$20 each. JKS charges an origination fee of 2–5 percent, an early savings withdrawal fee of 5 percent, and a charge from M-PESA of K Sh 10 (approximately US12 cents) per transaction. Repayments for both P9 and JKS can be made as often as desired and in any amount.

However, the products are not without their challenges. The variable costs to clients can be quite high, and securing appropriate banking licenses and satisfying regulatory requirements will be key to their growth.

Source: Ashriul Amin.

Time Deposits

Time deposits—also called fixed deposits, term deposits, or certificates of deposit—are savings products in which a client makes a one-time deposit that cannot be withdrawn for a specified period or term without penalty. At the end of the term, the client can withdraw the entire amount with interest or roll over the deposit for another term. Financial institutions offer a range of possible terms and usually pay a higher interest rate on time deposits than on passbook or contractual savings accounts because these accounts offer the institution larger amounts of money for longer periods of time at lower costs (see box 8.7).

Long-Term Savings and Micropensions

Poor people are vulnerable because low and irregular incomes combined with insufficient financial tools often leave them with little to no savings as they age. In many developing countries, particularly in poor communities, children and grandchildren will take financial responsibility for older family members and provide them shelter and financial resources. In addition to family support, there are financial services that facilitate savings for long-term goals and/or retirement, including long-term savings, micropensions, and savings combined with insurance products.

Pensions

Although not highly prevalent among poor communities, pensions are a type of savings product that provides a regular flow of payments from retirement to death. Sometimes these payments transfer to a surviving spouse. Pensions are primarily provided by employers. Benefits accumulate based on earning level and years of service; the more years of service and the higher the employee's earnings, the greater the amount of payments. Pension funds can be internally managed by the company or outsourced to an investment manager and can be fully funded by the employer (*defined benefit pension*) or a *defined contribution pension* funded by both the employer and employee, with the employer matching the employee's contributions using a formula such as 2:1 or 0.5:1.

Even less prevalent—and, in fact, so far there is very little long-term experience to draw from—micropensions provide a form of income security, enabling voluntary savings for old age and aimed at lower income populations (Sterk 2011). They require fixed contributions over time, which are

---

Box 8.7 Nicaragua—Promoting Agriculture Savings

The Central de Cooperativas de Ahorro y Crèdito Financieras de Nicaragua (CCACN) is a second-tier network of Nicaraguan credit unions. CCACN developed a time deposit product called "Agriculture Salary" with a twist. Rather than receive all the proceeds of an annual or semiannual harvest as a lump sum all at once, the goal of the product is to smooth the flow of income farmers receive. Credit unions work with farmer members to open a savings account and deposit the proceeds from each harvest and then work with each farmer to identify his or her individual expenses and determine an appropriate "salary"—a portion of harvest proceeds on deposit combined with interest—to be withdrawn from the credit union each month.

Source: WOCCU 2003.

invested in term savings accounts, group term savings accounts, or physical assets such as property, land, and livestock, to create a consistent flow of income when the micropension holder can no longer generate income. Micropensions offer an option to invest in a financial asset over time that produces a flow of income—either as a lump sum, on a periodic basis, or through the purchase of an annuity—beginning at a predetermined age (Sterk 2011). Micropensions can also be informal whereby money is invested in the businesses or education of family members in exchange for future income or subsistence support (Rutherford 2008).

Long-Term Contractual Savings

Similar to micropensions, long-term contractual savings (LTCS) products can be used to prepare for retirement and to build resources for life-cycle events anticipated in the future. LTCS products work much like other contractual savings products whereby clients make small regular deposits over time and then withdraw either the lump-sum amount or, like micropensions described above, with an annuity allowing a regular stream of payments over time after a certain age (see box 8.8). Although clients appreciate the illiquid nature of LTCS products as well as the benefits of discipline (like other contractual savings products), they necessarily compare the options of investing elsewhere and the associated risks. In particular, if available, clients need to consider the benefits of saving long term versus buying insurance. The risk of LTCS products is that the person may die before the savings goal is reached. This risk is addressed with retirement and life products offered by insurance companies (Frankiewicz and Churchill 2011).

Finally, retirement planning can also involve the combination of savings and insurance products, specifically, savings completion insurance, endowment plans, or annuities. This is discussed under insurance products in chapter 11.

Box 8.8 Grameen's Deposit Pension Scheme (GPS)

In 2001 Grameen Bank began to offer long-term savings products for the poor. Terms are 5 or 10 years, and equal monthly deposits are made in sums as little as US$1. Interest on the 10-year term is paid at 12 percent per annum. This is about 8 percent in real terms and generous compared with rates offered by commercial banks for similar products. (This has led to increased demand from nonpoor households to obtain Grameen membership and brings into question the profitability of the product.) The depositor gets almost twice the amount of money she saved at the end of the period. The matured sum may be taken in cash or as monthly income. Savers may also transfer the sum into one of Grameen's fixed deposits.

Deposits are made during the weekly meetings that all Grameen members are obliged to attend. Grameen thus uses its own "agents," because the agents are also credit officers. After five years, in 2005 GPS had attracted more than 3 million accounts holding approximately US$83 million. By the end of October 2011 the balance was Tk 38.87 billion (US$513 million).

Understanding precisely why the product is so popular is complicated by the fact that all borrowers with a loan of more than US$125 are required to hold a minimum-value GPS account. Nevertheless, many savers hold more than one account, suggesting that the product is valued for its own sake.

Source: Frankiewicz and Churchill 2011, adapted from Roth, McCord, and Liber 2007; http://www.grameen-info .org/index.php?option=com_content&task=view&id=26&Itemid=0.

Notes

1. The willingness of poor women and men to pay for deposit collection demonstrates the value of saving services and the overall need for both the ability and discipline to save small amounts frequently.
2. This section is summarized from Robinson (2006).
3. This description of products draws substantially from Gilsovic, El-Zoghbi, and Foster (2010).

References and Further Reading

* Key works for further reading.

Ashraf, Nava, Dean Karlan, and Wesley Yin. 2006. "Tying Odysseus to the Mast: Evidence from a Commitment Savings Product in the Philippines." *Quarterly Journal of Economics* 121: 635–72.

*CGAP (Consultative Group to Assist the Poor). 2005. "Microfinance Consensus Guidelines Developing Deposit Services for the Poor." CGAP, Washington, DC.

*Christen, Robert Peck, and Ignacio Mas. 2009. "It's Time to Address the Microsavings Challenge, Scalably." *Enterprise Development and Microfinance* 20 (4): 274–85.

Dupas, Pascaline, and Jonathan Robinson. 2011. "Savings Constraints and Microenterprise Development: Evidence from a Field Experiment in Kenya." NBER Working Paper 14693. NBER, Cambridge, MA, October 27.

*Frankiewicz, Cheryl, and Craig Churchill. 2006. *Making Microfinance Work: Managing for Improved Performance.* Geneva: International Labour Organization.

*———. 2011. *Making Microfinance Work; Managing Product Diversification.* Geneva: International Labour Organization.

*Gilsovic, Jasmina, Mayada El-Zoghbi, and Sarah Foster. 2010. "Advancing Saving Services: Resource Guide for Funders." CGAP, Washington, DC.

*Karlan, Dean, and Jonathan Morduch. 2009. "The Economics of Saving. Access to Finance: Ideas and Evidence." Financial Access Initiative and Innovations for Poverty Action, New York and New Haven, CT.

*McKee, K. 2005. "Prerequisites for Intermediating Savings." In *Savings Services for the Poor*, ed. Madeline Hirschland, 27–42. Bloomsfield, CT: Kumarian.

Robinson, Marguerite. 2004. "Mobilizing Savings from the Public: Basic Principles and Practices." USAID, SPEED Network, and Women's World Banking, Kampala, Uganda.

*———. 2006. "Mobilizing Savings from the Public." In *Transforming Microfinance Institutions: Providing Full Financial Services to the Poor,* ed. Joanna Ledgerwood and Victoria White. Washington, DC: World Bank.

Roe, Alan, Robert Stone, Stephen Peachey, and Abigail Carpio. 2008. "Increasing the Number of Deposit Accounts: A White Paper for Discussion." Oxford Policy Management, Oxford.

Rosenberg, Rich. 1996. "Microcredit Interest Rates." CGAP Occasional Paper 1. CGAP, Washington, DC.

Roth, Jim, Michael McCord, and Dominic Liber. 2007. *The Landscape of Microinsurance in the World's 100 Poorest Countries.* Appleton, WI: MicroInsurance Centre.

Rutherford, Stuart. 2008. "Micropensions: Old Age Security for the Poor?" In *New Partnerships for Innovation in Microfinance,* ed. Ingrid Matthäus-Maier and J. D. von Pischke, 241–64. Berlin: Springer.

*———. 2009. *The Poor and Their Money: An Essay about Financial Services for Poor People.* New Delhi: Oxford University Press.

Sadana, Mukesh, et al. 2011. "Deposit Assessment in India." IFC, MicroSave, and Ministry of Foreign Affairs, March. http://www.microsave.org/sites/default/files/research_papers/Microsave_IFC.pdf.

*Sterk, Boudewwijn. 2011. "Micro Pensions: Helping the Poor to Save for the Future." Aegon Global Pensions, The Hague, May 31.

WOCCU (World Council of Credit Unions). 2003. "A Technical Guide to Rural Finance: Exploring Products." Technical Guide 3. WOCCU, Madison, WI, December.

CHAPTER 9

Credit

Joanna Ledgerwood and Julie Earne

Credit products offer clients the ability to borrow money in exchange for an agreement to repay the funds with interest and/or fees at some future point(s) in time. Credit products range from working capital loans, emergency and consumption loans, to leasing products and housing loans. They are found at the core of the financial market system.

This chapter provides a brief overview of lending products including product characteristics, pricing, methodologies for determining the effective cost of borrowing, and the most prevalent credit products accessed by poor people today. It will be of interest to practitioners, donors, and others wanting to support outreach of credit to the poor.

Characteristics of Credit Products

Loans are structured based on client demand, capabilities of the provider, and risk management

requirements (to ensure repayment). The core components of a loan are size, term, repayment terms, lending methodology, collateral or security, and pricing.

Loan *sizes* vary depending on need and can be as low as US$5 from a community-based provider to upwards of US$20,000 or more for an individual business loan or housing loan. Loan sizes can increase over time based on client needs, debt capacity, and credit history; loans should not increase simply as a function of continued borrowing.

Loan *term* (or *tenor*) refers to the length of time the loan is intended to be outstanding. Most microfinance loan terms range from three months to one year, although terms can be up to three years or longer. Group loans tend to have short maturities given they are normally small and sometimes provided to clients without a credit history. Agriculture loans may have longer terms

---

Contributions to this chapter were made by Liz Case.

to match the planting and harvest period, while housing loans may be even longer due to their larger size and purpose. Given the higher risk associated with a longer term, loan terms can increase as clients establish a track record.

Repayment terms affect the credit risk, transaction costs, and accessibility of loan products. Loans are usually designed to be repaid in periodic (often equal) installments over the loan term or at the end as a lump sum, ideally matched to the borrowers' cash flows. Loan payments (usually comprising principal plus interest but can be interest only if the principal is paid all at the end) can be made in weekly, biweekly, or monthly installments depending on the loan structure, or can be a lump-sum payment at the end of the term. The frequency of loan payments depends on the needs of the client and the ability of the provider to ensure repayment and manage liquidity. A grace period (period of time between the disbursement and first repayment) may also be provided, especially with agriculture loans to allow for planting.

More frequent repayments serve to reduce credit risk but in turn can increase the transaction costs and may make loans less accessible for borrowers in remote areas or those with infrequent cash flows. Depending on how, when, and where payments are made, the risk of default may increase if the borrower is not able to manage larger installments or a final lump sum.

Loan products must be well structured to meet client needs and provided in a safe, transparent manner. For example, it is imperative that providers effectively assess debt capacity to ensure that clients borrow amounts they can afford to repay on time. When clients are unable to repay, providers should have policies that support delinquent borrowers and limit further harm while still ensuring a strong repayment discipline.

Lending Methodology

Lending methodologies differ with respect to whether loans are made to groups or to individuals and, in some cases, whether they must adhere to Islamic banking principles. The lending methodology chosen greatly influences product design, client selection, the application and approval process, loan repayment, and monitoring and portfolio management. Lending methodology also impacts the institutional structure and staff requirements, including training and compensation.

Group Lending

Group-based approaches lend either to the group itself as one loan, to individuals who are members of a group, or to groups who then on-lend individually to the members. Group lending reduces transaction costs and risks to providers and often facilitates greater access to financial services for those who are difficult and expensive to reach, including remote, rural populations, those with low debt capacity, and those who have no collateral or credit history. The group mechanism effectively shifts the bulk of the responsibility for screening, monitoring, and enforcement from the provider to the borrowers, and thus some of the costs.

Some of the most well-known group lending methodologies include the following:

- Grameen—five-person subgroups, six of which make up a center of 30 individual borrowers; the subgroups guarantee each other's loans, and the center provides a secondary guarantee.

- Solidarity groups—three to 10 people per group, each guaranteeing each other's individual loans.

- Village banks—15 to 50 people who form a "village bank" that makes individual loans to the members of the village bank. In some cases pooled member savings may be loaned to members within the group; such loans are referred to as "internal account" loans.

Disadvantages of the group approach include higher transaction costs for clients due to time spent in group meetings (and away from productive activities or household responsibilities), a relatively limited product offering, a lack of privacy, and of course the risk a fellow group member will default. Covariance risk—the tendency of group members to be affected by the same risk at the same time as a result of similar production activities or event—can also exist, resulting in higher risk for both the provider and borrowers. Group training costs can be high because of the importance of quality group formation and related consumer education. Furthermore, group members sometimes feel pressure to borrow even if they do not need a loan or are unsure of their ability to repay. This may also happen in Savings Groups or Self-Help Groups even though loans are made by the group to individuals.

Individual Lending

Individual lending requires greater up-front analysis of clients and their cash flows, sometimes physical collateral, and frequent and close contact with clients during the term of the loan. Loan approvals and amounts are based on an applicant's eligibility and debt capacity, which in turn are dependent upon a number of factors, including personal and business characteristics, for example, age, gender, or reputation, sources and amount of income, age of business (if applicable), cash flow, and available collateral. Historically many providers also considered the purpose of the loan as part of the loan approval decision, but this is less and less common as providers begin to understand client cash flows, their needs, and the fact that money is fungible within households and microenterprises.

Cash flow analysis is used primarily for individual loans and focuses on the overall cost structure of the household or microenterprise, including all revenues flowing in and expenses flowing out, anticipated cash flows during the term of the loan, and the absorptive debt capacity of the borrower. Many individual providers have designed streamlined worksheets that guide loan

officers' cash flow analysis. These worksheets enable a loan officer to create a basic balance sheet and income statement based on revenues, expenses, turnover, and value of stock and supplies in the household or enterprise.

A cash flow analysis can be supplemented with other tools such as credit ratings, credit scoring, and psychometric evaluations, depending on their availability in a given market. A credit rating is obtained from a credit bureau and provides information on a borrower's history of repayments and delinquencies from all providers participating in the credit bureau (see chapter 18).

For clients without a credit history and without formal employment, providers use other data to better assess risk and help currently unbanked clients develop a formal credit history. Such data can include the following:

- Bill payments (electricity, gas, or water)
- Phone bills (mobile and fixed, post- and prepaid)
- Rental payments
- Transaction data (remittances, withdrawals, deposits, or transfers).[1]

These data are sometimes put into a credit scoring that uses historic payment data to mathematically predict the probability of a client defaulting. Instead of conducting extensive analysis of financial statements, credit scoring uses simple predictive variables, such as length of time in business, bill payments, and length of time with the financial institution, to generate a score that represents the probability of future repayment (Frankiewicz and Churchill 2011). The increasing use of electronic channels by lending institutions (for example, mobile banking, ATMs, or banking agents) increases the ability to track and utilize clients' payment and transaction histories to predict payment capacity and creditworthiness.

Psychometric testing is a newer form of client evaluation and is in the early stages of development. Psychometric evaluations involve asking a series of questions that evaluate the potential borrower's attitude and outlook, ability, and character in an effort to predict creditworthiness.[2] These tests are processed by specialized companies and attempt to measure credit risk without depending on formal financial accounts, business plans, or collateral.

Islamic Lending

Islamic banking requires special lending methodologies.[3] Islamic (or Sharia-compliant) financial principles strictly prohibit giving or receiving any fixed, predetermined rate of return on financial transactions (Karim et al. 2008). Because Islamic law forbids gains on lending money, Islamic loans are often treated more like equity than debt with lenders considered investors rather than creditors. Other Islamic banking principles state that (1) all financial transactions must be linked to a "real" economic activity involving tangible assets and (2) funds may not be invested in activities inconsistent with Sharia (alcohol, pork, or gambling). Furthermore, contracts must reflect mutual agreement; all parties must have precise knowledge of the product or service being bought or sold (Karim et al. 2008).

There are various types of Islamic microfinance lending contracts. *Murabaha sale* is a cost-plus-markup sale contract that requires the financial service provider to purchase the asset, as requested by the client, and sell it to them at a predetermined markup to pay for the service provided (see box 9.1). Contracts can also be developed as profit and loss sharing schemes: *Musharaka* refers to equity participation in a business with parties sharing the profits or losses according to a predetermined ratio. *Musharaka*

Box 9.1 Islamic Finance in Practice

Akhuwat was established in 2001 in Pakistan with the aim of providing interest-free microcredit to the poor. Akhuwat dispenses small interest-free charitable loans *(qard al-hasan)* with an administration fee of 5 percent. Administrative procedures and activities are coordinated through mosques and the community. There are no independent officers; rather, loans are disbursed and recovered in the mosque. The Islamic provider relies on collateral-free and individual financing based on mutual guarantees. Anecdotal evidence suggests that disbursing loans in a mosque attaches a religious sanctity to borrowers' oaths to repay them on time.

Islamic Relief, a Muslim international relief and development organization, provides Islamic microfinance services in Pakistan using *murabaha*-based financing principles to individuals, based on a combination of personal guarantors, group savings accounts, cosigners, and community recommendations to ensure repayment. In 2009 Islamic Relief partnered with HSBC Amanah, the Islamic finance arm of the commercial bank HSBC, to provide financing to its microfinance projects in Rawalpindi. HSBC Amanah also assists in developing the Sharia structure for financing models and contracts and providing Islamic finance training to Islamic Relief staff. In turn, Islamic Relief staff manage the microfinance projects, including setting out eligibility criteria, screening potential beneficiaries, and reporting to HSBC Amanah.

Source: Allen and Overy LLP 2009.

can be used to fund assets and/or for working capital. *Mudaraba* is trustee financing in which one party provides funding while the other party provides the managerial expertise in managing the business, and they share in the profit or loss. Profit-and-loss sharing schemes require vigilant reporting and a high level of transparency for profits and losses to be distributed fairly (Karim et al. 2008).

Loan Collateral

Low-income clients often have minimal assets to pledge for loans; property, land, machinery, and other capital assets are often not available. Because of this, collateral substitutes and alternative collateral are used to reduce the risk to the lender.

Collateral Substitutes

One of the most common collateral substitutes is peer pressure, either on its own or jointly with group guarantees.

Group guarantees: Many providers facilitate the formation of groups whose members jointly guarantee each other's loans. Guarantees are either implicit guarantees, with other group members unable to access a loan if all members are not current in their loan payments, or actual guarantees, with group members liable if other group members default on their loans.

Some providers require group members to contribute to a group guarantee fund, which is used if one or more borrowers fail to repay. Use of the group guarantee fund is sometimes at the discretion of the group itself and sometimes decided by the provider. If it is used at the group's discretion, the group will often lend money from the guarantee fund to the group member who is unable to pay. The member who "borrows" from the group fund is then responsible for paying the fund back. If use of the group guarantee fund is managed by the provider, the fund is seized to the extent of the defaulted loan, with other group members making up any shortfall. Failure to do so

means that the entire group no longer has access to credit.

Character-based lending: Some providers lend to people based on a good reputation. Before making a loan, the credit officer visits various establishments in the community and asks about the potential client's character and behavior.

Frequent client visits: Provided the branch or credit officers are within a reasonable geographical distance from their clients, frequent visits help to ensure that the client is able and willing to repay the loan. Frequent visits also allow the credit officer to understand his or her clients' cash flows and the appropriateness of the loan (amount, term, frequency of payments, and so forth). Visits also contribute to developing mutual respect between the client and the credit officer as they learn to appreciate and understand each other's commitment to their work, which can lead to stronger relationships that benefit both the clients and providers. However, more frequent client visits entail additional costs that need to be considered.

Alternative Forms of Collateral

Commonly used alternative forms of collateral include compulsory savings and personal guarantees.

Compulsory savings: Many providers require clients to hold a balance (stated as a percentage of the loan) in savings (or as contributions to group funds) for first or subsequent loans (or both). Compulsory savings differ from voluntary savings in that they are not generally available for withdrawal while a loan is outstanding. In this way compulsory savings act as a form of collateral.

By being required to set aside funds as savings, borrowers are restricted from utilizing those funds. Usually the deposit interest rate paid (if any) on the savings is lower than the return earned by the borrowers if the savings were put into their business or other investments. This results in an opportunity cost equal to the difference between what the client earns on compulsory savings and the return that could be earned otherwise. This needs to be considered in calculating the cost of the loan for the borrower. Compulsory savings, however, also provide a means of building assets for clients; not all providers view compulsory savings as strictly an alternative form of collateral.

A variation of compulsory savings is for borrowers to pay additional interest each month and, provided they have made full, on-time payments each month, the additional amount is returned to them. For example, at the Bank Rakyat Indonesia, this is referred to as a "prompt payment incentive" and results in the borrower receiving a lump sum at the end of the loan term. This benefits the borrower and provides a concrete incentive to repay the loan on time, thus benefiting the bank as well.

Personal guarantees: If borrowers do not have the ability to guarantee their loans, they are sometimes able to enlist friends or family members to provide personal guarantees (sometimes referred to as cosigners). This means that in the event of the inability of the borrower to repay, the person who has provided a personal guarantee is responsible for repaying the loan.

Loan Pricing

Revenue on loans is, for the most part, generated from interest and fees, including in some cases penalties for late payments. Revenue needs to cover various expenses, including operating costs, loan loss provisions, and the cost of capital, ideally leaving a surplus (profit). Pricing requires a balance between the need to cover costs through revenue with the need for simplicity, transparency, and affordability for clients. For community-based lenders who have minimal if any costs, the price for loans is usually set based on demand and supply. If the price is set too high, there will be little demand and therefore minimal returns; if it is set too low, demand will exceed supply.

The price of loans is normally stated as a nominal interest rate—a percentage of the loan amount. Interest rates can be flexible and change depending on market conditions, or, more often,

be fixed for the term of the loan. The effective price is increased when a fee is charged in addition to interest. Fees are generally charged on the initial amount of the loan disbursed and may be expressed as a percentage of the loan amount or an absolute amount to cover the cost of making the loan. Other costs to the client such as transport costs to visit the provider, costs to obtain documentation such as identification or property rights, child care, and time away from business all contribute to the total cost of credit for the borrower but are generally not expressed in the price of the loan and do not generate revenue for the lender.

Calculating Interest Rates

Interest rates can be stated using a declining balance method or a flat-rate method. The declining balance calculates interest as a percentage of the amount outstanding during the loan term. As the amount of principal declines with each periodic payment, the interest is calculated only on the remaining amount owed. The flat-rate method calculates interest based on the original disbursed amount (sometimes net of fees). The flat-rate method is sometimes preferred by providers for the sake of simplicity in calculation; because the interest payment is the same amount each repayment period, some providers argue that using the flat-rate method is easier for staff and clients to understand (see box 9.2).

Although many providers use the flat-rate method because it is simple to calculate, it results in higher effective rates of interest (and thus higher costs for the borrower) for the same stated rate compared to interest calculated on a declining balance. For example, by month 6 of a 12-month loan for 1,000, the borrower will owe only 500 (approximately) if he or she has paid in regular weekly installments. At that point, if the loan price were to be calculated using the declining balance method, interest would be charged on only 500 rather than 1,000. (Note that with interest paid on the declining balance, a greater

Box 9.2 The Flat-Rate Method

The flat-rate method calculates interest as a percentage of the initial loan amount rather than the amount outstanding (declining) during the loan term. Using the flat-rate method means that interest is always calculated on the total amount of the loan initially disbursed, even though periodic payments cause the outstanding principal to decline.

To calculate interest using the flat-rate method the interest rate is simply multiplied by the initial amount of the loan. For example, if a provider charges 20 percent interest using the flat-rate method on a 1,000 loan, the interest payable is 200.

For example, loan amount: 1,000; 12-month loan term; monthly loan payments: 100; interest rate: 20 percent.

Month	Payments	Principal	Interest	Outstanding balance
0	—	—	—	1,000.00
1	100	83.33	16.67	916.67
2	100	83.33	16.67	833.34
3	100	83.33	16.67	750.01
4	100	83.33	16.67	666.68
5	100	83.33	16.67	583.35
6	100	83.33	16.67	500.02
7	100	83.33	16.67	416.69
8	100	83.33	16.67	333.36
9	100	83.33	16.67	250.03
10	100	83.33	16.67	166.70
11	100	83.33	16.67	83.37
12	100	83.33	16.67	0.00
Total	1,200	1,000.00	200.00	—

Source: Ledgerwood 1998.

portion of the monthly payment is paid in interest during the early months of the loan and a greater portion of principal is paid toward the end of the loan. This results in a slightly larger amount than half of the principal remaining outstanding at the midpoint of the loan. In the example in box 9.3, in month 6, 524.79 is still outstanding, not 500.)

The declining balance method is a fairer way to price loans but more difficult to calculate and may be confusing to borrowers (box 9.3).

However, providers should realize that regardless of the nominal rate quoted, it is important that all interest calculations are transparent.

The examples in boxes 9.2 and 9.3 illustrate that with all other variables the same, the amount of interest paid on a loan with interest calculated on a declining balance is much lower than that on a loan with interest calculated on a flat-rate basis, for the same stated rate. To compare rates of interest calculated by different methods it is necessary to determine what interest rate would be

Box 9.3 Declining Balance Method

To calculate interest on the declining balance, a financial calculator is required. On most financial calculators, present value and payment must be entered with opposite signs; that is, if present value is positive, payment must be negative, or vice versa. This is because one is a cash inflow and one is a cash outflow. Financial calculators allow the user to enter different loan variables as follows:

PV = Present value, or the net amount of cash disbursed to the borrower at the beginning of the loan

i = Interest rate, which must be expressed in same time units as n below

n = Loan term, which must equal the number of payments to be made

PMT = Payment made each period.

In the example above, a one-year loan of 1,000 with monthly payments and 20 percent interest calculated on the declining balance is computed by entering the following:

PV = –1,000 (enter as negative amount, as it is a cash outflow)

i = 20 percent a year; 1.67 percent a month

n = 12 months

Solve for PMT:

PMT = 92.63.

Total payments equal 1,111.56 (12 months at 92.63).
Total interest is 111.56.
Loan amount: 1,000; 12-month loan term; monthly loan payments: 92.63; interest rate: 20 percent.

Month	Payments	Principal	Interest	Outstanding Balance
0	—	—	—	1,000.00
1	92.63	75.96	16.67	924.04
2	92.63	77.23	15.40	846.79
3	92.63	78.52	14.21	768.29
4	92.63	79.83	12.81	688.46
5	92.63	81.16	11.48	607.30
6	92.63	82.51	10.12	524.79
7	92.63	83.88	8.75	440.91
8	92.63	85.28	7.35	355.63
9	92.63	86.70	5.93	268.93
10	92.63	88.15	4.49	180.78
11	92.63	89.62	3.02	91.16
12	92.63	91.16	1.53	0.00
Total	1,111.56[a]	1,000.00	111.76[a]	—

Source: Ledgerwood 1998.
a. Difference of 0.2 is due to rounding.

required when interest is calculated on the declining balance to earn the same nominal amount of interest earned on a loan with a flat-rate basis calculation (see box 9.4).

Fees and Other Service Charges

In addition to charging interest, many providers also charge a fee or service charge when disbursing loans. Fees or service charges increase the financial costs of the loan for the borrower and revenue to the provider. Fees are often charged as a means to cover initiation costs or to increase the yield to the provider instead of charging higher nominal interest rates.

Fees are generally charged as a percentage of the initial loan amount and are collected up-front rather than over the term of the loan. Because fees are not calculated on the declining balance, the effect of an increase in fees is greater than a similar increase in the nominal interest rate (if interest is calculated on the declining balance).

Calculating Effective Rates

The total cost of a loan is often expressed as the "effective interest rate." The effective rate of interest refers to the inclusion of all direct financial costs of a loan in one rate. Effective interest rates differ from nominal rates by incorporating interest, fees, the interest calculation method, and other loan requirements into the financial cost of the loan. The effective rate also includes the cost of compulsory savings or group fund contributions because these are financial costs to the borrower. Other transaction costs, both financial and nonfinancial, incurred by the borrower to access the loan, such as opening a bank account, transportation, child-care costs, or opportunity costs, are not included when calculating the effective rate because these can vary significantly by borrower. The effective rate of interest is useful for determining whether the conditions of a loan make it more or less expensive for the borrower than another loan and the effect of changes in pricing policies.

Box 9.4 Equating Declining Balance and Flat-Rate Methods

A 1,000 loan with 20 percent interest calculated on a declining balance for one year with monthly payments results in interest of 112 (rounded from 111.56). The same loan with interest calculated on a flat-rate basis results in interest of 200. To earn interest of 200 on a loan of 1,000 with interest calculated on the declining balance, the interest rate would have to increase by 15 percentage points to 35 percent (additional interest revenue of 88 based on interest on a 1,000 loan at 35 percent declining balance results in a total interest cost of 200, rounded from 199.52).

	Interest 20% declining balance	Interest 20% flat	Difference	Interest 20% flat	Interest 35% declining balance
Actual costs	112	200	88	200	200

Source: Ledgerwood 1998.

When interest is calculated on the declining balance and there are no additional financial costs to a loan, the effective interest rate is the same as the nominal interest rate. Many providers, however, calculate the interest on a flat-rate basis, charge fees as well as interest, or require borrowers to maintain savings or contribute to group funds (guarantee or insurance funds).

Variables of microloans that influence the effective rate include the following:

- Nominal interest rate

- Method of interest calculation: declining balance or flat-rate

- Payment of interest at the beginning of the loan (as a deduction of the amount of principal disbursed to the borrower) or over the term of the loan

- Service fees either up front or over the term of the loan

- Contribution to guarantee, insurance, or group fund

- Compulsory savings or compensating balances and the corresponding interest paid to the borrower either by the provider or another institution (bank or credit union)

- Payment frequency

- Loan term

- Loan amount.

When all variables are expressed as a percentage of the loan amount, a change in the absolute amount of the loan will not change the effective rate.

Calculation of the effective rate demonstrates how different loan product variables affect the overall costs and revenues of the loan. Box 9.5 illustrates the effect that a change in the loan fee and a change in the loan term have on the effective rate (the examples are calculated on both a flat-rate and a declining balance basis).

Given all the possible variables when structuring loans, numerous examples could be provided and the permutations are many. Various sources are available that explain in more detail how to calculate effective rates, including Rosenberg (1996), Ledgerwood (1998), and mftransparency. org. In particular, mftransparency.org provides a downloadable Excel spreadsheet called the "Calculating Transparent Pricing Tool."[4]

In reality, it is possible for all providers, even without sophisticated systems, to calculate the declining balance interest rate and communicate the effective interest rate to clients. Using several widely available tools, a provider can amortize the loan repayment so that each installment is the same, thus maintaining simplicity for clients who want to pay the same installment each period. It is used by most, if not all, formal financial institutions. Also, if all providers used the declining balance method, it would enable price competition based on transparency.[5]

Loan Products

As we now know, poor women and men have a multitude of financial service needs. In addition, more and more providers acknowledge that money is *fungible*; that is, loans intended for a specific purpose may be used for something else within the household or business. In response providers have expanded their credit product offerings to include more than the standard microenterprise loan for working capital or fixed assets. Loans are beginning to be made available for different purposes, including the following:

- Cash flow management (working capital and consumption loans)

- Risk management (emergency and top-up loans)

- Asset building and productive investment (fixed asset loans, leasing, housing loans).

Box 9.5 The Effect of a Change in Loan Fees and Loan Terms

With all other variables the same, the effective rate for a loan with interest calculated on a flat-rate basis will be higher than the effective rate for a loan with interest calculated on a declining balance basis. Fees also increase the effective rate, and if fees are charged, the effective rate is further increased when the loan term is shortened. This is because fees are calculated on the initial loan amount regardless of the length of the loan term. If the loan term is shortened, the same amount of money needs to be paid in a shorter amount of time, thus increasing the effective rate. (This difference is greatest when a fee is charged on a loan with interest calculated on the declining balance. The shorter loan term increases the *relative* percentage of the fee to total costs.) Similarly, a fee that is based in currency (such as US$25 per loan application) will change the effective rate if the loan amount is changed; that is, smaller loan amounts with the same fee (in currency) result in a higher effective rate.

Fee/Term	Calculation 20% annual rate	Service fee (%)	Loan term (months)	Effective cost per month (%)	Change (%)
3% fee; 12-month term	Flat-rate	3	12	3.5	
Raise fee to 8%	Flat-rate	8	12	4.3	↑ 0.8
Lower term to 3 months	Flat-rate	3	3	4.0	↑ 0.5
3% fee; 12-month term	Declining balance	3	12	2.1	
Raise fee to 8%	Declining balance	8	12	2.9	↑ 0.8
Lower term to 3 months	Declining balance	3	3	3.2	↑ 1.1

Note that the effect of an increase in the fee by 5 percent (to 8 percent) has the same effect (an increase of 0.8 percent per month in effective rate) whether the loan is calculated on a declining balance or flat-rate method. This is because the fee is calculated on the initial loan amount.

Source: Ledgerwood 1998.

Cash Flow Management

Working capital loans for microenterprises were among the first microcredit products to be developed during the industry's initial growth phase in the 1970s. Working capital loans (often termed microenterprise loans) are provided to either start or expand enterprises with the assumption that additional business revenue will be used to repay both principle and interest at predetermined intervals. Working capital loans are, for the most part, used for cash flow management to support productive investment.

Lines of credit are often used for working capital and/or household cash flow management. Rather than receiving a set amount of a loan that is then repaid, lines of credit allow the borrower to access credit as needed up to a certain amount. Repayment is often very flexible as well. Interest and fees (if applicable) are paid on the amount borrowed (or "drawn down") for as long as it is outstanding. Lines of credit, however, require management systems that accurately track withdrawals and payments of the line of credit as well as the ability to ensure adequate liquidity at all times; they are typically available only from commercial providers.

Consumption loans: Many households face cash management challenges related to both daily consumption and larger expenditures for life-cycle events such as marriages and funerals, or to address emergencies or education needs. These needs are often best addressed through savings, but if not available or if cash flows are insufficient, consumption loans with appropriate loan amounts and repayment terms can be useful. The primary purpose of these loans is to help households to smooth cash flows so that daily consumption becomes less dependent on income, particularly when income is erratic (Frankiewicz and Churchill 2011). Consumption loans may not be available if providers are used to assessing microenterprise cash flows to determine debt capacity. Frequently when consumption loans are not readily available, borrowers will take a working capital loan and use it for consumption.

Salary loans are made to clients with a regular source of income through salaried employment. The borrower's salary provides collateral for the loan, and repayments are usually debited directly through the employer at the time of payroll. Salary loans may or may not be required to be used for specific investments or purchases and are often used for consumption. Salary loans, however, are relatively rare for low- and very low-income populations because most do not have salaried employment.

Education loans are used to finance primary or secondary education. These loans can have more flexible repayment schedules and collateral requirements to accommodate students' lack of regular income and assets, and in some cases, payment may be delayed until schooling ends. Education loans are increasingly linked with financial education for youth with the view to develop financial capable consumers.

As more stakeholders begin to acknowledge the need for education funding, innovative products are being developed (see box 9.6)

Risk Management

Emergency loans provide funds on short notice for unanticipated events. They are generally offered by community-based providers but are becoming more prevalent with institutional providers. Banks sometimes make emergency loans to clients with whom they have long-term relationships, often by adding to existing loans As with any loans, the debt capacity of the borrower must be ensured.

Top-up loans: Many providers, both formal and informal, offer "top-up" loans where the outstanding loan amount can be increased if the amount requested is relatively small. Top-up loans were introduced to provide flexibility to traditional working capital loans and are generally processed very quickly with decisions largely based on a borrower's repayment history.

Asset Building and Productive Investment

Fixed asset loans are used to finance a specific asset such as a sewing machine or motorcycle; generally the assumption is the asset will contribute to an income-generating activity or enterprise, increasing the borrower's cash flow and, thus, capacity for debt. However, as mentioned above, stated and actual use may vary fundamentally. It is important thus to assess cash flows and debt capacity without the asset in case the loan proceeds are not used to purchase the asset. Acknowledging that this sometimes happens and that altogether the poor may want to purchase assets that are not productive, some providers are beginning to make loans to purchase household assets as well.

Box 9.6 Financing Education through Human Capital Contracts

Education finance has long been an area of interest for financial service providers. One new tool—the Human Capital Contract (HCC)—provides an innovative approach to some of the key challenges associated with lending for higher education.

More like equity then debt, the HCC is not technically a *credit* product. Participants apply for and receive a given amount of funding to help cover costs associated with higher education. In exchange, each student commits a fixed percentage of their income for a fixed period of time after graduation. There is no set principal associated with the transaction—the student's obligation ends after the designated number of payments (generally defined as a percentage of their income over a set number of years paid monthly) have been made regardless of the total sum paid. The percentage of income commitments never exceeds 15 percent and is set for each individual based on the expected earnings for his or her degree. As a result, some students will ultimately repay more than others, but all students face

affordable payments upon graduation regardless of their level of income. Graduates are not required to make payments when unemployed, and they make smaller payments during periods of underemployment, reducing the risk of unmanageable debt servicing associated with traditional student loans.

Although the HCC lowers risk for students, lenders must cope with variable repayment streams, income verification, and legal barriers to implementation. One Latin American firm, Lumni, is successfully overcoming these and other challenges. Lumni smoothes the risk inherent in such variable repayment schemes by pooling student contracts and bringing actuarial and labor market expertise to bear in its fund design and contract pricing work. To ensure success for both parties, students have access to career development services and networking activities.

By 2012, Lumni had financed over 3,000 students with operations in Chile, Colombia, Mexico, and the United States and is currently planning expansion into Peru.

Source: Noga Leviner, education finance specialist and former CEO, Lumni USA.

Leasing

Leasing is a form of financing that allows businesses or individuals to make use of equipment and other assets without having to own them or purchase them outright at the beginning. The user (the lessee) pays specific regular amounts to the owner (the lessor). Commonly leased assets include machinery (such as plows or shovels), vehicles, farming equipment, and livestock. Separating the use and ownership of an asset eliminates the need for a business or household to commit scarce capital to purchase assets (Wakelin et al. 2003). Broadly there are two different types of lease

agreements, financial and operating, with some variations.

Financial leases are leases in which the risks and rewards associated with ownership of the leased equipment are substantially transferred from the lessor to the lessee. A financial lease has the following common aspects:

- Amortization of the asset price—includes a purchase option for an agreed amount of payments or at the end of the lease period

- Maintenance—lessee is responsible for maintenance and all risks usually associated with ownership without actually owning the asset

- Noncancellation—the agreement is generally fixed at the time of the contract (Kloeppinger-Todd and Sharma 2010).

For farmers or enterprises constrained by a lack of assets for collateral, financial leases overcome this constraint, and in some cases, the lessee owns the asset outright at the end of the lease period (see box 9.7).

Financial leases are often beneficial to providers who may not have specific knowledge about the equipment being leased. Under a financial lease, the lessor takes the financial risk of the leased product without having to assume the technical risk associated with product performance. Financial leases are sometimes called capital leases, lease to purchase, or hire-purchase leases (with a hire-purchase lease, part of the ownership of the asset is transferred with each payment, and upon payment of the last installment the lessee becomes the full owner).

A variation on financial leases are sale and lease-back leases; the asset is sold initially to the lessor, with the agreement that the lessee will purchase back the asset over the life of the lease agreement (Deelen et al. 2003).

Operating leases are structured so the responsibility associated with ownership of the leased asset rests with the lessor who owns the asset. Generally operating leases are for terms substantially less than the economic life of the asset, and the lessee pays to use it for a finite period of time. An example of an operating lease includes the use of livestock or a vehicle for a few days in exchange for payment. With operating leases, the lessor takes responsibility for the upkeep and ongoing operations of the asset.

Leasing can also be provided under Islamic banking. *Ijarah* is a leasing contract typically used to finance small equipment. The term of the lease and the payment schedule must be determined in advance to avoid speculation and comply with

---

Box 9.7 Cow Leasing

K-Rep Development Agency in cooperation with Swisscontact developed a cow-leasing product. Under the lease, a farmer is loaned a pregnant cow and a chaff cutter used for producing milk. Various alternative forms of collateral and risk mitigation mechanisms are used to protect the provider and the farmer. First, as a lease, the asset itself is collateral, because the provider may take the cow back if the farmer does not make the agreed payments. Second, the farmer must belong to a group with other farmers who cross-guarantee each other. Third, the farmer has to take insurance coverage for the cow and for himself. The attached credit life product, the cost of which is built into the amount of the lease, ensures that all the risks to both

the microleasing company and the farmer's family are covered. In the event of death of either the farmer or the cow, the leasing company is paid the outstanding amount of the loan.

Under the microleasing contract, the farmer has the benefit of a grace period of up to three months. After this period, the farmer has to begin repaying the cost of the cow plus interest. The farmer can also choose to repay in 9, 12, or 18 months. The farmer uses income from milk sales to repay the loan. When the farmer completes payment for the cow and the chaff cutter, he owns both outright and reaps double benefit; because the cow is already pregnant, the farmer owns the cow and its calf.

Source: Baumgartner and Kamau 2010.

Sharia principles. For the transaction to be considered Islamic (and not a sale camouflaged with interest), the *ijarah* contract must specify that the ownership of the asset, and responsibility for its maintenance, remain with the funder. An *ijarah* contract may be followed by a sales contract, whereby the ownership of the asset is transferred to the lessee (Karim et al. 2008).

To date, however, leasing services have not been readily available given the difficulties of offering leasing products and the need for special licenses and expertise.

Housing Loans

Housing loans have become more popular in the last decade as providers acknowledge the need for adequate shelter and the value of building assets.[6] Housing loans differ from traditional mortgages in that mortgage finance refers to long-term loans to purchase real estate where the property acts as collateral. Mortgages are generally offered by commercial banks and mortgage companies at market interest rates; however, up to 80 percent of the global population cannot access conventional mortgage finance because of affordability issues, informal incomes, lack of clear land ownership, insufficiently deep financial markets, and/or weak housing finance institutions (Daphnis and Ferguson 2004). The World Bank estimates that only 3 percent of the population of Africa can afford a mortgage (Centre for Affordable Housing Finance in Africa 2011).

CGAP (2004) defines *housing microfinance* as "loans to low-income people for renovation or expansion of an existing home, construction of a new home, land acquisition and basic infrastructure." Some institutional providers have begun, most notably over the past 5 to 10 years, to develop housing loans for low-income populations. These products combine elements of both conventional mortgage finance and microcredit. Housing microfinance provides relatively larger loans (up to US$5,000) and longer terms (one to eight years) and may require compulsory savings as collateral. Interest rates are often lower than for microenterprise loans. Like other microcredit products, housing loans make use of group guarantees, localized collection efforts, and minimal collateral, often other than the house or land itself; providers generally do not require a land title to guarantee the loan, making products more accessible to low-income borrowers. Even where specific housing finance products are not available, there is evidence that up to 20 percent of all microfinance loans intended for working capital is used for housing and upgrading purposes (Ferguson 2008).

Housing support services, such as expertise from architects, engineers, and construction supervisors, are sometimes offered with housing loans. For example, Prodel in Nicaragua and the Patrimonio Hoy program of Cemex in Mexico offer specific technical assistance to both ensure high-quality results and confirm that loan funds are used for housing improvements or construction. Although many argue they help ensure quality housing (Ferguson 2010; Vance 2010), these services can be costly and complicated to deliver (see box 9.8).

The vast majority of housing loans have so far focused mainly on progressive building improvements, where individual households take a series of loans to improve their homes incrementally given the costs involved and low incomes. Furthermore, the poor do not show much appetite for larger loans with terms beyond five years;[7] they are well aware they will have other needs—for education, weddings, funerals—that will require their resources. Lastly, few providers show significant appetite for providing finance for new house construction for the poor, or slum-upgrading financing overall, because of increases in risk and costs that this kind of larger project entails. Incremental lending, and the housing improvements that go with it, are an easier "fit" into the existing delivery models of most providers seeking financial viability (Ferguson 2010; McLeod and Mullard 2006).

Box 9.8 Affordable Housing in Ghana

In 2007 UN-Habitat, supported by the governments of Sweden, Norway, and the United Kingdom, established a local finance facility institution in Tema-Ashaiman, near Accra, which was designed to provide credit enhancement (in this case, cash-collateral guarantees) and technical support to develop "bankable" low-income housing or slum upgrading projects, that is, projects that are able to secure and repay commercial housing loans. The TAMSUF institution has now delivered on a challenging but thus far successful project that resulted in the construction of a mixed-use low-income housing project in the heart of the informal settlement of Amui Djor. The three-story building, constructed on land provided by the Tema Traditional Council, has 32 residential units on the upper floors, which were sold to low-income residents at a reduced rate. This was made possible through the construction and operation of 15 shops and a commercial toilet and shower operation on the ground floor that delivered cross-subsidy. Financing and funding arrangements included a commercial loan that was guaranteed by TAMSUF, community down payments, subsidy from partner nongovernmental organizations, subsidy from government, and the commercial cross-subsidy being generated by the shops and the toilets and showers. Thus far, the community, all of whom are informally employed, have been paying the commercial loan with a 100 percent repayment rate.

Although a complex project, which required significant structuring and negotiation, the Amui Djor building has served as a positive example that communities can repay commercial loans and can ensure and manage group repayment. TAMSUF is working on further phases of this project, which received an award of excellence in December 2011 for innovation in social housing from ConsultASH and the UK Charted Institute of Housing.

Source: Liz Case, UN-Habitat.

Notes

1. CGAP Technology—Alternative Data to Develop a Credit Score, http://www.cgap.org/p/site/c/template.rc/1.26.2144/.
2. The Entrepreneurial Finance Lab, http://www.efinlab.com.
3. Adapted from Karim et al. (2008).
4. See http://www.mftransparency.org/resources/calculating-transparent-pricing-tool/.
5. Contributed by mftransparency.org, October 2011.
6. This section was contributed by Liz Case.
7. Pierre Giguere, private communication with Liz Case, Manager, Housing Finance, Développement International Desjardins, Canada, June 2010.

References and Further Reading

* Key works for further reading.

*Allen and Overy LLP. 2009. "Islamic Microfinance Report." Report for the International Development Law Organisation, February. http://loganswarning.com/wp-content/uploads/ 2010/12/Islamic-Microfinance-Report.txt.

Baumgartner, P., and P. Kamau, eds. 2010. "How Can a Farmer Get a High Yielding Cow?" *Organic Farmer* no. 56, January, Nairobi, Kenya.

Centre for Affordable Housing Finance in Africa, FinMark Trust. 2011. "2011 Yearbook." FinMark Trust, Parkview, South Africa. http://www.housingfinanceafrica.org/wp-content/uploads/2011/09/2011-Housing-Finance-Year-book.pdf.

CGAP (Consultative Group to Assist the Poor). 2004. "Helping to Improve Donor Effectiveness in Microfinance: Housing Microfinance." Donor Brief 20, CGAP, Washington, DC.

Daphnis, Franck, and Bruce Ferguson, eds. 2004. *Housing Microfinance: A Guide to Practice.* Bloomfield, CT: Kumarian Foundation.

*Deelen, Linda, Mauricio Dupleich, Louis Othieno, Olivier Wakelin, and Robert Berold, eds. 2003. *Leasing for Small and Micro Enterprises: A Guide for Designing and Managing Leasing Schemes in Developing Countries.* Geneva: International Labour Organization.

Ferguson, Bruce. 2008. "A Value Chain Framework for Affordable Housing in Emerging Countries." *Global Urban Development Magazine* 4 (2), November. http://www.globalurban.org/GUDMag08Vol4Iss2/FergusonValueChain.htm.

———. 2010. "Financing Slum Upgrading and Slum Prevention for the Poor." Presentation at the conference Sustainable Housing Microfinance in Sub-Saharan Africa: Turning Loans into Homes," April 12–15, Nairobi.

*Frankiewicz, Cheryl, and Craig Churchill. 2011. *Making Microfinance Work: Managing Product Diversification.* Geneva: International Labour Organization.

*Karim, Nimrah, Michael Tarazi, and Xavier Reille. 2008. "Islamic Microfinance: An Emerging Market Niche." Focus Note 49, CGAP, Washington, DC. http://www.cgap.org/gm/document-1.9.5029/FN49.pdf.

Kloeppinger-Todd, R., and M. Sharma. 2010. "Innovations in Rural and Agricultural Finance." Focus Note 18, World Bank, Washington, DC.

Ledgerwood, Joanna. 1998. *Microfinance Handbook: An Institutional and Financial Perspective.* Washington, DC: World Bank.

McLeod, Ruth, and Kim Mullard, eds. 2006. *Bridging the Finance Gap in Housing and Infrastructure.* Urban Management Series. Rugby, Warwickshire: Practical Action Publishing.

Vance, Irene. 2010. "Housing Support Services in Central America: Status and Challenges." Presentation at the conference Sustainable Housing Microfinance in Sub-Saharan Africa: Turning Loans into Homes, April 12–15, Nairobi.

Wakelin, Oliver, Louis Otheno, and Kirugumi Kinuya. 2003. "Leasing Equipment for Business: A Handbook for Kenya." Report, Enterprise Development Innovation Fund, September. http://practicalaction.org/microleasing/leasing.htm.

*Wright, Graham A. N. 2010. "Designing Savings and Loan Products." Report, MicroSave, Nairobi. http://www.microsave.org/research_paper/designing-savings-and-loan-products-0.

CHAPTER 10

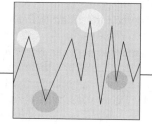

Agricultural Finance

Calvin Miller

Rural finance refers to financial services provided in rural areas for agricultural as well as nonagricultural purposes. Agricultural finance, primarily a subset of rural finance, is dedicated to financing agriculture-related activities such as inputs, production, storage, processing, and marketing of goods. In addition to funding for working capital, agricultural finance also funds investment and infrastructure, such as irrigation systems, storage facilities, and machinery. It includes a variety of products including credit, savings, insurance, and transfer payments. Agricultural finance is provided in various forms (cash and in-kind) to agroenterprises and farmers operating small, medium, and large farms. It also includes financial services such as warehouse receipts systems, savings or other capitalization mechanisms, as well as insurance and forward contracts that are

specific to agriculture. This chapter focuses primarily on credit products for agriculture and will be of interest to practitioners, policy makers, and regulators who want to understand the financial service needs of individuals and businesses working in the agriculture sector and to develop appropriate products for addressing those needs.

The Context of Agricultural Finance

Governments have tended to promote agricultural finance, providing credit to low-income farmers through government-owned agricultural banks and special agricultural loan programs. After relatively dismal results of agricultural credit programs due to systemic or covariant risks (risks that affect many at the same time, such as

The author thanks Linda Jones and Emilio Hernandez for their contributions. The views expressed here are those of the author(s) and do not necessarily reflect the views of the Food and Agriculture Organization of the United Nations, for which the content of this chapter was written.

droughts), high costs of operations, and unsustainable subsidies, the focus of financing changed from agricultural credit to financial services serving other rural activities in addition to agriculture. Financial services were more efficient by serving the entire rural population, while reducing risk by moving beyond a sole focus on agriculture. However, without incentives, many private and even public financial institutions have grown increasingly hesitant to fund agriculture due to the difficulties involved in managing an agricultural portfolio. Given the shift of government financing away from agriculture, significant gaps now exist in the availability of both rural and agricultural financial services.

Since many microfinance institutions (MFIs) were founded to serve the poor and agriculture is a critical source of rural employment, income, and food security, addressing the financial needs of poor agricultural households fits within their mission. However, due to the typical nature and cost of their services, MFIs have tended to provide rural financial services that are most appropriate for nonagricultural purposes. While product innovation has allowed MFIs to reach impoverished rural households with savings and loan products and, in many cases, with training and other services, financial services for agricultural finance have generally remained a small portion of their portfolios.

Today, development concerns and market potential are driving renewed interest in both agriculture and agricultural financial services. Recognizing that the majority of poor people in developing countries reside in rural areas and depend on agriculture for their livelihoods, many governments and development agencies have specifically included increased access to agricultural finance in their national development strategies. Furthermore, a drop in global food reserves has raised concern for food security; short-term increases in food prices are causing unrest, while growing demand increases vulnerability over the long term. At the same time, higher food prices improve the profitability of agriculture and the returns to investment in the sector, thus creating demand for agricultural financial services.

In addition to the rise in prices and long-term growth prospects in agriculture, an even more fundamental change has been occurring in how agriculture is organized and operates. Agriculture has become more commercial, catalyzing more integration between buyers and sellers to meet higher consumer demand. The relationships between buyers, sellers, and other participants in agricultural value chains have changed in an effort to improve efficiency, meet tighter standards of agroindustries, and satisfy market demand for consistent quality, timely delivery, and differentiated products. These changes have had a major impact on how the agriculture sector is or could be financed.

New technologies in information and communication have opened new opportunities for improved financial and value chain services. All types of financial institutions, including most MFIs, now have management and information systems that can handle multiple, customized credit, savings, and payment products, including point-of-sale transactions and direct transfers. They also have improved communication with agricultural clients. Furthermore, improved access to information facilitates pricing, direct sales, and deliveries as well as forward buying and selling of contracts and lowers the transaction costs of doing business, making agricultural enterprises good clients.

One aspect of agricultural finance that has not changed is the effect of political intervention, which in some countries can be significant. Governments often intervene in agricultural prices, either through price controls or through import and export restrictions or regulations that affect market prices for agriculture and hence repayment capacity of agricultural borrowers. In addition, governments and even donors are often tempted to control interest rates for lending to agriculture, especially to smallholder farmers, which can be disruptive for those lending to the sector. Policy makers in some countries may also directly intervene in agricultural finance with policies to provide subsidized credit through a variety of channels or loan write-offs at election time or after poor harvests. Such programs often create more problems than they solve and make private financial institutions wary of lending to the sector. The provision of subsidized funding to farmers or cooperatives often creates disincentives for private providers to get involved (van Empel 2010). For example in India, the government provided an agriculture debt waiver scheme for smallholder farmers in 1990 and again in 2008, adding to the banks' reluctance to lend to these farmers (Das 2012).

One reason for political and development intervention in smallholder agri*culture* financing is that it is often perceived as agriculture rather than agri*business* or agro*enterprise*. However, for financing, especially lending, agriculture must be treated as a business. "Credit is not appropriate, nor viable, for subsistence farming, although some financial services such as savings for income 'smoothing' and insurance can be useful. Despite both the important development role of aiding smallholders as they transition from subsistence farming into the market economy and the social emphasis of many microfinance organizations, it is not the role of a financial services provider to lend where there is not a market-linked business case to do so" (Miller 2011, 4).

The Challenge of Agricultural Credit

Farmers often live in areas that are hard to reach with traditional financial services. In addition, they face climatic and price risks, seasonal demand for products, and fluctuating labor and capital. Many of these risks and challenges such as droughts, floods, pests, or diseases are beyond the control of farmers; within a region, they are often subject to the same weather and climate risks, making it hard for financial service providers to hedge them. Consequently, providers find it difficult to finance agricultural activities.

The nature of the flow of capital is a further challenge to both borrowers and lenders. Because agricultural production (crops and livestock) in general has a slower turnover than other microenterprise ventures traditionally funded by MFIs, agricultural credit generally requires longer loan terms and is vulnerable to unpredictable and potentially lower returns on capital. Consequently, it entails higher risk and is much more sensitive to interest rates than traditional microfinance (Miller 2011).

Agricultural credit requires adjustments that differentiate it from a typical microenterprise loan. Because cash outflows for inputs, capital, and some labor occur at the beginning of the season and cash inflows occur primarily at harvest time, agricultural loans often require the loan principal to be paid at maturity rather than throughout the loan period. Interest may also be paid at maturity, at the beginning of the loan, or periodically (either at fixed or flexible intervals) throughout the loan period.

In agriculture, land is often used as collateral. However, there are frequent problems with land title and property rights for smallholder families, especially women-headed households that often do not have title to land (in some cultures women are not allowed, either formally or informally, to own land). Furthermore, small loans rarely justify the legal costs to process a land claim. Movable assets such as livestock and equipment are also fairly high risk, as farmers often have no proof of ownership or insurance coverage for them. Personal and group guarantees have weaknesses, since group members often are also farmers and likely to face the same risks. Therefore, such guarantees work best when the group or its members do not depend on similar sources of income such as crop agriculture. Poor financial literacy rates of farmers also contribute to inefficient agricultural finance markets.

The following factors apply primarily to rural and agricultural markets and constrain both the supply of and demand for financial services (Christen and Pearce 2005):

- Generally lower population density, dispersed demand, low literacy rates, and inadequate transportation and communication infrastructure

- Limited economic opportunities for local populations

- High risks faced by potential borrowers and depositors due to the variability of incomes, exogenous economic shocks, and limited tools for managing risk

- Seasonality of crops and production schedules, leading to spikes in loan demand and shortages in both funding and labor in certain periods

- Heavy concentration on agriculture and agriculture-related activities, exposing clients and providers to multiple risks, both idiosyncratic (one household) and covariant (entire region or country)

- Women farmers, who are constrained by lack of land, loss of land when the husband dies, or inability to borrow without the husband's permission

- Lack of reliable information about borrowers

- Lack of market information and market access

- Weak institutional capacity, including poor governance and operating systems and insufficient skills among staff and management of service providers

- "Crowding out" effect of subsidies and directed credit.

While there is no one simple solution to successful agricultural finance, an array of proven processes, approaches, and tools work within their respective contexts. These extend well beyond loans, savings, and other financial services to include insurance, hedging, embedded finance from nonfinancial entities, and investment finance. There are also guiding principles of agricultural finance that can be considered universal better practices.

Agricultural risk assessment includes both the risks of the particular client or group of clients themselves and their relationships with the persons or groups with whom they buy and sell. Thus the assessment goes well beyond what is common in microfinance. The emphasis of microfinance is placed on knowing the clients, their character, and their capacity, demonstrated, in part, by their repayment history. Assessment is quick but generally only provides a cursory overview of the household or enterprise activity. In traditional banking, collateral is the most important and often determining factor for lending. As long as the loan is secured, often with a collateral value much higher than the loan amount, there is little interest in fully understanding the business or household. Collateral requirements are often prohibitive for agricultural borrowers, who generally do not have the type of mortgage collateral most banks request.

When financing agriculture, fully understanding the needs and risks of the client, business activity, and sector is crucial. Lending solely on the basis of the client's character or the group's track record is inadequate, as is the traditional collateral-based banking approach. Each of the *5 Cs of loan analysis*—namely, character, capacity, collateral or capital, conditions, and cash flow—must be well understood for each borrower as well as for their agricultural activity. It is important to assess the capacity of the borrower and, if relevant, the strengths and weaknesses of his or her agribusiness partners with regard to their financial, managerial, and technical capacity. There must also be a level of confidence in both the character of the borrower and his or her relationship with the various participants in the value chain. And while character and collateral remain important, agricultural credit places much greater weight on cash flows and conditions (Miller and Jones 2010).

Cash flow analysis is the most important *C* for determining the amount and timing of loans, repayment schedules, and repayment capacity. The diversity of agricultural activities on even a small farm makes it seem complicated, but the cash flow of a household or agribusiness must be assessed. The lender can assess cash flow either directly or indirectly using information from the farmer's buyers or sellers. Some of the farm's cash flow will be regular, while some will be irregular; for agricultural producers, most production-related cash flow is irregular—that is, seasonal in nature (Heney 2011).

Conditions are a second critical factor. Conditions are not simply the conditions of the loan, which must work well for the borrower, but the short- and long-term conditions of the entire value chain and sector. Collateral remains important, but the emphasis shifts from reliance on mortgage collateral and toward collateral based on products, contracts, and processes.

These characteristics of agricultural lending require a deeper assessment and understanding for planning and monitoring loans and thus are prohibitively costly for small loans, which is a major reason why MFIs and banks are typically not interested in them. However, the changing nature of agriculture is providing ways to use the agricultural value chain to accomplish much of this risk assessment and monitoring. For this, a new approach—*agricultural value chain finance*—has emerged to address finance in agriculture. It is not new in its elements or new to those who have taken a comprehensive approach to agricultural lending, but it is quite new to many. It is an approach that seeks to reduce costs and lower the risks of lending by understanding risks and structuring financing (that is, fitting the conditions) to fill the needs of participants within a value chain.

Agricultural Value Chain Finance

Agricultural lending requires risk assessment well beyond the agricultural borrower to include an analysis of market dynamics that determine the fluctuations of prices and production in the agriculture sector. This is because the ability of farmers to produce, sell their products, and profit from their farming activities is influenced by the economic performance of individuals or businesses from whom they buy and sell. Farmers' cash flow is linked to the competitiveness and reliability of their suppliers, buyers, and service providers. These farmers, businesses, and individuals are interdependent actors participating in the transformation of agricultural products, each one of them adding value through their efforts to produce products that the end consumer will purchase. The total set of interactions between all of these actors to produce a specific agricultural product is often referred to as a *value chain*.

A value chain is the path that a product follows from raw material to consumer, from input supplier to producer, and on through the various actors (private or public) that take ownership of the product before it arrives at its final condition and location. The path may be very short—from farmer to household—or may follow a complex path of value addition and geographic movement from farmer to aggregator or cooperative, to raw materials processor, to value added production, to retailer (Miller and Jones 2010). In the expanded definition of the term, a value chain and its analysis also embody support service providers, sociocultural constraints, enabling environment, and relationships among stakeholders.

Value chain finance refers to the flow of funds *to* and *through*, or among, the various actors in a value chain. It uses an understanding of production, value added, and marketing processes to determine financial needs and provide financing to those involved. The strength of value chain finance lies in understanding the risks of the business by understanding the risks and competitiveness in the value chain, using that information for investment decisions, and then providing financial services tailored to current and potential clients within the value chain. Competitive agriculture is connected agriculture—linking participants in a sector or within a value chain in which everyone involved has a vested interest (Miller 2011).

Lenders need to understand the nature of relationships and the capacities and limitations of the persons and companies participating in a particular value chain in order to assess the level of risk that may affect the ability of a specific client to repay a loan. With this awareness, lenders also need to consider the cash flow and interests of the other participants within the value chain or chains of the borrower (Miller and da Silva 2007). In addition, providers need to improve their data management to capture and use production and marketing data for the most important agriculture sectors of their clients and region.

Value chain finance can be either *internal* or *external* to a value chain. For example, when a dealer supplies inputs on credit to a producer, or a wholesaler makes an advance payment to a trader for the purchase of raw materials, these constitute *internal* value chain finance. Internal financing between value chain actors is often "embedded" with other services. Common forms of embedded finance are trader credit, input supplier credit, marketing company credit, and lead firm financing. The flow of funds from an outside provider to a business or a category of businesses (producers, traders, input suppliers) in the value chain is defined as *external value chain finance*. For example, when a bank lends money to a buyer for production purchases, or when a provider extends credit to a farmer using a warehouse receipt as collateral, these are examples of *external* value chain finance.

If a provider, for example, offers general loans to rural and agricultural borrowers, and some of them use the funds to generate income related to specific crops or value chains, this is not value chain finance. However, if the same provider lends to coffee producers so they can purchase inputs—because they are known to be part of a viable coffee value chain with a reliable buyer and market—this is value chain finance. These relationships often give external financiers the confidence to extend credit to those who would not be able to obtain credit on their own. Additionally, medium or large firms may be able to obtain financing for their partners farther down the chain. For example, a bank may not be geared to serving small-scale producers and agroenterprises, but might provide a loan to a large buyer with the understanding that the large buyer will on-lend to those in their value chain. Such on-lending could enable these smaller producers and agroenterprises to purchase inputs so that they can produce or manufacture goods and sell them to the large buyer. Knowledge of a value chain and how it operates can improve repayment and reduce risk.

The interplay between a value chain and the financial market strengthens both the value chain and the financial market system. Access to credit helps participants in the value chain to overcome bottlenecks and supports the smooth functioning of the value chain. The existence of a viable value chain reduces risk and instills confidence in lenders, thereby deepening outreach. However, agricultural value chains often are poorly organized, lack transparent pricing, and are fragmented—all of which results in higher transaction costs. In many cases, the market is distorted by stakeholders, including donors, governments, and development banks, that regard agriculture as a social problem rather than as an economic activity.

Value chain financing not only analyzes the flow of funds between participants in the value chain and financial institutions, but also is cognizant of the support services[1] that are provided and those that are needed in order to strengthen the weakest links in the chain, as shown in figure 10.1.

Figure 10.1   Using the Value Chain for Agricultural Financing

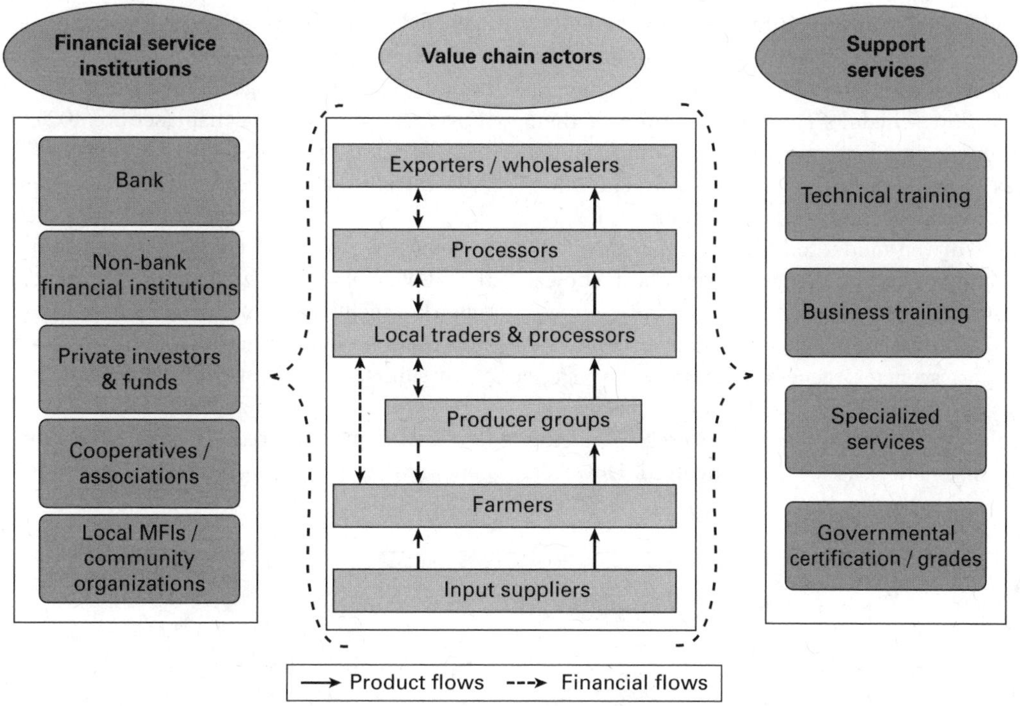

Source: Miller and Jones 2010.

Value Chain Business Models

The nature of the product, cash flow dynamics, type of relationships, and risks associated with a value chain are influenced by various business models defined by who is the "driver" of the value chain. There are several types of models:

- Producer-driven
- Buyer-driven
- Facilitated
- Integrated.

In *producer-driven* models, the producer organization is the driver and the principal decision maker. Producers and even governments often envision this model as the most desirable because it gives producers the greatest power. But this model generally brings greater exposure to risk, requires greater productive and managerial capacity of farmers, and entails the need to access more sophisticated financial services. Many, and in some countries a majority, of small producer organizations do not have the capacity and market knowledge for sustainable success and growth without some support. One disadvantage is that market demand is driven by consumers, who are the farthest from the producers in the value chain. However, for producer organizations with good capacity and value chain partners, the model can be successful.

In *buyer-driven* models—for example, contract farming—buyers contract producers to supply the product and offer them direct or indirect credit to enable them to meet delivery requirements. Financing conditions are set to fit the producer's cash flow schedule. For smallholders and their producer organizations, *contract farming* or the less formal arrangements called *outgrower schemes* are becoming the most common form of buyer-driven model today for linking finance to the value chain and securing inputs, technical assistance, and market access.

Facilitated value chain models use outside support agencies (generally development agencies acting as facilitators) to build capacity and broker partner relationships, thereby reducing the costs and risks for those involved. However,

since this model depends on subsidies from nongovernmental and governmental development agencies, it must be conceived as a catalytic short- to medium-term model. The facilitator does not become directly engaged in product flows or transactions in the value chain (see box 10.1).

In *integrated* models, the lead agribusiness has full control over and responsibility for coordination. This is common with larger conglomerate agribusiness firms and can allow them to lower their financing and business risks. This model is much less inclusive of small producers and agroentrepreneurs, making it harder to reach the poor.

In summary, understanding business models and how they are organized helps lenders to know how best to provide credit to value chain participants, with the financing often coming through or

---

Box 10.1 The DrumNet Project

The DrumNet Project in Kenya establishes relationships with key actors along a supply chain—a buyer, a bank, and several retailers of farm inputs—and links them to smallholder farmers through a dedicated transaction platform and a fully integrated finance, production, delivery, and payment process. The targeted use of information and communication technologies across the platform makes the process efficient, cost-effective, and practical in the African context.

The process begins when farmers (organized into farmer groups) sign a fixed-price purchase contract with an agricultural buyer. The contract allows farmers to approach a partner bank, obtain credit, and receive farming inputs from a local, certified retailer. At harvest, the contracted produce is collected, graded, and sold to the buyer at designated collection points. A successful transaction triggers a cashless payment through a bank

transfer. DrumNet serves as the intermediary in the flow of payment to ensure that credit is repaid before earnings reach the farmers' accounts. A master contract governs the entire process, and DrumNet's information technology system monitors compliance.

The process creates an enabling environment for agricultural finance in several ways. First, banks are assured at the time of lending that farmers have a market for their produce and the means to serve that market—two building blocks of a healthy revenue stream. Second, banks minimize the problem of loan diversion by offering in-kind credit to farmers for inputs and directly paying certified (and monitored) retailers after the inputs are distributed. Finally, cashless payment through bank transfers reduces strategic default, since farmers cannot obtain revenue until their outstanding loans are fully repaid.

Source: Campaigne and Rausch 2010

---

in coordination with the value chain driver, who can then pass on funding through to its partners. However, many agribusiness firms that buy or sell products prefer not to manage credit and look to outsource credit management, thus creating an opportunity for financial service providers. By working in partnership with input suppliers and buyers, they can provide financial services with lower market risk and greater efficiency, as loans can often be repaid at the point of sale through coordination with warehouse managers and processors. Working with specialized financial institutions (rather than suppliers and buyers doing it themselves) often improves the delivery and lowers the cost of financial services to the value chain partners. Agribusinesses finance their suppliers or buyers as a way to secure products or markets, but they are often less equipped to manage financing and find it more efficient to concentrate on their core business and let financial institutions manage loans. At the same time, these participants in the value chain often have more knowledge about agricultural inputs, markets, and the persons and organizations they work with than external financial institutions. This gives them a comparative advantage.

Trade Finance

Trade and product-related finance refers to credit provided by traders, input suppliers, and agribusiness processors and buyers. Trade finance has traditionally been the most prevalent form of agricultural financing, especially for small producers. It is common in both well-structured agricultural value chains and in informal and fragmented ones. These farmer-trader or buyer-trader relationships play a critical role in connecting farmers to markets. They provide farmers with funds for inputs, harvest, or other needs such as family consumption and emergencies. In more organized value chains, a trader or buyer may give an advance to a producer so the producer can purchase inputs and cover costs until harvest. The trader then deducts the

advance (with interest as agreed) from the purchase price. A supplier may offer a producer inputs on credit, with the understanding that the producer will pay the supplier once the crop is sold. In some cases, these arrangements can involve a third party such as when a buyer pays the supplier for inputs and deducts the cost from the price paid to the producer.

Marketing companies and lead firms that aggregate products from producers often advance payment for goods prior to production, which is a form of trade credit embedded in the value chain. Similarly, contract farming exists when a wholesaler provides credit to producers based on a contract specifying that the farmer must provide a specific volume and quality of produce to the wholesaler at a specific time. While there may not be an explicit interest rate, a discount on the selling price is usually built into the contract. With contract farming arrangements, the wholesaler may also offer technical assistance to ensure quality products.

Traders are most often members of the rural community or from within the region. They not only have capital and have or can arrange transportation, but, which is most important, often also have specialized knowledge of markets and contacts that enable them to operate effectively in their region. Traders are therefore able to advance funds with the guarantee that the crop to be harvested will be available to them for resale according to a price that is fixed at the time of financing. In regions where there is little competition, prices offered by traders are often low to compensate for risk, costs of embedded interest, and profit; traders may be opportunistic and take advantage of smallholder farmers who need cash.

For financial institutions, especially MFIs and government banks, it is often assumed that financing must be provided directly to the micro and small agricultural producers and households. This may or may not be the most feasible way to finance agricultural activities due to the costs and risks involved. Hence, financing institutions also need to consider alternative ways to finance suppliers, traders, and agribusiness buyers who can advance the supplies or funds needed by those producers. For example, when sufficient competition among traders or buyers helps to keep their prices realistic in relation to market prices, then indirect financing of smallholder farmers through such traders and buyers may be the most cost-effective manner of financing them.

Bill Discounting and Factoring

Input suppliers that sell on credit as well as agribusinesses or producer organizations that sell products on consignment or on delayed payment (for example, 60 days) often struggle with liquidity. This limits the amount of sales they can make on credit, which, in turn, limits the ability of smallholder farmers to obtain inputs on credit to be paid upon delivery of their harvest. Bill discounting and factoring can help to improve cash flow without requiring additional collateral (which is often not available). Bill discounting and factoring are both financial transactions whereby a business or producer organization sells its accounts receivables (that is, invoices) at a discount. Both are forms of credit, which allows a business to obtain immediate cash without waiting for invoices to be paid. This cash advance credit is especially important for small enterprises that need operating capital for purchasing goods or advancing cash or inputs to their clients.

Factoring is a special form of bill discounting that works through specialized factoring agencies (see box 10.2). Buyers and wholesalers or input suppliers sell their invoices at a discount to the factoring agency, which provides a credit advance (for example, 80 percent of invoice value) to the business or producer organization. The agency collects the receivables when due and makes a final settlement payment to the business, minus a factor discount (administrative fee and interest). Factoring speeds the turnover of working capital and provides services such as accounts receivable bookkeeping and bill collection. In addition, it provides some protection from credit risk in that the factoring agency conducts a due diligence assessment of the buyer from whom it must collect.

Box 10.2 Factoring to Support Agriculture

In Kenya, De Derby Green Ventures Capital (DGV) is a limited-liability company, whose focus is value chain financing through factoring, both in agriculture and in manufacturing. Its mission is to facilitate business linkages by eliminating the financial stress experienced by businesses. DGV gives priority to the agriculture sector, which represents 80 percent of its portfolio.

DGV allows agricultural suppliers to convert approved invoices and delivery documents into instant cash by discounting them at an agreed fee. DGV then collects the face amount of the invoices from the buyers. On the due date, the buyers pay DGV the full amount of the invoice, and DGV discounts its fees and pays the remainder to the supplier as previously agreed (Obara 2011).

In Guatemala, the MFI Summa provides short-term bridge financing to producer organizations and their members while they wait for buyers to pay them. Even more important, it also collects the accounts receivable, which can be very difficult and costly for producer organizations to handle directly, especially when they operate far from cities.

Source: Miller 2011.

Factoring differs from credit in three main ways. First, the emphasis is on the value of the receivables, not the creditworthiness of the agribusiness or producer organization. Second, factoring is not a loan; it is the purchase of an asset—the receivables. While not directly financing producers, it allows input suppliers or buyers to access funding, which can benefit farmers who receive advances. The factoring agency provides the collection service, which can even make other financial service providers more willing and able to extend inputs on credit or provide advances to farmers. Also, producer organizations who sell to supermarkets or other buyers on consignment not only have to wait for payments, but often find that collection is difficult. Due to their location and collection experience, it can be more effective to have a factoring agency manage this.

Warehouse Receipts Systems

Warehouse receipt systems (sometimes called warrants or warrantage) are a form of inventory credit that originated during the nineteenth century among European farmers. Warehouse receipts involve a tripartite agreement between (a) producers (or often producer organizations operating on behalf of farmers), who borrow using stored produce as collateral; (b) local financial institutions, which lend to producers or organizations; and (c) a warehouse manager, who provides storage services. The stored produce is then sold when prices are generally highest and potential revenue can be maximized. Agribusinesses also can use warehouse receipts as long as the goods are stored securely by an independently controlled warehouse. Farmers or other participants in the value chain receive a receipt from the warehouse stating that they have deposited goods of a particular quantity, quality, and grade, which they then pledge as collateral to access a loan from a third-party financial service provider, such as a cooperative or an MFI (see figure 10.2).

Warehouse receipt systems can help to smooth seasonal price variations throughout

Figure 10.2 The Warehouse Receipts Financing System

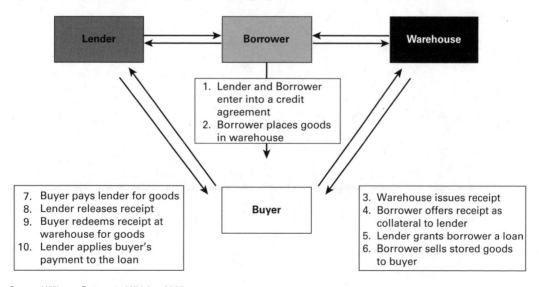

Source: Höllinger, Rutten, and Kiriakov 2009.

the year, as they help consumers and sellers to know that supply is available in warehouses. This can help to forecast demand and revenue, leading to a more stable and developed market overall. However, for products and commodities for which prices do not generally rise in a predictable, seasonal fashion, there is little incentive or need to store and use warehouse receipts.

While many warehouse receipt programs are formally structured, informal credit systems involving village granaries or regional storage centers are common in many developing countries. In Latin America, MFIs have begun using "micro-warrants" as a form of warehouse receipt financing for their agricultural microentrepreneurs, and in Africa, credit cooperative federations use a "warrantage" system (Miller 2011; see box 10.3).

Agricultural Leasing

As discussed in chapter 9, a financial lease, also called a lease-purchase agreement, is a viable loan alternative for financing equipment and durable assets. Leasing uses the agricultural equipment and machinery acquired as its own collateral, thus providing an alternative for clients who do not have the traditional collateral needed to purchase directly. Leasing is a specific financial product governed by distinct legislation. Leasing and micro leasing have become common in some countries, but are still relatively new. Leasing is sometimes available from banks or MFIs, but quite often is available from

---

Box 10.3 Warehouse Receipt Systems: Lessons from Niger

In Niger, local farmer organizations and MFIs have adapted the warrantage concept. Since its beginnings in the mid-1990s, the warrantage system has created a relatively popular financial product offered by all MFIs in the country. Producer organizations provide their members with storage facilities and also handle their loan transactions. The loans enable farmers to finance several of their household's income-generating activities during the storage period, allowing for smoother cash flows. Revenues from the activities financed often enable farmers to pay back the loan without using revenue from the eventual sale of the stored produce.

Several conditions need to be met for warehouse receipt financing to work. Some important ones include detailed lender knowledge of the dynamics of the agricultural value chain, the stability of borrowers' agribusiness opportunities, the enabling regulatory framework, the existence of proper storage management and facilities, and sound governance within producer organizations. Lessons from Niger highlight the relative importance of these conditions. The constant demand for cereal imports from neighboring Nigeria has created stable business opportunities for farmers in Niger. Through their organizations, farmers have taken advantage of these opportunities by building storage facilities and requesting joint loans backed by cereal stocks. Lenders understand the worth of these stocks and accept them as collateral. Even though the court system in Niger makes credit contracts difficult to enforce, the combination of stable agribusiness opportunities, strong farmer organizations, and lenders familiar with agricultural markets makes warehouse receipt financing work in the country.

Source: Interview with Emilio Hernandez, May 2012.

specialized leasing companies, which may or may not be linked with banks or MFIs.

Addressing Client Risk through Financial Services

Agriculture is subject to production, price, and marketing risks. These can affect all clients in a region. While these risks are determined by uncontrollable factors, their effects on income and loan repayment can be mitigated. Financial service providers working with low-income clients, like any financial institution, must mitigate these systemic risks through portfolio and sector diversification and, where possible, regional diversity and insurance. In addition, MFIs can also make better agricultural lending decisions when they improve their management of data to capture and use production and marketing data for the most important agriculture sectors of their clients and regions.

Agricultural Insurance

Weather and related natural events affecting agricultural production are unpredictable, and risks are increasing with climate change. Insurance can reduce these risks. While various types of insurance described in chapter 11 are important for farm households and enterprises, insurance products are available specifically for agricultural risk.

Agricultural insurance products can be classified as four principal types (Kang 2007; Roberts 2007):

- *Damage-based insurance.* Indemnity payments are triggered by the occurrence of a specific type of damaging event, such as hail, fire, or death of animals. These products tend to be used when there is a low correlation between events occurring within a given area and payment is subject to the value of the loss.

- *Yield-based insurance.* Indemnity payments are made when the client's yield is below a predefined level, independent of the damage that is measured after the defined loss event. It is suited to perils where individual attribution to the crop loss is difficult to measure.

- *Crop-revenue insurance.* The timing and amount of indemnity payment are defined based on a predefined combination of yield and commodity prices, set according to historical norms in a subarea.

- *Index-based insurance.* A predefined index is used to estimate the timing and value of losses suffered by the insured client. The index is calculated based on historical meteorological and production data. Examples include some combination of temperature, rainfall, wind speed, yields, and mortality rates averaged over a subarea. Use of an index avoids the need to verify the value of losses, and its deviation from a specified level defines the value of the indemnity payment. Examples of indexes include (a) a specified minimum temperature for a minimum period of time (for frost); (b) a specified amount of rainfall in a certain period of time (for excess or lack of rain); and (c) a certain wind speed (for hurricanes).

Although agricultural insurance is quite common in developed countries, it is much less so in the developing world. The institutional mechanisms to obtain relevant data, verify losses, develop appropriate indexes, or distribute insurance products are limited in many countries, making it costly for insurance companies to provide services and difficult for them to offer prices that farmers are willing to pay. However, if a proper index can be determined, delivery costs can be significantly reduced because payment for damage does not have to be verified but is automatic according to the index. The use of an index also avoids the risk of moral hazard. This is because neither the insurer nor the client can influence the index measurements, usually collected by a third party such as a government ministry. However, like all types of insurance, index-based insurance depends on reliable, historical data. While data collection is improving, it remains a major drawback for insurance in developing countries. A related challenge is building indexes that represent losses and avoid the risk of not providing payment when it is due or of providing payment when it is not due (IFC 2010; see chapter 11 for more on index-based insurance).

In addition, agricultural households face limited market opportunities and have little access to complementary services such as credit, savings, agricultural inputs, or communication infrastructure. Insurance services bring little additional value to these households, and their willingness to pay for them tends to be low, even if subsidies are provided.

For agricultural insurance for smallholder farmers, it is useful to bundle insurance with other financial products like loans and savings products. Bundling greatly reduces the transaction costs of delivering payments, deposits, and premiums. Insurance product management is often beyond the capacity of most MFIs, but it can be delivered effectively through them or in conjunction with loans through links with insurance providers.

Forward Contracts

Forward contracts commit the issuer to sell a product with delivery at a future date, such as at harvest. The sale price is fixed at the time of the contract. Forward contracts are useful for smallholder farmers, traders, and agroenterprises to mitigate or "hedge" the price risk, which helps to mitigate the risk for lenders, since future income is more secure. Forward contracts can also be used as collateral for loans (see box 10.4).

Guarantee Funds

In some countries, governments, donors, or commercial companies offer guarantee funds for agriculture or for specific sectors or target groups of farmers or agroenterprises. These are meant to reduce the risk of lending. A typical example is a fund that guarantees approximately 50 percent of the loan in the event of default (either shared equally or the first loss) for a fee of 3 to 5 percent annually. Lowering the risk gives the lender an incentive to lend to new or risky sectors and to lend more. The loan guarantee fund manager also provides an additional risk review as part of its due diligence. The weakness of loan guarantee programs is the cost, which is unsustainable

---

Box 10.4 Crop Receivables

The government of Brazil created the rural finance note, called the *cedula produto rural*, for loans to agribusinesses and producers. The note is not a typical forward contract; it is a hybrid of forward contracts and warehouse receipts. Its mechanism is very simple—farmers issue a rural finance note to a buyer that commits the farmer to deliver a specific quantity and quality of product at a given future date and location. In exchange, the buyer pays in advance a certain amount of money that corresponds to the quantity of product specified. In effect, the buyer provides an unsubsidized loan backed by the note.

Source: Miller and Jones 2010.

unless subsidized by the government or a donor (Zander, Miller, and Mhlanga 2012).

Lending for Livestock

While much of the previous description has focused on crop agriculture, attention must also be given to animal husbandry. Providing financial services for small animals as well as livestock is common in microfinance and does not pose the same risks as crop financing. Small animal raising and dairy are often carried out by women. Animals provide a means to increase women's assets, while also being relatively liquid in times of emergency or need. In addition, raising animals can diversify income and risk to farmers and make them more creditworthy.

Credit for livestock and other animals is not without risks, however. Small animals such as chickens, pigs, or cows are often raised at a very small scale under rustic conditions without proper care. Poor animal hygiene, lack of proper pasture and feed, as well as lack of disease control can lead to animal losses, sickness to the family, or exclusion from markets (animals that are sick or do not meet quality requirements are difficult to sell). In addition to capital, farmers raising livestock could benefit from other inputs (see box 10.5).

The Role of MFIs in Agricultural Finance

All financial institutions that provide agricultural financial services need to understand agriculture and related small and medium agroenterprises in order to be effective. Inclusive finance acknowledges the role that agriculture plays in the lives of the rural poor. Agricultural finance requires an array of financial and nonfinancial services. MFIs alone cannot deliver the breadth of financial services and nonfinancial technical support needed in the agriculture sector. It is thus more effective for them to work with other service providers to deliver the comprehensive financial services that agricultural households need. For MFIs, understanding the agricultural needs of their clients and linking with partners that complement their services are keys to making a significant contribution to livelihoods.

Continual innovation is important if financial institutions are to succeed in reaching smallholder farmers and agroentrepreneurs in a cost-effective and sustainable manner. MFIs have been successful in applying innovative products and approaches to reach the needs of the poor; they can and are innovating to serve agricultural clients better. For example, in Bolivia FONDECO (Community Development Fund), an MFI, has

---

Box 10.5 Heifer International

Heifer International and BRAC have long recognized that promoting animal husbandry may require more than finance. Heifer International gives loans in kind, with recipients repaying the loan with offspring. Its success over 60 years around the world has been intricately linked to its support for group formation, pasture improvements, para-veterinary training, vaccination campaigns, and other services. To increase the success of its many clients raising chickens, BRAC instituted hatcheries to supply day-old chicks and supported access to improved feeds.

Source: Miller 2011.

moved beyond simply lending for agricultural production to offering multiple financial products for different parts of the value chain, as shown in box 10.6.

In summary, new approaches to agricultural finance reduce costs and risks. Some of these have been facilitated by increased value chain linkages and improved management, communication, and technology systems. Even so, the three Rs of finance remain critically important for agricultural finance: the *risk* of clients and their agricultural businesses, generation of sufficient *returns* to capital of the clients, and *repayment capacity*. There is no substitution or shortcut for assessing clients and their businesses accurately. Cash flow analysis, product value chain assessment, and tailoring of loans with the appropriate conditions are critical.

Even with the best assessment, agricultural credit should be accompanied by insurance and safety cushions. While insurance products can help to mitigate losses, the most important insurance is built through *savings* and *accumulation of assets*, which can be liquidated easily in times of need. Easily accessible savings services support farmers.

Agricultural finance depends on the success of the agriculture sector as a whole and the competitiveness and risk profile of the client and the value chain. Long-term investments are needed to improve production and quality as well as to build human capacity (skills and relationships) and physical infrastructure (irrigation, storage, equipment, and technologies). All are required for a healthy agriculture sector capable of generating economic growth and higher incomes for farmers.

Note

1. These support services are market-based, supporting functions within the market system, not facilitation.

References and Further Reading

Becerra, N., M. Fiebig, and S. Wisniwski. 2010. "Agricultural Production Lending: A Toolkit for Loan Officers and Loan Portfolio Managers." Rural Finance Learning Center, FAO, Rome.

Campaigne, Jonathan, and Tom Rausch. 2010. *Bundling Development Services with Agricultural Finance: The Experience of DrumNet.* Innovations in Rural and Agriculture Finance Focus 18, Brief 14. Washington, DC: International Food Policy Research Institute and World Bank, July.

Christen, Robert P., and Douglas Pearce. 2005. "Managing Risks and Designing Products for Agricultural Microfinance: Features of an Emerging Model." Occasional Paper 11, CGAP, Washington, DC.

Das, P. K. 2012. "Agricultural Credit Policy in India." Unpublished research paper, Bhubaneswar, India.

Heney, J. 2011. "Loan Appraisal: Agricultural Lending; Self-Study Guide for Loan Officers." Rural Finance Learning Center, FAO, Rome.

Höllinger, Frank, Lamon Rutten, and Krassimir Kiriakov. 2009. "The Use of Warehouse Receipt Finance in Agriculture in Transition Countries." Working paper, FAO Investment Centre, FAO, Rome.

IFC (International Finance Corporation). 2010. "Indexed-Based Agricultural Insurance: A Product Design Case Study." IFC Advisory Services, Washington, DC.

Kang, M. G. 2007. "Innovative Agricultural Insurance Products and Schemes." Agricultural Management, Marketing, and Finance Occasional Paper, FAO, Rome.

Miller, Calvin. 2011. "Microfinance and Crop Agriculture: New Approaches, Technologies, and Other Innovations to Address Food Insecurity among the Poor." Workshop paper commissioned for the 2011 Global Microcredit Summit, Valladolid, Spain, November 14–17.

Miller, Calvin, and Carlos da Silva. 2007. "Value Chain Financing in Agriculture." *Enterprise Development and Microfinance* 18: 95–108.

Miller, Calvin, and Linda Jones. 2010. *Agricultural Value Chain Finance.* Rugby: FAO and Practical Action Publishing.

Obara, Beatrice. 2011. "De Deby Green Ventures Capital in Kenya." In *Agricultural Value Chain Finance*, ed. Rodolfo Quirós. Rome and San José: FAO and Academia de Centroamérica.

Roberts, R. A. J. 2007. "Livestock and Aquaculture Insurance in Developing Countries." Bulletin 164, FAO, Rome.

Van Empel, Gerard. 2010. "Rural Banking in Africa: The Rabobank Approach." In *Innovations in Rural and Agricultural Finance,* ed. R. Kloeppinger-Todd and M. Sharma. Focus 18, Brief 4. Washington, DC: International Food Policy Research Institute and World Bank.

Vargas, Edwin. 2010. "Innovaciones financieras en la cadena productiva." PowerPoint presentation at the conference "Agricultural Value Chain Finance," FAO and Academia de Centroamérica, Rome and San José, Costa Rica. http://www.academiaca.or.cr/presenta-cion2010/presentaciones/edwin_vargas.pdf.

Zander, Rauno, Calvin Miller, and N. Mhlanga. 2012. *Credit Guarantee Systems for Agriculture and Rural Enterprise Development.* Rome: FAO.

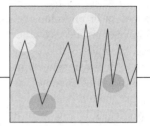

CHAPTER 11

Insurance

Craig Churchill

Low-income people live in risky environments, vulnerable to numerous perils—illness, accidental death and disability, loss of property due to theft or fire, agricultural losses, and disasters of both the natural and manmade varieties.[1] They are also the least able to cope when a crisis does occur. For example, an estimated 150 million people are adversely affected by out-of-pocket spending on health care services each year. More than 90 percent of these individuals live in low-income countries. For approximately 100 million people, out-of-pocket payments for health services are so financially devastating that they are pushed below the poverty line (Xu et al. 2007).

Microinsurance is much younger than other financial services for the poor. In the original *Microfinance Handbook* (Ledgerwood 1998), it received only a passing mention, two paragraphs and a box. At the time, there was very little experience or innovation around insurance services for the poor. Over the past decade, however, microinsurance has been on a steep growth and learning curve, in part because of work by the Microinsurance Network and the International Labour Organisation's Microinsurance Innovation Facility. Thanks to their efforts, the experiences of microinsurance providers around the world have been documented and analyzed, creating new waves of lessons and guidance.

This chapter describes the need for insurance and key product design issues that need to be considered to make insurance relevant for low-income households. It provides an overview of the types of products, including life, health, property, and agriculture insurance, and describes how insurance can be integrated into the financial inclusion agenda. It will be of interest to practitioners, funders, and other stakeholders interested in understanding how microinsurance can help poor women and men better manage risk.

The Need for Microinsurance

Stakeholders in microfinance often focus their attention and resources on the productive side of finance, particularly micro- and small enterprise lending. Yet any development gains achieved—such as increased incomes, assets accumulated, and jobs created—can quickly be lost if the entrepreneur's business or household experiences a peril. Consequently, productive investments must be balanced with similar attention and resources on promoting protection.

Although people in different countries are concerned with different risks, low-income households consistently identify the loss of an income earner and sickness of a family member as their greatest concerns (Cohen and Sebstad 2006). The dominance of illness is not surprising, especially because of its double impact. An inability to work results in lower income opportunities and additional expenses to cover health care costs. For families with sick children, small expenses can quickly mount and have a large financial impact. Accidents, as well as chronic illness such as malaria and HIV/AIDS, require relatively large sums. These overwhelming financial pressures frequently fall on women, many of whom assume primary responsibility for the welfare of their families.

Although poor households may have informal means to manage risks, these strategies generally provide insufficient protection. Many risk-management strategies, such as spreading financial and human resources across several income-generating activities, result in low returns. Informal risk-coping strategies, such as borrowing from friends and family, tend to cover only a small portion of the loss, so the poor have to patch together support from a variety of sources. Even then, informal risk protection does not stand up well against a series of perils; before the household has a chance to fully recover from one crisis, they are often struck by another.

Microinsurance is emerging as a complementary tool to help low-income people manage risks more effectively. It provides protection against specific perils including death, disability, hospitalization, or crop failure, in exchange for regular payments proportionate to the likelihood and cost of the risk occurring. Often the term "insurance" is used loosely to refer to general risk-prevention and management techniques. For example, savings set aside for emergency purposes might be referred to as an insurance fund. This book, however, uses a narrower definition in which microinsurance, like traditional insurance, involves a risk-pooling element, which allows large groups of insured entities to share the losses resulting from the occurrence of an uncommon event (see box 11.1 for definitions of key insurance terms).

The insured entities—such as persons, businesses, households, communities, or even countries—are therefore protected from risk in exchange for a fee known as a premium. The premium amount is determined by an estimation of the frequency and severity of the event occurring. Those in the risk pool who do not suffer a loss during a particular period essentially pay for the losses experienced by others. Insurance reduces vulnerability as households replace the uncertain prospect of peril with the certainty of making small, regular premium payments and receiving a payout if the peril occurs. This risk-pooling function makes insurance more complicated than savings, credit, or payment services.

Despite features similar to those of traditional insurance, microinsurance requires a fundamentally different approach to be relevant for the low-income market and viable for providers. The products generally available from insurers are not designed to meet the specific characteristics of the working poor, particularly the irregular cash flows of households with bread winners in the informal economy. Other key product design challenges include inappropriate insured

Box 11.1 Key Insurance Terms

Actuary: A person who calculates insurance and annuity premiums, reserves, and dividends.

Adverse selection: The tendency of higher-risk individuals to seek out more insurance coverage on average in anticipation of a greater probability of experiencing the insured event(s).

Agent: An insurance company representative who solicits, negotiates, or effects insurance contracts, and provides service to the policyholder for the insurer, usually for a commission on the premium payments.

Basis risk: The chance that an insurance payout does not match the loss experienced by the policyholder. This is a particular concern with index insurance, which pays out based on a measurable indicator, such as too much or too little rain, but that indicator may or may not correlate well with the policyholders' actual losses.

Beneficiary: The person or financial instrument (for example, a trust fund), named in the policy as the recipient of insurance money if an insured event occurs.

Benefits: The amount payable by the insurer to a claimant or beneficiary after the occurrence of the insured event.

Capitation: Method of payment whereby a physician or hospital is paid a fixed amount for each person in a particular plan regardless of the frequency or type of service provided.

Claim: A request for payment of a loss that may come under the terms of an insurance contract.

Claim verification: The process whereby the microinsurer verifies and processes claims for payouts.

Copayment: Mechanism used by insurers to share risk with policyholders and reduce moral hazard, which establishes a formula for dividing the payment of losses between the insurer and the policyholder. For example, a copayment arrangement might require a policyholder to pay 30 percent of all losses while the insurer covers the remainder.

Covariant risk: The tendency for either (1) many households to be affected by a risk at the same time or (2) several risks to consistently occur together.

Coverage: The scope of protection provided under a contract of insurance, and any of several risks covered by a policy.

Deductible (or excess): Mechanism used by insurers to share risk with policyholders and reduce moral hazard, which establishes an amount or percentage that a policyholder agrees to pay, per claim or insured event, toward the total amount of an insured loss.

Endowment: Life insurance payable to the policyholder if living, on the maturity date stated in the policy, or to a beneficiary if the insured dies before that date.

Lapse: The termination or discontinuance of an insurance policy due to nonpayment of a premium.

Moral hazard: A risk that arises when people with insurance engage in more dangerous behaviors or use more services because they know they are protected. An example might include failing to take preventative health care measures or making unnecessary visits to a doctor.

Preexisting conditions: These are health conditions that are often excluded by insurance policies as a means of controlling adverse selection. To control for this, insurance programs may

(continued next page)

require a health checkup before enrollment, or ask prospective policyholders to answer a health questionnaire.

Premium: The sum paid by a policyholder to keep an insurance policy in force.

Rider: An amendment to an insurance policy that modifies the policy by expanding or restricting its benefits or excluding certain conditions from coverage.

Risk pooling: The spreading of losses incurred by a few over a larger group, so that in the process, each individual group member's losses are limited to the average loss (premium payments) rather than the potentially larger actual loss that might be sustained by an individual. Risk pooling effectively disperses losses incurred by a few over a larger group.

Self-administration: Maintenance of all records and assumption of responsibility by a group policyholder for those covered under its health insurance plan. Responsibilities include preparing the premium statement for each payment date and submitting it with a payment to the insurer. The insurance company, in most instances, has the contractual prerogative to audit the policyholders' records. An alternative is *third-party administration*, whereby a specialized company performs the administrative function.

Underwriter: (1) A company that receives the premiums and accepts responsibility for the fulfillment of the policy contract; (2) the company employee who decides whether or not the company should assume a particular risk; or (3) the agent that sells the policy.

Waiting period: The period whereby policyholders cannot access certain benefits for some time after they enroll. A waiting period has essentially the same effect as excluding preexisting conditions except the insurer does not have to incur the claims verification costs.

Source: Adapted from Roth et al. 2007.

amounts, complex exclusions, and indecipherable legal policy language, all of which conspire against effectively serving the poor.

Another major challenge in extending insurance to the poor is educating the market and overcoming its bias against insurance. Many poor persons are skeptical about paying premiums for an intangible product with future benefits that may never be claimed. Insurance providers are seen as quick to take one's money, but slow to pay it out. In fact, this bias goes in both directions. People who work for insurance companies are usually unfamiliar with the needs and concerns of the poor. In addition, the culture and incentives in insurance companies reward and encourage salespersons to focus on larger policies and more profitable clients.

Microinsurance is just one of several risk-management tools available to low-income households, and so organizations truly concerned about helping the poor to manage risks should assess whether the provision of microinsurance is the most appropriate response. For risks that result in small losses or for risks with a high likelihood or high frequency of occurrence, savings and emergency loans would be more appropriate risk-managing financial services. Savings and credit are also more flexible than insurance because they can be used for a variety of different risks (and opportunities). Insurance, on the other hand, provides more complete coverage for large losses than poor households could provide on their own. For these larger risks, participating in a risk pool is a more efficient means of accessing protection than if households try to protect themselves independently.

Like other financial products, insurance programs for the poor have to balance three competing objectives: (1) provide coverage to meet the needs of the target population, (2) minimize operating costs for the insurer, and (3) minimize the price (including transaction costs) for clients to enhance affordability and accessibility. The goal is to strike a balance between broad inclusion, sufficient benefits, low premium rates, and sustainability.

Product Options

When designing insurance products, various options need to be considered. Will the insurance be offered to groups or individuals? Will it be mandatory or voluntary? What are the coverage terms and prices? How will premiums be collected? And how will benefits be paid?

Group or Individual Insurance

The primary feature distinguishing group insurance from individual insurance is that under group insurance, many people are insured under one master policy. The group policyholder decides what type of coverage to buy for the members of the group and is responsible for enrolling members, collecting premiums, disseminating certificates of insurance and product information, and assisting members to file claims. The policy describes and defines the eligible members of the group.

Underwriting guidelines for group insurance generally begin by specifying the fundamental requirements that define a group. The main criterion is that the group must have been formed for reasons other than to obtain insurance. This mechanism should limit the scope for adverse selection and allow for easier underwriting and risk management; particular care needs to be made to implement it properly, as illustrated in box 11.2. Examples of groups suitable for group insurance include employees in a company, labor union members, borrowers of a microfinance institution (MFI), and affinity

---

Box 11.2 AKAM's Experience with Village-Based Health Microinsurance in Pakistan

In 2006 the Aga Khan Agency for Microfinance (AKAM) launched a microinsurance program in Pakistan to test an innovative health microinsurance to protect low-income families from the often ruinous effects of catastrophic health care expenditure. The program attempted to make insurance possible among villagers in the rugged Northern Areas by dramatically reducing transaction costs through group policies and designing insurance products that meet the target market's needs.

Based on thorough market research, microinsurance experts designed a remarkable product and innovative processes. The product covered not only inpatient hospitalization cost (up to US$400 per year), including a follow-up visit and medication needed after discharge, but also one outpatient consultation for every insured person and life insurance for the family's bread winner. The product had few exclusions and no age limits, waiting periods, copayments, or deductibles. Both normal and

(continued next page)

Box 11.2 *(continued)*

complicated maternity was covered from day one. The general intention was to provide coverage for US$5 per year that addressed people's needs in a way that would allow them to understand, appreciate, and embrace formal insurance.

Because cases of catastrophic health costs of one villager can affect the entire community, the insurance purchase was intended to be a community decision. Applying the principles of group insurance to villages would allow AKAM to insure larger numbers by selling the product through village organizations—thereby reducing the transaction cost per person—and protect the program against the risk that only unhealthy people would buy insurance.

Market research indicated, however, that the insurance purchase could not be imposed on every person in a village: Some were too poor, and the initial assumption that the better off would subsidize the premium of their neighbors proved unrealistic. So departing from one fundamental principle of group insurance, the minimum take-up rate was reduced from 100 percent (everybody is insured) to 50 percent of households in a village organization, but with the additional condition that those households that decided to buy the coverage had to include every household member.

The outcome of this careful design was not as expected. Fewer people than anticipated bought the coverage, and the families who did were smaller than the average household size.

In addition, insurance utilization greatly exceeded expectations; claims exceeded premiums by several hundreds of thousands of dollars between 2007 and 2011. The main reason was an erroneous assumption regarding membership in village organizations, which was neither universal nor static. Although the insurance design assumed that every person was already a member of a village organization when they were offered insurance, instead people who intended to use the insurance because of current pregnancies or preexisting illnesses could choose to join one village organization or another specifically to access insurance. Market research confirmed the opportunistic attitude. When asked why she had not renewed her policy, one woman answered, "Last year I was pregnant, but this year I don't plan to have a baby, so why insure?"

Other factors aggravated this behavior: Not all of a family's children were insured, insurance was bought after the sales window was officially closed, and claims control could have been more rigorous. Given that much larger premium volumes and much larger numbers of insured persons were needed to cover expenses and reduce the cost per person, management's main focus for several years was on increasing scale. It was expected that by insuring more people, automatically more healthy people would be insured, reducing the unsustainable utilization rates. But this did not happen, and in the end restrictive product redesign was necessary to contain losses.

Source: Peter Wrede.

groups such as professional or community associations.

Individual microinsurance requires a high participation rate among the potential target market to make the provision of individual insurance

financially sustainable. Individual insurance is often twice as expensive as group coverage because of higher sales, underwriting, administration, and claims costs. The cost for individual insurance claims can be reduced through more

The New Microfinance Handbook

rigorous underwriting, such as medical screening (because bad risks are identified and filtered out or are limited to lower coverage). However, for microinsurance additional screening may not make economic sense because coverage amounts are very low; moreover it may run counter to the social agenda of the microinsurer.

A key advantage of individual insurance is that the coverage can continue with the individual once group membership ceases, for example, for MFI borrowers who no longer require loans. Group coverage can be converted into individual policies using continuation options. To the extent that the group coverage relies on infrastructure supporting the group (such as using an MFI for premium collection), continuation policies may require additional charges and administration.

Voluntary or Mandatory Insurance

Mandatory insurance is the most common type of microinsurance and refers to a situation in which an organization requires all of its clients to purchase insurance or it is provided as a loyalty incentive to customers (see box 11.3). Mandatory participation ensures a broad cross section of people participate and can help to limit adverse selection. To be demand driven and client focused, one would expect that voluntary coverage would be the most appropriate. Yet in the field of insurance—microinsurance in particular where affordability is so important—a strong case can be made for mandatory coverage because it performs the following:

- Enables insurers to reach scale, which increases the accuracy of predicting future claims

Box 11.3 IFFCO-Tokio's Bundled AD&D Coverage

In India the *Sankat Haran* Policy sold by IFFCO-Tokio provides accidental death and disability (AD&D) coverage, which is obtained when clients buy a 50 kg fertilizer bag of IFCCO and Indian Potash brands. The receipt for the fertilizer bag acts as proof of payment, and the policy document is printed on the fertilizer bag. The amount of coverage is US$90 in the event of an accidental death and US$45 for certain categories of dismemberment and disability. The insured is the purchaser of the fertilizer bag, and a single person can hold multiple policies up to a maximum of US$2,260 in coverage. More than 3.5 million farmers are covered by this program.

Essentially the program sells prepaid insurance, in the sense that the retailer buys the fertilizer, including its insurance component, from a wholesaler. The *retailer prepays the insurance premium*, so there is no need for the insurer to collect premiums from the client or, indeed, from the retailer.

On the face of it, in a competitive market for fertilizer and AD&D insurance, it is hard to imagine what value is offered to the consumer by this type of embedding. Any consumer who wanted either fertilizer or AD&D insurance could buy it separately in the required quantities without needing to buy the two together. However, the rural Indian market is not competitive, and this may be the only means of distributing such insurance. It is also possible that the addition of AD&D insurance provides an incentive to purchase a particular brand of fertilizer (in much the same way some Visa cards come with similar coverage linked to travel). The insurance is compulsory, which in theory should control adverse selection.

Source: Adapted from Roth and Chamberlain 2006.

- Reduces costs due to higher volumes and lower enrollment, administration, collection, and underwriting costs

- Improves claims ratios because it brings in lower-risk individuals, which is known as positive selection, who may otherwise opt out or postpone their participation and

- Reduces vulnerability to staff fraud because it reduces the chance for agents to sell policies and keep the premiums.

Community groups, such as women's associations and other community-based organizations, financial cooperatives, MFI borrowers, and small business associations, can be leveraged as distribution channels and as a mechanism to protect against adverse selection. One of the biggest disadvantages of mandatory coverage, besides the fact that people are required to buy something that they may not want, is that the distribution system tends to overlook the consumers' need for information. Such products generally have excessively low claims ratios, seemingly the result of people not knowing that they are covered. As one rural banker in Ghana noted, "If we tell people all about the cover, we'd be flooded with claims." When offering mandatory coverage, microinsurers (or their agents) need to ensure that clients are constantly educated about buying an intangible service that provides security and peace of mind to ensure that they can appreciate the benefits, and thus lead to the creation of an insurance culture.

Microinsurance providers can combine the advantages of mandatory and voluntary coverage by making insurance mandatory for all members of an existing group (which minimizes adverse selection), while providing two or three options to choose from. This allows members to opt for the coverage level they would prefer and increases the likelihood they will receive sufficient information to make informed decisions. Some microinsurers use groups more effectively than conventional insurers by enlisting the support of the groups in

member selection to reduce the risks of overusage and moral hazard, but as shown in box 11.2, such an approach is not always successful.

Terms of Coverage and Pricing

Many microinsurance products have terms of 12 months or less. Short-term policies are generally preferred by insurers because long-term insurance involves longer-term commitments and thus higher risk—it is easier to predict the likelihood of an insured event in the next year than in the next 10 years. For the insured, however, the opposite is true: The advantage of long-term coverage is that he or she will have protection over the long term without having to reapply for insurance every year.

To address the need to balance long-term risk with client preferences for long-term coverage, short-term policies can have a *renewable term arrangement* whereby the policyholder can continue to have coverage up to a maximum age without the need to reapply, as long as premium payments are made. Renewable terms combine the advantages of short- and long-term coverage. The insured are guaranteed to receive continued coverage, yet the insurer can adjust the pricing, up or down for each renewal term, depending on its experience.

Although insurance companies tend to exclude high-risk persons, or charge them higher rates than others, microinsurance programs generally strive to be inclusive. Because the sums insured are small, the costs of identifying high-risk persons, such as those with preexisting illnesses, may be higher than the financial benefits of excluding them in the first place. Consequently, instead of pricing products for an individual's risk profile, microinsurance generally uses a group pricing method. Limiting the number of exclusions and restrictions lowers administrative costs and increases efficiency, and the group provides some means of controlling insurance risk.

Besides using groups, insurance plans incorporate various mechanisms to protect against adverse selection and overusage, including deductibles, copayments, and benefit ceilings. With a deductible, all claims below a specified amount are paid by the insured. Copayment arrangements mean a portion is paid by the insured and a portion by the insurer and are normally structured as a fixed fee, usually a specific amount per office visit. Benefit ceilings limit the overall amount of coverage to a specified amount, normally on a per person basis over a fixed period. Instead of using waiting periods or screening for high-risk persons, microinsurance programs often will include graduated benefits that start small during initial months of coverage and increase over time, which also creates an incentive to renew.

Premium Payment Mechanisms

Methods for paying premiums must minimize administrative costs for the insurer and transaction costs for clients. In general, the best time to collect premiums is when policyholders have cash, for example, at harvest time, or when they receive a loan or a government cash transfer.

To streamline premium payments, a common strategy is to "piggyback" the premium on top of another financial transaction. Linking the premium payment to a loan is a good example of this strategy; when clients receive a loan, they have cash to pay the premium. This strategy is also one of the easiest ways to achieve high renewals. Its downside is that only clients who receive a loan can obtain insurance coverage.

Alternatively, a link between savings and insurance provides more continuous coverage than the credit-insurance link, and it can significantly reduce the transaction costs. This can be done by deducting the premium from a savings account (although there is a public relations risk that depositors may not be aware that the money is being deducted). Another more innovative link between savings and insurance is to establish a fixed deposit account and allow the interest to pay the insurance premium. One challenge with this method is for the poorest clients to save up enough money to deposit in the account. From a management perspective, there is the risk the interest rates that are payable on the account may change and not be sufficient to pay the premiums.

More recently, insurance is being linked to other financial transactions, such as buying groceries or cell phone minutes or paying an electricity bill (see box 11.4). The emergence of more

---

Box 11.4 Collaborating with a Utility Company in Colombia

In response to increased competition, CODENSA, the largest electricity distribution company in Colombia, has developed a customer loyalty program to strengthen its customer base. A core component of the strategy is to offer alternative, nonelectricity products, including insurance, which can be paid through the electricity bill. With this objective, CODENSA entered into a partnership with MAPFRE Insurance in 2003 and currently offers five products: life, personal accident, funeral, home, and vehicle insurance. As an equal partner with a significant investment in the project's success, CODENSA is committed to maximizing profitability and developing an effective microinsurance business model. Because of aligned interests and good project management, the project has enabled more than 300,000 families to manage risk more efficiently by paying insurance premiums together with their electricity bill.

Source: Adapted from Smith et al. 2012a.

effective payment services, for example, through smartcards and point-of-sale devices or by mobile phones themselves, creates a new platform for premium collection and dramatically expands potential outreach.

Eligibility

When designing an insurance product, it is also necessary to determine who is eligible to be covered. Generally it is better to have more people covered by one product, and therefore a family benefit approach, which may include spouses, dependents, and even parents, creates a number of advantages for microinsurers:

- A family is a group of sorts, and consequently family coverage carries many of the same advantages as group coverage, including larger numbers and lower adverse selection risk. All other things being equal, the price for a family unit is generally lower than the sum of individual premiums.

- Family coverage can have a positive selection effect by purposefully enrolling very low-risk persons.

- Family coverage often has a better marketing effect because the claims are more frequent, and thus there are many more examples to demonstrate the value of microinsurance.

- Lenders concerned about protecting their loan portfolio realize that borrowers have repayment problems when death or illness strikes family members.

The downside of family benefits is that not everyone has a family, or that some people have larger families than others. To deal with the size of the family, microinsurers either ask the policyholder to identify a specific number of dependents who are covered by the policy or they offer different prices for different sized households. To ensure that women and children are not left out,

it is preferable to require family coverage where possible.

Even more important than defining which dependents are eligible is to identify them in advance. To minimize claims fraud, each person covered by the policy must be individually identified using official documents (where possible) and/or with photographs. It is not sufficient to specify which persons are covered without explicit identification of the additional persons. It is also important to control movements of dependents on or off the policy. For example, to control adverse selection, clients may have an option of adding newborn children on to the policy within a specified time frame, but not subsequently.

Claims

The best opportunity to demonstrate the value of insurance is to pay claims. *When* the benefits are paid is equally as important as *how* they are paid. Some products pay benefits in phases rather than in one lump sum to cover ongoing expenses. The provision of benefits over a period of time after the insured event may have greater development impact than a lump-sum payment because demands on the receiver of the payment can be significant; if the insurance payout is spent, for example, on an elaborate funeral, it is no longer available to help the household cope with the loss of income from the deceased.

Generally claims are paid only when the claim has been verified through a claim verification process. Policyholders have the right to efficient claim processing to ensure they receive tangible benefits for the premiums paid. A claim verification process consists of (1) an insured event leading to a notification of loss, (2) collection of required documents, (3) presentation of the claims application to an intermediary or the insurer, (4) claim adjustment to verify the claim and the amount, and (5) claim settlement.

In general there must be enough checks and balances to ensure that fraudulent claims are not paid. Effective controls center on ensuring the

Table 11.1   Two Long-Term Insurance and Savings Products in India

	Max Vijay	Grameen Shakti
Insurance	Max New York Life Insurance Company, Ltd	SBI Life Insurance Company, Ltd
Term	10 years	5 or 10 years
Premium	First payment from Rs 1,000 to 2,500 (approximately US$22–55); subsequent premiums of Rs 10 (US$0.20) to Rs 2,500 per day are voluntary	Annual payment of Rs 301 for a sum assured of Rs 25,000 (approximately US$6.50 for US$532 of coverage); grace period of 30 days from the premium payment due date
Sum assured	Five times premiums paid subject to a limit of Rs 50,000 to 100,000 (limit depends on amount of first premium payment)	Rs 5,000 to 50,000 (in multiples of 5,000); group decides the sum it wishes to assure
Maturity benefit	Maturity = (sum of premiums paid + investment return – account fees)	5-year term = 50% of premium paid net of service tax guaranteed; 10-year term = 100% of premium paid net of service tax guaranteed
Death benefit	Natural death = account value plus sum assured; accidental death = account value plus two times sum assured	Sum assured
Withdrawal/ surrender	Surrender and partial withdrawals possible after 3 years	Surrender possible after 3 years

Source: Adapted from Rusconi 2012.

target savings amount. A major difference between the endowment and savings completion insurance is that with the latter, the insurer does not hold the savings—rather, the financial service provider does. From the insurer's perspective, this is a very simple product: just basic term life with a declining benefit amount. However, it may be less attractive to insurers than an endowment policy because insurers generally prefer to hold the savings so they can invest and earn additional revenue. Alternatively, savings completion insurance may provide better value to clients, because their savings are not used to pay an agent's commission (see box 11.5).

For all long-term insurance products, policyholders need to trust that the insurer will exist 10, 20 or 30 years later when benefits are expected to be paid out. Insurers thus need to be managed (and supervised) so they continue to operate and can fulfill their commitments, especially in times of inflation and currency devaluations.

Health

Health insurance is one of the most highly demanded insurance products and among the most difficult to provide to low-income households. It is in big demand because health risks occur frequently and costs can be catastrophic. Health problems cause expenses for treatment but also result in the loss of income due to reduced productivity. The benefit of having health insurance is that people do not have to delay care because they cannot pay, which in turn can reduce the loss of income and lead to better health outcomes. If subsidies are not available, to make the coverage affordable to the poor, benefits are often rationed to a limited range of treatments. The effectiveness of health insurance is highly dependent on the health care system and the availability of quality services, whether public or private. Health insurance can be complicated and difficult to price and manage given the involvement of a third party (health care providers) and the number of potential risks, including over-usage and fraud.

Box 11.5 Savings Completion Insurance Offered by TUW SKOK

TUW SKOK, the primary provider of insurance to Polish credit unions, offers savings completion insurance to encourage credit union members to save regularly. The member determines a savings goal and time period, up to a maximum of 10 years. The credit union then calculates the amount of the member's required monthly deposit to achieve his or her savings target. It also calculates the monthly premium for insurance coverage. In the event of the member's accidental death, TUW SKOK pays the beneficiary the difference between the savings target and the savings balance at the time of death. This insurance product is of particular interest to credit unions because it is closely integrated into their core business and helps them achieve their own goals by making the contractual savings product more attractive.

Source: Adapted from Churchill and Pepler 2004.

Health insurance benefits are often paid on a reimbursement basis; the policyholder pays for the health care and then submits the receipts for reimbursement. Such an arrangement is generally less appropriate for poor clients who do not have regular cash flows. Some health insurance programs use a third-party or cashless payment system whereby the microinsurer pays the health care provider directly so the insured does not experience any out-of-pocket expenses, except perhaps for a copayment or transportation, which is sometimes also reimbursed by the insurer (for more details see LeRoy and Holtz 2012).

As with life insurance, there are several different ways of structuring health insurance benefits, and not all of them actually cover health care costs.

The most basic version, *critical illness* coverage, is essentially a life insurance policy that pays benefits early, that is, before the person dies, if the policyholder is diagnosed with a specified critical or terminal illness. In the context of microinsurance, this benefit is unlikely to cover the cost of treatment, but would assist with the financial hardship of not being able to work.

Hospital cash pays the insured a daily rate for the number of days in the hospital, as well as sometimes an additional payment for transportation. Such a product is also not linked to the actual medical expenses, and therefore claims processing does not require medical expertise. Such a product is particularly relevant where the poor have access to good quality care in government or other low-cost hospitals (see box 11.6).

Inpatient coverage pays for the actual costs of being in the hospital and is linked directly to the medical costs incurred. Hospitalization is a good example of an insurable risk because it is a large expense that occurs infrequently, so it is possible for the risk pool to function effectively. However, inpatient-only coverage does not typically include preventative care and early treatment, encouraging the insured to wait until an illness is so serious that it requires hospitalization before seeing a doctor when the illness may have been treated more effectively if it had been addressed earlier.

Pharmaceutical coverage pays for medicine either on its own or as an additional benefit to other health insurance.

Outpatient coverage pays for outpatient visits to the doctor or clinic. Because it occurs fairly often and is not a major expense, risk pooling does not work as well. Consequently, some organizations experiment with health savings accounts for outpatient expenses, with possible links to insurance for hospitalization. The advantage of covering outpatient expenses in an insurance product is that policyholders are likely to use the benefits and thus appreciate the value of renewing their policies. With inpatient coverage, in contrast, generally fewer than 5 percent of policyholders are likely to experience a claim, and therefore many may feel they have wasted their money.

In many countries, both developed and developing, there is ongoing debate about the role of government in providing health insurance benefits to the public, particularly the poor. Although universal health insurance coverage is certainly an ideal objective, governments that cannot afford it may have to ration benefits in some way, perhaps by limiting coverage to the poor, or by subsidizing health care providers to lower costs for consumers. In some developing countries, including Rwanda, Ghana, and India (see box 11.7), the government is providing leadership in efforts to extend health insurance coverage to workers in the informal economy (Leatherman et al. 2012). Indeed, microinsurance lies at the crossroads between financial inclusion and social protection; sometimes it is offered by insurers on a purely market basis, sometimes it is completely subsidized by governments, and often the reality lies somewhere in between.

Property

Property insurance provides coverage for tangible assets such as housing and contents as well as machinery and other equipment. For low-income households and businesses, such coverage can be difficult to underwrite and verify claims, because ownership may not be clear and actual losses can be difficult to verify. With the exception of agriculture insurance, there are few examples of stand-alone property coverage for the low-income market, although it is included in some composite products. Perhaps the most common type of property microinsurance is a rider on a credit life policy that would pay specified benefits if a borrower's business burns down. Such a risk is common among MFI clients who work as vendors in large markets.

Agriculture

In rural areas, concerns about drought, death of livestock, and other agricultural risks tend to be high for low-income households. Without protection against agricultural risks, financial service

Box 11.7 Public-Private Partnerships and Health Microinsurance in India

What is particularly interesting about health microinsurance in India is the emergence of state-driven mass programs. These programs are considered under the broad heading of microinsurance, even though they are heavily subsidized, because they generally involve some sort of user fee and they are often implemented by the insurance industry through public-private partnerships.

From 75 million people covered under such programs in 2007, it is estimated that 302 million people had health microinsurance in 2010. Three of these programs—Aarogyasri in Andra Pradesh, Kalaignar in Tamil Nadu, and the national Rashtriya Swasthya Bima Yojana (RSBY) program—reportedly insured 54 million families by the end of 2010 (PHFI 2011). Backed by political will and the ability

to aggregate huge numbers, these programs are transforming health microinsurance by addressing key challenges such as data creation, investment in identification technology, and setting industry standards for health care provision.

For RSBY, the successful implementation on such a scale can be attributed to the public-private partnership and the use of technology. Whereas Aarogyasri and Kalaignar collaborated with one insurer, Star Allied Insurance, RSBY in its first year worked with eight insurers and 16 third-party administrators to implement the program. To control fraud, RSBY uses biometric cards that are issued in "real time," which improves customer service and controls any rent-seeking behavior by the card-issuing agency.

Source: Adapted from Ruchismita and Churchill 2012.

providers may be unwilling to lend for agricultural inputs. Even if poor farmers have funds to pay for seeds and fertilizer in one growing season, a crop failure may ruin their ability to plant the following season. These risks tend to be covariant, affecting many farmers in the same region at the same time, causing particularly large risks for local lenders. When an entire community is affected, this also limits the ability of farmers to help each other.

Agriculture insurance generally covers crop failure and the death of livestock. However, it is wrought with challenges, particularly moral hazard (for example, having insurance may give the farmer an incentive not to follow appropriate farming practices), covariant risk (for example, a natural disaster affects many of an insurer's policyholders at the same time), fraud (for example, the farmer may fake crop

loss or pay off the claims adjuster), and expensive claims verification processes, especially for smallholder farms.

As described in box 11.8, an innovation to overcome these problems is index-based insurance whereby policyholders in a particular geographic area receive a benefit regardless of whether or not they experience a loss if a predetermined measurable outcome occurs, such as too much or too little rain, temperatures above or below certain thresholds, or excess wind speeds. The big advantage of an index approach is that it helps to eliminate fraud and moral hazard and minimizes the costs of claims processing. A key limitation, however, known as basis risk, is that farmers may experience a loss even though the index is not triggered, or alternatively do not experience a loss and still receive a benefit (for more details, see World Bank 2011).

Box 11.8 Index Insurance and Technology: The Case of Kilimo Salama, Kenya

Kilimo Salama is an index-based agriculture insurance product that was piloted in March 2009, initially covering only 200 maize farmers and drawing on data collected by two weather stations. The project has since grown and now uses 30 weather stations and covers 22,000 farmers who grow maize, sorghum, cotton, beans, and coffee.

Kilimo Salama (which means "Safe Agriculture" in Kiswahili) is a partnership between the Syngenta Foundation, Safaricom, the largest mobile network operator in Kenya, and UAP, a large general insurance company. The product covers farmers' agricultural inputs (for example, fertilizer, seed, and pesticides) in the event of drought or excessive rainfall. The product is index based, meaning that payouts are triggered by rainfall amounts. During the planting season, actual rainfall is measured using a solar-powered weather station in each area. If rainfall is below or above predetermined thresholds, a payout is made. The value of the payout is a function of how much the recorded rainfall deviates from the threshold.

To distribute the product, Syngenta involves agro-dealerships and an innovative technology system. The administrative backbone of Kilimo Salama is a fully automated, paperless technology that uses mobile phones with tailor-made Java software as registration devices at the points of sale. The mobile phones transmit customer information to a central server, and the server in turn communicates with the insured farmer via SMS (text messaging). The "backbone" technology is linked to Safaricom's M-PESA mobile payments platform to facilitate payment of premiums and settlement of claims. The following steps highlight how technology supports enrollment:

- Farmers visit a local agro-dealer who offers Kilimo Salama for a premium related to their expected harvest or the cost of inputs purchased from the agro-dealer.
- If a farmer decides to buy Kilimo Salama, the dealer scans a bar code on the bag of seeds using a specially designed mobile phone application.
- The application then informs the dealer of the premium the farmer should pay, which is currently between 5 and 15 percent of the cost of inputs.
- The agro-dealer captures the farmer's details—name, mobile number, and coverage amount—on the dealer's mobile phone and transmits this information via GPRS to the insurer through a central communications server.
- The farmer then receives a text message with the policy number and coverage details. Provision has been made for farmers who do not have mobile phones: The policy number and coverage details are sent instead to the dealer's phone, and the dealer then passes them on to the farmer.

Kilimo Salama uses the amount of rainfall as a trigger for claims. During the planting season, weather stations send the precipitation data via a general packet radio service connection to UAP. The insurer enters it into a weather-index application that outlines the rainfall requirements for each crop. The application calculates the claim percentage, if any, and then UAP transfers the claim amount to the M-PESA account of the farmer or dealer.

Although reasonably effective, the use of technology has posed certain challenges. The weather station technology allows for the design of a viable insurance product, but it also makes

(continued next page)

Box 11.8 *(continued)*

the product more complex to understand. Farmers are on average 20 kilometers away from the nearest station, which could lead to a misunderstanding by farmers as to whether they are entitled to a payout if the rainfall recorded on their farms differs from the local weather station. This basis risk increases the need for appropriate and extensive client education.

Multiple technologies are required to minimize the error margin in constructing weather indices. Reliance only on weather station data is unlikely to provide an accurate picture of the rainfall patterns experienced in a particular area. This is all the more difficult if weather stations are few and far apart. To overcome this challenge, Kilimo Salama is experimenting with satellite mapping systems and devising better ways to collect and track yield data. This will allow for the cross-validation of weather data and the selection of more accurate product parameters.

Source: Adapted from Smith et al. 2012b. http://kilimosalama.wordpress.com/about/.

Composite Insurance

Offered in some low-income markets, composite insurance combines multiple benefits into one integrated insurance policy. Benefits can come from two or more different insurance companies and are bundled together into one comprehensive product. The rationale is that composite insurance delivers a more comprehensive risk protection package at a lower cost (that is, it would be more expensive to sell three separate products). The marginal cost of adding benefits to many insurance products is minimal. In addition, when selling the product, a cost-effective solution to diverse risk-management needs can be offered.

For example, VimoSEWA, the insurance arm of the Indian trade union the Self-Employed Women's Association (SEWA), offers life, hospitalization, and property coverage for individuals and families all in one product. However, because insurance regulations require companies to have separate licenses for life and general insurance, the risks are underwritten by two different companies, the Life Insurance Corporation of India for life insurance and the New India Assurance for non-life insurance.

A challenge with composite insurance is that the benefits can be complicated, which runs counter to a primary tenet of microinsurance: simplicity. A related issue is the potential lack of transparency. The contribution of each individual benefit relative to the total price may not be communicated, nor are clients normally allowed to choose the specific benefits they want. Because different risks may be managed by different companies, a potential problem also exists when the service provided by one component of the product is inadequate and negatively affects the perception of the entire product.

Microinsurance and Financial Inclusion

A unique aspect of microinsurance is the willingness to be broadly inclusive. The method by which commercial insurers typically limit their exposure by excluding high risks, such as older persons or those with preexisting conditions, naturally excludes large numbers of vulnerable people. The microinsurance challenge is to find ways to inclusively serve vulnerable households at affordable rates over the long term.

Broader inclusion means lower operating costs by reducing the costs of screening, while accepting higher-risk persons and their accompanying claims costs. However, significant scale is required to justify this approach. High-risk individuals can be included if the benefits are limited or, alternatively, if premiums are correspondingly higher for risky members than for the rest of the group. Both of these approaches reduce the cross-subsidization of the higher-risk individuals by the rest of the members to support broader inclusion on a sustainable basis. There is a solid economic rationale at play as well: The costs of monitoring and enforcing complex exclusions must be weighed against the claims avoided; the small sums insured and premiums of microinsurance products cannot support complex screening and claims validation.

Another challenge in getting broader microinsurance inclusion is that in developing countries, information for actuarial calculations, such as mortality and morbidity rates, is at best unreliable and generally not available. Garand et al. (2012) propose some solutions for actuaries to price insurance products with limited data, but only once programs have sufficient experience can they accurately predict claims incidents and costs.

Although programs may be willing to accept high-risk members, they might not be so inclined to keep older policyholders. Most have age ceilings whereby members may be asked to leave the program just when they really need the benefits. In these cases, some microinsurers provide a withdrawal payout. Insurers may use exclusions for a number of reasons:

- Controlling adverse selection, for example, preexisting condition exclusion

- Reducing moral hazard, for example, suicide exclusions

- Reducing the cost of insurance by removing high-frequency or common claims and targeting only specific causes of claims, for example, accident-only coverage, which excludes death due to illness

- Controlling covariant or catastrophe risk, for example, riots or weather catastrophe exclusions

- Reducing the extent of initial underwriting, for example, one-year HIV/AIDS exclusions applied to life coverage to eliminate the need for testing.

Microinsurers, however, may adopt a different approach to exclusions than traditional insurers. Although the moral hazard exclusion is justifiable regardless of the type of insurance, a microinsurer may allow typically excluded conditions for covariant risk and certain adverse selection risks in the spirit of social protection. Where covariant risks are taken on, it is essential that appropriate risk management strategies exist, such as reinsurance. Otherwise, the only consequence of dropping the catastrophe exclusion will be the insolvency of the program in the event of a catastrophe, which benefits no one.

The argument against exclusions for preexisting conditions is not quite as clear. If a microinsurer offers voluntary individual insurance, then the high-risk people are most likely to sign up; if only high-risk people join, the insurer cannot effectively pool the risk. However, if it is group coverage, especially if it is mandatory, or the microinsurer recruits large volumes of policyholders, then it can be more inclusive with regard to preexisting conditions. This additional risk is highest at product launch. If renewal rates can be kept high as the program matures, the risk associated with preexisting conditions becomes more manageable because new insured members become a smaller proportion of the entire portfolio.

A microinsurance-friendly alternative to exclusions is the waiting period where benefits are not accessible for some time after enrollment. For example, HIV/AIDS-related adverse selection is managed using six-months to one-year accident-only waiting periods. If the insured event occurs during the waiting period, the claim is rejected; the insurer does not have to check with doctors and review medical records to determine if the policyholder already had the problem, as it has to do with exclusions for preexisting conditions.

Another alternative to exclusions which is more in line with the spirit of microinsurance is to offer benefit schedules with gradually increasing benefits. For example, if the insured event occurs in the first year, the benefit is small; but if it occurs after the first year, the benefit is much larger. Such an approach is an effective way to control adverse selection while creating an equitable microinsurance program that encourages long-term participation and renewal.

Moving Forward

The rapid growth of microinsurance means that many more low-income households have insurance coverage, but it does not necessarily mean that they have quality coverage. A growing body of evidence shows that it is possible to design and deliver insurance services to low-income households and enterprises, and it can be viable for providers, but the next step is to increase the value that those products provide to the insured and their beneficiaries. In this context, the concept of value includes a range of dimensions, including affordability, accessibility, covering risks that are relevant, paying claims quickly, and a substantial portion of the premium paid by policyholders coming back to the risk pool in the form of claims (see Matul et al. 2011). To achieve these objectives, critical issues need to be addressed, including the following:

- *Improve insurance literacy:* Low levels of insurance literacy make it difficult for clients to understand policies and use them properly, which undermines client value. Financial education is especially important with mandatory insurance and subsidized offerings.

- *Improve efficiency:* Administrative costs for microinsurance continue to be high for many products, making it difficult for sufficient premiums to return to policyholders as claims. To support scale, insurers need to efficiently process huge volumes of data. At the same time, front-office technology, from handheld and point-of-sale devices to mobile phones, are beginning to improve sales, premium collection, and even claims settlement. There are great expectations that technology will facilitate paperless insurance processes that will streamline systems and provide greater value to policyholders.

- *Innovate with voluntary products:* Much of the scale that has been achieved to date can be attributed to mandatory coverage or automatic benefits. The next step is to experiment with voluntary products and sales mechanisms to better understand how to unlock the latent demand for microinsurance.

- *Engage new players:* Insurance companies have been increasingly attracted to microinsurance, but outreach has dramatically increased in part because of the involvement of new players, such as governments, mobile phone companies, retailers, and banking correspondents. Greater competition does not automatically lead to better quality products, but these new entrants are likely to contribute to both scale and client value.

- *Develop better data:* Insurance is a data-intensive industry, and one of the drawbacks inhibiting the expansion of microinsurance is the lack of data, including information about mortality and morbidity for people and animals, property loss, and weather. Institutional performance data are also limited. Where microinsurance is not considered a business line for insurance companies, they often cannot assess their own performance in the low-income market segment.

- *Enter new markets:* Various countries, including India, South Africa, and the Philippines, can boast about significant microinsurance accomplishments. But for every developing country that is experiencing significant growth, there are at least three or four that are stagnant or have limited microinsurance activity.

A patient approach is required for microinsurance because the demonstration effect will take some time to sink in. The findings from Matul et al. (2011) illustrate that products mature over time, and as they do they become more efficient and provide better value. A critical challenge in building a market is to create conditions that encourage low-income households to turn to insurance naturally as part of their risk-management toolkit. In environments where microinsurance is prevalent, and providers are cultivating the trust of that market through efficient claims payments, such conditions are emerging. However, microinsurance providers need to continue to recognize that their most important function is to pay claims, and build on the emerging demonstration effect.

Notes

1. This chapter draws heavily from Churchill (2006), especially chapters 1.1 and 3.1, and various chapters in Churchill and Matul (2012).
2. One might also consider accident and disability insurance, but they could also be considered as subsets of life and/or health. They are perhaps most useful as part of a composite product or as a rider on a life insurance product.

References and Further Reading

Churchill, C., ed. 2006. *Protecting the Poor: A Microinsurance Compendium.* Geneva and Munich: International Labour Organization and Munich Re Foundation.

Churchill C., D. Liber, M. J. McCord, and J. Roth. 2003. *Making Insurance Work for Microfinance Institutions: A Technical Guide to Developing and Delivering Microinsurance.* Geneva: International Labour Organization.

Churchill, C., and M. Matul, eds. 2012. *Protecting the Poor: A Microinsurance Compendium, Vol. II.* Geneva and Munich: International Labour Organization and Munich Re Foundation.

Churchill, C., and T. Pepler. 2004. "TUW SKOK, Poland." CGAP Working Group on Microinsurance, Good and Bad Practices Case Study 2, ILO Social Finance Programme, Geneva.

Cohen, M., and J. Sebstad. 2006. "The Demand for Microinsurance." In *Protecting the Poor: A Microinsurance Compendium,* ed. C. Churchill, 25–44. Geneva and Munich: International Labour Organization and Munich Re Foundation.

Frankiewicz, C., and C. Churchill. 2011. *Making Microfinance Work: Managing Product Diversification.* Geneva: International Labour Organization.

Garand, D., C. Tatin-Jaleran, D. Swinderek, and M. Yang. 2012. "Pricing of Microinsurance Products." In *Protecting the Poor: A Microinsurance Compendium, Vol. II,* ed. C. Churchill and M. Matul, 464–83. Geneva and Munich: International Labour Organization and Munich Re Foundation.

Hougaard, C., and D. Chamberlain. 2012. "Funeral Insurance." In *Protecting the Poor: A Microinsurance Compendium, Vol. II,* ed. C. Churchill and M. Matul, 217–36. Geneva and Munich: International Labour Organization and Munich Re Foundation.

Leatherman, S., L. J. Christensen, and J. Holtz. 2012. "Innovations and Barriers in Health Microinsurance." In *Protecting the Poor: A Microinsurance Compendium, Vol. II,* ed. C. Churchill and M. Matul, 112–30. Geneva and Munich: International Labour Organization and Munich Re Foundation.

Ledgerwood, Joanna. 1998. *Microfinance Handbook: An Institutional and Financial Perspective.* Washington, DC: World Bank.

LeRoy, P., and J. Holtz. 2012. "Third-Party Payment Mechanisms in Health

Microinsurance." In *Protecting the Poor: A Microinsurance Compendium, Vol. II,* ed. C. Churchill and M. Matul, 132–55. Geneva and Munich: International Labour Organization and Munich Re Foundation.

Matul, M., C. Tatin-Jaleran, and E. Kelly. 2011. "Improving Client Value from Microinsurance: Insights from India, Kenya, and the Philippines." Microinsurance Paper Series 12, International Labour Organization, Geneva.

PHFI (Public Health Foundation of India). 2011. *A Critical Assessment of the Existing Health Insurance Models in India.* New Delhi: PHFI.

Roth, J., and D. Chamberlain. 2006. "Retailers as Microinsurance Distribution Channels." In *Protecting the Poor: A Microinsurance Compendium, Vol. II,* ed. C. Churchill and M. Matul, 439–51. Geneva and Munich: International Labour Organization and Munich Re Foundation.

Roth, J., M. J. McCord, and D. Liber. 2007. *The Landscape of Microinsurance in the World's 100 Poorest Countries.* Appleton, WI: MicroInsurance Centre.

Ruchismita, R., and C. Churchill. 2012. "State and Market Synergies: Insights from India's Microinsurance Success." In *Protecting the Poor: A Microinsurance Compendium, Vol. II,* ed. C. Churchill and M. Matul, 427–60. Geneva and Munich: International Labour Organization and Munich Re Foundation.

Rusconi, R. 2012. "Savings in Microinsurance: Lessons from India." In *Protecting the Poor: A Microinsurance Compendium, Vol. II,* ed. C. Churchill and M. Matul, 176–96. Geneva and Munich: International Labour Organization and Munich Re Foundation.

Smith, A., H. Smit, and D. Chamberlain. 2012a. "New Frontiers in Microinsurance Distribution." In *Protecting the Poor: A Microinsurance Compendium, Vol. II,* ed. C. Churchill and M. Matul, 486–502. Geneva and Munich: International Labour Organization and Munich Re Foundation.

Smith, A., E. Gerelle, M. Berende, and G. Chelwa. 2012b. "The Technology Revolution in Microinsurance." In *Protecting the Poor: A Microinsurance Compendium, Vol. II,* ed. C. Churchill and M. Matul, 528–47. Geneva and Munich: International Labour Organization and Munich Re Foundation.

Wipf, J., E. Kelly, and M. J. McCord. 2012. "Improving Credit Life Microinsurance." In *Protecting the Poor: A Microinsurance Compendium, Vol. II,* ed. C. Churchill and M. Matul, 197–256. Geneva and Munich: International Labour Organization and Munich Re Foundation.

World Bank. 2011. *Weather Index Insurance for Agriculture: Guidance for Development Practitioners.* Washington, DC: World Bank.

Xu, Ke, D. B. Evans, G. Carrin, A. Mylena Aguilar-Rivera, P. Musgrove, and T. Evans. 2007. "Protecting Households from Catastrophic Spending." *Health Affairs* 26 (4): 972–83.

CHAPTER 12

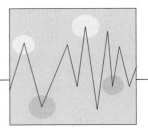

Payment Services and Delivery Channels

Joyce Lehman and Joanna Ledgerwood

Payment services refer to the electronic transfer of funds, sometimes called money transfers, transfer services, transactions, mobile money, or simply payments. Although nonelectronic payment services exist, in this chapter these terms refer to the electronic transfer of funds between two parties, whether either party consists of an individual person, a business, a government, or any other organization. Referring to electronic money rather than using the more common terminology of mobile money reflects the fact that most, if not all, payment services can be accessed using devices other than a mobile phone.

With electronic payment services, it can be difficult to distinguish between the product (for example, when a transfer is conducted on a

mobile phone) and the channel (for example, when the mobile handset is connected to a bank account, referred to as mobile banking, discussed under delivery channels below). These distinctions are important to note when discussing electronic money.

Payment services involve both a provider of the services and the service or product itself. The provider can be any one of a variety of financial service providers, including money transfer companies, banks or other formal financial institutions, post offices, and now mobile network operators (MNOs) (see chapter 7). The product can be a remittance from one individual to another, a social welfare payment from a government to an individual, a bill payment by an individual to a business, a salary deposited directly

---

Contributions to this chapter were made by Joakim Vincze and Geraldine O'Keeffe.

into a bank account, or a payment for goods purchased from a merchant. The term "payment services" is used in this chapter when discussing the product.

A payment service is not the same as a payment system. Also known as a clearing or settlement system, a payment system is the infrastructure that enables the transfer to occur. Clients initiate payment services but are not involved in payment systems, which are discussed in chapter 18.

Delivery channel refers to the mechanism by which financial services are delivered to clients and is distinct from both the product and the provider. For example, a money transfer (the product) can occur over a mobile phone (the delivery channel) through a service offered by an MNO (the provider). Or a client can make a deposit (the product) by giving cash to a savings officer in the field with a point-of-sale (POS) device (the delivery channel) connected to the back-end technology of a bank (the provider).

In the developed world, individuals with bank accounts have the ability to conduct most financial transactions electronically. In the developing world, most poor people are trapped in a cash-only world and pay a high cost in both time and money to conduct financial transactions. As more alternative delivery channels develop to allow poor women and men to access services through agents in their own community, the cost to conduct personal financial transactions, whether deposits, withdrawals, payments, or transfers, can be greatly reduced.

This chapter describes various payment services used by the poor followed by a discussion of the channels available to deliver all financial products. And whether they are MNOs, financial institutions, or independent third parties, a key part of many delivery channels is a network of agents who conduct transactions on the behalf of providers and brand the network accordingly. The issues and operational challenges involved in setting up an effective and efficient agent network are also discussed.

Payment Services

Payment services or electronic transfers can occur between two people, between a person and a business (or vice versa), or from the government to a person (or vice versa).[1] Transfers can be made using a negotiable instrument such as a check, a direct debit through a bank account, an electronic funds transfer (EFT), a POS device, an ATM, or a mobile phone. The terms commonly used are P2P for a person-to-person transfer, P2B or B2P for transfers between a person and a business, and G2P for transfers from the government to a person. Although these terms are most commonly used in the context of mobile money, they can also apply to payments using POS devices and other channels.

All electronic transactions generally involve a fee levied by the provider doing the transfer. For example, banks charge fees for drawing a check on a current account or sending a wire transfer. Services can be priced as a percentage of the transaction amount or on a sliding scale based on the transaction size, with a fixed fee assigned to each size range or simply a flat fee.

Person-to-Person Transfers

The bulk of money transfers in the low-income sector consist of remittances from migrant or seasonal workers sending money back home to family and friends.[2] Many of these are domestic remittances as a family member migrates to an urban area and sends money back to family in the rural village. International transfers are also common but require a provider with cross-border settlement capabilities. Money transfers can also occur between two private parties for general purposes. Taxi drivers in Nairobi, for example, prefer to be paid with M-PESA electronic money rather than with cash to reduce the risk of theft.

Because the senders and receivers of remittances are often low-income people and the amounts remitted are small, the price of the services, which can be quite high, is a major consideration (see box 12.1).

Box 12.1 Trends in the Average Cost of Remittance Services

Remittances Prices Worldwide (RPW), a World Bank initiative launched in 2008, monitors the costs of cross-border remittances, measuring the progress of a 2009 G-8 goal to reduce the global average cost by 5 percent in five years. By 2011 RPW was monitoring prices in 213 remittance corridors to and from 31 sending countries and 91 receiving countries. The findings here are based on an analysis of third-quarter 2011 data.

Commercial banks charge about 14 percent of the amount remitted and are the least transparent in disclosing exchange rates. Post offices are less costly at 7.1 percent, but transparency is also an issue. Money transfer companies, at 7.4 percent, are similar in cost but notably more transparent, with 99 percent of those in the RPW database disclosing full price information to their clients.

The cost of remittances also varies depending on where the money is being sent. South Asia (6.2 percent) and Latin America and the Caribbean (7.7 percent) are the least costly, whereas Sub-Saharan Africa (12.4 percent) and East Asia and Pacific (9.8 percent) are the most expensive. These variations are likely due to the level of competition as well as contextual factors such as local costs of doing business.

A comprehensive analysis of the average price by product found the following results:

- Cash products are available at an average price of 7.6 percent.
- Account-to-account services are very costly at 14.5 percent, but the price drops to 6.5 percent if the two accounts are in the same or a partner bank.
- Online services cost on average 8.8 percent but are generally not available to the senders.
- The least expensive services are prepaid cards and account-to-cash products, at 4.2 and 2.9 percent, respectively.

Source: World Bank 2011.

Although most P2P transfers have traditionally been through money transfer companies or transacted through informal channels, this is beginning to change with the advent of mobile money.

Transfers between Individuals and Businesses

P2B transfers include bill payments made by an individual to a business such as a utility or telephone company as well as payments to a merchant for goods purchased. Depending on the arrangements made between the utility, telephone company, or merchant receiving the payment and the bank or MNO, the transfer can be made either through a POS device and a card or a mobile phone. Some organizations allow customers to pay for services such as health care premiums using mobile money (see box 12.2). The agreements for P2B transfers typically do not entail a fee to the consumer; instead, the business or merchant pays the provider an agreed amount per transaction. Throughout the developing world, numerous financial service providers are experimenting with having their credit clients repay loans or make deposits using mobile money rather than transacting with cash at a branch.

B2P transfers are increasingly used by companies to pay salaries to their employees. These salary payments are made through direct deposits to

Box 12.2 Mobile Money Innovations in Microinsurance in the Philippines

Health care financing is one of the biggest constraints to improved health care around the world. In the Philippines, a national health insurer enables clients to pay microinsurance premiums though a mobile phone and receive claims into the mobile financial services account. They can also use text messages to pay premiums on a

weekly or monthly basis, as opposed to quarterly or half-yearly. Participation has increased as convenience has increased and costs (financial and opportunity costs) have decreased. The ability to make small payments through a mobile phone gives individuals greater opportunities to manage insurance payments.

Source: Gencer and Ranck 2011.

the employees' bank account, if they have an account, or onto their mobile phones. Some credit providers are beginning to use mobile payments to make loan disbursements as well, although the size of the disbursement may exceed the maximum size of transaction allowed.

Government Transfer Payments

G2P payments include government employee salaries, pensions, health and social welfare benefits, and one-off payments for emergencies. Such government transfers are increasingly being linked to bank savings accounts or to mobile phones, facilitating access to the financial system and encouraging recipients to save a portion of the funds received. The recipient can then choose when and how much of the money received to take as cash (through an agent, ATM, or branch office). As the entire electronic ecosystem develops and more governments, businesses, and merchants begin to use electronic technology, customers have an opportunity to keep an increasing amount of value in electronic form rather than converting it to cash.

Proximity of the cash outlet (an agent, for example) to the recipient clearly leads to both time and cost savings for receiving and making payments, transferring and withdrawing money, and storing

value (see box 12.3). And although it has the potential to put formal savings options within reach, there are little or no data demonstrating a clear correlation between agent proximity and an increase in both the uptake of savings accounts *and* deposit balances over time (Alvarez 2010).

From the government's perspective, however, upgrading G2P payment mechanisms can substantially reduce administrative costs as well as limit opportunities for fraud and leakage. In Brazil, switching just one financial institution to electronic benefit cards helped to reduce the cost of delivering Bolsa Familia grants from 14.7 to 2.6 percent of the grant value disbursed. Moreover, there is growing recognition that financial inclusion efforts, particularly if driven by promoting access to savings, can be highly complementary to a range of social protection objectives (Almazan 2010).

Value of Payment Services

Some payment service products are more appealing than others. The price of services is important, perhaps more so than for other financial services; particularly when small amounts are involved, fees can represent a significant cost. As technology develops, the price of payment services will decline, particularly as competition and

Box 12.3 Mobile Money in Papua New Guinea

Improvement in mobile money networks in Papua New Guinea contributes to improved health care and education by reducing the need for nurses and teachers to travel to cash points to collect their pay. The government and private sector, often based in urban areas, employ thousands of individuals across the country, most often in rural areas. The difficulty of transferring money from urban to rural areas can have real consequences for the country's education and health care systems. Teachers and nurses are the largest groups of government employees, but the education and health care systems are some of the weakest, in large part because of absenteeism. Teachers, for example, have a 15 percent absentee rate, primarily because of the need to travel to collect wages. The opportunity cost is children in school with no teachers or patients in hospitals with no nurses. Mobile money reduces absenteeism and improves federal and private services, particularly in rural areas.

Source: Bruett and Firpo 2009.

efficiency increase; however, this will require a level of scale not yet reached.

An important feature of payment services is the time it takes to effect the payment or transfer. Generally the shorter the time, the higher the price, but this is not always the case, depending on the service used. Transfers can be instantaneous, within a few hours, or take several days. Depending on their needs, clients may be willing to pay additional fees to ensure a quick transfer.

Convenience is also important—both for the sender and the receiver. If either needs to incur substantial costs for transport, identification, or time away from home or business, these additional costs need to be considered. In addition, although security of cash is likely increased through electronic money, particularly with new delivery channels, using technology, agent networks, or both may lack the level of confidence and trust embedded in more traditional services. Clients need to be sure that the money they are sending will get to the right person at the right time and in the intended amount. If conducting the transfer themselves is too complicated—for example, on their mobile phone—or is prone to errors, with no checks and balances in place, clients may be less likely to use the service. The risk of losing money or having the receiver claim it never arrived is a concern, especially for new users. These risks need to be mitigated as much as possible by the provider, enabling clients to trust the service and see value in using it.

Delivery Channels

Transactions can occur over a range of channels either in person at a branch or with technology-enabled alternatives. Financial service providers traditionally operate through branch networks, requiring face-to-face meetings with clients either at the branch or in the field. As discussed in chapter 1, to reduce costs, increase convenience, and reach more clients, providers are exploring alternative channels such as ATMs, mobile branches, agent networks (using POS devices and mobile phones), and Internet banking. In most alternative channels, the "face-to-face customer experience" with the institution changes significantly, a factor that may alter products and how they are marketed or designed. Box 12.4 provides a glossary of terms related to alternative delivery channels.[3]

Box 12.4 Glossary of Terms Related to Alternative Delivery Channels

- *Agent.* Any third party acting on behalf of a bank or other financial service provider (including an e-money issuer or distributor) in its dealings with customers. The term agent is commonly used even if a principal-agent relationship does not exist by law in the country. Agents may (if permitted under local law) engage subagents to carry out the activities on behalf of the financial service provider. A financial service provider may also engage an agent network manager to help select, train, manage, and oversee agents.
- *Automated teller machine.* An unattended electronic machine usually located in a public place, connected to a data system, and activated by a client with an electronic payment card connected to an account; it is used to make cash withdrawals or deposits and conduct other banking services.
- *Branchless banking.* The delivery of financial services outside conventional bank branches, using ATMs, mobile branches, agents, or other third-party intermediaries as the principal interface with customers and relying on technologies such as card-reading POS devices and ATMs, mobile phones, or Internet-connected computing devices to transmit the transaction details.
- *Cash-in.* In the context of e-money, the exchange of cash for electronic value.
- *Cash-out.* In the context of e-money, the exchange of electronic value for cash.
- *Credit card.* An electronic payment card allowing the holder to purchase goods and services on credit.
- *Debit card.* An electronic payment allowing the holder to deposit or withdraw funds to or from a bank account; it may be used with an ATM or in conjunction with a POS device.
- *Electronic funds transfer or e-payment.* Transfers initiated through an electronic terminal, telephone, computer, or magnetic tape for the purpose of ordering, instructing, or authorizing a financial institution to debit or credit a consumer's account.
- *Electronic money (e-money).* A type of stored-value instrument or product generally understood to have the following attributes: (1) issued upon receipt of funds, (2) consisting of electronically recorded value stored on a device (for example, a chip, prepaid card, mobile phone, or computer system), (3) accepted as a means of payment by parties other than the issuer, and (4) convertible into cash.
- *E-money account.* An account of a holder of e-money held with the e-money issuer. If the e-money issuer is a bank, the account could be a "regular" transactional bank account; if the e-money issuer is a non-bank, then the account is a recording of the e-money issued by the issuer and held by the customer. The funds backing the amount may be pooled with other customers' funds of the same non-bank e-money issuer and held in a bank account or accounts. In some cases, a trust account is established for such customers.
- *E-money issuer.* An entity that initially sells or issues e-money against the receipt of funds; some countries permit only banks to issue e-money; other countries also permit non-banks to issue e-money.
- *E-wallet.* Electronic money held on a mobile phone, smartcard, or the Internet.
- *Internet banking (e-banking).* The use of an Internet browser to perform financial transactions over the Internet, via the provider's website.
- *Interoperability.* The ability of diverse information technology systems to work together so that services can be provided across multiple providers.

(continued next page)

Box 12.4 *(continued)*

- *Mobile banking.* The use of a mobile phone to access financial services and execute financial transactions connected to a bank account. This covers both transactional and nontransactional services, such as viewing financial information on a customer's mobile phone (Chatain et al. 2011).
- *Mobile branches.* Sometimes referred to as mobile vans or as minibranches, vehicles equipped with a portable ATM that are staffed by a teller equipped with a small laptop, mobile phone, or POS device linked to the provider's core banking system that travels to remote areas at specified times to conduct financial transactions, primarily cash-in, cash-out services.
- *Mobile financial services.* The use of a mobile phone to access financial services and execute financial transactions. Mobile financial services can also include mobile branches. As mobile branches are relatively few, the term most often refers to accessing financial services and executing transactions via a mobile phone.
- *Mobile money.* A type of e-money that can be transferred by an MNO. As with other e-money issuers, the issuer of mobile money may (depending on the local law and the business model) be an MNO, a bank, or a third party.
- *Mobile network operator.* A company that has a government-issued license to provide a mobile phone service.
- *Mobile payment.* An e-payment made through a mobile phone.
- *M-wallet.* A mobile-based account for storing electronic money on the mobile device.
- *Payment terminal.* A stand-alone terminal similar to an ATM, providing retail cash-in access points, but not cash-out capabilities.
- *Point-of-sale device.* A small, portable device that facilitates an electronic financial transaction.
- *Prepaid cards.* Also called stored-value cards, plastic cards that are preloaded with value and used for purchases or payments where they are accepted. They typically do not require a bank account, and they can be reloaded with funds.
- *Smartcard.* A payment card with a machine-readable embedded chip that stores information about the customer and his or her accounts.
- *Smartphone.* A highly portable personal computer that has a built-in mobile phone.
- *Third-party provider.* Agents and others acting on behalf of a financial service provider, whether pursuant to a service agreement, joint-venture agreement, or other contractual arrangement.

Source: CGAP, draft glossary of mobile financial services terms; Center for Financial Inclusion 2010; CGAP 2011.

Branches

In a branch, a teller or customer service officer conducts transactions, including cash-in, cash-out services. These brick and mortar branches are the most expensive channel to operate. A properly functioning branch needs accessible roads, electrical power, Internet connectivity, and telecommunications access. Operationally there are staff costs, security provisions, and backup power sources, as well as internal controls and other risk management and monitoring costs. Because of the high costs of setup and operations, branch networks are not generally conducive for reaching remote, rural areas or lower-income consumers in urban areas. For customers in rural areas, visiting a branch can involve traveling long distances, paying for transportation, and often waiting in long lines once they reach the branch.

As technology continues to transform the core brick and mortar bank functions, the relative space allocated to front- and back-office functions is changing, with branches becoming primarily sales offices, while alternative delivery channels are increasingly being used to conduct transactions.

Some providers address cost issues by establishing minibranches or outlets that are staffed only one or two days a week or by setting up kiosks in marketplaces equipped with POS devices or laptop computers that allow access to the provider's core banking system for entering client transactions and generating ministatements. In this way, outreach is increased without incurring the costs of operating a full branch. For example, Kshetriya Gramin Financial Services (KGFS) branches in India are set up to be welcoming meeting points for villagers (bright colors, an awning, and benches in front to encourage people to linger and chat) and are powered in the back by a technology infrastructure. In some way, KGFS branches are similar to branch innovation in the United States and Europe, where branches sometimes double as Internet cafes.

Field Officers

As part of their outreach strategy, financial service providers often send staff to the field to meet clients (either individually or in groups) close to their place of business or residence. Using field officers is a common practice, often associated with early initiatives in microfinance such as Grameen, solidarity group lending, or village banks. The model has proven resilient in many countries but is still relatively inefficient and expensive compared to some of the newer channels being developed. Field officers traditionally record transactions with paper and pen, and each transaction is later entered into the provider's core banking system when the field officer returns to the branch. This is changing as field officers take advantage of technological innovations and facilitate transactions on behalf of clients via handheld devices (mobile phones, POS devices, tablets, or laptop computers) to increase efficiency. Although more expensive, sometimes field officers are able to provide other services in the field such as information or technical support that can help both clients to increase productivity and providers to decrease risks (see box 12.5).

Automated Teller Machines

ATMs perform many of the same functions as a cashier or teller at a branch, but customers carry out transactions using the ATM and a card. ATMs are generally located in high-traffic areas close to clients and function 24 hours a day, providing convenient access points for basic transactions, including withdrawals, transfers, and bill payments. In some cases they accept deposits as well. ATMs increase convenience through better locations or, in some cases, inside or next to the branch, which reduces congestion in the branch and results in shorter wait times. However, they are still relatively scarce. In 2009 there were only 8 bank branches per 100,000 adults in developing countries versus 24 in developed countries. There were only 23 ATMs per 100,000 adults in developing countries versus 78 in developed countries (Mylenko et al. 2009).

Although most ATMs guide clients through the steps of a transaction using written instructions displayed on the device's screen, some ATMs developed for populations with minimal literacy use pictures or spoken instructions for this purpose. Some ATMs have also incorporated biometric technology to either replace cards or verify client identity. As soon as the machine recognizes the client's identity and retrieves the account information, the client can conduct a range of transactions.

Although less expensive than a branch, ATMs can still be relatively expensive for providers to own and operate. In addition to infrastructure

Box 12.5 Expanding Rural Finance in Sri Lanka

The Hatton Nation Bank (HNB) of Sri Lanka is a well-established commercial bank that was forced to embark on rural and agricultural finance in the mid-1970s when the government restricted private commercial banks from opening more branches in urban areas. By the late 1980s, HNB had implemented a strategy for serving the largely underserved rural market. It had downscaled its regular operations, established a dedicated rural banking division, and offered extension services to its new rural clientele. To support the new strategy, HNB invested in new delivery channels to reach rural customers more

effectively—customer service centers, microfinance units, ATMs, and mobile vehicles.

The bank also invested in a large network of field officers, hiring qualified people who not only understand finance but also have expertise in agriculture and creating a network of 250 "barefoot bankers" who work in the villages and normally come from the community. They act as field officers and also mentor, guide, and provide technical assistance to clients, encouraging and guiding farmers to become commercially viable. With the barefoot bankers providing technical expertise and guidance close to clients, the bank has reduced its risk.

Source: Lahaye 2011.

costs (machines, cards, vehicles for moving cash), they require appropriate theft-proof installation structure, data network connectivity, reliable power, and regular service to replenish or collect cash. Furthermore, regulations also mandate that rigorous information management and internal control systems are in effect and may restrict the use of ATMs by providers such as MFIs that may be lacking in those systems.

Electronic Payment Cards

Clients access ATMs through electronic payment cards using a password or personal identification number (PIN) that allows personal information to be verified and transactions carried out. Cards can be debit cards, where the amount available for withdrawal depends on the amount of accessible funds in the corresponding bank account, or credit cards, with a maximum amount of credit available to the holder, which, if used, is repaid at a later date with interest. They can also be branded with merchant or other organization logos or a card association such as Visa or

MasterCard, which gives clients the ability to use them at ATMs or with an agent.

The electronic cards store customer information on a magnetic stripe or an embedded chip. Cards with an embedded chip are referred to as smartcards. Although not an access point in and of themselves, smartcards facilitate access to different transaction points and increase the security of information. Chips enable detailed transaction records to be stored offline and to perform transactions without a real-time link to the customer's account. They can also store biometric information. Smartcards can function as debit cards, credit cards, or prepaid (or stored-value) cards.

Prepaid cards differ from traditional debit cards in that they are preloaded with value (and can be reloaded) and typically do not require a bank account. Prepaid cards come in various formats and can be single- or multiple-use cards. They are cheaper to issue and to host than conventional debit or credit cards. They are increasingly used for government transfer payments and can be issued by banks or retailers. For example, UBL in Pakistan issued cards to recipients of government payments after realizing that many low-income women beneficiaries did not have their own mobile phone (see box 12.6).[4]

Smaller providers without sufficient capital and technical capacity can enter into partnerships to give their clients access to the ATMs of a larger, more established provider. This arrangement is referred to as a "white label" arrangement in which the smaller institution obtains specially printed bank cards, PIN mailers (sealed envelopes with the client's assigned PIN), and access to a telephone-based customer support center that deals with ATM issues (for example, unreadable cards).

Some ATMs do not require users to have an electronic payment card, but rather are linked to mobile phones as cash points, allowing customers with or without a bank account to use e-wallets to access cash through the ATM (see box 12.7). For this to work, the ATM needs to be placed in a location with Global System for Mobile (GSM) network coverage and the client must have access to a GSM phone with a charged battery, a subscriber identity module (SIM) card, and airtime credits.[5]

Payment Terminals

Payment terminals are retail cash-in access points located in local shops and markets or in stand-alone kiosks along streets, often two to three on a single city block.[6] Customers use payment terminals to pay bills for services such as electricity, Internet, and water. Where utility company main offices or branches may be located far from a customer's home or place of work, terminals are particularly convenient. Depending on the license granted to the terminal operator, payment terminals can also be used to top up mobile airtime as well as facilitate domestic and international person-to-person transfers (see box 12.8).

Like ATMs, payment terminals can be relatively expensive for operators to install and maintain. Data network connectivity, reliable power sources (some have solar panels where regular power is unstable), and cash handling all result in substantial costs for terminal operators. Similarly, some terminals necessitate that clients have electronic cards. Cards may be purchased only with proper identification, and in most cases registration is required.

Regulatory supervision of payment terminals varies by country as well as by specific terminal functions. Some terminals accept cash deposits, an activity that requires a banking license or partnership with a bank. In some countries, simple bill payments require regulatory supervision.

Point-of-Sale Devices

POS devices are small special-purpose portable computing devices that facilitate payments, deposits, withdrawals, money transfers, voucher distributions, account balances, and printing of mini-statements. Unlike an ATM, transactions on a POS device are performed in conjunction with an agent or retailer or a mobile field officer who supports the successful completion of the transaction, provides cash-in, cash-out services (if applicable), and provides a printed receipt with the client's card once the transaction is complete. POS devices generally include a facility to read information from a card (magnetic strip or smart card),[7] which allows the device to work with prepaid or stored-value cards. These can be used to pay for goods or services, withdraw cash, and, if used with an agent or field officer, deposit cash.

POS devices are generally located at fast-moving consumer goods retail outlets where a retailer acts as the agent for an MNO or bank. Retailers are often affiliated with a bank card brand (for example, Visa, MasterCard, or Maestro) and can serve clients from any financial institution that is also affiliated with the bank card brands that the retailer represents.

Although the cost of a POS device is higher than a mobile phone, the device offers a larger screen, higher-quality keyboard, superior data

Box 12.6 World Food Programme Card Pilot, 2009

United Bank Limited (UBL), one of Pakistan's largest private banks, has a branchless banking channel called Omni, which launched in early 2009 and was fully rolled out in April 2010. In 2009 several million residents of the Swat Valley in Pakistan were displaced from their homes following a period of intense conflict between security forces and militants, making them dependent on emergency supplies and cash transfers from the World Food Programme (WFP). UBL approached the WFP with an offer to pay out the cash transfers of Rs 4,000 (US$47) in each of two monthly payments using a prepaid card as a means of piloting this way of paying cash. The WFP designated 12,000 beneficiaries to participate, and UBL staff issued the cards.

A total of 24,000 cash payments were made, amounting to just over US$1 million using a network of 15 Omni agents. The WFP transferred the funds in bulk to the UBL, which credited each of the underlying limited-mandate bank accounts set up for each beneficiary. Thereafter, beneficiaries could withdraw their money by presenting the card and using their PIN at an Omni agent. For each withdrawal, agents received the standard Omni cash-out fee of 1–1.5 percent. An NGO, Save the Children, provided extensive support to the beneficiaries, training them on how to use their card and PIN and even accompanying them to make their first withdrawal. This spared UBL staff from having to provide support to previously unbanked beneficiaries.

Based on the UBL's experience and subsequent feedback from the WFP and customers, all parties involved were extremely satisfied with and confident in the process. One enormous benefit was that the program mobilized the local economy and generated employment and business opportunities in the affected communities.

The biggest benefit was that the total cost of distributing aid was the 5 percent commission that the WFP paid to UBL plus the minor administrative cost of its monitoring staff. If other development agencies adopt the process, the aid distribution structure could be made more efficient, because in the current system about 60 percent of aid is spent in the distribution chain and does not translate into any benefit for the intended recipients.

Source: CGAP 2010.

Box 12.7 Cardless ATM Transactions

Paynet Kenya developed the world's first software that allows cardless transactions at ATMs. In March 2005, PesaPoint was founded to provide convenient ATM locations countrywide. Through the integration of financial institutions, as of 2012 the PesaPoint network had grown to more than 500 ATMs nationwide, enabling Kenyans to withdraw cash, pay bills, access their M-PESA accounts, inquire about their bank balance, and more.

PesaPoint is a "white label" ATM network. One year after its launch, M-PESA partnered

(continued next page)

Box 12.7 *(continued)*

with PesaPoint. Customers can now retrieve money from any PesaPoint ATM. To do so, they must select "ATM withdrawal" from their M-PESA menu. They then receive a one-time authorization code, which they enter on the ATM keyboard. No bank card is needed for

this transaction. By accessing the PesaPoint ATM network, M-PESA customers can now make withdrawals from their stored-value accounts at any time without having to go to an M-PESA agent.

Source: Mas and Radcliffe 2010.

Box 12.8 Payment Terminals in the Russian Federation

The payment terminal is a grassroots Russian invention. Terminals take in, but do not disburse, cash—their main limitation and major distinguishing characteristic from ATMs. Payment terminals came about as a convenient means to top up mobile phones. Customers enter their phone number into the machine and insert cash into the terminal. The paid amount net of commission is automatically added to their mobile account.

Currently, payment terminals can also be used to pay for utilities, traffic tickets, and movie tickets, to transfer money to bank cards, as well as to pay a variety of other services. In 2009, Qiwi, the leading operator in Russia, offered payment services for more

than 1,300 companies through its terminals. Qiwi is expanding internationally and works in 22 countries in Europe, Asia, Africa, and the Americas.

There were approximately 250,000 terminals in Russia as of early 2011, and the number is growing. In places where people have limited access to the Internet or agents, payment terminals remain the best way to pay for services without going to a bank (Boris 2011).

In 2010, the average payment size was Rub 132 (US$4.20), and the total volume of transactions was Rub 772.2 billion (US$24.7 billion), implying approximately 5.8 billion transactions (Qiwi Channel 2011).

Source: Jenya Shandina. For information on Qiwi, see http://tv-technopark.ru/index.php?option=com_content&view=article&id=479&catid=11 and http://qiwi.ru/about/world/ (both in Russian).

security, and the option of generating a printed transaction receipt.[8] Retailers, providers, or their agents can use this feature to issue ministatements showing, for example, the last 10 transactions on a client's account.

Multiple models of POS devices cater specifically to development finance markets by being

portable and equipped with biometric scanners and wireless connection capabilities, including Bluetooth,[9] Wi-Fi,[10] GPRS,[11] and even a dial-up modem to allow data connections over analog phone lines (similar to fax machines). Rechargeable batteries typically allow several hundred transactions to be performed between charging.

POS devices have their own proprietary operating systems that can be configured to operate with essentially any core banking system or transaction-processing platform.

The physical POS device operates software that allows it to establish a secure data connection with the back-end systems of a bank. An encrypted data connection is used to protect the client's private information, including account numbers, balances, and access code. Data communications protocols[12] used by the POS device to communicate with the core banking system are robust and involve multiple exchanges of data between the device and the banking platform to ensure that the transaction has been successfully completed. Should the communications link be severed during a transaction, the POS transmission protocol will ensure that the transaction is voided in a way that protects the client's account balance.

Some manufacturers have experimented with turning POS devices into "cashless ATMs." In this operating mode the POS device is used as a self-serve terminal, typically located in a retail outlet that is the primary source of liquidity for the device. To use the POS device, clients insert their access card, enter their PIN, and then select a transaction from the device display. For withdrawals, the device generates a bar-coded receipt that the client then takes to a retailer cash point where the receipt is validated and the retailer provides cash to the client.

Mobile Branches

Mobile branches operate either as mobile ATMs loaded onto a van or, within the van, as a mini-branch staffed by a teller equipped with a small laptop, mobile phone, or POS device linked to the provider's core banking system and often by a security guard. These models are designed to enable transactions in sparsely populated rural areas where distances make travel inconvenient and costly and there are no alternative access points (box 12.9). Mobile branches generally have fixed schedules, arriving at remote villages on market days when clients regularly gather. They

---

Box 12.9 Urwego Opportunity Bank's Mobile Bank and Open Sky System

In an effort to reach rural populations in Rwanda, Urwego Opportunity Bank launched a mobile banking service in 2010. A vehicle was equipped with networks, modems, and an application called Open Sky, which enabled a low-bandwidth real-time connection to the core banking system operating at the head office. With this technology, key banking services were available in the communities visited, including teller transactions, new client registration, and loan applications. A schedule was determined and advertised so that customers knew when to expect the mobile bank visits.

When the mobile bank was launched, it appeared to be one of the more attractive methods for reaching rural clients, but after the pilot phase, it was determined to be too costly. The vehicle itself was expensive to purchase and set up, as were the operational costs related to vehicle maintenance, fuel, and secure cash transit.

At the same time, more options became available for using mobile money to extend outreach. Although the initial vehicle remains in use, the bank shifted its focus to mobile phone technology.

Source: Geraldine O'Keeffe, Software Group.

---

provide cash-in, cash-out services and can be used to update accounts instantly if the systems can connect to the Internet.

Mobile Phones

Similar to POS devices, mobile phones can facilitate basic transactions: withdrawals, deposits, payments (through agents), and account inquiries. The mobile phone does not have to be connected to a bank account. If the customer has a bank account, then the mobile phone becomes the device for conducting transactions in and out of the account. If the customer is unbanked, then the mobile phone simply provides electronic money services or "mobile payments." The provider of mobile payments may, depending on local law, be the MNO itself, a commercial bank, or a third party (the distinction as to whether a deployment is bank-led, MNO-led, or provided by a third party lies with which party "owns" the customer and builds out the network of access points). In each case the mechanism is the same: using a mobile phone to conduct the transfer.

A mobile phone can also become a "mobile wallet" for storing monetary value or "e-money" (referred to as stored value), for depositing additional value by giving cash to a cash-in, cash-out agent, or for transferring funds to another individual or a business. The mobile wallet has the same value to the customer as a low-balance bank account. Some clients deposit funds onto their mobile account purely for security without the intention of transferring them to another person or bank account (Kumar, McKay, and Rotman 2010). For example, Savings Groups may use a mobile e-wallet to store excess group liquidity as well as to save for specific purposes such as bulk purchases of fertilizer. Given the risks of theft, some members believe that storing money in a secure mobile e-wallet is better than using the traditional lockbox kept in their homes.

Many electronic money schemes have been tried in developed countries, but with the exception of debit cards, they have routinely failed to open up enough space within the crowded set of payment service options for customers and merchants. While there are various ways to carry out electronic transfers, mobile payments using mobile phones may be the game changer. From 2010 to 2012, the number of people with access to a mobile phone but not to traditional financial services is expected to have grown from 1 billion to 1.7 billion (Baptista and Heitmann 2010). Although only a few of the mobile money deployments in the developing world have reached scale, those that have demonstrate the significant potential for mobile phones to revolutionize access to financial services for poor people living in developing countries who have few alternatives to cash (see chapter 1).

In Kenya the MNO Safaricom developed M-PESA, an e-money transfer and payment product, becoming the first mobile money deployment to reach scale (see box 12.10). M-PESA is an MNO-led deployment, and customers are not required to have a bank account. Rather, customers can choose to retain electronic value on the mobile device itself, sometimes referred to as stored value. The rapid uptake of the payment and stored-value services of M-PESA, and the fact that the service is increasingly being used by poorer clientele, shows its value to customers.

Mobile phones can potentially replace a bank card and a POS device. GSM phones hold account and transaction information on each customer's SIM card.[13] Clients can apply for a SIM card directly from an MNO retail outlet or from an issuing bank working in partnership with an MNO, which ensures that some form of identification is provided to satisfy the know your customer/anti-money-laundering regulations for bank accounts.

The customer's PIN and bank account number are recorded on the SIM card or in the phone's memory, and in this way the phone acts as a virtual card (Mas and Kumar 2008). Once recorded, the customer can move funds to and from the account using a menu on the mobile phone as

Box 12.10 M-PESA Reaching Scale with Mobile Money

M-PESA, a Safaricom-led mobile money service in Kenya, was launched in 2007 with the simple proposition to "send money home." M stands for mobile, and PESA means money in Swahili. By the end of 2009, more than 70 percent of households in Kenya and, more important, more than 50 percent of the poor, unbanked, and rural populations were using the service (Jack and Suri 2010). By June 2010, 70 percent of all financial transactions in Kenya were done using M-PESA, but the total value of these transactions represented only 2.3 percent of the total transaction *value,* demonstrating the demand for a great many very small transactions (Jack and Suri 2010). As of November 2011, M-PESA had more than 14 million subscribers and well over 28,000 agents across Kenya.

M-PESA's perceived safety and convenience are major reasons that early adopters chose to use it. In the fall of 2008, researchers completed a survey of 3,000 randomly selected Kenyan households to gain further insight into M-PESA use. Within the sample, 26 percent of M-PESA users reported that safety was their main motivation for adopting the service, whereas 45 percent stated ease of operation as their reason. About 12 percent of users stated that they use M-PESA for emergencies (see Jack and Suri 2010 for full survey results). Additionally, the vast majority of users viewed M-PESA to be faster, more

convenient, and more secure than the informal methods they had previously used to send and receive money (Rotman 2010). The 2008 survey also found that among nonusers the lack of adoption was due to inadequate access to network agents.

Overall, M-PESA's success has demonstrated that leveraging mobile technology to extend financial services to large segments of unbanked poor people is possible, largely because cell phone technology is becoming ubiquitous in the developing world. In contrast to traditional banking models that rely on the debt capacity of borrowers to generate revenue from interest and fees charged on loans, M-PESA's revenue model is based on usage fees. This usage-fee model has proven to be profitable despite targeting a client segment of hard-to-reach poor. In addition, M-PESA has demonstrated the importance of offering low-cost payment services.

The early support of Kenya's central bank for the pilot M-PESA and the fact that Safaricom held a dominant position in the market at the time of the launch were key factors that led to the rapid uptake. Even so, the M-PESA results demonstrate that low-income clients sufficiently value the ability to make payments for payment services to be considered a financial product (along with credit, savings, and insurance) that helps poor people to manage their financial lives.

Source: Jack and Suri 2010; Rotman 2010.

---

defined by the MNO. Cash-in, cash-out services still need to be performed in a branch, at an ATM, or with an agent.

MNOs offer three types of transaction messaging protocols to perform financial transactions over GSM mobile networks:

1. *Short messaging service (SMS).* The client sends a specially coded SMS message to the intended recipient. This is usually referred to as texting or a text message.

2. *Unstructured supplementary service data (USSD).* The client begins the session by

typing in an MNO-defined code on the phone and pressing "send." A transaction menu prompts the client to choose the desired action. USSD messages create a real-time connection, which makes them more responsive than SMS messages, and do not store the customer's data, unlike the SMS protocol.

3. *Custom-built application.* The provider uses a purpose-built application software program on the SIM card or in the phone's internal memory to enable the user to launch the financial transaction menu directly from the handset.

Although each option has both positive and negative characteristics, the customer generally does not get to choose among them. When an MNO, a bank, or a third party launches an electronic payment platform, the protocols have already been decided. Whatever the functionality, the most important factor is to ensure that the

staff or agents working with the consumer are well trained and can assist the customers in how to use the service.

These technical decisions on message protocols, encryption standards, and software platforms can have a great effect on the customer experience (Mas and Kumar 2008; see box 12.11). Technology choices can also affect the relationship between the bank and the MNO. Applications using the SIM card require the active support of the MNO to install the menu and enable the encryption keys. Likewise, applications based on USSD may require the MNO to allow access to its USSD server to send and receive messages to and from the clients' mobile phones. Other applications, including those that are purpose built, do not require support of the MNO or even the MNO's knowledge that mobile banking transactions are taking place. These variations in dependency can create a delicate balance of power between the bank and the

---

Box 12.11 Banking with a Mobile Phone: The Customer Experience

To open a bank account, the customer visits a bank branch or an agent accredited by the bank where she is properly identified as required by law. She fills out a form, supplies her name, address, and mobile phone number, and presents an acceptable form of identification. If she already has a bank account, she can use her phone to sign up for mobile banking by sending a text message to a particular number. Once the account is opened, the bank transmits the mobile banking application wirelessly to the customer's phone, where it appears on the main menu. The customer registers her phone number and selects and types in a PIN. She can now begin transacting. She will be able to receive her salary, remittances, and other transfers into this

account and be able to make payments—for example, pay utility bills (P2B) or transfer money to others (P2P).

If she wants to withdraw cash from her account, she can do so through an agent who represents her bank. She simply selects the application from the phone's menu, enters her PIN, and selects "withdraw" from the menu. She will be prompted to select the account from which she wants to withdraw, enter the amount, and then enter the phone number of the agent. The next screen prompts her to confirm the transaction. Both the customer and the agent then receive a message confirming that the customer's account is debited, and the amount is transferred to the agent's account. At this point the agent gives her the cash.

Source: Mas and Kumar 2008.

MNO that can ultimately affect the pricing structure to the clients.

Figure 12.1 shows the relationship between the customer, the agent, and a bank in conducting a mobile banking transaction. After the agent opens a bank account and the account is operational, the agent can assist the client in opening an account so that the client does not have to go to the bank at all.

More and more financial service providers are using mobile phones to create greater efficiencies for themselves and for their clients. Some use mobile phones to send transaction confirmation messages as well as other information to clients via SMS or USSD. Some use basic SMS messages to remind borrowers that a loan installment is due. For example, rather than having a loan officer visit a client when a payment is overdue, the provider can send an SMS the day before the payment due date as a reminder, lowering costs for the provider, helping the client stay on track, and potentially reducing portfolio risk.

Clients can also use phones to check their account balances and recent account activity, allowing them to detect fraud if they do not recognize recent transactions or to increase their balance if necessary.

Internet Banking (e-Banking)

Financial service providers around the world allow clients to transact on their account via the Internet. To do so, the client must have some form of Internet-connected access device, such as a personal computer, tablet,[14] or smartphone. Users connect to the provider's Internet platform via a browser or an application installed on their device. As always, cash-in, cash-out transactions must be performed with an agent or at an outlet. However, given the high costs of dedicated broadband infrastructure and the cost of the connection devices as well, Internet banking does not yet have significant outreach in developing countries.

Enabling clients to perform financial transactions via smartphones is a huge step forward

Figure 12.1 Relationship between the Customer, the Agent, and a Bank in Conducting a Mobile Banking Transaction

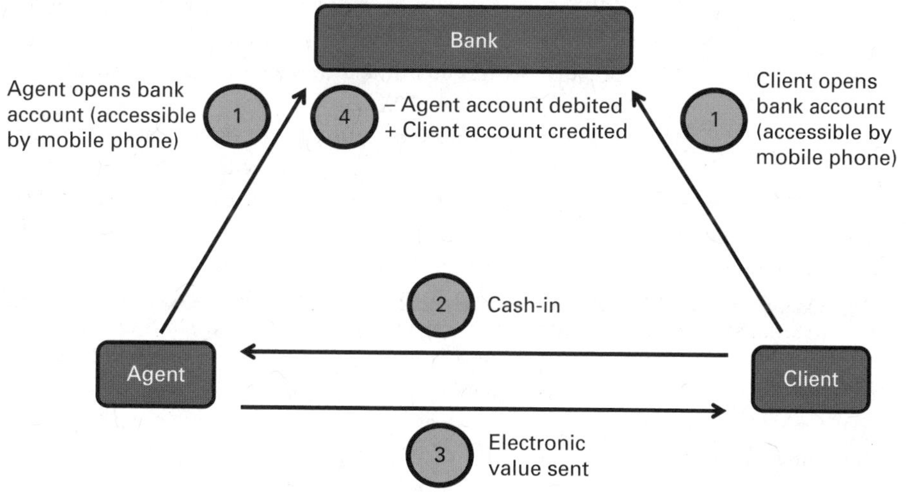

Source: Adapted from CGAP.

in terms of accessibility and convenience. Smartphones, like personal computers, have random access memory and local storage that can be used to install small purpose-built software applications, typically just called "apps." Banks and other financial service providers develop and distribute apps to give clients with smartphones access to their accounts.

Transacting on a smartphone provides a higher-quality experience than transacting on a regular mobile phone, but smartphones are significantly more expensive. In addition, the data plans that enable Internet connectivity are a "premium service" for which the client pays more. For poor women and men in rural areas, the benefits of a smartphone may be moot (at this point) given that many mobile telephone data networks do not operate reliably outside of metropolitan areas. A smartphone also requires more frequent battery charging than a regular mobile phone. This may not be a major consideration for people living and working in an area with reliable electricity, but rural populations in many developing countries frequently live off-grid and have to pay someone to charge their mobile phones.

As a practical matter, smartphones are perhaps best suited for interacting with clients in the field, that is, by the provider's staff or agents to access information and services traditionally available only from branches.

Interoperability

A major challenge facing mobile banking is the need for interoperability so that providers within the same sector can recognize each other.[15] Banks and MNOs have negotiated interoperability agreements that allow their customers to transact beyond the markets they directly serve (ATMs for banks and "roaming" for MNOs, for example) but are hesitant to do so for mobile banking. In the case of mobile banking, providers often want to recoup the substantial investments in developing

services and related infrastructure before interoperating their systems with others.

The hesitancy of providers to "interoperate" has given rise to third-party payment platforms that allow clients from any mobile network (or any bank) to transact using the same interface. With some notable exceptions such as United Bank Limited (UBL) in Pakistan, which developed its own technology to create a payment platform for providing the service known as Omni and a national network of Omni agents, most banks do not have their own platform and instead partner with third-party providers—independent companies that provide the platform giving access to bank customers (see box 12.12).

Third-party platform providers may initially negotiate a nonexclusive contract with one MNO but then are free to market to other MNOs and banks. This is particularly useful for smaller banks and MFIs, which can access a platform without having to negotiate individual relationships with MNOs or to develop their own platform. For example, bKash in Bangladesh is an independent entity that developed the payment platform and has the brand and the agent network, but a commercial bank holds the customer balances to comply with central bank regulations. The bKash service has agreements with multiple MNOs that enable their customers to become customers of bKash (see box 12.13).

Interoperability can be defined at the platform level, where a customer with an account with one service provider can transact with the account of a customer with a different service provider; the agent level, where agents can serve customers for more than one service provider (as long as the platforms are interconnected); and the customer level, where a customer can access his or her account using any phone with a SIM card on the same network or access multiple accounts on one SIM (Kumar 2011).

The incentive for providers to interconnect depends on the size of their relative market

Box 12.12 Third-Party Providers: New Business Models

In some countries, third-party technology companies are developing "technology-enabled business models" in partnership with banks and non-banks. Examples of these include FINO, Eko, ALW, and SubK in India and Wizzit in South Africa.

FINO and ALW and several similar companies in India use card and card-reader systems, usually focusing on G2P payments. The accounts are held by banks, and all transactions must be done with an agent. These companies manage agents and their acquisition of and interaction with customers, but banks "own" the customers and are fully liable for meeting all know your customer, documentation, and other requirements. FINO's agents are not stationary; instead they set up temporary disbursement sites on payment days.

FINO and ALW use smartcard technology with biometrics, which is relatively expensive (both cards and the readers) and does not link into the national payments system. Eko uses cell phone technology that requires the customer to be familiar with numbers. SubK (a subsidiary of BASIX Group) uses a voice biometric system that might work better for poor people; its system could be linked into the national payments system. Some of these companies have both their own platforms and a separate not-for-profit *business correspondent* company that manages the customer and agent relationship. FINO claims to be the largest branchless banking business in the world, with more than 45 million customers, and is still growing. Eko's customers can transact via cell phones without going to an agent, unless they want a cash transaction. Most of Eko's transactions are person to person (P2P) and not government to person (G2P).

Wizzit has a platform company called Wizzit International with contracts in several countries and a business in South Africa also called Wizzit. All Wizzit accounts are held in the South Africa Bank of Athens, which is responsible for meeting central bank know your customer and risk management requirements. Wizzit is a P2P transaction business in which customers get both a debit card and a SIM card that are linked to the same bank account and use both for transactions (transactions on the two channels were about half and half at the time of writing). For the most part, Wizzit has recruited, trained, and managed its own agents, called Wiz Kids, an innovative sales approach that other providers have copied. It has tried to work with retail networks, the post office, and fast-moving consumer goods companies, but with little success so far. None of these start-up companies is profitable yet, and some have struggled to find equity investors and to grow to scale. But they have demonstrated new business models, and this has influenced regulators to open up space and attracted other businesses to invest.

Source: Steve Rasmussen and Kabir Kumar, CGAP.

shares and their strategy for maintaining a geographic presence. To become comfortable sharing platforms or agent networks, providers need to (1) understand the power of broad client reach versus exclusive operational control over fewer agents and (2) the necessity of competing on the basis of superior products and service rather than trying to establish exclusive geographic zones with high barriers to entry (Mas 2008).

Box 12.13 bKash Ltd.

bKash was created in 2010 to develop a national payments platform accessible to a majority of the poor in urban and rural Bangladesh. bKash functions as a third-party network that aspires to work with multiple MNOs and multiple banks. The components include the following:

- An interoperable mobile money software platform that allows customers to make deposits, withdrawals, transfer funds, pay bills, and store funds through a mobile wallet account
- An extensive agent network that registers customers, assists them with transactions, and serves as cash-in, cash-out points
- A mobile operator through which bKash uses a USSD channel to conduct secure transactions over the air (initially bKash partnered with Robi, but recently Grameen Phone, the MNO with the largest market share in the country, has signed on to permit its customers to use the bKash platform)
- A bank that will hold customer accounts; the first bank partner was BRAC Bank, but bKash is looking to add additional banks in the future
- Other platform participants, such as governments, merchants, bill-pay services, and credit and insurance providers.

Since the official launch in July 2011, customers are able to receive electronic money into their bKash accounts through salaries, loans, domestic remittances, and other disbursements and eventually can cash out at any of the thousands of bKash agents, hold the money in the account for safe keeping, or make electronic payments.

The bKash mobile wallet is a Visa technology platform, fully encrypted to ensure secure transactions. Money can be deposited into and withdrawn from this account or used for various services.

Source: Author interview with b-Kash.

In places where interoperability is limited, consumers respond by opening multiple mobile money accounts and swapping SIM cards in and out of their phones. This arrangement, although workable, is far from ideal because the client is required to maintain a much larger aggregate amount of on-deposit funds than if a single fully interoperable account were possible. Allowing clients to access their accounts via other SIM cards increases not only the potential size of the market but also the likelihood that the clients will choose another MNO as their primary service provider. MNOs may fear that a service accessible to their subscribers will cannibalize their own service (CGAP n.d.).

Agent Networks

Financial services can be delivered to a majority of poor households only if the service providers—banks and MNOs—use retail distribution channels to get closer to where the poor live at a fraction of the cost of traditional banking (see box 12.14). These agents who convert cash to electronic money (e-money) or convert e-money to cash are the human face of all agent banking systems. Therefore, when building, incentivizing, and managing a network of retail agents, providers must address the operational challenges in a way that fosters a positive and consistent customer experience that will create

Box 12.14 Branchless Banking in Brazil

The market for payments, whether it is people paying utilities, taxes, or credit card bills (P2B) or the government making welfare payments (G2P), has been tapped most successfully by the larger banks in Brazil. The country now has more than 130,000 outlets acting as agents of the bank (although only 39,000 of these outlets offer full banking services) and serving about 13 million new bank customers who have been added since 2002.

As a result, Brazil is the first developing country with at least one banking outlet in every municipality. The success of the Brazilian model hinges on country-specific factors. On the demand side, two factors created captive markets for new banking agents setting up in areas previously unserved by banks.

First, the government embraced the early use of bank accounts to distribute welfare benefits (under the Bolsa Familia program), and most of the new bank account holders are welfare recipients. Second, bill payment is

treated as a regulated banking service, so utility companies cannot sign up local shops as agents for bill collection points, as is commonly done in other countries.

On the supply side, two factors helped to create a distributed network of agents. First, state resources were used effectively. State-owned Banco do Brasil and Caixa Federal led the charge in signing agents (the latter using a major lottery chain), and the extensive postal network was auctioned off as an exclusive banking agent (won by Banco Bradesco, which then created the Banco Postal as a joint venture with the postal service). These became three early and powerful agent networks that prompted other banks (Banco Real, HSBC, Unibanco) to join in. Second, a special retail payment technology infrastructure allows agents to deposit and withdraw from their account at the branch of any bank. This enables banks to provide service to agents who are far from their own branches.

Source: Mas 2009.

and maintain trust in the system (Lehman 2010).

Building an Agent Network

An effective agent is well trained, trusted by customers, strategically and conveniently located, and properly incentivized to follow procedures, keep sufficient float on hand, and serve customers. Banks typically select larger and more established retail stores, whereas mobile networks are more inclined to use smaller retail outlets such as roadside stands, "mom and pop" shops, or kiosks (Mas and Siedek 2008). Some providers choose to outsource agent recruiting and training altogether. Either way, the size and growth of the agent network has to be planned carefully to ensure that

there are enough agents to serve customers and enough customers to keep the agents interested in providing the service (see box 12.15).

Safaricom, the single most successful mobile money deployment to date, invested heavily in developing the M-PESA agent network with a focus on a consistent customer experience. Each one of its more than 20,000 agents provides the same services (that is, signing up new customers and facilitating cash-in, cash-out transactions), follows the same procedures, and has the same branding. Other providers have assigned different roles to different agents, which has resulted in difficult trade-offs. For example, MTN Uganda separated the "field-based" account-opening function from the "static" cash-in, cash-out

Box 12.15 From Payment Terminals to Multiple Services

Inspired by a network of payment terminals in Russia, Express Pay—an unregulated payment service provider—started in Tajikistan in 2007 and now offers a web of financial services for numerous providers. According to Express Pay's co-founder, Dilshod Niyazov, a forward-thinking representative of the National Bank of Tajikistan discovered Express Pay's first terminals within the busy markets of Dushanbe and insisted that Express Pay set up a licensed microdeposit organization in 2009 to carry on business. In response, FG Vavilon was established allowing Express Pay to capture savings legally as well as to make transfers and bill payments.

Today, Express Pay manages 800 terminals, small street-side machines that resemble a one-way ATM, providing cash-in but not cash-out. Through these terminals, users can pay bills, make domestic money transfers to other account holders, top up mobile airtime, and, in some cases, repay loans. Express Pay is convenient for clients. Bill pay services are free. Utility providers (water, electricity, Internet) and other financial service providers

pay a commission to Express Pay for processing transactions. For money transfers, customers pay a maximum 3 percent of the transaction amount.

In addition to payment terminals, Express Pay has extended its network to include 1,600 agents, most of whom are local shopkeepers located throughout Tajikistan. Agents perform the same functions as terminals but also offer "cash out" services to customers and soon will be able to register new accounts. (Currently, customers must register for a new account at a central office.)

Niyazov estimates that 25 percent of Express Pay's business comes through agents and 75 percent comes through terminals. That will change as its presence expands geographically and the company deepens its offerings, particularly to utilities, where company employees travel from home to home to invoice customers, collect payments, and issue paper receipts. It is not difficult to imagine a time when certified, roaming Express Pay service agents will perform this function for a variety of companies.

Source: Kim Wilson, Fletcher School, Tufts University.

function to speed up the acquisition of new clients. However, this created a situation in which customers signed up even though they did not need the service or could not find an agent with which to transact (Davidson and Leishman 2010).

When an agent can both open accounts and facilitate transactions, not only does the agent have an incentive to provide services to customers, but customers are encouraged to use the service. If customers cannot transact immediately upon opening an account, they lose the instant gratification of being able to use the service. This situation is well illustrated by the deployment of

Orange Money in West Africa, which has a registration process that takes up to a week. As a result of this long wait time, only 6,000 of its first 120,000 customers, or 5 percent, actively used the account.

Managing Liquidity

An agent is essentially an aggregator for the cash requirements of a community. It is a cash-storing and transfer business that absorbs the risk inherent in handling cash. An agent must maintain adequate cash and e-money float balances to meet customer cash-in, cash-out requests. If too much cash is taken in, the agent may run out of e-float and not be able to accept more deposits. If there are too many withdrawals, the agent will accumulate e-float but run out of cash. In either case, customers will get discouraged if the agent cannot provide the services they need when they need them. In addition, a secure mechanism needs to be in place to transport cash to and from an agent.

When agents provide a range of services (for example, account opening, deposits, withdrawals, or bill payments), they are able to generate volume and more easily maintain liquidity. Providers have developed a variety of mechanisms to ensure agent liquidity and assist the agent in handling cash. The options available depend to a great extent on the banking infrastructure in the markets where the agents operate and the willingness of banks to take charge of secure cash transport.

Vodacom Tanzania, for example, tested multiple strategies and settled on using "aggregators" both to recruit agents and to manage their floats, transporting cash for the agent if necessary. The aggregator receives a flat fee for each new agent and a percentage of the agent commissions. This provides the incentive to sign up high-quality agents who actively conduct transactions (Davidson and Leishman 2010).

Banco de Crédito del Perú (BCP) found outsourcing management of its 2,300 agents to be less efficient, so it chose to use in-house agent executives to identify, prepare, and manage each retail outlet. In densely populated areas, BCP agents have a sufficient mix of transactions to balance cash-in, cash-out, but in more remote areas, the agents themselves need to travel to the bank branches more frequently. BCP is finding it hard to train and manage rural agents, a challenge that will require added incentives for the agents and adjustments to the agent management model (see box 12.16).

Box 12.16 Cost of Managing Agent Liquidity

Managing agent liquidity is the critical piece in ensuring the viability of the agent system. Regardless of how providers and agents share the burden of cash management, a burden that is too heavy will compromise the sustainability of the entire system or price the transactions beyond the poor's ability to pay.

Emerging data from the Bansefi-Diconsa correspondent banking pilot program in Mexico indicate that handling cash may amount to anywhere from 35 to 60 percent of total system costs. Most cash-handling costs are outlays for secure transport services and insurance premiums, and about 10 percent are the opportunity costs of holding cash and reserves for theft.

The central factor influencing cash-handling costs is the ability to minimize the amount of cash that needs to be moved between the bank and the retail agents—the ideal agent being one that is fully "cash neutral" at the end of every day. Because cash-handling costs are typically proportional to the volume of cash in transit (secure transport firms charge close to 1 percent of cash volume in Mexico, for example), the notion that a large number of transactions per agent ensures viability of the system comes into question. If the volume of transactions involves the transport of large amounts of cash to the retail payout point, then the net effect on system viability is uncertain. Large social payments programs (G2P) present a special challenge in this respect.

Source: Lehman 2010.

Managing the Channel

Agents will not provide quality service to customers without ongoing on-site supervision and in-store training to ensure they are liquid, consistently branded, and following the prescribed business processes. Providers need to decide how to divide the various management functions and whether to keep those functions in-house or outsource them to an independent service provider. As the networks grow, it is increasingly difficult for the provider to cover the "last mile" of the distribution chain, so most use third parties for part or all of the channel management functions.

Providers need a system of regular site visits to ensure that agents are in compliance with the business processes and maintain proper branding and merchandising. There is a choice of models:

- *Use existing airline sales and marketing staff in the field for MNO-led models.* Zain in Tanzania used this method for budgetary reasons but found that its marketing teams were unwilling to focus on agent training and management.

Even if a proper incentive structure were developed, it is unclear whether a sales representative would have the skills to manage and train agents.

- *Build a new team of dedicated staff solely focused on monitoring and training agents.* MTN Uganda created a new in-house team with the sole responsibility for training and monitoring agents. It works well but requires a major increase in payroll.

- *Outsource the monitoring function to a third party.* Safaricom in Kenya uses a third party, Top Image, to keep direct and centralized control over key elements of the customer experience, including store selection and agent training and supervision.

Agent Costs and Fees

Agent banking systems are much less expensive to operate than bank branches. As shown in figure 12.2, the monthly costs associated with five savings account transactions (two deposits, two

Figure 12.2 Monthly Costs in Dollars Associated with an Illustrative Transaction Account

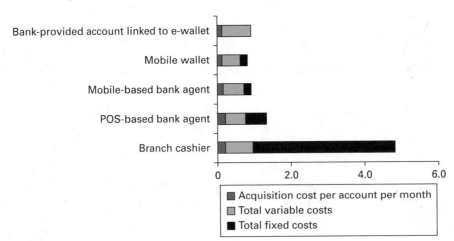

Source: Veniard 2010.

withdrawals, one transfer in the agent channels) ranged from less than US$1 for a mobile wallet to almost US$5 for a bank cashier.[16]

There are several reasons for this differential in costs:

- Agent banking minimizes fixed costs by leveraging existing retail outlets and reduces the need for banks and other financial service providers to invest in their own infrastructure. So although agent banking incurs higher variable costs for commissions and communications, the fixed costs per transaction are significantly higher in branches than through agents.

- Acquisition costs are lower for mobile-enabled agents. By using mobile phones instead of electronic payment cards and POS devices, mobile wallets and bank accounts linked to a mobile phone are able to acquire customers at less than 70 percent of the cost of a branch or POS-enabled agent.

- Agents receive a commission only if transactions are realized, while the fixed costs of a branch remain even though the branch may be underused.

It is a delicate balance to set both the agent commissions and the prices charged to customers at a level that incentivizes the behavior wanted by providers. For example, M-PESA paid its agents the equivalent of about US$1 for every new account (another factor for the rapid uptake of customers) in addition to paying a commission for every transaction, whether or not the customer was charged; M-PESA clients pay only for "cash-out" transactions and transfers to other accounts because those transactions carry the greatest value for the customer.

Commission structures are adjusted over time to match the state of the agent network. Initially when there are few clients, agents need to be compensated for signing up new clients; as the number of clients grows, the commission structure needs to be based more on the number of transactions and less on the number of new clients.

Common methods for calculating agent commissions include (1) a fixed percentage of the transaction value (easy to understand), (2) a flat fee per transaction (easy to understand but discourages small transactions), or (3) a flat fee per tiered transaction values (allows appropriate incentives for all transactions but is more complicated to understand and calculate).

By bringing the channel closer to clients, agents may benefit from additional revenue associated with transactions such as bill payments. Although customers can pay bills at a branch for no charge, agent proximity may increase their willingness to pay for these services in that customers are already willing to pay for remittance and other transfer services. A recent study found that households using M-PESA doubled the number of remittances they sent between 2008 and 2009 (Jack and Suri 2010). This is especially relevant when serving poor customers with low-balance accounts, because it is hard for the provider to cover the operational costs of the account on financial margin alone and because the provider needs to move to a transaction-driven revenue model.

Notes

1. In some cases transfers can also occur between two communities.
2. When people migrate for work, they need to send money back home. This type of transfer is called a remittance because it involves a labor component and some sort of redistribution of wealth between members of the same family or community.
3. These definitions were provided by CGAP, with some variation and additions made by the authors.
4. Interview with UBL, March 2012.
5. See the discussion under mobile phones for definitions of GMS networks.

6. This section was contributed by Kim Wilson, The Fletcher School, Tufts University.

7. Ultra-low-cost POS-like transaction terminals without card-reading capabilities do exist, but lack the security features associated with bank cards (see, for example, www.movilway.com).

8. The printing technology on most POS devices is thermal paper printing, which means that the receipts become illegible if they are exposed to direct sunlight or other forms of heat; however, many mobile devices use a Bluetooth printer to ensure that receipts are available irrespective of the paper used.

9. Bluetooth is a proprietary, open wireless technology standard for exchanging data over short distances (http://en.wikipedia.org/wiki/Bluetooth).

10. Wi-Fi is a technology that allows electronic devices to exchange data wirelessly over a computer network. A device enabled with Wi-Fi, such as a personal computer, video console, smartphone, tablet, or digital audio player, can connect to the Internet via a wireless network access point (http://en.wikipedia.org/wiki/Wi-Fi).

11. General packet radio service (GPRS) is a packet-oriented mobile data service on the 2G and 3G cellular communication system's GSM. It provides moderate-speed data transfer, by using unused time division multiple access channels in the GSM system (http://en.wikipedia.org/wiki/Gprs).

12. Data communication protocols are hardware and software standards that govern data transmission between computers. In the banking sector, this is usually XBRL (eXtensible Business Reporting Language). The term "protocol" is used for hundreds of communications methods. A protocol may define the packet structure of the data transmitted or the control commands that manage the session, or both.

13. The two main mobile phone technical standards are GSM or code division multiple access (CDMA). One of the key features of GSM is the SIM card, a detachable smartcard containing the user's subscription information and phone book. This allows the user to retain his or her information after switching handsets. Mobile phones based on CDMA technology do not have removable SIM cards and are not prevalent in developing countries.

14. A tablet computer is a highly portable computer, larger than a mobile phone or personal digital assistant, which is integrated into a flat touch screen and operated primarily by touching the screen rather than using a physical keyboard. It often uses an onscreen virtual keyboard, a stylus pen, or a digital pen (http://en.wikipedia.org/wiki/Tablet_computer).

15. This section draws on CGAP (n.d.).

16. This is based on a confidential analysis of the costs of six financial service providers by Veniard (2010).

References and Further Reading

*Key works for further reading.

AFI (Alliance for Financial Inclusion). 2010. "Mobile Financial Services: Regulatory Approaches to Enable Access." AFI, November.

Alexandre, Claire. 2010. "10 Things You Thought You Knew about M-PESA." CGAP Technology Blog, CGAP, Washington, DC, November.

*Alexandre, Claire, Ignacio Mas, and Dan Radcliffe. 2011. "Regulating New Banking Models That Can Bring Financial Services to All." *Challenge Magazine* 54 (3, May-June): 116–34.

Almazan, Mireya. 2010. "Beyond Enablement: Harnessing Government Assets and Needs." Brief written for the Global Savings Forum, Bill and Melinda Gates Foundation, Seattle, November.

Alvarez, Gabriela Zapata. 2010. "Turbocharging the Client Proposition through Proximity: Agent Banking in Latin America." Brief written for the Global Savings Forum, Bill and Melinda Gates Foundation, Seattle, November.

*Baptista, Piya, and Soren Heitmann. 2010. "Unleashing the Power of Convergence to

Advance Mobile Money Ecosystems." Report, IFC and Harvard Kennedy School, Washington, DC, and Cambridge, MA.

Boris, Kim. 2011. "Payment Terminals Do Not Want to Die Off [in Russian]." *Digit.ru*, November 22. http://www.digit.ru/opinion/20111122/386574218.html.

Bruett, Tillman, and Janine Firpo. 2009. "Building a Mobile Money Distribution Network in Papua New Guinea." IFC and UNCDF, Washington, DC.

Center for Financial Inclusion. 2010. "Glossary of Terms." Draft, Center for Financial Inclusion, Washington, DC.

CGAP (Consultative Group to Assist the Poor). 2010. "Case Study: United Bank Limited Supports Cash Transfer Payments." CGAP, Washington, DC.

——. 2011. "Global Standard-Setting Bodies and Financial Inclusion for the Poor: Toward Proportionate Standards and Guidance." White Paper prepared by CGAP on behalf of the G-20's Global Partnership for Financial Inclusion. CGAP, Washington, DC, September.

——. n.d. "Interoperability and Related Issues in Branchless Banking: A Framework." PowerPoint presentation. CGAP, Washington, DC. http://www.cgap.org/gm/document-1.9.56025/CGAP_Interoperability_Presentation.pdf.

Chatain, Pierre-Laruent, Andrew Zerzan, Wameek Noor, Najah Dannaoui, and Louis de Koker. 2011. "Protecting Mobile Money against Financial Crimes." World Bank, Washington, DC.

Davidson, Neil, and Paul Leishman. 2010. "Building, Incentivizing and Managing a Network of Mobile Money Agents." Global Savings Forum.

Dolan, Jonathan. 2009. "Accelerating the Development of Mobile Money Ecosystems." IFC and Harvard Kennedy School, Washington, DC, and Cambridge, MA.

Eijkman, Frederik, Jake Kendall, and Ignacio Mas. 2010. "Bridges to Cash: The Retail End of M-PESA." *Savings and Development* 34 (2). http://ssrn.com/abstract=1655248.

*Frankiewicz, Cheryl, and Craig Churchill. 2011. *Making Microfinance Work: Managing Product Diversification*. Geneva: ILO.

Gencer, Menekse, and Jody Ranck. 2011. "Advancing the Dialogue on Mobile Finance and Mobile Health." Country Case Studies, mHealth Alliance. Draft.

GSMA. 2009. *Mobile Money for the Unbanked: Annual Report 2009*. http://www.gsma.com/developmentfund/wp-content/uploads/2012/03/annualreport200927.pdf.

Ivatury, Gautam. 2006. "Using Technology to Build Inclusive Financial Systems." In *New Partnerships for Innovation in Microfinance*, ed. Ingrid Matthäus-Maier and J. D. von Pischke, 147–72. Berlin: Springer.

Jack, W., and T. Suri. 2010. "The Economics of M-PESA: An Update." Georgetown University, Washington, DC.

*Kendall, Jake, Phillip Machoka, Clara Maurer, and Bill Veniard. 2011. "An Emerging Platform: From Money Transfer System to Mobile Money Ecosystem." School of Law Research Paper 2011-14, University of California, Irvine.

Kumar, Kabir. 2011. "Banks Have Some Good News ... Are They Listening?" CGAP Technology Blog, CGAP, Washington, DC, September 21.

*Kumar, Kabir, Claudia McKay, and Sarah Rotman. 2010. "Microfinance and Mobile Banking: The Story So Far." Focus Note 62, CGAP, Washington, DC, July.

Lahaye, Estelle. 2011. "Rural Finance: Let's Crack the Nut!" CGAP Microfinance Blog, CGAP, Washington, DC, August 16.

Lehman, Joyce. 2010. "Operational Challenges of Agent Banking Systems." Brief written for the Global Savings Forum, Bill and Melinda Gates Foundation, Seattle, November.

Mas, Ignacio. 2008. "Being Able to Make (Small) Deposits and Payments, Anywhere." Focus Note 45, CGAP, Washington, DC.

——. 2009. "The Economics of Branchless Banking." *Innovations* 4 (2): 57–75. http://ssrn.com/abstract=1552750.

——. 2010a. "Banking for the Poor: State-of-the-Art Financial Offerings for the Developing World." *The International Economy* (Fall, November 14). http://ssrn.com/abstract=1709164.

——. 2010b. "Savings for the Poor: Banking on Mobile Phones." *World Economics* 11 (4). http://ssrn.com/abstract=1663954 or http://dx.doi.org/10.2139/ssrn.1663954.

——. 2010c. "The Utility of Retail Payments in Addressing the Financial Inclusion Gap in Developing Countries." *Lydian Payments Journal* 1 (November). http://ssrn.com/abstract=1694867.

*Mas, Ignacio, and Mireya Almazan. 2010. "Transactional Models to Bank the Poor." *The American Banker,* November 15.

*——. 2011. "Banking the Poor through Everyday Stores." *Innovations* 6 (1, Spring). http://ssrn.com/abstract=1719580.

*Mas, Ignacio, and Gautam Ivatury. 2008. "Early Successes in Branchless Banking." Focus Note 46, CGAP, Washington, DC.

*Mas, Ignacio, and Kabir Kumar. 2008. "Banking on Mobiles: Why, How, for Whom?" Focus Note 48, CGAP, Washington, DC.

Mas, Ignacio, and Dan Radcliffe. 2010. "Mobile Payments Go Viral: M-PESA in Kenya." http://papers.ssrn.com/sol3/papers.cfm?abstract_id=1593388.

Mas, Ignacio, and Sarah Rotman. 2008. "Going Cashless at the Point of Sale: Hits and Misses in Developed Countries." Focus Note 51, CGAP, Washington, DC, December.

*Mas, Ignacio, and Hannah Siedek. 2008. "Banking through Networks of Retail Agents." Focus Note 47, CGAP, Washington, DC.

Mylenko, N., et al. 2009. *Financial Access 2009.* Washington, DC: World Bank.

Pickens, Mark. 2010. "Where Will the Next Mobile Money Innovation Come From?" CGAP Technology Blog, CGAP, Washington, DC, November 18.

——. 2011. "Which Way? Mobile Money and Branchless Banking in 2011." CGAP Technology Blog, CGAP, Washington, DC, March 9.

Qiwi Channel. 2011. "NAUET Summarizes 2010 on Vimeo [in Russian]." *Vimeo,* March 30. http://vimeo.com/21697639.

Rotman, Sarah. 2010. "An Alternative to M-PESA? Orange and Equity Bank Launch Iko PESA." CGAP Technology Blog, CGAP, Washington, DC, December 6.

——. 2011. "So Where Are We in the Link between G2P and Financial Services?" CGAP Technology Blog, CGAP, Washington, DC, July 28.

Veniard, Clara. 2010. "How Agent Banking Changes the Economics of Small Accounts." Brief written for the Global Savings Forum, Bill and Melinda Gates Foundation, Seattle, November.

World Bank. 2011. "An Analysis of Trends in the Average Total Cost of Migrant Remittance Services." *Remittance Prices Worldwide* 3 (November): 1–6.

CHAPTER 13

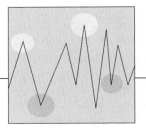

Beyond Products: Building Integrated Customer Experiences on Mobile Phones

Ignacio Mas

The previous four chapters have discussed individual financial products and ways in which institutions might deliver them. In this chapter we argue that, for customers to make sense of all these products, they must be embedded within a financial planning tool. The use of all financial services should logically flow from a customer desire to organize payments to meet present and future needs.

Financial services are a means to an end, and a full financial service is one where customers are presented with various options to achieve their objectives. For instance, an objective might be buying a motorcycle, which a customer might get by setting some money aside and by borrowing the remainder and repaying it over time. This suggests that the most useful way of offering financial services should be in relation to clients' objectives, with the various financial options presented in a consistent way so customers can select the option that most suits them, or indeed mix and match between them. In this fashion, the service transcends the constituent financial service elements and becomes an integrated customer experience—one that allows users not only to choose but also to construct their own bouquet of services based on their specific circumstances and needs.

Such a customer experience should permit, and indeed require, a high level of interaction between customers and their money. The personal, always-with-you, connected nature of the mobile phone presents a unique opportunity to conceive financial services as a conversation between the client and the provider.

The principal challenge in designing these expanded, flexible customer experiences is in developing an intuitive, easy-to-access mobile user interface. A good user interface lets customers discover and try out new services with relatively little prodding or guidance, it prompts customers to reveal more about themselves to the provider, it induces customer loyalty through sheer familiarity, and it offers a diversity of branding and cross-selling opportunities.

With today's mobile money platforms, the value proposition for keeping money digital and driving up usage of digital payments is still thin. Mobile money is built on speed (real-time clearing) and liquidity (thousands of merchants where you can cash in and out). It is *ready cash* (an immediately accessible mobile wallet), *cash to go* (person-to-person money transfers, bill pay). But mobile money is a flexible tool that can be expanded from *making payments now* to helping people earmark funds for and build up to the things they want to pay for *tomorrow*. Savings and credit enable a shifting of expenditures in time. Therefore, savings and credit services are a logical extension of a payments service.

The chapter is in three parts. The first section describes the need to put personal financial management at the heart of financial service propositions. It argues for embedding the kind of mental models and psychological discipline tricks that people engage in informally within formal financial services. The second section describes the basic elements of a mobile financial service delivery platform, emphasizing the role of the user interface as the key link between clients' mental representation of money and the digital representation embodied in formal financial services. The third part illustrates how an integrated mobile financial service fulfilling a broad variety of needs might be constructed, simply by recasting shorter-term savings as a set of payments to oneself and permitting a range of early liquidity options. By giving providers a more meaningful window to

client's financial profiles, such a service ought to allow providers to extend advances to clients on the fly.

This chapter will be of interest to mobile banking and mobile money players who are eager to build a fuller value proposition to address the low take-up and especially the low usage that we are currently seeing with many such systems. Regulators might also note the potentially crippling effects of pigeonholing providers into narrow product sets: payment providers, storage of electronic money, credit issuance, banking, and the like.

Putting Personal Financial Management at the Heart of Financial Service Propositions

Setting money aside for planned future expenditures or for a rainy-day fund is tough if you are poor and you feel like you have a whole backlog of things you would like to buy today. Poor people need to be quite deliberate in planning what they are saving for, what expenditures to forgo, and how they build up assets over time. In this section we look at the psychology of savings, in terms of how poor people define and set spending and financial goals, and how they assign savings vehicles to these goals.

The Psychology of Savings and Goal Setting

People's notions of spending goals are quite diverse. Some goals are explicit, a typical one being paying for school fees at the beginning of each school term. There is a clear amount that needs to be paid and a clear due date; let us call these *objectives*. But oftentimes the goals are aspirational and without a clear timeline—things such as buying a motorcycle, a "permanent" (for example, brick) house, or a plot of land. There is a clear desire, but no clear plan to get there; let us call these *intentions*. The key difference between objectives and intentions is the degree of earmarking of money to the specific, stated goal.

A continuum is found between objectives and intentions, and in fact goals can transform between these categories. Goals may be recalibrated based on circumstances. For instance, building an emergency fund for unplanned health or funeral expenses may look more like an intention (no specific target amount, no clear timeline for its consumption), but it turns into a very tangible objective the moment someone falls ill or dies. Or I may be saving for a bicycle, but if the roof starts leaking I will shift the goal to fixing that. In other words, some goals must be understood as a proxy for a category of potential expenditures. The individual might be quite clear about what *kinds* of expenditures he or she is saving for, but for an observer these might appear as shifting goals.

The next question then is how people assign savings vehicles to (classes of) goals. People will consider tensions along three key dimensions:

- *Liquidity versus discipline.* Liquidity is about having the flexibility to meet changing goals and circumstances, for instance, by being able to dispose of saved balances quickly in the event of an emergency or when a good investment opportunity arises. Yet people know that if money is too accessible, there is a constant temptation to spend it. Saving and keeping money saved becomes an active decision that must be revisited every time there is a spending opportunity. These little decisions that prevent depletion of savings can grow exhausting, and once decision fatigue sets in, self-control flies out the window. Discipline is therefore about making it hard for people to revisit prior savings decisions, in terms of how much and how often to forego current expenditures and set money aside (we can call this *discipline in*) as well as at any time subsequently when you

decide not to raid your savings for current expenditures (*discipline out*).

- *Certainty versus surprise.* People want to know that the money they have set aside is accounted for and safe. They like to be able to check at any point in time how much they have saved (hence the popularity of passbooks and check balance capabilities on mobile-enabled solutions), and they want to know what return they can expect. On the other hand, people also like to surprise themselves about how much they have saved, to feel the elation of breaking the (real or virtual) piggybank. They may also embrace surprises as savings rewards, either by investing in schemes with higher although uncertain returns or by participating in a lottery mechanism. While certainty creates confidence, an element of surprise carries more of a prospect of a different future, and that can be more motivating.

- *Privacy versus social display.* People may have a strong preference to keep larger amounts of savings private given social pressures to share bounties. On the other hand, saving publicly helps create the commitment of regular savings which members find so important, and it can also be used to signal success or claim social status.

The choice of savings vehicle will therefore depend on the nature of the goal in question. School fees, which I—and everyone else around me—need to pay one way or another, might be saved in a mechanism that involves more discipline/less liquidity, more certainty, and more social contact. A village-level savings scheme might meet these criteria. The motorcycle that I aspire to might be saved for in a mechanism that involves more liquidity/less discipline (I might want to change my goal, after all), more surprise (I will take a gamble on it), and less privacy (announcing that I am working toward a bicycle). Buying a couple of pigs might meet these criteria.

Informal Discipline-Building Mechanisms

People have attached a remarkable range of informal discipline-building mechanisms to their savings practices, among them the following:

- *Fragmentation* of savings across multiple pots, assigning a clear purpose to each. Creating a tight mental association between savings objectives and instruments (for example, the goats are to pay for school fees and uniforms, the rotating savings and credit association account is to buy a sewing machine) helps keep savings goals always in view (you are reminded of your children's future every time you see the goats) and makes it more difficult to justify to oneself tapping into these savings on a short-term whim.

- *Indivisibility* of individual savings pots to prevent casual raiding. People often save in gold jewelry rather than small pieces of gold; they convert a pile of small banknotes into fewer larger ones; and they trade up from chickens to goats to cows. One might be tempted to take out a one-dollar bill from under the mattress or sacrifice a chicken to fulfill some small desire, but everyone would hesitate to break a hundred-dollar bill or sell a cow unless there is a strong reason. There is a higher guilt factor about tapping into a high-ticket savings item.

- *Mental labeling* of broad savings categories, for instance, drawing a sharp distinction between savings and investments, or calling certain forms of savings heirlooms. All these represent *not-consumed* assets, but calling something an investment or an heirloom removes it from contention for meeting day-to-day needs. They seek to reinforce these distinctions by putting different expectations on them, for instance, expecting investments to yield higher returns (and correspondingly accepting higher risks).

- Vesting savings with *social meaning and constraints*. People often seek to add a social dimension to their savings in order to increase the stakes of failing to save or actually dis-saving. This can be done for instance by embracing peer pressure as a way of making regular savings contributions through community-based savings groups, or by displaying savings publicly and linking that to social status.

The end result is a compartmentalized, almost ritualized treatment of savings, where unconscious mental processes substitute for conscious ones.

The Trouble with Banks: Inflexible Products

Banks typically structure their mass-market offerings into a few standard products. Their communications strategy with their clients is centered on explaining to customers when, why, and how to use each product. That works well with the formally employed who have larger, regular, and stable income streams. Products involving a rigid structure of payments over time (whether a loan schedule, regular pension plan contributions, or a term deposit) are easy to analyze in the context of one's income.

But the informally employed face a more bewildering range of risks because they do not have regular, guaranteed income flows. Poor people naturally find it harder to build steadily toward their goals; they need more help. But banks' rigid products rarely work for them; they are not seen as relevant. Banks could offer more diversity of products or more flexible terms for poor people in the informal sector, but that would make their service complex to market, sell, and manage. Instead, they fall back to the single product, the catch-all liquid account, which simply does not connect with people's mental model around money and discipline.

Rather than confronting poor people with a barrage of separate financial products, each with its own set of conditions and rules, we need to envelop them within a consistent customer experience that blurs the boundaries between the various constituent products. Whether it is by providing electronic payments, savings, or credit, the objective is to help customers buy the things they aspire to. We also need to blur the boundary between formal and informal financial services by bringing in elements of self-discipline, peer pressure, and social capital that serve people well today. Even more fundamentally, presenting mobile financial services as means for planning expenditures involves a blurring of the notions of savings and consumption. *Buy that bicycle you have long desired* can be as much a call for consumption as for saving—you will manage to buy the bicycle by not buying other (supposedly less important) things in the meantime. That is why the ability to plan is at the heart of the savings problem.

An Interesting Experiment

The most ambitious project to date in this regard is the *private banking for the poor* model of KGFS

in India (see box 13.1). KGFS's strategy entails high-touch individualized service and product recommendations based on thoughtful analysis of livelihood sources and asset portfolio analysis. It may seem counterintuitive to provide high-touch services for the poorest persons, but the KGFS premise is that private banking seems right for the very affluent (who have complex wealth management choices to make) as much as for the very poor (who have vital risk management choices to make). It is the people like you and me in between who feel adequately served by helping ourselves from a menu of off-the-shelf banking products.

Building a high-touch channel reaching millions of poor people is an expensive proposition, involving steady investment in staff training. Any staff-centric model is also likely to suffer from inconsistent quality of service as it grows, because quality will become harder to measure and financial measures of success will tend to dominate. This chapter is an attempt to visualize what a *virtual KGFS* model might look like—one that achieves the same level of customer support but with a higher element of self-service and remote interaction.

Box 13.1 IFMR Trust in India

Since 2008 a new microfinance model has been tested in three remote rural regions of India under the franchise name Kshetriya Gramin Financial Services (KGFS). Sponsored by IFMR Trust, the goal of KGFS is to provide complete financial services to all individuals and enterprises in a predefined area. The operations of each franchise organization are limited to between two and three contiguous rural districts with total populations ranging from 4 to 5 million; within its catchment area, each branch is responsible for understanding

and addressing the financial needs of the approximately 10,000 people and 2,000 households living in the area. Work begins with a financial well-being assessment that collects household-level data in household visits; these data are entered into a series of preset formulas for easy analysis. Based on that assessment, frontline staff (called wealth managers) recommend a tailored combination of financial products for each household. Each KGFS unit is "product agnostic," advising clients on the right combination of savings,

(continued next page)

credit, insurance, and pension services for that particular household's current needs. Financial well-being assessments and recommendations are updated on a regular basis as household needs change.

Achieving this vision requires the capacity to deliver a full range of services. KGFS focuses primarily on establishing a "front-end" presence with close client relationships. Staff members visit households to conduct assessments and provide financial advice, whereas services are provided only in branch offices, which are within walking distance of all households in the catchment area. Management and staff incentives are geared toward understanding and catering to the needs of the population, not toward delivering products.

KGFS partners with a range of commercial banks, pension funds, brokerages, and insurance agencies. A central (shared) product design unit sources and designs appropriate products. KGFS does the heavy lifting of extending services to remote rural areas, sign-

ing up clients, and completing transactions. However, most services are contractually between the clients and actual providers (large partner financial institutions). This arrangement is necessary to deliver a full range of services that is being adjusted constantly, but KGFS also believes that a larger specialized financial institution is better placed to manage systematic and actuarial risks than a relatively small microfinance organization. The one exception to this model is credit. In most cases, KGFS provides loans directly from its own resources. This is to ensure that the incentives of KGFS to underwrite and monitor loans are intact and that the relationship with the financial institution is not one of a pure agent.

Three KGFS franchises have already been launched in very different regions of India, all significantly underserved rural areas, and more franchises are being incubated. Franchises adapt to their local environment but are tied together through a common culture and brand.

Source: Greg Chen and Steve Rasmussen, CGAP.

Delivering Financial Services over Mobile Platforms

What might a financial system that includes everyone look like? We can guess at some of the constituent elements of the solutions by looking at what has been successful in various related sectors. Box 13.2 ascribes two success factors or lessons to each of microfinance, informal finance, mobile money, mobile telephony, and the Internet.

The sheer magnitude of the financial inclusion gap—70 percent of households in developing countries are unbanked—calls for pretty radical solutions. We need to overcome an *access* barrier (last mile infrastructure), a *relevance* barrier (right-sized products and services), and a

usability barrier (friendly and intuitive customer experience).

What makes these problems particularly difficult is that they cannot be thought of separately or tackled sequentially. These three aspects must come together at the marketing level to answer the three main questions customers will have: (1) what is it, what does it do; (2) why should I use it, what are the benefits; and (3) how does it work, where can I use it?

Elements of a Mobile Financial Service Proposition

We can distinguish between three basic elements of a mobile financial service proposition. First,

Box 13.2 What Are the Attributes of Success in Adjacent Sectors?

Microfinance success stories are many and diverse, but two common factors stand out across all of them. The first is the value of *proximity:* They all found ways to get physically close to the customers they wanted to serve. The second is *simplicity:* They focused on streamlining the product set and standardizing features.

There are now high hopes for mobile money as a new platform for financial inclusion, following M-PESA's success in Kenya. One lesson is the importance of cultivating the edge of the electronic payment network: Make *conversion in and out of cash* easy and reliable. The other major lesson is that profitability in financial services need not come from credit alone: There is substantial *willingness to pay* for some types of payment services that are costly or inconvenient for people to do today.

The rampant growth of mobile telephony even in the poorest countries has shown us the power of two additional drivers of demand. The first one is the *immediacy* of the service, which is inherent in the technology: being able to communicate here and now, on demand. The second one, slashing *price barriers,* came with the shift to prepay: introducing tiny top-up amounts (as low as US20 cents) and eliminating fixed fees and usage commitments.

From the internet, we have learned about two new key sources of value enabled by digitization of services. The first one is the packaging of individual offerings into a fuller, friendlier, customizable *customer experience.* The second one is the *customer information* that can be gleaned from their transactions or interactions with the service, which can be used in turn to tailor products and further optimize the customer experience.

The informal money management practices that people use in their daily lives have two characteristics that set them apart from what banks normally conceive. First, they *blur the boundaries* between savings, credit, and insurance (for instance, savings-led groups or lending money among friends). Second, they use a range of *discipline devices* beyond sheer time commitments (fragmentation by purpose, indivisibility of savings vehicle, creating habits, peer pressure, and assigning social/family value).

Let us now connect all the emphasized keywords: To crack the financial inclusion problem all we need to do is to design a customer experience that (1) combines features of savings, credit, and insurance and offers a variety of self-discipline tools, (2) is manageable by the customer within a simple-to-use, logically consistent framework, (3) is delivered as and when people need it in any amount they need, and (4) has convenient local liquidity options.

there needs to be an infrastructure to *exchange* physical cash for electronic value (most commonly, branches and ATMs). This is not banking per se because it merely enables exchange between two forms of money, just like one might exchange notes for coins. But it allows people to easily combine the forms in which they are paid their wages, store money, and spend it. There needs to be a much more dense and cost-effective network of cash in/out points that people can incorporate into their daily routines. These points need to be near where people live and work, located in retail environments that want to serve poor people like them, and offering two-way services (deposits and withdrawals) in small amounts.

The most promising approach is to engage everyday stores as cash in/out points, where they offer to buy and sell electronic money to or from their customers against cash (constituting a withdrawal and deposit, respectively), much like they would sell rice by exchanging their holdings of rice for their customers' holdings of cash. This can be made secure as long as stores operate on a fully prepaid basis (it holds balances in both cash and electronic value), and the electronic transactions between stores and their customers are authorized securely in real time using a digital communications network.

Second, there needs to be a digital payments ecosystem which makes electronic money directly useful for people, by allowing easy *transfer* of value within the electronic cloud. This is more immediately convenient than cash for larger payments (where cash presents a significant risk), remote payments (cash is costly to transport), business-related payments (cash leaves no evidence trail), and at unattended points of sale (cash fills and jams ticketing machines). Over time, electronic payments naturally come to be seen as increasingly convenient for smaller, face-to-face, everyday transactions (for example, at retail shops) between people who have (are *long*) electronic money and do not wish to incur the hassle of converting back to or from cash.

We need to find mechanisms to induce more payments in the informal economy to be made electronically, such as for the sale of day labor, goods, or services, in order to get as many people as possible *long* electronic money. This is a more direct method of access than through cash-in networks. One priority should be on electronifying the *sources* of money rather than making it convenient for people to use electronic money, as the latter will follow naturally from the former. The second priority should be to connect all the electronic accounts and wallets into one interconnected network: No one should be relegated to an island. This is about catalyzing and speeding the transition from the legacy payment system—cash—to new interconnected electronic payment platforms.

Finally, there needs to be a set of financial services that map simply and directly into people's mental models of their money. These services allow people to *plan* how to achieve their investment and spending goals and how to manage certain risks. Whereas the functions of exchange and transfer work best the more immediate they are, planning is by definition something that occurs over time.

Building a Platform That Balances Specialization and Scale

Successfully fulfilling these elements requires building a costly infrastructure and supporting a complex service delivery chain. There is a need to redesign the institutional structure and the value chain within which financial services are offered to the mass market of poor people in developing countries. Most financial institutions have neither the proper cost structure to scale nor the marketing capabilities to cater to customers' diverse needs. Figure 13.1 shows a schematic of the journey that is required.

Today most microfinance institutions serving the poor tend to offer a limited number of discrete products (often just one, for example, group-based lending or ordinary savings accounts) within a proprietary delivery structure (they manage their own cash points, treasury and investments, loan evaluations and recovery, and the like). Many interventions in support of financial inclusion entail creating new unconnected, vertically integrated institutions in un- or underserved areas. These institutions are often mission based and develop very good affinity and proximity with their target customers. But because they combine all functions (some scalable, some not) into a single structure, they tend to operate at very high unit costs, and their systems and procedures cannot handle geographic expansion well.

Figure 13.1 A Platform Perspective

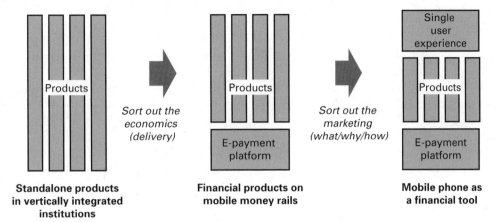

Standalone products in vertically integrated institutions → *Sort out the economics (delivery)* → Financial products on mobile money rails → *Sort out the marketing (what/why/how)* → Mobile phone as a financial tool

Balancing customer intimacy and scale is generally achieved through institutional specialization. One approach, shown in the middle of figure 13.1, is to separate the operation of the basic payment platform from the development and marketing of value-adding financial services that ride on that platform. The *e-payment platform* box in figure 13.1 refers to the basic *exchange* and *transfer* functions described above. This service could be supplied by larger banks through interoperable switches or by mobile network operators (MNOs) under mobile money schemes.

Although it is possible that these players might operate such platforms as a closed loop, one would expect that over time they would open them up to an ecosystem of specialized financial institutions that wish to offer a fuller set of services to their customers. These specialized institutions riding on the scalable platforms could operate as *cashless banks*, because they would collect and return value to their customers through third-party electronic payment platforms. Freed from the operational challenges of handling cash and electronic payment networks, they would be in a position to focus more fully on marketing and

product development, through which they could develop deeper and richer relationships with their customers.

Creating a Single-User Experience

This separation of functions would go a long way to put financial service providers on a more sound economic footing, but the proliferation of services running on these rails presents significant marketing challenges of their own. Communicating *what* each product does (features and terms), *why* or in what circumstances it might be relevant for people (benefits), and *how* it is used (procedures) requires a level of attention from poor customers that providers may not be able to garner, and even if they did, it may entail a cost which providers are not able to bear.

There is a need to create a simple framework through which people can discover, learn about, and manage a diverse set of services. That is represented by the *single-user experience* box on the right-hand side of figure 13.1. Customers might avail themselves of many products and services, but all are presented and managed in a consistent, seamless way through common interfaces.

Note that here we are talking about a single-user experience *per customer*, but different classes of customers might be presented different user experiences based on their sociodemographics and level of familiarity with financial services. In fact, one could imagine customers having their user interfaces upgraded over time to deliver a richer and expanded set of potential services, commensurate with their growing financial capabilities and needs.

The customer experience box would be made consistent by the following elements:

- A *user interface* available on customers' electronic access devices (mobile or web), which allows them to find, contract, and interact with their services on a self-serve basis.

- A *customer relationship management* system, which allows the provider to create a detailed picture of each of their customers based on the history of interactions they have had through the user interface, as well as any other available sociodemographic data that can be cross-referenced from external sources. This system would also have a *customer analysis and proposition engine,* which evaluates the suitability of customers for certain services (for example, credit scoring) and triggers relevant outbound messages to customers (for example, to reinforce goals or propose a new service that the customer is likely to want).

- An *assisted sales and service channel,* which customers can use when they want to interact with people. This might be a chain of dedicated stores, an outbound sales force, or a call center.

Why Mobile?

There is much promise of using mobile phones, in combination with retail shops acting as cash in/out points, in solving the access barrier. There are two key advantages of using mobile phones: (1) they enable secure *real-time* communications from increasingly remote locations, a key ingredient for building trust; and (2) they are cheap and already *out there*, thus slashing deployment costs in comparison with other technology platforms.

Mobile phones not only represent the key to unlock access, they are also the key to increase usage. Promoting financial inclusion involves developing customer experiences that help people plan for and achieve their goals, whether these relate to concrete planned expenditures or looser financial cushions. That requires two things: (1) extracting information from clients as to what their goals are and in what timeframe they aim to achieve them, and (2) presenting the various available financial services (savings, credit, payments, and insurance) in the context of those goals.

Both these things are hard to do when customer interactions are infrequent and not very consistent. In one month, a bank client typically listens to one bank advertisement on the radio or TV and walks over to a branch once, which means that communication is very limited and mostly one way. In this setting, the bank's promotion has to be as simple as possible, and that means making it product driven.

But when banks (or alternative financial service providers) and their clients are connected by mobile phones, the potential exists for the relationship to be much more frequent and interactive. With this in place, the bank can start thinking about having a conversation with their customers based on their goals (whether based on aspirations or fears) rather than on the bank's standard list of products. There is less pressure to propose the right products to customers from the outset, because customers will guide banks on an ongoing basis as to what they need. The mobile user interface should draw customers into this conversation, so it must be structured around people's goals. It is up to the bank to fit their products to these goals. The interactions would also be bank initiated: to remind people of their stated goals, congratulate them when they work effectively toward their goals, and propose new ways in which they can achieve their goals.

Mobile phones can be used as a lower-cost alternative to rolling out cards and point-of-sale terminals. But, beyond cost, the real opportunity with mobile phones is for the bank to establish a direct, on-demand connection with its customers. Mobile phones make it possible to think of a future where banks and their customers have daily interactions that are based less on the banks' products and more on the customers' goals. In a successful mobile banking relationship, clients would be reaching for their phone every time they have money coming in. How do I assign this money across my goals? Banks' offerings then go from being productized (offering choices within a set à la carte menu) to being mass customized (where customers interact uniquely although using the same set of tools).

The key challenge in visualizing the single-user experience box is in imagining how multiple, apparently disparate services might be presented within a single logical framework and common user interfaces.

The Mobile Money Journey Thus Far

Mobile money today mostly offers a basic *transactional account*. In Kenya and elsewhere, we have seen customers taking up this service in large numbers. But these accounts largely fulfill a *means of payment* function: They are not generally used to store significant amounts of money over long periods of time, and they are generally not linked to other financial products such as credit or insurance.

As a result, financial inclusion enthusiasts have tended to look at mobile money as providing low-cost *transactional rails*; once those are in place, we can then devise the right products to *ride* on those rails. But that leap is proving hard. Without the necessary range of products, we cannot ensure sufficient usage of the rails, which undermines the case for the necessary infrastructure and marketing investments. Yet it is not clear

how to get people who are new to banking to understand and use such a variety of financial services on a simple mobile phone.

Overcoming these challenges probably requires integrating the rails and the products more tightly, from early on. On the other hand, optimizing the mobile money environment by adding higher-level financial services (savings commitment features, credit, insurance) runs the risk of making the concept of mobile money more complex to market and practically unwieldy to manage on simple mobile phones.

To break out of this dilemma, what we need is a single mobile-enabled customizable experience that puts customers' goals and needs as the basis for the interactions between the bank and its customers. The key driver for this experience will be less the underlying financial products that fulfill the service and more the user interface and customer information management systems that guide the interactions.

Telecommunication companies and banks will certainly play a role in enabling such integrated service concepts, but perhaps what we really need is a third party playing an Amazon.com–like role: managing customer insight, presenting relevant offers, and organizing the service delivery chain behind them.

This is the area explored in the next section. The aim is to examine how one could offer a rich menu of money management services in a way that is appealing to the bulk of poor people in developing countries.

Turning the Mobile Phone into a Financial Management Tool

So far we have developed two core ideas. First, from a usability point of view, mobile financial services need to be conceived as a single customer experience that integrates across a range of underlying financial services. This makes it possible to design a simple mobile user interface logic that guides customers to appropriate financial services and usage patterns. Second, from a relevance point of view, people interpret the use of various financial options within the context of deeply entrenched mental models of financial management. This presents the opportunity of designing the integrated mobile user interface fundamentally as a financial management tool, one that incorporates the psychological discipline mechanisms that people engage in instinctively. This section illustrates how this might be done in a simple fashion.

Introducing the Time Dimension into Mobile Money

Mobile money, as it is currently conceived, works best when there is a coincidence of timing between sources and uses of funds, because then the transaction can be realized immediately. But when there is separation in time between when money is available and when it needs to be paid out, mobile money has so far proved less useful.

The separation in time can occur for two main reasons: (1) if the payment needs to be made on a future date (for example, rent, school fees, electricity bill, seeds for planting) or (2) if the payment is sizable relative to income flows, such that there needs to be an accumulation of funds before the commitment of the expenditure (for example, buying a motorcycle or new farming implement). These desired future expenditures thus create goals.

Bridging that gap in time between money inflows and expected outflows is the role of the stored-value account in a mobile money system, except that it appears that most people do not leave much value in there. That is to a significant extent because, for regulatory reasons, mobile money is usually not marketed as a savings vehicle. But it could also be that people find mobile money too liquid, too easily available: Like cash in the pocket, it is best gotten rid of in favor of something that will *stick*, lest it comes to be used for something superfluous.

Deferred Payments

Because spending goals represent future expenditures, one could use a system of deferred payments to apply current income to future goals (Mas and Mayer 2011). One could therefore present savings services as an extension of payments: In the same way that you can use mobile money to send money immediately to someone else, you ought to be able to send money to yourself to be received at a future date. Think of these as self-payments ("Me2Me," across time), instead of the garden-variety person-to-person payments ("P2P," across space, in real time), as illustrated in figure 13.2.

All it takes to create these deferred payments is one additional optional field in the standard money transfer menu: the date when the transaction is to take effect. (Immediate execution could be the default, if no date is specified.) Users can then associate future dates with goals and commit money to those goals as and when they earn it.

When customers check their mobile money balances, the provider would provide a fuller description of saved balances: total amount in the account, available or liquid balance, and value of deferred payments (which could be split between deferred payments to others and to oneself, that is, savings).

With these services, users would be able to allocate or *deal* their money across their various goals each time they come across some income. The various dates would operate like earmarked savings receptacles. Consider two examples:

- Casual laborers would be enticed to reach for their phone every time they have money coming in—which happens unpredictably but often daily. Thus, if I had a good day and made US$5 today, I will cash in the US$5, send US$2 to myself for February 28 because that is when school fees are due, and another US$2 to myself June 30 because that is when I aim to buy a bicycle; the remaining US$1 I will keep

Figure 13.2 Transactions in Space and Time

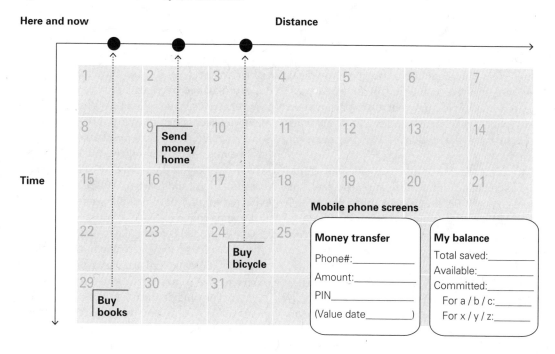

in my liquid mobile money account for daily expenditures.

• Farmers have the opposite problem: All their money comes at once, at harvest time. Thus, I could deposit the entire value of the crop and send large parts of it to myself on those dates when I need to pay for the rent of the land for the next season, and pay for soil preparation and seeds at planting time. With the remaining value, I could even create monthly payments to myself emulating a salary until the next harvest.

Remember the previous discussion on goals: Some, like school fees, are clear objectives, whereas others, like buying a motorcycle, might represent a more fuzzy category of intentions. Thus, future payment dates to oneself might sometimes be interpreted to be not necessarily exact dates when certain payments are planned but rather future financial decision points. Thus, I might push money to April 1 simply so that I do not have to think about how to use that money until then; on April 1, I might decide to do something with it, or simply roll it over to, say, July 1.

Me2Me payments to future dates are functionally equivalent to commitment savings subaccounts, each of which is associated with a particular future date. Through this scheme, there is no need to predefine or open multiple accounts. In the customer's mind, each date, and hence each subaccount, would be associated with a goal.

Most people save because they want to buy something. Applying a payments logic to savings behaviors makes it more tangible and relevant for people. It is "parking" money for a purpose, it is pushing money forward. From a marketing point of view, it reinforces the positives (the spending goals) rather than the sacrifices (savings).

Where there is a very common goal, such as school fees, that could be a useful prototypical use case to drive marketing of deferred payments, for example, "pay yourself to pay for your kid's school," much like "send money home" was used to drive the notion of P2P payments in Kenya.

Enabling Me2Me payments could offer significant added value for mobile money providers. But more importantly, it can help soften the brutal network effects that are inherent in the early phase of development of P2P networks. With Me2Me, mobile money may be very useful even when few other people are on the network, because it helps people manage their own money. If people were comfortable keeping higher balances, it would likely increase the activity rate on mobile money transfers, as well as reduce the proportion of transfers that are converted back into cash—a costly step.

Harnessing Customer Information

The interactions could also be bank initiated and evolve into an ongoing conversation. If the customer is saving money for March 31, why not contact her (by SMS/text message or a call from the contact center) to find out what her goal is and how much she needs? If she does not seem to be following through on a pattern of set-asides for her March 31 goal, why not reach out to her to remind her of her goal or find out why she is having trouble?

Each of these interactions is an opportunity to capture information that can be useful in two ways. First, the bank can play back this information to the customer and show that it listens and cares about her. Receipts for deposits, for instance, can now refer to how far the customer is from getting her motorcycle. Second, knowing how people manage their money and observing how

regularly they meet their objectives constitutes valuable information for credit scoring.

Liquidity versus Commitment

We noted above that when people make financial or investment choices they must strike a delicate balance between liquidity (being able to access funds if and when I wish) and commitment (not accessing funds until I really need to). So far, the deferred payment scheme has shown how people might commit by pushing money forward to certain dates. But what if they need to access their funds earlier? How can a bank be expected to offer both flexibility and discipline, at the same time?

One approach is for banks to position a portfolio of products, some catering to the liquidity objective (current and savings accounts) and others to the commitment objective (deferred payments or time deposits). Users can then segment their wealth and treat part of it as a liquidity reserve and part of it as a commitment fund. But the choice seems unnecessarily artificial and removed from most people's daily worries. Remember that no one is guaranteeing them a periodic income; they are exposed to deep crop price fluctuations and crop failures, and no one is underwriting their health risks. They may want to put away some savings for the future, but they will want to retain access to their money if a new business opportunity arises, or if they get sick.

Instead of assigning each dollar I save to either a liquidity pool or a commitment pool, I would like to assign a measure of liquidity and a measure of commitment to each dollar I save. I want to strike a balance between flexibility and discipline with each dollar I resolve to set aside, based on what I think I am setting it aside for and how much uncertainty I have in my life. I may want more commitment if I am setting aside money for school fees (which I need to pay one way or another) than for a bicycle (which I can defer if a more urgent need arises).

Early Liquidity Options

What we need is more of a continuum in liquidity-commitment options. This would need to be supported, functionally, by having the user assign a priori an early liquidity option to each savings goal (which might be associated with a date or subaccount). This option would logically be composed of two key choices: (1) under what conditions can the customer request early liquidity (that is, what are the liquidity triggers) and (2) how is the early liquidity facility provided (such as early withdrawal or as a loan).

In terms of the liquidity triggers, six options are available. The two extreme options, at either end, are the following:

- *Free disposal* (full liquidity): The user is entirely free to withdraw any amount saved at any time even before the specified due date. The deferred payment still contains a mental discipline element, insofar as one can mentally associate a purpose and a timeframe to a particular pot of money. This can be reinforced by the provider with every early withdrawal made (for example, on a small withdrawal: "Are you sure you want to set back your motorcycle fund by US$10, when it is not even March?"). But there is nothing stopping users from accessing their money.

- *Time-locked* (illiquidity): The account is illiquid until a defined point in time in the future, the deferred payment date. This offers full commitment on amounts saved.

In between, there might be the following four early liquidity options. Their objective is to make it a little hard for customers to dip into their savings prematurely, but falling well short of blocking access:

- *All-or-nothing* (indivisibility): Early withdrawals are allowed, but they must be for the entire balance. The intention is to raise the stakes of dis-saving, thereby providing liquidity for large emergencies but preventing casual account raiding. Of course, if the full amount is not required for the emergency, the user can still liquidate the deferred statement and set up a new one to the same forward date for the unused balance.

- *Waiting period:* Users must preannounce an early (partial or full) withdrawal, and the funds will become available one or two days later, which gives the user an opportunity to rethink whether the early withdrawal is justified or not. This seeks to avoid impetuous financial decisions.

- *Peer pressure:* The user must nominate one person they trust upfront who will act as their "savings buddy." The buddy is informed of, or even must agree to, any (partial or full) early withdrawal. The buddy would readily agree if she knows there has been an emergency and can talk to the saver if she feels the saver is being rash. The sheer notion that the savings buddy would be notified may by itself discourage hard-to-justify early withdrawals. The consultation with the savings buddy would occur automatically by SMS/text message.

- *Financial penalty:* There is a financial cost to exercising early liquidity, which might be a flat fee (to disproportionately punish small temptations) or a percentage of the amount withdrawn.

These triggers are intended to be deterrents—but not outright barriers—to dis-saving. If these selected trigger conditions are met, the early liquidity facility can be provided in two ways:

- *Liquidating savings balances:* This is the straightforward reduction of saved balances following an exercise of early liquidity. This is easiest to implement, but has the drawback that the continuity of the savings goals is compromised or may even be extinguished when clients exercise early liquidity.

- *Borrowing against one's savings:* Savers can request a loan up to the value of what they have stored to a certain date. An amount equal to the unpaid balance of the loan is frozen from that deferred payment balance, so the loan is riskless. There might be fixed or flexible repayment terms on the loan, which in effect offers clients a path to rebuild their savings. There might be an interest cost to the loan, which we can map to the *financial penalty* option above, but equally there might be no interest if other discipline mechanisms are used instead. Providing early liquidity in this fashion gives savers an opportunity to meet unforeseen needs while preserving savings goals. It is often observed that poor people save and borrow at the same time, and that is because they are simultaneously juggling goals and needs.

Thus, for a bank, helping discipline savers goes beyond extracting time commitments and can include a variety of other planning devices that customers might be free to choose from. It may not be necessary to offer all these options: With appropriate market research, this can be boiled down to the essential set of options that people consider most useful.

Regardless of how this is implemented, here is the key: People yearn for ways to commit to themselves and possibly to each other in the community, but not to outsiders and much less to banks. In their informal savings mechanisms, they do not commit to the savings medium itself: They make no promises of long life to the cow. Bank commitment mechanisms (recurring deposits, time deposits) are all about committing, in the first instance, to the bank. That does not feel right to poor people: No one is guaranteeing them anything; why should they be guaranteeing money to the bank?

Adding Credit to the Mix

Mobile money so far has been a pure prepay product, acting like a *debit card*. The absence of credit in the system allowed it to be sold through third-party, mass-market retail channels, without requiring any customer screening. But its usefulness will grow when it evolves into being also like a *credit card*. To do so scalably requires reliable credit scoring, which will come from either capturing more relevant financial information from people or harnessing community-level information.

Credit is important because it expands customer's payment opportunities. The deferred payment scheme outlined above allows people to build their own prepaid installment plans—accumulate money, then use it. Credit offers different means for the same purpose: It can be thought of as a postpaid installment plan. Credit is also important because customer willingness to pay is higher for credit (payout now, discipline later) than for savings (discipline now, payout later) and hence is often a key driver of profitability for banks and microfinance institutions. The possibility of credit is also an important hook for people to choose formal over informal savings in the first place (Johnson et al. 2012).

We can incorporate credit into our framework in three ways:

- *Credit collateralized by user's own savings.* As mentioned earlier in the liquidity section, it ought to be possible for users to request credit against a deferred payment or savings balance. If the user's savings are frozen until the credit is repaid, this is fully collateralized credit and hence should be riskless for the institution and cheap for the user. This mechanism gives liquidity to users without breaking their mental model of how and why they save.

- *Personal credit scoring based on user's past financial behavior.* The deferred payment scheme gives providers a good perspective on how people manage their money. If the bank knows how often I set goals (number of deferred dates I use), how regularly I contribute to them (number of deferred payments I make), how often I exercise early withdrawal options, and the purpose and extent of achievement of my goals (based on information obtained from the user through outbound calls from the provider's contact center, as mentioned above), then the bank has a pretty good handle on my financial habits. That ought to translate into automatic credit based on a behind-the-scenes credit-scoring engine. The provider can now offer the customer to advance the rest of the money the customer needs to achieve a particular goal. The promise of the advance itself can induce the customer to set aside some more money ("if you get to 50 percent of your goal within a month, we will advance the rest of the money you need for your motorcycle").

- *Social credit scoring based on the quality of users' social network.* A user soliciting credit might be able to extend his personal credit score by asking peers to vouch for him. Peers need not be guaranteeing the debt; they could simply be endorsing the borrower. People would be assigned a social credit score based on the repayment track record of people they have vouched for in the past. They could build up social capital with their social network by vouching for them, but their social credit score would reduce and eventually vanish if they vouched for people who end up not repaying their loans.

Taking Advantage of Social Capital

Microfinance has shown the power of leveraging social capital within communities and invoking peer pressure. This generally operates at two levels: to induce and screen new joiners into groups, and to impose loan repayment discipline. But the use of peer pressure has generally been limited to people living in proximity and to the management of credit.

The deferred payment scheme can take advantage of social capital and peer pressure in three ways, two of which have already been mentioned:

- *Vouching for other users' credit requests.* Users can develop a reputation with the bank for reliably vouching for the integrity of other borrowers. Each time they do so they are putting their reputation (but not necessarily their money) on the line. Building up this reputation allows them to help their peers when they require credit, which helps them build social capital within their community.

- *Managing early liquidity.* People who have set money aside for a future date may opt to nominate someone they know as a savings buddy. A savings buddy helps you keep your savings intact, either because she will not agree that you are justified in withdrawing your money early, or because you might be shy to ask her in the first place unless you have a good reason. This brings the notion of peer pressure to work for savers.

- *Incentivizing community-level savings.* Imagine that when a bank is opening a new outlet in a rural area and announcing that when the whole village saves a certain amount, it will do something to benefit the whole community: repaint the school, purchase medical supplies for the local hospital, or build a new football field for the youngsters.

The objective is to endow mobile financial services with as much richness of interpersonal interactions as possible. But it will certainly be impossible to capture electronically the subtlety of informal financial relationships. Johnson et al. (2012) note that there is an underlying logic of *give and take* and social connections in people's transactions. *Giving* money to others is a form of saving, of putting money beyond immediate reach: Although there is no explicit demand for payback, there is an implicit expectation that it might be returned in some way, eventually.

Customer Service Channels

Figure 13.3 maps the four channels mentioned above along two key dimensions: How much of a heavy investment do they require from the promoting financial institution, and how much service support do they offer. The objective is to place as many customer interactions as possible through the top-left quadrant—involving low customer support through a direct channel.

Business Model

The business model would build on top of the model already in place for mobile money, namely, charging per transaction fees on P2P money transfers and cash-out. Account registration and cash-in tend to be free to customers, although the provider generally pays agents a commission for both. Cash-in commissions are generally recouped by the provider at the time of cash-out (the cash-out fee payable by customers is roughly equal to the commissions payable to agents for both cash-in and cash-out). Thus, the business model works for mobile money providers as long as there is a rough balance in the number of cash-in versus cash-out transactions.

With the expanded service proposed here, it is envisioned that Me2Me transactions would be free, that is, customers would not be charged for reallocating their money across subaccounts. However, new direct revenue sources would open up:

- *More savings mobilization.* The fragmentation and commitment features would result in higher average customer balances, which should result in a funding-cost advantage for the bank holding the funds. Raising deposits from poor people will never be an overly profitable business, but it could definitely make a nice business.

- *Margin on loans.* The system ought to result in good quality credit being placed, which would generate additional interest income (and possibly fees) for the provider.

Figure 13.3 Channel Mix

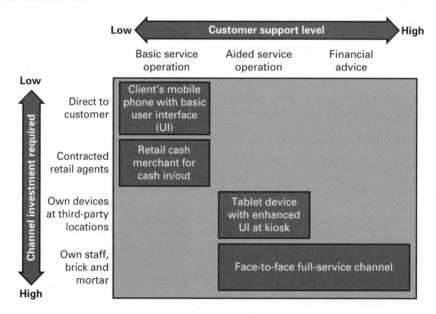

To benefit from these two additional revenue streams, the mobile money provider would need to structure its offering in such a way that a bank is the customer account issuer of record and negotiate some kind of revenue sharing with the bank.

A separate benefit of increasing customer balances is to reduce the number of withdrawal transactions taking place. This would reduce the total cost of operating the mobile money service, because agent commissions represent a significant share of the cost of the service. On the other hand, the mobile money provider might find itself funding agent commissions on cash-in without these being compensated by customer charges upon cash-out. Thus, the provider would need to monitor carefully the impact of this service on the ratio of cash-in to cash-out transactions.

On the cost side, the business case for this service would need to factor in the increased burden on marketing and contact center resources, because of the more sophisticated nature of the offering.

Some Final Thoughts: Financial Information *Is* Financial Access

The notion that we cannot count on brick-and-mortar investments to massively expand access to finance in developing countries is now widely accepted. We need to go branchless, and to do so safely we have an opportunity to leverage mobile phones that are increasingly ubiquitous. That is clear at an infrastructure level, but there is insufficient understanding of what that means at the service level.

The starting point is recognizing that financial services are primarily about *information*. Mechanically, financial services are about recording numerous credits and debits: how much you would like to transfer to whom, how much you have, how much you owe, how much you will be owed if certain events occur. More fundamentally, financial services are about trusting or being trusted, and that is a function of the information you have on the other party.

Viewing finance as an information service has five implications. First, money needs to be digitized—turned into pure information—as much and as quickly as possible. I am not saying going cashless, I am saying that we need to create a cheap and extensive infrastructure that allows poor people to convert cash into electronic value on demand, in small amounts that are relevant to them, as close as possible to where they live and work. How many physical points do banks make available for poor people to cash in their meager wages? (ATMs do not count; those are still mainly about de-digitizing money, that is, withdrawals.)

Second, information about money has value in and of itself. Financial service providers must try to extract as much information value as possible from each interaction they have with their clients, and indeed they must seek to maximize the number of interactions so that they can create a fuller picture of each client. That can power service propositioning and credit-scoring algorithms.

Third, we need to get over the obsession with finding silver-bullet financial products and focus much more on the *platforms* that create the basis for proper service innovation and delivery of whatever it is that customers need. Mobile money needs to be enhanced with a framework that puts customers in control of how they think about their financial needs and aspirations, that collects relevant insights from customers, that presents all the information that is pertinent to customers in a simple framework, and above all, that makes transactions commercially viable so that they become the friend rather than the enemy of the bank.

Fourth, information commands a premium if it is *immediate*—available here and now. Convenience is just a precondition: finding the channels through which I can find service. Immediacy is about being able to take action the moment I make a mental decision (pay the electricity bill, set some money aside for that bicycle I want to buy). Exercising responsible finance is about having discipline, and putting hassles and delays in front of the customer is an excellent excuse to avoid it.

Fifth, information wants to be accumulated, but mostly it wants to be shared. We need to look at poor people's money in the same way. The microfinance worldview has been mostly about accumulation: helping microentrepreneurs build up the capital they need. But what poor people need most is to be *connected*. With connections come opportunities. Financial inclusion is then about connecting poor people to a digital payments grid that allows them to transact more cheaply and broadly with each other (support networks across friends and families), larger service providers (utilities), their business relationships (clients and suppliers), government entities (getting social welfare payments or pensions), and, yes, financial institutions. Primacy has to be given to the network; financial products will follow if that network allows for efficient distribution.

Banks tend to do none of these three things when it comes to the poor: They do not go near where poor people live and work, and when poor people go to them they tend to discourage transactionality through charges and long lines. Indeed, in providing banking to the poor two key service attributes are often neglected: convenience and immediacy. Formal financial service providers lose out to a range of informal services or practices mostly because they are not so easily and reliably available.

It is not surprising that MNOs have taken the lead in branchless banking in developing countries. They have seen the power of letting people communicate and share pictures *here and now*.

They reworked their distribution around prepay arrangements to allow people maximum buying convenience. They know they are payment layer enablers rather than packaged product providers.

But MNOs' role may remain limited. In their core voice and data services, MNOs deliver basic connectivity but struggle to supply the value-added platform layers on top (content management, unified communication, or business support services). In the same way, other financial service providers will need to ride on MNOs' mobile money systems to build the kind of rich, tailored customer experiences that people and entrepreneurs at the base of the pyramid want.

What we will need is precisely the opposite: nimble players that are specialized in horizontal segments of the value chain. That is what being a platform player means: You do only a small part of the total job, but you feel secure doing that because you can do it better and more cheaply than others, and you come up with frequent innovation. These are players who will think more in terms of customer interfaces and tools rather than in terms of financial products and education.

References and Further Reading

Johnson, Susan, Graham Brown, and Cyril Fouillet. 2012. "The Search for Inclusion in Kenya's Financial Landscape: The Rift Revealed." Report. Financial Sector Deepening Trust of Kenya, Nairobi, March. http://www .fsdkenya.org/pdf_documents/12-03-29_Full_ FinLandcapes_report.pdf.

Mas, Ignacio, and Colin Mayer. 2011. "Savings as Deferred Payments." http://papers.ssrn.com/ sol3/papers.cfm?abstract_id=2018807.

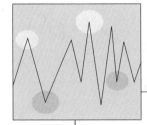

PART IV

INSTITUTIONAL MANAGEMENT FOR SCALE AND SUSTAINABILITY

CHAPTER 14

Monitoring and Managing Financial and Social Performance

Joanna Ledgerwood, Geraldine O'Keeffe, and Ines Arevalo

This chapter addresses data and financial management for planning, reporting, and monitoring of social and financial performance and financial risk. This is different than measuring financial inclusion at the national, regional, or global level discussed in chapter 5. This chapter is about managing data and monitoring performance and risks of individual institutions providing financial services—primarily credit and savings. It does not address insurance providers or payment service providers. It focuses on institutional providers, as community-based providers generally do not require sophisticated levels of data collection or financial management of the type discussed here.[1] It will be of interest to practitioners, funders, regulators, and others interested in understanding performance management metrics.

Different stakeholders require data and information for different purposes: managers rely on financial and social performance information at the institution and unit level to understand areas of operations that may require attention or focus; investors use financial information to measure value and determine institutional performance relative to business plan targets and other potential investments; other funders use information on financial and social performance to allocate funding for specific interventions or to monitor existing grants or debt; regulators use financial information primarily to measure compliance and support their oversight of financial service providers within their area of jurisdiction; policy makers use aggregated information on institutional financial performance to structure and protect the financial sector and to ensure

---

Contributions to this chapter were made by Julie Earne.

that policies and laws are appropriate and support increased financial inclusion.

Financial management and reporting requirements reflect the level of sophistication of the product offering as well as the size and scope of operations. Nongovernmental organization (NGO) providers tend to adopt standard measures of performance and reporting standards to both self-regulate and enable external comparative analysis. Formal structures such as deposit-taking microfinance institutions (MFIs) or state banks generally have complex operating policies and procedures set out by regulatory authorities, including specific reporting requirements.

While performance indicators vary depending on the type of financial service provider, overall the industry has developed an increasingly standardized list of measurements. The standardization of indicators improves transparency by enabling comparisons and benchmarking.[2] Several frameworks are used to organize social and financial indicators; first it is necessary to collect and manage data through information systems.

Information Systems for Financial Service Providers

A system that manages information is often referred to as a management information system (MIS) or a core banking system (CBS), depending on the nature and size of the provider. These systems fulfill various functions ranging from transaction processing to basic portfolio reports to real-time financial statements required by regulators and investors. As providers grow in size and their operations become more formal, the systems they require generally become more complex and are typically at this stage referred to as CBS. Smaller, unregulated entities typically adopt the term MIS.

Community-based providers such as Savings Groups (SGs) or Self-Help Groups (SHGs) need to consider two levels of information: the information that the groups need to manage their interactions with each other and the higher-level management information that the facilitating agency or external lender (if applicable) needs to assess group performance and the overall intervention. Typically, group-level data are handled with manual records (passbooks, ledgers) maintained by the groups themselves, although with the emergence of low-cost smartphones, some initiatives are aiming to help groups replace their manual recordkeeping with an automated system. For example, mobile applications can allow groups to keep records, helping to develop the sector and to support linkages.

For facilitating agencies or lenders, a more complex system is needed to enable periodic assessment of the group and its obligations based on agreed indicators. This information must be easy to collect and ideally should allow the facilitating agency to generate core ratios that reflect the state of the group and the program (see box 14.1). Microsoft Excel is typically used, although more complex systems are evolving, including those that allow the submission of data collected via mobile devices. For example, in 2010, the Savings Groups Information Exchange (SAVIX) developed an online reporting website to aggregate data from the MIS on a quarterly basis. The next generation of this tool aims to replace the Excel-based system and move users to an online system that is integrated more closely with the SAVIX website but is still easy to use.

Small NGO MFIs require a basic system for credit-only operations, which is often either a manual Excel-based system or an off-the-shelf software developed for microfinance. The simplest systems track client loan portfolios and generate reports for management. Some systems also integrate a general ledger function facilitating the automation of financial statements.

Mid-size providers with more than 10,000 clients, multiple products, and multiple locations require a more robust system to ensure effective management. The capacity to handle increasing volumes of transactions and accounts becomes

Box 14.1 Performance Monitoring of Savings Groups

To support the periodic assessment of groups, VSL Associates and Software Group, have made available an open-source, Excel-based MIS that stores information collected from each SG and generates core ratios. The adoption of a common MIS has advanced the standardization of reporting in the sector and enabled all practitioners and donors to adopt a stand-alone MIS that would otherwise be prohibitively costly and time-consuming to develop separately. No data are collected on individual members. Rather the focus is on (a) group profile and member satisfaction; (b) group financial performance and sustainability; (c) efficiency and productivity of facilitating agencies; (d) sustainability of service delivery, post-project; and (e) the cost per member, measured both during the life of a project and in the long term.

The MIS is structured around three primary reports:

- *Performance ratios.* A quick overview of the program based on 16 key indicators of performance (see table B14.1.1)
- *Overall project performance.* A detailed summary of performance including 48 metrics covering outreach and profile of members, financial performance of the group, and operational and financial efficiency of the facilitating agency
- *Portfolio performance comparison.* A report providing consolidated portfolio performance data for each facilitator based on 13 key indicators of performance to identify differences across facilitators, to allocate resources and efforts more efficiently, and to resolve weaknesses.

Table B14.1.1 Key Indicators of Performance for Savings Group Facilitation

Ratio	Formula	Purpose
Member satisfaction		
Attendance rate	Number of members attending meeting/number of active members	Indicates short-term relevance and value of services and appropriateness of methodology
Retention rate	Number of active members/ (number of active members + number of dropouts)	Indicates long-term relevance and value of services and appropriateness of methodology
Membership growth rate	(Number of active members – number of members at start of cycle)/number of members at start of cycle	Indicates long-term relevance and value of services and appropriateness of methodology
Financial performance of groups		
Average savings per member	Value of savings/number of active members	Indicates level of member confidence in the system and demand for savings

(continued next page)

Box 14.1 *(continued)*

Table B14.1.1 *(continued)*

Ratio	Formula	Purpose
Return on assets	Net profits/total assets	Measures profits in relation to member investment
Annualized return on assets	(Net profits/total assets) x (52/average age of groups in weeks)	Measures profits in relation to member investment; allows for comparisons across projects of different ages and maturity
Return on savings	Net profits/value of savings	Measures profits in relation to member savings
Average outstanding loan size	Value of loans outstanding/number of loans outstanding	Indicates the ability of the system to meet the credit needs of members
Portfolio at risk	Unpaid balance of late loans/value of loans outstanding	Indicates quality of loan portfolio
Average write-off per graduated group	Value of write-offs/number of graduated groups	Indicates quality of loan portfolio
Operating efficiency of groups		
% of members with loans outstanding	Number of loans outstanding/number of active members	Indicates degree to which loan access is equitable
Loans outstanding as a % of total assets	Value of loans outstanding/total assets	Indicates operating and financial efficiency of loan activities and member demand for credit
Efficiency of facilitating organization		
Caseload: groups per trainer	Number of supervised groups/number of trainers	Indicates outreach and operational efficiency
Caseload: members per trainer	Number of active members/number of trainers	Indicates level of staffing efficiency
Ratio of trainers to total staff	Number of trainers/number of project staff	Indicates level of staffing efficiency
Cost per member assisted	Total expenditures to date/cumulative number of individuals assisted by the project	Measures financial efficiency and the cost of service delivery

Source: Adapted by David Panetta based on the Community-Managed Microfinance Management Information System of VSL Associates; SEEP Network 2008; and program materials developed by the Aga Khan Foundation and Freedom from Hunger.

Source: Panetta 2012; www.thesavix.org.

critical at this point, and many providers find that their original systems no longer cope efficiently, necessitating new ones. Real-time reporting and accessibility of reports also become more critical as institutions grow.

At this size and scale, some MFIs may become regulated entities; those undergoing this transformation generally must either upgrade or replace their systems to comply with regulations and meet the demands associated with their new status. For example, deposit mobilization requires a new level of regulatory reporting with a commensurately higher-integrity system. If the regulated entity offers current accounts with checks or other negotiable instruments, it may require modules for administering checks and clearing (although many will either not offer current accounts or will clear checks and other negotiable instruments via a correspondent commercial bank already participating in a clearing system; see chapter 18).

The information requirements of financial cooperatives largely overlap with those of other deposit-taking institutions; cooperatives may require specialized functions for calculating member dividends and payments. They often segregate their systems into front-office and back-office administration, although for many this is just a logical segregation of functions within the same system.

Larger, more advanced institutions that are regulated and intermediate deposits use systems developed for banks capable of regulatory and real-time reporting. For example, commercial banks require functionality including clearing, money markets, treasury, current accounts, and the capacity to calculate floating interest rates. Many deposit-taking MFIs and specialized commercial microfinance banks use bank systems tailored to microfinance.

Over the years, several tailored systems have been developed to cater to financial service providers working in low-income markets. The Consultative Group to Assist the Poor (CGAP)

and the Microfinance Information eXchange (MIX) both provide a listing of such providers on their websites.[3]

The following section focuses on the capabilities required of a CBS and the process of selecting and installing a new system.

Functions of Core Banking Systems

The required functions of a CBS differ for each financial service provider depending on the nature of its products and services and its organizational structure. However, some common functions are typically available in most systems:

Customer Information Systems

Customer information systems create and manage customer records. This includes the capture of data such as name and address as well as other information. Many systems also support the capture of photos, signature scans, and possibly biometrics, all of which help to verify the customer's identity. Within this module, it is common to have the ability to capture "user-defined" fields that are specific to the individual provider's needs, such as social performance tracking or other unique data.

Group Management

For providers offering products based on a group lending methodology, the system needs to provide the functionality to create and manage group membership. Many systems offer this within the customer information system by specifying a type of customer as a solidarity group. Irrespective of how the functionality is included, the system should allow validation of group size (minimum-maximum), identify group leaders, have an option for identifying subgroups, track exits from the group, and ideally track meeting attendance.

Loan Portfolio Tracking

A loan portfolio tracking module is used to define loan products and support the processing of loans from application through to repayment and settlement. To support these requirements, the system needs to offer a large amount of flexibility with regard to product definition, with multiple options for calculating interest, associated fees, and other parameters to ensure that the system can enforce loan policies. For providers working with groups, the system should support bulk or group-based loan processing. Information derived from this module is used by various stakeholders and supports a range of decisions, from granting repeat loans to assessing portfolios.

Deposit Account Management

For providers offering deposit products, the system needs to support the definition and management of liability accounts. These may be in the form of voluntary savings accounts, mandatory or guarantee funds linked directly to a loan, fixed or term deposits, or current accounts. For all liability products, the system needs to support the method of calculating interest as well as of handling fees and other charges.

Transaction Processing

Support is required to process transactions to and from customer accounts. These modules should enable efficient data capture, both for individuals and for groups. Financial service providers offering full teller services require cash management support to monitor teller and vault floats. Transaction processing should also consider automation of receipts and potentially authentication of user identity via biometrics.

Accounting

The extent and functionality offered by an integrated accounting module can vary considerably. At a minimum, one should expect basic general ledger support to ensure that all transactions are summarized in the general ledger. Additionally, it should be possible to post basic journal entries to the general ledger to manage all noncustomer-related transactions. More complex systems can also offer submodules, such as bank reconciliation and budgeting. Lastly, while large providers require additional support for accounts payable and receivable, payroll, and fixed assets, it is rare to find this as part of an integrated CBS; if it does exist, the functionality may be quite limited.

Audit Support

All systems should provide some basic functionality for managing the provider's audit functions, including interfaces or possibly reports for auditing user interactions, particularly those considered high risk. Audit support should also consider the general security of the system, which can range from user access rights to logical controls preventing unauthorized access to the system (see box 14.2).

Reporting

The reporting module overlies all other modules to provide end users with the reports necessary to conduct their business. Reports can range in detail from a listing of accounts or transactions to summary management reports that show the overall performance, both financial and social, of the provider. Users of these reports can be internal or external, such as regulatory bodies or rating agencies. For larger providers with more complex reporting requirements, a dedicated reporting system is often deemed necessary. These dedicated reporting systems can be in the form of either a reporting warehouse that simply stores reports or more complex systems capable of extracting data from multiple sources and aggregating the information into a consolidated set of reports. Irrespective of what type of reporting system is used, whether bundled or separate, reporting tends to require ongoing investment because the need for information is never static. The most successful systems have the capacity to add and edit reports over time.

Box 14.2 Software Application Controls

Software application controls are *preventive*, *detective*, and *corrective* in nature. Automation enables and facilitates a range of such controls very effectively. All software applications contain some generic controls. Regardless of whether the software is purchased or developed, application-based controls should be in place to ensure that the following objectives are fulfilled:

- *Input controls.* Check the integrity of data entered into a system, regardless of when, where, or how, to ensure the information is within specified parameters. Examples include the sequential entering of receipts, prevention of entering duplicate transactions, controls around the entry date, and prevention of entering duplicate loan numbers.
- *Processing controls.* Ensure that processing is complete, accurate, and authorized. An example is ensuring that the sum of all debits and credits posted by the system on any given day are always equal. Processing controls also include user access for various activities and levels of authority to carry out those activities.
- *Output controls.* Address what is done with the data or the transactions. Output controls compare output results with the intended results and outputs with inputs. An example is verifying receipt batch entries and their allocation to principal, interest, and fees with the database report summary.
- *Integrity controls.* Monitor data in process or in storage to ensure that data remain consistent and correct.
- *Management trail.* Provide a historical traceable record of transactions and processes. The "audit trail" enables management to track transactions from the source to the ultimate results reported and to trace backward from results to the events and activities they record.

Source: Richards, Oliphant, and Le Grand 2005.

Identifying a System Provider

The process for identifying a new information system is critical. No one system will satisfy all of an institution's requirements. Experts generally suggest that if a system can cover 75 percent of requirements, the remaining needs can be "plugged" with supporting applications. Following are steps for identifying a core system:

- *Business case development.* Identify and come to agreement about the need for a system and procurement requirements to source it.

- *Requirements analysis.* Conduct mapping and documentation of existing systems, products, and processes and identification of "future" processes and products. This phase should produce a list of functional, technical, and other system requirements. This is one of the most important steps. If a provider does not have the in-house capacity to carry out this step, it should consider hiring a technical consultant.

- *Request for proposal.* Translate the requirements into a request for proposal that will prompt suppliers to describe how their systems meet the requirements of the specific provider. Each requirement should be rated in terms of importance to the provider, as some will be "must have," while others will be "nice to have." Requests should be sent to an agreed shortlist of providers.

- *Evaluation.* Evaluate all proposals received and list questions for clarification, followed by demonstrations and site visits. Supplier demonstrations should be used to confirm answers received in the request for proposal and obtain an overall sense of the system; they also provide an opportunity to interact with and assess supplier staff. Site visits and references are the best way to evaluate the quality of supplier support and implementation. A standard list of questions should be developed for reference. At this stage, it may be useful to assess the gaps between the institution's stated requirements (output from the "requirements analysis" stage) and the standard functionality of the systems being proposed.

- *Negotiation and selection.* Review contracts, finalize negotiations, and make the final selection. This process should yield clear contracts with service-level agreements for support.

Installing a Core Banking System

The first step for installing a new system is to create a team of representatives from all key departments. Change management and broad-based buy-in are crucial. Similarly, staff members need to understand why the system is changing and how the institution will benefit from the change.

Data Preparation and Extraction

If moving from one system to another, information needs to be extracted from the old system and put into the new system. Data converted to a new system must be accurate and free of errors. Suppliers will differ in the extent to which they assist with the extraction of data. Whoever performs the extraction and conversion must have an intimate knowledge of the structure of both the old and new systems. Undertaking multiple sample data conversions before moving to the new system is strongly recommended to ensure that both systems fully reconcile with each other. Many providers will need to include a "data-cleaning" stage at this point to rectify any inconsistencies identified during the extraction and conversion process.

Customization

Customization involves tailoring the system to the specific needs and products of a provider. Staff members need to understand the system before any changes are made to ensure that customized elements reflect the institution's operations. In many cases, the institution will find a standard feature perfectly adequate, albeit not identical to the functionality envisioned by the end users during the scoping of requirements. During these discussions, it is important to ask whether clients or other stakeholders will derive significant additional value from customization. Setting aside personal preferences, if no objective measure of incremental benefit can be identified, the institution will save both money and implementation time by accepting the standard feature already programmed into the system. These savings will compound with each new release of the software that does not have to be customized. Customization can create significant complications and should be done only for high-priority, significant changes. All customization should be fully documented, with clear agreement between the supplier and the provider on exactly how it will work. Where customization is required, additional time will have to be allocated for testing.

Training

The mantra of experts and those who have installed a new system is "train, train, train, and then train some more." All levels of staff need to be trained on the new system, from end users to senior management. Training should occur at various stages, including the pilot stage before customization, before full rollout, and continuously after rollout. Follow-up training is particularly important after staff have used the system to allow them to ask specific questions. Training typically is done using a "core team" and a train-the-trainer approach. This has the benefit of building capacity in-house to support the system and can also help to bridge cultural and institutional differences that may exist between the supplier and the end users.

When training is not conducted thoroughly, field staff may continue to keep parallel manual records or continue to use the old system. Reasons for this usually stem from a lack of trust in the (new) system or a lack of direct access to it. When two parallel systems are running, it is impossible to know which is the correct version and whether data entered into one system have been entered into the other. Engaging staff in data verification exercises and ensuring that all field staff have access to the system as well as effective training will increase buy-in and ownership.

User Acceptance Testing
After the system has been installed, configured, and (potentially) customized, financial service providers need to confirm that it is functioning to their requirements. This is typically done during a user acceptance testing phase whereby a series of test cases or scenarios is run on the system to confirm that it operates as required. This critical phase should not be rushed, as it is much easier to resolve issues arising at this point than when the system is live. Ideally, user acceptance should be tested by a team of primary users or the core team that was trained, as testing often consolidates what was learned in theory-based training.

Delivery Channel and Systems Upgrading
The development of new technologies and channels of delivery is becoming increasingly relevant for expanding outreach and access. However, if the information systems are not stable or scalable,

introducing new channels can add significant risk. The first step is to ensure that transactions can be processed reliably and that the data with which to monitor new channels are available in regular reports.

A CBS has two primary user components. The "front end" of the system facilitates client transactions and is what is accessible to the end users of the system, including tellers, loan officers, and accountants. The "back end" refers to the database that stores the data and is typically only accessed by the information technology department. As providers deliver services through increasingly diverse delivery channels, an interface is required to enable the system to receive transactions electronically from a source other than its own front end. Two primary options are available for posting transactions to and from delivery channels:

1. *Manual system.* Some providers opt to interact with branchless delivery channels via the use of batch files that are manually uploaded or downloaded between the system and the delivery channel. For example, payments made to an e-wallet service could be downloaded periodically in a format compatible for uploading to the system, such as Excel or CSV.[4] This method is by far the cheapest, but it is associated with several security issues because data may be manipulated during the transfer process. Further, it does not process transactions in "real time," so there will always be a delay before payments are reflected in the accounts of the customer. For these reasons, manual systems are typically only used when the volume of transactions is low or the provider does not have enough revenue to invest in an automated system.

2. *Automated system.* To allow two or more systems such as a CBS and an e-wallet service to communicate with each other in real time, some type of middleware software is required to sit between the two systems. The most

commonly used software of this type is referred to as a "bridge" or "switch," which could be provided either by the CBS supplier or by a third party (see chapter 18). These applications enable the two systems to communicate with each other using an agreed language, or protocol, to structure the transaction data into a machine-readable format (such as ISO, NDC, JSON, XML). Messages are then sent in the preferred protocol using an agreed interface, which could be a published application program interface, a Web service, a simple object access protocol (SOAP), or a transmission control protocol (TCP) socket. Using this type of technology, multiple systems can communicate seamlessly in real time. This approach provides many clear benefits for the financial service provider, including automated handling of errors, a full audit trail, real-time processing, and lower risk of transaction fraud because no manual intervention is required.

The increased use of branchless banking has also created new security requirements, and security technology has evolved accordingly. Whereas a branch teller could ask to see a photo identification, technology-enabled transactions require alternative forms of verification and security. Security usually is broken down into three types: (1) something you know (password), (2) something you have (bankcard), or (3) something you are (biometric).[5] Biometric verification measures an individual's unique physical characteristics to recognize and confirm identity.

Mobile banking transactions use a combination of traditional personal information number codes, real-time alerts, and approval verification codes. Real-time alerts are notifications or messages that inform customers of a certain event, such as a deposit or a withdrawal. The alerts are delivered across a wide variety of channels and devices, including e-mail, text messages, personal digital assistants, and fax. Alerting technology is expected to grow rapidly, particularly as customers realize that it offers them more control over their interaction with providers (Rao 2009).

Data from the CBS form the basis for analyzing social and financial performance and for managing financial risk. Data captured via these systems also support other operational processes, such as human resource management, product management, and operational risk management, which are discussed in chapter 15.

Financial Management

Financial management involves a continual process of recording, measuring, monitoring, assessing, and managing financial performance and financial risks.[6] Financial management extends beyond simply reporting and managing accounts; rather it is a comprehensive process that includes business planning, financial reporting and analysis, performance management, and profitability analysis. Financial management also includes the management of financial risks, including asset quality, capital adequacy, asset-liability management (ALM), and liquidity management.

Responsibility for sound financial management rests primarily with the board and senior management. The board determines the broad strategy and financial objectives, including limits on the level of acceptable financial risk. Senior management then determines how to operationalize these goals and remain within acceptable risk parameters. If applicable, regulators often stipulate the level of financial risk allowed for different types of providers and, as such, influence how and which financial risks should be monitored and assessed.

Business Planning

The business planning process incorporates three primary stages: strategic or long-term planning, annual operational planning, and budgeting.

Strategic planning is normally embodied in a *strategic plan* (generally covering a three- to five-year period) approved by shareholders (if applicable), the board or management committee, and senior management. A strategic plan outlines the provider's medium- to long-term goals and highlights its plan with regard to markets served, growth, product offerings, product delivery, channel development, marketing, staffing, funding, risk management, and related systems. The strategic planning process should be undertaken at least once every three years and is used to guide providers through a comprehensive review of operations and to achieve widespread buy-in from all stakeholders.

Operating plans are created on an annual basis and provide detail on outreach, projected revenues, expenses, and capital expenditures, while the *budgeting* process provides more detail. Budgets generally present financial information on a month-by-month basis, including line-by-line details of revenues and expenses for the entire organization. Budgets can usually be disaggregated by location and by time period. Often when developing a new product, a budget is prepared that details staff and training costs, required funding (including market research, marketing, and capital costs), and related revenues based on projected outreach. Budgets provide a benchmark against which to assess performance.

Financial Reporting

While budgeting and planning predict future activity, financial reporting is concerned with tracking and observing historical results. Financial reporting refers to the timely production of *financial statements* based on up-to-date and accurate financial records (SEEP Network 2005). Financial reporting summarizes financial transactions and aggregates them by category or at a certain point in time.

Various stakeholders use financial reports to understand performance and identify risks. The board assesses information to determine whether the overall financial and operational strategy is being achieved and to identify risks, opportunities, and challenges for discussion with management. External stakeholders, including donors, investors, and regulators, examine financial statements closely to assess financial performance and to determine future engagement. Internally, financial reports inform management of the financial performance and financial condition for the period or at a point in time (SEEP Network 2005).

An organization's *accounting system* continuously collects, summarizes, and updates data on assets, liabilities, equity, revenues, and expenses. Although different accounting standards are used around the world, the International Financial Reporting Standards are emerging as the primary accounting system in most countries.

The *chart of accounts* is the core of the accounting system. The structure and design of the chart of accounts ultimately determines the type of financial information that can be accessed and analyzed by management or reported to external parties. In most regulatory frameworks, the central bank or other regulatory bodies provide specific guidelines for an institution's chart of accounts. For unregulated providers, accounting software packages provide charts of accounts that follow industry standards for microfinance.

An accounting system (and the related chart of accounts) is normally linked to an organization's CBS. To minimize potential errors, the portfolio quality information system should be integrated directly with the accounting system. Accounting systems produce financial statements on a systemwide basis, and most can also produce financial statements for geographic or functional areas, depending on the provider's organizational structure.

Financial Statements

Financial statements contain both *stock* data (information on data at a moment in time) and *flow* data (information on the flow or summary of transactions over a defined period of time). They generally include the following:

- Income statement (profit and loss statement)
- Balance sheet (financial position)
- Cash flow statement (sources and uses of funds)

The *balance sheet* represents the financial condition of a provider at a point in time (that is, stock data) and is divided into three primary categories: assets, liabilities, and equity. Assets are on the left-hand side of the balance sheet, and for most financial service providers the loan portfolio is the largest asset. It changes over time as loans are repaid and new loans are made. The balance sheet normally shows the gross loan portfolio—all outstanding principal amounts including current, delinquent, and renegotiated loans—but not loans that have been written off. The gross loan portfolio is reduced by the amount of loan loss reserve (or impairment loss allowance), resulting in the net loan portfolio. When loans are written off, the gross loan portfolio and the loan loss reserve are reduced by the same amount, leaving the net loan portfolio unchanged.

Other assets include cash, deposits with other financial institutions, amounts due to the financial service provider but not yet received, and property and other capital assets. Capital assets decline in value over time through the depreciation expense, which is recorded on the income statement. Assets are funded by liabilities and equity.

Liabilities and equity together equal the total amount of assets. Liabilities represent what is owed by the provider and include client deposits (if applicable) and borrowed funds (debt) or payments due but not yet paid. Assets minus liabilities equals equity—or the *net worth* of a provider. Equity includes retained earnings as well as any invested funds (that is, start-up capital either through donor grants or through shareholder

purchases, plus any subsequent equity investments). The greater the proportionate amount of liabilities versus equity, the greater the leverage of the provider. As leverage increases, so does risk, as liabilities are borrowed funds and must be repaid. For regulated providers, the degree of leverage is mandated by the regulator to ensure that the institution is financially secure and, in particular, that the funds on deposit are not at undue risk.[7]

The *income statement* is a flow statement and reflects the financial results of operations over a specified period of time by aggregating all revenues and deducting all expenses. The result is *net income*. Net income represents the primary link between the income statement and the balance sheet. The net income (or loss) is added to (or deducted from) equity through the retained earnings account on the balance sheet. Equity increases (or decreases) as net income is recorded and transferred from the income statement. At the beginning of each income period, the income statement begins at zero. In contrast, the balance sheet is cumulative over time.

For most financial service providers, the primary revenue-generating asset is the loan portfolio. While cash is an asset, it generally does not earn revenue. Revenue from interest, fees, and commissions on loans plus any other earnings are recorded on the income statement. This includes not only interest received, but also interest accrued and not yet received. Expenses include salaries and other staff costs, funding costs (that is, interest and fees paid on debt), loan loss provisions (or impairment loss expense), rent, depreciation, other operating costs, and taxes (if applicable).

A *cash flow statement* provides information about the cash receipts and cash payments during a period of time. Some cash flow statements classify cash flows resulting from operating, investing, and financing activities. *Operating activities* are the activities carried out in the course of operations and include cash inflows, such as interest received on loans or repayment of principal, and cash outflows from expenses incurred, such as staff costs or loan disbursements. *Investing activities* refer to the investment of money into return-generating instruments such as treasury bills or other investments. *Financing activities* involve cash inflows through either infusions of equity (from shareholders or grants, for example) or borrowed funds (short- or long-term debt) and cash outflows when debts are repaid or dividends declared.

Portfolio Reports

Portfolio reports provide detail on lending activities by disaggregating the loan portfolio into sectors, geography, and overdue amounts. They are used to analyze asset quality and composition as well as outreach. Sector breakdowns are used to evaluate concentration in a given subsector and to evaluate the diversity of a loan portfolio. A geographic breakdown is helpful for analyzing the performance of the portfolio by branch or region and for pinpointing any issues associated with location, including staff or contextual factors.

The most common disaggregation of portfolio reports involves grouping the principal amount of loans according to how many days a payment has been missed; such reports are used to analyze the quality of a portfolio. From the portfolio report, providers can then calculate the *loan loss reserve* and *loan loss provision*. The loan loss reserve represents the amount that institutions set aside to cover projected bad debt. The amount of the loan loss reserve is calculated by splitting the loan portfolio into time buckets, which refer to the number of days a loan is past due (that is, current, 0–30, 31–60, 61–90, and over 90 days). Regulations, if applicable, and local or international standards often stipulate how much an institution should provision.

(In an effort to be conservative, many providers provision 1 or 2 percent of current loans even though they are not past due.) The total amount of the required loan loss reserve is determined by multiplying the total portfolio outstanding in each time bucket by the provision percentage and adding each amount together for a total. This is calculated on a periodic basis, generally as balance sheets are updated. The amount of the new loan loss reserve is compared to the amount of the existing loan loss reserve on the balance sheet to determine if additional reserve is required. If so, this amount—the difference between the amount of new loan loss reserve and the amount of reserve currently on the balance sheet—becomes the amount of loan loss provision on the income statement (recorded as an expense). The loan loss provision, in turn, reduces the net income (because expenses increase) transferred to the balance sheet and thus keeps the balance sheet balanced—that is, both sides of the balance sheet are lower because assets are reduced by the increase in the loan loss reserve (a negative asset) and equity is reduced by the reduction in net income transferred to equity (retained earnings).

Similarly, the value of capital assets (for example, vehicles) on the balance sheet is reduced over time by recording a depreciation expense on the income statement. Most capital assets are depreciated over a period of years matched to the anticipated life of the asset, which is generally stated in accounting principles or by the accounting regulatory body. The amount of the capital asset (on the balance sheet) is decreased by the amount of the periodic depreciation expense (on the income statement), which again keeps the balance sheet balanced since net income is reduced by the amount of the depreciation expense (that is, the value of capital assets is reduced by an amount equal to the reduction of net income transferred to equity).

Financial Performance Monitoring and Risk Management

Several standardized frameworks help to monitor and manage financial performance, including financial risk. Some have been developed by rating agencies and others by networks or other stakeholders to standardize performance reporting of MFIs. Commonly used frameworks include ACCION's CAMEL, Planet Rating's SMART GIRAFE rating system, and the SEEP Network's Microfinance Financial Reporting Standards (MFRS). While these frameworks suit most institutional providers of credit and savings, the World Council of Credit Unions developed PEARLS specifically for credit unions and other financial cooperatives.[8] Each has a core set of ratios used for analyzing financial and risk management, depending, to some extent, on the type of provider. The indicators are similar, however, and generally fall into six categories: efficiency and productivity, profitability, asset quality, capital adequacy, and liquidity. CAMEL also includes qualitative measures for management, while MFRS includes indicators for outreach. Each framework can be used to assess the performance of individual institutions or to assess performance across institutions.[9]

The MFRS is a framework developed by the SEEP Network for institutional financial service providers, including NGO MFIs, deposit-taking MFIs, various types of banks, and others providing credit and savings, and in some cases, payment services (see SEEP Network 2010). Updated in 2010 from the SEEP Network's original "sweet 16," the MFRS framework includes a core set of ratios. It also has a set of "noncore" ratios for the growing number of regulated financial service providers that intermediate deposits and have complex financial structures.[10] Because the MFRS framework applies to a wide range of providers, the MFRS ratios are used throughout the rest of this section on financial performance and risk management.

Financial Performance Monitoring

Financial performance is a function of two primary areas: revenue and cost. Revenue is received through interest and fees (and, if applicable, other financial services provided by the institution).[11] Expenses consist of funding costs (interest paid on debt and to depositors), operational costs such as staff, insurance, transportation, and premises, among others, and loan loss provisioning expenses. Often costs are measured as a percentage of the portfolio. Given that the loan portfolio is the primary earning asset, it is useful to understand how much it costs to originate and manage the portfolio. Financial performance is measured by looking at efficiency and productivity, and profitability.

Efficiency and Productivity

Ratios that measure *efficiency and productivity* provide information regarding the rate at which providers generate revenue to cover expenses (see table 14.1). Efficiency refers to the cost per unit of output. Productivity refers to the volume of business that is generated (output) for a given resource or asset (input). Both productivity and efficiency ratios can be used to compare performance over time and to measure improvements in a provider's operations.

Profitability Indicators

Profitability indicators provide information on returns generated on assets, particularly the loan portfolio, and on equity (see table 14.2). They also indicate profit margins.

Financial Risk Management

Financial analysis and risk management are structured around four core areas: asset quality or credit risk, capital adequacy, liquidity management, and asset-liability management. Capital adequacy, liquidity, and ALM are often managed jointly within treasury management. The main rationale for a comprehensive approach stems from the fact

Table 14.1 Efficiency and Productivity Ratios (MFRS)

Ratio	Formula	Explanation
Portfolio to assets	Gross loan portfolio/assets	Measures the provider's allocation of assets to its lending activity; considered to be the core activity for a microfinance lender
Operating efficiency ratio	Operating expense/revenues	Highlights personnel and administrative expenses relative to total revenues
Operating expense of deposits ratio (cost per unit of deposits mobilized)	(Direct + indirect operating expenses allocated to deposits)/average savings balance (average deposits)	Evaluates whether deposit mobilization is cost-effective. Can guide the provider on how to price its deposit products. Requires a disaggregation of all direct and indirect deposit-related costs. Only relevant for deposit-taking providers
Cost of funds ratio	Financial expense on funding liabilities/average (deposits + borrowings)	Calculates a blended interest rate for all of the provider's funding liabilities
Financial expense ratio	(Interest + fees on funding liabilities)/average gross loan portfolio	Measures the total interest expense a provider incurs to fund its portfolio
Financial expense of deposits ratio (cost of deposits)	Total interest expense of deposits/average savings balance (average deposits)	Allows providers to compare the cost of funds of deposit activities directly to borrowing opportunities in the market. Does not factor in the benefits of deposits as a product for clients. Only relevant for deposit-taking providers
Cost per active client	Operating expense/average number of active clients	A simple but effective measure of the average cost of maintaining an active client. Costs per client may vary significantly depending on the type of product. "Client" should be interpreted as "unique client" for this ratio, since a client may access multiple products. Providers should clearly define "active client"—for example, a client who has used a financial product from the provider in the last 12 months
Borrowers per loan officer	Number of active borrowers/number of loan officers	Measures the average caseload of the average number of borrowers managed by each loan officer
Active clients per staff member	Number of active clients/total number of personnel	Measures the overall productivity of staff who are managing clients, including borrowers, depositors, and other clients. Client should be defined as "unique client." Varies both by productivity and by the nature of the product mix

Source: SEEP Network 2010.

Table 14.2 Profitability Ratios (MFRS)

Ratio	Formula	Explanation
Portfolio yield	Cash received from interest, fees, and commissions on loan portfolio/ average gross loan portfolio	Indicates the provider's ability to generate cash from interest, fees, and commissions on the gross loan portfolio. Excludes revenues accrued but not paid in cash
Operating profit margin	Net income before taxes and donations/operating and nonoperating revenue	Measures a provider's profitability in terms of its effectiveness in managing costs
Return on assets (ROA)	Net income after taxes and before donations/average assets	Measures how well the provider uses its assets to generate returns. Is net of taxes and excludes donations
Return on equity (ROE)	Net income after taxes and before donations/average equity	The definitive measure of commercial profitability. Calculates the rate of return on average equity for the period. The numerator does not include donations and is net of taxes

Source: SEEP Network 2010.

that most financial risks are interrelated. For example, liquidity risk could easily lead to credit risk if borrowers begin to lose confidence in the provider's ability to satisfy their demand for loans. Similarly, credit risk may aggravate liquidity risk and capital adequacy.

Asset Quality

Credit risk is a well-known and well-understood risk for financial service providers, particularly since lending is the prime source of revenue in most contexts. Credit risk is essentially the risk faced by lending one's resources to others. There is an inherent risk that loans will not be repaid; for this reason, institutions design eligibility criteria, loan policies, and procedures and guidelines to assess and analyze a client's ability and willingness to repay and the appropriateness of the size and term of the loan. Portfolio analysis—with reports segmented by branch, loan officer, product, and aged delinquency—is one of the best ways to understand and manage a loan

portfolio over time. Visits to clients—to authenticate their existence, verify loan balances, and gather feedback on satisfaction—are also an essential part of understanding and managing both credit and fraud risk in the loan portfolio.

Asset quality refers to the quality of the loan portfolio, the cost and impact of nonperforming loans, and the percentage of nonearning assets (see table 14.3). Credit risk is the core risk affecting asset quality. In general, many providers offer relatively few products, which for the most part focus on credit for investment in productive activities. This often results in homogeneity of borrowers, either geographically or by livelihood, resulting in covariance risk. Because the loan portfolio usually constitutes a proportionately large share of overall assets, difficulties affecting a large number of borrowers, such as a poor harvest, can have a substantial effect on overall performance. As providers expand their loan products or target sectors, covariance risk may decline.

Table 14.3 Asset Quality (Portfolio Quality) Ratios (MFRS)

Ratio	Formula	Explanation
Nonperforming loans as of 30 days past due (NPL30)	(Nonperforming loans > 30 days + value of renegotiated loans)/gross loan portfolio	90 days overdue is the most common international measurement of a nonperforming loan; for microfinance, 30 days is a more appropriate time horizon for this ratio
Renegotiated loans ratio	Value of renegotiated loans/gross loan portfolio	Includes all rescheduled, restructured, refinanced, and renegotiated loans. Because renegotiated loans are sometimes not disclosed or cannot be identified separately within NPL30, this ratio discloses the risk level of the renegotiated loan portfolio
Write-off ratio	Value of loans written off/average gross loan portfolio	The percentage of loans that have been removed from the balance of the gross loan portfolio because they are unlikely to be repaid; write-off policies vary; it is recommended that managers calculate this ratio on an adjusted basis
Nonperforming loans as of 30 days past-due + write-off ratio	(Average nonperforming loans > 30 days + value of renegotiated loans + value of loans written off)/average gross loan portfolio	Gives the most comprehensive measure of asset quality. Includes all NPLs > 30 days, all renegotiated loans, and write-offs. In the past, troubled loans could be shifted among these categories. Shows the combined impact of these three components of asset quality
Loan loss rate	(Write-offs − value of loans recovered)/average gross loan portfolio	Provides a true picture of loan losses from write-offs by including the offsetting value of recovered loans. Tends to vary far more than the write-off ratio, since loan recovery tends to be sporadic and occurs irregularly in time and amounts
Risk coverage ratio	Loan loss reserve/(nonperforming loans > 30 days past due + value of renegotiated loans)	Measures how much of the nonperforming loans as of 30 days past due plus the value of renegotiated loans is covered by the loan loss reserve
Loan loss reserve (impairment loss allowance) ratio	Loan loss reserve/average gross loan portfolio	Measures the loan loss reserve as a proportion of the gross portfolio. Can also be measured as a proportion of NPL30, with NPL30 in the denominator
Loan loss provision (impairment loss expense) ratio	Loan loss provision/average gross loan portfolio	Indicates the expense a provider incurs to ensure an adequate loan loss reserve, which will increase as the portfolio grows

Source: SEEP Network 2010.

Capital Adequacy

Capital adequacy management involves determining if the amount and type of capital a provider has is sufficient and working as efficiently as possible (see table 14.4). Financial service providers have different sources of funding, primarily equity, debt, and deposits (if regulated as a deposit-taking institution). Equity is the most permanent source of funding. A financial institution leverages its equity by taking on debt. Debt can be obtained in three primary ways: (a) borrowing from institutions (bank debt) or government, (b) mobilizing deposits from the public or members, and (c) borrowing from the public through issuing a bond. Debt funding can be short term or long term. Long-term debt, which has a term greater than one year, is often borrowed from other banks or accessed from the capital markets in the form of bonds. Short-term debt has a term of less than one year. Deposits can be short term or long term.

Capital structure policy involves a trade-off between risk and return and reflects the organizational mission, appetite for risk, and regulatory requirements. The appropriate degree of leverage for a provider ultimately depends on its ability to manage the risk (Ledgerwood and White 2006). Higher leverage indicates a higher level of risk, as an institution may have limited ability to absorb unexpected losses or may have borrowed more than it can repay based on cash flows. Leverage that is too low may indicate that an institution is not using an adequate amount of debt to generate an increase in revenue. If an institution can generate greater returns on its operations (that is, return on assets or return on equity) than the cost of debt, it may make sense to increase leverage, albeit in a conservative manner.

Liquidity Management

Liquidity management involves effectively managing liquidity to finance daily operations

Table 14.4 Capital Ratios (MFRS)

Ratio	Formula	Explanation
Debt to equity (leverage)	Liabilities/equity	Measures the overall financial leverage (or gearing) of an institution and how much cushion the provider has to absorb losses after all liabilities are paid
Equity to assets ratio	Total equity/total assets	A measure of the solvency of a provider. The information derived from this ratio helps a provider to assess its ability to meet its obligations and absorb unexpected losses. The denominator should exclude goodwill and intangible assets
Capital adequacy ratio	Total capital/risk-weighted assets	Measures the amount of capital in relation to risk-weighted assets (risk weights are generally provided by the regulator). It is a more finely tuned indicator of a provider's solvency and its ability to meet its obligations and absorb unexpected losses. The denominator should exclude goodwill and intangible assets
Uncovered capital ratio	(Nonperforming loans > 30 days + value of all renegotiated loans – impairment loss allowance)/total capital	Indicates how the provider is managing its level of loan portfolio risk relative to the amount of capital it has. The lower the ratio, the better. Nongovernmental organizations and other nonregulated providers may substitute equity for total capital in the denominator

Source: SEEP Network 2010.

(including withdrawals, if applicable), while minimizing the costs of holding idle cash (see table 14.5). Assets are considered liquid if they are easily accessible and convertible into cash. When evaluating a provider's liquidity and its liquidity risk, it is important to look at the structure of the balance sheet, the different types of funding sources, and the assets they fund.

Asset-Liability Management

ALM analyzes the structure of the balance sheet and the risks and returns inherent in this structure vis-à-vis the relationship between pricing and the cost of funds, maturity of assets and liabilities, and the currency of funding versus the currency of lending.[12] ALM seeks to manage the balance between risk and return by maintaining a positive spread between the interest rates earned (on loans and other interest-earning assets) and the interest rates paid (on borrowed funds). The goals of ALM are to protect shareholders and depositors, maintain sufficient liquidity to cover cash flow requirements and invest idle liquidity profitably, manage the interest rate gap to maximize earnings with risk limits, generate attractive foreign exchange earnings within risk limits, and price products to support asset and liability management and maximize earnings (Ledgerwood and White 2006). ALM does not rely on ratios; instead, ALM tables are included in the MFRS (see SEEP Network 2010).

An asset and liability committee (ALCO) is often set up to manage exposure of the balance sheet to market risks. It generally consists of members of the management team. Their responsibilities include (a) decisions with regard to the provider's exposure to market risks and supervision of their implementation, (b) development and adoption of medium- and long-term financial and liquidity plans, (c) identification of funding

Table 14.5   Liquidity Ratios (MFRS)

Ratio	Formula	Explanation
Liquid ratio (quick ratio or acid-test ratio)	(Cash + trade investments)/ (demand deposits + short-term time deposits + short-term borrowings + interest payable on funding liabilities + accounts payable + other short-term liabilities)	Indicates level of cash and cash equivalents the provider has to cover short-term liabilities. Short-term liabilities refer to assets or liabilities, or any portion thereof, that have a due date or a maturity date or may be readily converted to cash within 12 months
One-month stressed liquidity ratio	Current assets/(current liabilities + one-month operating expenses + one-month net portfolio growth)	A forward-looking ratio that measures whether there is sufficient liquidity for one month of disbursements, including portfolio growth. Can be modified to measure three or six months
Liquid assets to total assets	Cash/total assets	Measures the percentage of total assets supported by fully liquid assets
Savings liquidity	(Reserves against deposits as required by regulators + unrestricted cash)/total demand deposits	Provides information on the cash available to meet withdrawals in demand deposit accounts. Regulators generally require a statutory reserve against demand deposits that may directly affect this ratio
Loans to deposits ratio	Gross loan portfolio/deposits	Measures the relative portion of the portfolio funded by deposits. Provides information on the role of deposits as a funding source

Source: SEEP Network 2010.

needs and strategies for meeting those needs, and (d) continuous review of market conditions and adaptation of business operations (Ledgerwood and White 2006). Some boards have a board-level ALCO that sets higher-level strategies for managing financial risk.

A provider suffers from *maturity mismatch* if the maturity of its assets differs substantially from the maturity of its liabilities. For example, a bank could have substantial long-term assets (in the form of long-term loans or mortgages), funded by short-term liabilities (such as demand deposits that can be withdrawn on short notice) or short-term commercial paper (a money market security issued by financial institutions to meet short-term debt obligations). Issues of maturity mismatch are often compounded in developing countries where a broad range of financial securities (negotiable financial instruments holding value) is often not available to match maturities.

Interest rate risk represents repricing risk, defined by the difference in the time frame in which interest rates on assets and liabilities reset and may reprice. For example, an institution could have all of its liabilities in floating interest rate bonds (bonds whose interest rate can fluctuate with market conditions usually related to lending risk), but all of its assets in fixed-rate loans. If interest rates were to rise, the cost of its funding could rise above the fixed rate it earns on its loans.

Given the large volume of cross-border, fixed-income investments denominated in foreign currencies (currencies other than the currencies in which providers are operating), some providers have significant foreign exchange exposure. *Foreign currency risk* considers assets and liabilities held in foreign currencies relative to total equity and measures the risk of exchange rate fluctuations. If the institution holds a currency that depreciates, foreign exchange losses are incurred when repaying the source of foreign funding. *Liquidity risk per foreign currency* measures the foreign exchange risk for each loan

term, detailing the maturation of assets and liabilities for each currency and an institution's exposure to foreign exchange risk in each time frame.

Social Performance Management

For many institutional financial service providers as well as their funders, social performance and development impact are as important as financial performance. Social performance is the effective translation of an institution's mission into practice in line with accepted social goals (Social Performance Task Force 2012). If social performance refers to whether or not an institution achieves its mission, social performance management (SPM) refers to *how* an institution achieves it mission—the operational systems that allow the institution to create benefits for clients.

Social performance management has increased in importance in recent years, in large part as a result of ongoing concerns of mission drift as many institutions begin to serve higher-income clients in the move toward commercialization and profitability. Similarly, global debates about the effectiveness of microfinance as a poverty alleviation tool (increasingly brought to light through impact assessments) has reinforced the importance of ensuring that financial service providers are assessing the social impact of their operations and making changes as needed to improve social performance. Concerns of over-indebtedness highlight further the importance of responsible finance, which does not equate to but is a fundamental part of social performance management (see chapter 3). Overall, social performance management helps to ensure that the industry's mission of helping poor people to manage their financial lives remains intact in the face of evolving market conditions (Social Performance Task Force 2012).

Managing social performance is the process of integrating the mission into the day-to-day business of an institution. It involves setting clear social goals and objectives, defining a strategy for achieving them, monitoring and assessing progress toward achieving them, and using this information to improve performance and align organizational systems to the social mission (Campion, Linder, and Knotts 2008). The Universal Standards for Social Performance Management produced by the Social Performance Task Force define the key practices that constitute a strong social performance management system (see box 14.3).

Managing social performance requires that an institution actively manages its progress toward achieving its social goals. Financial service providers generally have the following social objectives (Social Performance Task Force 2012):

- Serve increasing numbers of poor and excluded people in an ongoing, sustainable way both by broadening and by deepening outreach

- Improve the quality and appropriateness of the financial services available to clients through the systematic assessment of their specific needs

- Create benefits for clients, their families, and communities related to strengthening social capital and social links, empowering women and other disadvantaged groups, increasing assets and income, and reducing vulnerability

- Improve the social responsibility of providers toward employees, clients, and the communities served.

Balanced Performance Management

For institutions to manage and align operations with their social goals, a system is needed for collecting and analyzing information on the

---

Box 14.3 Universal Standards for Social Performance Management

In June 2012, the Social Performance Task Force launched the Universal Standards for Social Performance Management, which is "a set of management standards that apply to all microfinance institutions pursing a double bottom line. Meeting the standards signifies that an institution has 'strong' social performance management practices." The standards are divided into six sections:

1. Define and monitor social goals
2. Ensure board, management, and employee commitment to social performance
3. Treat clients responsibly
4. Design products, services, delivery models, and channels that meet client needs and preferences
5. Treat employees responsibly
6. Balance financial and social performance.

The standards were developed in consultation with industry players, including MFIs, investors and donors, social rating agencies, networks, and associations. They build on previous initiatives in the industry, including those of the ImpAct Consortium, MicroSave, and the Smart Campaign. The standards seek to guide institutions in the self-evaluation and implementation of their social performance management. It is also expected that MIX Market, social rating agencies, and funders will incorporate them into their reporting, rating tools, and due diligence processes.

Source: http://www.sptf.info/sp-standards#1; Social Performance Task Force 2012.

---

institution's performance in relation to these goals. Financial data alone are not sufficient to allow managers to make operational and strategic decisions or to permit funders to assess the social value of investment choices. A balanced approach to performance management uses information on both financial and social performance to inform and shape the strategy and operations of the institution (see table 14.6).

Several recent studies show the existence of both synergies and trade-offs between social and financial performance (González 2010; Bédécarrats, Baur, and Lapenu 2011; Guarneri, Moauro, and Spaggiari 2011). Using regression techniques to analyze and quantify potential relationships (both positive and negative) between indicators of social and financial performance, they seek to establish both causality and correlation between the variables. Findings indicate that, overall, social and financial performance not only are compatible, but also reinforce each other: "The overall social rating score is closely associated with several dependent variables and above all, with the PAR 30 [portfolio at risk more than 30 days] and FSS [financial self-sufficiency]. This means that social performance, in general terms, is strongly linked to financial profitability and the two exist in a mutually reinforcing relationship" (Guarneri, Moauro, and Spaggiari 2011).

The Social Performance Process

In order to satisfy the need to measure social objectives and be responsive to clients, a framework was developed for managing social performance by the Social Performance Task Force, an industry-wide working group composed of industry stakeholders, including practitioners, donors, investors, national and regional networks, technical assistance providers, rating agencies, academics, and researchers (see figure 14.1).

In March 2005, the Social Performance Task Force agreed to the following dimensions of performance:

- *Intent and design.* What is the mission of the institution? Does it have clear social objectives?

- *Internal systems and activities.* What activities does the institution undertake to achieve its social mission? Are systems designed and in place to achieve and measure those objectives?

Table 14.6 Balanced Performance Management

Scope	Financial performance management	Social performance management
Main goal	Solvency and growth of the financial institution	Benefits for clients, their families, and the wider community
How is it assessed?	Systematic bookkeeping and accounting	Routine monitoring of scope, outreach of services, and changes in client conditions plus periodic more in-depth understanding of the reasons behind patterns and trends observed through monitoring
How is it used?	To influence decisions about prices, products, service delivery systems, and strategies	To influence decisions about prices, products, service delivery systems, and strategies
How is it validated?	Internal and external audits; financial ratings	Internal cross-checks and external reviews; social ratings

Source: Social Performance Task Force 2012.

The New Microfinance Handbook

Figure 14.1 The Social Performance Process, Indicators, and Assessment Tools

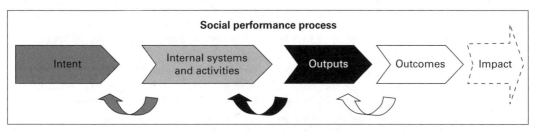

Social performance process

Intent → Internal systems and activities → Outputs → Outcomes → Impact

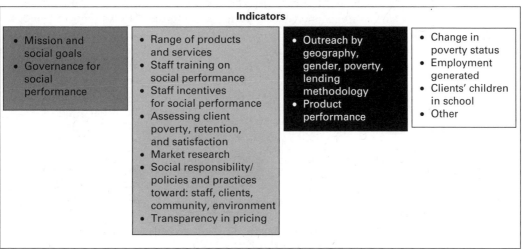

Indicators

• Mission and social goals • Governance for social performance	• Range of products and services • Staff training on social performance • Staff incentives for social performance • Assessing client poverty, retention, and satisfaction • Market research • Social responsibility/ policies and practices toward: staff, clients, community, environment • Transparency in pricing	• Outreach by geography, gender, poverty, lending methodology • Product performance	• Change in poverty status • Employment generated • Clients' children in school • Other

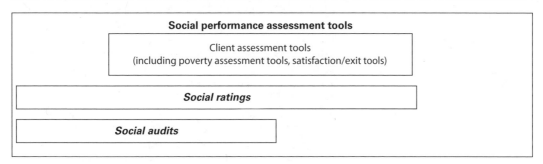

Social performance assessment tools

Client assessment tools
(including poverty assessment tools, satisfaction/exit tools)

Social ratings

Social audits

Source: Adapted from Social Performance Task Force 2012.

- *Output.* Does the institution serve poor and very poor people? Are the products designed to meet their needs?

- *Outcome.* Have clients experienced social and economic improvements? Can these improvements be attributed to institutional activities?

Social Performance Indicators

SPM does not focus on proving impact; rather it focuses on gathering information that allows providers to understand their clients' needs and behaviors and to improve the appropriateness and effectiveness of financial services (IFAD 2006). A range of qualitative and quantitative indicators is available for assessing each dimension of social performance (as shown in figure 14.1). Measuring aspects of a provider's social performance provides information that can influence the institution's products, policies, or even mission (illustrated by the feedback loops in figure 14.1). For example, if clients are poorer than expected, the provider may design products that are more suitable to that segment of the population. Low levels of educational attainment among clients' children may make the case for developing an education loan or a contractual savings product for clients who have school-age children (Social Performance Task Force 2009). For each

step in the social performance process, MIX Market and the Social Performance Task Force have jointly developed a set of core indicators of social performance (middle panel of figure 14.1).

The Social Performance Standard Report

Most of the social performance indicators included in figure 14.1 have been brought together in a report on social performance standards, which allows institutions to report their social performance to the MIX Market (Pistelli 2010). The indicators included in the report were chosen according to the following criteria: (1) relevance for use in social performance management decisions; (2) clear link to a specific desired result; (3) testable; and (4) easily validated by a third party (see table 14.7). The reporting framework increases social performance transparency and

Table 14.7 Indicators in the Social Performance Standard Report

Indicator category	What the indicators measure
1. Mission and social goals	The MFI's stated commitment to its social mission, its target market, and development objectives
2. Governance	Whether members of the board of directors have been trained in social performance management and the presence of a formal board committee that monitors social performance
3. Range of products and services	Both financial and nonfinancial products and services offered by the MFI.
4. Social responsibility to clients	The number of Smart Campaign Client Protection Principles applied by the MFI
5. Transparency of cost of services to clients	How the MFI states its interest rates
6. Human resources and staff incentives	The MFI's policy regarding social responsibility to staff, including human resource policies, board and staff composition, staff turnover rate, and staff incentives linked to social performance goals
7. Social responsibility to the environment	Whether the MFI has policies and initiatives in place to mitigate the environmental impact of financed enterprises
8. Poverty outreach	Poverty levels of clients at entry and their movement out of poverty over time
9. Client outreach by lending methodology	The type (or types) of lending methodology employed by the MFI
10. Enterprises financed and employment created	The number of enterprises financed by the MFI and employment opportunities created by the enterprises financed
11. Client retention rate	The client retention rate of the MFI

Source: http://www.themix.org.

The New Microfinance Handbook

accountability and enables grand-scale social performance benchmarking (MIX 2011).

Social Performance Assessment Tools

The industry has developed and continues to develop tools that financial service providers can use to measure and assess their social performance. Different tools focus on different steps in the social performance process (see bottom panel of figure 14.1). Certain tools focus specifically on institutional processes and internal systems by assessing intent and activities. Others help to assess the institution's outreach (outputs) and whether clients are experiencing changes in their lives, in line with the social mission of the institution (outcomes). Social performance assessment tools are used to assess clients and institutional processes.[13]

Client Assessment Tools

Client assessment involves looking at three main types of client data: (1) the socioeconomic profile of clients, (2) their experience using financial services and their needs and preferences for products, and (3) whether their lives are changing in line with the objectives of the financial provider. Collecting information of this sort can help institutions to design better products for their clients (in terms of affordability and utility) and to improve service and client retention. Client assessment tools help institutions to investigate clients' needs, satisfaction, and reasons for leaving.

Poverty assessment tools, such as the Progress out of Poverty Index (PPI)[14] of the Grameen Foundation or the poverty assessment tool (PAT) of the U.S. Agency for International Development,[15] assess the level of poverty of clients (see chapter 5). This information helps providers know who their clients are and whether they fit the target profile. It can be analyzed against operational aspects of interest to the provider, for example, by product, branch, or other aspect.

Formally assessing customer satisfaction and investigating reasons for exit can shed light on who is using the institution's products and services, who is not (that is, those who leave), and why. This involves investigating how clients and former clients use products to meet various household needs (education, health, business); their opinion on product characteristics (cost, loan size) and institutional features (time required for transactions, distance to branch); their perceptions of whether the provider's services meet their needs; and why they stop using the institution's products (for former clients only). These issues can be investigated through focus group discussions, participatory tools, and surveys. The toolkits of MicroSave, the ImpAct Consortium, and the SEEP Network include client satisfaction and exit tools that can be used to assess client satisfaction and client exits.[16]

Social Ratings

Social ratings measure the likelihood that a financial service provider will create the social value that it aims to create (social performance) and the social risk of not achieving its social mission (SEEP 2008, 112). Social ratings are undertaken by an external party. They provide a score or rating, which is based on a scale of performance. At the time of writing, four rating agencies conduct social ratings: Micro Credit Rating International, MicroFinanza Rating, MicroRate, and Planet Rating (see chapter 16). While each rating agency has its own methodology, they all use the process and indicators presented in figure 14.1 as the analytical framework of reference.

Social Audits

A social audit is an internal assessment of an institution's intent (mission) and internal systems and activities conducted for the purpose of improving its existing systems and procedures to enhance social performance. The result of a social audit is, unlike a social rating, a set of recommendations on how to enhance social performance; it does not

Box 14.4 Social Audit Tools

The CERISE social audit tool uses a questionnaire and guide to examine (1) outreach to the poor and excluded populations, (2) adaptation of products and services for target clients, (3) improvement in social and political capital, and (4) corporate social responsibility. Given its focus on organizational systems and processes, CERISE determines outreach to the poor through indirect means rather than through client assessments. It analyzes the mission statement, board and staff commitment, and targeting methods to approximate whether poor clients are being served. Rather than analyzing client empowerment at the household and community level, it assesses the social and political capital of clients by looking at their involvement in MFI decision making and at the transparency of financial transactions.

The quality audit tool was developed by the Microfinance Centre and Imp-Act. It can be implemented either internally by staff or externally by a consultant. It identifies the strengths and weaknesses of the processes and management systems vis-à-vis the institution's social mission and goals through a four-step procedure: (1) a gap analysis with management, (2) interviews and group discussions with key stakeholders of the financial provider to get more in-depth information on the systems and processes, (3) a summary of findings that are summarized in a report, and (4) a discussion of the findings with an internal audit panel of key stakeholders. This last feature is thought to be useful in validating the results of the assessment and building understanding within the institution of the various aspects of social performance. The final output of the assessment is an action plan for the actions that could help the institution to improve its current social performance.[a] As such, it is a good entry point into social performance management for financial service providers that are new to social performance management, but it is also good for institutions wanting to improve their current practices.

Source: http://www.cerise-microfinance.org/publication/impact.htm; SEEP Network 2008.
a. For more information on the tool, see SEEP Network (2008); http://www.mfc.org.pl/. For a user's review, see http://api.ning.com/files/S6i7J1FpYVkkMGKF4TG901dP2qw2vr7x8FDcMyztLOMw7tHVp9mhE1a5lU6BFgsc/UserReviewVol1No6QAT.pdf.

seek to obtain a valuation of existing social performance within the institution.[17] Various organizations have developed social audit tools including CERISE (Comité d'Echanges, de Réflexion et d'Information sur les Systemes d'Épargne-crédit), MFC (MicroFinance Centre), EDA, and MicroSave. The social audit tools of CERISE and MFC are described briefly in box 14.4.

Notes

1. The exception is organizations that facilitate Savings Groups using a standardized management information system and thus it is discussed briefly in this chapter.

2. For example, the uniformity of measurement across countries and markets allows for benchmarking and comparison, helping to inform investment decisions. This information is a vital part of the due diligence of any investor and sends important signals to the market regarding the current value and anticipated performance of a given financial service provider.

3. The lists can be found at http://www.cgap.org/p/site/c/template.rc/1.11.160192/1.26.3104/ and http://www.mixmarket.org/service-providers.

4. Comma-separated value, like Excel, but in a more basic format.

5. Interview with Joakim Vincze, October 14, 2011.

6. Parts of this section were contributed by Julie Earne.

7. If a provider were to collapse, its assets would be sold to pay off its liabilities and the remaining amount would be distributed to its owners (or, in the case of an NGO, to some other civil society body or, less likely, the donors).

8. The six categories of analysis in the PEARLS framework are similar to those in the MFRS framework, but are organized differently. Protection refers to a cooperative's ability to protect depositors and focuses on loan loss reserves and the impact of write-offs on capital and deposits. *Effective financial structure* focuses on a cooperative's sources of funds (savings, shares, external credit, and institutional capital) and use of funds (loans, liquid investments, financial investments, and non-interest-earning assets). *Asset quality* focuses on portfolio at risk and overall delinquency. *Rates of return and costs* evaluate profitability. *Liquidity* measures a cooperative's ability to respond to member-client demands for withdrawals and disbursements. *Signs of growth* measure member satisfaction and appropriateness of product offerings.

9. The primary tools for analysis include ratio analysis, trend and common size analysis, and variance analysis. A ratio expresses a relationship between one quantity and another. Some ratios are used to evaluate performance vis-à-vis a standard number, such as the capital adequacy ratio, for example, which has a specific target set by regulators. Others are used to compare the performance of one institution to that of another or one performance period to another. Trend analysis is used to analyze direction and growth and can be applied to a single indicator such as a ratio or to a range of items in a financial statement. Common size analysis is used to determine the proportion of a single item in the total group or subgroup. For example, the proportion of the portfolio to total assets is useful for understanding the amount of loan portfolio relative to total assets. Common size analysis is also used to evaluate a provider's capital structure. Variance analysis is used primarily to compare the budget to actual costs, but also to assess the achievement of targets, such as growth projections, outreach to a particular sector, or percentage of women reached. Budget to actual variances are used to highlight areas that may require closer evaluation.

10. In addition to noncore ratios, a set of ALM tables is included focusing specifically on liquidity risk, repricing risk, foreign exchange risk, and foreign exchange liquidity. These tables are useful for providers with complex funding structures and those seeking to undertake a broader analysis of how an institution's funding structure is sensitive to market risks. See http://www.seepnetwork.org/pocket-guide-to-the-microfinance-financial-reporting-standards-measuring-financial-performance-of-microfinance-institutions-resources-180.php.

11. Nonfinancial services, if any, should be tracked separately.

12. This section was contributed by Julie Earne.

13. For information on tools, see http://www.sptf.info/sp-task-force/online-trainings; SEEP Network (2008); IFAD (2006); http://www.sptf.info. For a review of some tools, see http://www.sptf.info/page/user-reviews-of-sp-tools.

14. PPI is a poverty scorecard that measures absolute poverty. It can be used to estimate the likelihood (probability) that a household has expenditure or income below a given poverty line, to estimate a group's poverty rate at a point in time, to track changes in a group's poverty rates over time, and to target clients. It derives the indicators from national income and expenditure surveys and the national poverty line using the logit regression model. The PPI is also calibrated to other poverty lines. The result is a 10-indicator scorecard that is country-specific, expenditure-based, objective, and with known accuracy. Field staff

can fill in the scorecard in the client's home in five to 10 minutes. Results can be computed using an Excel spreadsheet provided by the developer. Training and quality control are fundamental to ensure the quality of the data collected.

15. PATs, developed by the IRIS Centre, measure absolute poverty. They are country-specific scorecards comprising 16–30 indicators derived from nationally representative household surveys. They use one or more poverty lines to calculate the incidence of poverty and assess changes in poverty levels for a group. Unlike the PPI, the PAT cannot be used to assess the poverty level of an individual. The PAT scorecard is collected through a 15- to 20-minute interview with clients (individuals). Results are entered into a software program either by hand or with a handheld device. To ensure accurate results, the individuals who collect and process the data should be trained on the specific requirements of the PAT scorecard and the software used to analyze the data.

16. MicroSave (http://www.microsave.org), the ImpAct Consortium (http://www.imp-act .org), and the SEEP Network (http://www .seepnetwork.org).

17. For an excellent resource on social ratings and social audits and all social performance information, see http://www.sptf.info/images/ spm%20essentials%20resource%20hand book.pdf.

References and Further Reading

* Key works for further reading.

Aga Khan Foundation. 2010. "Monitoring, Evaluation, and Learning Plan for Savings Initiatives." Internal document, Aga Khan Foundation, Geneva.

Bédécarrats, F., S. Baur, and C. Lapenu. 2011. "Combining Social and Financial Performance: A Paradox?" Workshop paper commissioned for the 2011 Global Microcredit Summit, Valladolid, Spain, November 14–17.

*Campion, Anita, C. Linder, and K. E. Knotts. 2008. *Putting the "Social" into Performance Management: A Practice-Based Guide for Microfinance.* Brighton: Institute for Development Studies.

*CGAP (Consultative Group to Assist the Poor). 2003. "Microfinance Consensus Guidelines: Definitions of Selected Financial Terms, Ratios, and Adjustments for Microfinance." Report, CGAP, Washington, DC.

———. 2010. "Rewarding Innovation in Social Performance Reporting." Report, CGAP, Washington, DC.

*Ekka, Rashmi, and EDA Rural Systems. 2011. "Risk Management: Integrating SPM into Microfinance Capacity Building." Guidance Note, Imp-Act Consortium, Washington, DC.

*González, Adrian. 2010. "Microfinance Synergies and Trade-offs: Social vs. Financial Performance Outcomes in 2008." Report, MIX, Washington, DC.

Guarneri, M., A. Moauro, and L. Spaggiari. 2011. "Motivating Your Board of Directors to Actively Promote and Deepen the Social Mission." Workshop paper commissioned for the 2011 Global Microcredit Summit, Valladolid, Spain, November 14–17.

*Hashemi, Syed, and Laura Foose. 2007. "Beyond Good Intentions: Measuring the Social Performance of Microfinance Institutions." Focus Note 41, CGAP, Washington, DC.

*IFAD (International Fund for Agricultural Development). 2006. "Assessing and Managing Social Performance in Microfinance." IFAD, Rome.

*Ledgerwood, Joanna, and Victoria White. 2006. *Transforming Microfinance Institutions.* Washington, DC: World Bank.

MIX (Microfinance Information eXchange). 2011. "MIX Brings Social Performance to the Forefront of Microfinance." Press release, MIX, Washington, DC.

*Panetta, David. 2012. "Performance Monitoring." In *Savings Groups at the Frontier.* ed. Candace Nelson. Washington, DC: SEEP Network.

Pistelli, Micol. 2010. "Social Performance Standards." Report, MIX, Washington, DC.

Rao, S. 2009. "Real-Time Alerts a Big Step Forward in Collaborative Banking." Report, Infosys Technologies, Bangalore.

Richards, David A., Alan S. Oliphant, and Charles H. Le Grand. 2005. "Information Technology Controls." Global Technology Audit Guide, Institute of Internal Auditors, Altamonte Springs, FL.

*Rosenberg, Richard. 2009. "Measuring Results of Microfinance Institutions: Minimum Indicators That Donors and Investors Should Track: A Technical Guide." CGAP, Washington, DC.

Saltzman, S., and D. Salinger. 1998. "The ACCION CAMEL: A Technical Note." Microenterprise Best Practice Report, ACCION International, Boston.

*SEEP (Small Enterprise Education and Promotion) Network. 2005. "Measuring Performance of Microfinance Institutions: A Framework for Reporting, Analysis, and Monitoring." Financial Services Working Group, SEEP Network; Alternative Credit Technologies, Washington, DC.

*——. 2008. "Social Performance Map." Social Performance Working Group, SEEP Network, Washington, DC.

*——. 2010. "Pocket Guide to the Microfinance Financial Reporting Standards Measuring Financial Performance of Microfinance Institutions." Report, Financial Services Working Group, SEEP Network, Washington, DC.

Social Performance Taskforce. 2012. "What Is Social Performance?" http://www.sptf.info/what-is-social-performance.

*Yamini, Veena. 2010. "The Overlap between Customer Service and Social Performance Management." Briefing Note 91, MicroSave.

CHAPTER 15

Governance and Managing Operations

Peter McConaghy

Chapter 14 discusses data management and financial and social performance monitoring for institutional providers. This chapter provides an overview of governance and other issues related to the management and operations of institutional providers, including human resource management, product management, and operational risk management. It will be of interest to practitioners, funders, and board members wanting to improve their understanding of the governance and operations of financial service providers.

Governance

Governance is the system of people and processes that defines and upholds the organization's goals and mission, guides major strategic decisions, manages risks, and ensures accountability. Good governance provides management with the proper incentives to pursue objectives that are in the interests of the organization. Governance structures also facilitate effective monitoring and feedback of information, encouraging providers to make good decisions and use resources effectively.

The ownership and governance of a financial institution depend largely on its legal form, its primary stakeholders, and if and how it is regulated or supervised. The legal form could be a shareholding company licensed by the government, such as a bank or insurance company, a member-owned cooperative registered locally, or a nonprofit such as a company limited by guarantee, or a nongovernmental organization (NGO)

Contributions to this chapter were made by Ruth Dueck-Mbeba.

microfinance institution (MFI). Most institutional providers have a board of directors (or a similar structure) who are either elected or appointed and provide the primary governance mechanism:

- NGOs and companies limited by guarantee do not have owners and are normally overseen by boards, which, unlike shareholder boards, do not have a fiduciary responsibility, but rather a responsibility to protect the organization's assets and fulfill its mission.

- Financial cooperatives and other member-based organizations are by definition owned by their members, usually with each member having one vote. They are generally governed by a board elected by the members with oversight provided by a government body.

- A shareholding company can be government owned (such as state or postal banks) or privately owned (such as specialized microfinance banks, commercial banks, and some NBFIs) and possibly publicly traded; it is normally governed by a board of directors and often regulated by the central bank.

Board of Directors

A board of directors oversees management and is largely focused on (a) upholding the mission and vision of the organization and providing strategic guidance, (b) ensuring the adequacy of resources (financial, leadership, and reputation), and (c) designing and implementing policies to achieve the institution's strategy and ensure management accountability (Council of Microfinance Equity Funds 2005).

The board selects the head of the institution and approves his or her compensation. While the board supports management and monitors performance, it does not have a direct role in managing the day-to-day operations (other than in times of extreme crisis). The board ensures effective organizational planning, including succession planning at both the board and executive levels, and

monitors the deployment of human and financial resources to ensure that they are used effectively and efficiently. In addition, it identifies risks and ensures that the provider operates prudently to mitigate them. To this end, the board also approves external audits and ensures proper internal controls; generally the internal auditor reports to the board or the board's audit committee.

While the board should not be directly involved in managing the organization, it should be confident in the senior management team and the policies and procedures in place for monitoring performance. Management accountability should be monitored through both a robust reporting system to measure progress against benchmarks and third-party reviews. Benchmarks should correspond to operational and business mandates of the provider and be measurable, transparent, and fair. Well-designed benchmarks highlight potential deficiencies in management performance and help to identify operational issues that require attention from senior management or the board.

External reviews conducted by third parties, including (a) bank supervisors, (b) internal auditors, (c) external auditors, (d) legal counsel (internal and external), and (e) rating agencies and consultants, can provide additional information that helps boards to monitor and supervise management and to ensure compliance with board policies as well as applicable laws and regulations. Boards and management should ensure that all relevant parties see the reports submitted by external agencies. Furthermore, boards should have direct access to a provider's internal legal counsel or other experts, if applicable.

Building and Growing an Effective Board

The number of board members normally ranges from five to 25, with most falling in the range of seven to nine members.[1] The ideal size for a board depends on its organizational responsibilities as well as the strategic direction and funding needs of the organization. The board should be large enough to complete work effectively, secure funding as needed, provide continuity, and ensure that quorums are easily met for meetings. Simultaneously, however, it should be small enough to allow for substantive decisions to be made and for board members to establish a relationship of trust and accountability with each other. The board should have an odd number of seats to avoid the possibility of a tied vote.

The composition of a board is perhaps more important than its size. It is not unusual for bank laws and specialized non-bank laws to authorize supervisors to review the qualifications of each board member, typically known as the "fit and proper test." As a general rule, this kind of supervisory assessment is focused on screening out individuals who are inappropriate to direct the activities of a regulated financial intermediary rather than to find ideal members. A fit and proper test assesses the integrity, honesty, and reputation of a potential board member through an in-depth background check. The purpose is to ensure that directors do not have a history of fraud or criminality and are not politically exposed, subject to adverse findings or settlements in civil or criminal proceedings, or involved in a company or organization that has contravened any requirements or standards of the regulatory system. See box 15.1 for the specific board requirements for an NGO MFI transitioning into a regulated institution.

Board members should be skilled professionals who can devote intellectual resources, practical experience, and commitment to improving the organization. Similarly, it is useful if board members have networks to help source funding and ensure the organization's good standing within the financial services industry. Achieving diverse gender, ethnic, and cultural backgrounds can ensure that the board has a broad perspective.

Board members should be free from political exposure and other conflicts of interest that could influence their decisions and prevent them from acting in the best interests of the organization. Ineffective boards are often composed of individuals chosen based on political or social patronage, rather than skill and dedication to managing the strategic direction of the organization.

When there is a vacancy, the board (or its nominating committee, if applicable) is responsible

Box 15.1 Board Consideration for NGO MFIs Transforming into Regulated Institutions

Specific governance considerations exist for NGO MFIs that are in the process of becoming regulated deposit-taking microfinance institutions. One crucial challenge facing such institutions is how to incorporate old board members into an updated governance structure. Board members of the NGO MFI prior to its transformation face an important and in some ways unique challenge—they must provide continuity to the institution, including a reminder of its history (and dedication to its social mission), acknowledge and respond to the very different challenges and risks faced by a deposit-taking institution, as well as meet regulatory requirements. This includes understanding the role and time commitments of board members of regulated MFIs. Some transforming MFIs secure training to help board members to comprehend the roles they may be asked to play in the new governance structure. In other cases, members leave the board (or do not join the new board) as the MFI transforms.

Source: Ledgerwood and White 2006.

for identifying one or more candidates to fill the vacancy, investigating each candidate, and making recommendations for election. Potential board members are evaluated based on their previous experience on boards, leadership ability, diversity, knowledge of financial services for the poor, and, perhaps most important, specific skills such as microfinance, financial management, audit, legal, or project management experience. Despite the fact that new board members may be recruited by fellow board members or other stakeholders, once appointed or elected they serve the organization and not the body or person that nominated them.

Directors may be held personally liable for their actions as board members, and if their actions are found to fall short of the "standard of care" expected of them (which is often defined in local law), they may be subject to civil and criminal penalties. Many financial service providers procure directors and officers insurance, which provides an indemnity to cover any civil penalties that might be imposed on directors or to pay legal costs should directors be sued for alleged misbehavior, although protection is not available when criminal liability is an issue. The extent to which such insurance or indemnity is available varies greatly with local practice and laws.

Board committees are often formed according to the needs of the provider and, if applicable, the requirements of the regulator, which may mandate the presence of certain types of committees. The following are the most typical board committees and their functions:

- *Executive committee.* Authorized by the board to act on problems or make decisions between board meetings, with such decisions to be ratified later by the full board

- *Audit or finance committee.* Oversees expenditures and budgets, ensures internal control and financial analysis, recommends expenditure power within a board-approved budget, and hears reports of internal and external auditors

- *Personnel and compensation committee.* Reviews strategic personnel issues and overall compensation policy and recommends compensation for senior management

- *Risk management committee.* Monitors the adequacy and implementation of risk policies

- *Nominating committee.* Develops board member responsibilities, identifies and evaluates potential board members, and provides orientation to new members

- *Ad hoc committees.* Respond to specific issues, usually for a limited period of time.

Strategic Governance Considerations

Governance is complex because of the double (or triple) bottom line implicit in financial inclusion. Governance structures have evolved to adapt to industry developments, including the introduction of diversified products (for example, leasing and microinsurance), a significant increase in private investment, and, in many cases, exponential growth in financial activities. This growth has made the operational processes of most financial service providers more complex, further reinforcing the need for strong and relevant governance structures and practices. In particular, governing bodies need to pay special attention to strategic risks.

Strategic risks include *internal* risks, such as adverse business decisions or improper implementation of decisions, poor leadership, or ineffective governance, which can result in *reputational* risk—the risk of losing value as a provider because of negative public opinion (Ekka and EDA Rural Systems 2011). Commensurate with managing reputational risk, a crucial challenge for governing bodies is balancing the need for both financial and social performance (see chapter 14). Regulated institutions are often required by law to maintain solvency and protect deposits of the public. Shareholders expect financial institutions to produce a return on investment. Given this financial mandate, an important aspect of governance is ensuring that providers also focus on social goals.

The ability of boards to balance financial and social performance is facilitated by the development of social performance metrics that help to assess the social impact of providers. Some boards create a social performance management committee or at least have a social performance champion on the board.

Strategic risks also include *external* risks such as changes in competition or in the political environment. The entrance of new players places competitive pressures on providers to match innovations and operational processes. This can stimulate innovation, which can benefit clients, but also can create predatory practices in the search for new clients and market share. The imposition of interest rate ceilings could potentially limit outreach. In some countries, governments have forced providers to forgive loans outstanding to certain groups of clients or related to a particular occurrence, such as a natural disaster or a political event. Politicians are increasingly questioning tax exemptions for NGO MFIs as commercially viable microfinance becomes more prominent. Boards need to be aware of competitive pressures and political developments and work with management and other stakeholders to mitigate external risks.

Human Resource Management

Human resource management is the process through which an institution recruits, develops, and motivates people to accomplish its mission (Frankiewicz and Churchill 2006).[2] Human resource management supports efforts to give staff and management the appropriate skills, incentives, and compensation (financial and nonfinancial) to achieve institutional mandates.

The organizational structure determines human resource requirements and functions, clarifies reporting and accountability channels, and structures information flows, allowing for maximum efficiency while supporting social and financial goals. Large, regulated providers generally have more complex structures, while others purposely have flat and nimble structures. Organizational structures are also influenced by the provider's intended target market, product offering (structured by type of client or by business line or product units), delivery channels, available technology and infrastructure, and whether decision making is centralized or decentralized. The organizational structure is generally commensurate with the size and level of sophistication of a provider's product offering. For example, a provider with a broad geographic footprint may have systems and procedures to support decentralized decision making and ensure the integrity of data across different outlets and channels.

An organizational structure should support increased accessibility to clients and lower transaction costs and risks. Accessibility for clients means that staff members are able to visit clients and clients can easily use services or receive required support. Close proximity to the poor makes it easier for providers to understand client needs, develop trust with the communities in which they operate, and develop and offer products and services in line with the financial needs of intended target markets. Improving accessibility often implies increasing the number of access points that serve the poor either by opening new branches or by entering into agent relationships and using the associated technological platforms.

Flat organizational structures—as opposed to hierarchical or matrix structures—generally allow providers to interact more often with clients and respond quickly to their demands and changing needs. However, flat organizational structures require the ability of frontline staff to make decisions without reverting to senior management. This requires sound training of frontline staff or agents, trust between various levels of the organization, and appropriate supervision and information feedback that allows decentralization to occur without compromising service quality and outreach.

Human Resource Policies

Most providers have human resource policies that provide coordination and procedures for managing staff and respecting local labor laws. Human resource policies usually include general policies, such as recruitment, training, and compensation, as well as corporate policies regarding conflicts of interest, harassment, and security.

Recruitment and Screening

A critical component of any human resource strategy is hiring a sufficient number of individuals at the appropriate time who have the adequate skills, attitudes, and motivation to complete their responsibilities on time and in an effective manner. To identify and recruit the best staff, a financial service provider may want to consider qualitative assessments such as written tests, diagnostic tools such as psychometric tests, and role-playing exercises that test the character and aptitude of applicants. Many providers hire staff with very basic skill sets and provide training to build their skills and capacity over time. Institutions dedicated to providing poor women with financial services often hire large numbers of women. This is particularly important in cultures where it is uncommon for men and women to engage in professional or interpersonal activity outside of the home. If a provider cannot hire a sufficient number of women, it is important to screen male applicants for their attitudes toward women. Finally, staff members who believe in an organization's mission are more likely to be satisfied and productive long-term employees.

Training and Development

Training is used to update skills, reinforce the institutional culture and values, promote teamwork, and motivate staff. Training and staff development include training for a specific skill, development of leadership abilities, coaching or mentoring, and on-the-job training. Human resource development focuses on the knowledge, skills, and attitudes necessary for long-term achievement of an individual's career goals as well as the provider's objectives.

While training is fundamentally about equipping staff with the knowledge and capacity to ensure the social and financial performance of a financial service provider, these mandates will be achieved more easily when training incorporates a client-specific lens. Organizations may have to modify their training or turn to external trainers to incorporate knowledge of client behavior into their curriculum.

Salary and Incentives

An important objective of human resource management is to retain well-performing and experienced employees and to provide incentives to achieve results. Financial compensation includes a base salary and possibly additional incentives, either financial or nonfinancial. Financial and other incentives should align the goals of the institution with the employee's personal goals, encouraging desired behavior. This is particularly important in a decentralized organizational structure where employees work in remote and rural areas. Incentive schemes should reward both quantity and quality. For example, for loan officers, this involves balancing rewards for the number of borrowers, the volume of portfolio, and the quality of portfolio (for example, percentage of on-time repayments). For agents, incentives should encourage adequate liquidity and the accessibility of services as well as the number of transactions and, above all, customer service.

Financial incentives must be crafted carefully to discourage staff from engaging in aggressive sales techniques or behavior aimed at maximizing their earnings at the expense of the safety and respect for the client and the security and culture of the institution (see box 15.2). A financial incentive scheme that does not balance safety of clients and the provider with maximization of individual profits can prevent an institution from achieving its mandate.

Other incentives can include additional benefits, such as increased vacation time, sabbaticals, staff development grants or external training programs, pensions, or employee loans. Cultivating a positive working environment where people feel they are making an important contribution and are respected also provides intangible rewards that foster commitment and loyalty. For example, impact studies and client success stories can remind staff why they do what they do. To keep them interested and engaged, employees can be invited to participate in committees or task forces working on innovations or improvements, engaging in market research, or assessing impact.

Performance Management

Performance management is the process of setting performance objectives to achieve operational and outreach mandates. It is the method by which managers delegate, monitor, and evaluate responsibility (Pityn and Helmuth 2007). An effective performance management strategy requires managers to set performance objectives and evaluation criteria with each employee for a specified period of time; supervise employee performance; support successful performance and discipline employees whose performance or behavior is unacceptable; and evaluate the degree to which employees achieve their goals so performance can be rewarded, adjustments can be made, and goals for the following period can be set (Frankiewicz and Churchill 2006). A well-designed performance management process establishes sound communication principles, including providing and receiving feedback, and

Box 15.2 Principles of Well-Designed Incentive Schemes

- *Gradually introduce incentives.* Especially when base salaries are high, the ratio of salaries to incentives can be decreased over time by gradually increasing incentives. Incremental introduction of incentives also allows for impacts to be monitored and adjusted as needed.
- *Adjust incentives to account for inequalities.* Incentives should be adjusted for different environments. For example, urban loan officers may have different targets than rural staff, or expectations for staff may be different in established than in new branches.
- *Reward healthy growth.* Incentives should encourage loan officers to grow at a steady and stable pace until they reach (but do not exceed) maximum productivity levels.
- *Encourage innovation.* Monthly staff bonuses for innovative ideas tend to fuel creative thinking.
- *Keep it simple.* To achieve its goals, a scheme should be simple; having too many variables will make it more difficult for staff to allocate their time and resources to maximize financial return.
- *Promote teamwork with group incentives.* To promote teamwork, consider a combination of group and individual incentives based on the performance of the branch or the organization as a whole. Group incentives include profit sharing, whereby a percentage of any surplus is distributed to staff members, and employee stock ownership programs.

Source: Frankiewicz and Churchill 2006.

provides the opportunity for staff to participate in planning and monitoring their own work (Pityn and Helmuth 2007).

Team and individual performance objectives should be set to attain objectives that are SMART: specific, measurable, achievable, realistic, and time-bound. Objectives should not only be quantitative in nature, but also incorporate objectives for quality, such as customer service, attitude, teamwork, and overall commitment to meeting the mandate of the provider. Performance objectives should be set for all staff within an organization, not only for frontline staff dealing in revenue-generating activities or interacting with clients.

Product Management

Product management is not limited to the development of new products or refinement of existing products; rather it is the sum of institutional processes that result in an understanding of client needs and thus an appropriate mix of products coupled with appropriate delivery and, which is important, customer service. The ability of financial service providers to offer quality products rests on their ability to understand complex client needs. Although efforts have been made to offer products tailored to local economic and sociocultural contexts, many providers simply replicate successful models, offering products based on assumptions rather than a good understanding of client needs through market research. Tailoring products to the specific needs and consumption habits of clients can improve client satisfaction and retention as well as profitability (see box 15.3).

The ability of providers to offer various products depends on the needs of the target market and the capacity of the provider itself. For example, some products (savings, insurance) require specific regulatory status, while others require specific skills and access to information (housing loans, index-based insurance), while still others require specific technologies and access to infrastructure (settlement systems, communication technology). Providers must determine an appropriate mix of products that will meet the needs of their current and potential clients as well as achieve their stated objectives and mission.

Providers can determine the most strategic mix of products in various ways, including taking a market segment approach (offer a combination of products to meet the needs of specific target markets), a client life-cycle approach (offer products that meet client or business needs during each stage of development), or a developmental approach (offer products that help clients to transition out of poverty; Frankiewicz and Churchill 2011). Depending on the specific mix, some products may be more profitable than others; less profitable products may still be important for retaining clients or having the ability to cross-sell more profitable products. Overall, a financial service provider must understand the margins of each product and monitor trends to understand profit (or loss) drivers.

In addition to ensuring an overall appropriate product mix, managing products involves developing new products, product costing and pricing, and product marketing.

Product Development

Product development begins with market research followed by product design and testing, product launch, and then rollout.[3] It considers a range of potential products and successively narrows the choice of products as project feasibility is researched and analyzed (Brand et al. 2009). Increasingly, providers are placing client needs at the forefront of product design, developing products only after studying the complex set of activities used by the poor to manage their financial lives (see box 15.4).

Understanding client needs, forecasting demand, and segmenting the market can be done through a variety of market research methods, from surveys and client feedback forms to close

Box 15.3 Client-Focused Product Design in Practice

Grameen Bank began as a project to deliver credit to poor rural Bangladeshis in 1976. Led by its managing director, Mohammad Yunus, it steadily developed what it now calls classic microcredit. Poor villagers (means-tested through land and asset ownership) formed groups and participated in weekly meetings where savings were collected, loans were disbursed, and joint liability or support was provided should they fall into difficulty. Loans were repaid over one year in weekly installments. By 2000 almost 2 million members—the majority women—were served by Grameen's credit program. That same year, work began on Grameen II, known formally as the Grameen Generalized System. Grameen II represents a series of important changes to the product offering, consolidating many of the lessons learned during years of providing services. Important changes include the following:

- *Public deposit services.* The bank became a true intermediary by mobilizing deposits from the general public, not just from members, whose mandatory deposits were part of the bank's credit methodology.
- *Extended member deposit services.* It introduced a wider range of savings opportunities for members, including a commitment-savings account known as Grameen pension savings. Personal savings accounts were made far more flexible, and group savings accounts largely disappeared. Passbook savings accounts and contractual savings products were added.
- *Improved loan products.* It introduced a wider range of loan products with variable terms and repayment schedules. Larger loans for business use are available. Loans may be "topped up" mid-term or paid off early. There is no obligation to borrow. Borrowers in repayment difficulties have their loans rescheduled (into "flexi" loans). Joint financial liability among group members is formally not allowed (although members still undertake to help each other).

The introduction of a wider range of financial services and options help customers to manage their complex financial lives. Top-up loans allow members to maintain capital in their businesses or to manage unforeseen challenges or shortfalls and to extend repayment periods in a structured manner where necessary. Grameen II also offers special terms for the very poor and makes education grants and loans.

Grameen II has achieved significant results. After a difficult period of stagnation and compromised portfolio quality, the bank has grown significantly both in the number of customers and in profitability. Grameen took 27 years to reach 2.5 million members and then tripled that with Grameen II. Between 2002 and 2005, Grameen's deposit base tripled and its loans outstanding doubled. As of October 2011, Grameen had 8.35 million borrowers, 96 percent of whom were women; 42 percent of the branches had borrower deposits equal to 75 percent or more of outstanding loans of the branch. According to senior managers, the improvement in the bank's performance is related to the attractiveness of Grameen II's wide range of consumer-focused loan products.

Source: Rutherford 2004; Wright 2010. Statistics are from http://www.grameen-info.org/.

analysis of financial and social monitoring information.[4] Depending on organizational resources, market research can range from having a full research department to lighter-touch techniques involving ongoing feedback such as rapid surveys administered by staff to monitor client experience, client-focused discussions at staff meetings, suggestion boxes in branches, or simple questions on account forms. Further information can be gathered by reviewing industry trends and by disaggregating the existing client base by product, size, and term to begin to segment the market and potentially expand the product mix. More purposeful research can be carried out through periodic focus group discussions or surveys with current, potential, and former clients, through feasibility studies and pilot projects, or through detailed competition analysis.

For financial service providers interested in operating in or expanding their services, key market research questions center on understanding the financial service needs of potential clients, determining the level and quality of infrastructure (if moving to a new area), and understanding sociocultural and historical issues. For well-established providers with experience operating in a particular area, market research often focuses on improving client outreach, market positioning, staying ahead of the competition, and enhancing delivery channels of products and services.

Traditional product design builds off market research findings to identify gaps in service delivery and unmet client demand. In the design process, product characteristics such as eligibility, terms, price, and accessibility need to be determined, operational procedures outlined, risks identified, and cost analysis and revenue projections estimated (Frankiewicz and Churchill 2011). This will help to determine if the product is potentially viable or not based on assumed market size. If the product seems viable, the next stage is the pilot test.

Piloting involves the introduction of a *prototype* on a limited scale to determine acceptance and refinement of needs. *Pilot testing* helps to predict how different clients will respond to the new product, to assess potential demand, and to get a sense of operational processes. It includes selecting test sites (size, location), establishing test duration, and setting landmarks during the pilot phase for analysis and product refinement.

The 10 steps of pilot testing include (Wright 2010):

1. Define the objectives
2. Compose the pilot test team
3. Develop the testing protocol
4. Prepare all systems
5. Model the financial projections
6. Document product definitions and procedures
7. Train relevant staff
8. Develop product marketing plans and materials
9. Commence the pilot test
10. Monitor and evaluate.

This phase provides crucial information that is used to determine product expansion by considering the financial, competitive, methodological, and institutional issues involved with revising the product design (Wright 2010).

Success in the pilot test phase will be defined differently for each provider based on context and stage of institutional growth; once it has been deemed successful, the next step is to launch the product officially and then roll it out broadly. Closely tied to a product launch is a sound marketing plan. Providers must anticipate needs in terms of staff training, incentives, information systems, and infrastructure (see box 15.5).

Product Costing

Product costing analysis allows a financial service provider to assess products that are profitable on a consistent basis versus products that,

---

Box 15.5 The Cost of Failure: Equity Bank's Painful Lesson

Equity Bank in Kenya is a strong proponent of a market-led approach that embraces pilot testing as a core step in developing successful financial products. Its exponential growth in 2003–04 and its transformation from a building society to a bank challenged management to find ways of giving adequate attention to the changes taking place. With the potential of 100,000 customers per year, the bank decided to roll out an apparently straightforward salary-based loan product without testing it. In the words of the CEO James Mwangi, "We thought it would be a quick win."

There was enormous demand for the product. It was easy to administer at low volume, so the bank scaled up, reaching a portfolio of US$3.75 million in only nine months. Then the trouble started. The amount of staff time required to complete an employer assessment and manage relationships daily had been underestimated. Soon one Equity employee was managing a portfolio of 5,000 clients.

Post transformation, it took more than three months for Equity to connect to the central payment system. This caused several months of arrears to pile up quickly as customers' loan payments fell due, but their salaries were yet to be credited. Portfolio at risk greater than 30 days rose (from 7 to 18 percent in three months). Equity Bank quickly reviewed and reengineered the product, identified and mitigated risks, purchased and installed a robust core banking system, and launched a major collections effort. By November 2005 recovery had risen to 90 percent. The key lesson is that pilot testing is absolutely essential to forecast demand and address risks.

Source: Wright 2010.

---

while important to the product mix, are unprofitable. Cross-subsidizing products may allow providers to balance financial sustainability with expanding access to hard-to-reach customer segments.

There are two primary methods for allocating costs: traditional cost allocation and activity-based costing.[5] Traditional cost allocation methods use allocation bases to distribute costs among products, such as direct labor hours or total account balances of a specific financial product. Traditional cost allocation generally relies on volume-related metrics, such as portfolio volume of staff time dedicated to a particular product. This method may overestimate the costs of products with higher volumes and, in general, fails to capture the full and complex picture of specific product costs.

Activity-based costing (ABC) traces the costs of activities before linking them to products. For each major process, a costing team identifies the main activities performed by staff at both the branch and headquarters—for example, processing a loan application or opening a savings account. These particular activities are "used" or "consumed" by different products, depending on specific attributes that drive activity costs (for example, number of housing loan applications received, number of passbook savings accounts opened). A given product consumes many different activities; when these activities are added up, the total cost of delivering the product is revealed (see figure 15.1). An important challenge with ABC is the level of detail required, which may exceed the scope of available information of many financial service providers.

To maximize accuracy and effectiveness, product costing should be conducted at least once a year. While conducting more regular costing exercises may provide insight into seasonality issues, tracking costs over time will provide insight into whether efforts to increase the efficiency of internal operations are effective. In general, providers should complete the identical set of activities as much as possible, each time a costing exercise is undertaken.

Product Pricing

Product pricing is the process through which financial institutions analyze costs, assess competitive trends, and forecast demand in order to set prices for products. Correct pricing is crucial to ensure that adequate revenue is generated to cover the full costs of operations. Providers set prices using a wide variety of metrics and strategies. Prices may be based on each transaction, such as opening a savings account or transferring money, or may include higher up-front fees and unlimited access to services. A product's price should normally reflect the product's complexity and relative value proposition. For example, a savings account that can be accessed on an unlimited basis is more convenient for clients than one that can only be accessed three times a month. However, the cost of offering the unlimited savings account is higher than that of the limited savings product. Thus the fees associated with the unlimited savings account will generally need to be higher and the interest rates paid will likely be lower.

There are three primary methods for pricing products. Under the *cost-based method*, prices are based on the cost of the product plus a particular margin or markup. This method can ensure that all costs are covered, but it may be difficult to link direct and indirect costs to each specific product.

Using the *competition* or *market-based method*, prices are based on the prices charged by competitors and industry comparables.[6] This approach is quite common in markets where service offerings are relatively standard or the number of competitors is limited. Competition-based pricing can be inexpensive, quick, and easy to adjust as conditions in the market change. Pricing based on competitive trends, however, may not fully cover costs, depending on the provider's efficiency. Similarly, given that the market for financial services for

Figure 15.1 Traditional Cost Allocation versus Activity-Based Costing

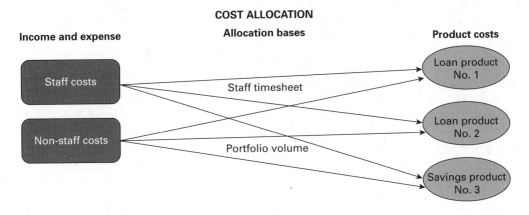

COST ALLOCATION

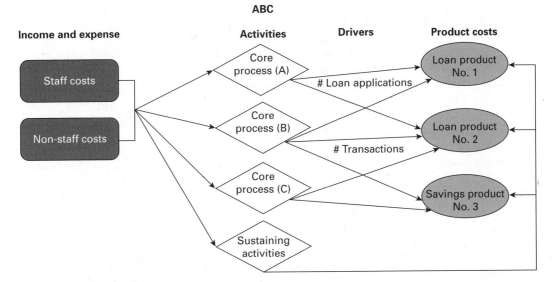

Source: Grace and Helms 2004.

low-income and remote populations often has significant information asymmetries and few providers, it can be difficult to select appropriate competitive benchmarks. In addition, certain providers may receive subsidies from donors and therefore may price their products at prices that are not sustainable. This can lead to substantial distortions in pricing.

Finally, with *demand-based* pricing, prices are determined based on the customers' willingness and capacity to pay. This method sets prices based on the value proposition of the product to the customer. Value is a function of the benefits that come from using a particular product, such as quality, convenience, safety, or commitment features that create discipline to save or repay on time.

Most providers use a combination of all three strategies to price products. For example, an institution can set a price that covers the full cost of delivering a product or service. It can then compare this price with that of competitors and analyze what makes its specific product unique, helping it to understand what clients would be willing to pay and thus to adjust the price based on demand.

Product Marketing

Providers use marketing to inform consumers of the products on offer and to communicate their value and differentiate them from those of their competitors.[7] They typically communicate value to potential customers through the five components known as the marketing communications mix: personal selling, advertising, sales promotions, public relations, and direct marketing. Providers can draw from any or all of these strategies to create a sales strategy that is appropriate for their products, target market, and available resources.

Branding is an important tool for positioning within the marketplace and communicating key value propositions to existing and potential clients. A *brand* represents a collection of information about a product or an institution and typically consists of a name, identifying mark, logo, and distinguishing visual symbol and image (Brand 2006). Financial service providers focus on developing brands that are associated with the provision of quality services that meet the needs of their target clients. They use brands to generate knowledge and awareness of core products in order to expand outreach, build loyalty with existing clients, target new clients, and inform clients of new services.

As discussed in chapter 3, responsible finance in the microfinance industry attempts to ensure consumer protection by developing financial capabilities and ensuring transparent and fair pricing. Institutional providers may also be subject to regulatory review of their marketing practices, requiring full disclosure of all terms and conditions and preventing misleading or dishonest claims about products. Ensuring that clients understand all the conditions and risks of the financial products they are using can safeguard against misleading marketing practices.

Risk Management

In light of the commercialization of microfinance, recent reputation challenges, and rapid diversification of service providers and delivery channels, good governance, risk management, and internal control and audit are essential regardless of whether the provider is a mobile money operator, a participant in the agricultural value chain, a commercial bank, a credit union, an MFI, or a bank.[8] The degree of professionalization and complexity will vary, ranging from very sophisticated, tightly supervised or controlled methods in regulated entities to much less-structured approaches in more informal providers.

Risk is the possibility that current and future events—expected or unanticipated—may have an adverse or harmful impact on an institution's objectives, capital, or earnings. Risk is measured in terms of impact and likelihood. Financial service providers face many risks—both internal and external. Risk is an inherent part of business in general and of the environment and operations, in particular.

Risk management is the systematic process of identifying, assessing, managing, and controlling potential events to provide reasonable assurance of achieving objectives. Risk management includes balancing risk taking against a well-designed control environment. It effectively reduces the likelihood that a loss will occur, minimizes the scale of potential losses should they occur, and adds value by helping the provider meet its objectives. Risk management must be proactively led by a provider's board and senior management through approval of policies, oversight of the internal audit function, and monitoring of management and operations (see table 15.1).

Table 15.1 Roles and Responsibilities for Risk Management

Institutional role	Responsibilities
Board	Approve policies and monitor adherence to them
Senior management	Identify risk and develop policies, procedures, systems, and guidelines to reduce risk
Branch management	Implement procedures and monitor adherence to policies and procedures
Operational staff	Comply with policies, procedures, and risk-mitigating controls. Offer suggestions for and provide feedback on proposed operational changes and new, emerging risks
Internal control staff	Monitor compliance and verify that policies and procedures are followed accordingly
Internal audit	Test and verify that policies and procedures are followed, assure management that risk-mitigating approaches are adequate, and determine the extent to which risks remain uncontrolled

Source: Adapted from Campion 2000.

Risk should also be evaluated in light of the opportunities to create value—financial and social—that risk taking represents. Successful risk taking and a well-managed appetite for risk should be evaluated periodically relative to the rewards and results they bring. This approach implies that the response to risk—whether avoiding, accepting, transferring, or controlling risk—is a careful process that evaluates the trade-offs in developing risk-mitigating strategies. Controlling risks affects costs, efficiencies, and the client experience and must be weighed against the expected benefits.

A common framework presented to understand risk management is the risk management "feedback loop," which incorporates risk management activities throughout an organization. The risk management feedback loop has six key components: (1) identify, assess, and prioritize risk, (2) develop strategies and policies to measure risks, (3) design policies and procedures to mitigate risks, (4) implement and assign responsibilities, (5) test effectiveness and evaluate results and efficiently communicate the findings, and (6) revise policies and procedures as necessary (Campion 2000). Risk management is an ongoing process, as vulnerabilities change over time and improvements to risk mitigation strategies prove effective.

Providers take a variety of approaches to implementing risk management. Many institutions establish a risk department (or officer) or a risk and compliance department (or officer). A risk manager's role is to support the effective and efficient governance of a provider and the implementation of an enterprise-wide risk management strategy. This individual continually monitors and measures the institution's evolving external and internal risks, generally in conjunction with board member(s) or board appointees charged with risk management. Other institutions form a risk management committee composed of senior managers from all operating units and areas. A strong committee will ensure that a risk management strategy is well incorporated into all of the provider's business activities. As the provider grows in size, scale, and complexity, its board may choose to appoint a risk committee or a risk officer. Most small- to medium-size institutions do not have a risk manager and, until one is appointed, the entire role of risk assessment and reporting often falls to the internal audit department, a task that compromises the objectivity and independence of its internal audits.

Neither risk management nor internal auditing should be confused with internal controls; however, the three are interconnected in current best practices and should be well understood and coordinated to maximize their efficiency and effectiveness (see figure 15.2).

The role of an internal auditor is to test and assess independently and objectively the effectiveness of risk management strategies and internal controls. Therefore, the role of an internal audit in the risk assessment process needs to be managed carefully in order to maintain audit independence. Internal auditors may perform an advisory role in the identification and management of risks, but they should not be involved in implementing a provider's risk management policies.

Risks faced by financial service providers generally include credit risk, liquidity risk, market risk (including interest rate risk), operational risk (including fraud, systems, transaction, and error risks), compliance and legal risk, reputational risk, strategic risk, governance risk (including commercial and social mission risks), human resource risk, and insurance and counterparty risk (if relevant).

Although they have limited control over them, organizational managers and directors must also assess the *external risks* to which they are exposed. An institution with relatively strong management and staff and adequate systems and controls may still experience major problems due to the environment in which it operates. These risks include regulation, competition (part of

strategic risk), natural disasters and other physical risks, and political and macroeconomic risks, such as high inflation or devaluation.

Credit, liquidity, and market risks are discussed in chapter 14; the risk and risk management approaches discussed in this chapter focus on operational risks.

Operational Risks and Risk Management

Operational risks are the vulnerabilities that a provider faces in its daily operations—fraud and theft, systems and human errors, portfolio integrity, and security—all of which can undermine its financial and reputational position. Through oversight, effective processes, and risk-mitigating controls, management has some degree of control and influence over operational risks. The core activities in financial service intermediation involve transactions of value through cash, documentation (receipts, vouchers, and negotiable instruments such as checks), accounting entries, and electronic entries or messages that are negotiated or exchanged between customers and staff. Risk mitigation strategies for operations are designed to protect assets, protect information and systems, assure the integrity of transactions, and assure the reliability of financial reporting.

Several inherent risks are related to the entry and processing of transactions in financial services delivery. Transactions may be incomplete, inaccurate, or omitted from processes or records. For example, a loan that is not repaid results in a loss for the provider and potentially a negative credit rating for the borrower. This is a result of incomplete information, inaccurate information, interruption in transaction handling or processing, or the lack of capacity of the client or the provider to complete the transaction.

Another inherent risk in all of these areas is that humans—staff, management, and clients—are ultimately conducting business transactions.

Figure 15.2 Relationship between Risk Management and Internal Control

Source: Campion 2000.

The New Microfinance Handbook

The risk of fraud refers to the potential loss of cash or revenue as a result of intentional deception by an employee or client. Cash theft by loan officers or other staff members is one of the most common incidences of fraud. Others include creating false financial statements or other documents, engaging in bribery, bypassing computer software or application controls, manipulating systems' data input, and recording borrowers or loans that do not exist.

Having an honest, well-qualified, competent, and motivated staff is the best way to manage and control operational risks, as staff members implement control procedures, policies, and processes. Controls are designed to limit the opportunities for staff to make deviant or fraudulent choices in order to take advantage of situations for personal, rather than organizational, gain.

An Internal Control Framework

Internal controls are the integrated set of components and activities to address the risks, challenges, and issues faced by providers in the pursuit of both financial and social objectives. The integrated internal control framework developed by the Committee of Sponsoring Organizations of the Treadway Commission (COSO) is a commonly accepted model of internal control, although other reliable models also exist. The COSO framework defines internal control as follows:

> Internal control is broadly defined as a process, affected by an entity's board of directors, management, and other personnel, designed to provide reasonable assurance regarding the achievement of objectives in the following categories: effectiveness and efficiency of operations; reliability of financial reporting; and compliance with applicable laws and regulations.[9]

Figure 15.3 illustrates an internal control system consisting of five interrelated components

Figure 15.3 Components of Internal Control

Source: http://bibiconsulting.homestead.com/coso_s_internal_control.ppt#260.

that support the achievement of a provider's mission, strategies, and related business objectives.

Control Environment

The control environment is the *overall attitude, awareness,* and *actions* of the board of directors and managers regarding the internal control system and its importance. If top management appears to give just lip service to internal control or to apply double standards and policies for themselves, it is almost certain that the control environment will not be effective for organizational staff.

A strong control environment is generally characterized by the following:

- Involvement of the board of directors and its committees, particularly the audit committee

- Philosophy and operating style of senior management as well as its commitment to competence

- Commitment of senior management and staff to integrity and ethical values

- Organizational structure and the methods used to assign authority and responsibility within this structure

- Design of the control system and control methods, including the internal audit function, by senior management

- Human resource policies and procedures, including segregation of key duties

- Senior management's awareness of and attention to external influences.

Risk Assessment

Periodic risk assessments help to identify, measure, and prioritize risks. A risk assessment exercise generally recommends acceptable risk parameters, risk reporting, and means of monitoring specified risks on a periodic basis. It begins with the first two components of the risk management feedback loop: (1) identify, assess, and prioritize risk and (2) develop strategies and policies to measure risks. Some providers appoint an independent consultant or evaluator to conduct an objective, independent assessment; such an evaluator reports directly to the board. In other providers, the risk management committee or a risk officer is responsible for conducting regular risk assessments.

Prioritizing and measuring risks are perhaps the most challenging parts of the process, in that the assessment considers risk tolerance and risk rewards. It is usually a subjective, evaluative activity that articulates and shapes the institution's response to risk. Numerous tools are used to provide a systematic approach to assessing all aspects of risk, including both quantitative and qualitative measurements. However, most institutions find that risk assessment is an iterative learning process that is strengthened over time if undertaken thoughtfully and objectively. Another common approach to identifying, analyzing, and prioritizing operational risks is through "process mapping."[10]

Risks are usually prioritized through a ranking exercise that categorizes risks as increasing, stable, or decreasing. Increasing risks that have both the potential and likelihood of significant impact are generally considered a priority that should be addressed through risk-mitigating strategies and controls. This process helps to determine the most appropriate and cost-effective approach to determining control activities, since financial service providers must continually focus on operational efficiencies.

Control Activities

Based on the risk assessment, providers can choose to avoid risks (change business processes that have inherent risks), transfer risks (purchase insurance if available), accept risks (and thereby do nothing to manage, mitigate, or eliminate risks), or seek to control risks. A risk-based approach to internal control links specific controls to the provider's objectives. This section describes the most common approaches to control activities and procedures in a financial service provider.

Control procedures are the policies and procedures that guide staff to process transactions, manage assets, and conduct their work. They also enhance and strengthen the consistency and reliability of data and information in the accounting system. Accounting and transaction controls are designed to meet management's objectives of profitability or sustainability, compliance with policies, safeguarding of assets, prevention and detection of fraud and error, accuracy and completeness of accounting records, timely preparation of reliable financial information, discharge of statutory responsibilities, and protection of staff members against disinformation. The integrity of the entire financial and accounting system, including the financial reports, depends on the internal control procedures that assure the integrity and consistent treatment of individual transactions—including their validity, accuracy, timeliness, classification, and authorization.

Control procedures are *preventive* or *prescriptive*, *detective* (the internal audit), and *corrective* in nature. They may include, but are not limited to, any of the following elements:

- *Segregation of duties.* Segregation of duties among different departments and individuals to reduce the risk of inappropriate action and to ensure that no specific individual or entity has a concentrated amount of responsibility that can threaten transparency. Segregation of duties pertains to responsibilities for authorizing and recording transactions and handling related assets including cash.

- *Dual controls.* Dual or triple controls for access or oversight, such as access to cash vaults, system changes, reconciliations, and independent review and verification.

- *Human resource controls.* Rotation of duties, mandatory vacation policy, and authorization of overtime.

- *Signature requirements and approval authorizations.* Requirements for transaction approvals, transaction limits, report reviews, and approvals by a third party, adding a level of transparency to critical activities and functions.

- *Accounting, administrative, reporting, and financial policies and procedures.* Clear, accessible, and current policies and procedures that support the correct and consistent treatment of transactions and operational activities.

- *Budgets and comparative reports.* A means of exercising fiscal control. When actual expenses are reported regularly against budgets, they become an effective management control tool.

- *Limits on cash or expenditures.* Policies designed to safeguard and prevent abuse when using cash, such as authorizing designated personnel to handle cash, including cash limits, and a series of documentation procedures to trace the flow of cash in and out of the provider.

- *Design and use of adequate documents and records.* Prenumbered documents, document registers, multiple copies, sequential and numerical documents, and a chart of accounts that organizes the accounting transactions in the general ledger.

- *Physical control of assets.* Safes and lockboxes where three people are required to access cash to ensure that assets are safeguarded and used appropriately. In addition, having more than one employee transport assets, particularly cash, between branches or from a provider branch or outlet to the client can help to minimize the risk of fraud and theft.

- *Accounting controls.* Daily postings and monthly reconciliations, including full and timely bank reconciliations to inform management and the board of the financial position. Sequential numbering of items such as cash receipt vouchers and checks reduce staff fraud or exposure. All transactions should leave an audit trail to ensure transparency. Portfolio accounts (loans, savings, and other subsidiary accounts) should be reconciled regularly to ensure that discrepancies are found quickly.

- *Information technology (IT) general controls.* Commonly understood as "standards" in IT management control. These controls are intended to ensure the appropriate development and implementation of applications as well as the integrity of programs, data files, and computer operations generally. The most common IT general controls are logical access controls over infrastructure, applications, and data, system development life-cycle controls, program change management controls, physical security controls over the data center (including climate controls and electricity supply and control), system and data backup and recovery controls, computer operation controls, password security controls for varying levels of access, use, and application, and system protection, such as antivirus, registration, and updates of licenses, firewall, and version-configuration compatibility (see box 15.6).[11]

Monitoring

Internal control is a continuous process whereby the board or management committee and senior management monitor the (a) efficiency and effectiveness of activities; (b) reliability, completeness, and timeliness of financial and management information; and (c) compliance with applicable laws and regulations. Internal control structures facilitate the constant flow of information critical to the monitoring and mitigation of all business risks and vary depending on the type and size of the provider and regulatory requirements (if applicable).[12] Formal financial institutions, such as commercial banks, often structure the internal control function according to central bank guidelines and must have their internal control structure approved and monitored by the regulatory body. Nonregulated

and informal providers have self-governed internal control and monitoring functions.

Part of the management function involves *supervision and monitoring* on a day-to-day basis. Through segregation of duties and independent checks and verification, an element of ongoing monitoring takes place in everyday operations of a financial service provider. Budgets and comparative reporting are also a regular means of monitoring operations. Perhaps the strongest and most effective monitoring in the internal control process takes place through the internal audit function (discussed below).

Information and Communications

The information and communications component of an internal control system is not a standalone component. It intersects, interacts with, and is part of each of the other four elements just discussed. Staff and management must be fully informed and aware of the policies and procedures of the provider. Policies that are not available to staff cannot be implemented. Business

---

Box 15.6 IT Disaster Recovery and Business Continuity Management

The more an institution relies on information technology, the more important are the development, testing, and comprehensiveness of an IT disaster recovery and business continuity plan. However, all institutions should develop a plan, regardless of their size or dependence on technology.

A very basic, simplistic approach includes the following:

- Regular documented system of backups—whether twice a day, daily, or weekly (not recommended)
- A revolving backup system, where several days' data are maintained
- Off-site storage of backup data
- Occasional testing of backup restoration and an efficient time period for recovery (ideally within one to two days)
- Plans for alternate or remote work locations and equipment.

Source: Ruth Dueck-Mbeba.

strategies and objectives must be communicated throughout all channels in the provider as well. Without information and communication, providers cannot prioritize risks, detect fraud, comply with legal and statutory requirements, monitor performance with regard to budget, or make data-driven, informed decisions about performance and operations.

Communication channels between staff, management, and internal audit must also be a continuous, efficient means of ensuring the effective implementation of internal controls. The reports and results of internal audits, monitoring activities, external evaluations, and assessments should be shared in a timely manner to address risks and concerns early. Regular meetings between supervisors and individuals or work teams, meetings of the management team, and an "open door policy" should help to foster a culture of open and honest communication.

Limitations of Internal Controls

Internal controls are developed and used by management to support them in achieving objectives. However, controls can only be implemented as far as is practical. The following limitations to internal controls must be considered in the design process:

- *Cost versus benefit.* The cost of implementing a control must be evaluated relative to the probability of the risk of loss and the size of loss. Most benefits are difficult to determine since institutions are dealing in loss probabilities.

- *Abnormalities.* Controls are typically directed toward normal, everyday transactions; abnormal and unusual transactions are generally not covered primarily because of cost-benefit issues.

- *Human error.* This factor is always present to some degree, as humans are prone to error and impaired judgment.

- *Staff turnover.* Staff who have worked in an area for some time are normally more efficient than new staff; rapid turnover or growth of staff may diminish the effectiveness of controls.

- *Workload volume.* Compliance with policies and procedures may become weak when workloads are large, given competing priorities for attention and effort.

- *Collusion.* If a control depends on the segregation of duties, internal controls can easily be circumvented when two or more of those responsible decide to defraud the institution.

- *Staff irresponsibility.* Persons responsible for a control may also neglect or abuse that responsibility; this limitation normally arises when employees are not satisfied or are bored with their jobs.

Internal Audit

The Institute of Internal Auditors defines internal auditing as "independent, objective assurance and consulting activity designed to add value and improve an organization's operations. It helps an organization accomplish its objectives by bringing a systematic, disciplined approach to evaluate and improve the effectiveness of risk management control and governance processes."[13]

The internal auditor is independent of other business processes, reports to the board of directors (usually the audit committee), and focuses on *detective controls*—testing for compliance with policies, procedures, and controls, the reliability of financial reports, the effectiveness of risk management strategies, and the presence of previously unidentified risks.

Ideally, the board will appoint an audit committee that operates as a subcommittee of the board with a specific mandate to oversee the internal and external audit functions. The audit committee is preferably composed of a qualified accountant or auditor, a treasurer (if the board has such a position), and perhaps another individual well versed in accounting and auditing matters. The audit committee reports to the board. A direct reporting line to the audit committee establishes the internal auditor's independence and objectivity, although he or she retains an indirect line to senior management for coordination of work and communication.

Large, formal financial intermediaries normally have an audit department, staffed by a senior, experienced professional (see box 15.7). Small or informal providers may not have a dedicated audit function, in which case the task can be outsourced to an external consultant or audit firm that does not have responsibility for the external audit. In larger, more formal institutions, the audit function is based on an annual audit plan that is reviewed and approved by the board or its audit committee. A typical audit plan entails audits of all headquarter departments, including IT systems, human resources, and of branches at regular intervals (usually ranging from once a quarter to once a year). Its scope may also expand to risk and governance functions. An audit manual, outlining policies and procedures, guides the audit function. While most departmental audits can be carried out by the internal auditor, specialized skills are sometimes required for audits of more advanced systems, and an external specialist may be hired.

Branch audits often form the core task of the audit function, regardless of the size of the provider. Key areas of branch audits include cash, loans, provisions, write-offs, savings, transfers, IT systems, fixed assets, and financial and operational reporting. Audit officers

---

Box 15.7 Audits Performed by the Internal Audit Department

The internal audit department or function performs various types of audits:

- Financial audits assess the reliability of the accounting system, data, and financial reports.
- Compliance audits assess the quality and appropriateness of the system established to ensure compliance with relevant laws, regulations, policies, and procedures.
- Operational audits assess the quality and appropriateness of operational systems and procedures, analyze the institution's organizational structures with a critical mind, and evaluate the adequacy of operational methods and resources.
- Management audits assess the quality of the approach of managers to risk and control within the framework of organizational objectives.
- Reviews evaluate the means of safeguarding assets and, as appropriate, verify the existence of assets.
- Evaluations of internal control systems assess the deterrence and detection of fraud and alertness to indications of fraud.
- Periodic audits of computer systems and post-installation evaluations determine whether major data-processing systems meet their intended purposes and are capable of fulfilling their objectives.
- Special reviews are conducted at the request of the CEO or the board (for example, fraud investigations, efficiency reviews, risks related to new branch openings, new products, or delivery channels).

Source: http://www.seepnetwork.org/filebin/pdf/resources/Board_Audit_Guide_2010_final.pdf.

typically also visit randomly selected clients to verify credit files. The results of audit findings and analysis are documented in audit reports and include management response to the recommendations submitted to the board of directors or audit committee.

While primarily relevant for institutional providers, internal audits do exist in the informal sector. For example, Savings Groups employ a regular audit function called an "action audit." Action audits require the group to distribute all of the group's savings and earnings from interest and fees periodically to the members. The audit is usually timed to occur during an important time of year when members require larger lump sums, such as the start of the agricultural planting season or the school year. At the end of the action audit (or "share-out"), groups normally reconstitute and begin the savings and loan process again, but with "clean books."

An increasing number of financial service providers are now integrating checks on social performance metrics into their internal audit function to ensure compliance with the social mission.[14]

External Audit

An external audit is a formal, independent review of a provider's financial records, transactions, and operations, performed by professional accountants. The objective of an external audit is to express an opinion on the fairness and reliability of the financial statements of the provider's position and results. External audits also establish the credibility of financial statements and other management reports. Through an objective review and analysis of an institution's operations and performance, external audits assure that the provider is reporting reliable information internally (to staff and the board) as well as externally (to donors, investors, or regulators). External audits usually occur annually, following the fiscal year end.

For many financial service providers, the *financial statement audit* is the most common type of external audit. It includes an assessment

of the provider's balance sheet (or statement of financial position), income (profit and loss) statement, cash flow statement (or statement of changes in financial position or cash flow), and statement of changes in equity. Financial service providers generally undergo an external audit because managers, donors, investors (if applicable), and the board want assurance that the statements fairly reflect the state of operations. Normally, regulators require an audit of financial statements; licensed financial intermediaries may also be required to publish audited financial statements. Most countries require providers licensed as NGOs to produce audited financial statements.

External financial audits assess whether information in the financial records is congruent with the accounting standards adhered to—generally accepted principles or International Accounting Standards and International Financial Reporting Standards. The accounting principles of financial service providers are tested to ensure that financial statements are free of *material misstatement*—claims or misrepresentations of the financial information that are substantive enough to affect decision making. Audits are governed by auditing standards developed under the International Accounting Standards. Based on the results of the audit, external auditors provide an *audit opinion* on the financial statements. The audit opinion can be *unqualified* (clean), *qualified,* or *adverse.*

External audits are an important component of the control environment and risk management. External auditors make assessments and observations about internal control and the procedures and policies that are designed to mitigate risks through the management letter. However, the role of the external audit is not to identify fraud or risks. That responsibility lies squarely with management.

The work of the external audit—from the development of terms of reference, request for proposals, selection of auditors, agreement of the scope of work and terms of contract, supervision of the work, and receipt of the auditor's management letter—is the responsibility of the board or its designated members, such as the audit committee. Financial service providers draw on a range of other audit services as necessary, including special-purpose audits, operational audits, agreed-upon procedures, and reviews and compilations.[15]

As financial services and providers diversify, particularly with technological innovations and the possibilities they bring, the nature of operational risks will no doubt evolve as well. Practitioners and support professionals in the fields of risk, control, audit, IT, and management disciplines in governance, change management, human resources, and organizational development will need to maintain relevance and deepen capacity to meet the changes and the challenges that those changes will bring to financial services for the poor.

Notes

1. This section draws on Ledgerwood and White (2006); http://microfinance.cgap.org/2010/10/14/getting-back-to-governance/.

2. This section draws on Churchill, Hirschland, and Painter (2002).

3. This section draws on Wright (2010) and Frankiewicz and Churchill (2011).

4. Chapter 5 provides an overview of research methods with a focus on understanding consumer needs and behavior and the financial sector as a whole. Here the term "market research" is used to describe research conducted by financial service providers directly to develop new or modify existing products, to understand clients, to understand their financial service needs and their perceptions of the provider and its services or products, to analyze problems such as an increase in loan defaults or a decrease in market share, to develop and monitor customer service strategies, or to analyze the depth of outreach.

5. This section draws on Grace and Helms (2004).

6. Using this method, pricing is not necessarily set directly by mimicking the competition. Rather, prices are set after conducting a detailed investigation of the pricing structures and charges of major competitors (Frankiewicz, Wright, and Cracknell 2004).

7. This section draws on Frankiewicz and Churchill (2011).

8. This section was contributed by Ruth Dueck-Mbeba.

9. http://www.cpa2biz.com/AST/Main/CPA2BIZ_Primary/InternalControls/COSO/PRDOVR-PC-990009/PC-990009.jsp.

10. See www.MicroSave.org for tools to support process mapping to document work flows, identify risks in those work processes, and suggest ways in which to manage those risks while retaining efficiencies.

11. Adapted from Bellino et al. (2007, 2).

12. This definition is based on guidelines outlined by the Basel Committee on Banking Supervision, which is a group of supervisory authorities established by the central bank governors of the G-10 that developed a framework for evaluating financial institutions' internal control systems. http://www.bis.org/publ/bcbs40.pdf; BCBS (1998).

13. The definition is from https://na.theiia.org/standards-guidance/mandatory-guidance/Pages/Definition-of-Internal-Auditing.aspx.

14. http://spmresourcecentre.net/iprc/assets/File/internal_control_guidance_note.pdf; Ekka (2012).

15. For more information on external audits in the microfinance industry, see CGAP (1998).

References and Further Reading

*Key works for further reading.

*BCBS (Basel Committee on Banking Supervision). 1998. "Framework for Internal Control Systems in Banking Organisations." BCBS, Basel. http://www.bis.org/publ/bcbs40.pdf.

*Bellino, Christine, Jefferson Wells, Steve Hunt, and Crowe Horwath. 2007. "Auditing

Application Controls." Global Technology Audit Guide. IIA, Altamonte Springs, FL.

*Brand, Monica. 2006. "Marketing and Competitive Positioning." In *Transforming Microfinance Institutions: Providing Full Financial Services to the Poor,* ed. Joanna Ledgerwood and Victoria White, 95–129. Washington, DC: World Bank.

Brand, Monica, et al. 2009. *Product Development for Microfinance Institutions*. Course manual. Washington, DC: CGAP.

*Burge, Jennifer F. 2008. "Embedding Enterprise Risk Management into the Internal Audit Process." IIA, Altamonte Springs, FL.

*Campion, Anita. 2000. "Improving Internal Control: A Practical Guide for Microfinance Institutions." MicroFinance Network and GTZ, Washington, DC, and Frankfurt.

*CGAP (Consultative Group to Assist the Poor). 1998. *External Audits of Microfinance Institutions: A Handbook*. Technical Tool Series 3. Washington: CGAP.

Churchill, Craig, Madeline Hirschland, and Judith Painter. 2002. *New Directions in Poverty Finance: Village Banking Revisited*. Washington, DC: SEEP Network.

Cohen. n.d. "Listening to Clients: How to Better Serve Your Customers." MicroSave and Microfinance Opportunities, Washington, DC. http://microfinanceopportunities.org/docs/ Listening_to_Clients_How_to_Better_Serve_ Your_Customers.pdf.

COSO (Committee of Sponsoring Organizations of the Treadway Commission). 1992. "The Internal Control: Integrated Framework." COSO, Chicago.

———. 2004. "FAQs for COSO's Enterprise Risk Management: Integrated Framework." COSO, Chicago. http://www.coso.org/ erm-faqs.htm.

*Council of Microfinance Equity Funds. 2005. "The Practice of Corporate Governance in Shareholder-Owned MFIs." Consensus statement, Council of Microfinance Equity Funds, Boston.

Ekka, Rashmi. 2012. "Internal Control and Audit: Integrating SPM into Microfinance Capacity Building." Guidance Note, Imp-Act Consortium, Washington, DC.

Ekka, Rashmi, and EDA Rural Systems. 2011. "Risk Management: Integrating SPM into Microfinance Capacity Building." Guidance Note, Imp-Act Consortium, Washington, DC. http://spmresourcecentre.net/iprc/assets/File/ internal_control_guidance_note.pdf.

*Frankiewicz, Cheryl, and Craig Churchill. 2006. *Making Microfinance Work: Managing for Improved Performance*. Geneva: ILO.

*———. 2011. *Making Microfinance Work: Managing Product Diversification*. Geneva: ILO.

*Frankiewicz, Cheryl, Graham Wright, and David Cracknell. 2004. *Product Marketing Toolkit*. Nairobi: MicroSave. http://www.microsave.org/ toolkit/product-marketing-toolkit.

Grace, Lorna, and Brigit Helms. 2004. "Microfinance Product Costing Tool." Technical Tools Series 6, CGAP, Washington, DC.

Grameen Bank. 2012. "Grameen Bank: Introduction." Grameen Bank, Dhaka. http:// www.grameen-info.org/index.php?option= com_content&task=view&id=26&Itemid=0.

IIA (Institute of Internal Auditors). Various years. "Tone at the Top," no. 18 (June 2003); no. 28 (November 2005); no. 30 (March 2006). IIA, Altamonte Springs, FL.

———. 2008. "GAIT for Business and IT Risk." IIA, Altamonte Springs, FL.

———. 2009a. "Adding Value to the Organization: Questions and Answer Recommendations." IIA, Altamonte Springs, FL.

———. 2009b. "Audit Committees and Boards of Directors." IIA, Altamonte Springs, FL.

———. 2009c. "Fraud Prevention and Detection in an Automated World." Global Technology Audit Guide, IIA, Altamonte Springs, FL.

———. 2010. "International Standards for the Professional Practice of Internal Auditing." IIA, Altamonte Springs, FL.

*Ledgerwood, Joanna, and Victoria White. 2006. *Transforming Microfinance Institutions:*

Providing Full Financial Services to the Poor. Washington, DC: World Bank.

*Pityn, Kim, and Jennifer Helmuth. 2007. "Human Resource Management: Toolkit." MicroSave.

*Rutherford, Stuart. 2004. "What Is Grameen II? Is It Up and Running in the Field Yet?" Grameen II Briefing Note 1, MicroSave. http://www.microsave.org/briefing_notes/grameen-ii-1-what-is-grameen-ii-is-it-up-and-running-in-the-field-yet.

*SEEP (Small Enterprise Education and Promotion) Network, and Jeane Wehlau. 2010. "Microfinance Internal Audit Toolkit and Resources." Financial Services Working Group, SEEP Network, Washington, DC.

*Wright, Graham A. N. 2010. "Designing Savings and Loan Products." Report, MicroSave, Nairobi. http://www.microsave.org/research_paper/designing-savings-and-loan-products-0.

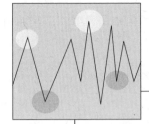

PART V

SUPPORTING FINANCIAL INCLUSION

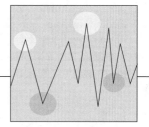

CHAPTER 16

Funding

Julie Earne and Lisa Sherk

This chapter examines the role of funding, the various types of funders, and the funding tools available for providers within the core market system. This content will be most useful to microfinance providers and investors. Chapter 4 addresses the role of funding for support functions in the market system in greater detail.

Funders are largely differentiated by their roles and purpose, which reflect in part their own source of funding as well as the tools they use. In the early days of microfinance, funding generally came from philanthropic or development-focused donors such as foundations, bi-lateral and multilateral agencies, and development finance institutions. As the industry has developed and grown, the types of funders have expanded significantly to include private sector institutional investors, commercial banks (both local and international), private equity funds, and individuals.

The commercialization and professionalization of the microfinance industry has attracted increasing and varied investors and has also allowed various providers to serve more clients in diverse areas with a variety of products. The proliferation of microfinance investment intermediaries demonstrates the view that financial service providers (FSPs) can be good and profitable investments while still satisfying double-bottom-line agendas. More recently the emergence of "impact investing" has brought funders actively seeking investments that explicitly include a social development goal.

While there is a range of funder types, there is also a range of *funding tools,* including grants, various types of debt, guarantees, and equity. Member deposits and fees have, historically, funded the operations of savings-based cooperatives small and large. Nongovernmental organization microfinance institutions (NGO MFIs) for the most part have relied on grants for operations and loan fund capital until achieving financial sustainability, at which point many access loans from international and/or local lenders to expand their operations. Deposits and other forms of debt, equity, and retained earnings are the main sources of funding for more formal regulated providers. Public listings of financial service providers and keen involvement from profit-oriented investors in the sector have expanded funding sources to include capital markets.

Given the increasing complexity of funding in microfinance and the entrance of many new actors and terms, a glossary of funding terms is provided in box 16.1.

Box 16.1 Glossary of Funding Terms

Bond: A bond is tradable debt security, in which the "issuer" (borrower) owes the "holders" (creditors) a debt and, depending on the terms of the bond, is obliged to pay periodic interest (a coupon) for the life of the bond and repay the principal on the maturity date. A bond is a formal contract to repay borrowed money and differs from a loan principally in that it can be easily traded or transferred from one holder to another whereas a loan is a contract between two specific parties: the borrower and the lender.

Capital: In general, capital represents all the accumulated assets—including cash, accounts receivable, and fixed assets—of a company. Sometimes, however, the term capital is used synonymously with equity, representing the accumulated wealth of a business, represented by its assets less its liabilities (as in tier 1 capital or tier 2 capital). It is important to know the context in which the term is being used to determine which sense is being used.

Capital markets: A capital market is a market for securities (debt or equity), where companies and governments can raise long-term funds. It is defined as a market in which money is provided for periods longer than a year. The capital market includes the stock market (equity securities) and the bond market (debt).

Convertible debt: Convertible debt is a type of bond that the holder can convert into shares of common stock in the issuing company or cash of equal value, at an agreed-upon price. It is a hybrid security with debt- and equity-like features. Although it typically has a coupon rate lower than that of similar, nonconvertible debt, the instrument carries additional value through the option to convert the bond to stock, and thereby participate in further growth in the company's equity value.

Correlation: Correlation is the degree to which two or more measurable items show a tendency to differ at the same time. In financial markets, it is usually used to describe how the returns of two or more different investments move together (or not). A correlation between two investments means that the two investments always move in the same direction, and a correlation of −1 means that they always move in the opposite direction.

Covenants: Covenants are contractual agreements in debt (loan or bond) agreements requiring or forbidding certain actions of the debtor. Positive covenants require actions, whereas negative covenants forbid them. In microfinance loan agreements, there are often covenants related, for example, to the level of a provider's portfolio quality, profitability, or capital adequacy that must be maintained by the borrower over the life of the loan. The exact terms of a covenant must be written in the loan agreement/bond indenture. If the terms of a covenant are not met, then the debt holder may declare the borrower/issuer in default and require repayment of the loan/bond.

(continued next page)

Box 16.1 *(continued)*

Currency swap: A currency swap is an agreement between two parties to exchange cash flows in two different currencies over a predefined period of time, in order not to take on the risk of fluctuations in the other currency.

Diversification: In finance, diversification means reducing risk by investing in a variety of assets. If the asset values do not move up and down at the same time, a diversified portfolio will have less risk than the weighted average risk of its constituent assets, and often less risk than the least risky of its constituents. Therefore, any risk-averse investor will diversify to at least some extent, with more risk-averse investors diversifying more completely than less risk-averse investors.

Equity: Equity is equal to a company's assets after all outstanding liabilities have been paid (or assumed to be paid). In a for-profit company, it also represents the ownership of the company: Shareholders' equity (or stockholders' equity, shareholders' funds, shareholders' capital, or similar terms) represents the remaining interest in assets of a company, spread among individual shareholders of common or preferred stock. Shareholders are the most junior class of investors in assets and can be paid only after liabilities are satisfied.

First-loss tranche: A first-loss tranche is a high-risk investment that accepts first loss of principal in a portfolio of assets, represented as a percentage of the total portfolio. For example, an investor that has a first-loss tranche equal to 5 percent of a portfolio of US$100 million in assets will lose all principal if there are loan defaults, or other losses (due, for instance to currency depreciation) in excess of US$5 million.

Hedging: A hedge is an investment position intended to offset potential losses that may be incurred by an associated investment. For example, if a European investor makes a loan in Mexican pesos to a Mexican FSP, it may hedge movements on the euro versus the Mexican peso in order not to incur exchange rate losses if the peso devalues against the euro.

Institutional investor: An institutional investor is an investor, such as a bank, insurance company, or retirement fund, that is financially sophisticated and makes large investments, often held in very large portfolios of investments.

Liquidity: The degree to which an asset or security can be bought or sold in the market without affecting the asset's price. Liquidity is characterized by a high level of trading activity. Assets that can be easily bought or sold are known as liquid assets.

Mezzanine: Mezzanine refers to a subordinated debt investment that is senior only to that of the common shares.

Private placement: Private placement means direct sale of securities to a small number of investors that meet certain eligibility criteria.

Retail investors: Retail investors are individual investors, members of the general public, who buy and sell assets for their personal account, and not for another company or organization.

Secondary market: Secondary market refers to the market for any existing financial asset to be bought and sold. A secondary market can be a formal exchange, such as a stock exchange, or an informal one (often called "over the counter") where buyers and sellers negotiate directly on the terms of any transaction. If an active secondary market exists, then investors may buy or sell their assets easily.

Securitization: Securitization is the financial practice of combining various types of

(continued next page)

Box 16.1 *(continued)*

debt investments and selling bonds to investors that are repaid by the proceeds from these debt investments.

Senior debt: Senior debt is debt that takes priority over other debt owed by a borrower. Senior debt has greater seniority in the borrower's capital structure than subordinated debt. In the event the borrower goes bankrupt, senior debt theoretically must be repaid before other creditors receive any payment.

Structured products: Structured products are investment structures that combine a portfolio of assets that are funded by notes of various risk tranches, usually to different types of investors with different risk/return appetites.

Subordinated debt: Subordinated debt is debt that ranks after other debts should a company become bankrupt. Such debt is referred to as subordinate, because the debt providers (the lenders) have lower status in relationship to the normal, senior debt. Because subordinated debt is repayable after other debts have been paid, they are more risky for the lender of the money.

The Role of Funding

Funding is required by all financial service providers to finance expanded outreach, to develop new products and channels, or to move into new regions and market segments. The majority of direct funding to microfinance is to support portfolio growth,[1] although this may vary depending on the stage of development of the provider being financed. For a greenfield or early stage institution, a greater proportion of funding—typically equity and grants—will be required for start-up costs, infrastructure, and capacity building, versus portfolio funding for a more mature institution already able to generate sufficient income to cover its costs.

The type of provider a specific funder will support depends particularly on their return expectations, mandate, and the importance of social vis-à-vis financial return. Patient capital from double-bottom-line investors with longer investment horizons provides investees the time they need to grow through a start-up phase or transformation and become profitable. Other funders may have liquidity and/or return requirements

and will be more interested to fund more mature, developed institutions.

Different types of funding support different objectives. Debt financing is typically extended to fund portfolio growth or refinance maturing debt. Equity is often used as a foundation to support regulatory requirements and to secure other types of financing by acting as a financial cushion that provides greater comfort for lenders to provide debt. Increasingly the type and structure of funding available is designed with the needs of the actual microfinance client in mind. Innovations in structured finance allow investors with different risk and return appetites to participate in the same funding vehicle with some investors taking "first loss" while others have a more secured position. This helps to increase the term and amount of funding available, which in turn facilitates different products such as longer term leasing and housing credit. Local currency debt allows a provider to borrow in the same currency it uses to serve its clients.

Investments that require a return generally instill greater discipline and accountability for the investee. Here, in a very tangible form, debates on subsidy and sustainability come to a head. Although subsidies aligned with investment can support frontier projects and organizations initially unattractive to the private sector, such subsidies should also result in a public good beyond the specific company, such as new institutions or products coming to market facilitating greater access.

Types of Funders

A wide variety of funders support financial service providers. Important distinctions to note when discussing the types of funders include the difference between funders and intermediaries, public and private funders, and cross-border and local funders.

Funders allocate or provide funds directly to financial service providers, and *intermediaries* receive funds from various sources and then invest them in individual providers. The distinction between these two groups is not always completely clear: Banks, for example, intermediate (on-lend) funds they receive as deposits and are therefore usually considered "intermediaries." For the purposes of this chapter, however, banks are included as "funders," because it is the bank's board or management that has made the decision to allocate funds to microfinance (in whole or in part).

Intermediaries include microfinance investment vehicles, microfinance holding companies, local apex organizations, and peer-to-peer aggregators. Intermediaries are themselves funded by both public and private investors.

Public funders include (1) bilateral agencies, (2) multilateral agencies, (3) development finance institutions (DFIs), and (4) local governmental agencies. Private funders include (1) foundations, (2) NGOs, (3) private institutional investors, and (4) private individual investors, both retail (the general public) and high-net worth individuals (see table 16.1).

Cross-border funders are foreign funders that allocate or invest funds in other countries, whereas local funders allocate or invest funds within their own country. The primary sources of funding in local markets are deposits, local banks, and capital markets. Cross-border financing is increasing and reached US$24 billion in commitments as of December 2010, with about 70 percent from public funders and 30 percent from private funders (CGAP 2011).

The 20 largest microfinance funders provided approximately US$15 billion in funding in 2010 and include 10 DFIs, 5 multilateral agencies, 3 bilateral agencies, 1 institutional investor, and 1 foundation. The top five largest funders include KfW with 18 percent of overall funds invested, followed by the World Bank with 11 percent, the Asian Development Bank with 11 percent, IFC at 9 percent, and EBRD 7 percent (CGAP 2011).

Although the amount a funder commits to microfinance is one indication of its role in the sector, a funder's effectiveness depends on its staff capacity, local presence, and relationship to its partners, including governments, cofinanciers, and clients. Many of the largest cross-border funders have a presence in many countries and increasingly a decentralized operating model.

Despite this, in many markets, particularly those in Sub-Saharan Africa, deposits are the largest source of funding for most providers (CGAP 2012). Figure 16.1 provides the funding proportions by funder type and whether funding was direct or through intermediaries. Note that financing from local sources—deposits, local banks, and capital markets—is not included in this graphic.

Motives and return expectations vary considerably by funder type, from public good to pure profit and many combinations in between. Although private investors make up a smaller percentage of microfinance funding than public funders, the amount of private funding is growing more quickly. This growth is predominantly driven by large foundations and institutional

Table 16.1 Public and Private Funders

Public funders	Bilateral agencies	Multilateral agencies	DFIs
Examples	Canadian International Development Agency (CIDA), Gesellschaft für Internationale Zusammenarbeit (GTZ), Swedish International Development Cooperation Agency (SIDA), Swiss Development Corporation (SDC), U.K. Department for International Development (DFID), U.S. Agency for International Development (USAID)	African Development Bank (AfDB), Asian Development Bank (ADB), European Commission (EC), International Bank for Reconstruction and Development (IBRD of the World Bank), International Fund for Agricultural Development (IFAD), United Nations Capital Development Fund (UNCDF)	Agencia Española de Cooperación Internacional para el Desarrollo (AECID), Belgian Investment Company for Developing Countries (BIO), Corporación Andina de Fomento (CAF), Dutch Development Agency (FMO), European Bank for Reconstruction and Development (EBRD), European Investment Bank (EIB), Inter-American Investment Corporation (IIC), International Finance Corporation (IFC), KfW Entwicklungsbank (KfW), Multilateral Investment Fund (MIF IADB)
Tools used	Grants, guarantees	Grants, guarantees, debt, equity	Debt, equity, guarantees, grants

Private funders	Foundations	NGOs	Institutional investors	Individuals
Examples	Bill & Melinda Gates Foundation, Ford Foundation, Grameen Foundation, Grameen Jameel, MasterCard Foundation, Michael & Susan Dell Foundation	ACCION, ACP, FINCA, Opportunity International, SEPAR	Pension funds, insurance companies, private equity firms, commercial banks	High-net-worth individuals, retail investors, individual donors
Tools used	Grants, debt, equity	Grants, debt, equity	Debt, equity	Debt, equity, donations, deposits

Note: DFI = development finance institution; NGO = nongovernmental organization.

investors, two groups with often different motivations. Where foundations often provide funding, primarily grants, to achieve development goals, individuals and institutional investors invest for both social and financial reasons and usually look for a financial return.

The motivations of funders are increasingly focused on scale, commercialization, and broad-based financial inclusion. As discussed in chapter 4, public funders tend to focus on the facilitation of market development, providing an example to private investors with the aim of "crowding in" or attracting private investors to underinvested markets. Private funders are more split, with foundations focusing more on market development and investors targeting a double bottom line where financial returns are balanced with objectives to improve financial access and impact.

Some funders specify what funding may be used for. This is often detailed explicitly in the case of grant funding. For debt financing, the use of proceeds is often not stipulated, although in some cases lenders may require that funds be used only to fund a specific product (for example, agricultural loans or loans below a certain size) or target market (for example, women or clients in rural areas).

Figure 16.1 Sources of Microfinance Funding

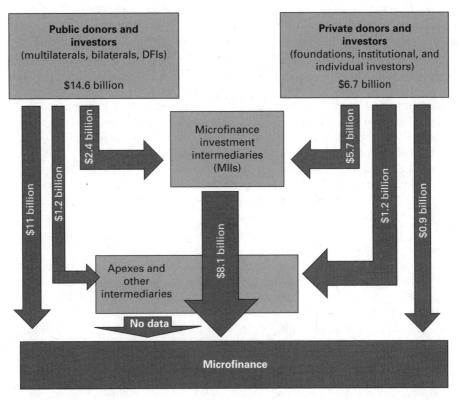

Source: Adapted from El-Zoghbi et al. 2011.
Note: DFI = development finance institution. In line with CGAP's definition, apex institutions are intentionally separated from micro-finance investment intermediaries because they tend to be funded publically and are generally local intermediaries only.

Public Funders

Public funders provide funding to achieve development goals and have clear social objectives underlying their activities. They are funded from national budgets in the case of bilateral agencies such as USAID or SIDA, and from country contributions in the case of multilateral agencies, including the World Bank or United Nations. Development finance institutions (such as the German development bank KfW, FMO in the Netherlands, or IFC, the private sector arm of the World Bank Group) are funded by a combination of initial country shareholder contributions and retained earnings, and they also often issue bonds on capital markets. Ultimately these institutions are accountable to the public at large and seek a double-bottom-line return. Public funders are therefore active through a variety of different tools, including grants, guarantees, debt, and equity. Public funders generally provide support where the private sector cannot or will not participate, to help create conditions that will ultimately encourage private sector involvement.

Bilateral and Multilateral Agencies

Bilateral development agencies are country-specific government agencies that work directly with governments in developing countries and other organizations. Bilateral strategies are often linked to foreign policy initiatives of the donor country. Funding from bilateral agencies is frequently directed to developing markets through either supporting individual financial service providers or funding the development of supporting service markets. If not provided directly to the government, bilateral funding is given to local or international NGOs to support capacity development. Because of their strong credit standing, bilateral agencies are also well placed to provide guarantees for providers to issue debt purchased by private sector participants.

Multilateral and UN agencies provide financial support (grants, guarantees, and debt)[2] and professional advice for economic and social development activities in developing countries. The term multilateral development bank (MDB) typically refers to the International Bank for Reconstruction and Development (IBRD, commonly referred to as the World Bank, the public sector arm of the World Bank Group) and other regional development banks such as the African and Asian Development Banks. These banks are characterized by broad ownership, including both governments of developing countries and governments of developed countries. Most multilateral funding organizations are organized to interact with a target country's government,[3] and funds are largely provided as loans to governments. Governments then use the funds to on-lend to various provider types and to support capacity-building initiatives of providers or to support market infrastructure and policy development (El-Zoghbi et al. 2011). Given MDBs' extensive relationships with governments, they are well placed to influence policy makers. In 2011 the top five multilateral funders of microfinance were the IBRD, the Asian Development Bank (ADB), the International Fund for Agricultural Development

(IFAD), the European Commission (EC), and the African Development Bank (AfDB) (CGAP 2011).

Development Finance Institutions

Development finance institutions (DFIs) differ from MDBs in that they largely focus on the private sector. DFIs invest funds both directly in financial service providers and increasingly through intermediaries such as investment funds or holding companies (discussed below). Some of the primary DFIs investing in microfinance include KfW, the European Bank for Reconstruction and Development (EBRD), the International Finance Corporation (IFC, the private sector arm of the World Bank Group), and FMO (the Dutch development bank).

As quasi-government, DFIs are double-bottom-line investors and, as such, have dual objectives of profitability and development impact. DFIs generally allocate resources to projects and companies that may not initially be appealing to the private sector. Many DFIs attempt to crowd in the private sector by investing in frontier projects, demonstrating that these providers are investable, and exiting once greater confidence in a given market is built. However, in economies where there is a vibrant or emerging private investment sector, DFIs must be careful not to crowd out the private sector by providing more lenient terms or unnecessarily subsidizing well-performing institutions. In particular, the choice of countries and funding tools as well as the timing of a DFI's exit from its investments is key to ensure effective development of financial markets.

Private Funders

Most private funders in the financial service market are driven by both social and profit motives. Impact investment, double-bottom-line investment, triple-bottom-line investment, or sustainable investment is defined as investment in businesses or funds that intentionally set out to generate social or environmental good alongside financial returns. It has been driven by various factors including the recognition that government and charities alone do not have sufficient capital to solve the world's social and environmental problems, the corporate social responsibility (CSR) considerations of private companies, and in some cases interest in a risk profile that is seen to provide greater social and financial rewards (Reille et al. 2011). These return expectations are becoming increasingly interwoven in terms of both the investment tools used and the metrics used for defining success.

Foundations

Foundations are endowed with capital from (generally) private sources, often from very successful multinational corporations such as Microsoft (the Bill & Melinda Gates Foundation) or the Ford Motor Company (the Ford Foundation). Foundations contribute to development by supporting global philanthropic initiatives, recognizing that private money can significantly help to address global poverty.

Funding provided by foundations to microfinance can take a wide variety of forms, although it is primarily in the form of, for example, grants for training, capacity building, or product development, or as seed capital for start-up institutions. Foundations often also act as "catalytic" investors, agreeing to take the first loss in an investment portfolio to create a cushion for other, more risk-averse investors (that is, certain investments can be set up in such a way that if there is a default in a portfolio, the foundation would absorb this loss, and other investors would be protected). Some foundations also invest in microfinance investment vehicles (discussed below).

NGOs

Many NGOs, both local and international, are involved in funding microfinance. They obtain funding from multiple sources in the public and private sectors and also raise funding directly from individuals through targeted fundraising efforts. Many are also active in areas other than financial inclusion, such as health, women's empowerment, children's issues, or humanitarian relief. NGOs typically provide grants to assist product development, the provision of non-financial services, or seed capital for operations to serve specific, underserved groups that fall under their general mission/target clientele. NGOs that have helped to start up local MFIs (and often remain on as shareholders after transformation) include such entities as ACP (Acción Comunitaria del Perú, founder of MiBanco); FIE NGO, founder of Banco FIE in Bolivia; Separ, founder of Confianza in Peru; Urwego, founder of UOB in Rwanda; and Acleda, founder of Acleda in Cambodia.

Institutional Investors

Pension funds and insurance companies are increasingly investing in financial service markets for both social value and diversification in returns with other investments that they typically make. "Impact investing" has emerged in the past few years as an overall investment theme within the socially responsible investing (SRI) sector and involves making investments that are specifically intended to have a positive social impact. This differentiates them from other types of SRI investments, which screen out investments in companies or products that may have a negative impact, such as those that pollute the environment or produce cigarettes and firearms. As of 2011, financial services was the sector that received the largest allocation of investments within impact investing (Saltuk et al. 2011).

Most investments in microfinance from pension funds and insurance companies have been made through intermediaries. Although institutional investors may have both social and financial motivations, they do require a financial return. As a result, the majority of their funding goes to established, profitable providers. Institutional investors also generally have various requirements on reporting standards that have influenced the way providers and intermediaries gather and provide information on their operational, financial, and social results. The entry of institutional investors into the field of financial inclusion has been an important development in the evolution of the industry, resulting in microfinance being more in the mainstream of investment alternatives with more standardized reporting, ratings by mainstream rating agencies, and other more formal sector characteristics. Box 16.2 provides an overview of the size of the institutional investor market in microfinance and examples of noteworthy transactions.

Banks

Local commercial bank funding to microfinance providers varies significantly by country; in some countries they are not active at all, whereas in others they are key funders in financial services for the poor. They are typically present only when both the local banking industry and the microfinance industry are well developed and/or if government mandates exist. In India, for example, local banks are actively encouraged by a regulation that requires banks to lend to "priority sectors" to help achieve national development goals.

Commercial banks invest in microfinance to achieve both commercial and socially responsible

---

Box 16.2 Institutional Investors in Microfinance

The market for institutional investors in microfinance is relatively new. Institutional investors are the fastest growing investment group in microfinance, having increased their outstanding investment in microfinance from US$1.2 billion in 2006 to US$3.5 billion in 2010 (CGAP 2011). A December 2011 survey conducted by J. P. Morgan and the Global Impact Investing Network on "impact investing" as a whole (with microfinance constituting approximately 40 percent of current investment in impact investing) reported that institutional investors who responded to the survey expected to allocate approximately 5 percent of their total investments to impact investing over the next 10 years.

A diverse set of institutional players are dedicating investment resources to microfinance. Institutional investors include international banks, pension funds, and insurance companies. For example, in 2006 TIAA-CREF, a leading pension fund with US$453 billion in combined assets under management, launched a US$100 million Global Microfinance Investment Program. The program has since invested in ProCredit, a German holding company with microfinance banks in 21 developing countries. Similarly, in April 2010, Dutch pension fund ABP invested US$30 million in global private equity fund Grassroots Capital. The investment brought ABP's total debt and equity holdings in microfinance to US$215 million. The Swiss Post Pension Fund dedicated CHF 130 million to microfinance in 2011 and stated "our analysis of microfinance assets has shown that this asset class fulfills our set selection criteria: it offers an attractive risk/return ratio and can be expected to enhance our portfolio diversification." Likewise, insurance companies with long-term funding have begun to invest in microfinance. The Sonam insurance company in Senegal has invested in MicroCred Senegal directly.

Source: Reille et al. 2011; Saltuk et al. 2011; *Responsible Investor* 2012.

---

goals. Although most banks initially engaged in microfinance by providing donations to achieve CSR goals, many have now incorporated microfinance activities to achieve both financial and social business goals. Local commercial banks sometimes sell cash management services to smaller microfinance providers, and after building a relationship begin to extend credit and other investment services such as credit lines or term loans. However, conditions tend to be more conservative than other lenders, for example, by requiring collateral or offering shorter term financing. Local commercial banks also sometimes provide equity to local providers or establish cobranded, specialized subsidiaries with the aim of expanding the financial sector locally or to reach a new market segment. Box 16.3 provides examples of commercial banks' investment in microfinance.

Individual Investors

Individual investors are driven by the dual trends of retail investing and high-net-worth investing. Where some high-net-worth individuals have made direct investments in financial service providers (typically as equity), the vast majority invest via microfinance investment vehicles, whereas smaller retail investors channel funds through donations to foundations or NGOs, peer-to-peer aggregators (discussed below), or increasingly, through microfinance investment vehicles.

Intermediaries

Although many public and some private funders directly fund individual providers, a large portion of funding to microfinance is channeled through intermediaries. Microfinance investment intermediaries (MIIs) are attractive to investors because they can provide economies of scale, diversified portfolios, and dedicated regional and industry expertise that direct investors may not have the budget or scope to build in house. MIIs come in many forms and include microfinance investment vehicles, networks and holding companies, apex institutions, and peer-to-peer aggregators.

Microfinance Investment Vehicles (MIVs)

Approximately half of all microfinance investment from DFIs, individuals, and institutional investors is channeled through MIVs (El-Zoghbi et al. 2011). MIVs are private investment funds managed by specialized investment managers. They play an increasingly important financial intermediation role between investors (usually foreign) and financial service providers. Increasingly, MIVs target

---

Box 16.3 Commercial Bank Investment in Microfinance

Commercial banks invest both debt and equity in microfinance providers. Bank of Africa and BFV-SG (Société Générale) are minority equity investors in greenfield microfinance institutions. As minority investors, the banks have board seats, help in the licensing process, and provide complementary services to some SME clients as they grow larger.

Deutsche Bank was one of the first global banks to establish a socially motivated microfinance fund in the late 1990s. Led by their development finance group as part of the bank's overall corporate social responsibility commitment, Deutsche Bank provides debt, equity, and limited philanthropic grants to the microfinance sector. Between 2002 and 2012, Deutsche Bank microfinance had invested $215.5 million in capital in over 50 countries benefiting an estimated 2.8 million poor entrepreneurs (https://www.db.com/us/content/en/1077.html).

---

underserved markets and rural areas that other funders may not have the capacity to engage with directly. Symbiotics, a fund manager based in Geneva, estimates there were more than 102 MIVs as of 2011, managing US$6.8 billion. The majority of MIVs are focused on debt investments. A smaller, but growing, proportion focus on equity investments, and some provide both (so-called mixed or hybrid funds) (Symbiotics 2011). Box 16.4 provides aggregated data on the MIV segment.

Debt and Hybrid MIVs

Although MIVs are largely funded by institutional investors, some debt and hybrid MIVs are open to retail investors, such as the Dexia Micro-Credit Fund, responsAbility Global Microfinance Fund, Dual Return Fund, and Triodos SICAV. These are set up as *mutual funds* and allow investors to buy or sell their shares in the funds usually on a monthly or quarterly basis. Because of this liquidity feature, and because loans made by MIVs to financial service providers cannot easily be sold, loans provided by these funds are usually short to medium term (usually averaging about two years, with maximums in the three- to five-year range). Typically such funds target established, well-performing institutions, although to varying degrees they also invest in smaller institutions, and some may also offer equity in addition to debt.

Most MIVs are global in nature to maximize diversification and geographical outreach. Although the investment funds themselves are denominated in hard currency (usually dollars or euros, with some also in Swiss francs), most also make loans in local currency to providers. The majority use currency-hedging instruments so that their investors are not exposed to foreign exchange risk and receive a more predictable return. The funds typically target a stable return,

---

Box 16.4 Aggregating Data on MIVs

Since 2008, CGAP, and then Symbiotics, has conducted annual surveys of the MIV market, analyzing data and industry trends. For the 2011 survey, 70 MIVs, representing 87 percent of the total estimated MIV market, responded to the survey. Some of the key findings were as follows:

- Fixed-income funds are the main type of MIVs, accounting for 64 percent of the total participating MIVs and 83 percent of the total assets under management.

Microfinance investment vehicles (MIVs)	Number of MIVs	Assets under management ($ million)	% of total
Fixed-income funds	45	4,881	83
Mixed funds	13	667	11
Equity funds	12	358	6
Total	**70**	**5,906**	**100**

- Private institutional investors represent the largest share of investors in each MIV peer group (figure B16.4.1).

(continued next page)

Box 16.4 *(continued)*

Figure B16.4.1 Source of MIV Funding

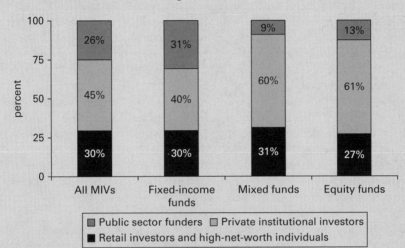

- Geographical focus is concentrated in Eastern Europe and Latin America, although trends are for MIVs to expand their investments in underserved areas, such as Africa and the Middle East.

Microfinance investment vehicles (MIV)	% of portfolio invested in			
	Eastern Europe and Central Asia	Latin America and Caribbean	East Asia and Pacific, South Asia	Africa and Middle East
Fixed-income funds	45	34	14	8
Mixed funds	27	39	27	8
Equity funds	6	47	45	2
Total	**40**	**35**	**17**	**7**
2010 growth across all funds	*5*	*12*	*26*	*32*

Source: Adapted from Symbiotics 2011 MIV Survey.

usually somewhat higher than investors would receive on three- to six-month bank deposits.

Other, similar MIVs are private placement debt and hybrid funds, such as the European Fund for Southeast Europe (EFSE), the Microfinance Enhancement Facility (MEF), and the Rural Impulse Microfinance Fund, with the main difference being that only "qualified" investors who meet certain regulatory requirements are able to invest in these vehicles through private placements, and they may also be closed to new investors. They are also more likely to have regional or sectoral focuses than funds that are open to retail investors and usually also do not provide regular liquidity. These vehicles are funded principally by institutional investors and DFIs.

Other MIVs are cooperative/NGO structures, such as Oikocredit or Alterfin funds. The differences with these funds are that these structures are owned by their members and tend to target smaller institutions, with a more explicit focus on social performance than other funds. As a cooperative MIV, Oikocredit in the Netherlands has a different structure than other MIVs in that its members provide the capital and vote on the size of the annual dividends they receive annually, which has historically been 2 percent or less. Members are principally churches, church-related organizations, and support associations (www.oikocredit.org).

Other debt funds are set up as *structured finance vehicles,* often called collateralized loan obligations (CLOs) or collateralized debt obligations (CDOs). Structured finance vehicles are established for a fixed period of time and, in their simplest form, fund a portfolio of loans to providers. They are funded by issuing "notes" to investors whose repayment comes from the repayment of loans in the portfolio. They can also act as a means to "securitize" loans within the providers' portfolio itself, combining a large number of loans made to provider clients into an overall structure and then selling notes to investors that are repaid by repayment proceeds on these loans.

Structured finance vehicles issue various classes of notes that appeal to different types of investors. In a typical structure, there are three or more different classes of notes, which are paid sequentially (in a so-called payment waterfall) as the loans that the structured vehicle has made to providers are repaid. For example, the most senior "A" notes would be paid first and are therefore the lowest risk tranche in the structure. Typical investors in these "senior" notes are private institutional investors. Next in line for repayment are so-called mezzanine "B" notes, which are higher risk but also provide higher return. These are often bought by DFIs willing to support greater developmental return or private investors willing to take greater risk for a higher return. The third class—the first-loss "equity" tranche—is paid back last and are generally bought by foundations and bilateral and multilateral development agencies that may not expect a return on their investment but are willing to provide the catalytic investment to allow the structure itself to go forward. Given the development of different types of structured funds, box 16.5 provides examples of the evolution of structured funds in the market.

Equity Fund MIVs

Equity fund MIVs are also usually of a fixed duration and, because of the long-term nature of the investment, do not generally allow investors to sell their interest in the fund until the end of the fund's term. Typically they have a "ramp-up" investment period of several years, followed by another multi-year "exit" or divestment period. They are a heterogeneous group with varying return targets typically offering a blend of equity and convertible debt to high-growth providers in emerging markets. The first generation of equity MIVs were set up largely by DFIs or international NGO networks. Private investors—first high-net-worth and then institutional investors—have been increasingly involved, with regionally focused funds such as Bellwether in India, global funds such as the BlueOrchard Private Equity Fund, and traditional venture capital funds such as Sequoia Capital. The Symbiotics 2011 MIV survey showed equity funds to be the fastest growing segment of MIVs.

One of the first equity funds dedicated to microfinance was ProFund, incorporated in 1995 as a for-profit investment fund, with funding principally from NGOs, DFIs, and multilaterals. The fund was created both to provide returns to investors and to act as an example for future

Box 16.5 The Changing Character of Structured Funds

The nature of structured funds has changed along with developments within the wider market of collateralized debt obligations (CDOs), a US$1.3 trillion global industry in 2007, which all but dried up in the 2008/9 global financial crisis. (In 2009 only US$4 billion in CDOs were issued globally, compared with US$455 billion at the market's peak in 2007, according to the Securities Industry and Financial Markets Association.)

In microfinance, the first large CDOs came to market in 2004–7 (for example, BlueOrchard Microfinance Securities, BlueOrchard Loans for Development, and Microfinance Securities XXEB) and were focused mostly on lending to top-tier financial service providers, with high country diversification. These funds were viewed as a way to bring mainstream institutional investors into microfinance and were structured in the same way as mainstream financial market CDOs, with the highest target return going to the highest risk equity tranche. For example, BlueOrchard Loans for Development 2007 had its two senior tranches rated by Standard & Poor's.

Changes in the market conditions in 2008, however, meant that such products were difficult to sell to institutional investors after the crisis. More recent CDOs have been smaller focusing on tier II and tier III FSPs, with public donor funds taking the first-loss equity pieces, often with no expectation of return, and also tend to be regionally focused. The Regional MSME Investment Fund for Sub-Saharan Africa (REGMIFA) is one of this latter group.

REGMIFA is meant to build, over time, a public-private partnership for Africa that leverages donor funds with private capital and supports the economic growth and job creation in the region. The fund is a partnership between various European member states, DFIs, and, through its tiered risk-sharing structure, aimed to attract private institutional investors. Figure B16.5.1 illustrates REGMIFA's structure and flow of funds.

The objectives of REGMIFA are (1) to offer and encourage additional but market-based financing—with an emphasis on local currency—to financial entities serving micro- and small businesses ("microfinance institutions"), (2) to help establish microfinance as an asset class with mainstream investors and leverage donor funds with private capital, and (3) to support medium-term capacity building among financial entities serving micro- and small businesses. REGMIFA provides local currency debt financing to smaller banks, nonbank institutions, and commercially oriented NGOs that serve small and microbusinesses. A parallel technical assistance facility provides capacity-building support to investees.

Figure B16.5.1   REGMIFA's Structure and Flow of Funds

Source: Adapted from International Finance Corporation.

private, commercial investors. ProFund invested in 10 MFIs in Latin America and was liquidated, as planned, in 2005, providing an overall 5.1 percent annual return to investors.

Microfinance Holding Companies

Many international microfinance "networks" are set up as NGOs or holding companies. These networks, with their own donors or investors, channel funds to affiliate operations globally, providing grants, equity, debt, and parent guarantees depending on the requirements of the affiliate (table 16.2). Notable NGO actors in this realm include ACCION International and Opportunity International, although the NGO network model is shrinking in favor of more formal institutional models.

The holding company model was pioneered by ProCredit Holding and has been replicated successfully by AccessHolding, MicroCred, and the Advans networks, among others. The holding company is usually the majority founding shareholder and sponsor of network banks. It effectively acts as the investment vehicle for DFIs to set up and manage new providers in underserved markets. Given that most holding companies have DFI shareholders, they effectively create public–private partnerships that demonstrate scalable and replicable commercial microfinance models in nascent markets.

Table 16.2 Holding Company Investment Examples

Holding company	Assets	Number of investments	Area of investments	Investors
Access Holdings founded 2006 in Germany	€479.8 million (as of December 2011)	7	Primarily in Sub-Saharan Africa and Central Asia	CDC Group plc, European Investment Bank (EIB), International Finance Corporation (IFC), KfW Entwicklungsbank (KfW), LFS Financial Systems GmbH, MicroAssets GbR (MA), Omidyar-Tufts Microfinance Fund (OTMF), the Netherlands Development Bank (FMO)
Advans SA founded 2005 in Luxembourg	€133.5 million (as of December 2011)	6	Sub-Saharan Africa and Cambodia	CDC, EIB, FISEA (Proparco), FMO, Horus Development Finance, IFC, KfW
MicroCred SA founded 2005 in France	€108.7 million (as of December 2011)	6	Primarily in Sub-Saharan Africa and China	AXA Belgium, Developing World Markets (DWM), EIB, French Development Agency (AFD), IFC, PlaNet Finance, Société Générale
ProCredit Holding founded 1998 in Germany	€5.4 billion (as of December 2011)	21	Eastern Europe, Latin America, and Africa	BIO, DOEN, FMO, Fundasal, IFC, IPC GmbH, IPC Invest GmbH & Co., KfW, Omidyar-Tufts, PROPARCO, responsAbility, TIAA-CREF

Source: Holding company websites: www.accessholding.com; www.advansgroup.com; www.microcredgroup.com; and www.procredit-holding.com.

For example, FINCA, one of the world's largest microfinance networks, announced the launch of a subsidiary called FINCA Microfinance Holdings (FMH) in July 2011. The holding company was created to enable a US$74 million capital investment from socially responsible investment institutions to strike the right balance between attracting capital needed for expansion and protecting the integrity of FINCA's charitable mission. The goal of FMH is to increase outreach as well as introduce new products such as savings and insurance products to existing clients (FINCA press release, Washington, DC, June 17, 2011).

Some holding companies have a number of shareholders at the holding level, with the holding company owning 100 percent of the subsidiaries, as is the case of FMH and most ProCredit subsidiaries. Other holding companies have a number of investors at the holding level and at the subsidiary level to facilitate local shareholders and other strategic investors.

Local Apex Organizations

An apex is a pool of funds constituted domestically to lend to providers that, in turn, disburse loans to low-income people. Apexes distribute funds to providers mostly in the form of subsidized loans and occasionally as grants. Apexes are funded with public money but take various institutional forms, such as development banks, nongovernmental organizations, donor programs, private commercial banks, and special government or donor programs. CGAP mapped 76 apexes in 2009 and found the largest 15 apexes had a total gross loan portfolio of more than US$3 billion as of 2009. Although apexes exist in all regions, they are most prevalent in Latin America and South Asia (Duflos and El-Zoghbi 2010). The 15 largest apexes lent to 1,650 retail microfinance providers in 2009, across a wide variety of institutional types, including NGOs, cooperatives, microfinance banks, and other commercial finance companies (Forster et al. 2012).

Peer-to-Peer Aggregators

Peer-to-peer lenders such as Kiva, MicroPlace, Globe Funder, Babylon, and Good Return provide an opportunity for individuals to "invest" money directly in microfinance institutions. They act as retail aggregators, by creating Internet-based platforms that leverage technology to facilitate direct investment from individuals on a small scale. Disadvantages for providers include the fact that most peer-to-peer aggregators do not normally provide local currency funding and reporting requirements are significant and costly. Financial service providers that use these funds are generally second- and third-tier providers that do not have access to more commercial sources of funding. Proponents of the model claim there is a facilitation role these aggregators play by providing funding deeper in the sector. Given the often limited recourse between the aggregator and the provider receiving the funds, providers may use these funds to finance risky clients and/or to fund pilots for new products. Although acting as a first-loss facility is not necessarily the proclaimed strategy of peer-to-peer lenders, it is a potentially useful, if unintended, use of their funds.

Box 16.6 addresses the consequence of funding concentration in the microfinance sector.

Funding Tools

Funding is provided through various tools. The mission and scope of the funder, the investee's (financial service provider) performance, its ability (or inability) to mobilize deposits, the regulatory framework, and the openness and level of development of the financial system all impact the choice of funding tools used. In general, however, as financial service providers mature, an increasing number of funding options are available to them. Whereas NGOs traditionally rely on subsidized grants to fund portfolio growth, sustainable and profitable institutions are able to attract equity investors, issue longer term and unsecured debt, and raise funds on capital

Box 16.6 Funding Concentration

Funding is crucial to improving financial access because it ensures that providers have the resources needed to expand, through either increasing the volume of clients served, moving into new geographic areas, or introducing new products into the market.

With debt and equity investments from public and private investors alike, providers have moved from donor-dependent projects to sustainable financial service providers. Between 2007 and 2010, foreign investment in microfinance (including both debt and equity) quadrupled to reach US$24 billion (CGAP 2011). Additionally, top-tier providers are increasingly accessing financing through capital markets, as development oriented investors are looking at tier 2 and tier 3 providers as possible investments.[a]

Although the benefits of increased funding are well established, there are those who argue that a large surge of microfinance investment is now struggling to find appropriate institutions to invest in, with most money still flowing to the same top-tier providers.

Microfinance investment is concentrated both geographically and increasingly through intermediaries. From a geographic perspective, funding is concentrated mainly in Latin America and Europe and Central Asia. Ten countries with a combined population of 100 million receive more than 60 percent of all foreign lending.

There is similarly a great deal of concentration among investee institutions. As of December 2010, DFIs committed US$9.1 billion with half of this funding going to 30 recipients: 12 MFIs with an average investment of US$120 million per institution and 18 MIVs, holding companies, local banks, and funds with an average investment of US$160 million.

Investment concentration is a challenge to truly expanding financial access and reflects the lack of viable MFIs in many markets. Diversification in recipient institutions and countries is important to ensuring markets are not flooded with capital, which may prompt irresponsible lending behaviors by providers.

Source: Peter McConaghy drawing from El-Zoghbi et al. 2011.

a. Tier 2 providers are often defined as successful, but smaller, younger, or simply less well-known providers. They are typically at or near profitability. Tier 3 providers are those approaching profitability that have understandable shortcomings due to, for example, being a young organization, lacking capital, or having weak information systems.

markets, and deposit-taking institutions are able to intermediate savings from the general public.

Funding is transferred either through a direct investment between a funder or intermediary and a provider or through public capital markets where institutions and governments raise funds in the form of financial securities such as bonds and stocks. Both bond (debt) and stock (equity) markets are part of the capital markets. Microfinance is increasingly tapping into capital markets, both as a fundraising tool for providers and as an exit mechanism for investors. Accessing capital

markets enables providers to diversify funding sources, reduce foreign exchange risks (via sources of local, rather than foreign, capital), and support growth and loan product diversification (for example, housing loans) through longer-term funding (Women's World Banking 2006).

Capital markets provide investment access to the public at large and are regulated given the presumed lack of sophistication of retail public investors. The securities laws of many countries require the issuer to register the offer of securities with a national securities regulatory authority before making public offers and sales. These registration requirements impose a high standard of disclosure on the issuer. Through engaging with capital markets, providers also develop capacity as they satisfy the demands of investors and the process of becoming "investment ready." Thus, a secondary benefit of drawing on capital markets is professionalization and skill building of the financial service provider.

Grants

Grants are primarily used to encourage financial service providers to deepen their outreach, to develop new products and channels, or to support the development of the market. Grants are generally nonreimbursable, meaning the donor does not expect the funds to be returned.

Grants can be used to fund technical assistance or as a tool to enable investment in riskier frontier markets and projects.[4] When used to support frontier investments, grants can be used to provide an equity-type first-loss cushion, which allows a provider to take more risk initially, enabling deeper outreach and innovation. A first loss can take the form of a cash reserve where the first losses from a pilot or experiment are covered by a grant, or it can be part of a more structured facility or vehicle, taking the form of an equity tranche in a structured finance vehicle or risk-sharing facility as described above. Likewise, first-loss funds can be used to facilitate financial service providers to invest in underserved sectors such as health and education.

When used as a tool to fund technical assistance, grants are increasingly performance based. Performance-based grants are structured to incentivize desired behavior by the grantee and are paid conditionally based on results. They often have a cost-sharing component and time-bound targets. Payment of performance grants can be structured where financial service providers pay for technical services up front and are reimbursed once targets are met. They may also receive performance bonuses for over achievement of targets. Performance-based grants help ensure the subsidy is no greater than necessary to induce the required performance and do not simply increase the profits for the provider.

Debt

Debt represents funds lent over a fixed period of time and must be repaid, normally with interest. Debt is often defined by its level of seniority, or, in other words, which lender is paid first in the event that the issuer runs into financial problems and cannot repay all of its obligations. At the top are public depositors, who bear the least risk and consequently generally earn the lowest return. At the bottom are subordinated lenders, who bear the most risk and typically therefore earn the highest return.

Debt can be secured or unsecured. Secured debt is collateralized by the borrower pledging an asset. In the event that the borrower fails to repay according to the original terms, the lender can take legal action to claim and, if necessary, sell the collateral. Conversely, unsecured debt is backed only by the creditworthiness and willingness of the borrower to pay and is not supported by collateral.

Senior Term Loans

Senior term loans are loans that have a fixed maturity and are repaid first after depositors. Loan characteristics include the currency of the funds borrowed, the term or length of the loan, pricing, which can be fixed or variable, and principal repayment terms, which can include a grace period in which no principal payments are due, staggered amortizations of principal, or a bullet repayment at maturity. Sometimes loans are credit enhanced, whereby the borrower (the financial service provider) provides collateral, usually in the form of portfolio or fixed assets, or a third party provides some form of guarantee that could be called upon in case of default. Term loans often also include "covenants," which are conditions that the borrower must comply with to remain in good standing. These often include, for example, limits on delinquency, related party lending, and capital adequacy ratios. If these covenants are breached, then the lender has the right to demand early repayment of the loan. The majority of international debt funding to financial service providers comes in the form of term loans from MIVs, DFIs, or banks.

Syndicated Loans

A syndicated loan is a senior term loan for which there is a primary or lead lender of record and other commercial banks/lenders acquire participation, that is, lend part of the value of the overall syndicated amount. Participants share risks with the lead lender on a pari-passu basis (meaning all lenders have equal rights). Syndicated loans are used when the amount of debt required by an institution is larger than the exposure any single lender can manage. Through syndication, a group of investors agree to the same structure and terms, reducing the amount of bilateral negotiation necessary to raise a large amount of debt. In this way a provider is able to negotiate with the lead syndication firm once, rather than individually with all lenders.

Citigroup and a consortium of local banks in Pakistan provided the first local currency syndicated transaction for the microfinance sector in 2007. The syndication enabled the Kashf Foundation, a leading commercial provider in Pakistan, to access wider commercial financing. The landmark US$22 million term financing package provided funding to support Kashf Foundation's significant growth plans. (Citi Microfinance Business Unit, http://222.citigroup.com/citi/citizen/data/cr07_ch08.pdf)

Subordinated Debt

Subordinated translates as to "below" or "inferior to," and *subordinated debt* is therefore below all other claims of debt. In the event of bankruptcy, liquidation, or reorganization, subordinated debt can claim assets only after senior debt (senior term loans and all other debt) has been paid off. Because of its higher risk, such debt typically carries a higher interest rate. Raising subordinated debt is advantageous for institutions to help them meet capital adequacy requirements, because in some cases it can count as equity for regulatory calculations. Box 16.7 outlines the Basel regulations associated with subordinated debt.

Subordinated debt instruments are also often convertible into equity. *Convertible debt* is debt with an option to convert part or all of the loan to common shares of the borrowing organization. Although convertible debt usually carries a lower interest rate than nonconvertible debt, convertible debt offers investors a chance to participate in the profitability of the borrower in exchange for the lower rate. In some environments, however, having an option to convert debt into equity limits the debt's qualification as tier 2 capital (Ledgerwood and White 2006).

Bonds

Bonds are essentially transferable or "securitized" versions of loans: that is, debt obligations that can be easily transferred from one lender, or "bondholder," to another. Similar to loan agreements, the borrower, or "issuer" agrees to make payments of interest and principal on specific dates to the holders of the bond.

Private bond placements offer providers an opportunity to tap a broader range of investors than straight loans from commercial banks but are more limited than issuing a bond on a public market (Ledgerwood and White 2006). Private placements are investments that are offered to specific investors, rather than through the capital market, and can be either debt or equity. Private placements are sold directly to institutional investors, such as banks, mutual funds, insurance companies, and pension funds.

Public bond issuances are available through the capital markets and thus evaluated by the financial markets in terms of yield (return) versus risk. Public bonds can be issued on local capital markets or international capital markets. A local bond issuance will provide funding in the local currency of the country it is issued in. International bond issuances can be denominated in different hard currencies, usually associated with the country in which they are issued, but not always. Box 16.8 provides examples of private placements and public bond issuances in microfinance.

Significant administrative, regulatory, and reporting requirements are related to issuing bonds, including ratings, and bonds are therefore typically only a feasible option if the amount of money being borrowed is significant, or if the provider is looking to establish its name in the market for future, larger issuance. Only a handful of providers use this funding option because few have reached the scale that would make this an economically attractive alternative and/or are present in markets that allow for bond sales.

Local Currency Funding

Local currency funding is important to the health of a financial service provider because it allows an institution to borrow in the same currency it lends. Matching the currency of assets and liabilities reduces exposure to foreign exchange risk. This is a critical issue in financial services for the poor because the vast majority of funders (except for depositors) are based in developed countries and access funds in U.S. dollars and euros, but providers located in developing countries require local currency. The consequence of foreign currency mismatch is discussed in box 16.9. Although some MIVs and direct lenders will take on some amount of local currency risk (sometimes diversifying across different currencies to lower their risk), most local currency financing from international lenders is hedged in some manner, by either the funder or the borrower.

Numerous tools have been developed to facilitate local currency funding, including hedging using back-to-back lending, swaps, forwards, partial credit guarantees, and specialized foreign currency funds.

The simplest form of a hedge is for a provider to take the hard currency it has borrowed, deposit it into a local commercial bank, and use it as cash collateral to borrow local currency. This is known as "back-to-back" lending. Although conceptually straightforward, a cash hedge like

Box 16.8 Bond Issuance in Financial Services for the Poor

Private Placements

The first private placement of bonds in the microfinance world was made by BancoSol in 1996 and 1997 for a total of US$5 million. Both issues were backed by a 50 percent guarantee from USAID and were relatively short-term two-year maturities. Since then BancoSol's funding structure has evolved as the funding products available have increased relative to the institutions growth and formalization. Shortly after issuing partially guaranteed private placements, BancoSol moved on to issuing certificate of deposits. Although also short term in nature, these were less expensive than private placements.

Bonds can also be issued in international markets outside of the country a provider is domiciled. AccessBank Azerbaijan issued a US$25 million Eurobond during 2007 and 2008. The bond was rated BB+ by Fitch, in line with the bank's (issuer) rating. Unlike a local bond, a Eurobond is an international bond denominated in a currency other than the currency of the country or market in which it is issued. The bonds were issued in Luxembourg by MFBA Bond I, a special-purpose legal vehicle. The proceeds of the bond were defined to provide a senior loan to MFBA for financing its portfolio growth. The bond issue was sponsored and arranged by Developing World Markets (DWM), a U.S.–based socially responsible financial group. DWM assists micro- and small businesses throughout emerging markets to enter the international capital markets.

Public Issuance

Because of the expense and administrative requirements of issuing bonds, this type of funding is usually sought only by the largest financial service providers. MiBanco in Peru had its inaugural bond issue in 2002, raising S/. 20 million (US$5.8 million) as part of a multiyear program. Financiera Compartamos in Mexico raised US$19 million in 2005 as part of a US$50 million public issue program and after three private bond placements. After its conversion to a bank, Banco Compartamos had one of the largest public issues in microfinance, raising Mex$1 billion (US$81 million) in 2010 in local markets.

It is not a requirement that a bond issuer be a for-profit, regulated institution, however. Indeed, one of the largest bond issues in microfinance came from the NGO WWB Cali (although it has since transformed into a bank), a member of the Women's World Banking network, which raised Col$120 million (US$52 million) in 2005.

Source: Ledgerwood and White 2006; Microcapital.org and Women's World Banking (www.swwb.org).

---

this can be very expensive because the provider has to pay interest on both the dollar loan and the local currency loan. The deposit of hard currency earns some interest, and the local currency loan should theoretically be priced lower to reflect the limited risk the local currency lender is taking with a 100 percent collateralized loan, but often the price is not adjusted well enough. As commercial banks become more comfortable with microfinance providers and understand microfinance better, hard currency cash deposits can be leveraged, and a provider can borrow multiple amounts in local currency vis-à-vis the amount of hard currency it has deposited.

A *swap* is a transaction in which two parties agree to exchange one set of future cash flows for another. A currency swap facilitates the exchange of cash flows denominated in one currency for

Box 16.9 Quantifying Foreign Exchange Risk for Currency Mismatch

In June 2008 a financial service provider in Kyrgyzstan borrowed US$1 million for two years with repayment due in June 2010. Upon receipt of the dollars, the provider converted it into Kyrgyz soms and used the proceeds to on-lend to its clients in soms. On June 30, 2008, the dollar/som exchange rate was 35.92. Upon conversion of the US$1 million, the provider received som 35.92 million. On June 30, 2010, the dollar/som exchange rate was 46.71, and the provider needed som 46.71 million to repay the US$1 million. It therefore cost the provider an extra som 10.8 million (equivalent at the time to US$233,000), reflecting a currency depreciation of more than 20 percent over two years.

Source: All historical exchange rate sources from www.oanda.com.

cash flows denominated in another currency. For every swap there is a counterparty who wants the opposite currency. The lender usually initiates the swap on behalf of the provider and then lends the local currency directly to the provider. Some currencies have well-developed swap markets with many potential parties interested in swapping a certain currency. Other currencies have less liquid swap markets, where there are fewer interested swap partners. Many currencies in developing countries are too thinly traded to develop a functioning swap market.

In countries where swaps are not available or the swap market is not liquid enough, *partial credit guarantees* (discussed in more detail in the Structured Finance section) can provide good local currency solutions. For a partial credit guarantee (PCG) set up to manage local currency risk, a well-rated institution such as an AAA-rated DFI or bilateral donor guarantees a loan between a commercial bank and a financial service provider. A PCG can also be used to guarantee a bond issued by a financial service provider on a capital market. The amount of the guarantee can be any percentage of the underlying loan; however, the usual range is anywhere from 80 percent down to 10 percent. The guarantor is paid a fee commensurate with the level of guarantee. For example, if a guarantor prices the risk at 5 percent for a certain institution in a certain country, then the price of a 50 percent guarantee fee would be 2.5 percent of the amount borrowed. The more comfortable the lending institution is with the risk of the financial service provider, the lower the guarantee required. When a provider has a good track record of on-time repayments and reporting during a first loan, the level of guarantee typically declines as the local currency lender becomes more comfortable with the risk.

Specialized foreign currency funds have been created to address the lack of hedging instruments for many local currency markets. They are typically based on a diversification principle whereby the lender tries to diversify its lending across a basket of currencies. Sometimes these funds are set up as structured finance vehicles (discussed in more detail in the next section), where risk is managed through a tiered investment structure and "first-loss" investors bear the brunt of currency losses, cushioning more senior investors. These funds act as counterparties to borrowers who do not want to take on foreign currency risk, or to lenders who lend directly in local currency but wish to offload the currency exposure. DFIs and multilaterals have played a crucial role in the development of these funds and in this capacity have kept very much with their mission to catalyze rather than replace private sector capital. Box 16.10 provides examples of foreign currency funds.

Deposits

Deposits play a dual role for an institution. On the one hand, they are an important service to clients. On the other hand, deposits are also a source of local funding for financial service providers that are licensed to accept them. A portion of deposits are held aside as liquid assets to ensure clients can withdraw their funds when desired, and a larger portion are used by the institution to fund its loan portfolio (intermediate).

Because of the importance of protecting public depositors' funds, strict regulations are in place to ensure the soundness of institutions allowed to mobilize deposits. These regulations vary significantly from country to country, but usually include minimal capital ratios, minimal standards on information systems and reporting, and other requirements (see chapter 17). Although deposits typically have very short maturities—demand deposits can be withdrawn

at any time, and term deposits tend to be only a few months in maturity—in practice they are usually quite stable as a source of funding, with long holding periods and frequent rollover of term deposits. An exception to this is if depositors suddenly feel that their money is no longer safe, because of either institution-specific problems or economic instability, and a "run on deposits" occurs whereby large numbers of depositors demand their savings at the same time, potentially jeopardizing the health of the institution.

Licensed providers that take deposits are less dependent on external sources of funding and generally have more liquidity. A deposit-taking institution is able to raise deposits in local currency and loan out or intermediate those funds in the same currency, thereby matching its sources and uses of funds and reducing foreign currency risk.

Structured Finance

Structured finance facilitates access to funding for providers that would not otherwise be credit

---

Box 16.10 Specialized Currency Funds

The Currency Exchange Fund N.V. (TCX), based in the Netherlands, has a mandate to provide local currency and interest rate hedging products in emerging markets to its investors and their clients. TCX was launched in 2007 by FMO, KfW, other DFIs, and commercial banks, and the capital structure includes a first-loss component provided by the Dutch and German governments. The initial shareholders were later joined by development banks, multilaterals, and MIVs, and as of September 30, 2011, TCX had US$650 million in capital and was rated A– by S&P. TCX enters into medium- to long-term swap agreements and can transact in more than

60 currencies. As of October 2011, it had outstanding exposure to 43 different currencies for an aggregate amount of US$835 million.

Importantly, only shareholders or specified clients of shareholders can access the hedging services of TCX. To expand accessibility to the services of TCX, "Microfinance Currency Risk Solutions" or "MFX," was created in January 2008 by a group of lenders, investors, networks, and foundations. With a US$20 million credit guarantee from OPIC, MFX became a shareholder of TCX, allowing it to offer the hedging services from TCX to its clients, who would have been unable on their own to commit the capital required for direct access.

Source: https://www.tcxfund.com/partners/investors/mfx-solutions.

worthy on their own and facilitates investment from funders who would not otherwise be willing to take exposure to an institution without added credit protection. Structured finance includes guarantee structures for debt instruments (bonds and loans) through partial credit guarantees, risk-sharing facilities, and participation in securitizations.

Guarantees

If a provider is unable to attract financing on its own, either because it is a start-up with a limited track record, is located in a country that is deemed too risky, or for some other reason is not seen as "investable" on a standalone basis, guarantees are sometimes provided by creditworthy institutions: multilaterals, DFIs, or, often, the network to which the provider belongs. In this way, debt can be extended directly to the provider under the condition that if it is unable to pay, its guarantor will be called upon to repay the debt. Although it is unusual to have a full guarantee covering 100 percent of principal and interest, this is sometimes offered in the case of networks guaranteeing debt issued to affiliate providers. Depending on the relationship between the guarantor and the financial service provider, the provider benefiting from the guarantee usually pays a guarantee fee to the guarantor.

Guarantees are tailored to meet the needs of both borrowers and creditors. In general, the objective of the guarantor is to offer the minimum amount of guarantee necessary to facilitate a successful transaction. Guarantees have several advantages, allowing (1) the borrower in most cases to achieve a lower overall cost of funds, (2) investors to maximize their return given their risk tolerance, and (3) the guarantor to mobilize the maximum amount of financing for the borrower for a given level of credit exposure.

More common are PCGs, discussed briefly above, which represent a promise of timely debt service payment up to a set amount that is lower than the full amount of the debt in question.

Typically the sum the guarantor pays out under the guarantee reimburses creditors for the loss irrespective of the cause of default. The guarantee amount, as a percentage of the loan being guaranteed, may vary over the life of the transaction based on the borrower's expected cash flows and creditors' concerns regarding the stability of these cash flows. Guarantors for PCGs are typically highly rated international DFIs or bilateral agencies backed by highly rated countries. For example, IFC and KfW have AAA ratings that can be levered for guarantees. PCGs benefit clients by allowing a guarantor to absorb part of the credit risk of a lesser known entity. Overall PCGs facilitate improved market access, longer-term funding, and a broader investor base.

Partial guarantees can be in either local currency (for domestic transactions) or foreign currency (for cross-border transactions). Local currency partial guarantees are most applicable for a provider that has local currency revenues but lacks access to local currency financing of the desired term. Cross-border partial guarantees are best for a provider that cannot access international markets on its own because of the high-risk premium associated with the country in which it is domiciled. With a cross-border partial guarantee a provider may gain access to international markets by mitigating the sovereign risk associated with the borrowing.

Although a PCG is a guarantee between a guarantor and a financial service provider, *risk-sharing facilities* allow a financial service provider to share the risk of a specific portfolio of loans (for example, loans made to the agriculture sector, or to borrowers located in a specific high-risk region). In this case, the assets typically remain on the provider's balance sheet, and the risk transfer comes from a partial guarantee provided by a highly rated institution. In general, the guarantee is available for new assets originated by the provider using an agreed upon underwriting criteria, but in certain situations may also be used for assets that have been already originated.

Typically a provider's purpose in entering into a risk-sharing facility is to increase its capacity to make more loans within a specific "high-risk" area without increasing the risk it incurs.

Securitization

Securitization is a form of financing that involves the pooling and transfer of financial assets to a special purpose vehicle (SPV). This SPV then issues securities that are repaid from the cash flows generated by the pooled assets. In general, any asset class with relatively predictable cash flows can be securitized. The most common assets include mortgages, credit card debt, auto and consumer loans, corporate debt, and future revenues. This type of transaction allows financing to be based primarily on the risks of the asset pool rather than solely on the risk of the institution that originated the assets.

Securitization can be a valuable tool to increase liquidity, spread credit risk, gain access to new investors, lower the cost of funds, and remove assets from balance sheets, thereby reducing the FSP's debt/equity ratio. A lower debt/equity ratio can be beneficial to an FSP to meet minimum regulatory capital adequacy requirements, and generally to improve its overall creditworthiness. Securitization structures are most appropriate for a provider that seeks financing but is unable to tap funding sources for the desired length of time (term) and funding cost because of its perceived credit risk. It is important to note, however, that only providers that have sound credit risk management techniques and a well-performing portfolio and have demonstrated capable lending practices should consider securitization. Box 16.11 highlights key microcredit securitization transactions.

Equity

Equity is an ownership interest in a financial service provider through the form of shares that

---

Box 16.11 Microcredit Securitization

One of the first microloan securitizations was with BRAC in 2006. BRAC received US$12.6 billion Bangladesh taka (US$180 million) in financing over six years from a microcredit securitization structured by RSA Capital, Citigroup, FMO, and KfW. One billion Bangladesh taka (US$15 million) was disbursed to BRAC every six months, with a maturity of one year. During the transaction, a special purpose trust was created to purchase BRAC's receivables from its microcredit portfolio and issue certificates to investors. The issuance received the highest quality credit rating (AAA) from a local rating agency, Credit Rating Agency of Bangladesh, and succeeded in attracting two local banks as key investors.

Similarly, in May 2006, ProCredit Bank Bulgaria securitized US$47.8 million of its euro-denominated microfinance loans. Enhanced by guarantees provided by the European Investment Fund and KfW, these securities received a BBB credit rating, considered "investment grade" from the global credit rating agency Fitch.

In June 2009 Banco Solidario in Ecuador securitized US$60 million of its loans by creating a special purpose trust that took title to these loans and issued five classes of notes to investors with maturities of up to 85 months. The notes were purchased by local banks, the apex organization Corporación Financiera Nacional, national pension funds, and MIVs. After the success of this program, the bank issued another US$30 million securitization in 2011/2012.

Source: Adapted from www.microcapital.org.

---

represent a claim on the providers' assets in proportion to the percentage of the class of shares owned. Initial equity is often provided by local NGOs or investors, international networks—either NGOs or holding companies—and/or multilateral agencies and DFIs. Equity for cooperatives comes from the members (depositors, who to open an account at the cooperative also contribute equity through purchasing shares). DFIs play an active role in providing equity to many providers, while private equity funds have become increasingly active participants. It is important to note that although NGOs also have equity (the difference between their assets and liabilities), it does not represent "ownership" per se, because the NGO cannot be owned. Here equity is provided as a donation from private and/or public funders that may or may not ultimately be converted to actual transferrable equity, depending on whether the NGO transforms into a for-profit institution.

On rare occasions, some providers have given their clients an opportunity to become owners through the purchase of shares.

A closed private placement can be an innovative tool to promote client ownership. Family Bank in Kenya, a financial institution committed to serving the lower end of the Kenyan banking market through microfinance and mobile-banking products, in 2008 issued a private placement in which microfinance clients participated in a closed private placement and now own shares in "their" bank. The bank added more than 7,000 new shareholders and raised more than K Sh 500 million (US$5.6 million) through this process (http://www.familybank.co.ke).

As owners, equity shareholders take on the highest level of risk and are the last to be paid out in the case of institutional failure. Along with this higher level of risk comes a higher level of expected reward. Unlike debt, where most returns are fixed, equity owners can earn unlimited returns through *dividends* or gains made from selling their shares. Earnings made by the

provider are either retained, increasing the equity on the balance sheet, or they are distributed in the form of dividends to owners.

Like debt, equity investments are made through private placements or public issuances (figure 16.2). A public offering is an issue of securities that is offered to institutional and individual investors through a securities house such as a stock exchange. When an institution raises funds for the first time on a capital market, it is called an initial public offering (IPO). An IPO is a key opportunity for investors who have invested in an institution in the early stages of its development to exit or liquidate some of their investment. It is also an opportunity for financial service providers to raise additional funds from the public, resulting in a far more diverse set of potential investors. It allows providers to raise capital, gain increased market visibility, and potentially achieve or attain liquidity of the issuing securities depending on the level of secondary market activity in a given market (Women's World Banking 2006). Relatively new to microfinance, IPOs have received keen interest of various stakeholders (see box 16.12)

There are two primary classes of shares: *common shares* and *preferred shares*. Common shares are units of ownership that entitle the shareholders to voting rights. In the event that a provider is liquidated, the claims of depositors, secured and unsecured creditors, and preferred shareholders take precedence over the claims of those who own common shares, in that order. Preferred shares are units of ownership with preferential rights over common shares with respect to dividends and in liquidation. Preferred shares can be voting or nonvoting and typically pay dividends at a specified rate.

A provider's shareholding structure can be made up of majority and minority shareholders. The largest shareholder is usually the sponsor or primary operator. The sponsor is responsible for the operational and financial success of the

Figure 16.2   Three Main Stages in the Processing of Large Public Issues

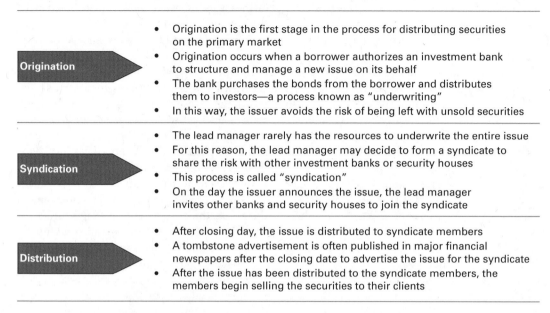

Origination
- Origination is the first stage in the process for distributing securities on the primary market
- Origination occurs when a borrower authorizes an investment bank to structure and manage a new issue on its behalf
- The bank purchases the bonds from the borrower and distributes them to investors—a process known as "underwriting"
- In this way, the issuer avoids the risk of being left with unsold securities

Syndication
- The lead manager rarely has the resources to underwrite the entire issue
- For this reason, the lead manager may decide to form a syndicate to share the risk with other investment banks or security houses
- This process is called "syndication"
- On the day the issuer announces the issue, the lead manager invites other banks and security houses to join the syndicate

Distribution
- After closing day, the issue is distributed to syndicate members
- A tombstone advertisement is often published in major financial newspapers after the closing date to advertise the issue for the syndicate
- After the issue has been distributed to the syndicate members, the members begin selling the securities to their clients

Source: Women's World Banking 2006.

institution. Minority shareholders own less than 50 percent of an institution's equity and often less than 20 percent. Typically, larger shareholders also play an active governance role and often require one or more seats on the board of directors (relative usually to their share of ownership), rights to vote on board decisions, and other privileges.

One of the largest risks for equity investors is exit risk. Once an investor holds shares in a provider, the only way to liquidate the investment is to find a willing buyer. Although the microfinance market is increasingly diverse and global, the vast majority of investments are in private, unlisted companies, and as such, equity investments are not very liquid. Equity exit mechanisms include private trade sales to another investor or provider, selling shares through the capital market, or a preagreed option arrangement.

A preagreed option arrangement involves negotiation at the time of the initial investment of an option to exit called a *put option*. A put option provides the unilateral right to sell shares in a provider to a preagreed buyer under prearranged terms. Conversely a *call option* is the right to buy shares in a provider at a preagreed price or formula. Sometimes debt funders are interested in becoming equity holders. In these cases, sometimes a lower coupon (interest) rate is negotiated in exchange for *warrants*. Warrants are essentially options to buy, usually issued in conjunction with another financial instrument, conferring the right, but not the obligation, to buy stock at a stated price within a specific period.

Responsible Investing Practices

With the strong growth in funding for financial service providers in the past decade and the expansion in the types of funders to the sector, many participants in the industry have worked to codify principles and establish best practices to maintain a healthy, sustainable, and inclusive financial system.

Box 16.12 Access to Capital Markets

Although numerous financial service providers have issued bonds, as of December 2011 only three microfinance stocks have been listed on equity capital markets: Compartamos in Mexico, Equity Bank in Kenya, and SKS in India. The IPOs of SKS and Compartamos, both of which were approximately 13 times oversubscribed, drew keen interest from not only public and private actors in the microfinance industry but also the mainstream public.

Supporters argue that IPOs offer a crucial funding source that can help a microfinance organization fully commercialize and scale operations, thereby enhancing the volume and reach of the unbanked. Many supporters also suggest that an IPO is an ultimate demonstration of the commercial potential of the microfinance model. The prospect of an IPO has drawn keen interest from countries with major microfinance industries such as Bangladesh, Mexico, Kenya, and India, as well as private equity firms that have recently moved into the sector.

Critics, however, made up of a diverse set of stakeholders, including NGO FSPs, civil society, and consumer protection advocates, see IPOs as a tool that promotes mission drift as they attract stakeholders with varied objectives and afford investors the opportunity to cash in on profits. They argue that IPOs make a very small number of people very rich and, overall, promote institutional incentives that go against microfinance's larger mission of addressing vulnerabilities and extending financial access among the poor.

One particular component of the IPO debate is whether IPO prices are based on intrinsic value or whether the lack of capacity in the market is bidding up the asking price. Critics point out that the high valuation of both SKS and Compartamos were not in line with market peers at the time of their IPOs. In emerging markets, banks are valued at three times book value on average, although finance institutions serving low-income customers are trading at 2.6 times book value. SKS, on the other hand, was valued at 6.7 times the company's post-issue book value, and about 40 times the company's fiscal year 2010 earnings. At listing, Compartamos was valued at 13 times book value and 27 times the company's historical earnings.

Another critical concern is that investors buying at such a high level may pressure management to increase profitability, at the expense of clients' interests and long-term company sustainability. The short-term and profit-focused interests may in fact clash with longer-term interest of the clients, noticeably to access affordable and accessible financial products.

Source: Reille 2010; Women's World Banking 2006.

This is related to concerns of over-concentration and over-indebtedness: If funders are all drawn to providing their funds to the same small number of profitable providers, or to certain specific regions that are easier to access, there is a risk that these providers or regions will have more funding than they can on-lend in a sustainable manner, and in turn can lead to over-indebtedness of their own clients. Linked to this are concerns related to issues of transparency of pricing on loans and other issues of client protection.

Many initiatives have occurred on this front in the past several years, including the United Nations Principles for Responsible Investment[5] and the Principles for Investors in Inclusive Finance.[6] Guiding principles have also been established by the International Association of Microfinance Institutions to help creditors and other stakeholders in cases where a provider is either in default or in a distressed situation that may lead to default. Underlying these principles and guidelines is the basic idea that funding within the sector should be done in a responsible manner that takes into account the interests of the end client and the health of the overall system. Box 16.13 provides an overview of responsible investor principles.

Ratings

The prevalence and importance of ratings in microfinance have grown exponentially since they were first introduced in the mid-1990s. Used primarily by funders, including both donors and investors, ratings are evaluations of institutions' operational, financial, and more recently, social performance based on standardized methodologies.

Microfinance institutional ratings[7] provide an opinion on long-term institutional sustainability and creditworthiness through a comprehensive assessment of risks, performance, market position, governance, and responsible finance practices. They measure the probability that a provider will continue to operate and remain a "going concern," even in the case of an external shock. They have a strong focus on governance, on the quality of the microfinance operations and systems, and on alignment of decisions with stated social goals and client protection, which are considered core assets for long-run sustainability.

A *credit rating* is the product of conventional rating agencies (Standard & Poor's, Fitch, and Moody's are the best known rating agencies) and has a narrower focus than general performance ratings. Credit ratings focus specifically on whether a provider is able to meet its credit obligations, assessing the default risk during a given period of time. The methodology applied to a microfinance credit rating is the same as that applied to any financial institution—its purpose is primarily to make an opinion regarding the institution's default risk at a given time. Although many market players take interest in credit ratings as objective third-party assessments of provider's

---

Box 16.13 Responsible Investor Principles

Institutional investors that adhere to the Responsible Investor Principles acknowledge they have a duty to act in the best long-term interests of investment beneficiaries. In this fiduciary role they believe that environmental, social, and corporate governance (ESG) issues can affect the performance of investment portfolios (to varying degrees across companies, sectors, regions, asset classes, and through time). They also recognize that applying these principles may better align investors with broader objectives of society. By adhering to the principles, investors have agreed to the following:

1. Incorporate ESG issues into investment analysis and decision-making processes
2. Be active owners and incorporate ESG issues into ownership policies and practices
3. Seek appropriate disclosure on ESG issues from investees
4. Promote acceptance and implementation of the principles within the investment industry
5. Work together to enhance effectiveness in implementing the principles
6. Report on activities and progress toward implementing the principles.

Source: www.unpri.org.

creditworthiness, they are also used by investors and supervisory authorities as part of the compulsory requirements to comply with regulations.

A *social rating* is an independent assessment of an organization's social performance using a standardized rating scale (SEEP 2006; see chapter 14). A social rating typically assesses both social risk (the risk of not achieving social mission) as well as social performance (the likelihood of contributing social value). The social rating evaluates practices, measures a set of indicators and scores them against benchmark levels and generally accepted standards. A social rating assesses how the processes and performance of a provider have contributed toward specific desired goals, with an analysis of overall outreach and quality of services provided. A social rating cannot in itself determine whether a provider has achieved a particular social impact. What a social rating contributes to, however, is whether the processes undertaken by a provider have moved the institution closer to achieving its particular social mandate.

Mainstream rating agencies tend to rate debt and the probability of default on a continuous basis, upgrading and downgrading ratings accordingly. In contrast, the timing of updates for microfinance ratings is more fragmented, because ratings tend to be valid for an extended period of time (see box 16.14). Repeat ratings demonstrate maturity in the market, as financial service providers have the resources and expertise at their disposal to commission another rating.[8] The

---

Box 16.14 Microfinance Institutional Rating versus Mainstream Credit Ratings

Since 1997, of providers that have been rated, the vast majority had microfinance institutional ratings conducted, rather than traditional credit ratings, provided by such agencies as Standard and Poor's, Moody's, and Fitch. A microfinance institutional rating is often more adapted to MFIs given that mainstream credit ratings usually automatically see negatively unregulated financial institutions with a relatively small asset size (small when benchmarked to mainstream financial institutions or banks) and uncollateralized loan portfolios.

This has started to change as more MFIs transform into banks, and the rating agencies themselves have developed more in-house expertise on the sector. MFIs that are operating as regulated financial institutions and/or are sourcing their funding on local or international financial markets are more likely to use standard credit ratings, rather than microfinance institutional ratings. For many MFIs, a credit rating represents an important milestone, because it is the mainstream product when seeking external investments in capital markets.

In addition to ratings for institutions, bond issuances and securitizations are also rated. Ratings for issuances are usually prepared by mainstream rating agencies. Ratings of issuances are important because they enable regulated investors such as pension funds and insurance companies to purchase investment products meeting certain regulatory investment grade criteria.

Issuances generally have a long- or short-term rating, reflecting the tenor of the paper issued. A bond will have a long-term rating, and commercial paper will have a short-term rating. Long- and short-term ratings usually relate closely to the rating of the issuer. Ratings for securitizations may differ from the issuers rating because they are based on the quality of the portfolio securitized, not the issuer itself.

Box 16.15 Ratings for MIVs and Funds

Just as providers are rated, so too are MIVs and funds. The Luxembourg Fund Labeling Agency is an independent, nonprofit organization created in 2006 to support microfinance and environmental related investments. The LuxFLAG Microfinance Label is a mark of quality signifying to investors that a fund invests the majority of its assets in the microfinance sector and does so with transparency, responsibility, sustainability, and independence.

In partnership with MicroRate, LuxFlag also offers Luminis, an online analytical platform on microfinance funds. Luminis offers analysis based on performance, risk, social, and management data. The Internet-based platform enables investors to compare basic data and analysis on 80 microfinance funds at no charge, with full fund profiles and reports available on a smaller subset for a fee.

CGAP and the United Nations Principles for Responsible Investment, a network of international investors, in 2010 established criteria for measuring the nonfinancial performance of microfinance investment vehicles. These criteria include environmental (carbon emission compensation, environmental exclusions, and exposure to natural disasters); social (average loan size, client protection principles, breadth of services, percentage of consumptions loans, percentage of female and rural borrowers, and percentage of activity relating to health, education, and women's empowerment); and governance (reporting, staff training, investee corporate social responsibility policies, investee anti-corruption policies, whistle-blowing protections, and seats on investee board of directors).

Source: www.LuxFLAG.org, www.microcpaital.org June 2012 issue, and www.CGAP.org.

frequency of repeat ratings also demonstrates that ratings are seen as a tool to improve governance or motivate change within the organization to continue to reach organizational mandates, both financial and social. Typically the rated provider itself pays for the rating, as is standard practice in mainstream ratings. Funding has been given to providers to obtain their first ratings on a cost-sharing basis by multilateral agencies and DFIs; however, this funding is being phased out.[9] Ratings for MIVs and microfinance funds are also available (see box 16.15).

Notes

1. A study by CGAP showed that in 2009, 88% of funding to microfinance was destined for on-lending, versus 12% for capacity building (8% at the retail level, 2% at the market infrastructure level, and 2% at the policy level) (El-Zoghbi et al. 2011),

2. The United Nations Capital Development Fund (UNCDF) provides a small amount of equity to some MFIs, but it is generally an exception for multilaterals.

3. In order to engage with the private sector, some MDBs have separate departments that focus on private sector clients; however, this is generally not their primary focus.

4. The term "frontier" denotes less developed and postconflict countries as well as rural and underserved regions of countries with otherwise robust microfinance sectors.

5. See www.unpri.org/piif.

6. See www.iamfi.org.

7. The term "Microfinance Institutional Rating" was first introduced and defined in "Global Microfinance Ratings Comparability" by Abrams (2012). M-CRIL, MicroFinanza Rating, MicroRate, and Planet Rating all agreed to adopt it as a common rating product name.

8. In 2010, 34 percent of the 396 MFIs having performed at least one rating was a repeat rating (ADA and PwC Luxembourg 2011, 29).

9. In May 2001, the Inter-American Development Bank (IDB) and the Consultative Group to Assist the Poor (CGAP) launched a joint initiative called the Microfinance Rating and Assessment Fund. The European Union subsequently joined the Rating Fund in January 2005. In February 2009, the MIF of the Inter-American Development Bank and the Development Bank of Latin America (CAF) launched the Rating Fund II. www.ratingfund2.org

References and Further Reading

*Key works for further reading.

*Abrams, Julie. 2012. "Global Microfinance Ratings Comparability." Multilateral Investment Fund (MIF), Member of IDB Group, Washington, DC.

ADA and PwC Luxembourg. 2011. "Microfinance Rating Market Review 2011." ADA and PwC Luxembourg, Luxembourg, September.

Basel Committee on Banking Supervision. 2006. "International Convergence of Capital Measurement and Capital Standards: A Revised Framework Comprehensive Version." Basel Committee on Banking Supervision, Basel, June.

Burand, D. 2009. "Microfinance Managers Consider Online Funding: Is It Finance, Marketing, or Something Else Entirely." CGAP, Washington, DC.

CGAP (Consultative Group to Assist the Poor). 2009a. "Focus on Deposits and Consumer Protection: A Silver Lining to the Crisis?" Article based on podcast interview with Elizabeth Littlefield, May 28.

———. 2009b. "Microfinance Funds Continue to Grow Despite the Crisis." CGAP, Washington, DC.

———. 2009c. "MIV Performance and Prospects: Highlights from the CGAP 2009 MIV Benchmark Survey." CGAP, Washington, DC.

———. 2011. "2010 MIV Survey Report." CGAP, Washington, DC, December.

———. 2012. "2011 Sub-Saharan Africa Regional Snapshot." CGAP, Washington, DC, February.

Dieckmann, R. 2007. "Microfinance: An Emerging Investment Opportunity: Uniting Social Investment and Financial Returns." Deutsche Bank Research, New York, December 19.

DiLeo, P., and D. Fitzherbert. 2007. "The Investment Opportunity in Microfinance: An Overview of Current Trends and Issues." Grassroots Capital Management, New York.

Duflos, E., and M. El-Zoghbi. 2010. "Apexes: An Important Source of Local Funding." CGAP, Washington, DC, March.

*El-Zoghbi, M., B. Gahwiler, and K. Lauer. 2011. "Cross-border Funding of Microfinance." Focus Note 70, CGAP, Washington, DC, April.

Forster, S., E. Duflos, and R. Rosenberg. 2012. "A New Look at Microfinance Apexes." Focus Note 80, CGAP, Washington, DC, June.

Freireich, J., and K. Fulton. 2009. "Investing for Social and Environmental Impact: Executive Summary." Monitor Institute, Cambridge, MA.

Gahwiler, B., and A. Negre. 2011. "Trends in Cross-Border Funding." CGAP Brief, CGAP, Washington, DC, December.

*Goodman, P. 2007. "Microfinance Investment Funds: Objectives, Players, Potential." In *Microfinance Investment Funds: Leveraging Private Capital for Economic Growth and Poverty Reduction,* ed. Ingrid Matthäus-Maier and J. D. von Pischke, 11–46. Berlin: Springer.

Harford, T. 2008. "The Battle for the Soul of Microfinance." *Financial Times*, December 6.

Ivory, G., and J. Abrams. 2007. "The Market for Microfinance Foreign Investment: Opportunities and Challenges." In *Microfinance Investment Funds: Leveraging Private Capital for Economic Growth and Poverty Reduction,* ed.

I. Matthäus-Maier and J. D. von Pischke, 47–65. Berlin: Springer.

Ledgerwood, J., and V. White. 2006. *Transforming Microfinance Institutions: Providing Full Financial Services to the Poor*. Washington, DC: World Bank.

Mahmood, A. 2009. "Social Investment Matters." Deutsche Bank, New York.

Market Data and Peer Group Analysis. 2010. "2010 MIV Benchmark Survey." CGAP, Washington, DC, August.

Matthäus-Maier, I., and P. J. von Pischke, eds. 2006. *Microfinance Investment Funds: Leveraging Private Capital for Economic Growth and Poverty Reduction*. Berlin: Springer.

McKay, C., and M. Martinez. 2011. "Emerging Lessons of Public Funders in Branchless Banking." CGAP, Washington, DC.

MicroRate. 2011. "The State of Microfinance Investment 2011: MicroRate's 6th Annual Survey and Analysis of MIVs." MicroRate, Arlington, VA.

*———. 2012. "Microfinance Investment: A Primer." MicroRate, Arlington, VA.

Miller-Sanabria, T., and T. Narita. 2008. "MIF Retrospectives Investing in Microfinance: Making Money, Making a Difference." Multilateral Investment Fund, Washington, DC.

Platteau, S., and H. Siewertsen. 2009. "Trends in Microfinance: 2010–2015." Triodos Facet, Bunnik, the Netherlands.

Portocarrero Maisch, F., A. Tarazona Soria, and G. Westley. 2006. "How Should Microfinance Institutions Best Fund Themselves?" Sustainable Development Department Best Practices Series. Inter-American Development Bank, Washington, DC.

Puillot, R. 2007. "Governance, Transparency, and Accountability in the FSP Industry." In *Microfinance Investment Funds: Leveraging Private Capital for Economic Growth and Poverty Reduction,* ed. Ingrid Matthäus-Maier

and J. D. von Pischke, 147–74. Berlin: Springer.

Reille, X. 2010. "SKS IPO Success and Excess." CGAP blog, August 11. http://microfinance.cgap.org/2010/08/11/sks-ipo-success-and-excess/.

Reille, X., and S. Forster. 2008. "Foreign Capital Investment in Microfinance: Balancing Social and Financial Returns." Report 44, CGAP, Washington, DC.

*Reille, X., S. Forster, and D. Rozas. 2011. "Foreign Capital Investment in Microfinance: Reassessing Financial and Social Returns." Focus Note 71, CGAP, Washington, DC, May.

Responsible Investor. 2012. "How One of Switzerland's Largest Pension Schemes Invested CHF130m into Microfinance." March 14.

Saltuk, Y., A. Bouri, and G. Leung. 2011. "Insight into the Impact Investment Market." J. P. Morgan Social Finance and the Global Impact Investing Network. J. P. Morgan, New York, December 14.

Sapundzhieva, R. 2011. "Funding Microfinance—A Focus on Debt Financing." Microfinance Information eXchange, Washington, DC, November.

SEEP Network. 2006. "SEEP Network Social Performance Glossary." Social Performance Working Group. SEEP Network, Washington, DC, October.

Stauffenberg, D., and D. Rozas. 2011. "Role Reversal Revisited: Are Public Development Institutions *Still* Crowding Out Private Investment in Microfinance?" MicroRate, Washington, DC.

Symbiotics. 2011. "2011 MIV Survey Report: Market Data & Peer Group Analysis." Symbiotics, Geneva, August.

*Women's World Banking. 2006. "Women's World Banking Capital Markets Guide for Microfinance Institutions (MFIs)." Women's World Banking, New York, New York, November.

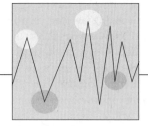

CHAPTER 17

Regulation

Kate Lauer and Stefan Staschen

Chapter 3, "The Role of Government and Industry in Financial Inclusion," discusses at a high level the role of policy makers in financial inclusion and the role of governments as "rule makers." This chapter is more technical in nature and focuses on the how and what of regulation—the rules that govern the financial system and the various actors within. It will be of interest to policy makers new to microfinance, practitioners wanting to better understand how regulation works, and other stakeholders interested in understanding how formal rules affect the financial ecosystem and how they can support markets that work better for the poor.

Definitions and General Discussion

Regulation: The term *regulation* is used in this book to refer to different types of formal legal edicts and pronouncements by government, all of which are published or otherwise made public. This includes primary legislation (that is, laws adopted by the legislature), secondary legislation (that is, circulars, regulations, or guidelines issued or adopted by the regulator), executive orders, declarations, decrees, and other similar enactments and issuances. Typically primary legislation designates and authorizes a government authority to issue secondary legislation. For example, the banking law may designate the central bank as the regulatory authority for banks. A microfinance law may designate a specialized financial authority as the body responsible for regulating microfinance institutions (MFIs). Primary legislation typically can be changed only by the legislature, whereas secondary legislation (such as regulations) can be changed by the regulatory authority. Some regulation may be enforceable in court by private parties; some may be enforceable only by a government agency.

Many areas of law and regulation impact financial services, financial service providers, and clients: Banking law (that is, primary and secondary legislation) applies to banks and sometimes to other depository institutions (in which case other possible names may be used, such as "financial institutions law"); nonprofit law is often relevant to nongovernmental organization (NGO) MFIs; financial cooperatives are often subject to a specific law on cooperatives, although in some countries they may also be subject to a specific finance law (for example, non-bank financial institutions law); insurance law governs insurance companies; leasing law covers leasing companies; the commercial code or companies law will typically apply to for-profit financial entities as well as nonprofit companies (where they exist); and payment systems law generally governs the payment infrastructure (and may also cover payment service providers and e-money issuers, either directly or as elaborated in regulations adopted under such law). Financial consumer protection regulation should apply ideally to all financial service providers. Other areas of law that may be relevant to financial service providers include competition law, secured transactions/collateral registries, anti-money laundering and combating the financing of terrorism (AML/CFT), insolvency, capital markets, property rights, and foreign direct investment. The regulatory environment can have significant impact on the particular models of financial service delivery and the possibility of developing innovative approaches.

Registration and licensing: Registration typically involves filing basic information with a government body designated as the registrar (for example, nonprofit registrar, MFI registrar, or cooperative agency). Basic information includes the provider's name, address, and constituent documents (for example, articles of association or foundation, by-laws) and sometimes the names of the founder(s) or owners, senior management, and members of the board of directors.

Licensing may be required to operate as a specific type of institution. (Some jurisdictions use the term "permit" instead of license.) Banks and other deposit-taking institutions, e-money issuers, and payment service providers are required to be licensed. In some countries, lending-only institutions are also required to be licensed or "permitted."

To be licensed, an application must be submitted to the regulator that oversees or supervises the specific institutions that are licensed. The application usually involves submission of various documents, including a three- or five-year business plan, operational policies and procedures, evidence that proposed senior management, board members, and significant owners (that is, those with an ownership interest exceeding a specified percentage) meet fit and proper criteria, and demonstrated ability to meet the regulatory minimum capital requirement. In some cases a deposit of funds must be made at the time the application is submitted. An applicant for a banking or similar license may also be required to demonstrate that it meets the following requirements: well-designed and implemented risk management policies and procedures, an effective audit function, secure branches, contingency plans, diverse ownership, and evidence that the core banking system and other technology requirements are adequate. A licensed institution in some countries may be required to seek additional licenses to engage in certain activities (for example, foreign currency trading).

Supervision: The term "supervision" with respect to financial institutions is most often used to refer to prudential supervision of banks and other deposit-taking institutions, although it can also include supervision of nondepository institutions, such as non-bank e-money issuers and payment service providers. The main objective of banking (or prudential) supervision is to promote the safety and soundness of banks and the banking system.[1] This does not mean preventing all bank failure but rather reducing the "probability and impact of a bank failure."[2] Effective supervision is critical to ensuring a well-functioning financial sector. When a provider is subject to prudential supervision, the implication is that a governmental body is ensuring that the risks being taken by the institution (and, for banks and other depository institutions, the risks being taken with the public's deposits) are not subject to undue risk of loss.

Supervision of financial institutions typically includes licensing, ongoing review of the institutions' reports and operations (which constitutes a part of off-site supervision and can inform decisions about on-site supervision, such as whether the supervisor should conduct on-site supervision of a particular institution), issuing compulsory instructions and corrective actions, temporary administration, and mandated closure.

The supervisor may document in detail the tasks to be performed and the specific approach to be taken by individual supervisors. These documents may or may not be available to the public. Some supervisors use the "relationship management technique" that involves an in-depth understanding of the particular industry and the individual firms, their business, and their risks. Other supervisors rely on reports and computer analysis. Some supervisors apply relationship management only to those providers that present systemic risk.

The two most common approaches to organizing the supervision of financial institutions are (1) unified or integrated approach, with one supervisor handling both prudential regulation and supervision and conduct of business regulation, and (2) twin peaks, which has one government agency responsible for prudential regulation and supervision and another agency responsible for conduct of business regulation. In general, unified supervision benefits from having the knowledge and understanding under one roof but is subject to criticism for lack of rigor on prudential regulation. The twin-peaks structure benefits from enabling the prudential supervision to be (theoretically, at least) more intensive and focused but can suffer from lack of coordination and communication between the two regulators (although there can also be a similar problem between two departments of the same regulator).

Self-regulation and delegated supervision: Self-regulation and delegated supervision both place a nongovernmental body in charge of monitoring. In the case of self-regulation, this body may be an association of financial service providers; the "rules" that are being enforced may be a charter drafted by members or an industry code of conduct (see chapter 3). Although self-regulation may on the surface be preferable to no regulation or supervision, it is often difficult to establish a system that is free from influence and enforceable; that is, the regulator can enforce standards against one of the members, especially if such member is influential.

In the case of delegated supervision, the delegated authority could be a governmental agency or nongovernmental entity (for example, an apex institution), existing or established specifically for the purpose of supervising a category of financial service providers. In comparison to self-regulation, a delegated authority may have the advantage of enforcement power, especially if the delegator retains ultimate responsibility for effective supervision. Although the problem with improper influence is less in the case of delegated authority, problems remain of both capacity (both of the delegator and the delegatee) and funding. This is an area in which time-bound donor support to develop capacity can be critical.

Rationale and Objectives of Regulation

Imposing regulation on market participants requires a clear justification, which can best be found in the theory of market failures. Although substantial experience exists to date regulating microfinance, there is certainly no "one size fits all" approach. In most countries the financial services industry is the most heavily regulated industry. Why is this the case, even though most countries subscribe to the principles of a free market system? In other words, what is the economic justification or rationale for regulation? In economic theory, it is assumed that the financial sector is subject to *market failures* and that this provides a rationale for government interventions in the form of regulation—the public interest view of regulation.[3]

The most important market failures that provide a rationale for imposing regulation are the result of information asymmetries and externalities:

- Information asymmetries in deposit mobilization result in depositors lacking incentives and the means to sufficiently monitor the utilization of their funds by the deposit-taking institution. In such a case, a regulator operates as a "delegated monitor" on behalf of depositors and can monitor the provider more cheaply and more effectively.

- In lending, borrowers hold superior information about their capacity and willingness to repay and use borrowed funds, which makes it difficult for the provider to choose the most creditworthy clients. One potential outcome of this is credit rationing.

- With insurance, again information asymmetries exist because of the complexity of the business and the inability of clients to assess the viability of the insurer. Regulating to reduce risk of failure of the insurer is of particular importance given the specific vulnerability of the client: If the insurer fails to perform under the contract, the client will suffer the loss at the moment when he or she or the beneficiaries most need the proceeds.

- Payment systems will—without regulation—generally favor first movers and can result in the exclusion of competitors that can potentially serve broader populations and offer more effective and efficient payment mechanisms. Regulation is also necessary to address the risk that would result from one payment system participant's failure to perform (that is, failure to settle its obligations by paying the other participants what is due), whether as a result of an operational failure or a contractual breach.

- Negative externalities cause the risk of "bank runs" (many depositors withdrawing their funds at the same time), which can cause otherwise healthy institutions to deteriorate, and contagion leading to a system-wide panic (the systemic risk).

The objectives of regulation are either directly targeted at removing these market failures (for example, by disclosure requirements that mitigate information problems) or at alleviating negative consequences of market failures (for example, by protecting clients). In financial regulation the burden of proof should always be on the rule maker; only if there is a clear economic rationale for imposing regulation is regulatory intervention justified.

Table 17.1 summarizes the main regulatory objectives for financial services for the poor. Each of the objectives is based on an economic reason for regulation and can be addressed by a specific type of regulation. The most widely discussed types of regulation in microfinance are prudential regulation, which is about the safety and soundness of financial institutions, and conduct of business regulation, which focuses on how providers conduct business with their clients (see, for example, Christen et al. 2012). The term "enabling regulation," which is often used in relation to access to finance, refers to the objective that microfinance regulation should not unduly restrict access to finance, but rather remove current bottlenecks and enable its provision in a safe and sound manner. The five regulatory objectives are subject to trade-offs (for example, strict safety and soundness rules curtailing access), but also to

Table 17.1 Regulatory Objectives for Microfinance

Objective	Main reasons for including objective	Type and scope of regulation	Examples for regulatory measures
Promote safe and sound financial service providers	Information problems in deposit and lending business and negative externalities affect safety and soundness of providers	*Prudential regulation* required only for deposit-taking institutions	Capital, liquidity, and provisioning requirements; management and governance standards
Guard against systemic risk	Risk of contagion exists among providers caused by negative externalities both among deposit-taking institutions and—to a lesser extent—among credit-only institutions	*Systemic regulation* mostly for deposit-taking institutions	Lender of last resort; deposit insurance; payment system oversight
Establish a competitive market	Regulation can establish barriers to entry, and providers might benefit from market power when operating in unsaturated markets	*Competition regulation* considering market power in certain locations and newly created entry barriers	Mergers and acquisition, interoperability, anticartel, and anticollusion rules
Protect consumers	Negative consequences of market failures may hurt loan and savings clients	*Conduct of business regulation* for all types of financial institutions	Disclosure and fair treatment rules; recourse mechanisms
Improve access	Transaction costs, information problems, and externalities as well as regulation itself are all reasons for lack of access	*Enabling regulation* for all types of financial institutions	Removal of existing barriers; adjusting norms to suit microfinance

Source: Adapted from Staschen 2010, table 2.2.

supportive relationships (for example, safety and soundness rules improving the safety of clients' deposits and thereby contributing to the consumer protection objective).

Regulation can play a role in pushing the "access frontier" outward over time and thereby bring new clients into the formal financial sector (Porteous 2006). However, in a country with very little capacity of providers to push the access frontier, changes in regulation are likely to have only a limited impact. Regulation (and supervision) primarily supports the development and expansion of the core, that is, transactions between providers and clients (as opposed to a market-creation role). Rules will be most effective if they follow the market.[4]

Principles of Regulation and Supervision

In designing an appropriate regulatory and supervisory framework for an inclusive financial sector, various guiding principles can be identified:

- *Proportionality:* The principle of proportionality advocates an approach to regulation and supervision that (1) is tailored to the specific risks of a provider type, an activity, or a product and (2) aims to keep the costs imposed on providers, regulators, and consumers proportionate to the benefits. This approach can have significant implications on various regulatory and supervisory initiatives targeted at providing the poor with financial services, especially given that most existing regulations and supervisory structures may not have taken the specific needs of the poor sufficiently into account. However, assessing the costs and benefits is not an easy task, and different views often will be found among stakeholders (regulators, providers, consumers) on the risks as well as the quantification of costs and benefits. Regulatory impact assessment can be a practical tool for implementation of this principle (see box 17.1).

• *Competitive neutrality:* To establish a level playing field, the same activity should be subject to the same rules, regardless of which type of institution is being regulated. This is also referred to as activity-based regulation rather than institutional regulation. This has important implications because many countries have chosen to establish a separate legal framework for microfinance, but at the same time allow mainstream banks to provide the same or similar products. Following the principle of competitive neutrality, various types of institutions' microloan portfolios should be subject to the same asset quality and provisioning rules. The same is true for conduct of business rules, which should equally apply to all types of lending institutions no matter whether they are prudentially regulated or not. However, prudential regulation and supervision is mostly targeted at the solvency of institutions, and thus an institutional approach is more appropriate. For example, minimum capital requirements

Box 17.1 Regulatory Impact Assessment

Regulatory impact assessment (RIA) is a methodology to measure the success of specific regulatory reforms. This can either be done *ex ante*, that is, as an estimation of the *expected* impact of a regulatory change, or *ex post*, that is, after regulation has been changed. RIAs have gained in popularity in developed countries but are also slowly picking up in developing countries (Kirkpatrick and Parker 2007). As an instrument, they can play an important role in creating a proportional regulatory framework.

An RIA measures the impact a particular regulatory change has on the achievement of regulatory objectives (effectiveness) and the cost of implementing the new regulation (efficiency) (Staschen 2010). The regulatory change could be either broad (for example, the creation of a new institutional type such as a deposit-taking MFI or a non-bank e-money issuer) or narrow (for example, the change of a specific prudential standard). An RIA can compare different options of regulatory change or assess one particular reform proposal in comparison to a situation without any regulatory change. Both qualitative and quantitative indicators can be used to measure the impact.

One of the advantages of an RIA is that it requires policy makers to clearly articulate the objectives of a regulatory change and the expected impact it will have. It thus increases the accountability of regulators and explicitly acknowledges the costs imposed on the sector.

are targeted at the institution as a whole and should be tailored to the risk profile of its entire business (which could include microfinance as one of its activities).

- *Flexibility:* The history of microfinance is primarily about financial innovation and "thinking outside the box." Without a certain amount of flexibility in revising existing rules to make them more appropriate for financial services for the poor or to remove existing bottlenecks, much of the growth of microfinance might not have happened. Principles-based regulation rather than rules-based regulation has been advocated as an approach that provides more flexibility for financial service providers, but it is more challenging for less experienced regulators and has also been criticized for being lax (Black 2008). The degree of flexibility also depends on to what degree rules are stipulated in primary legislation (requiring legislative change) or in secondary legislation such as regulations (can be changed by the regulatory authority).

Regulatory Structures for Microfinance Institutions

Most regulatory frameworks are not designed with a view to allowing for innovative approaches of financial services provision to the poor: For example, only commercial banks might be allowed to mobilize savings, only branches licensed by the regulator might be permitted to be used as customer service points, and non-banks such as mobile network operators might be prohibited to offer financial services.

With regard to microfinance regulation, one of the challenges is how to integrate MFIs into the existing regulatory framework for banks. Three broad approaches can be distinguished:

- *Accommodate microfinance under existing banking law:* Some of the largest providers of financial services to the poor in the world are regulated as commercial banks. Depending on the flexibility of the banking law, it might be possible to also integrate deposit-taking MFIs under the same law, perhaps with some amendments. This is easiest if the specific prudential standards for microfinance are prescribed in the secondary legislation (as opposed to the primary legislation).

- *Create a special law:* Various countries have promulgated a separate law for microfinance. (A few have instead adopted regulations, that is, secondary legislation, for microfinance.) Although this permits the law to be tailored to the specific risk profile of microfinance, harmonization with the existing framework for banks is more challenging. Such a law typically either covers only deposit-taking institutions or microlending institutions as well. The permitted activities for institutions regulated under this law must be clearly defined to prevent "regulatory arbitrage," that is, providers being issued with a license that were not supposed to come under this law (for example, consumer lenders or other financial service providers taking advantage of lower barriers to entry).

- *Issue an exemption under the existing law:* With this approach, MFIs are exempted from the banking law as long as they comply with certain conditions. These conditions define the specific regulatory measures applicable to MFIs.

A *tiered approach* allows different financial service providers to be under different institutional forms, each with different permitted activities and subject to different regulatory standards. The different tiers could be defined in a single piece of legislation or in separate legislative acts. The advantage of such an approach is that the intensity of oversight varies with the risks posed by different providers, and as well, providers can graduate from one tier to the next in line with their stage of development.[5] For example, the top tier may be commercial banks with the power to engage in all types of activities from intermediating deposits to entering into international and foreign currency transactions. A second tier may limit the scope of activities by allowing deposit intermediation but not international transactions, while a third tier may allow only credit activities (see box 17.2).

Regulation of Financial Service Providers

Financial service providers are subject to different regulations based on their activities and their specific legal form. For example, banks and other depository institutions are subject to prudential regulation. In contrast, nondepository institutions may be subject to certain limited nonprudential requirements, such as basic reporting.

In all cases, taking a proportionate approach to regulation helps to focus attention on the relevant risks and involves an assessment (ideally by both providers and the regulator) of what activities, products, and services involve what risks and why. A primary objective of regulating for financial inclusion—regulating so that markets work better for the poor—is ensuring that regulation is appropriately crafted and not unduly burdensome, and that it gives a clear signal to the market that financial services for the poor are a basic component and priority of the regulatory scheme.

Box 17.2 Examples of Tiered Approaches

In 2002 the Economic and Monetary Community of Central Africa (including Cameroon, the Republic of Congo, the Central African Republic, Equatorial Guinea, Gabon, and Chad) adopted a microfinance law that divides MFIs into three tiers: credit-only institutions, institutions that take savings from members only, and institutions that take deposits from the general public. Mozambique divides institutions into two categories: those that are licensed and are prudentially regulated ("microbanks" and credit cooperatives) and those that are registered and are monitored by the central bank (credit programs and savings and loan associations).

Within Europe and Central Asia, countries including Bosnia and Herzegovina, Kyrgyzstan, and Tajikistan have adopted specialized tiered microfinance laws. These laws typically differentiate institutions that provide only credit service from institutions that accept deposits. In 2002 Kyrgyzstan passed its law regulating microfinance organizations. Kyrgyzstan separates all microfinance activity into three tiers/types: (1) microfinance companies, (2) microcredit companies, and (3) microcredit agencies that offer microfinance on a nonprofitable basis.

Uganda was one of the first countries in Africa to adopt a separate law for deposit-taking MFIs. In addition to commercial banks (tier 1) and credit institutions that cannot take deposits (tier 2), a new tier (tier 3) was created pursuant to the Microfinance Deposit-Taking Institutions (MDIs) Act in 2003. In the first five years after the law was passed, four NGO MFIs received a license under the new law. However, since then, a commercial bank bought one of the four MDIs, leaving only three MDIs after nine years.

Banks

Banks engage in the risky business of financial intermediation: They take deposits from the public (both legal entities and individuals) and lend these deposits (with and without collateral) and other funds, including capital and borrowed funds to borrowers (who are likely not to be net depositors). Basic banking activities typically include but are not limited to opening and servicing clients' accounts as well as correspondent accounts; payment and money transfer operations, including the issuance of credit and debit cards and other payment cards; safekeeping; trust operations; issuing guarantees and stand-by letters of credit; and discounting bills of exchange and other promissory notes.[6] Given these various activities and the two basic concerns presented by banks—the stability of the financial system and the potential loss of the public's funds—they are subject to prudential regulation (and supervision).

Prudential regulation includes requirements to comply with specified ratios (for example, liquidity ratios and capital adequacy ratios) and other limits, including minimum capital requirement and capital reserves, credit exposure limits and unsecured lending limits, restrictions on insider lending, and open positions on foreign exchange (see box 17.3). Banks are often also permitted to hold only a specified percentage interest in other legal entities. These rules and requirements are intended to provide parameters for managing the risks of banking business.

Savings banks differ from commercial (or universal) banks by more limited activities and their smaller size. Savings banks, and often rural banks, are generally regulated differently from commercial banks and typically by a different regulator. Regulation for savings banks should be differentiated from regulation of large international financial institutions;[7] however, with respect to *microlending activities* these should

---

Box 17.3 Certain Prudential Requirements

Minimum capital is the regulatory requirement for the minimum capital that a financial institution must have. By requiring investors to put their own money at risk, capital should ensure that shareholders oversee the activities of the institution, which in turn should promote good management. To facilitate entry of institutions and promote access, prudential regulation can serve as a balance against a lower minimum capital requirement.

Capital adequacy sets a framework for how banks and deposit-taking institutions are capitalized or funded. Regulated institutions are required to hold a certain amount of capital relative to assets. Assets are risk weighted; that is, the riskier the asset, the more capital is required to be held.

Ownership, board, and senior management requirements typically include certain fit and proper criteria (owners may be subject to a financial capability standard; senior management and at least some board members will likely have to meet certain requirements regarding experience and expertise). Some countries may have certain additional requirements for significant owners.

Maximum shareholding limits (which may be set at 20 percent, 25 percent, 50 percent, or higher) are intended to address diversification interests.

Source: Ledgerwood and White 2006.

be regulated similarly to other institutions engaged in microfinance (Christen et al. 2012).

Agent banking (that is, a bank's use of agents to provide various services to clients and potential clients) has been advancing in several countries as a means for reaching and serving rural populations and others living in low-populated or hard-to-reach areas where bank branches do not operate. Agents may engage in various services, including cash-in/cash-out, account opening or facilitation of account opening, collection of other information (for example, loan application form) on behalf of the provider, effecting payments and transfers, and providing account balances. In general, agent banking is a type of outsourcing and should be regulated as such. However, in many countries, the lack of specific regulatory permission regarding banks' use of agents has been a barrier. It is critical to consider that rules are in place to ensure optimal and effective use of agents. These include (1) permitting the use of agent network managers and a tiered retail structure (for example, agents and subagents) to enable cost-effective rollout of agent networks, (2) permitting a wide range of institutions (including retail outlets and small shops) to serve as agents,[8] and (3) permitting agents to effect or facilitate account opening and perform other actions required to ensure the bank's compliance with AML/CFT rules.[9] In addition, it is important to ensure consumer protection rules also address the risks introduced by the use of agents.[10]

Non-Bank Deposit-Taking Institutions

Typically, non-bank deposit-taking institutions are permitted to engage in a subset of banks' permitted activities. Lending activities may be limited (entirely or in part) to microloans, and activities other than lending and deposit-taking may be restricted. Other complex or risky activities such as foreign currency exchange or derivatives may not be permitted. Prudential requirements should be evaluated by the regulator—which may be the banking regulator or a separate body—to ensure

their application to deposit-taking MFIs is proportionate. Certain prudential requirements applicable to banks and other deposit-taking institutions—minimum capital, capital adequacy, ownership requirements and maximum shareholding limits, loan-loss provisioning, and liquidity requirements—should be adjusted to accommodate the specific risks and benefits of microfinance activities[11] (see box 17.4).

Financial Cooperatives

The term "financial cooperatives" refers to member-based institutions with each member having one vote. Financial cooperatives include a wide variety of institutions of different size, membership criteria/composition, and operations, including credit unions, savings and credit cooperatives, *cajas*, *caisses*, and cooperative banks. In some countries financial cooperatives are found with more than 100,000 members and total assets exceeding the equivalent of US$20 million. In other countries, the financial cooperatives are local and small (fewer than 100 members) and geographically dispersed.

Much less uniformity in approach to regulating (and supervising) financial cooperatives is found than there is for banks, non-bank financial institutions, and insurance companies. In some countries financial cooperatives are subject to prudential regulation; in other countries, they are not. In many countries the regulatory body in charge of all cooperatives is also the regulator of financial cooperatives (and in some cases, although perhaps very few, the nonfinancial regulator is asked to supervise compliance with prudential regulations). In other countries one may find either an apex (or federation of cooperatives) or a separate financial regulator for financial cooperatives.

For small financial cooperatives, the common bond among members allows for a much less intrusive regulatory approach, especially if they take deposits only from members (although for many financial cooperatives, the distinction

Box 17.4 Adjustments to Prudential Requirements to Accommodate Microfinance Activities

- Minimum capital requirements are typically lower for microfinance providers given their more limited scope of activities and the nature of their business. The minimum capital—which is often used as a rationing tool (to avoid overburdening the supervisor)—should be sufficient to cover start-up costs as well as start-up losses.
- There has been much debate about whether specialized MFIs should have a higher capital adequacy requirement (CAR) than diversified commercial banks. Although a higher CAR lowers profits (and hence may deter potential investors from investing), it may not hamper growth of a new MFI in its initial years, because a typical MFI will require more time to build its microloan portfolio than a commercial bank will require to build a conventional loan portfolio.
- Ownership, board, and senior management requirements (that is, fit and proper requirements with respect to experience and ability to respond to capital calls) should be tailored to the specific business and risks of a deposit-taking MFI.
- Maximum shareholding interests have been adjusted in some countries and in certain instances to permit the founding nonprofit MFI to be a sole shareholder or to hold in excess of the specified limit. If not adjusted, the limit can be problematic for a transforming NGO MFI that must find investors—and, specifically, investors who share the NGO's commitment to the mission.
- Provisioning requirements imposed on microfinance providers are often higher than those for banks to reflect the lack of or different collateral requirements, the shorter loan terms, and the more frequent repayment schedules of microloans. However, a strong argument can be made for having similar provisioning requirements *until* a microloan becomes delinquent; after a certain period of time, a short-term unsecured microloan should then be subject to a more aggressive provisioning than a secured bank loan.
- Providers may need higher liquidity requirements because of the risk of contagion in borrower payment defaults, the ineffectiveness (for the typical MFI) of imposing stop-lending orders (that is, because microborrowers' incentive to repay is largely dependent on an expectation of a follow-on loan), as well as the lack of access to a lender of last resort facility.

Source: Christen et al. 2012.

---

between deposits of members and nonmembers is not significant given the ease of becoming a member by paying a small fee). Supporting this approach is the underlying reality that it is difficult to create a sustainable system for the prudential regulation and supervision of small (for example, 100-member) cooperatives; a large number of small institutions can overwhelm a regulator's capabilities. Furthermore, these small cooperatives generally do not have the capability (in terms of staff and information systems) or the funding to comply with prudential requirements. The alternative—to close down all financial cooperatives that are not prudentially regulated and supervised—would deprive many people of financial services that they need. However, there are clear situations in which financial cooperatives need to be prudentially regulated and supervised, specifically, when they are big (as measured by number of members and asset size) and/or take deposits from nonmembers. These institutions are often engaged in activities similar to those of microfinance banks and should be regulated similarly.

Microlending Institutions

Microlending institutions may be nonprofit or for-profit and may take different legal forms, including associations, foundations, companies, or corporations. A microlending institution's activities are typically limited to lending—which it does using capital provided by donors, private investors, and other lenders including commercial banks—and other ancillary services, such as providing business development services.[12]

Given the basic nature of credit-only operations (which by definition do not introduce risk of losing deposits), there is no reason to impose the burdensome and difficult prudential regulation that is applied to banks and other depository institutions.[13] Instead, a credit-only institution should be subject to certain fundamental requirements (in addition to registration): conduct of business (that is, consumer protection) rules, basic reporting, and perhaps fit and proper criteria for senior management, board members, and, in the case of a company, owners. The reporting requirement (if any) should be shaped by the legitimate objectives of the regulator. It is always important not to impose burdensome or unnecessary requirements.[14]

Some credit-only MFIs take cash collateral (also referred to as "compulsory" or "forced" savings) from clients and intermediate or on-lend such funds. Nondepository institutions should arguably be required to hold such funds in a bank account or other safe and liquid investment and should not be permitted to intermediate (that is, on-lend) them. However, many would argue forcefully against such a requirement, citing two reasons: (1) MFIs often depend heavily on the availability of such funds for their business and (2) the risk of loss of customer funds is limited to the amount by which (for any customer) the cash collateral exceeds outstanding loans owed by such customer.

Although credit-only institutions do not raise issues requiring prudential regulation, some countries have placed the bank regulator in charge of these institutions (typically using a newly created department). Other options include establishing a delegated body, a separate regulator, or self-regulation by an association or apex. Some countries may have only a registrar that holds the basic registration information of credit-only providers.

Many credit-only MFIs wish to *transform* into a deposit-taking MFI in order to offer clients savings services and also to access additional capital.[15] Taking deposits is a complicated business, and the new (or transformed) entity should be subject to the applicable licensing criteria and the relevant regulatory requirements applicable to such type of deposit-accepting institution. There should also be clear rules regarding how such a transformation is affected. Those rules should at a minimum permit the transfer by the credit-only MFI (including nonprofits) of its microloan portfolio to the new institution in exchange for assets of equivalent fair market value.[16] Some of the other issues to consider and address include (1) whether to permit inclusion of the loan portfolio to satisfy a part of the initial capital requirement,[17] (2) permitting an NGO to have an ownership interest in a for-profit company, and (3) permitting an NGO to hold a significant interest in a deposit-taking institution.[18]

In some countries the transformation of an NGO MFI into a deposit-accepting institution (or a for-profit microlending company) is prohibited because of a concern regarding the transfer to private actors of assets intended for public benefit. This is a complicated topic, but the concern can be addressed by ensuring that (1) the NGO MFI receives fair value for the assets transferred (as determined by an expert valuation) and (2) the NGO continues to operate under applicable nonprofit law or dissolves pursuant to such law. Whether the transformed institution continues to serve the same population as the NGO MFI will depend on the specifics of the transaction and the governing documents of the transformed institution.

Payment Service Providers and E-Money Issuers

Non-banks such as payment service providers (PSPs) and mobile network operators (MNOs) providing e-money play an increasingly important role in delivering financial services to the poor. Typically these institutions are not subject to prudential regulation for deposit-taking institutions, nor do they have to be as long as they comply with certain risk mitigation measures. They normally offer a much more limited range of services (that is, only payments and/or e-money), and risks are therefore also more limited. Following the principle of proportionality, it is best to bring PSPs and MNOs under a specific regulatory framework for non-bank financial service providers.[19]

A growing number of countries have a dedicated law for payments systems. Often the central bank has regulatory authority; sometimes such power is vested with another regulator. In many countries, this power is implied as a part of the regulator's responsibility for ensuring the safety and soundness of the financial system.

Providers that engage only in payment services would generally be covered under this law or secondary legislation (for example, regulations or guidelines) adopted thereunder. In some countries, e-money issuers are subject to the same regulatory requirements as PSPs; in other countries, one finds distinctions, including in particular the specified minimum capital requirement (if any), where customer funds must be held, and how

long a PSP may hold a customer's funds before effecting a payment.[20]

Unlike payments or transfers, which typically have to be cleared and settled within a specified period, e-money (in most jurisdictions) can be held indefinitely.[21] Its "redeemability" (withdrawing against cash) and thus its similarity to a deposit has made regulators at times uncomfortable with allowing non-banks to issue e-money.[22] Yet an increasing number of countries as diverse as the EU member countries, Malaysia, the Philippines, Indonesia, the BCEAO West African countries, and Afghanistan have created specific rules for non-bank e-money issuers. In other words, they have permitted a non-bank-based model of branchless banking (Lyman et al. 2008). The two most important regulatory measures to mitigate the risks of such models are the following (Tarazi and Breloff 2010):

- *Fund safeguarding:* The "e-money float," which are the funds received in exchange for e-money issued by the provider, has to be kept in safe assets so that it is available at all times. This could either be in accounts with commercial banks (in some cases subject to diversification requirements to minimize residual risks) or in safe assets such as government securities.[23] The float also cannot be used for any purpose other than paying it out to the clients.

- *Fund isolation:* The e-money float has to be isolated from claims against the issuer. This can be a problem if the funds are held in the name of the non-bank and the non-bank goes bankrupt. Some countries have used trust or escrow accounts to shield the money against creditor claims.[24]

Non-banks might be subject to other risk mitigation measures such as a prohibition to engage in other activities (in particular lending), transaction limits for e-money accounts, and minimum capital requirements. Furthermore, if non-bank agents are used, the same rules for bank agents should generally apply to non-bank agents to ensure a level playing field between both models.

Questions about payment system interoperability (the ability of clients of competing financial service providers to transact with each other) and agent exclusivity (the ability of a customer to use the agents of different providers for cash-in/cash-out services) challenge policy makers to develop rules that will facilitate fuller financial inclusion (Ehrbeck et al. 2012) (see box 17.5).

Microinsurance

Insurance companies are typically subject to a distinct supervisory regime because the risks of insurance are different from those presented by lending or deposit-taking institutions.[25] Normally insurance underwriters are prohibited from engaging in other financial services; similarly, banks and other depository institutions are generally prohibited from underwriting insurance. As stated by the International Association of Insurance Supervisors, the primary purpose of supervision of insurance providers is to promote a "fair, safe and stable" sector for the benefit and protection of policyholders (IAIS 2011, p. 15, sec. 1.3). This implies that providers of microinsurance are licensed and supervised by the insurance supervisor.[26]

As with many other aspects of microinsurance such as innovative product development or delivery, good practice in the regulation of microinsurance is emerging in terms of regulatory and supervisory options. First, there is recognition of the leading role of the insurance supervisor in supporting microinsurance and the relevance of a clear development mandate for the supervisor: Access to insurance should be included in financial inclusion strategies. Furthermore, regulation should be risk based and proportionate to the nature, scale, and complexity of the risks inherent in the individual business. Last but not least, supervisors should build their capacities in terms

---

Box 17.5 Financially Inclusive Ecosystems

"Interoperability and nonexclusive agents can expand financial access by opening more access points to a greater a number of customers. They could also increase competition that could drive costs down, though this ultimately depends on pricing—freely negotiated or government imposed—for cross-network transactions. But what is the best path to interoperation?

"Permitting exclusive platforms and agent networks can ultimately allow first movers or large actors to dominate the market, with the possible result of limited competition and artificially high prices. However, mandating interoperability too early in the growth of the market may discourage actors from entering the market due to concerns that competitors could 'piggyback' off of a large start-up investment. A few governments have imposed mandatory interoperability *ex ante,* sometimes even requiring connection to a state developed and/or -owned central switch for funds transfer processing. Such efforts have often achieved lackluster results. Other countries are considering mandating interoperability *ex post*—often upon evidence that the dominance of large players is suppressing competition. And other governments have taken a less direct approach—encouraging the private sector to interoperate voluntarily, with the tacit understanding that the government can impose interoperability on perhaps less favorable terms if the voluntary approach does not produce the desired results."

Source: Ehrbeck et al. 2012, pp. 7–8.

---

of the different client segment, business model, and internal challenges they face in their authority to accommodate microinsurance.

Existing insurance regulatory frameworks often show numerous barriers to inclusion, including the following:

- Product regulation

- Demarcation between life and non-life lines of business

- Market conduct regulation to ensure that the interests of the insured are adequately safeguarded

- Rules for claim payment or redress

- Capital adequacy, solvency, and technical provisions

- Prescribed standards on investment activities

- Prescribed risk management systems

- Prescribed underwriting systems and processes.

Regulatory areas beyond insurance also often impact microinsurance provision, including banking laws (which may impede bancassurance), telecommunication laws (which can impede mobile-phone based delivery), and cooperative laws (which may provide different standards for this type of entity).

Insurance supervisors should develop a regulatory solution that considers both insurance and other legal areas, encourages industry innovations, and clearly defines insurance providers and those that can act only as intermediaries.

Insurance supervisors have been pursuing a variety of actions to advance inclusion in their jurisdiction. Some countries (for example, the Philippines and South Africa) have established a tiered regulatory structure for microinsurance to facilitate entry as well as growth and formalization. This approach strives to make capital requirements proportionate requirements relative to the nature, scale, and complexity of the

risk. Creating a second tier of insurance license with entry and other regulatory requirements tailored to microinsurance supports the entry of new providers. It can facilitate the formalization of member-based organizations, which are highly prevalent in microinsurance and often not formalized under the insurance law. This regulatory approach can be necessary in the case of a significant number of informal providers.

An increasing number of insurance supervisors allow innovative distribution channels to reach low-income populations through known and trusted providers (for example, public utilities, MFIs, pawnshops, religious groups, trade unions, or retail shops).

There are more options for how the insurance supervisor can help to spur microinsurance, among them, lowering the regulatory burden that insurers and distribution channels incur, for example, by allowing the bundling of life and non-life insurance in one insurance policy, or by simplifying requirements of product registration and agent training. Box 17.6 provides more information on the policy, supervisory, and regulatory options supervisors can pursue to stimulate sound microinsurance provision and broad-based industry engagement by a variety of insurers and intermediaries.

Supervision of Banks and Other Non-Bank Institutions

Institutions subject to prudential supervision generally include banks and other deposit-taking institutions, although not all deposit-taking institutions are subject to supervision. Other nondepository financial service providers engaged in activities that are similar to accepting deposits (such as non-bank e-money issuers) may be subject to supervision by the financial regulator, although typically more limited than that of banks given the key distinction (that is, no deposits).

Credit-only institutions are typically *not* supervised. There may be a regulator that oversees

Box 17.6 Making Insurance Markets Work for the Poor—Emerging Guidelines for Microinsurance Policy, Regulation, and Supervision

- *Take active steps to develop a microinsurance market*—Confer a market development mandate on regulators over and above their normal supervisory mandate; understand the existing as well as potential market; consider both formal and informal providers; place information including market surveys about unserved market segments within the public domain; make a public commitment to the growth of microinsurance; allow space for market experimentation while monitoring risk to the market and consumers.
- *Adopt a policy on microinsurance as part of the broader goal of financial inclusion*—Formulate a policy appropriate to the circumstances of the country; consult formal and informal market players and relevant government departments; locate the policy within government's approach to financial inclusion; base the policy on sound information about the market and its evolution.
- *Define a microinsurance product category*—Determine the extent to which the current regulatory burden inhibits the underwriting and/or distribution of microinsurance; if the regulatory burden inhibits the growth of microinsurance, define a microinsurance product category with systematically lower risk that will justify reduced prudential and market conduct regulation; define microinsurance as wide as possible in terms of risk events covered and maximum benefit levels; restrict the contract term of microinsurance polices; ensure simplicity of terms and easy communication.
- *Tailor regulation to the risk character of microinsurance*—Consider the specific regulator provisions that restrict the growth of microinsurance; decide whether appropriate exemptions to key provision will be sufficient or if a new tier of regulation is required; design microinsurance regulatory tier to be attractive to existing insurers and potential new entrants; develop risk-proportionate rules for microinsurance providers; consider the need to maintain the strict demarcation between life and non-life insurers and if possible allow a microinsurance license holder to underwrite both.
- *Allow microinsurance underwriting by multiple entities*—Allow multiple legal forms to underwrite microinsurance, including cooperatives and other mutual types of member-based legal forms; ensure institutions that underwrite the same products are subject to the same regulatory requirements; ensure all institutions are subject to corporate governance and accounting and public disclosure standards adequate to ensure compliance; enable all microinsurance providers to access reinsurance.
- *Provide a path for formalization*—Allow new institutional forms to underwrite insurance; provide a tiered minimum capital and solvency structure; make underwriting mandatory of all or certain lines of business by larger insurers or reinsurers coupled with capacity-building requirements; coordinate formalization with other government agencies.
- *Create a flexible regime for the distribution of microinsurance*—Allow multiple categories of intermediaries; avoid prescriptive regulation that restricts potential intermediaries; provide ease of consumer recourse.
- *Facilitate the active selling of microinsurance*—Apply the lowest possible levels of market conduct regulation without comprising consumer protection; develop standard simplified

(continued next page)

compliance with regulatory requirements, including basic reporting, fit, and proper requirements
(applicable to senior management, board members, and significant owners), as well as consumer
protection rules.

In many countries one finds institutions that
collect savings and intermediate them but are
subject to no prudential supervision at all.
Technically these institutions may not be taking
"deposits" (as defined under the law), but their
activities involve risks similar to those of other
deposit-taking institutions. These institutions
should probably be prudentially regulated and
supervised if they exceed a certain size, measured
by assets (or in the case of financial cooperatives,
number of members).[27] However, supervisors may
not have the staffing or capacity to take on such
responsibility, and the institutions themselves
may not have the staffing or funding to comply
with prudential requirements. Policy makers need
to assess the situation and determine which is
preferable: institutions engaged in unsupervised
deposit-taking (or depository-like) activities or the
cessation of such institutions or such activities.

Banks

The supervisor of banks is usually the central
bank, although there may be more than one
supervisor; that is, the central bank may be

responsible for monetary issues, a separate regulator responsible for systemic risk and prudential issues, a deposit insurance supervisor, and
different regulators of state banks, private banks,
smaller banks, and other banks (for example,
savings banks or rural banks).

The focus of supervision for banks is risk management and should ideally be shaped by the
application of a proportionate approach. This
should serve to increase financial inclusion
because it advocates regulating according to risk
(of both the institution and the particular activities) and accordingly can serve to encourage and
enable innovations with confined scope (focused
on specific clients and products) and risk.

Prudential supervision of banks involves
(1) monitoring (both off-site through reports
and on-site) to ensure banks are complying with
prudential regulations, (2) issuing compulsory
instructions, (3) taking other measures to influence banks' activities and actions, and (4) imposing sanctions. Supervision of banks' agent
activities should be approached similarly to
supervising other outsourcing by a bank.[28]

Non-Bank Depository Institutions

The supervisor of non-bank depository institutions may be the same as the bank supervisor
(although typically there will be a separate

department for non-bank depository institutions) or it may be a separate financial regulator. In some situations, supervision is conducted by a nongovernmental agency, acting either pursuant to delegation by a regulatory (governmental) authority or as part of a self-regulatory scheme. Certain supervisory practices may not work well with respect to institutions with loan portfolios predominantly comprising microloans. First, the off-site and onsite supervision techniques need adjustment because microloan portfolios are relatively light on documentation and cannot be assessed by reviewing a sample of large loans. Rather, supervision should focus on compliance with the lending and collection policies as well as performance of the portfolio. Second, certain supervisory actions—specifically, stop-lending orders and forced assets sales and mergers—may not work for such institutions. Given clients' reliance on follow-on loans, a stop-lending order can result in widespread defaults (Christen et al. 2012), and with the often close relationship between loan officers and clients, an asset sale or merger that cuts such a relationship may also cause clients (who may also conclude that there is less likelihood of a follow-on loan) to default.

As stated above, less uniformity in approach is found in supervising financial cooperatives than other non-bank financial institutions. Often the financial regulator with responsibility over the banking system has neither the required staff nor familiarity with financial cooperatives to take on supervisory responsibility. This is a difficult challenge, and policy makers must decide whether to impose the responsibility on such regulator, create a delegated structure, bring them under a separate supervisory body, or seek to impose self-regulation.

Regulation of Financial Infrastructure

Well-functioning and inclusive financial infrastructure is key to financial inclusion, including credit information, payment and clearing systems, deposit insurance, and collateral/secured transactions.

The regulation of the *credit information* market is usually tied to data privacy and bank secrecy laws.[29] To transmit information about clients to an outside party (such as a credit bureau), without a separate regulatory provision permitting such activity, a provider would typically need to have customers' permission. (In some countries, regulation specifically requires providers to have customer's consent to such activity.) In countries where there is low participation by non-banks in credit reporting, the regulator may decide either to require participation or to create incentives to participate (for example, by applying lower provisioning requirements for loans that were extended based on review of the customer's credit report). To ensure customers are not subject to mistreatment as a result of inaccurate information in credit reports, there is typically a requirement to keep information up-to-date and remove stale information, to provide customers' access to the information on file, and to correct information upon notification of error.

Although regulators have traditionally focused on *payment and clearing systems* between financial institutions (for example, SWIFT), increasing attention and time is devoted to retail payments and transfers because of their increasing importance. Oversight includes promoting efficient, secure and reliable systems, addressing operational and other risks, and promoting fair and open access. Access to a particular payment system is usually determined by agreement among participants who decide which institutions may have access and at what cost. Ideally the participants of a payment system will set requirements (for example, proof that internal controls are sufficiently robust to address and cope with various risks) designed to ensure the system's integrity and stability. The reality is that formal payment systems are typically dominated by large commercial banks that have little interest or incentive to serve the poor. In some countries, because of concerns about dominant players or out of an interest in promoting interoperability, regulators have mandated access (or intervened in the case of anticompetitive pricing) and regulated fees (although these steps can be counterproductive for financial inclusion purposes if they serve to inhibit innovation). An important factor in determining whether to regulate *ex ante* or take *ex post* regulatory enforcement or intervention (which may involve the competition regulator) is the state of maturity of the particular payment system: in general, *ex ante* regulation is difficult to craft when the implications are little known or understood, as may be the case with a new payment system.

In the majority of countries, prudentially regulated commercial banks have to participate in the *deposit insurance* scheme. A few countries require or permit non-bank deposit-taking institutions to participate (either in the same scheme or a similar scheme), although usually this applies only to those institutions that are prudentially regulated and supervised. Supervision of the deposit insurance scheme and its participants may in some cases be undertaken by a separate regulator, in which case coordination with the bank regulator is critical. In all events it is essential to ensure that such a scheme can be funded and that the covered institutions are *effectively* supervised.

Although collateral is typically not a feature of most microloans, effective use of collateral (that is, secured transactions) requires clear regulation on what can be used as collateral, how such collateral is registered, and how a security interest in collateral is "perfected." In addition to having accessible *collateral registries* (either physically accessible or accessible electronically), it is critical to have a functioning enforcement mechanism. However, establishment of registries and capacity in the courts to enforce creditors' rights is time consuming and costly.

AML/CFT Requirements

Although a number of countries do not have dedicated AML/CFT laws, many countries have established requirements that follow the recommendations and guidance of the Financial Action Task Force (FATF).[30] The basic AML/CFT measures include customer due diligence (CDD) (often synonymous with "know your customer" [KYC]), monitoring and maintaining records of customer transactions, and notifying the appropriate authorities in case of suspicious transactions. (The AML/CFT CDD requirements may overlap with the KYC measures identified by the Basel Committee on Banking Supervision as an essential part of a bank's risk management practices. However, there may also be differences because the two sets of requirements serve different purposes.)

As articulated in the new 2012 FATF recommendations, CDD measures should comprise the following, subject to a risk-based approach that permits simplified measures for lower-risk products and services and exemption from certain requirements for proven low-risk products and services:

- Identifying and verifying a customer's identity using reliable documents, data, or other information

- Identifying the beneficial owner and taking reasonable steps to verify such identity

- Understanding the purpose and intended nature of the business relationship

- Conducting ongoing due diligence on the business relationship.

Because of the difficulty that poor customers may have providing proof of identification and proof of address in the absence of a national identification (ID) program, a country's AML/CFT requirements can negatively impact financial inclusion efforts.[31] The risk-based approach supported by FATF is critical to addressing this potentially significant and negative impact of AML/CFT rules. Low-value savings accounts and mobile money wallets particularly benefit from this flexibility (Bester et al. 2008; Isern and de Koker 2009).

Notes

1. Basel Committee on Banking Supervision (2011), para. 16, p. 4.

2. This in turn means working with resolution authorities so the handling of the failure is done in an orderly manner. Ibid., para. 16, p. 4.

3. The public (as opposed to private) interest view of regulation assumes that regulation benefits the society as a whole (and not only particular interest groups). See, for example, Barth et al. (2006). On market failures in microfinance, see Staschen (2010).

4. In rare cases, regulation might also spur the market, but only if it is closely tailored to what the market needs. A case for this are the Branchless Banking Regulations in Pakistan, which were issued before any of the providers had launched a product, but have since facilitated a vibrant market.

5. This approach was first described in van Greuning et al. (1998).

6. Additional activities that may be permitted but in some cases require an additional license include investment banking operations, foreign exchange operations, custody and sale of precious metals, leasing, factoring and similar activities (that is, buying and collecting claims), and conducting operations outside country borders. Each country will have its own list of permitted activities that may include some or all of the activities listed as well as others.

7. WSBI-ESBG message to the G20 Leaders' meeting at the Cannes Summit in November 2011, http://www.wsbi.org/uploadedFiles/Position_papers/WSBI%20and%20ESBG%20message%20to%20the%20G20%20Leaders.pdf.

8. Many countries permit individuals to be agents. Appropriate criteria should be designed in light of the activities that the agents will engage in. See further discussion of this and other regulatory issues relevant to bank agents in Tarazi and Breloff (2011).

9. For a discussion of these issues and others, see Lyman et al. (2008).

10. See further discussion on the consumer protection issues raised by the use of agents in Dias and McKee (2010).

11. See Christen et al. (2012) for a detailed discussion of the special prudential regulatory standards and the particular supervisory actions that should be applied to depository microfinance institutions. See also Basel Committee on Banking Supervision (2010).

12. Some microlending institutions also engage in financial education activities as well as nonfinancial activities, such as providing services related to education and health.

13. Generally credit-only institutions do not introduce systemic risk, although in a few countries, the microlending institutions have grown so large and have such significant borrowings that their failure can cause systemic instability. These risks, however, should ideally be addressed through prudential regulation of the banks that lend to the microlending institutions.

14. Reporting may include updating basic elemental information on ownership, board membership, address, and names of senior management. Requiring some financial reporting can be justified if it is made available to the public or if the regulator will use such information to better understand and monitor the financial system as a whole. However, requiring reporting for the purpose of "training" the MFIs is more appropriately set forth in private arrangements, for example, with a donor or a lender.

15. The terms "transform" and "transformation" in this case do not usually involve the conversion of an institution from one type into another but

rather involve the transfer of a microlending business to another institution.

16. Ideally such a transfer should be subject to an expert evaluation, especially if the loans are permitted to be counted as capital for purposes of satisfying the initial capital requirement of the deposit-taking institution.

17. There are alternative mechanisms for using the loan portfolio to satisfy the minimum capital requirement, including giving the transformed institution time to satisfy the requirement provided that it does not engage in taking deposits during the period before the date on which the capital has been contributed in full.

18. See Lauer (2008) for a further discussion of issues to be considered.

19. To ensure competitive neutrality, payment services and e-money issuance by banks and other depository institutions can be brought under similar rules.

20. The second and third requirements are related. If the funds may be held for only a short period, the requirement applying to e-money issuers regarding "fund safeguarding" may not apply or may be less restrictive.

21. E-money can be defined as electronically stored value issued on receipt of funds for the purpose of making payment transactions. It can be redeemed against cash or used for payments and transfers.

22. In fact, it has been argued that the money held in e-money accounts should also pay interest and be covered by deposit insurance. This, however, is not the current practice. See Ehrbeck and Tarazi (2011).

23. Even if these deposit accounts are subject to deposit insurance, the value of funds in the account is typically much higher than the coverage limit. The EU E-Money Directive also permits as an alternative to cover the full amount of the e-money float by an insurance policy.

24. It depends on the specific legal system what structure is best used for fund isolation.

25. Contributed by Martina Wiedmaier-Pfister, member of the Advisory Committee and

Technical Team of the Access to Insurance Initiative, on behalf of BMZ/GIZ.

26. Only one legal body should be responsible for supervision of insurance regardless of the provider and its size.

27. In its Model Regulations for Credit Unions, the World Council of Credit Unions takes the position that all credit unions (that is, financial cooperatives) should be prudentially regulated and supervised, and it suggests a minimum requirement of 300 founding members (WOCCU 2008).

28. For a more detailed discussion of such supervision, see Lauer et al. (2011).

29. This discussion addresses the regulation of private credit bureaus as opposed to credit registries, which are typically housed in the financial regulator and are permitted by applicable financial regulation (that is, the banking law or the microfinance bank law) to collect information from its regulated institutions as a part of the regulator's activities.

30. Depending on the country approach, the regulator responsible for enforcing AML/CFT rules (referred to as the financial intelligence unit [FIU]) may be housed in the financial regulator. If the FIU is an independent government agency or housed in another government agency (such as the police), coordination with the financial regulator(s) will be important.

31. A national ID program can also enable non-face-to-face account opening and the use of agents for KYC purposes.

References and Further Reading

*Key works for further reading.

Access to Insurance Initiative. http://www.access-to-insurance.org.

Barth, J. R., G. Caprio Jr., and R. Levine. 2006. *Rethinking Bank Regulations: Till Angels Govern*. Cambridge: Cambridge University Press.

Basel Committee on Banking Supervision. 2010. "Microfinance Activities and the Core

Principles for Effective Banking Supervision."
Report, Bank for International Settlements,
Basel.

———. 2011. "Core Principles for Effective Banking
Supervision—Consultative Document." Bank for
International Settlements, Basel, December.

Bester, H., D. Chamberlain, L. de Koker, C.
Hougaard, R. Short, A. Smith, and R. Walker.
2008. "Implementing FATF Standards in
Developing Countries and Financial Inclusion:
Findings and Guidelines," FIRST Initiative,
World Bank, Washington, DC.

Bester, H., D. Chamberlain, and C. Hougaard.
2008. "Making Insurance Markets Work for the
Poor—Executive Summary and Emerging
Guidelines." Focus Note 2, Microinsurance
Network, Luxembourg.

Black, J. 2008. "Forms and Paradoxes of Principles
Based Regulation." LSE Legal Studies Working
Paper 13. http://papers.ssrn.com/sol3/papers
.cfm?abstract_id=1267722.

Chatain, P.-L., R. Hernandéz-Coss, K. Borowik, and
A. Zerzan. 2008. "Integrity in Mobile Phone
Financial Services: Measures for Mitigating
Risks from Money Laundering and Terrorist
Financing." World Bank, Washington, DC.

Chatterjee, A. 2012. "Access to Insurance and
Financial Sector Regulation." In *Protecting the
Poor: A Microinsurance Compendium, Vol. II,*
ed. C. Churchill and M. Matul, 548–72. Geneva
and Munich: International Labour
Organization and Munich Re Foundation.

*Christen, R., K. Lauer, T. Lyman, and R. Rosenberg.
2012. *Microfinance Consensus Guidelines: A
Guide to Regulation and Supervision of
Microfinance.* Washington, DC: CGAP.

CGAP. 2011. *Global Standard-Setting Bodies and
Financial Inclusion for the Poor – Toward
Proportionate Standards and Guidance.* A White
Paper prepared on behalf of the G20's Global
Partnership for Financial Inclusion.
Washington, DC: CGAP, October.

Committee on Payment and Settlement Systems.
2005. "Central Bank Oversight of Payment and
Settlement Systems." Basel: BIS. http://www
.bis.org/publ/cpss68.pdf .

Cuevas, E. Carlos, and Klaus P. Fischer. 2006.
"Cooperative Financial Institutions: Issues in
Governance, Regulation and Supervision."
World Bank Working Paper No. 82.
Washington, DC: World Bank.

De Koker, L. 2009. "The Money Laundering Risk
Posed by Low-Risk Financial Products in South
Africa: Findings and Guidelines." *Journal of
Money Laundering Control* 12(4).

Dias, D., and K. McKee. 2010. "Protecting
Branchless Banking Consumers: Policy
Objectives and Regulatory Options." Focus
Note 64, CGAP, Washington, DC.

Ehrbeck, T., M. Pickens, and M. Tarazi. 2012.
"Financially Inclusive Ecosystems: The Roles
of Government Today." Focus Note 76, CGAP,
Washington, DC.

*Ehrbeck, T., and M. Tarazi. 2011. "Putting the
Banking in Branchless Banking: Regulation and
the Case for Interest-Bearing and Insured
E-Money Savings Accounts." World Economic
Forum, Geneva.

Financial Action Task Force. 2012. "International
Standards on Combating Money Laundering
and the Financing of Terrorism and
Proliferation – The FATF Recommendations."
Paris: FATF.

IAIS (International Association of Insurance
Supervisors). 2011. "Insurance Core Principles,
Standards, Guidance and Assessment
Methodology." International Association of
Insurance Supervisors, Basel.

Isern, Jennifer, and Louis de Koker. 2009. "AML/
CFT: Strengthening Financial Inclusion and
Integrity." Focus Note 56, CGAP, Washington,
DC. http://www.cgap.org/gm/document-
1.9.37862/FN56.pdf.

Kirkpatrick, C., and D. Parker. 2007. *Regulatory
Impact Assessment: Towards Better Regulation?*
Cheltenham: Edward Elgar.

Lauer, Kate. 2008. "Transforming NGO MFIs:
Critical Ownership Issues to Consider."
Occasional Paper 13, CGAP, Washington,
DC, May.

*Lauer, Kate, Denise Dias, and Michael Tarazi.
2011. "Bank Agents: Risk Management,

Mitigation, and Supervision." Focus Note 75, CGAP, Washington, DC, December.

Ledgerwood, Joanna, and Victoria White. 2006. *Transforming Microfinance Institutions: Providing Full Financial Services to the Poor.* Washington, DC: International Bank for Reconstruction and Development and the World Bank.

*Lyman, T. R., M. Pickens, and D. Porteous. 2008. "Regulating Transformational Branchless Banking: Mobile Phones and Other Technology to Increase Access to Finance." Focus Note 43, CGAP and DFID, Washington, DC, and London.

*Porteous, David. 2006. "The Regulator's Dilemma." FinMark Trust, Johannesburg. www.finmarktrust.org.za.

*Porteous, David, Daryl Collins, and Jeff Abrams. 2010. "Prudential Regulation in Microfinance." Policy Framing Note 3, Financial Access Initiative, Cambridge, MA, January.

*Staschen, Stefan. 2003. "Regulatory Requirements for Microfinance: A Comparison of Legal Frameworks in 11 Countries Worldwide." GTZ, Eschborn.

——. 2010. *Regulatory Impact Assessment in Microfinance: A Theoretical Framework and Its Application to Uganda.* Berlin: Wissenschaftlicher Verlag.

Tarazi, M., and P. Breloff. 2010. "Nonbank E-Money Issuers: Regulatory Approaches to Protecting Customer Funds." Focus Note 63, CGAP, Washington, DC.

*——. 2011. "Regulating Bank Agents." Focus Note 68, CGAP, Washington, DC.

Trigo Loubière, Jacques, Patricia Lee Devaney, and Elisabeth Rhyne. 2004. *Supervising & Regulating Microfinance in the Context of Financial Sector Liberalization: Lessons from Bolivia, Colombia and Mexico.* Somerville: ACCION.

van Greuning, H., J. Gallardo, and B. Randhawa. 1998. *A Framework for Regulating Microfinance Institutions.* Washington, DC: World Bank.

WOCCU (World Council of Credit Unions). 2008. *Model Regulations for Credit Unions.* Madison, WI: WOCCU.

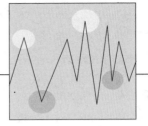

CHAPTER 18

Infrastructure and Outsourced Support Services

Geraldine O'Keeffe, Julie Earne, Joakim Vincze, and Peter McConaghy

In many developing countries, infrastructure is lacking or degraded, limiting efficient scale and broad-based access to financial services. Physical infrastructure such as accessible roads, reliable power, and efficient data and voice communication systems are all required to provide financial services. Financial infrastructure, such as clearing and settlement systems, deposit insurance, and credit bureaus, facilitates transactions between individuals and institutions and supports the efficient functioning of financial markets, enabling financial service providers and others (including regulators) to exchange information and settle payments. Reliable and efficient infrastructure fosters financial stability and is imperative for the successful operation of modern, integrated financial markets.

Outsourcing support services to third-party providers can improve the efficiency of operations by allowing financial service providers to specialize in their core expertise while paying outside specialists to fill gaps. It can also streamline the services offered by minimizing unforeseen costs and maximizing operational performance thus allowing for greater focus on providing services. As the industry expands, more and more service markets are developing for outsourced services including, for example, call centers, cash-in-transit, audit services, or software as a service.

This chapter briefly addresses some of the more crucial infrastructure required for the provision of financial services and various outsourced support services becoming available in the financial market system. It will be of interest primarily

---

Contributions to this chapter were made by Candace Nelson.

to providers and policy makers as well as donors interested to support the development of strong supporting functions.

Physical Infrastructure

Roads are among the most basic infrastructure and are used by all financial service providers, their agents, and clients. While most relevant for branch networks, even branchless banking requires accessible roads for providers to service automated teller machines (ATMs), for agents to replenish their liquidity, and for mobile branches to reach remote villages. Clients who need to make deposits and withdrawals, apply for and receive loans, or attend group meetings all use roads. In rural or mountainous areas, road infrastructure is often limited, and in high-density urban areas heavy traffic can mean that a disproportionate amount of time is needed to travel even short distances. This has implications for both clients and providers: "In rural Africa women often walk ten miles or more every day to fetch water. In the dry season it is not uncommon for women to walk twice this

Box 18.1 Lighting Africa

When the sun sets in rural Kenya, about 96 percent of households light up their homes with candles and kerosene lamps. These sources of lighting are expensive, inefficient, and unhealthy. On average, a rural household spends approximately US$18, or 20 percent of their total monthly income, on kerosene per month. To overcome this obstacle, Lighting Africa, a program of the International Finance Corporation and the World Bank, has been helping to develop commercial off-the-grid lighting markets. TechnoServe, a nongovernmental organization (NGO) dedicated to building businesses that create income and economic growth, has capitalized on this work and established a sustainable method whereby rural farmers participating in its dairy program can access affordable lighting resources.

To supply lighting products at an affordable price, TechnoServe linked rural stores to leading global solar lighting companies such as d.light, Barefoot, and Green Planet. These rural businesses, known as agrovet stores, which sell everything from livestock feed and drugs to motorbikes and water tanks, were able to supply portable solar lighting technologies at affordable prices by purchasing lights in bulk. The solar lamps also double as phone chargers.

While making this product available for purchase was a great start, smart financing solutions were necessary to ensure that rural communities could take advantage of this new efficiency. The cost of each solar lamp is anywhere from US$22 to US$97 and is guaranteed to last without replacement costs for five years. While the up-front costs are significant, the dairy cooperatives agreed to introduce a loan product through the village bank, something that was made possible by the security of the dairy business.

Households realize the monetary benefits of having a solar light after just four months. Assuming that a light lasts only five years (the minimum life span), the household will save US$144 over the course of the first year and more than US$800 for the remaining four years, a total of nearly US$1,000 in savings for rural Kenyan farmers.

Source: Keepper 2011.

distance."[1] Although the need for water is more critical than the need for financial services, many people, especially women, spend a large amount of time in transit in order to obtain the basic necessities of life; at the same time, there is significant potential for branchless delivery of financial services, for example, via mobile phones, with clients being able to transact right in their village.

Electrical power is critical to the operations, data integrity, and security of providers. In areas where electricity sources are irregular and unreliable, providers create their own electricity using a generator or an alternative source of energy such as solar panels. Clients also benefit from access to solar lighting (see box 18.1). Even in areas with electricity, unplanned power outages occur. If available, uninterruptible power supply devices or short-term back-up equipment, such as an inverter, can supply power long enough to support the proper shutdown of equipment and avoid the loss of data and incomplete posting of transactions.

Payment, Clearing, and Settlement Systems

Payment systems are the set of laws and regulations, procedures, and network infrastructure for transferring money between two or more financial institutions and their customers. They play a key role in the functioning of financial markets by facilitating communication between participants. These communications revolve around the clearing and settlement of transactions. Clearing refers to the transmission and reconciliation of payment orders and establishment of the final positions to be settled. Settlement is the event that actually carries out the obligations—that is, the debiting and crediting of the accounts of the parties within the transaction.

Payment systems can be either physical or electronic, with electronic systems growing the fastest with the emergence and wide-scale adoption of systems such as debit cards, electronic

fund transfers (EFTs), direct debits, mobile payments, and e-commerce payment systems. These electronic payment systems allow participating institutions to facilitate client transactions in multiple locations, perform electronic fund transfers, clear checks, and process card payments. Although this offers many potential benefits, participation is generally restricted to large, regulated financial institutions and their clients (Glisovic, El-Zoghbi, and Foster 2010).

Transactions between institutions or between clients using different providers require technology to allow one system to communicate with the other. This is generally referred to as *interoperability*. Interoperability can also refer to the linking of networks to allow users of one network to access the services of another (see chapter 12). Interoperability expands the number of ways and places in which money can be used and therefore is of value to consumers. An electronic payment system promotes interoperability between institutions, which, in turn, facilitates transactions between clients.

National and International Payment Systems

Banks and other depository institutions participate in electronic payment systems via message-routing systems that facilitate wholesale transactions. These systems exist both as global systems that facilitate international payments as well as national systems for in-country movements of funds (see box 18.2). At the international level, the Society for Worldwide Interbank Financial Telecommunication (SWIFT) network, a Belgium-based cooperative society, provides a global standard for fund transfers and processes payment orders on behalf of 9,000 financial institutions in more than 200 countries. SWIFT uses a unique number to identify the institution initiating and the institution receiving the transfer. In 2009 SWIFT introduced Alliance lite, a simplified product designed to facilitate the participation of smaller banks. Alliance lite affords low-cost access to the SWIFT network for institutions with a low volume of transactions.[2]

At the national level, several systems exist, including real-time gross settlement (RTGS), which is typically operated by the central bank to facilitate high-value, low-volume transactions. In an RTGS system, transactions are settled immediately using accounts held at a central bank, which eliminates credit risk associated with settlement time lag. At the national level, EFT switches also facilitate electronic payments via networks of ATM and point-of-sale (POS) devices. Switches can be either hosted by individual financial institutions or shared among a group of institutions, as is the case with national switching systems. Through these national switches, clients of all participating institutions can use shared ATMs and POS devices via debit or credit cards (see box 18.3).

Retail Payment Processors

Retail payment processors, such as Visa, MasterCard, Maestro, and CIRRUS, have their own settlement systems. Participating financial institutions issue branded cards to clients. When an institution issues a credit card, it evaluates the creditworthiness of the cardholder and provides a line of credit with a limit. Likewise, when it issues a debit card, it reviews the client's account to ensure that it holds sufficient funds for payment capacity. Clients can then purchase goods and services using the credit or debit card at retailers that accept the payment processor's brand. The payment processor facilitates the payment directly from the cardholder's bank to the retailer's bank. This process effectively transfers the repayment risk from the seller to the financial institution that issued the card, which should be more capable of analyzing credit risk than the retailer.

In addition to retail settlement systems, there is an increasing need for clearing payments originated by individuals or businesses outside of financial institutions. These person-to-person (P2P) payments, which are primarily facilitated by the Internet and mobile phones, require a system for settling accounts between a triangle of clients, mobile network operators (MNOs) or Internet merchants, and financial service providers. Some facilitate electronic payments over the Internet alone, some provide a combination of mobile and Internet access points, while others clear mobile payments only.

Box 18.3 Regional or National Switches

Shared regional or national switches have been developed to extend financial access in unbanked regions where access to international payment systems is limited or nonexistent. Examples of regional switches include Ferlo, the first electronic payment platform of the West African Economic and Monetary Union. Ferlo was founded as a partnership between Byte-Tech, a provider of electronic payment solutions, and AfricapFund, an investment fund owned by a pool of international investors. Ferlo has positioned itself as a provider of services and electronic payment solutions for microfinance institutions (MFIs), including integrated electronic payments at the community level.

Another example of a national switch in Africa is Ghana's e-switch, a national switch and smartcard payments system initiated by the Bank of Ghana. The system, which was launched in part through financing from international financial institutions such as Kreditanstalt für Wiederaufbau (KfW), can be used for savings, payments, and transfers, as well as for managing various business transactions. The technology is being deployed in rural areas through agent networks and merchants in order to extend financial access in rural areas. The technology permits offline transactions and fingerprint recognition, making it as accessible and as convenient as possible for the rural poor.

Source: CGAP 2011b; http://www.ghipss.net/.

Payment Integrators

To participate in an electronic payment system, a financial institution needs to consider how to integrate its core banking system with the payment system so that payments are processed in real time. This work is typically contracted to a payment integrator who supplies the technology that connects the systems in the financial institution with that of the payment system provider. Payment integrators can play a large role in promoting interoperability because having more financial providers connected to electronic payment systems means a greater ability for clients to transact with each other and access their funds from multiple locations.

The integration of systems involves the translation of banking instructions, or financial messages, from the technology that originated the transaction, which could be either a mobile (mobile banking, mobile money), POS, ATM, or Internet banking platform, to the core banking system of the financial institution where the client holds an account. The technology used to connect the two systems is often referred to as a "bridge" or EFT switch, which is a piece of software that connects multiple financial systems. Switches use industry standard communication protocols. The exact protocol used will depend on an agreement between the payment system provider and the financial institutions (see box 18.4). In some cases, where the two systems generate or require different formats, the EFT switch or bridge will translate from one format to another.

Voice and Data Communications Infrastructure

Telecommunications technology comes in two primary forms: fixed line and wireless. Traditionally provided by public entities, fixed telephone lines are sparse in many parts of the

Box 18.4 Payment Integrators

Two broad categories of companies provide payment integration services: core banking system providers and independent providers. Within this first category, core banking system providers bundle payment gateways with their own core banking system. These gateways are typically sold as optional modules and can be implemented either at the point of installing the core banking system or at a later point when the financial institution wants to connect to a payment system.

The second type of payment integrator is a company that provides other products and services to financial institutions and, either as part of these other products or as a standalone offering, also provides integration services. Included in this category are specialized software providers that enable financial institutions to connect to various payment systems or delivery channels via an EFT switch. This switch is sold either together with one of their front-end solutions (mobile, Internet) or on its own. Payment integrators may also offer integration as part of their mobile banking or commercial services. Both can offer integration services to a range of core banking systems.

Source: Geraldine O'Keeffe, Software Group.

developing world, as many governments have instead favored partnerships with private MNOs.

Wireless connectivity requires the end user to have a radio-equipped device, such as a mobile phone handset or a modem for connecting a computer to the Internet. The vast majority of the world's mobile phones and modems operate on a radio system called the Global System for Mobile (GSM) communications.[3] Users can access an MNO's network of radio towers by inserting an MNO-provided subscriber identity module (SIM) card in their device. A SIM card is a chip that stores client information. Coverage exists when a radio signal is picked up from a cell tower, allowing the client to make and receive calls and send text messages, also known as short messaging service (SMS) messages. GPRS, EDGE, 3G, and 4G are all wireless communications protocols that are advancements of the GSM technology, with the primary difference being speed of data

transmission.[4] Faster transmission speeds allow clients to receive confirmations more quickly and more reliably.

SMS messages are often used either directly by a financial institution or as part of an electronic payment system. Examples of direct communications include "push" SMSs, which the provider sends to remind a client that a loan repayment is due, for example, and "pull" messages, which the customer initiates to request their balance or a mini statement via a text message. The second category includes SMSs used within a payment system, such as when a mobile money provider sends an SMS confirmation after each transaction or after a transaction is done at an ATM.

Voice-based technology such as interactive voice response (IVR) is a phone technology that allows a caller to select options from a voice menu and interact with the phone system (Krugel 2007). While IVR was used prior to the emergence of mobile money, it is now being adapted for transaction services targeting illiterate populations.

Unstructured supplementary services data (USSD), a protocol used by GSM operators, is increasingly being used for mobile money services. Similar to SMS, it allows the phone user and the server to exchange a series of messages using a real-time connection. It is generally thought to be more user friendly than SMS because customers receive a series of prompts for information as they interact with the service.

Smartphones

Smartphones are the next step in mobile connectivity, adding computing, e-mail, and Internet functionality to a mobile phone. With the cost of smartphones becoming increasingly affordable for both clients and financial service providers (and their agents), they are becoming important business tools. The ability to run customized applications makes smartphones a viable channel for delivering financial services.

To take full advantage of smartphone applications as a delivery channel, the financial service provider needs to consider the availability and capacity of the data transmission network in their clients' locale. In many areas of developing countries, the only available Internet connection is via the GSM networks of MNOs (see table 18.1). Further, for cost reasons, many MNOs have only installed mobile data services on cell towers located in metropolitan areas. This means that mobile data services may not be available in rural areas where many financially excluded people live and work.

Internet Connectivity

Internet connectivity facilitates many functions in financial service provision. POS devices, tablets,

Table 18.1 Implications of Telecommunications Connectivity for the Provision of Branchless Financial Services

Connectivity level	SMS/USSD via mobile network	3G Internet via mobile network	Packet-switched broadband Internet (Wi-Fi) via Internet service provider
Incremental business benefit obtained through mobile data connectivity	Basic bank account control through a low-resolution menu system on a standard mobile phone display	Full bank account control (via mobile browser or app), e-mail access	Better performance of high-bandwidth applications (for example, customer support via live video link)
Client considerations	Low cost for access device, limited transaction functionality, lack of permanent transaction records	3G-capable phones relatively high cost compared to basic mobile handsets; cost of 3G data access (often quite expensive)	Smartphones relatively high cost compared to basic mobile handsets; Internet access mainly available via residences, schools, or offices; public Wi-Fi hotspots not common in rural areas
Availability (outreach)	High: urban, periurban, rural (most of the time)	Medium: urban, periurban, rural (less common)	Low: urban, periurban, rural (less common)

Source: Joakim Vincze, greenIP.co.uk.

and personal computers used in locations beyond the head office require access to the core banking platform of a financial institution. An excellent document developed by David Bridge and Ignacio Mas for CGAP ("Rural Connectivity Options for Micro-Finance Institutions") summarizes the Internet access options available for financial service providers, compares them with the types of uses, and comments on the viability of each option (see Bridge and Mas 2008).

Providers can use the Internet to establish a secure connection in the form of an encrypted VPN (virtual private network) connection of a branch outlet with its head office and then access the information system remotely. This allows for the secure exchange of operational data between branches, field offices, and the head office. Clients can also use an Internet browser to log onto their financial service provider's platform if the provider offers some form of Internet banking. From the browser, they can look up account information, conduct transactions, and pay bills. While many microfinance clients do not have direct access to the Internet, this is rapidly changing with the increasing availability of smartphones and declining cost of data communications.

By necessity, financial service providers almost always use a combination of communication technologies, depending on the location of their operations and the available infrastructure. Data transfer and connectivity solutions can use telecom or Internet infrastructure to connect headquarters or a central database with other operating points such as branches. A wide area network can be set up, allowing various operating locations to use the same central database. These point-to-point connections use a VPN that allows information and access only to private secured sites. When the Internet or telecom lines fail, some banking systems allow systems to continue processing transactions offline and then to upload and consolidate the transaction

details with the central database when conditions permit.

Deposit Insurance

Deposit insurance is normally established by the government to protect depositors and to support the stability of the overall banking system in a country. Deposit insurance protects depositors in full or in part from losses caused by the insolvency of a deposit-taking institution. Deposit insurance is needed because depositors cannot be expected to know the quality of a financial institution's loan portfolio and thus to evaluate the safety of their funds on deposit.

When developing deposit insurance schemes, there are three primary dimensions to consider: the extent to which the system relies on private management or private funding, the breadth of formal and informal coverage, and the susceptibility to the shifting of hidden risk by insolvent banks.[5] Deposit insurance can be financed by the central government through tax revenue, by participating financial institutions, or by a combination of both. The most common is to combine private and government sources. A typical premium paid by banks is in the range of 0.1 to 0.5 percent of insured deposits. Deposit insurance is most commonly administered through the government. In almost all countries, membership in a deposit insurance scheme is compulsory for regulated banks (Demirgüç-Kunt and Kane 2001).

The level and scope of coverage provided by deposit insurance should be commensurate with the level of risk clients are exposed to in the banking system. A key feature of deposit insurance is coverage limits, or the maximum amount for which each individual deposit account or depositor is guaranteed. The amount of coverage is important because it affects both the behavior of clients and the market discipline of depositors (Demirgüç-Kunt, Karacaovali, and

Laeven 2005). Some countries offer 100 percent deposit coverage regardless of size—that is, no coverage limits; other countries offer deposit insurance set at a level higher than the average deposit account, while others offer coverage at a relatively low level that protects only the most vulnerable depositors.

Credit Bureaus

Credit bureaus and credit registries collect individual credit histories from various sources such as banks, non-bank lenders, mobile companies, and public court records.[6] They cross-check and merge this information to produce a comprehensive credit report that is usually available to the market for a fee. The availability of this information benefits both lenders and borrowers; it contributes to lenders' ability to assess the creditworthiness of borrowers and motivates clients to adopt good payment habits that translate into better access and service by establishing a "credit record." Credit bureaus support the expansion of credit, reduce information asymmetries in the market, and increase transparency among all participants.

Credit bureaus collect various types of information, including

- Applicant demographics (age, marital status, sex, profession, residential status, education, status, employment, microenterprise history)

- Client credit behavior and loan history (number and types of previous loans, historical arrears)

and if applicable,

- Enterprise profile (business type, size, history, projected profits, business property)

- Enterprise financial statements (profit margin, net profit, assets, liabilities, expenses, equity, inventory turnover).

Most credit bureaus collect both negative and positive information. The former, often referred to as "black lists," focuses only on a client's current and past delinquency and defaults. Positive information, including details on all outstanding and previous loans as well as repayment behavior, can be more helpful in gaining a broader understanding of the client. Some bureaus include other data on clients such as tax information, history of guarantors and cosigners, business delinquency, bounced checks, and legal suits. In some countries, credit bureaus produce credit scores.[7] A credit score is a numerical expression—a rank order number or "score"—based on a statistical analysis of a person's credit history that indicates customers' relative creditworthiness (or alternatively, risk). Components of a credit score typically include payment history, outstanding debt, length of time managing credit, and types of credit.

Operation and Oversight

Credit bureaus are established and owned by both public and private entities.[8] The role of government includes (a) licensing and monitoring credit bureaus, (b) providing regulatory incentives for credit reporting, (c) mandating the sharing of data between credit bureaus and providers, and (d) requiring the sharing of credit data among all licensed credit bureaus, which is typically accomplished by having the public credit registry share its data with the private credit bureaus on a low- or no-cost basis (Christen et al. 2011).

Sharing client credit information has occurred primarily among mainstream banks and consumer lenders (see box 18.5). Informal sector providers and the low-income consumers they serve remain largely outside of this information infrastructure (CGAP 2011a). As a result, in some countries, MFIs and their networks have set up their own specialized bureaus. Some argue against specialized microfinance bureaus because clients often borrow from several types of institutions; instead,

Box 18.5 The Evolution of Credit Reporting in Ecuador

The Ecuadoran Rural Finance Network (RFR) looked at alternative approaches to credit reporting and settled on a partnership with Credit Report, a privately operated credit bureau. It selected the firm because of the strength of its technology platform, financial soundness, ownership by the international credit reporting firm Equifax (representing experience), and the price per report that the bureau guaranteed for RFR members. When the deal was struck, six privately owned credit bureaus were operating in Ecuador.

In 2011, after years of intense competition and bare-bones pricing—reports cost less than US$0.10 each—only Credit Report is left. Its unique access to data on borrowers at the base of the pyramid through RFR's members is one of the key factors contributing to its success. For RFR and the lenders it serves, working with a privately owned credit bureau provided access to data from other parts of the credit market, to related tools, such as credit scoring, and to quality data— all at a very attractive price.

Source: CGAP 2011a.

they advocate incorporating microfinance into mainstream credit bureaus as being more beneficial to both the client and the institution.

Credit bureaus must be credible enough both to enforce participation and to ensure that sensitive data are protected. An effective credit bureau requires consistent, reliable, and trustworthy data collected from and for both regulated and non-regulated providers. All relevant lenders in a given market need to participate. Information security and appropriate disclosure to authorized parties is critical to ensure equitable delivery of information (Helms 2006).

The Benefits of Credit Bureaus

Although credit bureaus primarily minimize lenders' risk, leading to a healthier portfolio, they are linked to a range of benefits for both providers and clients. Credit reports facilitate better, faster credit decisions. By making it easier to identify loan applicants with poor repayment histories, credit bureau data reduce lenders' transaction costs and increase efficiency. By identifying those with loans in multiple institutions and providing

a more complete picture of a client's obligations, credit bureaus can facilitate the measurement and mitigation of over-indebtedness. Knowledge of negative or positive payment behaviors, coupled with the ability to assess the probability of default, helps providers to calculate how much money to lend for how long. They can use the information to set appropriate interest rates and other loan terms according to risk-based pricing. In short, sharing credit histories reduces risk, increases efficiency and profit, and supports credit growth, leading to expanded access to financial services (Simbaqueba 2006).

Having a system in place for collecting consistent and reliable data will motivate clients to develop good payment habits, especially as they experience the power of their credit report. A positive credit history is an asset for clients as they try to access more and different types of financial products. It may help them to secure more flexible terms or lower rates, and it may enable them to seek other sources of finance rather than being tied to one provider. Timely credit histories can also reduce client over-indebtedness, as the system can identify those applying for multiple loans before they result in delinquency or default.

Challenges to Credit Bureau Growth

Today, only a handful of countries have functioning credit-reporting systems that include the range of bank and nonbank lenders serving the poor (see box 18.6).[9] The coverage of private credit bureaus is broader than that of public credit registries; however, there is great variation in the coverage of private credit bureaus globally. In Organisation for Economic Co-operation and

---

Box 18.6 Modern Credit Databases: Transforming Low-Income Financial Services in South Africa

South Africa has one of the most sophisticated and inclusive credit bureau infrastructures in the world. Mass-market credit reporting started through parallel initiatives by the Consumer Credit Association (representing the major retail merchants), the consumer microlending industry, and private credit bureau operators. The Microfinance Regulatory Council (since transformed into the National Credit Regulator) then took the initiative to regulate credit reporting and mandate full consolidation of the various data streams into a National Loans Register. The operation of the register is outsourced to two private credit bureaus—TransUnion and Experian. Other leading credit bureau operators in South Africa are CompuScan and Expert Decision Systems.

Building a positive credit history is becoming critical even for poor households, as the use of automated decision tools and credit scoring becomes ever more pervasive. Today, credit record checks not only are used in lending decisions, but also are built into many other routine processes, such as insurance underwriting, employment screening, rental background checks, and opening of utility accounts. At the same time, maybe unfairly, the belief that "no credit history is a bad credit history" has become entrenched in decision models. Hence, credit databases will increasingly play a gatekeeper role in the transition from poverty and into the economic mainstream.

Credit databases not only play a role in initial credit decisions, but are also a platform for collections. Databases provide address histories and current contact data; in addition, they track debt-related and other public filings, such as real estate transactions, death, marriage, and divorce. Thus credit bureaus offer lenders the functionality to put long-term trace orders on delinquent borrowers. A client whose loan has been written off and who is currently without revenues or assets, will automatically "pop up" for action if the name appears in a new credit transaction (indicating current revenues) or in a public record filing (possibly indicating economic activity or acquired assets). Although such uses of credit databases are entirely legal and legitimate, potential for abuse does exist, especially when powerful credit-reporting tools are introduced in the context of a fiercely competitive consumer credit gold rush. It is said that occasionally South African micro-consumer lenders will deliberately report well-paying clients as delinquent, so that they effectively "own" their borrowers and no competitor may legally lend to them or settle their high-rate debt.

Despite its many advantages, the adoption of sophisticated credit reporting calls for keeping an eye on the potential for exclusion and unfair discrimination that standardization of credit decision processes can bring.

Source: Contributed by Joachim Bald, consultant with Frankfurt School of Finance and Management.

Development countries, private bureaus cover 61 percent of the adult population, while in Latin America and the Caribbean they cover 31.5 percent and in Sub-Saharan Africa only 4.9 percent (CGAP 2011a). Credit bureaus face four principal challenges:

- *Market coverage.* It is difficult to establish credit-reporting systems that cover all types of lenders to the poor. In certain markets only regulated entities can access credit bureaus. MFIs may fall under specific MFI legislation that is separate from the laws governing other banks and financial institutions and, as such, are unable to access information from credit bureaus. Additionally, data on informal lenders are rarely captured at all.

- *Business model.* The small size of individual credit amounts poses a challenge as credit bureaus rely on high-volume sales of credit reports and economies of scale to cover their large up-front investment. Small loan volumes can be cumbersome and costly for traditional bureaus to handle. Providers may not have the information systems or data quality they need to meet bureau requirements and may find the costs of obtaining credit reports very high in relation to the size of the loans (Christen et al. 2011).

- *Identification.* Sometimes the lack of a national identification card, the absence of physical addresses, or variations in names among low-income clients can be hurdles to their inclusion in a credit-reporting database.

- *Consumer protection.* Protecting the privacy and accuracy of data at a reasonable cost is difficult given the high volume of transactions and small size of loans.

Unique Identification

Unique identification contributes to verifying identity and in doing so supports the integration of low-income clients into the formal financial system. In countries with national identification systems, the government normally issues and manages the identification cards, providing a unique number assigned to each individual. Identification cards are used to synthesize and track information about the public. They generally contain details such as the name, sex, address, and marital status of the individual and provide a unique identification number. The card can also include biometric information and smartchips. These cards are linked to electronic databases that can be accessed by authorized institutions such as regulated financial service providers or government entities. An individual's identity can be authorized by referencing the unique identification number back to the database, thus facilitating identity checks. With a nationwide unique identity system, individuals can establish their identity easily and effectively (Tiwari, Giri, and Mishra 2011).

In certain markets, a unique identification card can be used to open a bank account and is a valid document for satisfying know-your-customer standards. Furthermore, it can be used to verify customers and authenticate transactions. The ability to identify customers is a significant challenge for mobile banking; universal identification cards can help to confirm the identity of a mobile banking client. For example, the success of M-PESA, an e-money transfer and payment system in Kenya, can be attributed, in part, to the fact that Kenya has a national identification card (Tiwari, Giri, and Mishra 2011). Where the client is obliged to show a passport or proof of residency, mobile banking transactions can proceed more efficiently. Similarly, someone with a unique identification card may be more inclined to use financial services (mobile or otherwise) because establishing proof of identity is easier, significantly facilitating transactions (see box 18.7).

Box 18.7 India's New Unique Identification System

The Unique Identification Authority of India (UIDAI) was created in 2009 to issue a 12-digit unique number (called *aadhaar*) to all 1.2 billion residents. *Aadhaar* is linked to each individual's basic demographic and biometric information—a photograph, 10 fingerprints, and an iris scan—and stored in a central database. Individual identities can be verified using hand-held devices linked to the mobile phone network by sending the *aadhaar* and a fingerprint to the central database. The UIDAI verifies the individual's identity within eight seconds. Although possessing an *aadhaar* is not mandatory, obtaining one does require proof of identity, an address, and a date of birth. Individuals without identification documents may obtain an *aadhaar* if they are introduced to the issuing agency by a current participant in the scheme.

Source: Bhatnager 2011.

Collateral Registries

While somewhat less relevant for microfinance clients because loan methodology may be based on peer groups or other unsecured mechanisms, the ability to provide security for larger loans remains a tool for reducing risk.[10]

Secured lending refers to credit transactions in which a lender holds an interest in a borrower's land or movable property, such as inventory, account receivables, livestock, equipment, or machinery, as collateral to secure a loan. The interest in land or property is referred to as a security interest, pledge, or charge. In the developing world, 78 percent of the capital stock of businesses is typically in movable assets, and only 22 percent is in immovable property (Alvarez de la Campa et al. 2010).

Registries are publicly available databases where interest in or ownership of assets is registered. Different registries focus on different types of assets, including business registries, collateral registries, vehicle registries, leasing registries, ship or airplane registries, and land registries. Registries allow lenders to assess their ranking priority in potential claims against particular collateral. The use of reliable registries lowers the risks to lenders and reduces the costs of transactions by increasing transparency. Allowing a general (as opposed to a specific) description of collateral can make security agreements more flexible and does not require an update or new registration when, for example, movable collateral such as new inventory is ordered.

Clear secured lending laws that allow the use of movable collateral can significantly increase the level of credit because they enable borrowers who otherwise might not qualify for loans to leverage their movable assets to obtain credit. In developed economies, borrowers with collateral get nine times as much credit as those without it and also benefit from longer repayment periods and lower interest rates (Alvarez de la Campa et al. 2010). Secured lending laws improve competition in the financial sector by enabling both banks and non-bank financial institutions to offer secured loans. Using movable collateral also creates more space for the securitization of loan portfolios in secondary markets and enhances the ability of regulators to analyze portfolio risks.

For secured lending to operate efficiently, effective dispute resolution is required. Allowing out-of-court enforcement through, for example, arbitration, is a key mechanism for making enforcement more efficient. Court proceedings are often long and costly and therefore discourage lenders from engaging in secured transactions. Quick enforcement is particularly important for movable assets that depreciate over time.[11]

Outsourced Support Services

With the growth of financial services to the poor and particularly the growing complexity of products and providers, many services are outsourced to third-party providers. Supporting functions commonly outsourced include accounting services, training and technical assistance, management consulting, software as a service (SaaS), call centers, and security and cash-in-transit services. Mobile banking also outsources most customer transactions to agents or other third-party providers. Agent banking is discussed in chapter 12.

Auditing and Accounting Services

Adequate auditing and accounting services ensure accountability of financial records, comparability across institutions, and enhance overall transparency of financial institutions. Many providers engage external accountants to compile annual financial statements and to support their accounts and reporting activities. Most also engage auditors to conduct external audits (this is a requirement for most, if not all, regulated institutions), which provides an independent review of a provider's financial records, transactions, and operations (see chapter 15). External audits give credibility to financial statements and other management reports and can ensure accountability of donor or investor funds and identify weaknesses in internal controls and systems (Isern, Abrams, and Brown 2008). They act as a check on internal accounting and finance departments that are responsible for entering transactions, following accounting and control procedures, conducting appropriate reconciliations, and producing financial statements that can be used by senior managers.

Auditors and accounting firms need to understand the specific challenges and risks associated with auditing financial institutions serving the poor. These can include the ability to account properly for donor funds or partially subsidized investor funds as well as the need to work across multiple reporting standards if international investors or donors are involved (see chapter 14).

Training and Advisory Services

Specialized training organizations and management consulting firms provide training, strategic advisory, and management services. For example, NGO MFIs may seek external technical assistance to improve their financial management and other operational skills, while downscaling banks may bring in technical assistance to help them to adjust their systems, procedures, and staff skills to provide products for lower-income clients. Training and advisory services encompass a wide range of topics, including business optimization, financial management, strategic business planning, field staff training, product development, branding or marketing, and human resource training.

Training and advisory services can be provided on a commercial fee-for-service basis or may be subsidized by donors and investors. Particularly in parts of the world where the microfinance industry has grown rapidly, there is a shortage of technical service providers offering up-to-date services in line with the needs of market players. These services are often provided by international specialists. Numerous training programs have been developed to increase the capacity of providers, policy makers, and regulators (see box 18.8).

In addition, some organizations such as the International Labour Organisation (ILO) offer accreditation programs for trainers (see box 18.9).

Specialized consulting services are offered in a wide variety of areas within the financial services industry such as advising on the expansion of operations into new markets or supporting

Box 18.8 Training Courses for Capacity Building

Several ongoing training programs are offered annually, providing excellent opportunities for middle to senior management of financial service providers, policy makers, and regulators to develop their capacity and knowledge of financial inclusion. The following are some of the best-known programs.

The Sustainable Microenterprise and Development Program is held at the Carsey Institute at the University of New Hampshire in the United States. This two-week program emphasizes a livelihoods approach to microfinance, enterprise, and community economic development. The curriculum is built on a foundation of the five capitals of sustainable livelihoods—natural, physical, human, social, and financial. It emphasizes tools and strategies of transparency and good management practices that honor the triple bottom line (financial, social, environmental) of sustainability.

The Frankfurt School Micro and SME [Small and Medium Enterprise] Banking Summer Academy is held in Frankfurt, Germany. This one-week program is aimed at managers of microfinance institutions, commercial banks active in microfinance, and microfinance investors. Several electives are available. The program emphasizes the technical aspects of microfinance and leadership.

The Boulder Institute of Microfinance holds the annual Boulder Microfinance Training Program for three weeks from July to August

plus additional programs in Latin America and elsewhere. Offering training in English and French (and Spanish in Latin America), the program is one of the most popular and well-attended microfinance training programs. The extensive course selection is complemented by a daily symposium, where numerous industry leaders share their views on frontier issues.

The School of African Microfinance offers a two-week training program in Mombasa, Kenya, aimed at mid- and senior-level professionals working in microfinance. The program consists of plenary sessions covering key topics, electives (participants choose four out of 14 options), and moderated discussions. The courses aim to provide participants with the tools to develop market-focused strategies, deliver appropriate products and services, and lead high-performing institutions.

The European Microfinance Programme is a one-year master's degree program focused on microfinance. The program is jointly organized by four European universities and five NGOs. Classes are taught in English at the University Libre de Bruxelles in Brussels, Belgium. In addition to coursework, all students complete a two- to four-month internship at a microfinance institution in a developing country. To be eligible for the program, applicants must already have a master's degree.

Source: http://www.microfinancegateway.org/p/site/m/template.rc/1.26.19317?cid=PSD_MFGatewayBulletinEN_W_EXT.

the development of a strategic plan. Technical assistance may also be provided for the development of new products and channels, transformation to a deposit-taking institution, human resources and risk management, as well as regulatory compliance.

A growing number of consulting-based services (both for-profit and not-for-profit) are dedicated to helping providers to access capital markets. On the investor side, consulting services provide asset management services to institutional and commercial investors looking

Box 18.9 Making Microfinance Work: The ILO's MFI Management Training and Trainer Accreditation Program

As part of its Making Microfinance Work Program, the ILO offers a three-phase accreditation process for microfinance management trainers and a comprehensive set of training materials.

As of 2012, the ILO has accredited more than 100 trainers in Asia, Africa, the Middle East, the Americas, and Europe to deliver training to MFI managers using ILO training packages such as *Making Microfinance Work: Managing for Improved Performance* and *Making Microfinance Work: Managing Product Diversification* (Frankiewicz and Churchill 2006, 2011). Materials are available in a wide range of languages, including Arabic, English, French, Portuguese, Russian, Spanish, and Vietnamese.

Source: Peter Tomlinson, International Labour Organisation; http://mmw.itcilo.org/en/home/home-page.

---

to diversify their portfolios with socially responsible microfinance investments. Consulting firms that specialize in providing access to funding are generally centered in high-growth microfinance markets such as India or East Africa.

Some providers, particularly commercial banks entering the microfinance market, use a management service contract, whereby management is outsourced to a consulting firm specializing in microfinance. This is usually a time-bound relationship in which the consulting firm provides technical assistance to the subsidiary or greenfield institution on a fee-for-service basis. Technical assistance is greatest in the early stages, as the subsidiary or greenfield institution builds its internal capacity. Most greenfield institutions have ongoing management service contracts with their holding company (if applicable) to ensure standardization across a network of providers (see chapter 7).

Software as a Service

Many providers find it difficult to obtain the necessary skills in-house to manage their information technology (IT) environments. In these cases, they may choose to outsource some or all elements of their IT management. This could take the form of a core banking system based on an SaaS model, whereby the system is hosted on servers sitting at a remote location managed directly by the supplier or in the "cloud." Such arrangements relieve providers of the need to invest in hardware and skills to maintain and support the system in-house, reducing costs and the need for skilled technical personnel, who can often be difficult to find and expensive to hire.

SaaS options are increasingly available from suppliers and are often cost-effective. The supplier hosts the core banking system on its servers, which have been fully configured for the provider. Typically, costing of this type of service is either per client or per account and often does not require an up-front investment in a license. While many providers may find this attractive, the provider must have strong communication links to access the servers and must be fully assured of the quality of the day-to-day support of the supplier.

Other models of IT outsourcing also exist whereby the core banking system is hosted in-house, but third-party companies provide support in specific areas. In such cases, providers still need to have some IT resources available, but the number and skills of these employees could be lower than if the IT function were fully supported in-house. The following types of services are typically suited to this type of outsourcing:

- *Strategic IT inputs.* Help the institution to design and manage a high-level IT strategy

- *Hardware and networking.* Provide resources to manage the day-to-day work associated with running a network

- *Core banking system support.* Resolve issues and facilitate communication through a help desk with a dedicated staff

- *Core banking system audit.* Execute audit checks and report back to the provider's audit department. Technical checks focus primarily on the integrity of the database, security, and functionality of the backup system. Database audits help to ensure that the core banking system is working, provides accurate reports, and accounts for all transactions appropriately

- *Disaster recovery and backup.* Double as a backup data recovery site with a replica of the machines required to run the information system should there be a failure or loss of service

- *Custom developments.* Develop reports and implement supporting systems.

Outsourcing of IT is quite common among microfinance networks. For these organizations, a head office typically includes some elements of IT support, which helps not only to support country operations, but also to standardize the systems across all providers working within the same network. In these cases, the country operations typically still have in-house IT departments, but these tend to focus on the day-to-day operations, while the head office concentrates on special projects and more strategic inputs related to technology. Such support mechanisms work well provided that the head office maintains a good understanding of the challenges facing personnel operating in the field.

Call Centers

Financial service providers often rely on call centers to respond to client requests and communicate with clients about products and services. This is particularly true of mature MFIs and large institutional providers such as postal banks or savings banks. A call center is a centralized office that receives and transmits a large volume of requests by telephone. It generally is used to manage incoming inquiries from consumers for product and service support. Similarly, outgoing calls are also made to provide sales information or conduct telemarketing. Some may also support loan collection by calling clients with arrears and facilitating payment based on established procedures. Call centers are not limited to telephone technology; they may also handle letters, faxes, live chats, and e-mails. Call centers provide important physical and technological infrastructure because they provide the technology necessary to reach large numbers of clients.

Call and contact centers have increased in importance in recent years as more poor women and men have begun to use mobile technology (see box 18.10). The ability to attain support through a telephone call or text message greatly reduces the transportation and opportunity costs of visiting a physical location such as a branch. Similarly, call centers often process calls long after bank branches close for the day. Thus clients can communicate with providers in a more convenient manner at more flexible times.

Debt Collection

Many financial service providers outsource their collection practices to specialized agencies. Collection activities demand a significant amount of time and resources and require specialized skills if they are to be conducted well. Collection agencies have trained staff with experience in approaching clients and collecting past-due loans. Unlike frontline staff, they can dedicate the appropriate time to collection activities. Collection agencies often employ a variety

Box 18.10 Call Center at the First Microfinance Institution Syria

The First MicroFinance Institution Syria (FMFI-S) was interested in developing channels beyond its branch network for marketing its services. To improve services and expand outreach, FMFI-S established a call center to handle customer complaints and queries regarding products and services and also to disseminate information on promotional campaigns. By the end of 2010, seven promotional campaigns had been launched, resulting in 32 percent of those called having a conversation with an FMFI-S staff member. Of this 32 percent, about 10 percent visited a branch and received a loan. The overall number of loans being disbursed increased 3 percent and was expected to increase further as the campaigns continued. All of FMFI-S's branches say that the call center has played a role in attracting new clients.

Source: Aga Khan Agency for Microfinance 2011.

of strategies for receiving payment, including calling, collecting on-site, setting up payment plans, and offering various payment collection points. Collection agencies may be able to prompt payback in a more straightforward manner than loan officers because they do not have an ongoing relationship with the client. Thus a specialized agency may be able to secure payback while minimizing long-term damage to the relationship between the client and the financial institution.

However, there are risks and costs to relying on specialized collection agencies, and these must be assessed prior to deciding to outsource. Many collection agencies lack experience with the low-income sector. As a result, providers need to conduct a thorough due diligence of the collection agency and ensure that it understands the unique needs and behaviors of low-income customers. It also must ensure that outsourcing collections makes financial sense. Normally collection agencies take a percentage of the recovered debt, providing the incentive for increased recoveries. A full feasibility analysis including a multiyear cost-benefit analysis should be completed prior to outsourcing debt collection activities.

Outsourcing collection services can also disrupt the lines of communication between the provider and client. Procedures for contacting clients should be simple, consistent, and take into account the local context. Providers using collection agencies might find it useful to educate their clients on the role and authority of the collection agency. If the client fails to acknowledge the collection agency's authority, the agency may have a difficult time recovering loans and may damage the long-term relationship between the client and provider (ACCION 2008; see box 18.11).

Security and Cash in Transit

Specialized firms provide security and cash-in-transit services to minimize theft and fraud and ensure that clients can draw on deposit, credit, and mobile banking services safely. Outsourced security services generally involve the physical safeguarding of branches and ATMs to certified (and sometimes bonded) staff. Security staff is responsible for minimizing and preventing the possibility of robberies and for ensuring that security procedures for clients, staff, and other stakeholders are respected.

Box 18.11 In Practice: Paraguay Financiera El Comercio

The shareholders and board members of the Financiera El Comercio in Paraguay created their own external collection agency, called Gestión, which managed El Comercio's loans more than 180 days past due using specialized collections officers and lawyers. The company also provided call center services for loans up to 30 days past due to support loan officers in their collection activities. After some years of operations, El Comercio has reinstated its collections activities within the institution. The main reasons behind this decision were high operating costs to maintain two separate administrative structures (two accounts, two boards), and the absence of feedback channels between Gestión and the risk management unit of El Comercio for reviewing policies and procedures.

Source: ACCION 2008.

Cash-in-transit refers to the physical transfer of bank notes, coins, or items of value from one location to another. This can include the transport of cash and valuables from bank branches and smaller district offices to headquarters as well as the transport of cash from ATMs or agent locations. In some countries cash-in-transit companies fall under transport and security legislation, while in others they fall under municipal police or local authorities. Regulation often focuses on security and logistics. For example, cash-in-transit companies are often restricted in the number of firearms staff can carry, the types of vehicles used, and the number of staff per vehicle.

The importance of sound security and cash-in-transit procedures continues to increase as mobile banking becomes more prominent. Robbery and theft of agents are serious concerns. In a survey conducted by the Consultative Group to Assist the Poor of mobile banking agents in several key markets that included questions related to security, 93 percent of agents in Brazil reported that being an agent increases the risk of being robbed and 25 percent said that they had been robbed at least once during the past three years. One aggregator for M-PESA in Kenya reported that 10 percent of agents were robbed in 2009 (CGAP 2012).

Outsourcing security requirements can help to prevent the possibility of theft, although it can significantly increase the costs of doing business. The direct cost of outsourcing services must be balanced against the benefits accrued from additional security, mainly less money lost from theft or damage.

Notes

1. http://www.waterforafrica.org.uk/go/more-information/water-and-sanitation-facts/.
2. www.swift.com/alliancelite.
3. http://www.gsm.org/technology/gsm/index.htm.
4. Additional technical information on mobile technology can be found at http://www.gsm.org/technology/index.htm.
5. This section draws heavily from Demirgüç-Kunt and Kane (2001) and Demirgüç-Kunt, Karacaovali, and Laeven (2005).
6. This section was contributed by Candace Nelson.

7. Adapted from Campion and Valenzuela (2001); Making Finance Work for Africa (http://www.mfw4a.org/financial-infrastructure/credit-bureaus.html).

8. Credit bureaus tend to be private, while credit registries tend to be public or government-sponsored entities.

9. This section draws heavily from the following two sources: Making Finance Work for Africa (http://www.mfw4a.org/financial-infrastructure/credit-bureaus.html); CGAP (2011a).

10. Summarized from Making Finance Work for Africa (http://www.mfw4a.org/financial-infrastructure/collateral-registries.html).

11. https://www.mfw4a.org/financial-infrastructure/collateral-registries.html.

References and Further Reading

ACCION. 2008. "Best Practices in Collection Strategies." In Sight 26, ACCION, Boston, November.

Aga Khan Agency for Microfinance. 2011. "Case Study: Syria." Aga Khan Agency for Microfinance, Geneva.

Alvarez de la Campa, Alejandro, Everett T. Wohlers, Yair Barnes, and Sevi Simavi. 2010. "Secured Transaction Systems and Collateral Registries." IFC and World Bank, Washington, DC.

Bhatnager, Subhash. 2011. "India's Unique Identification System." East Asia Forum, October 22.

Bridge, David, and Ignacio Mas. 2008. "Rural Connectivity Options for Microfinance Institutions." CGAP, Washington, DC.

Campion, Anita, and Liza Valenzuela. 2001. "Credit Bureaus: A Necessity for Microfinance?" USAID, Office of Microfinance Development, Washington, DC, October.

CGAP (Consultative Group to Assist the Poor). 1998. "External Audits of Microfinance Institutions: A Handbook." Technical Tool Series 3, CGAP, Washington, DC.

———. 2011a. "Credit Reporting at the Base of the Pyramid: Key Issues and Success Factors." Access to Finance Forum 1, CGAP and IFC, Washington, DC, September.

———. 2011b. "Technology Program Country Note: West African Economic and Monetary Union (WAEMU)." CGAP, Washington, DC.

———. 2012. "Security Risk and Mobile Banking: Living with Robbery in Brazil." CGAP, Washington, DC. http://www.cgap.org/p/site/c/template.rc/1.26.15535.

Christen, Robert Peck, Kate Lauer, Timothy R. Lyman, and Richard Rosenberg. 2011. "A Guide to Regulation and Supervision of Microfinance." Microfinance Consensus Guidelines, CGAP, Washington, DC.

Demirgüç-Kunt, Aslı, and Edward J. Kane. 2001. "Deposit Insurance around the Globe: Where Does It Work?" Policy Research Working Paper 2679, World Bank, Washington, DC.

Demirgüç-Kunt, Aslı, Baybars Karacaovali, and Luc Laeven. 2005. "Deposit Insurance around the World: A Comprehensive Database." Policy Research Working Paper 3628, World Bank, Washington, DC.

Frankiewicz, Cheryl, and Craig Churchill. 2006. *Making Microfinance Work: Managing for Improved Performance.* Geneva: ILO.

———. 2011. *Making Microfinance Work: Managing Product Diversification.* Geneva: ILO.

Frederick, Laura I. 2008. "Information Technology Innovations That Extend Rural Microfinance Outreach." In *New Partnerships for Innovation in Microfinance,* ed. Ingrid Matthaus-Maier and J. D. von Pischke, ch. 10. Berlin: Springer.

Glisovic, Jasmina, Mayada El-Zoghbi, and Sarah Foster. 2010. *Advancing Savings Services: Resource Guide for Funders.* Washington, DC: CGAP and the World Bank.

Helms, Brigit. 2006. "Access for All: Building Inclusive Financial Systems." CGAP, Washington, DC.

Isern, Jennifer, Julie Abrams, and Matthew Brown. 2008. "Appraisal Guide for

Microfinance Institutions." CGAP, Washington, DC, March.

Ivatury, Gautam. 2008. "Using Technology to Build Inclusive Financial Systems." In *New Partnerships for Innovation in Microfinance*, ed. Ingrid Matthaus-Maier and J. D. von Pischke, ch. 9. Berlin: Springer.

Keepper, Kevin. 2011. "How to Save Rural Kenyan Farmers $200 per Year." *Next Billion*, March 22.

Krugel, Gavin Troy. 2007. "Mobile Banking Technology Options." August. FinMark Trust.

Matthaus-Maier, Ingrid, and J. D. von Pischke, eds. 2008. *New Partnerships for Innovation in Microfinance*. Berlin: Springer.

Simbaqueba, Lilian. 2006. "The Role of a Microfinance Bureau." PowerPoint presentation at the regional conference "Credit Reporting Systems in Africa," LiSim, Bogotá, Colombia. www.lisim.com.

Tiwari, Akhrand J., Anurodh Giri, and Priyank Mishra. 2011. "Leveraging Unique Identification (UID) for Mobile Banking in India." Focus Note 70, MicroSave India.

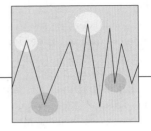

CHAPTER 19

Building Inclusive Financial Markets

David Ferrand

Over the last 18 chapters many aspects of financial inclusion have been discussed in depth. This chapter seeks to draw these various threads together and examine how the system as a whole develops and what can be done to influence it. In the Introduction the aspiration was established: "Full financial inclusion is a state in which all people who can use them have access to a full suite of quality financial services, provided at affordable prices in a convenient manner, and with dignity for the clients. Financial services are delivered by a range of providers, most of them private, and reach everyone who can use them, including disabled, poor, and rural populations."

The starting point here is to examine the empirical evidence on the development of markets and inclusion before turning to look, briefly, at some of the theory that seeks to explain what

drives the process. Building on this, the idea of "making markets work for the poor" is explored further and distinguished from the two diametrically opposed approaches to financial inclusion policy that have dominated debates in the past. One, belonging to a wider tradition of public intervention in the economy, advocates direct provision by government to substitute for the market. The other, based on a belief in the efficacy of unfettered markets in solving economic supply problems, urges governments to get out of the way of the private sector and focus on eliminating any putative distortion in incentives from regulation, taxation, or subsidy. By contrast a market systems approach seeks to harness the power-of-markets solutions to deliver services at scale and sustainably. Trying to resist or replace market forces is rarely effective. However, it also recognizes that how markets develop and who is reached is not predetermined. Much can be achieved by influencing the trajectory of market development toward a more inclusive direction. Systematic market development needs to be grounded in understanding the current state of the market, its dynamics, and potential futures.

Although the more pragmatic approach to building inclusive financial markets suggested by this analysis emphasizes the importance of examining the specific circumstances in each market system, various broad, generic challenges can be identified. These cover retail capacity, connected business services markets, the enabling environment, and coordinating market development. Based on a better understanding of the potential and challenges to market development, the more concrete questions of how practically to intervene effectively can be considered, and some practical principles are suggested.

Growth and Inclusion

Financial Depth

Evidence points to a strong relationship between economic development and the depth of financial markets. Examining the patterns of financial market development over different contexts and times shows very wide variations, as illustrated in figure 19.1, which plots domestic credit provided by the banking system as a percentage of gross domestic product (GDP) against gross national income (GNI) per capita. Despite a GNI per capita of US$7,650, Gabon has domestic credit provided by the banking system of only 8 percent; by contrast Bangladesh with GNI per capita of US$700 has domestic credit provided by the banking system of 47 percent. An important conclusion to be drawn from this evidence is that the state of financial market development is not a simple function of the wider state of economic development.

Figure 19.1 Variation of Credit Provision with GNI per Capita

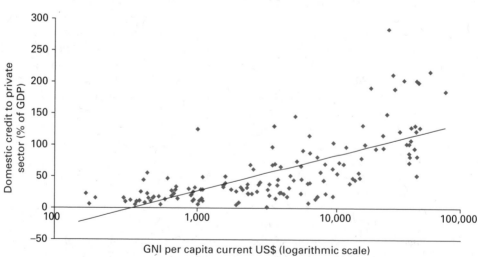

Sources: World Bank Global Financial Inclusion Database (2012): World Bank national accounts data, and OECD National Accounts data files; International Monetary Fund, International Financial Statistics and data files and World Bank and OECD GDP estimates.
Note: GDP = gross domestic product; GNI = gross national income.

Inclusion

Data on the development of financial inclusion are weak, but using proxies we again see very significant variations in the level of inclusion with economic development indicators, as illustrated in figure 19.2. Taking GNI per capita as a proxy for economic development, at a given level of economic development wide variations are found in the levels of financial inclusion measured by the proportion of the adult population with accounts at a formal financial institution. Sri Lanka has a GNI per capita of US$2,240 and has relatively high access with 68.5 percent of those aged 15 and over reporting having an account. By contrast Mexico with nearly four times the level of income per capita (GNI per capita of US$8,930) has only 27.4 percent reporting having a formal account. Although the data clearly show a strong association between rising levels of inclusion and

increased economic development, there is little to suggest that improved inclusion inexorably follows growth. The extent of the variation seen implies that there are other factors at work in determining a particular economy's level of financial inclusion.

It is important to be clear, however, that the data also leave little doubt that economic development and financial inclusion are associated. Attempts have been made to determine the direction of causality. Based on detailed econometric analysis of time-series data, the consensus view among economists studying financial markets is that there is a causal relationship; financial sector development helps to drive economic growth. Some, more tentative, evidence suggests that financial inclusion does also lead to improved economic development indicators. It certainly seems hard to avoid the conclusion that

Figure 19.2   Variation of Formal Financial Inclusion with GNI per Capita

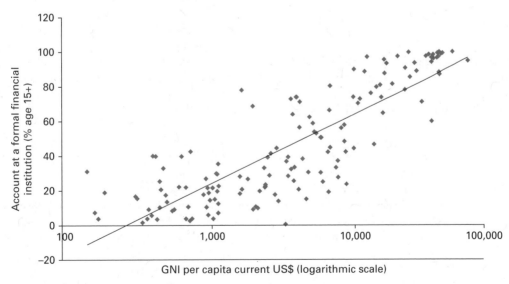

Source: World Bank Global Financial Inclusion Database (2012): World Bank national accounts data, and OECD National Accounts data files; International Monetary Fund, International Financial Statistics and data files and World Bank and OECD GDP estimates.
Note: GNI = gross national income.

there is an *interaction*. Drawing on the data available, we find no examples of industrially advanced economies that do not have both relatively well-developed financial systems and high levels of financial inclusion relative to developing economies. It would seem hard to argue that causality does not also run in the other direction. As economies expand and average wealth levels rise, inevitably more customers can be expected to become viable customers for banks and other financial service providers at a given level of efficiency of financial intermediation. It can be anticipated that inclusion will to some extent *naturally* tend to rise with wealth. The development of financial markets, and specifically the expansion of inclusion, has to be seen as endogenous to the market system. Nevertheless the important conclusion to be drawn from the data is that the future possibilities for market development are not foreclosed by a particular level of economic development.

Understanding Markets

At the heart of the market systems approach, in which this book is grounded, is the importance of trying to understand what is really going on in markets. Mainstream economic thinking centers on the role of decision making by participants in the economy. Incentives play a fundamental role. Where opportunities exist to profitably expand markets it is anticipated that players will invest to take advantage of these opportunities. Similarly on the demand side consumers will take advantage of financial products and services that are beneficial—in the language of economics, those that improve their utility. However, if the matching of supply and demand were all that mattered, then the result would surely be a much greater degree of convergence than currently seen across financial systems (and, indeed, economies more broadly). Not much evidence appears to exist of a simple relationship between economic growth and financial inclusion. What, then, accounts for

the differing levels of inclusion across economies? The weakness in detailed data (until recently) makes it difficult to rely on econometric techniques to isolate the potential drivers of variances across economies. Moreover even if the data were available, it is not obvious how much light could be shed on the story by simply looking at the aggregates. To understand what is going on it is necessary to consider the mechanisms of market development.[1]

An obvious starting point is to look more closely at the actions of providers and consumers of financial services and what determines that market behavior. To make modeling tractable, orthodox economic theory makes simplifying assumptions about the way in which participants in an economy behave. Rational economic man, *homo economicus,* is assumed perfectly rational—seeking to maximize his or her own utility on the basis of complete or perfect information regarding the available choices and, crucially, the implications. Although plainly unrealistic on any common-sense view, these assumptions were never intended to predict individual action but rather to approximate how, in aggregate, economic actors make choices. Unfortunately, as highlighted by the emerging and complementary behavioral and new institutional economics, these simplifying assumptions also lose sight of some of the important drivers of differences in markets and economic outcomes.

Behavior and Strategy

Behavioral economics focuses on the extent to which actual individual decision making departs from the earlier idealized notions of rationality. Although the field covers numerous aspects of behavior, three broad aspects are emphasized: the boundaries of rationality, willpower, and self-interest as a motivator. The first of these, the notion of "bounded rationality," is most immediately relevant to the question of understanding how markets develop. It simply reflects the impossibility of usefully processing the information available in a given situation. Although not necessarily always actively conscious of it, most consumers are familiar with the problem. For example, in well-developed financial systems, savers are confronted with a huge array of competing offers from saving providers, which change frequently. Trying to maximize interest earnings while balancing this with an unpredictable need for liquidity in the future can be surprisingly difficult. Often savers will simply choose one account and remain with it for a sustained period because trying to capture and process all the options is simply too hard. The assumption that consumers will necessarily be able to choose what is best for them has to be abandoned. This frequently interacts with the problem of willpower—in the example, self-enforcement of a resolution to scan the market periodically for better saving offers. Consumers often simply fail to take simple actions that would improve their financial position.

This limitation applies not only on the demand side but also to players on the supply side. Financial providers are guided in complex decision making by their business strategies that help them make sense of the wide array of information and uncertainties about the current and future state of the market in which they operate. Business strategies can be seen as implicitly representing applications of incomplete "theories" of how a market will respond to various offers and evolve over time. The incompleteness of the "theory" may arise from either the sheer complexity of a market at a given point in time or the impossibility of anticipating all possible future developments. Even the most apparently stable market will be susceptible to developments in technology. Financial markets in particular have undergone very considerable change as a consequence of developments in information and communications technology. The success or otherwise of a business strategy is rarely instantly tested by the market. Often it takes some time before it becomes clear whether a new strategy is succeeding or failing. Given the potential difficulty and risks

from developing an entirely new strategy, financial institutions frequently revert to adopting what looks to be a proven business strategy within a particular sector. Although much attention is often given to innovation, for many market participants replication of what has been shown to work is probably the norm. It is not uncommon to find commercial banks in developing economies adopting the basic business strategies and models of financial institutions from industrialized economies, despite the very considerable differences in the market circumstances.

The extent to which providers or consumers converge on broadly similar strategies can push markets in particular directions. Many different strategies can be conceived. How a particular dominant strategy emerges is likely to depend on particular historical circumstances. Crucially, potential market opportunities may be ignored simply because of the characteristics of the dominant sector strategy. The dominant business strategy found in commercial banks across many developing economies failed to support the type of services needed by many low-income consumers.

Rules of the Game: Institutions

The need to find ways to guide decision making and reduce uncertainty gives rise to the role of structure in markets. "Rules of the game," the institutions of the new institutional economics, play a key role in guiding economic decision making and improving the efficiency of markets. These rules range from formal institutions, such as laws and regulations, to informal social conventions and cultural norms.[2] From an economic point of view, obtaining reliable information (about both conditions today and in the future) to inform economic decisions is itself costly and contributes to the overall transaction cost in a market. Reliable institutions can help tackle the problem of limited rationality—often providing greater predictability and offering simplifications or "rules of thumb" to facilitate decision making. In providing structure to guide economic action, institutions help to address the problem of coordination and cooperation in markets.

Simple examples illustrate the significance of institutions for financial markets. State-enforced regulation and insurance of deposits in deposit-taking financial institutions allow savers to reliably assume that the risk to their savings placed with such organizations is (relatively) very low. Simply seeing that an institution is permitted to describe itself as a "bank" (usually reserved in law for use only by regulated financial institutions) allows a saver to reasonably confidently make a deposit without the need to undertake a detailed financial analysis of the institution concerned or monitor on a regular basis. Without this institution efficient small-value deposit taking at scale becomes impossible.

Another example, the sharing of information on loan defaulters, relates to solving a cooperation problem. It is in the *collective* interest of most market players, both credit providers and consumers (with the notable exception of the serial defaulter), to share information on credit defaults. However, it is only of real value in reducing the costs of credit risk assessment and discouraging default where the information covers most of the market and can therefore be relied on. The average consumer should obtain some modest benefit in improved access or cost of credit if the system is sufficiently comprehensive. However, this benefit may be hard to see and has to be set against the possible downside that if the borrower should default, he or she may not be able to obtain credit again. Without establishing rules (whether through state-backed regulation or an industry collective initiative) useful credit information sharing is unlikely to emerge spontaneously, foregoing the potential efficiency gains across the market.

Informal institutions—socially embedded rules and norms—are frequently more prominent in the economies of the poor, which are often beyond the reach of formal institutions. The efficacy of rotating savings and credit associations depends on norms to honor commitments made without reliance on legal contracts and prospective third-party enforcement through courts. Such norms are also drawn on by many microfinance institutions (MFIs) in solidarity group lending. More powerfully, the rules of reciprocity found in many communities in developing economies underpin more complex financial arrangements (see chapter 2). These can create forms of informal insurance that can help to significantly reduce vulnerability in low-income households.

Only rarely do formal institutions change rapidly, far less so than informal ones. Rather, changes happen at the margin, informed by the current rules of the game that set the incentives for the players involved. As a result there is path dependency; the options for where a financial system can go tomorrow depends on where it is today. This may seem an obvious point, but expectations as to how financial inclusion could evolve in a given context need to be considered in terms of viable *trajectories* of market development. Furthermore institutional change will often reflect the interests and relative bargaining power of the various key players. There can be no assumption that developments will *necessarily* result in more efficient arrangements either because it is not possible to see the consequences (another implication of limited rationality) or the balance of power favors changes to support particular narrow vested interests.

Making Markets Work for the Poor

The idea of making financial markets work for the poor builds on the premise that often real options exist for influencing how financial inclusion develops within a particular market. For markets to develop successfully it is necessary to understand what is going on at the heart of the market, where the incentives lie, and what may constrain participants from moving in a particular direction. This draws heavily on the insight that markets are structured by both formal institutions (rules)—established by laws, regulations, and their enforcement—and the informal norms, habits, and practices of market participants on both the demand and supply sides. Although participants are most often intentionally rational, seeking to improve utility, the capacity to make optimizing choices is limited by cognitive capacity, willpower, and the imperfect alignment of rules (whether formal or informal) with the task at hand. Furthermore the prospect for development of one market is often constrained by the state of development of linked markets, which similarly do not respond instantly and perfectly to opportunities. For example, the capacity of labor markets to provide the skills needed to expand pro-poor finance is often limited. It is, however, frequently possible to influence the trajectory or speed of development by intervening to address constraints or improve the incentives for players to move in a particular direction.

The idea is not to try to force a river to flow uphill. Taking this analogy further, the incentives of players in the market correspond to the force of gravity pulling water downhill. Trying to work against this will take considerable resources and is not sustainable; once the energy is removed the water will return to flowing downhill. Trying to make markets work better for the poor is about trying to take advantage of the fundamental "gravitational impulsion" of market incentives but looking to influence the direction of travel to move in a more advantageous way. At the right point even a relatively modest intervention can change the flow of a river; at another it may mean cutting an entirely new channel.

It is important to contrast the market systems approach with the major competing development approaches applied to financial inclusion, which can usefully be characterized here as broadly the interventionist and the laissez faire. Both have experienced their time in the sun in financial sector development theory and practice. The approach advocated here is motivated by a more nuanced view of markets. Confusion may arise, however, because often occasions arise when the policy prescriptions are similar. Where the impetus for market development has already been established, doing nothing may be entirely consistent with a market development approach. Or where there are no exemplars of how to address a particular market segment successfully, investing heavily in creating a demonstration case to market players could help to precipitate the market development process.

Interventionism

Interventionism in financial markets starts from the premise that if the market fails to reach particular target groups, then the appropriate response is simply to substitute for the market failure. If banks will not lend to smallholder farmers, then use public money (provided by development partners or host governments) to establish an agricultural lending institution that will. Alternatively if the banks claim that it is a risk problem, then guarantee the loans. At first blush all this sounds reasonable.

Rarely, however, does an interventionist approach pass what must be the two acid tests of effective development: sustainability and scalability. The developing world is strewn with expensive publicly funded agricultural finance schemes that either have failed or remain a significant fiscal drain. Causes of failure are varied and include governance failures in schemes resulting in corrupt lending practices, poor management and cost control, weak screening of borrowers, ineffective risk control, and politically motivated compromising of borrower incentives to repay.

At root there is usually a failure to start with the fundamental question: What is going on in the market? What would need to change for existing financial institutions to start addressing smallholder farmers? Not infrequently the politically determined decision to reach particular target groups overrules any consideration of whether the group actually has any debt capacity. Providing credit to agricultural businesses (farms) that are fundamentally unprofitable is unlikely to result in repayment rates that are viable for the lender. If the public policy objective is in fact simply to transfer resources to poor households, then providing loans that turn into grants is rarely an inefficient way to do it. Ironically it is also not infrequently regressive; it is the richer more empowered borrowers who are more likely to default while the poorer may further worsen their position by attempting to repay from other resources.

Laissez faire

Laissez faire, on the other hand, represents the opposite extreme. It supposes that any intervention in markets from public sector players beyond that of setting the minimum formal rules of the game is bound to leave the market and participants in it worse off. This would be the case if markets did indeed consist of rational, utility maximizing agents with perfect information operating within complete connected markets. Unfortunately only relatively rarely do market circumstances even begin to approximate to these conditions within developing economy contexts.

The market-oriented reforms of the 1980s, seeking to reverse long periods of financial repression found in many developing economies in the 1960s and 1970s, frequently produced disappointing results—certainly from the perspective of financial inclusion. Simply removing the legal and regulatory constraints to financial market development did not lead mainstream commercial bankers to suddenly see low-income households as a golden market opportunity. Where regulation had required banks to devote a proportion of activity to underserved sectors (agriculture being commonly targeted), liberalization often removed this requirement. Seen through the lens of business models firmly aimed at higher income groups and larger scale, formal businesses, these market segments were seen as highly unattractive, and banks often moved away from them with some relief.

Making Markets

A classic illustration of market development in practice can be found in the early history of modern microfinance. It started with a quite simple idea that had simply not been demonstrated in a way that was compelling to financial institutions—that it was possible to profitably lend to low-income women in Bangladesh. Perhaps most people in Bangladesh knew that the local money lender was able to lend on a viable basis by leveraging local knowledge and sometimes resorting to coercive practices to obtain repayment. However, the very high interest rates and sometimes dubious business practices associated with the relatively inefficient operation of the money lender scarcely encouraged formal providers to replicate this approach. Mohammed Yunus's great contribution was to simply demonstrate that a much more efficient form of lending was possible that relied on leveraging existing social institutions to create incentives to ensure a sufficient level of repayment at low delivery cost. It did not depend on the existence of any technology hitherto unavailable. The important point to note here is that the private sector in Bangladesh and pretty much every other poor country had failed to identify this market opportunity, which must have existed well before Professor Yunus's pioneering experiments. Although Yunus himself has tended to take a somewhat ambiguous position on the need for long-term subsidy in microfinance, the explosion of highly profitable microfinance has confirmed that there is indeed a real market opportunity. It illustrates the essential point that we cannot afford to take a Panglossian, deterministic approach to market development. Real market opportunities that can impact on the lives of the poor are often overlooked. Understanding why is the starting point for making markets work for the poor.

Market Potential

A wide range of reasons can be hypothesized as to why potentially profitable opportunities for expanding markets—and financial access—are not taken by either existing financial sector players or other investors. No attempt will be made here to enumerate all the possibilities. Rather, the aim is to look at the ways in which markets can be examined to understand where there may be potential and the constraints. Knowing what might stop a more rapid market expansion will help in identifying the opportunities for market development within a given economy.

The Challenge of Technology Transfer

Underpinning the potential for rapid growth in developing or emerging economies is the premise that the production or organizational technology required to improve productivity in the economy has already been developed in more advanced economies. Because it is not necessary to invent the technology, simply transfer it. High growth rates are there for the taking. Or so the argument goes. Of course, the experience from many late developing economies is that technology transfer is rarely that simple. Nevertheless, as recent history has shown in Asia, very rapid economic growth can be achieved—at rates unprecedented in any of the earlier industrializing countries.

A major challenge in transferring technologies from wealthier economies is that these technologies were developed to fit very different economic circumstances. These are often characterized by marked divergences in the relative prices of capital and labor, the availability of required skills and inputs from linked markets, and the characteristics of demand. One major hurdle faced in tackling financial exclusion in developing economies is the extent to which the core of the financial systems has been built from a straight transplant of western banking models. Viewed through the lens of such business models, many low-income households and smaller-scale informal businesses simply fail to register as potential markets: They are outside the scope. It may be less a case of risk aversion as simply not seeing the poor as a prospective market. Perhaps Yunus's greater contribution to financial inclusion was not Grameen Bank itself but helping to change the mind-set of the financial services industry across the developing world.

More tangibly, the business models of many financial institutions built to serve wealthier client groups will be poorly aligned with the needs of addressing lower-income groups. Cost structures will reflect much higher average unit transaction sizes. Delivery channels—archetypically centered on marble-clad banking halls—are constructed to meet the needs and aspirations of the upper income consumer. The mechanisms used to measure and appraise credit risk often reflect the livelihoods and behavioral norms of those in formal employment or running formal businesses. More than two decades of experimentation and development by MFIs were needed to find effective ways to tackle these challenges. Development of profitable microfinance continues to be hampered by the effective lock-in of financial markets geared toward a very different consumer base. Critical support service markets in areas as diverse as information systems, market research, training and human resource development, and management consulting have frequently developed in response to demand from financial institutions, which usually have very different needs from those of a typical microfinance provider.

In such a complex web of interdependencies one finds a temptation to quietism; the market system is so complex and interdependent that it is impossible to engineer any meaningful change. However, the recent history of financial market development shows frequent opportunities. Even where the surrounding market infrastructure or legal and regulatory environment is far from aligned with the needs of a new market it is possible to plant the seeds of change. When a new market segment emerges, the demands on efficiency or product design are usually far less exacting than when it matures, competition strengthens, and consumers become more demanding. The early experience of microcredit showed that it was possible to achieve sustainability on the basis of products that later evidence from market research showed were not especially well matched with the actual needs of many of the consumers targeted. However, in these early days of microfinance, in the absence of any better alternatives, simple short-term group based loans were taken on by many clients with considerable enthusiasm.

Mapping the Financial Landscape

An obvious but sometimes surprisingly neglected starting point for understanding the potential for market development is a detailed mapping of the market as it currently exists. This requires both a broad-based and detailed measurement and analysis of both supply and demand sides. Building on the points established in earlier chapters of this book, the analysis on the supply side should not be limited to a particular type of provider. In many developing economies informal finance provides a more significant source of services than the formal. Furthermore it may provide important insights into underlying needs not easily captured through an analysis focused on conventional formal sector–provided products. Although considerable caution is needed in attempting to leverage informal finance, effective ways to develop these mechanisms or link them to formal providers are starting to emerge.

Turning to the demand side, only looking at access to services or possession of an account gives a very limited picture of what is going on. It is not simply the *quantity* of access that matters in a market but its *quality*. Although a clear consensus has yet to emerge on cross-comparable indicators of quality, one simple proxy is to examine the level of usage. Finding that many low-income households have a transaction account may suggest progress in reducing exclusion. But if we then find that these accounts are used only a few times a year, it is clear that there can be little impact on managing the problem of smoothing day-to-day cash flows. This suggests an ongoing weakness in service provision and an opportunity to find improvements. Identifying the gaps in the market starts from this demand-side analysis.

Studies in various countries have revealed the prevalence of the use of a portfolio of financial services. For example, in Kenya, a demand-side survey showed that very few consumers rely on formal services alone. Interestingly, despite a significant expansion in formal service provision, the number of people using multiple sources, formal, semiformal, and informal, has increased in recent years. The rationale is not difficult to understand. Even in the most developed financial markets the needs of consumers or businesses are rarely best met by a single institution.[3] In a rapidly developing market, formal providers are just starting to reach many new market segments. Just as these markets may only still be marginally viable from the perspective of the provider, the added value to the consumer or business may also be marginal.

The Financial Access Frontier

Based on a clear measurement of what the existing demand and supply of financial services looks like today in a given market, the next step is to determine where the market development opportunities could lie. The financial access frontier (Porteous 2005) provides a useful way for thinking about the market as a whole (see figure 19.3). The usage frontier is obviously defined by those currently making use of financial services measured by demand-side studies. Beyond this are people who could potentially be reached now by the financial services industry as it presently exists (as measured by the supply-side research). This defines the access frontier. Market-enabling interventions (Porteous 2005) can be sought to help providers reach these prospective consumers, closing the gap between the usage and access

Figure 19.3 Financial Frontiers

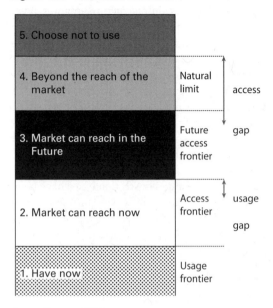

Source: Porteous 2005.

frontier. It is here that the (relatively) low-hanging fruit for market development should lie. Simply providing data identifying the market opportunities to existing players could produce an impact. The next step is to determine those consumers and businesses that could be reached in the future by pushing out the access frontier. Market development initiatives may be needed to expand in a number of directions. Typically this might entail expanding the geographical reach of the system, reducing delivery costs, or improving the relevance of service offers to new market segments. Beyond this future access frontier are those beyond the reach of the market—referred to by Porteous as the "supra-market" group. Bringing financial services to this supra-market necessarily involves some redistribution or net transfer whether through direct subsidy or embedded within government- or donor-financed social protection payments. Even in the wealthiest countries with some of the most advanced

financial systems, populations remain who cannot realistically afford to use financial services. Finally in any population there will be some (evidence from developed economies suggest a very small minority) who choose not to use financial services at all (category 5 in figure 19.3). This sets the overall natural limit for the market.

Scenario Analysis

Attempting to predict the future is usually a foolhardy undertaking. Rather than attempting to make definitive predictions, it is often more effective to look at the various directions in which the financial sector could evolve by considering potential scenarios. These can be used to help establish the scope of future possibilities and better understand what will influence these different paths. In seeking to peer into the future we need to understand what is likely to drive the development of markets. Both economic and noneconomic factors may impact on financial service access and usage. What will be the forces that could drive changes? First, clearly major political and economic forces can be identified that will shape the entire future of a country. Political and social stability, prudent macroeconomic management, or the avoidance of major environmental catastrophes simply have to be taken as background assumptions that cannot be readily influenced; nor is it possible to put in place meaningful strategic contingencies (at least in the context of tackling financial inclusion). Rather, there is a need to look at those forces that impinge more directly on the development of financial markets. These can be divided into those that are likely to change markets in ways that can be anticipated with a reasonable degree of confidence and those that although clearly set to impact could play out in very different ways. What determines the way the latter uncertainties play out will be at least in part exogenous to the financial system. Nevertheless identifying the prospective range of outcomes is useful in establishing broadly where market development needs to focus its search for opportunities to support positive change at scale.

Trying to exhaustively identify the full range of potential future scenarios for financial access in a given context will clearly be difficult even if a reasonable number of uncertainties have been identified (leave aside those that have not been anticipated). Nevertheless it is useful to consider how inclusion could develop over a period drawing on how the more significant uncertainties turn out. In many contexts technology is already starting to dramatically change markets. There seems to be little doubt that this will continue; the urgent task in many markets is to think about the ways in which technology could affect inclusion in the future. Necessarily this type of scenario analysis cannot attempt to cover all aspects of financial inclusion but only to provide a sense of how the existing dynamics of change could play out. Understanding this better can help point to possible opportunities for system-wide change.

Addressing the Key Challenges

Lack of Retail Capacity in the "Core"

The weakness in retail capacity is often seen as the central challenge of developing inclusive financial markets. At the outset, where there is little or no provision, demonstration models are needed to establish how low-income markets can be served on a sustainable basis. There is no single "best practice" here. The early history of microfinance was characterized by the creation of specialist MFIs. Mainstream commercial banks were typically very skeptical.[4] If it was possible to engage them at all, the involvement was seen as largely about corporate social responsibility rather than seriously seeking to develop a new strategic business area. It has often been found to be difficult to create effective microfinance within mainstream banking institutions. Frequently a misalignment is found between the businesses of microfinance and more mainstream banking, starting at the level of corporate culture and

reflected throughout in terms of human resources, delivery channels, infrastructure, market positioning, and branding. Trying to create the space for effective microfinance may sometimes be harder than creating an entirely new organization. Nevertheless it is important not to underestimate the challenges in establishing start-ups. In the early stages many of the resources needed to support rapid development are absent. Most obviously many of the necessary skills are simply not available in the market, and the organization has to develop its own staff.

Once the first demonstration cases have been established, the focus needs to shift away from individual institutions to working at an industry level. The long-term objective should not be to support specific champions—valuable those these are—but to create an environment in which competition and innovation will thrive. This is not easy. Human capacity frequently lies at the heart of driving industry development. Many of the skills can only be effectively developed through learning-by-doing within the framework of a retail organization, potentially pulling the attention back into specific institutions. Similarly innovation in the financial sector does not come through developing abstract patents but rolling out real products and services in the market. Continued effort is needed to take advantage of the opportunities for creating capacity by working with institutions but always looking to bring this back up to an industry level.

As microfinance has increasingly become understood as being about financial inclusion rather than a narrow focus on particular microcredit products or MFIs, the scope of organizations addressed has expanded dramatically (as discussed at length in earlier chapters). On the one hand, this has increased the potential capacity that can be drawn on to build a financial inclusive system; on the other, it creates the need to work with a much broader range of organizational types and needs. Retail commercial banks have started to realize the importance of reaching the next generation of clients with a need to find ways to adapt their existing products, operations, and channels to meet their needs. Credit unions or savings and credit cooperatives have often been serving a lower income market, but capacity and governance challenges tend to go hand-in-hand with their voluntarist roots. Community-based finance has the potential to reach many low-income consumers still far beyond the reach of formal or even semiformal finance. Training members in more robust models for community intermediation can significantly improve quality and safety. Finally entirely new players are now entering the field such as mobile network operators, large retailers, and technology-based start-ups. Although often coming with significant expertise in addressing mass retail markets, entering a whole new industry creates a wide range of needs from basic understanding of the market to compliance with regulatory requirements.

The form of an organization can have a profound impact on its ability to provide a particular type of service. There is no single type of organization that presents an optimal solution to reaching all market segments. According to market segment and product area, the key characteristics of organizational form have a varying impact on its competitive advantage. In the more remote rural areas the low-cost structure of user-owned and -managed community-based financial organizations constitutes a significant advantage over the more formalized centralized MFI or commercial bank. However, these organizations often struggle to meet the financing needs of a rapidly growing small business or the money management needs of extended families straddling rural and urban areas. Crucially, organizational forms continue to evolve with considerable crossover and cross-learning. Commercial banks with an orientation to the low-income market are busy developing lower cost agent outlets to reach poorer clients. MFIs have long understood the value of working with existing community-based groups to better reach more remote or rural clients.

Opportunities for market development at this level are increasingly about finding innovations that can drive market expansion. Achieving this usually means going beyond a simple design idea to working with market partners to providing credible demonstrations to the market. Focal areas for innovation that are often (and necessarily) tackled simultaneously include the following:

1. Organizational (for example, the creation of the form of the specialist MFI)

2. Production (for example, introduction of incentive systems for loan officers)

3. Channel (for example, development of viable agent banking models) and

4. Product/service (for example, index-based weather insurance).

Building Business Service Markets (Supporting Functions)

Individual organizations need to be seen as part of a wider "production system." Increased specialization, strategic alliances and partnerships, out-sourcing of noncore functions, and collaborative development of sectoral public goods (such as financial education)[5] or sectoral quasi-public goods (such as the FinScope market surveys)[6] all offer the potential for considerable gains in efficiency and effectiveness of service provision. Information is the lifeblood of financial markets, and its production and dissemination often depend on supports beyond the retail institutions themselves. The creation of this industry infrastructure can come from either linked markets or specialist organizations established to address a particular supporting function in the financial market. Examples of the former include business services that cover areas as diverse as training, market research, advertising, auditing, recruitment, information systems development, and management consultancy. Meanwhile classic examples of the latter are the industry membership organizations often established in the first instance to represent the common interests of an industry group—most obviously in dialogue with government.

As markets develop, the market-making agenda should logically start to shift to this level. The rationale for such a shift is related to both need and impact. In a nascent market the extent of collaboration and coordination between institutions can be anticipated to be weak. Bridging this gap can test options, deliver immediate benefits, and help demonstrate where opportunities lie. The prospective impact may be greater working at a sector level because any intervention is aimed at covering an entire industry group rather than with an individual institution. It also has the added benefit of reducing the execution risk and mitigates the inherent risk of market distortion associated with working with single players. Possible interventions at this mesolevel include the following:

1. Strengthening provision from support service markets (for example, service provider capacity building)

2. Building linkages within the financial system (for example, finite credit guarantees to build confidence in the inter-institution financial market)

3. Providing sectoral quasi-public goods (for example, building consumer financial capability, collating and publishing data in areas such as financial and social performance, and consumer product pricing) and

4. Investment in human resource development (for example, developing new curricula for savings and credit cooperative training).

Shaping an Enabling Environment (Rules)

All market activity takes place within the rules of the game that form the enabling environment. As discussed earlier these rules are both formal and informal. The focus tends to be on the former because these are seen to more immediately tractable, being shaped by government policy and the resulting formal institutions (laws, regulations, and enforcement practices). Nevertheless informal habits and norms play a critical role in the behavior of players in markets. There is now a growing consensus that behavioral factors played a significant role in creating the conditions that gave rise to the recent global financial crisis. Arguably the only realistic way to protect consumers from predatory or fraudulent financial schemes that have appeared in many markets is to develop societal norms that lead market participants to question the credibility of such "offers."

At the formal level the three areas that are likely to most directly impinge on financial market developments are prudential regulation, consumer protection, and competition policy. The last two have only relatively recently started to attract serious attention in many developing economies. Starting with policy formulation this is important not only insofar as it directly gives rise to specific laws and regulations but also because it helps to establish some predictability over the laws and regulations that have yet to be discussed. The latter is highly significant for prospective investors in financial markets.

Specific financial sector and related laws, regulations, and rules and their enforcement impact directly on the market. From a pro-poor market development perspective developing appropriate regulation is vital. Well-designed regulation can dramatically reduce transaction costs by improving predictability from the perspective of both financial service providers and consumers. The primary economic function of prudential regulation of financial institutions is to reduce potential instability and credibly signal this to the market. Mandating disclosure and transparency—a core pillar of consumer protection—significantly improves market functioning, enabling buyers to reduce their costs in identifying services appropriate to their needs.

Effective and efficient enforcement is vital in all cases. The development of rules therefore has to go hand-in-hand with the design of enforcement mechanisms. It seems doubtful, for example, that it would be viable to develop credible prudential supervision of community-based providers based on the current orthodox regulatory model. Reliable supervision and enforcement is simply difficult to achieve addressing a market of many thousands of small organizations distributed throughout a country.

The role of the facilitator is often related to know-how here: helping the authorities better understand the market—what it looks like and its specific challenges—with the aim of building long-term internal capacity. Establishing and brokering the linkages between a nascent industry and policy makers and regulators is especially challenging. In a young industry it is not unusual to find one or two institutions dominating, and inevitably their primary concern will be looking after their own needs rather than the wider industry. The facilitator has a role here in taking a longer term view.

This area is rightly emphasized as critical for wider market development and is clearly at the heart of a wider economic reform agenda. From the specific perspective of making financial markets work for the poor, various areas deserve attention:

1. Pro-poor policy analysis—supporting policy makers to understand the impact on financial access (for example, analysis of options for prudential regulation of bank channels)

2. Research—providing a real evidence base to support policy formulation (for example, research into losses and problems actually experienced by users of branchless banking services)

3. Regulatory design (for example, support for the development of new regulations and regulatory authorities) and

4. Broader public awareness and behavior change initiatives (for example, support for financial education targeting improved financial outcomes and greater dissemination of existing data and analysis).

It is important to emphasize that policy makers and regulators must be understood as a part of the market system. Because the enabling environment work may involve subsidizing a public entity with public good objectives there can be a tendency to apply less rigor. But this should not be the case: In forming part of the market system, policy makers and regulators need to have long-term capacity that does not depend on a facilitator or a nonsustainable subsidy (that is, one that does not have clear and reliable long-term public financing).

Coordinating Market Development

A final challenge is trying to align the various activities of international development partners, nonprofit organizations, and local governments around a market systems approach. In many markets this is not easy. The growing awareness of the significance of financial inclusion to economic and social development has attracted considerable interest from a wide range of actors. Poor practice in the way in which support is delivered can undermine the efforts of those seeking to support the emergence of long-term solutions through sustainable market systems. The global association of microfinance donors, the Consultative Group to Assist the Poor (CGAP), has invested heavily in raising awareness of good practice among its members. Most of the world's leading international donor organizations bound themselves to improve harmonization of efforts with the Paris Declaration of Aid Effectiveness. The so-called pink book on Good Practice Guidelines for Funders of Microfinance, which articulates a market systems approach, has been adopted by all 33 of CGAP's members. Nevertheless continued work is needed at country levels to ensure that these high-level commitments translate into reality on the ground. The temptation to take shortcuts is ever present.

Intervening to Build Markets

What then can be done practically to make financial markets work for the poor? A skeptic might insist that relatively little can be done to *make* markets work for the poor or indeed anyone else. This leads back to one of two diametrically opposed policy conclusions: *Either* development agencies and governments should simply get out of the way to allow markets to develop unhindered *or* accept that where markets are not working there should be direct substitution for them. Both these arguments can be rejected on the grounds that they fail to take account of the complexity of markets discussed earlier. Markets do not simply appear in a social and economic vacuum but are structured in complex ways and evolve gradually over time; a positive trajectory will move them toward lower transaction costs and greater inclusiveness. Starting with an understanding of how markets operate and where and how they fail provides a better chance of addressing these failures successfully.

Nevertheless the concern over causing more harm than good in intervening in markets is an important one. The role of those looking to facilitate market development should be to look for opportunities and undertake finite initiatives to push or—better—simply nudge the market toward a new more pro-poor trajectory. However, the first precept must be, following the Hippocratic Oath of doctors, to first do no harm.

A distinction must always be maintained between participation in the market and facilitation. Participants may be either on the demand side as clients or the supply side in various roles from retail providers through industry associations and players in linked markets to regulators and policy makers. It is important to note that although regulators and policy makers usually

need to be careful to avoid becoming players directly providing services in the core of the market, they are nevertheless still very much a part of the wider market system.[7] By contrast the role of the market facilitator is purely as a change agent or catalyst and should *not* become a long-term part of the system. Where the market facilitator starts to play a role that is within the market system, then sustainability is compromised. Market facilitation can, in principle, be sponsored by international donors, national governments, and nonprofit organizations of various kinds (including social impact investors). Regardless, an overriding need exists to be able to establish a clear degree of impartiality from any specific players in the market and a credible commitment to remaining outside the market (see chapter 4).

In advocating this approach it should be emphasized that there is no sense of a simple template or blueprint here for accelerating financial inclusion. Strategies for increasing financial inclusion need to be strongly conditioned by their contexts, and market facilitators should be wary of trying to be too prescriptive in their plans. The actual tools of engagement used in market systems approaches do not necessarily differ markedly from those that have long been used. Rather, it is a question of *how* they are used and to what end. A few key practical principles of how market facilitation can be achieved should help to clarify.

Identify the Exit

Perhaps the single most important practical principle of market facilitation is determining how to leave. The acid test of whether an intervention represents catalysis or not is whether there is a convincing exit strategy. If there is not, the chances are that the facilitator has become a player, and whatever role is being played must be regarded as a part of the market. An obvious problem is unwittingly creating dependency such that where the exit does inevitably occur, any progress achieved is compromised. Providing long-term technical assistance to market players often runs this risk with technical specialists becoming coopted into management teams. From a practical point of view there is also a danger of a growing reluctance to exit when things go well. Inevitably benefits are found for any organization in being associated with success, and the temptation is to continue. Here the problem can be a distortion of the market, creating a long-term advantage for a single player and ultimately undermining the development of effective competition—often likely to be essential to achieving the maximum impact on inclusion.

A relatively early exit can still produce good results. For example, the UK's Department for International Development (DFID) provided support to the mobile phone company Vodafone plc in developing mobile-based solutions for microfinance. At the end of the project period the basic technology for the now famous M-PESA mobile money system had been developed, but a convincing product had yet to be produced. It would have been tempting for DFID to remain engaged, but the terms of its challenge fund prohibited this and it was not necessary. The team at Vodafone and its Kenyan affiliate, Safaricom, had the technology and, crucially, had engaged with the market. Without further support they were able to develop the M-PESA money transfer product, which three years later is used in more than 70 percent of Kenyan households and is being rolled out in various other countries.

Defining the Underlying "Theory of Change"

Alongside the question of exit, it is important to be clear how we expect an intervention to bring about a change measured in market terms. A "theory of change" is needed that sets out how the market is expected to develop and the role of the intervention in bringing this about. The familiar economic concept of market failure is often useful here in analyzing where the challenges lie in a market, addressing the question of why the desired change should not simply occur without any support. However, analysis of market failure needs to be used with caution. It is not sufficient to simply identify why a market has failed, but how the failure can be addressed and a sustainable market-based solution created. If there is no way to credibly solve a particular failure, then intervention at this stage would slip back to the market substitution model with limited prospects for sustainability.

Proportionality

Nascent markets are frequently fragile, and it is important to avoid using hammers to crack nuts. Not only will this result in poor value for money in the use of scarce development resources, but it may also undermine the chances of achieving the objective. In general, very large scale interventions carry a substantial risk of distorting incentives and retarding the long-term development of sustainable markets.

Timing Is Everything

The market development process is necessarily dynamic, and whether a given type of intervention is appropriate depends strongly on the market's stage of development. In the early stages of developing microfinance around the world it was necessary to focus efforts on working with a relatively small number of MFIs. The aim was simply to develop the know-how to create sustainable institutions in many markets and provide the demonstration models for the next stage of development. As the history of microfinance showed in many contexts, this was not an easy undertaking. Attempting to support too many institutions at this point would have risked diluting the effort and failing to achieve the critical demonstration effect. However, once the demonstration has been provided, it is necessary to shift gears and look at what is needed to replicate the successes and build scale. Maintaining a narrow focus on individual institutions may no longer be appropriate, and the emphasis needs to shift to a broader, sector-wide approach. Maturation of markets will be associated with greater competition between players, and the risk grows of creating distortions in working closely with individual institutions.

Taking Chances

Pushing the frontier of financial inclusion frequently entails moving into unknown territory. The incentives are strong for prudent managers of financial institutions to target existing consumers rather than try to develop new products and services in order to reach unbanked populations. A potentially important role for market facilitation is to help explore and open up the frontier markets. Greater emphasis should be more on trying to tackle uncertainty rather than simply bearing known risks. The former refers to situations where even the drivers of performance may be unknown. Small-holder index-based weather insurance, for example, is currently in its infancy; what drives the cost-income structure for these products remains to be determined. Realistically, without support it is unlikely that providers will invest in exploring these techniques. By contrast, there is little need to help financial institutions enter the market for group-based, short-term microcredit. This is well understood, and although risk certainly arises for the institution involved, this is one for the investors to bear.

Pragmatism

It is important not to confuse the market systems approach with naïve or doctrinaire market fundamentalism. Markets frequently present effective opportunities to reach large numbers of poor people on a sustainable basis. The aim here is to make markets work for the poor, not the reverse. Some households may have such a poor endowment in financial, human, social, physical, natural, and political capital that they may be beyond the market for the foreseeable future—even for informal services. Opportunities can, however, arise to bring the poorest into the market. Where governments provide cash social transfers to the poorest

and most vulnerable, the financial system may offer the most efficient way to deliver these transfers. Although the costs here are ultimately met through a government subsidy, this still provides a potentially sustainable way to provide a service. A key question is whether the political will and fiscal capacity to provide subsidies on a long-term basis exists. Furthermore the emphasis should be on ensuring that government buys these services on a market basis—seeking the best offer from providers in the market and where possible providing choice to recipients.

Concluding Thoughts

Supporting a market systems approach to development simultaneously calls for a strong degree of ambition and modesty. Ambition is needed because developing markets is about achieving long-term permanent and significant change across an entire economy. Modesty because the market facilitator can work only within the possibilities offered by many forces of change over which there can be little or no direct influence and some of which may be very opaque. Finding routes to the end goal is not going to be about a one-off analysis of markets and identification of relevant constraints and opportunities. The whole market context is likely to change over time, initial evidence will turn out to be less accurate than originally hoped, experiments can reveal both failed ideas and unexpected successes, successful execution of even small initiatives will often throw up more challenges than anticipated, and the speed of change is almost entirely unpredictable. Technology is already revolutionizing the market, and based on current indications the pace of change is likely to accelerate rather than slacken.

To keep a market development strategy on track there has to be a constant process of measuring both market evolution and the actual success and impact of interventions. Only through creating an effective feedback loop between theory and practice can one expect that progress will be maintained. Research and analysis plays a significant role here and needs to be undertaken in a variety of ways, both quantitative and qualitative. Large national-level quantitative surveys mapping the landscape of access are essential to getting a good understanding of where the industry stands and what progress is being made. But in-depth studies such as financial diaries are needed to deliver insights from the field into the financial lives of the poor. Unless the market is grounded in the realities of its ultimate stakeholders it will founder.

Tremendous progress has been made over the last 30 years in developing financial inclusion. Although concerns will—quite rightly—persist over just how finance impacts on development, the evidence remains firm that financial inclusion is a vital part of bringing the poor into the economic and social mainstream. With a concerted effort to harness the power of markets it should be possible within far less than another 30 years to finally build financial systems that work for the poor.

Notes

1. This follows a methodological point made by Angus Deaton (2010).
2. Note that in this chapter, the term "institutions" is used in relation to new institutional economics, and not to refer to financial service providers as in previous chapters.
3. Large financial service groups have enthusiastically embraced cross-selling and attempting to meet a broad range of financial service needs of their customers. However, rarely will a single group provide the best offer to consumers across a diverse range of services. The emergence of "monoliners" focused on a single narrow business area supports the contention that efficiency gains can be achieved through such focus, and consumers are often best served by shopping around and choosing the best institution for a particular need (Kay 2009).

4. It should, of course, be noted that one of the standout successes in the early history of modern microfinance was Bank Rakyat Indonesia, a state-owned commercial bank. The success it achieved can, at least in part, be attributed to establishing a degree of separation between the microfinance element (in Unit Desas) and the main banking operation.
5. It is important to note the scope of financial consumer education can be very broad. Practically it is sometimes simply an element of marketing and therefore fails the test of a public good. However, the broader awareness of the value of how to use financial services appropriately and avoiding inappropriate behaviors passes the test. Interestingly, this does not necessarily entail that the best entry point for delivering financial education is through jointly funded programs. Recent evidence from a study of M-PESA suggests that financial capability may be most effectively built through use of appropriate products rather than more structured financial education processes (Zollman and Collins 2010).
6. The term *public good* is often misused. A minimum requirement is that it should be nonrival (consumption by one does not exclude consumption by others) and nonexcludable (if one person can consume, then it is not possible to exclude others). Much information is not strictly a public good insofar as it is excludable. For FinScope data this is the case. However, it can be argued that for the application of FinScope to public policy it must necessarily be available to all interested or potentially interested parties and is therefore nonexcludable. More difficult is human resource development. Here there is a free rider problem because it is not possible for an investor to secure the property rights to investment in human capacity in another individual (within the context of basic human rights). This produces a market failure. Only occasionally is this overcome through strong coordination among players who may invest from the perspective of the collective good. In a nascent market it provides an opportunity

for investment to encourage market development.

7. They are, to use the sports analogy, in the role of the sporting authorities and referees responsible for establishing and enforcing the rules of the game. Although a village football match can be guided by mutual consent among players who know one another, once the game becomes more serious and more is at stake, a form of disinterested third-party refereeing is inevitable if both sides are going to accept the result. In international matches rarely will the referee be of the same nationality of the teams playing as a means to help ensure impartiality.

References and Further Reading

Beck, T., S. M. Maimbo, I. Faye, and T. Triki. 2011. *Financing Africa—Through the Crisis and Beyond*. Washington, DC: World Bank.

Collins, D., J. Murdoch, S. Rutherford, and O. Ruthven. 2009. *Portfolios of the Poor: How the World's Poor Live on $2 a Day*. Princeton: Princeton University Press.

Deaton, A. S. 2010. "Understanding the Mechanisms of Economic Development." NBER Working Paper 15981, NBER, Cambridge, MA.

Demirgüç-Kunt, A., T. Beck, and P. Honohan. 2008. *Finance for All? Policies and Pitfalls in Expanding Access*. Washington, DC: World Bank.

Demirgüç-Kunt, A., and L. Klapper. 2012. "Measuring Financial Inclusion: The Global Findex." Policy Research Paper 6025, World Bank, Washington, DC.

Gibson, A., H. Scott, and D. Ferrand. 2004. "Making Markets Work for the Poor: An Objective and an Approach for Government and Development Agencies." ComMark Trust, Woodmead, South Africa.

Heyer, A., and S. Ouma 2011. "Financial Inclusion in Kenya: Results and Analysis from FinAccess 2009." FSD Kenya, Nairobi.

Jack, W., and T. Suri. 2010. "The Economics of M-PESA: An Update." Georgetown University, Washington, DC.

Kay, J. 2009. *The Long and Short of It*. London: Erasmus Press.

Khandker, S. R. 1998. *Fighting Poverty with Microcredit: Experience in Bangladesh*. New York: Oxford University Press.

Levine, R. 2004. "Finance and Growth: Theory and Evidence." NBER Working Paper 10766, NBER, Cambridge, MA.

North, D. 1990. *Institutions, Institutional Change and Economic Performance*. Cambridge: Cambridge University Press.

Porteous, D. 2005. "The Access Frontier as an Approach and Tool in Making Markets Work for the Poor." DFID Policy Division Paper. http://www.bankablefrontier.com/assets/pdfs/access-frontier-as-tool.pdf.

Ridley, J. 2011. "Facilitating Mobile Money for the Poor: The Contribution of Donors to Market System Development." M4P Hub Conference. http://www.m4phub.org/userfiles/resources/212201194742847-Jonathon_Ridley_-_Mobile_Money_Paper.pdf.

Roodman, D. 2012. "Due Diligence: An Impertinent Inquiry into Microfinance." Center for Global Development, Washington, DC.

Springfield Centre. 2008. *A Synthesis of the Making Markets Work for the Poor Approach*. Bern: Swiss Agency for Development and Cooperation.

Zollman, J., and D. Collins. 2010. "Financial Capability and the Poor: Are We Missing the Market?" FSD Insights 02, FSD Kenya, Nairobi.

INDEX

Boxes, figures, notes, and tables are indicated by b, f, n, and t following the page number.

slums in, 59
third-party platform providers in, 288, 290*b*
Bank Agroniaga, 189*b*
Bank of Africa, 389*b*
Bank of Ghana, 185, 191*b*, 441*b*
Bank of Tanzania, 84*b*
Bank of Uganda, 83*b*, 180
Bank Rakyat Indonesia, 188, 189*b*, 222
banks. *See also specific banks*
    "bank runs," 416
    banks-on-wheels, 127*b*
    funding and, 388–89, 389*b*
    as institutional providers, 183–93
    regulation of, 421–22, 421*b*, 423*b*, 427, 429
Bank Windhoek, 123*b*
Bansefi-Diconsa, 293*b*
Barclays, 114*b*
Barefoot (solar lighting company), 438*b*
"barefoot bankers," 279*b*
Basel Accords, 399*b*
Basel Committee on Banking Supervision (BCBS),
        81–82, 374*n*12, 431
Basel Core Principles (Core Principles for Effective
        Banking Supervision), 82
BCEAO West African countries, 425
BCP (Banco de Crédito del Perú), 293
behavioral economics, 462–63
Bellwether, 392
benefit ceilings, 257
Benin, financial service associations in, 169
BFV-SG (Société Générale), 389*b*
bilateral and multilateral agencies, 386
bill discounting, 244–45
biometrics, 278, 282, 289*b*, 325, 330, 448
bKash, 197, 288, 290*b*
"black lists," 445
BlueOrchard Loans for Development 2007, 393*b*
BlueOrchard Private Equity Fund, 392
Bluetooth, 282, 296*nn*8–9
board committees, 354
boards of directors, 352–54
Bolivia
    agriculture finance in, 249–50
    client focus in, 16
Bolsa Familia, 274
bonds, 398–99, 400*b*
borrowing to save, 211, 212*b*, 314

Bosnia and Herzegovina
    microfinance in, 102, 420*b*
    over-indebtedness and, 116*b*
Boulder Institute of Microfinance, 451*b*
Boulder Microfinance Training Program, 451*b*
"bounded rationality" concept, 462–63
BRAC, 22, 22*b*, 179, 249*b*, 290*b*, 404*b*
branches (banking), 277–78, 283–84, 291*b*, 318
branchless banking, 16, 38–44, 318
branding, 364
Brazil
    banking in, 68, 291*b*
    money transfer services in, 274
    robbery in, 455
    rural financing in, 248*b*
Bridge, David, 444
budgeting process, 331, 369, 370
Budget Law of 2010 (Mexico), 73*b*
burial societies, 58, 158
Burkina Faso, banking in, 43*b*
BURO (microfinance institution), 55
business case development, 327
business models
    for branchless banking, 41–44, 42–44*b*
    buyer-driven, 242
    credit bureaus and, 448
    for financial management, 316–17
    producer-driven, 241
    value chain, 241–47, 242*b*
Byte-Tech, 441*b*

C

CAF (Development Bank of Latin America), 411*n*9
Caixa Federal, 291*b*
"Calculating Transparent Pricing Tool"
        (mftransparency.org), 226
call centers, 453, 454*b*
call options, 406
CAMEL, 334
Cameroon, commercial banks in, 191*b*
capacity building, 36, 78, 102, 451*b*. *See also* financial
        capacity
capital adequacy requirements (CARs), 338, 338*t*,
        421*b*, 422, 423*b*, 433*n*17
capital markets, 396–97, 398–99
CARE, 98, 163*b*, 164*b*
CARs. *See* capital adequacy requirements

control groups, 134–36
convenience
    of financial tools, 63–64, 67–68
    of mobile money, 285*b*, 317
    of payment services, 275
convertible debt, 398
Co-Operative Bank of Kenya, 193*b*
coordination
    of facilitators, 107
    of financial inclusion, 82–86, 83*b*
    financial landscapes and, 36
copayment arrangements, 257
core banking systems (CBS), 322, 325–29,
    442*b*, 452–53
Core Principles for Effective Banking Supervision
    (Basel Core Principles), 82
Corporación Financiera Nacional, 404*b*
corporate social responsibility (CSR), 387, 389
correspondent banking, 192
COSO (Committee of Sponsoring Organizations of
    the Treadway Commission), 367
Costa Rica, Patrimonio Hoy in, 184*b*
cost-based method of product pricing, 362
costing of products, 361–62, 363*f*
covariance risks, 219, 235, 264
credit, 8, 217–33
    credit risk, 336
    creditworthiness, 219–20, 245, 409
    effective rates calculations, 225–26, 227*b*
    financial management tools and, 314–15
    information markets, 430
    product characteristics, 217–25
        character-based lending, 221
        client visits, 221
        compulsory savings, 221–22, 226
        fees and service charges, 225
        group guarantees, 221
        group lending, 218–19
        individual lending, 219–20
        interest rate calculations, 222–25, 223–25*b*
        Islamic lending, 220–21, 220*b*
        lending methodology, 218–21
        loan collateral, 221–22
        loan pricing, 222–25
        loan size and term, 217–18
        personal guarantees, 222
        repayment terms, 218

products offered, 226–32
    asset building and productive investment, 226,
        228–32
    cash flow management and, 226–28
    consumption loans, 228
    education loans, 228, 229*b*
    emergency loans, 228
    fixed asset loans, 228
    housing loans, 231–32, 232*b*
    leasing, 229–31, 230*b*
    lines of credit, 227–28
    risk management and, 226, 228
    salary loans, 228
    top-up loans, 228
    working capital loans, 227
    ratings, 404*b*, 408–9, 409*b*, 445
    scoring and history, 219, 314–15, 445–48, 446–47*b*
credit bureaus, 73, 445–48
credit cards, 314, 440
credit life insurance, 259
Credit Rating Agency of Bangladesh, 404*b*
Credit Report (credit bureau), 446*b*
credit unions, 65, 334, 440*b*
critical illness coverage, 262
crop insurance, 131, 247
"crowding in" of funding, 103, 110, 384, 386
"crowding out" of funding, 2, 103, 238
CSR (corporate social responsibility), 387, 389
Currency Exchange Fund N.V. (TCX), 402*b*
currency funding, 399–402, 401–2*b*
currency risks, 340
current accounts, 211
custom-built applications, 286
customer due diligence (CDD), 431
customers. *See* clients
customization of management information
    systems, 328
CVECAs (caisses villageoises d'épargne et de crédit
    autogérées), 158, 170

D
damage-based insurance, 247
databases, global, 118–19*b*, 118–20
data communications, 441–44
data preparation and extraction, 328
debit cards, 314, 440
debt collection, 453–54, 455*b*

Elektrafin, 183*b*
Elewa Pesa (Understand Your Money), 92*b*
El-Zoghbi, Mayada, 8, 97
embedded finance, 240
emergencies, financial, 56–58
emergency loans, 228
e-money, 284, 290, 292–93, 425–26, 433*n*21. *See also*
    mobile money
E-Money Directive (EU), 433*n*23
enabling environments, 472–73
endowment policies, 260–61
environmental, social, and corporate governance
    (ESG), 408*b*
e-payment platforms, 307
Equifax, 446*b*
equity
    funding, 392, 394, 404–6, 406*f*, 407*b*
    quasi-equity and, 109–10
Equity Bank, 43*b*, 164*b*, 361*b*, 407*b*
ESG (environmental, social, and corporate
    governance), 408*b*
e-switch system, 441*b*
Ethiopia, credit outreach data in, 117
Eurobonds, 400*b*
European Bank for Reconstruction and Development
    (EBRD), 383, 386
European Commission (EC), 386
European Fund for Southeast Europe
    (EFSE), 391
European Investment Fund, 404*b*
European Microfinance Programme, 451*b*
European Union, e-money issuers in, 425
evaluation of financial inclusion, 128–31
executive committees, 354
exit strategies, 474–75
Experian, 447*b*
Expert Decision Systems, 447*b*
Express Pay, 292*b*
eXtensible Business Reporting Language (XBRL),
    296*n*12
external risks, 355, 366

F
facilitated value chain models, 242, 242*b*
facilitators
    donors and, 103, 104–7, 106*b*, 110
    facilitating agencies, 161–62, 167

factoring in agriculture finance, 244–45, 244*b*
fair treatment in consumer protection, 75, 89
Family Bank, 405
family structures, 19, 19*b*
farming. *See* agriculture finance
FAS. *See* Financial Access Survey
FATF. *See* Financial Action Task Force
Faulu Kenya, 92, 92*b*
feedback loops, 365, 368, 476–77
fee-for-service models, 162, 163*b*, 192
fees
    in agent networks, 294–95, 294*f*
    effective rates and, 227*b*
    school, 211, 212*b*, 301, 312
    service charges and, 225
FEMSA, 44*b*
Ferlo, 441*b*
Ferrand, David, 9, 459
FG Vavilon, 292*b*
field officers, 278, 279*b*
FinAccess, 30, 114*b*, 125*b*
finance committees, 354
finance companies, 182, 182–83*b*
Financial Access Survey (FAS), 72, 78, 115,
    116–17, 122*b*
Financial Action Task Force (FATF), 81,
    82, 431–32
financial and social performance, 9, 321–49
    financial management, 330–33
        business planning, 330–31
        portfolio reports, 333
        reporting, 331
        statements, 331–33
    management information systems, 322–30,
        323–24*b*
        accounting, 326
        audit support, 326, 327*b*
        core banking systems, 322, 325–29
        customer information, 325
        customization, 328
        data preparation and extraction, 328
        delivery channel and systems upgrading,
        329–30
        deposit account management, 326
        group management, 325
        installation of, 328–29
        loan portfolio tracking, 325–26

FONDECO (Community Development Fund), 249–50, 250*b*
Ford Foundation, 360*b*
Ford Motor Company, 387
forward contracts, 248, 248*b*
Foundation for International Community Assistance (FINCA), 142
foundations as funders, 387
4G protocols, 442
fragmentation of savings, 302, 316
Frankfurt School Micro and SME Banking Summer Academy, 451*b*
FSAs. *See* financial service associations
funding, 9, 379–412. *See also* catalytic funding
    concentration of, 395, 396*b*
    "crowding in" of, 103, 110, 384, 386
    "crowding out" of, 2, 103, 238
    financial landscapes and, 36
    glossary of terms, 380–82*b*
    instruments, 103–4, 107–10. *See also specific instruments (e.g., grants)*
    investing practices, 406–8, 408*b*
    microfinance investment intermediaries (MIIs), 383, 389–95
        apex organizations, 395
        holding companies, 394–95, 394*t*
        microfinance investment vehicles (MIVs), 389–94, 390–91*b*, 393*b*, 410, 410*b*
        peer-to-peer aggregators, 395
    ratings, 408–10, 409–10*b*
    role of, 382–83
    tools for, 395–406
        bonds, 398–99, 400*b*
        currency funding, 399–402, 401–2*b*
        debt, 397–99
        deposits, 402
        equity, 404–6, 406*f*, 407*b*
        grants, 397
        guarantees, 403–4
        securitization, 404, 404*b*
        senior term loans, 397–98
        structured finance, 402–4
        subordinated debt, 398, 399*b*
        syndicated loans, 398
    types of, 383–89, 385*f*
        banks, 388–89, 389*b*
        bilateral and multilateral agencies, 386
        development finance institutions (DFIs), 386, 394, 405
        foundations, 387
        individual investors, 389
        institutional investors, 387–88, 388*b*
        nongovernmental organizations, 387
        private, 383–84, 384*t*, 386–89
        public, 384, 384*t*, 385–86
funeral insurance, 58, 260
fungibility
    of loans, 226
    in quantitative research, 132*b*, 136

G

G-20, 85, 85*b*
Gabon, domestic credit in, 460
Gähwiler, Barbara, 8, 97
The Gambia
    CVECAs in, 170
    family structures in, 19*b*
Garand, D., 267
Gates Foundation, 106
GDP (gross domestic product), 460
gender, 23–25, 24*b*, 25*t*. *See also* men; women
general packet radio service (GPRS), 282, 296*n*11, 442
Ghana
    banking in, 43*b*, 185, 185*b*, 191*b*
    debt collection in, 75
    e-switch system in, 441*b*
    financial capability in, 77*b*
    health insurance in, 263
    housing in, 232*b*
    insurance in, 256
    interest rates in, 75
    over-indebtedness and, 116*b*
    susu collectors in, 154*b*
Gibson, Alan, 8, 15
giro transfers, 196
Global Financial Inclusion (Findex), 3, 115, 121, 122*b*, 151
Global Impact Investing Network, 388*b*
Global Microfinance Investment Program, 388*b*
Global Partnership for Financial Inclusion (G-20), 83, 84–85, 114, 143*n*8
Global Policy Forum (2009), 114*b*
global supply surveys, 116–17

Global System for Mobile (GSM), 280, 284–85, 296n13, 442
Globe Funder, 395
GNI (gross national income), 460–61, 460–61f
Good Practice Guidelines for Funders of Microfinance, 473
Good Return, 395
governance and managing operations, 9, 351–76
    governance, 351–55
        board of directors, 352–54
        strategic considerations for, 354–55
    human resource management, 355–58
        control activities and, 369
        performance management, 357–58
        policies for, 356–57
        recruitment and screening, 356
        salary and incentives, 356–57, 357b
        training and development, 356
    operational risks, 366–74
        control activities, 368–70
        control environment, 367–68
        external audits, 373–74
        information and communications, 370–71
        internal audits, 366, 371–73, 372b
        internal controls, 365, 366–67f, 367–71, 370b
        monitoring, 370
        risk assessment, 368
    product management, 358–64, 359b
        costing, 361–62, 363f
        development, 358, 360–61, 360–61b
        marketing, 364
        pricing, 362–64
    risk management, 364–74, 365t, 366f
Government Savings Bank (Thailand), 186
government transfer payments (G2P), 73, 272, 274, 275b, 289b, 291b
GPRS. See general packet radio service
Grameen Bank
    "economically active poor" and, 49
    field officers and, 278
    financial inclusion and, 467
    group lending and, 66, 218
    loan top ups and, 56b
    long-term savings products from, 214b
    product management and, 359b
    repayment schedules of, 67, 68

Grameen Foundation, 142, 345
Grameen Generalized System (Grameen II), 359b
Grameen Phone, 290b
grants, 103, 108–9, 167, 179, 397
Grassroots Capital, 388b
greenfielding and greenfield institutions, 180, 188, 190–92, 191b, 382, 389b, 452
Green Planet, 438b
gross domestic product (GDP), 460
gross national income (GNI), 460–61, 460–61f
group guarantees, 221, 237
group lending, 218–19
Grupo Elektra, 182, 183b
GSM. See Global System for Mobile
G2P. See government transfer payments
guarantees
    in agriculture finance, 248–49
    as funding instruments, 103–4, 109
    as funding tools, 403–4
    group guarantees, 221, 237
    NGO microfinance institutions and, 179
    partial credit, 401, 403
    personal guarantees, 222, 237
Guatemala, factoring in, 244b
guidelines. See standards and guidelines
Guinea, financial service associations in, 169

H
Hatton Nation Bank (HNB), 279b
hawala systems, 155b
HCC (Human Capital Contract), 229b
health
    care costs, 250
    insurance, 193, 253–54b, 261–63, 263–64b, 274b
    money transfer services and, 275b
    out-of-pocket payments and, 249
    shocks, 206b
Heifer International, 249b
hire-purchase companies, 181
HIV/AIDS, 267–68
HNB (Hatton Nation Bank), 279b
holding companies, 190, 394–95, 394t
homeownership, financing of, 59
hospital cash, 262, 263b
housing loans, 231–32
HSBC Amanah, 220b
Human Capital Contract (HCC), 229b

human errors, 371
human resource management, 33b, 355–58

I

IAIS. *See* International Association of Insurance Supervisors
IDB (Inter-American Development Bank), 411n9
identification, unique, 448–49, 449b
IFAD. *See* International Fund for Agricultural Development
IFC. *See* International Finance Corporation
IFFCO-Tokio, 255b
IFMR Trust, 303b
ijarah leasing contracts, 230–31
Iko Pesa, 43b
ILO. *See* International Labour Organisation
IMF (International Monetary Fund), 116–17, 122b
impact assessments, 130–31, 132b, 418, 418b
ImpAct Consortium, 341b, 345, 346b
impact investing, 379, 387, 388b
incentives
    of donors, 101, 103
    financial, 356–57, 357b
inclusion, financial. *See* financial inclusion
income
    irregularity, 52, 53–55b
    levels, 19–22, 20f, 21b, 22b
    seasonal, 52–53, 55b
    statements, 332
income smoothing, 52–56, 53–55b. *See also* consumption smoothing
index-based insurance, 247–48, 264, 265–66b, 476
India
    agriculture debt waivers in, 237
    ASCAs in, 157b
    banking in, 68, 167, 185, 186b, 278, 303, 303–4b, 388
    chit funds in, 156
    community-based trainers in, 163b
    consulting services in, 452
    debt collection in, 75
    emergencies in, 57
    equity funds in, 392
    financial diaries in, 28
    financial inclusion in, 80b
    financial portfolios in, 50
    identification systems in, 449b
    income in, 55, 55b
    initial public offerings in, 407b
    insurance in, 255b, 260, 261t, 263, 264b, 266, 269
    microfinance market in, 5b, 102
    mobile network operators in, 197
    non-bank financial institutions in, 182b
    Rajan Committee in, 93n7
    religion and caste in, 23b
    savings patterns in, 205b
    self-help groups in, 3, 65, 152, 158, 164, 165, 165b, 168, 168b, 170nn7–9
    third-party providers in, 289b
indicator selections, 133
indigenous financial providers, 152, 153–58, 153t
individual investors, 389
indivisibility of individual savings, 302
Indonesia
    banking in, 185, 189b
    consumer protection in, 74
    e-money issuers in, 425
Indonesian Stock Exchange, 189b
information asymmetries, 99, 416
information technology (IT), 369–70, 370b, 452–53
infrastructure, 9, 437–50. *See also* outsourced support services
    for cash exchange, 305, 317
    collateral registries, 449–50
    credit bureaus, 445–48
        benefits of, 446–47
        challenges to growth, 447–48, 447b
        operation and oversight, 445–46, 446b
    deposit insurance, 444–45
    financial landscapes and, 36
    government support of, 73
    payment, clearing, and settlement systems, 439–41
        national and international, 439–40, 440b, 441b
        retail processors, 440
    payment integrators, 441–42, 442b
    physical, 438–39, 438b
    regulation of financial, 430–31
    unique identification, 448–49, 449b
    voice and data communications, 441–44
        connectivity and, 442–44, 443b
        smartphones, 443
initial public offerings (IPOs), 405, 407b
inpatient coverage, 262
Institute for Financial Management and Research, 156

Institute of Internal Auditors, 371
institutional investors, 387–88, 388*b*
institutional providers, 8, 173–99
    banks, 183–93
        agency relationships and partnerships and,
            192–93, 193*b*
        downscaling and, 188, 190
        greenfielding and, 188, 190–92, 191*b*
        postal savings, 186, 186–87*b*
        private commercial, 188, 190–93, 191*b*
        rural and community, 184–85, 185*b*
        savings, 185–86
        state, 186, 188, 189*b*
    characteristics of, 174–76, 175–76*t*
    deposit-taking microfinance institutions, 180, 181*b*
    financial cooperatives, 177–78, 178*b*
    insurance companies, 193–94
        commercial insurance providers, 193–94, 195*b*
        mutual insurers, 193
        NGO insurance providers, 193–94
    NGO microfinance institutions, 173–74,
        179–80, 181*b*
    other non-bank financial institutions (NBFIs),
        180–83
        finance and consumer credit companies, 182,
            182–83*b*
        leasing companies, 181–82
        suppliers and buyers, 182–83, 184*b*
    payment service providers, 194–97, 196*b*
    range of providers and, 174*f*
insurance, 9, 249–70
    agriculture and, 247–48, 263–66, 265–66*b*
    commercial providers, 193–94, 195*b*
    composite, 266
    crop, 131, 247
    damage-based, 247
    deposit, 33*b*, 431, 444–45
    emergencies and, 56, 57–58
    financial inclusion and, 122*b*, 266–68
    funeral, 58, 260
    future predictions, 268–69
    health, 193, 253–54*b*, 261–63, 263–64*b*, 274*b*
    index-based, 247–48, 264, 265–66*b*, 476
    informal, 158
    information asymmetries and, 416
    key terms in, 251–52*b*
    life, 259–61, 261*t*

mutual insurers, 193
need for, 250–53
NGO providers, 193–94
policy makers and, 76*b*
product options, 253–59
    claims, 258–59
    coverage terms and pricing, 256–57
    eligibility, 258
    group or individual, 253–54*b*, 253–55
    premium payment mechanisms,
        257–58, 257*b*
    voluntary or mandatory, 255–56, 255*b*, 268
product types, 259–66
property, 263
providers, 193
regulation of, 426–27, 428–29*b*
reinsurers, 194
savings completion, 260–61, 262*b*
savings groups and, 161
standards for, 82
sustainability of, 174
yield-based, 247
Insurance Core Principles (IAIS), 82
integrated value chain models, 242
interactive voice response (IVR), 442–43
Inter-American Development Bank (IDB), 411*n*9
interest rates, 222–25, 223–25*b*, 236, 340
internal controls, 365, 366–67*f*, 367–71, 370*b*. *See also*
    audits
internal risks, 354
International Accounting Standards, 373
International Association of Insurance Supervisors
    (IAIS), 81, 82, 426
International Association of Microfinance
    Institutions, 408
International Bank for Reconstruction and
    Development, 386
International Finance Corporation (IFC), 103, 191*b*,
    205*b*, 383, 386, 403, 438*b*
International Financial Reporting Standards, 373
International Fund for Agricultural Development
    (IFAD), 103, 169, 386
International Labour Organisation (ILO), 249,
    450, 452*b*
International Monetary Fund (IMF), 116–17, 122*b*
International Remittances Network (IRnet), 440*b*
Internet banking, 287–88

interoperability in payment services, 288–90, 289–90*b*, 439

interventionism, 465–66

interviews, in-depth, 134, 138

investments. *See* small-business investments

investors. *See* institutional investors; individual investors

IPOs (initial public offerings), 405, 407*b*

IRIS Centre, 348*n*15

IRnet (International Remittances Network), 440*b*

Islamic lending, 22–23, 34, 220–21, 220*b*

Islamic Relief, 220*b*

IT. *See* information technology

IVR (interactive voice response), 442–43

J

J. P. Morgan, 388*b*

jewelry as savings mechanism, 204–5

Jipange Kusave (JKS), 212*b*

Johnson, Susan, 8, 45*n*11, 49

Jordan, health insurance in, 263*b*

K

Kalaignar (health insurance program), 264*b*

Karim, Nimrah, 22

Kashf Foundation, 398

KDA (K-Rep Development Agency), 169*b*, 230*b*

Kenya
 agriculture insurance in, 265–66*b*
 ATMs in, 281–82*b*
 banking in, 43*b*, 114*b*, 186, 187*b*, 193*b*
 facilitators in, 106–7, 106*b*
 factoring in, 244*b*
 financial education in, 92*b*
 financial portfolios in, 30–31, 468
 financial service associations in, 169, 169*b*
 gender norms in, 24*b*
 identification cards in, 448
 initial public offerings in, 407*b*
 landscape research in, 129*b*
 microfinance market in, 102
 mobile network operators in, 197, 284, 285*b*
 person-to-person payments in, 312
 savings in, 162–63*b*, 206*b*, 212*b*
 solar lighting in, 438*b*
 supply chains in, 242*b*
 transactional accounts in, 309

Kenya Post Office Savings Bank, 187*b*

KfW. *See* Kreditanstalt für Wiederaufbau

Khan Bank, 189*b*

Kilimo Salama, 265–66*b*

Kiva, 395

Klapper, Leora, 121

know-how, 107–8

know your customer (KYC), 42, 431, 448

Kreditanstalt für Wiederaufbau (KfW), 191*b*, 386, 402*b*, 403, 404*b*, 441*b*

K-Rep Development Agency (KDA), 169*b*, 230*b*

Kshetriya Gramin Financial Services (KGFS), 278, 303, 303–4*b*

KYC. *See* know your customer

Kyrgyzstan
 currency depreciation in, 401*b*
 microfinance laws in, 420*b*

L

laissez faire, 465, 466

landscape data, 121*b*

landscapes, financial. *See* financial landscapes

Lauer, Kate, 9, 413

leasing, 181–82, 229–31, 230*b*, 246–47

Ledgerwood, Joanna
 on credit, 8, 217
 on effective rates, 226
 on financial and social performance, 9, 321
 on financial inclusion measurement, 8, 113
 on financial landscapes, 8, 15
 on institutional providers, 8, 173
 on payment services and delivery channels, 9, 271
 on savings services, 8, 203

legal mandates for financial inclusion, 79–81

legislatures, rule making and, 72–73

Lehman, Joyce, 9, 271

lending. *See* credit

leverage, 338

LFS Financial Systems GmbH, 191*b*

Liber, Dominic, 158

Liberia, microfinance banks in, 191*b*

licensing requirements, 414

life annuities, 260

life-cycle events, 52, 58–63, 60*b*, 65*b*, 77, 228

life insurance, 259–61, 261*t*

Life Insurance Corporation of India, 266

Lighting Africa, 438*b*

Nigeria, banking in, 185, 191*b*
Niyazov, Dilshod, 292*b*
nominating committees, 354
non-bank financial institutions (NBFIs), 29, 173–74, 180–83, 422, 429–30
nongovernmental organizations (NGOs)
    board of directors and, 353, 353*b*
    deposit-taking institutions and, 181*b*
    donors and, 98–99
    equity and, 405
    facilitated providers and, 152, 158
    as financial institutions, 29, 173–74
    financial statements and, 373
    funding and, 386–87
    global supply surveys and, 117
    governance and, 351–52
    holding companies and, 394
    as insurance providers, 193–94
    management information systems and, 322
    as microfinance institutions, 6, 173–74, 179–80, 181*b*, 424–25
    savings groups and, 65–66, 160, 161*b*, 170*n*2
    self-help groups and, 164
Norway, UN-Habitat and, 232*b*

O

OECD countries, 447–48
"OECD Principles and Good Practices for Financial Awareness and Education," 88
OIBM (Opportunity International Bank of Malawi), 127, 127*b*
Oikocredit, 392
O'Keeffe, Geraldine, 9, 321, 437
Omni, 281*b*, 288
on-lending, 101–2, 110, 167, 240
open door policies, 371
Open Sky, 283*b*
operating activities, 332–33
operating leases, 230–31
operating plans, 331
"operating self-sufficiency," 143*n*10
operational risks, 366–74
operations management. *See* governance and managing operations
Opportunity International, 179, 394
Opportunity International Bank of Malawi (OIBM), 127, 127*b*, 212*b*

Orange Money, 43*b*, 164*b*, 292
organizational structures, 355–56
Oriental Bank of Commerce, 165*b*
outgrower schemes, 242
outpatient coverage, 262–63
outreach in microfinance, 2, 3
outsourced support services, 9, 450–57. *See also* infrastructure; third-party platform providers
    auditing and accountancy, 450
    call centers, 453, 454*b*
    debt collection, 453–54, 455*b*
    efficiency of, 437
    security and cash-in-transit, 454–55
    software as a service (SaaS), 452–53
    training and advisory services, 450–52, 451–52*b*
over-indebtedness, 17*b*, 89, 90, 90*b*, 116, 116*b*, 152, 446
Overseas Private Investment Corporation, 104
ownership requirements for banks, 421*b*, 422, 423*b*
Oxxo, 43–44*b*

P

Pakistan
    branchless banking in, 43*b*
    health insurance in, 253–54*b*
    Islamic lending in, 220*b*
    payment platforms in, 288
    prepaid cards in, 280, 281*b*
    syndicated loans in, 398
Papua New Guinea, mobile money in, 275*b*
Paraguay, debt collection in, 455*b*
Paris Declaration of Aid Effectiveness, 473
partial credit guarantees (PCGs), 401, 403
participatory rapid assessments (PRAs), 134, 135*b*
passbook savings, 55, 64, 68, 211
path dependencies, 464
Patrimonio Hoy, 183, 184*b*, 231
PATs. *See* poverty assessment tools
pawnbrokers, 63, 154
payment and clearing systems, 430–31
payment integrators, 441–42, 442*b*
payment services and delivery channels, 9, 271–98
    agent networks, 290–95, 291*b*
        building of, 291–92, 292*b*
        costs and fees, 294–95, 294*f*
        managing channels, 294
        managing liquidity, 292–93, 293*b*
    delivery channels, 272, 275–88

pricing of microloans, 90
Principles for Investors in Inclusive Finance, 407
privacy of client data, 89
private funders, 383–84, 384t, 386–89
process mapping, 368
ProCredit, 191b, 388b, 395
ProCredit Bank Bulgaria, 404b
ProCredit Holding, 394
Prodel, 231
productive investment, 226, 228–32
product management, 358–64, 359b
profitability indicators, 334, 336t
ProFund, 392, 394
Progress out of Poverty Index (PPI), 142, 345,
    347–48n14
property insurance, 263
proportionality
    in financial markets, 475
    in regulation, 417–18
psychology of savings and goal setting, 300–302, 310
psychometric testing, 220
P2B. *See* person-to-business transfers
P2P. *See* person-to-person transfers
public funders, 384, 384t, 385–86
public goods, 471, 473, 477n56
public-private partnerships, 264b, 393b
put options, 406

Q
Qiwi, 282b
qualitative research, 132, 134, 138
quality of financial services, 115, 128–29
quantitative research, 132, 134–36, 138

R
randomized control trials (RCTs), 3, 120, 135–38,
    144n22
Rashtriya Swasthya Bima Yojana (RSBY) health
    insurance program, 264b
Rating Fund II, 411n9
ratings
    credit, 404b, 408–9, 409b, 445
    for funding mechanisms, 408–10, 409–10b
RCTs. *See* randomized control trials
real-time alerts, 330
real-time communications, 308
real-time gross settlement (RTGS), 440

recordkeeping, 167, 322. *See also* accounting
    systems
recruitment of staff, 356
Regional MSME Investment Fund for Sub-Saharan
    Africa (REGMIFA), 393b
registration requirements, 414
regulation, 9, 413–35
    AML/CFT requirements, 431–32
    enabling environments and, 472–73
    financial infrastructure, 430–31
    financial services providers, 420–30
        banks, 421–22, 421b, 423b, 427, 429
        financial cooperatives, 422–24
        microinsurance, 426–27, 428–29b
        microlending institutions, 424–25
        non-bank deposit-taking institutions, 422,
          429–30
        payment service providers and e-money
          issuers, 425–26, 426b
    overview, 413–15
    principles of, 417–19, 418b
    rationale and objectives of, 415–17, 417t
    structures for, 419–20, 420b
"regulatory arbitrage," 419
regulatory impact assessments (RIAs), 418, 418b
Reille, Xavier, 22
reinsurers, 194
reliability of financial tools, 63–64, 67–68
religion, 22–23, 23b
remittances, 19b, 272, 273b, 295n2, 440b
Remittances Prices Worldwide (RPW), 273b
renewable term arrangements, 256
repayment terms on loans, 218
replicability of savings groups, 162–63, 162b
reputational risks, 354
requests for proposals, 327–28
requirements analyses, 327
Reserve Bank of India, 80b, 168b
Reserve Bank of Malawi, 84b
responsAbility Global Microfinance Fund, 390
responsible finance, 2, 80b, 86b
Responsible Finance Forum, 84, 85–86
Responsible Investor Principles, 408b
retail capacity, 470–71
retail payment processors, 440
RFR (Rural Finance Network), 446b
RIAs (regulatory impact assessments), 418, 418b